THE NEW INTERNATIONAL COMMENTARY ON
THE OLD TESTAMENT — Edward J. Young, *Editor*

THE BOOK OF ISAIAH

THE BOOK OF ISAIAH

*THE ENGLISH TEXT, WITH INTRODUCTION,
EXPOSITION, AND NOTES*

by

EDWARD J. YOUNG
PROFESSOR OF OLD TESTAMENT
WESTMINSTER THEOLOGICAL SEMINARY

VOLUME I
Chapters 1 to 18

3279

WILLIAM B. EERDMANS PUBLISHING COMPANY
GRAND RAPIDS, MICHIGAN

PHOTOLITHOPRINTED BY GRAND RAPIDS BOOK MANUFACTURERS, INC.
GRAND RAPIDS, MICHIGAN
1965

TABLE OF CONTENTS

Contents

Preface

The present volume is the first in a series of three volumes on the prophecy of Isaiah. As the reader will discover, it is not primarily concerned with textual questions and problems but rather with commentary upon the Masoretic Hebrew text and the meaning of that text. Nor does the commentary seek to trace the history of each verse in the manner of some works. In it Isaiah is regarded as the author of the entire prophecy, and the purpose is to let him speak and to endeavor to understand what he says.

To accomplish this purpose I have devoted the main body of the commentary to exposition. I have tried to keep in mind the needs of the minister and Sunday-school teacher, and for that reason I have given very few Hebrew words in the main body of the text. The few exceptions are mainly examples of paranomasia and alliteration, which I have given in a loose transcription so that one unfamiliar with Hebrew will be able to understand them.

On the other hand, the commentary does endeavor to serve the ministers, teachers, and students who do know the Hebrew language. Therefore technical material has been included, but it has been placed in footnotes or in special notes. I would here call attention to the Hebrew vowel charts given in Appendix I. These charts really represent an advance in the study of Hebrew, and they undergird the explanation of many of the Hebrew words discussed in the commentary proper. That I may present them is due to the kindness of my friend Dr. Cyrus H. Gordon, who first introduced me to their significance. I would urge the reader who is acquainted with Hebrew to master these charts, and with their aid to study the notes to the text.

In footnotes and special notes I have also included material, such as archaeological discoveries, which throw light upon the sacred text. I have also endeavored to acquaint the reader with what I judge to be the more important ancient and modern literature on Isaiah. My goal throughout, however, has not been to make an exhaustive list of references, but to explain the Biblical text itself.

In this work I have made my own translation. The aim of this semiliteral translation is to bring out the force of the original so that the reader may be helped in his understanding of the original. Those readers who are unacquainted with Hebrew should compare this translation with the King James Version or whatever version they prefer. It is not my intention, of course, that this translation should supplant the accepted versions of the Scriptures.

I send forth this commentary on Isaiah with a sense of profound unworthiness. Great and mighty are the men who have labored in the exposition of this portion of God's infallible Word. Before me loom the names of Alexander, Delitzsch and Drechsler, and from another viewpoint, Rosenmüller and Gesenius. And behind them all stands Calvin. To modify a thought once expressed by Johannes Brahms, "I hear the tramp of the giants behind me." To all of these men I am greatly indebted, and in particular to Drechsler, whose work has deeply influenced me.

I would also express my gratitude to more recent writers, and in particular to Dr. James Pritchard for his helpful volume, *Ancient Near Eastern Texts* (1950). Grateful acknowledgment is made to the Princeton University Press for permission to quote from this volume, and also to T. & T. Clark, and Charles Scribner & Sons for permission to quote from George Buchanan Gray, *The Prophecy of Isaiah* (Edinburgh: 1926). My friend Donald Wiseman has been most gracious in reading over a portion of the material and in giving me the benefit of his profound knowledge of the historical situation of Isaiah's day.

To work with the Wm. B. Eerdmans Publishing Company has always been a pleasure and I would thank them for innumerable kindnesses and courtesies. To Mr. William B. Eerdmans, Sr. I am particularly grateful for the preface to this work. Mrs. Richard Marsh and Miss Dorothy Newkirk prepared the typescript and I am truly in their debt for their kindness.

If this work will in any way aid the reader in the understanding of this portion of Scripture, I shall feel amply repaid for the labor expended. My purpose in writing is to encourage men and women to read the Old Testament and to encourage ministers to preach therefrom. Isaiah brings us face to face with Him who sits upon the throne, high and lifted up, who controls the destinies of nations, and who sends to us a Child, even our Lord and Redeemer. The late Dr. J. Gresham Machen once spoke of the Old Testament prophecies as "full of the grace of God."

And as we read of that grace may our deepest gratitude be to Him who is the true Author of this prophecy, and who in the fullness of time sent to this earth Him whose name is Wonderful Counsellor, the Mighty God, the Everlasting Father, the Prince of Peace.

—EDWARD J. YOUNG

LIST OF ABBREVIATIONS

abs.	absolute	*DOTT*	Thomas: *Documents from Old Testament Times* (1958)
acc.	accusative		
adj.	adjective		
AfO	*Archiv für Orientforschung*	Egy.	Egyptian
Akk.	Akkadian	E.T.	English Translation
ANET	Pritchard: *Ancient Near Eastern Texts* (1950)	Eth.	Ethiopic
		f.	feminine
Ant.	*Antiquities* (Josephus)	*FAB*	*Festchrift für Alfred Bertholet* (1950)
Aq.	Aquilla		
Ar.	Arabic	*FI*	Rowley: *The Faith of Israel* (1956)
Aram.	Aramaic		
ARI	Albright: *Archives of the Religion of Israel* (1942)	fut.	future
		gen.	genitive
ATAT	Gressmann: *Altorientalische Texte zum Alten Testament* (1909)	Gk.	Greek
		GKC	Gesenius, Kautzsch, Cowley: *Hebrew Grammar* (1910)
AV	Authorized Version		
B	Codex Vaticanus	Heb.	Hebrew
BA	*Biblical Archaeologist*	HG	Green: *Hebrew Grammar* (1898)
BASOR	*Bulletin American Schools of Oriental Research*		
		HTC	Mowinckel: *He That Cometh* (1956)
BDB	Brown, Driver, Briggs: *Hebrew Lexicon*	*HUCA*	*Hebrew Union College Annual*
BH	*Biblia Hebraica*		
BK	Baumgartner, Köhler: *Lexicon in Veteris Testamenti Libros* (1953)	*IB*	*Interpreter's Bible* (1952-1956)
		imp.	imperfect
BT	Vos: *Biblical Theology* (1948)	imper.	imperative
		inf.	infinitive
CIS	*Corpus Inscriptionum Semiticarum*	*JAOS*	*Journal of the American Oriental Society*
CML	Driver: *Canaanite Myths and Legends* (1956)	*JBL*	*Journal of Biblical Literature*
col.	column	*JSS*	*Journal of Semitic Studies*
cons.	consecutive	*JTS*	*Journal of Theological Studies*
const.	construct		
Cyro.	Xenophon: *Cyropaedia*	*KAT*	Schräder: *Die Keilschriften und das Alte Testament* (1903)
Dio. Sic.	Diodorus Siculus		

KUB	Keilschrifturkunden aus Boghazkeui (1916, 1921)	subj.	subject
l.	line	Sym.	Symmachus
lit.	literally	Syr.	Syriac
m.	masculine	Targ.	Targum
M.	Masoretic Text	TAT	von Rad: Theologie des Alten Testaments (1958)
Met.	Ovid: Metamorphoses		
mss.	manuscripts	TGI	Galling: Textbuch zur Geschichte Israels (1950)
MSTP	Young: My Servants the Prophets (1952)		
		TLT	Jacob: Theologie de l'Ancient Testament (1958)
nom.	nominative		
NSI	Cooke: North Semitic Inscriptions (1903)		
		TPQ	Theologische und practische Quartalschrift
NT	New Testament		
obj.	object	TT	Driver: A Treatise on the Use of the Tenses in Hebrew (1892)
OS	Oudtestamentische Studiën		
OT	Old Testament	TTC	Pentecost: Things to Come (1958)
part.	participle		
perf.	perfect	TWNT	Kittel: Theologisches Wörterbuch zum Neuen Testaments
pl.	plural		
Pont.	Ovid: Ex Ponto		
pred.	predicate	Ug.	Ugaritic
prep.	preposition	UH	Gordon: Ugaritic Handbook (1955)
pret.	preterite		
PTR	Princeton Theological Review	VD	Verbum Domini
Q	Qᵉre	VPA	Watts: Vision and Prophecy in Amos (1955)
1Q	First Isaiah Manuscript, Qumran		
		VT	Vetus Testamentum
s.	singular	VTS	Vetus Testamentum Supplement
SAT	Die Schriften des Alten Testaments (1921, 1925)		
		Vulg.	Vulgate
SDK	Engnell: Studies in Divine Kingship (1943)	WHAB	Westminster Historical Atlas to the Bible (1956)
SII	Young: Studies in Isaiah (1954)	WThJ	Westminster Theological Journal
SOTP	Robinson: Studies in Old Testament Prophecy (1950)	ZAW	Zeitschrift für die alttestamentliche Wissenschaft

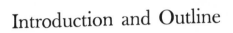

Introduction and Outline

Introduction

I. ISAIAH THE PROPHET

The name Isaiah means "The Lord is salvation," that is, "the Lord is the source of salvation." The two parts of the name seem to stand in the relation of subject and predicate. This construction is preferable to taking the first part as a construct, "the salvation of the Lord." Nor should the first part of the name be regarded as a verbal form, since the *Qal* of Ys[c1] does not occur. When this particular root appears in compound nouns, it is in the *Hif*[c]*il* stem (e.g., Jer. 42:1).

Concerning Isaiah's ancestry and parentage we shall speak in the commentary proper. Little is known about the man himself. He exercised his ministry in and about Jerusalem, and had ready access to the presence of kings. About him a number of legends have grown up. Thus, Beeri, the father of Hosea, is said to have left only two verses of prophecy, which Isaiah preserved in his own work, namely Isaiah 8:19, 20.[2]

Isaiah, the greatest of the prophets, and Obadiah, the least, did not prophesy until they had received permission from the Great Sanhedrin, and both uttered their prophecies in seventy-one tongues, which may be a reference to the seventy-one members of the "heavenly Sanhedrin."[3] Isaiah was regarded as a prophet as great as Moses, a tradition which shows that the Jews had no truly penetrating understanding of the position of Moses in the divine economy.[4] Isaiah was considered to be distinguished above all the other prophets, since he "prophesied from the mouth of the Almighty," whereas the others merely received the spirit of prophecy from their masters (e.g., Elijah's spirit came upon Elisha). Secondly, Isaiah was distinguished by repeating the introductory words of his prophecies, thereby indicating their certain fulfillment (e.g., 40:1; 51:9, 12, 16).[5]

---

1 ישע

2 *Midrash, Wayyiqra Rabba* 6:6; 15:2.

3 *Aggadat Bereshith* 14:32.

4 *Midrash, Pesikta Rabbathi* 4:14a.

5 *Pesikta de-Rab-Kahana* 16:25b; *Midrash, Wayyiqra Rabba* 10:2.

Adam, Jacob, Isaiah, and Jeremiah are said to be the four men in the Bible called creatures of God.[6] Isaiah and Ezekiel are compared as an inhabitant of the capital and a villager. Since Ezekiel was not accustomed to the divine glory, he gave a detailed description of what he saw, whereas Isaiah was used to it and so did not describe it.[7]

Isaiah is thought to have received his call on the day that Uzziah the king sought to sacrifice and was smitten with leprosy. He was in his study when the heavenly voice informed him that Micah had been sent and had been smitten on the cheek; Amos had been sent and had been reviled. Isaiah replied, "Here am I, send me."[8]

The legends respecting the martyrdom of Isaiah are quite interesting. According to one he is said to have been swallowed up by a tree which had to be sawed in pieces before he could be killed.[9] His hiding place was discovered by means of the fringes of his garment which the tree had not swallowed up.

In the pseudepigraphic work, *The Ascension of Isaiah,* there is the account of the prophet's martyrdom under Manasseh, who sawed him asunder with a wooden saw. False prophets mocked him, yet he neither cried aloud nor wept, but spoke with the Holy Spirit.[10]

Passing over these Jewish legends we may ask what the true significance of Isaiah was. Why should this man be a living embodiment of the truth that salvation is to be found in the Lord? What was the significance of his appearance upon the scene of history?

The answer is that Isaiah exercised his prophetic ministry at a time of unique significance, a time in which it was of utmost importance to realize that salvation could not be obtained by reliance upon man but only from God Himself. For Israel it was the central or pivotal point of history between Moses and Christ. The old world was passing and an entirely new order of things was beginning to make its appearance. Where would Israel stand in that new world? Would she be the true theocracy,

---

6 *Midrash, Pesikta Rabbathi* 26:129a; cf. 27:133b.

7 *Hagigah* 13b.

8 *Pesikta de-Rab-Kahana* 16:125b; *Midrash, Wayyiqra Rabba* 10:2.

9 *Yerushalmi, Sanhedrin* 10:28c; *Midrash, Pesikta Rabbathi* 4:14.

10 Cf. Josephus, *Antiquities,* 10:3:1; Justin Martyr, *Dialogue with Trypho,* 120; Tertullian, *De Patientia,* 14; *Visio Pauli,* 49; *Pseudo-Hippolytus,* 705; *Yebamoth,* 49b; *Sanhedrin,* 103b.

the light to lighten the Gentiles, or would she fall into the shadow by turning for help to the nations which were about her?

There had been a time when men had sought for salvation and deliverance wholly by material means. A great judgment had overcome the earth in the flood, and that they might not be scattered abroad over the face of the earth men sought to make a name for themselves by the Tower of Babel. This, however — their means of salvation — in reality became the occasion of their destruction in that they were dispersed and their tongues confounded. Thus, sin could not be concentrated in one place; mankind as a unit could no longer boast itself against God. A new order therefore set in. Mankind was scattered with the result that individual nations and peoples arose. From among them in the time of Moses God chose one people to be a nation for His name. It was to be a nation among nations, but one in which the righteousness of the righteous God would be justly exhibited in the judicial proceedings of the people and in their daily life.

Israel, however, in actual fact, showed herself to be little different from the other nations. It was an age of particularism, of various religions and cults, of various peoples. In such conditions salvation was not to be found, and the old spirit of Babel again asserted itself. As never before in the history of the world the idea of conquest gained ground, and one nation sought to subdue other nations and to make them a part of itself. Thus, the Assyrian king appeared upon the horizon, and his appearance signalized the striving for a new order of things. A reaching for universalism such as the world had never before known now began to appear, and a reaction against the old order took place. Again, the spirit of Babel was present, and again man began to exalt himself as he had tried to do at Babel. There would be no tower to reach into the heavens, but there would be a world empire. Mankind would not be concentrated in one spot; he would cover the earth but would belong to one kingdom, the kingdom of man. Man was to rule and to extend his sway, and man's kingdom was to cover the world so that man alone would be exalted through such universalism.

Where would Israel fit into this scheme? Was Israel to be swallowed up in the world kingdom, or would she, for some reason or other, resist the march of civilization? Opposed to the purposes of man was the plan of God. He had decreed to save His people (Gen. 3:15) and His purposes were not to fail. God's

5

purpose was the exaltation of Himself, and this purpose would be brought about by God's deliverance of man. Man must learn that his deliverance cannot come from himself. To God alone he must look. Israel was the chosen nation. Long before God had set before her blessing and cursing (Deut. 28; 30:15-20; Lev. 26), He had told her the consequences of choosing cursing. Israel, however, had acted as though she needed no God. Her desire for a king was prompted merely from longing to be like other nations; even a king like Saul would have satisfied.

Even though the curses were again spoken before Israel in the time of Solomon (1 Kings 9:6-9), she paid no attention. In reality Israel chose not the blessing of the Lord but the cursing. She might have remained in her land to enjoy its productivity and prosperity; the exile need never have come. But Israel chose cursing. She had therefore to learn that salvation could come to her only in the form of a servant. If ultimately she was to attain to life, she had first to pass through death. The exile, that period of God's great indignation, must come upon Israel in order that through the exile a remnant might pass and return and that from this remnant the Saviour might finally come.

The exile seemed to form the climax in human history of the curses that came upon the nation. Actually it was not the climax, for the cursing will reach its most severe point when world judgment shall fall upon all men and the Lord alone be exalted. Then, at that last day, which belongs to the Lord, it will appear that only the Lord is sovereign. His mighty arm will have gotten Him the victory. His people will be accepted into glory, and those who oppose Him cast into the outer darkness. The day of judgment is to bring the end to human history.

Not all at one stroke, however, did the curses come. They came gradually, and Israel continued her hardness of heart against the Lord. After the time of Solomon there were partial afflictions. The Philistines and the Arameans harassed Israel, but they did not accomplish her total defeat. But there was Assyria; the incursions of other peoples had been as nothing compared to the punishment Assyria brought about. Yet even Assyria was not the end. She was a fulfillment of the earlier punishments but she was also the preparation for the exile.

Even in Assyria's coming we can see gradation. There was first of all Tiglath-pileser, who harassed the northern kingdom and took some tribes into captivity. Then came Shalmanezer, and the northern kingdom was destroyed completely. Then came Sennacherib. Judah had been vexed, but not completely wiped out. Jerusalem remained, "like a booth in a cucumber field." Assyria was not able to overthrow Jerusalem. It was in Babylon that the Mesopotamian power reached its climax. Babylonia, the type or symbol of hostile opposition to God's people, finally overthrew Jerusalem. The people of God were then dispersed. Into the world-wide empire, into the universalism of that day, the people of God had to go.

Strange indeed are God's purposes. The theocracy was banished, and the period of indignation (Isa. 10:5) had come. The Jews had been dispersed by Babylon, but Babylon, like Assyria before her, was merely a tool in the hands of the Almighty God. Wherever the Jews were dispersed and scattered they exercised a leavening influence, and in time men became attracted by their insistence upon monotheism and their purity of doctrine. So there arose those God-fearers who were ripe for the gospel when the apostle Paul preached. Thus, in the universalism which man thought he was establishing, God exalted Himself.

The Jews, however, were compelled to go through the exile, and for them this was a period of indignation. They had to be in the form of a servant, a servant to Babylonia, that thus ultimately they might learn that life can come only from God. They must see that the bondage to Babylon from which Cyrus had freed them was but a type of the greater bondage, that bondage of a spiritual nature which had separated them from God and from which they could be delivered only by One who was truly a Servant, the Servant of the Lord. This One, whom Drechsler speaks of as the Unknown and yet the One so well known, is the Redeemer. He is the One who accomplishes the purposes of God as the nation itself could never have done.

To explain to the people of God that the old order was passing away and that the new era of universalism was approaching was the task of Isaiah, the prophet. It was this man whom God so highly exalted in choosing him to be the bearer of this message. Now, as possibly never before, Israel had to know that her help was in the Lord. The appearance of Assyria had to be explained, for the Jews could have made no greater mistake than to turn at this time to Assyria for help. Yet, the Jews did just this thing. They turned to the one who was to accomplish their destruction, and so the Lord, who overrules all things for His glory, brought upon them what they had asked for, even the king of

7

Assyria (Isa. 7:17).[11] The king of Assyria did come, and the whole course of human history was changed. Isaiah advised against dependence upon Assyria, but to no avail. It fell to him, therefore, to explain the course of events so that the Jews would understand what was occurring.

No man acting in his unaided strength could meet the challenge of the times. Only a prophet, directly raised up by God, who spoke the very words which God had placed in his mouth, could speak the message that needed to be heard. Such a man was Isaiah. He spoke of the Assyrian; he spoke of the sin of Judah, but he spoke also of Christ. He uttered predictive prophecy. If it be asked how Isaiah in the eighth century B.C. could predict Christ, the answer is that God revealed His words to the prophet and the prophet spoke them forth. Prophecy can really be understood only upon the presuppositions of true Christian theism, and such presuppositions undergird what has been written in this book.[12]

The prophet Isaiah himself was the author of the entire book; he himself committed it all to writing, and he was responsible for collecting his messages and placing them in the present book which bears his name. We shall point out the inner unity and connections of the various sections of the prophecy. And we shall not make any particular effort to defend the unity and authorship of the book until the completion of the entire work.[13]

Modern criticism which denies the essential unity and Isaiah's authorship of the book really regards the work as a library of prophetical pieces, coming from different ages. With respect to chapters 1-18, the following statement is fairly representative of present-day thought. Isaiah himself uttered certain oracles which had to do with Judah and Jerusalem. These were combined with his memoirs, of which chapter 6 is the more significant. At a later time additions and expansions were made to this original collection. After the death of Isaiah even further additions were made, and among these may be found the Messianic prophecies, particularly 9:1-6 and 11:1-9 and the foreign prophecies. These in turn received further expansion, including such passages as

[11] It is only a shallow and unpenetrating criticism that can explain these words as a gloss.

[12] This position has been developed more fully in my book, *My Servants the Prophets* (Grand Rapids: 1954).

[13] Those who are interested in this subject may consult my brief exposition, *Who Wrote Isaiah?* (Grand Rapids: 1958).

13:1-22; 14:1-23; 15:1—16:14.[14] When it seems necessary, we shall deal with the question of the authorship of the individual oracles. The wondrous unity which underlies the prophecy is one of the strongest arguments to show that there is purpose to the prophecy and that the work is best understood when regarded as a whole.

II. HISTORICAL BACKGROUND

It was the purpose of God to bring His people into the land of Palestine, to establish the city of Jerusalem as their capital, and to erect a kingdom from which in time the true King, the promised Messiah, would come (2 Sam. 7:12-17; 1 Kings 8:24-30; Isa. 2:2-4). This King was to accomplish the great mission of His life in Jerusalem in that there He would be crucified and buried and would rise from the dead. To prepare for His coming, the people of God must be formed into a nation so that they might occupy the land in which the Redeemer was to be born.

It was at Sinai that God formed His people into the theocracy. "And ye shall be unto me a kingdom of priests, and an holy nation" (Exod. 19:6a). Only gradually, however, did the people learn the meaning of these words. When the nation first entered Palestine it was scattered and not unified. Among other factors, the geography of the land served to keep the people apart from one another. This led to provincialism and to jealousies, some of which were never extinguished. Furthermore, external foes could attack a part of the nation at a time and weaken it. Thus it became apparent that to overcome both the internal difficulties and the external foes there was need for a king.

The request for a king, however, was made in a spirit and in the light of considerations which showed a lack of concern for the true nature of the theocracy. The people merely wished a king that they might be like the nations round about them (1 Sam. 8:5). It was because of the spirit in which the request was made that Samuel informed the people that they were rejecting the Lord (1 Sam. 8:7ff.). A king was given, but a fur-

---

14 For a fairly detailed survey of how the book supposedly "grew," consult the Introduction to the commentary in the *IB*. Cf. the analysis in H. Birkeland, *Zum Hebräischen Traditionswesen* (Oslo: 1938), pp. 26-41; and J. Eaton, "The Origin of the Book of Isaiah," *VT.*, XI, No. 2, 138-157. He suggests that Isaiah may have gathered about him a group of disciples who were spiritually united, and the book of Isaiah ". . . represents essentially the final fixation of a stream of developing tradition borne by this society from the fountainhead, their founder, Isaiah."

ther lesson had to be learned. The administration of Saul left the nation about where it was when he began to reign. There were many admirable qualities about Saul as a man, but he was not a man after God's heart. He leaned upon his own wisdom, and hence he had to be deposed. Saul had no true concern for the theocracy, and the theocracy could not be administered as though it were an ordinary kingdom. Its king must reign in righteousness so that in the administration of the government the righteous decrees of God would be carried out in strict justice. Thus under Saul the need for the proper kind of king appeared.

The man after God's heart was found in David. David built up the kingdom as none before him had been able to do. As a man he was truly great, but he was also very sinful. David suffered the consequences of his sins, but he was forgiven those sins. In his heart of hearts he desired to follow the Lord. Nevertheless, he was not permitted to build the Temple, for the kingdom of God is peace, and the outward manifestation of that kingdom is seen in the dwelling of God, the Temple. This Temple must be built by one who typifies peace in his reign (2 Sam. 7:1ff., 1 Kings 5:3-5, 1 Chron. 28:2-7).

It fell to Solomon therefore, whose name reminds us of the word šālôm (peace), to build the Temple. Thus, the theocracy, with the Temple at Jerusalem, was to serve as a light to lighten the Gentiles and to honor the name of the true God. But there were perils within the theocracy and perils without, and those within were the more serious. Solomon's policies were not wise with respect to the northern tribes, and consequently, after his death, these tribes revolted and renounced allegiance to the Davidic house. The schism became a great blot upon the theocracy. But schism was not all: formalism in the worship of the LORD crept in and with this formalism came an insensate materialism. This led to injustices in the social order, indeed to such a bad condition that the nation had to be removed from the land of promise.

We may thus say that in a certain sense the inward condition of the people gave rise to external foes. In His gracious providence God raised up a people that was to serve the purpose of removing the theocracy from Palestine. This was the great Mesopotamian power, which in the book of Isaiah stands as a symbol of the final enemy of God's people.

In Judah Uzziah was upon the throne. He was a good man who did much for his people. (2 Kings 14:21-15:7 and 2 Chron.

26:1-23 give accounts of his reign.) Under him the people enjoyed prosperity; it seemed to be a good time. But there were social injustices and inequities. The nation was sinning. Already the foe was on the horizon.

It was in the person of Tiglath-pileser III[15] (745-727 B.C.) that the Assyrian power reached its great height and became a dangerous threat to the theocracy. This warrior had probably been a usurper who set into practice the policies of Tiglath-pileser I (1115-1093 B.C.).[16] In his first year he turned his attention to Babylon, which for years had been in a weakened condition. Its present ruler, Nabu-nasir, had introduced a new era and had bought the support of the great Assyrian king.

With constant use of the first-person pronoun, Tiglath-pileser III relates how he entered the Babylonian territory. There he built a palace, Dur-Tukulti-apal-Esarra, and there he settled peoples of the lands which he had conquered. In his second year the king directed his attention to the northeast. Of particular interest is his comment with respect to Ramateia of Arazi, who, he says, "escaped like a mouse through a hole, and no one ever saw him again." In speaking of his conquests the king glories in his cruelty: "The gorges, and precipices of the mountains I filled with their bodies."[17] Once having made himself the undisputed master of the land of the two rivers he turned his attention toward the northwest, where lay Syria and Palestine.

The king's inscriptions are fragmentary and difficult to interpret. Two major phases of his westward expeditions interest us here. The first is his early incursions into the northwest territory,[18] and another is his dealings with Ahaz in 732 B.C. In

15 In 1 Chron. 5:26 the name appears as *pil-ne-tzer*. On the inscriptions it is *Tukulti-apil-esarra* (my help is the son of Esarra). B has θαγλαθφελλασαρ (2 Kings 15:29); θαγλαθφαλνασαρ (1 Chron. 5:26); Vulg., *Theglath-philasar* (2 Kings 15:29) and *Theglathphalnasar* (1 Chron. 5:26).

16 He too had made an incursion into Lebanon *(Labnani)*, bringing back beams of cedar for the temples of Anu and Adad. He says that he conquered the land of Amurru in its entire length. He sailed from Arwad to Zamuri in Amurru and mentions that he killed a *nahiru* (whale? seal?) in the midst of the sea. Cf. *ATAT*, I, 339; *ANET*, p. 275.

17 Luckenbill, *Ancient Records of Babylonia and Assyria* (Chicago: 1926), I, 272-73.

18 For a thorough discussion of the chronology cf. Edwin R. Thiele, *The Mysterious Numbers of the Hebrew Kings* (Chicago: 1951), pp. 75-98. For the texts see P. Rost, *Die Keilschrifttexte Tiglatpilesers III* (Leipzig: 1893). Cf. also Abraham S. Anspacher, *Tiglath Pileser III* (New York: 1912).

Syria Damascus had been becoming weaker and weaker, whereas Hamath had been growing in strength. Tiglath-pileser states that he received tribute from Rasunnu of Damascus,[19] Menihimme of Samerinaia,[20] Hirummu of Tyre,[21] Sipittibi'li of Byblos, and from many others in Syria.[22]

Menahem mentions that he paid tribute to Pul (2 Kings 15: 19, 20). That Pul is another name for Tiglath-pileser may be seen from the following considerations. Tiglath-pileser claims that he received tribute from Menahem, which would seem to show that the Assyrian king was a contemporary of Pul to whom Menahem says that he paid tribute. 1 Chronicles 5:26 really identifies the two: "And the God of Israel stirred up the spirit of Pul the king of Assyria even the spirit of Tiglath-pileser the king of Assyria and he carried them away."[23]

On a Babylonian king list Pulu appears following Ukin-zu, and two years is given for him. On the Babylonian Chronicle Tiglath-pileser follows Ukin-zu and dies in the second year.[24] It is clear that Tiglath-pileser III and Pul were one and the same person, and it was the payment of this large tribute, exacted by Menahem from his "mighty men of wealth" that turned back the Assyrian king.[25]

What is of interest in the Assyrian king's account is a reference to Azriyau of Yaudi (*Ya-u-di*). But who is intended by this designation? Is this Azariah (i.e., Uzziah) of Judah? Some have

[19] *Rasunu matDimaskai,* i.e., Rezin. Raṣunu would appear in Hebrew as *rāṣōn* which seems to be preserved in B ρασων and ρaaσων. But Tiglath-pileser also spells the name *ra-ḫi-a-ni,* which might appear in Hebrew as *ra-ḥin.* I cannot explain the present Hebrew form. Cf. Benno Landsberger, *Sam'al* (Ankara: 1948), p. 66, n. 169.

[20] *Minihimme aluSamerinai,* i.e., Menahem of Samaria.

[21] I.e., Hiram of Tyre, *ḥi-rām.* Heb. has *a* in the accented syllable whereas the cuneiform has *u.*

[22] As tribute he lists gold, silver, lead, iron, elephants' hides, ivory, colored garments, linen garments, blue and purple wool, maple, boxwood, royal treasure, lambs with dyed wool, birds with wings dyed blue, horses, mules, cattle, sheep, camels, female camels with their young (*ATAT,* I, 346; *ANET,* p. 283a).

[23] The translation of AV is incorrect, for it gives the impression that two different people are involved. See Thiele, *op. cit.,* pp. 76, 77.

[24] A table is given in Thiele, *op. cit.,* p. 77.

[25] Noth calls these "the free landowners in his State who were liable to military service" (*die heerbannpflichtigen freien Grundbesitzer in seinem Staate). History of Israel,* E.T. (London: 1958), p. 258; original edition (Göttingen: 1954), p. 233.

12

so maintained.[26] Uzziah was the head of a strong state, and it is somewhat difficult to assume that at such a time there would be another man with an identical name ruling over another kingdom with an identical name. If the reference is to the Biblical Uzziah, he would then be one of the leading figures of the time and a rallying point for opposition to Assyria. On the other hand, if Azriyau and Uzziah are the same person, why is there no immediate retribution on the part of Assyria? Would the death of Uzziah cause Assyria to leave Judah alone?

Many scholars believe that this Azriyau was a Syrian usurper heading a kingdom in Syria. The chief reason for this is the location of the campaign. What would Uzziah of Judah be doing in northern Syria? Gordon even states that the Assyrian king restored the old Yaudi dynasty under King Panamuwa II.[27]

Albright, on the other hand, points out that *Ya-u-di* is the normal genitive of *Ya-u-du* which in Hebrew would have not been identified with the *y'dy*[28] of the Shamal inscriptions (*ya'-di-i/ya*).[29]

A fragment of text has now been published which deals with Tiglath-pileser's excursion into Armenia in 735 B.C.[30] The king mentions Mt. Sizir in Urartu. He went to attack the Urartian capital Turuspa on the eastern shore of Lake Van and set up his royal statue opposite the city. Into the mountain towns he settled foreign peoples, following the practice of his predecessor Tiglath-pileser I.

The king then mentions certain places further west along the Armenian Taurus even to Sarduri (Sardebar on the Tigris?). This district was placed under the eye of a new fort Assur-iqisa, and the whole area was put under the border of Assyria. Towns further to the west are now mentioned, and mountains are identified as boundaries. These towns are added to the district of the

---

26 Cf. Thiele, *op. cit.*, chap. 5; and *Journal of Near Eastern Studies*, III (1944), 155-63; Wm. F. Albright, "The Chronology of the Divided Monarchy of Israel," *BASOR*, No. 100, p. 18, n. 8, and George E. Wright, *Biblical Archaeology* (Philadelphia, London: 1957), pp. 160-61.

27 Gordon, *The World of the Old Testament* (New York, 1958), p. 228.

28 In Hebrew script, יאדי

29 Wm. F. Albright, "The Chronology of the Divided Monarchy of Israel," *BASOR*, No. 100, Dec. 1945, p. 18, n. 8.

30 Donald J. Wiseman, "A Fragmentary Inscription of Tiglath-pileser III From Nimrud," *Iraq*, XVIII, Part II (1956), 117-29.

rab-saqe, which is probably the Jabal Tur region northeast of Mardin and east of Tusham.[31]

The king then speaks of towns near the headwaters of the Tigris and of places between the Euphrates and Harran.[32] The obverse of the tablet closes with a list of tribute taken from Bit-Arpad. On the reverse the description is continued with the statement that as far as Mt. Saue territory was brought back within the borders of Assyria. Syria and Israel are also mentioned. "The broad land of the house of Hazael in its circuit from . . . to the land of the house of Omri I returned to the borders of Assyria."[33]

Mention is then made of Hiram of Tyre and Rezin of Damascus. According to the king they did obeisance and brought gifts to him. It may be that part of Israel was actually taken, for a recently published fragment seems to suggest this.[34] This fragment (lines 1-9) appears to deal with a coastal region. The reference seems to be to Arwad a "city in the middle of the sea." This identification is supported by mention of Simirra (opposite the Nahr el-Kebir) which had already been annexed by Tiglathpileser in his earlier campaign[35] and in which the king had placed a governor.

Beginning with line 10 this fragment refers to a location other than Phoenicia. Inasmuch as Israel elsewhere is said to be near to Kašpunna, it may be that the king is here speaking of Israel.[36]

---

[31] *Ibid.,* p. 127. Wiseman here discusses the text.

[32] I.e., province of the turtan. Among these are Ura, a caravan center, which Wiseman suggests may be identified with Urfa (*op. cit.,* p. 128).

[33] Wiseman, *op. cit.,* p. 125.

[34] Wiseman, "Two Historical Inscriptions from Nimrud," *Iraq,* XIII, Part I, Spring 1951, 21-26. [The text may be rendered, "on dry land . . . I caused to pour out, that city . . . in the midst (*qabal*) of the sea I trod them down and unto . . . (5) . . . fel)l on him and his heart failed, in sackcloth did he clothe himself . . . of willow wood set with stones of gold together with . . . ivory, fine oil, all kinds of spices, horses from the land of . . . *ah,* from the city of Kash-punna (*ka-aš-pu-na*) which is by the sea (*ah tam-tim*) . . . in the hands of my official the governor (*šakin*) of Si (mirra) (I entrusted)."]

[35] Cf. Albrecht Alt, *Kleine Schriften,* II √(München: 1953), 152.

[36] In writing these lines I have followed the interpretation of Alt, *op. cit.,* pp. 152ff. The text may be translated as follows: "Like (gr) ass (with) bodies of their warriors I filled (the plain) . . . their (pos) sessions, their cattle, their flocks, their asses . . . in the midst of (i.e., within) his palace . . . their (tri) bute I received (from) them and their land . . . ." The text is found in Wiseman, "Two Historical Inscriptions from Nimrud," *Iraq,* XIII, Part I, Spring 1951, 23.

Possibly the Israelite king (Pekah?) had come out either to the plain of Akko or of Sharon to try to halt the Assyrian king on his southern march. Tiglath-pileser, however, was not checked.

On a stone tablet mention is made of the city Abilakka at the entrance to the house of Omri.[37] Tiglath-pileser had conquered Gaza whose king Hanun had fled to Egypt (Musri), took its possessions and gods, placed his own statue ("the picture of my kingship") in the middle of Hanun's palace, counted it as one of the gods of the land and imposed tribute.

The fragment to which we have just referred adds information concerning the Gaza campaign.[38] It would appear that the sudden approach of Tiglath-pileser caused Hanun to flee. The surprising defeat of Israel left him with no time for preparations. Naturally, Tiglath-pileser would head for Gaza without bothering about the other Philistine cities.[39]

Hanun was permitted to return to Gaza and to serve as a vassal king, his name appearing later in a list of Syrian and Palestinian vassals.[40] From the new fragment we learn that Tiglath-pileser pushed on or at least sent his soldiers on to the brook of Egypt.[41] Here he placed a certain Idibi'ilu as overseer (*qepūti*). Thus he made it impossible for the Palestinian states to have contact with Egypt; he could keep an eye on the Egyptian military situation and also on trade, border conditions and Egyptian movements.[42]

In 733 B.C. Damascus took the lead in combined resistance against the Assyrians. At this time we are probably to place the

---

37 *TGI*, p. 53, line 6 of text. Cf. *Abel-bet-maachah*, I Kings 15:20.

38 The text may be translated as follows: ["Ha] nun of the city of Gaza (*Ha-az-za-ta-a-a*) before the weapons of my might (i.e., my mighty weapons) was terrified . . . (15) gold, 800 talents of silver, peoples together with their possessions, his wife, (his) sons . . . the image of the great gods my lords, the image of my kingship of gold (i.e., the golden image of my kingship, myself) . . . I placed and he (i.e., Hanun) out of Musri like a bird (fled) . . . of Asshur I counted. The image of my kingship (i.e., a stele of my royal person, tr. by Wiseman) in the city of Naḥalmuṣur (the River of Egypt) (I erected) . . . the silver I tore out and to the land of Assyria (I carried it back)."] The text is found in Wiseman, "Two Historical Inscriptions from Nimrud," *Iraq*, XIII, Part I, Spring 1951, 23.

39 Ashkelon appears to have been taken later, cf. Luckenbill, *op. cit.*, p. 159.

40 Cf. Alt., *op. cit.*, p. 159.

41 Naḥal Muṣur, modern Wadi el-'arîsh. Possibly he went to Rapiḥu (*Tell er-refaḥ*) which Sargon later mentions. Alt suggests that it may be Sheik Ezzuwaiyid *op. cit.*, p. 160, n. 2).

42 Cf. *TGI* p. 51, line 226 of inscription.

Syro-Ephraimitic war. A general statement is given in 2 Kings 15:37 that the Lord began to send Rezin and Pekah against Judah.[43] These incursions evidently started while Jotham was still alive. When Ahaz became sole ruler they continued,[44] but at this time the foes were unable to overcome him. The purpose of the Syrian-Ephraimitic coalition was to depose Ahaz, thus overthrowing the Davidic dynasty and to place upon the throne the son of Tabael.[45]

It is held by some upon the basis of investigations of Hosea 5:8-11 by the late Albrecht Alt that the two northern enemies at first made good progress.[46] At any rate, when Ahaz learned that the two had taken evil counsel against him, he was greatly afraid. It was one of the most crucial moments in the history of

[43] This would allow for incursions earlier than that of Isa. 7:1 and 2 Kings 16:5. Cf. SII, pp. 146-49.

[44] Cf. יעלה 2 Kings 16:5.

[45] Cf. Albright, "The Son of Tabael," *BASOR*, No. 140, Dec. 1955, pp. 34, 35. He makes a very plausible identification of this personage. A letter written before the fall of Damascus in 732 B.C. from the Assyrian archives at Calah (this letter is from the 1952 finds at Nimrud) mentions the land of *Ṭâb-'el* (*kurṬa-ab-i-la-a-ia*). This Aramaic name points to a location north of Ammon and Gilead. Hence, son of *Ṭâb-'el* refers to a prince of Judah whose material home was in the land of *Ṭâb-'el* in northeastern Palestine or southeastern Syria. (Cf. Absalom, whose mother was a princess of Geshur, also northeast, and Rehoboam, whose mother was an Ammonite princess). The son of *Tâb-'el* may have been a son of Uzziah or Jotham by a princess of *Tâb-el*. Albright thinks that the phrase may possibly mean "house of *Ṭâb-'el*" and gives the following examples to support his contention. Hadadezer ben Rehob means Hadadezer of Beth-Rehob; Ba'sa son of Ruhub is Baasha of Beth-Rehob; Shamgar son of Anath is Shamgar of Beth-Anath and Jehu son of Omri is Jehu of Beth Omri. Cf. Alt, "Menschen ohne Namen," *Archiv Orientâlni*, XVIII (1950), 22ff.

[46] Alt, *Kleine Schriften*, II, pp. 163-87. Alt's argument may be summed up as follows. Hosea is not speaking of the Assyrians, as Wellhausen and the older scholars thought, but of the Syro-Ephraimitic war. The order in which the towns are mentioned, namely, Gibeah (*Tell-el Full*), Ramah (*Er-Ram*), Bethel (*Beitin*), all three of which appear to belong to Benjamin, points to a foe coming not from the north but from the south. Normally, Gibeah and Ramah belonged to Judah. That Hosea here regards them as Israelitic shows that at this time Israel had advanced this far south and taken possession of them. Apparently he expected a reprisal on Judah's part.

Verse 10 seems to show that this reprisal has occurred and that Judah has not only taken back her own territory but has also taken some of Ephraim. Apparently only Samaria remains of the northern kingdom. In vv. 12-14 Ephraim and Judah appear side by side. Israel like Judah must now side with Assyria, for Hoshea, not Pekah, is on the throne.

the people of God, and Isaiah was sent to calm the fear of the troubled king, and to urge him to put his trust in the Lord. With hypocritical wickedness Ahaz rejected the offer of the prophet and turned for help to the nation which eventually would bring about the destruction of the theocracy. It was a sad picture in Judah's history. Ahaz sent his messengers to no less a person than Tiglath-pileser himself. Where the king was at that time, however, we are not told. The message was a servile one. Ahaz sent gold and silver from the house of the Lord as a present for the Assyrian (2 Kings 16:7-9). Apparently he needed no urging from Ahaz, but the message served as a pretext for Tiglath-pileser to turn on Syria and Israel. The Bible stresses the capture of Damascus and the death of Rezin (2 Kings 16:9). In the eponym list for 733-32 B.C. the king has the note, "against the land of Damascus."[47] Inasmuch as Syria was the leader, it receives the stress in Scripture.

Earlier, Tiglath-pileser had conquered Hamath, but now for the first time he subdues Israel as a state. In his annals of 734-33 B.C. he says with respect to Israel: "The house of Omri, all of whose cities I had reckoned to the territory of my land on my earlier campaigns . . . as prisoners [I] had carried away, and the city of Samaria alone I had left remaining [These would be the campaigns of 734 and 733 B.C., Pekah was overthrown in 732 B.C.]. Pekah, their king, they overthrew . . . like a rain-storm. . . ."[48] The text is broken, but the inscription goes on to say, "Prisoners . . . from a district of the house of Omri . . . I took." Other cities are then mentioned. The king states that Mitinti of Ashkelon saw the overthrow of Rezin and fell into insanity.[49] The Bible recounts the coming of the Assyrian king and his capture of several cities, particularly the districts of Gilead and Galilee. These were the places that had been grievously afflicted (Isa. 9:1) and had seen the great light. First to feel the weight of deportation, they too first saw the Light, for the Lord left Nazareth and went down to Capernaum to dwell there (Matt. 4:13). Galilee and Jezreel were formed into the province of Megiddo;[50] the Israelitish coastal plain became the province of Dor (i.e., El-burj

---

47 Luckenbill, *op. cit.*, II, 436.
48 *ATAT*, p. 347; *ANET*, p. 283b.
49 *Ibid.*
50 Cf. Alt, "Galiläische Probleme," *Palästinajahrbuch* (1937), pp. 65-76. This article has also been printed in *Kleine Schriften*, II, 363-435.

near Et-Tantura) and the Israelite territory east of the Jordan was formed into the province of Gilead.

At this time Hoshea the son of Elah conspired against Pekah and slew him, reigning in the twentieth year of Jotham (2 Kings 15:30). Hoshea paid tribute to Tiglath-pileser and was made a vassal king by him. On the Small Inscription No. 1 the king proclaims: "The land of the house of Omri . . . the entirety of its people [and] its possession I led away to Assyria. They overthrew Pekah their king and I placed Hoshea in the kingdom over them. Talents of gold and talents of silver I received as their booty."[51] And again: "I set Hoshea as king over them."[52]

Thus Tiglath-pileser became the actual master of Syria which now consisted of a series of Assyrian provinces. Even those who still remained outside these provinces paid tribute to the great king. Among those who thus did pay tribute the king lists Sipittibi'il of Byblos, Eniel of Hamath, Panammu of Sam'al, Uassurme of Tabal, Sanipu of the House of Aman, Salamanu of Moab, Mitinti of Ashkelon, Iauhazi (i.e., Ahaz of Judah), Qausmalaka of Edom, Hanun of Gaza.[53] This situation continued, as far as we know, until the death of Tiglath-pileser.

Tiglath-pileser was succeeded by Shalmanezer V. For the purpose of establishing relations with the king of Egypt, Tefnakhte, who was at So (i.e., Sais), Hoshea now withheld the annual tribute to the Assyrians and sent messengers to Egypt (2 Kings 17:3ff.). Doubtless Israel was acting in concert with other Palestinian and Syrian states, but there are no actual details extant. At any rate the Assyrians came and imprisoned Hoshea, then turning their attention to the city of Samaria. The rebellion of Hoshea is probably to be placed in the year 724 B.C. and the final fall of Samaria in 722-21 B.C.

At this point a particular problem must be considered. 2 Kings 17:3 definitely states that Shalmanezer came up against Hoshea. Verse 4 says that "the king of Assyria" (Shalmanezer) found conspiracy in Hoshea. Then (v. 5) the "king of Assyria" (Shalmanezer) besieged Samaria for three years. In the ninth year of Hoshea the "king of Assyria" took Samaria (v. 6). Who was

---

[51] *TGI*, p. 53.

[52] Wiseman, "A Fragmentary Inscription of Tiglath-pileser III from Nimrud," *Iraq*, XVIII, Part II (1956), 126. He gives the text *au-si-i' ina šarr)u-ú-ti ina eli-šu-n(u aškun*.

[53] *ATAT*, p. 348; *ANET*, p. 282a.

this king of Assyria that took Samaria? Sargon, king of Assyria (722-705 B.C.) claims that he conquered Samaria. His text is fragmentary, but we can read that in his first year a city, Sama (Samaria) was apparently conquered by him.[54]

Another reference to the conquest of Samaria is found in 2 Kings 18:9-11. Here again it is stated that in the seventh year of Hoshea Shalmanezer came up against Samaria and then (v. 10) at the end of three years "they took it." Then follows the statement that "the king of Assyria" carried Israel away to Assyria. From a natural reading of the Biblical account it would seem that Shalmanezer had been the leading figure in the conquest of Samaria, whereas Sargon states that he himself took the city. Which is correct?[55] According to the Assyrian evidence the fall of Samaria took place in the ninth year of Hoshea's reign, i.e., 722/21 B.C. If this is so, then Samaria must have fallen before Nisan 722 B.C., but Sargon came to the throne about nine months later, the twelfth of Tebet 722 B.C. Hence, Sargon could not have captured Samaria at the beginning of his reign, as he claims.

On the other hand it is quite possible that Sargon may have been present at the fall of Samaria as a general rather than as king. He may in that sense have captured the city, as he himself states. What can be conclusively asserted is that the Scriptural account which attributes the capture to Shalmanezer is true to fact.[56] This brought to an end the state of Israel, which was deported by the Assyrians and its inhabitants located in distant places (2 Kings 17:6). In turn Samaria and Israel were themselves peopled with those whom the Assyrians had conquered elsewhere: "They possessed Samaria, and dwelt in the cities thereof" (2 Kings 17:24). Thus, new customs, new ways of life, and new religions were brought into Israel. From this conglomerate group the Samaritans eventually emerged.

In 720 B.C. we learn of uprisings in Syria and Palestine. Hamath rebelled and was turned, after the rebellion had been put down, into the Assyrian province Hamath. About this time also Hanun of Gaza and Re'e of Egypt, whose identity is really not known, apparently engaged in uprisings. They came into battle

---

[54] *ATAT*, p. 348; *ANET*, p. 284a.

[55] The argument is well presented by Thiele, *op. cit.*, pp. 123ff.

[56] Cf. Mowinckel, *The Old Testament as Word of God* (New York, Nashville: 1959), p. 14. He puts the language of the Bible with respect to the fall of Samaria in a list of supposedly erroneous statements to be found in the Bible.

with the Assyrians at Rapihu; Hanun fell into his enemy's hands and Re'e had to flee. Thus, the state of Gaza came back into Assyrian power. Noth comments that this is the first encounter between the Assyrians and the Egyptians.[57]

Respecting the battle Sargon himself relates: "Sib'u fled alone like a shepherd, who had been robbed of his herds, and went away. I took Hanun prisoner and brought him in bonds to my city Asshur. I destroyed, laid waste and burned the city Rapihu. I carried away 9033 people together with their rich possessions."[58] Indeed, Sargon boasts of this conquest as something of which to be proud. In his Cylinder Inscription he claims that he destroyed the broad house of Omri, attacked the land of Egypt in Rapihu and brought Hanun, the king of Gaza, in bonds to Assyria.[59]

From this time on Israel ceases to be of significance to the history of redemption. We know very little about life in the province. From a cuneiform document found in the ruins of Samaria we have the title "chief of the cities" (rab alâni), the reference probably being to an individual who served the Assyrian king by overseeing the conditions of the cities. During the excavations at Gezer two legal documents in cuneiform were found which throw some light on the ethnic arrangement of the foreigners who formed the upper class (cf. also 2 Kings 17:24).

What, however, happened in Judah? Isaiah had told Ahaz that inasmuch as Ahaz had rejected the promised sign, God would bring against him the king of Assyria. And indeed Ahaz had been compelled to pay tribute (2 Chron. 28:20, 21). We learn that Tiglath-pileser distressed him, but strengthened him not. According to 2 Kings 16:10-18 Ahaz went to Damascus to meet the Assyrian king and there saw an altar a copy of which he had constructed for use in Jerusalem. This took the place of the old Solomonic altar of burnt offering.[60] We may note particularly that Ahaz turned aside "the king's entry without." This entrance signified that the king had authority over the sanctuary. With the removal, therefore, of the "entrance of the king" Ahaz made clear his complete dependence upon Assyria. All this was done, we are told, "for the king of Assyria." Ahaz sacrificed to the gods

---

57 Noth, *op. cit.*, p. 262.

58 *ATAT*, p. 349; *ANET*, p. 285a, b.

59 *ATAT*, pp. 349-50; *ANET*, p. 285b.

60 Ahaz' taking over of the Assyrian altar may have been in accordance with the terms of the treaty imposed upon him by Assyria. Cf. D. J. Wiseman, *Vassal Treaties of Esarhaddon* (London: 1958).

of Damascus: "The gods of Syria help the inhabitants of Syria," so he reasoned, "therefore, I will sacrifice to them that they may help me" (2 Chron. 28:23). Having rejected the only One who could help him, the king now yielded to the folly of Assyrian imposed idolatry and polytheism. Judah, in other words, now had to become like other territories that were under Assyria. Together with the worship of Yahweh, the cult of the Assyrians was to be exercised in the temple. Indeed, it had to supplant the worship of the true God. But these gods did not help, for ". . . they were the ruin of him and of all Israel" (2 Chron. 28: 23). Thus Judah continued, weak and dependent upon Assyria, the result of the short-sighted and faithless policy of Ahaz, until finally there came upon the throne a man that did right in the sight of the Lord, even Hezekiah. In his days, Judah finally rebelled against the foreign yoke which Ahaz' hypocrisy had imposed.

Outline

I. THE CRISIS AND THE MESSIAH (1:1—12:6)

  A. Introduction to the Entire Prophecy (1:1—1:31)
    1. Judah's Sinful Condition (1:1-9)
      a. The prologue (1:1-3)
      b. The condition of the nation (1:4-9)
    2. God's Judgment upon Judah (1:10-31)
      a. Judah's hypocritical worship (1:10-17)
      b. An appeal to repentance (1:18-23)
      c. The announcement of coming judgment (1:24-31)

  B. Early Messages of Isaiah (2:1—5:30)
    1. God's Blessing and Judgment (2:1-22)
      a. A glorious future for God's people (2:1-4)
      b. Judah's present corruption (2:5-11)
      c. The Day of the Lord (2:12-22)
    2. Judah's Punishment and Glory (3:1—4:6)
      a. The removal of order (3:1-7)
      b. God pleads with fallen Judah (3:8-15)
      c. The women and their tragedy (3:16—4:1)
      d. The Sprout of the Lord (4:2-6)
    3. God and Judah (5:1-30)
      a. The parable of the vineyard (5:1-7)
      b. Analysis of Judah's sins (5:8-23)
      c. The judgment of abandonment (5:24-30)

  C. Judah's True Hope: The Messianic King (6:1—12:6)
    1. Isaiah's Vision of the Holy God (6:1-13)
      a. The vision itself (6:1-7)
      b. The mission of Isaiah the prophet (6:8-13)
    2. The Crisis and the Promise (7:1-25)
      a. Ahaz the fearful (7:1-9)
      b. The Lord's sign (7:10-17)
      c. The coming desolation (7:18-25)

3. The Assyrian Invader (8:1—9:7)
   a. Maher-Shalal-Hash-Baz (8:1-10)
   b. Confidence in God (8:11—9:1)
   c. The Messianic King (9:2-7)

4. The Threat of Assyria (9:8—10:34)
   a. The approaching destruction (9:8-17)
   b. The punishment (9:18—10:4)
   c. The boasting of Assyria (10:5-19)
   d. The deliverance by the Lord (10:20-34)

5. Judah's Hope in the Messiah (11:1—12:6)
   a. The shoot of Jesse (11:1-5)
   b. The coming peace (11:6-10)
   c. The future of Israel (11:11-16)
   d. A victorious song of praise (12:1-6)

II. THE THEOCRACY AND THE NATIONS (13:1—39:8)

A. JUDAH AND THE WORLD POWER (13:1—27:13)

1. The Growth of the Mesopotamian Power (13:1—14:32)
   a. The judgment will come (13:1-8)
   b. The outpouring of judgment (13:9-22)
   c. The fall of the Babylonian king (14:1-11)
   d. The end of the boastful king (14:12-21)
   e. The destruction of Babylon, Assyria, and Philistia (14:22-32)

2. The Downfall of Moab, Syria, and Other Nations (15:1—18:7)
   a. The oracle of Moab (15:1-9)
   b. Moab's suffering (16:1-14)
   c. Judgment over Syria (17:1-14)
   d. Distant effect of judgment (18:1-7)

Text and Commentary

1. The Crisis and the Messiah (1:1—12:6)

A. INTRODUCTION TO THE ENTIRE PROPHECY (1:1 — 1:31)

1. Judah's Sinful Condition (1:1-9)

a. *The prologue* (1:1-3)

1 The vision of Isaiah, the son of Amoz, which he saw concerning Judah and Jerusalem in the days of Uzziah, Jotham, Ahaz, Hezekiah, kings of Judah.

2 Hear, O heaven, and give ear, O earth; for the LORD speaketh, Sons have I reared and brought up, and they have transgressed against me.

3 The ox knoweth his owner, and the ass the crib of his master: Israel doth not know; my people doth not consider.

1 The first chapter is an introduction to the entire book, containing the basic themes of Isaiah's ministry, namely, the sinfulness of Judah and Jerusalem (vv. 3-8), the tender appeals of the LORD (vv. 16-19), the certainty of the coming judgment (vv. 24, 25, 29-31), and the blessedness of the salvation to come (vv. 26, 27). The heading over chapter 2 also supports the idea that chapter 1 is introductory to the entire book.

This verse is not a heading to the first chapter only, but to the entire collection of Isaiah's prophecies.[1] The mention of the four kings, whose combined reigns coincided with the entire period of Isaiah's ministry supports this interpretation (cf. Mic. 1:1; and Hos. 1:1). On the other hand, a heading such as Ezekiel 1:1 seems designed to introduce only the message following. Many scholars think that the title was added by editors or re-

---

[1] Ibn Ezra, Luzzatto, *et al.*, regarded the verse as a heading only for the first chapter and, to avoid applying the prophecy to the four reigns, rendered it as, "vision of Isaiah who saw, etc." This is grammatically possible but not natural. In 2:1 this rendering would be impossible.

27

dactors late in Israel's history after the exile. But Calvin suggested that after delivering his messages orally, the prophet would compose a written draft of them and post it on the gates of the Temple where all might become more familiar with it. This written draft would then have been taken by the priests, who preserved it for posterity, despite their ofttimes conflict with the prophets. They would have been the ones responsible for prefixing the title to the book.[2]

On the other hand it may be that Isaiah himself wrote the title after having delivered all his messages.[3] This verse is found in all the ancient manuscripts and versions. Furthermore, 2 Chronicles 32:32, although not quoting the entire verse, seems to have known the prophecy by its present title. The analogy of Jeremiah and Ezekiel would seem to indicate that the prophets themselves prepared and edited their own books. Indeed, the minor variations which appear among the different headings of the prophetical books do not point to a stereotyped stamp of an editor or redactor, but suggest an independency of procedure which could well be due to the individualism of the prophets themselves. If it does not actually come from the hand of Isaiah, it comes from very near his time.

Why, however, does the title limit the messages to Judah and Jerusalem when as a matter of fact Isaiah dealt so considerably with Ephraim and also with the heathen nations?[4] It was not

---

[2] Calvin's suggestion would explain the desultory character of the arrangement of some of the prophetical material and would also allow for the fact that the prophet might have uttered some of his messages many times, preserving for posterity what was essential for it to know, and what God desired posterity to have. Calvin's suggestion has more to commend it than Gunkel's view that the prophets were only interested in the spoken word and not in a written message (cf. *SAT*, 2. *Abteilung*, 2. *Band*, pp. xxxvi-lxxii; and *SII*, pp. 75ff.).

[3] If chaps. 40-66 were composed after Isaiah had retired from active life, the title might have been written at that time also. It is possible that Isaiah wrote the title together with his entire first chapter when he withdrew from active labors after Sennacherib had left the land.

[4] It has been held that v. 1 is a heading only for the first 12 chaps. Inasmuch as chaps. 13 and 14 have to do with Babylon, it is argued that they would not be adequately covered by the title. It should be noted, however, that even in chaps. 13 and 14 there are indirect references to Judah (e.g., 14:1,2,32). On the other hand, references to Samaria are found in 9:7-10:4, and if the words of the title, Judah and Jerusalem, are to be pressed, we should not expect treatments in chaps. 1-12 of other places or countries.

The following are the headings which are used for one oracle or for a small collection of oracles.

Isaiah's purpose to include in his heading all of the subject with which he intends to deal. As has often been pointed out, the title is an illustration of the principle, *a proximo fit denominatio*. Isaiah's purpose is to deal with the histories and destinies of Judah and Jerusalem, the elect people, the kingdom of God; and foreign nations, even the ten tribes, are considered only in so far as they develop the principal theme. If this were not the case, one might wonder why a supposed redactor would have inserted the present heading over the entire prophecy or even over the chapters 1-39.[5]

Calvin well illustrates the true force of the heading by calling attention to the ministry of Peter and Paul. Peter was the apostle to the Jews, but he did not go beyond his proper office in preaching to Cornelius (Acts 10:17; Gal. 2:8). Paul was the apostle to the Gentiles, but he also quite appropriately preached to the Jews (Acts 13:5; 14:1; 17:2; 18:4, 19). Likewise, Isaiah's main mission was to Judah, but he did not transgress his right limits when he prophesied to and about other nations.

2:1 "The word which Isaiah the son of Amoz saw concerning Judah and Jerusalem."

13:1 "The burden of Babylon which Isaiah the son of Amoz saw." (Only the subject of the burden is mentioned.)

14:28 "In the year of the death of King Ahaz was this burden."

15:1 "The burden of Moab."

17:1 "The burden of Damascus."

19:1 "The burden of Egypt."

21:1 "The burden of the wilderness of the sea."

21:11 "The burden of Dumah."

21:13 "The burden against Arabia."

22:1 "The burden of the valley of vision."

23:1 "The burden of Tyre."

All the above are particular messages, the title clearly indicating the principal subject matter. Inasmuch as the name of Isaiah is mentioned with the first burden (13:1) there is no need to repeat it in the nine subsequent titles.

38:9 "The letter of Hezekiah king of Judah." This heading applies only to the following vv., 10-20. Outside the book of Isa. we may note Ezek. 1:1 which applies only to particular visions, i.e., chaps. 1-3. Similarly Jonah 1:1; 3:1; Hab. 1:1; 3:1. Wherever a title has reference only to an individual oracle or section of the book, this appears to be clear from the title itself. On the other hand, headings which apply to the entire book, such as Hos. 1:1; Amos 1:1; Mic. 1:1 and Zeph. 1:1 are similar in form to Isa. 1:1.

5 Mic. 1:1 does not oppose this interpretation. Micah announces the destruction of Samaria (Mic. 1:6) and links her sins with those of Judah. Hence, Samaria is included in his title. This, however, is quite different from the situation prevailing in Isaiah.

The vision — The word *hazon* indicates specific visions (e.g., Isa. 29:7; Hos. 12:10; Hab. 2:2; 1 Chron. 17:15, etc.) and also revelation in general (e.g., 1 Sam. 3:1; Ezek. 7:26; 12:22, 23; Prov. 29:18, etc.). Here it has a collective force, for it includes a number of visions or revelations. It is the equivalent of the phrase "the words of," found in other headings.[6]

The word does not refer to inward sight or perception, nor is it a metaphorical name for the prophet's own insight, intuition or mental perception. It signifies rather the "sight" of what God had placed in the prophet's mind or had revealed to him. It here denotes all that is given in writing in the book before us, and thus clearly attests the supernatural origin of the entire prophecy. It is not human opinions or reasonings or the cogitations of Isaiah's own mind which are here presented, but a special revelation of God to Isaiah which in some sense inexplicable to us was "seen" by him.

of Isaiah — The genitive probably has possessive force, for it was truly a vision which belonged to the prophet. We are not to think that the vision of God had become flesh in Isaiah and therefore was subject to the fallibility and error which accompanies everything human. Rather, in His mysterious providential working, God prepared just this man to write just this prophecy, and revealed the prophecy to him. This "holy man of old" was borne of the Holy Spirit so that his words were "God-breathed" words. Thus, the vision is the revelation of God and at the same time the writing of Isaiah. How this could be, man cannot explain, for God has revealed very little as to the mode of prophetic inspiration, but what has just been stated is supported by the Biblical evidence.

the son of Amoz — This Amoz is not the prophet.[7] Kimchi says that he does not know from what tribe the prophet was, but

---

[6] In 1 Chron. 17:15 it stands as a parallel to "words" (cf. Amos 1:1; Hab. 1:1). חזון introduces an entire collection of oracles; it is actually an abstract and so does not form a pl. (Note, however, *hazôt* in 2 Chron. 9:29 and the Aramaic pl. in Dan. 7:1). The word is therefore to be taken as a collective (cf. Hos. 12:11). Marti's rendering, "the divine revelation concerning the end of time," is not correct.

[7] This identification was made by some of the church fathers who did not know Hebrew (cf. Clement, *Stromata*, 1:21; Pseudo-Epiphanius, *De Vitis Prophetarum* on Amos. Also Yahya, *Shalshelet hak-kabbalah* 99b). An inscription found on an ancient seal reads "Amoz the scribe" (*'mtz h[š]fr*). It is tempting to see here a reference to Isaiah's father, but caution is in order (cf. Diringer,

remarks that "our rabbis" identified Amoz as the brother of Amaziah, the father of Uzziah.[8] Such an identification would make Isaiah of royal lineage and a cousin of Uzziah, and it is true that Isaiah did have access to the king. Whether or not he was actually of royal lineage, there is something royal in his nature and bearing. Like Solomon among the kings, so he among the prophets towers in grandeur.

saw — Although *hazah* (to see) may be used of physical sight, it is generally employed of an inner sight, and here means, "he saw by revelation."[9] Such a revelation may be a vision in the narrower sense, but it may also be more general. In this latter sense it is employed of the seeing of words (Amos 1:1) and of a burden (cf. Hab. 1:1). The verb comprehends within itself a whole series of acts. The vision was not something which Isaiah saw at once in its entirety, but which he beheld in a number of revelations. He *saw* it over the reigns of four kings, and not all at one time.

Judah and Jerusalem — Herntrich takes the designation as not geographical, but as merely referring to the elect people. It is true of course that the prophecy does refer to the elect people, but in this specific heading it is Judah and Jerusalem as geographical entities which are in the fore.[10] This is shown by a

---

Le Iscrizioni Antico-Ebraiche Palestinesi [Firenze: 1934], p. 235; and Anderson, *JBL*, March, 1960, p. 58).

8 Cf. *Sota* 10b; *Megilla* 15a asserts that when the father's name is given, it is to show that the father also was a prophet (cf. also *Aggadat Bereshith* 14:32; *Midrash, Wayyiqra Rabba* 6:6). Basil says that the father's name is added to show that the paternal gift of prophecy is his. This is, of course, mere assumption.

9 See *MSTP*, pp. 61-65, for the relation between *rā'āh* and *hāzāh*.

10 The objection has been made that Isaiah always wrote "Jerusalem and Judah" and not "Judah and Jerusalem." 2:1 is denied to Isaiah. Five times (3:1, 8; 5:3; 22:21; 44:26 — note also 2 Kings 24:20; Ezra 2:1) we have "Jerusalem and Judah," (but the Greek of 3:1 and 5:3 reads "Judah and Jerusalem" in all mss.). In each of these instances Jerusalem is mentioned first because it is more prominent and must be emphasized. Thus, in 44:26 the building of Jerusalem is more important than that of the cities of Judah, and so Jerusalem is mentioned first. In a heading, however, the order "Judah and Jerusalem" is more suitable. The conjunction is the *waw* augmentum which emphasizes something included in the first term but not co-extensive with that first term (cf. Num. 31:6; Josh. 9:27). Isaiah's vision has to do with Judah generally, but in particular with Jerusalem (cf. also 2 Chron. 34:3, 5, 29; 35:24 and 36: 4, 10).

There is no fixed rigidity in the order of designation. Zion, for example, is

passage such as 5:3, "And now, O inhabitants of Jerusalem, and men of Judah, judge, I pray you, betwixt me and my vineyard."

Jerusalem was the capital city of the southern kingdom, Judah. Isaiah also calls it Ariel (29:1) and the city of righteousness (1:26). The connecting conjunction *waw* may be rendered as, "and specifically." It is thus Judah and in particular Jerusalem which form the principal and real subject of the prophet's message. During the course of the prophecy the mention of Judah fades more and more into the background, and Jerusalem stands alone.[11]

in the days of Uzziah, Jotham, Ahaz, Hezekiah — The specific temporal reference does not imply that the prophecy pertained only to a local situation. The vision was the truth of God; and although delivered at a particular time and under particular circumstances the vision was the Word of God that liveth and abideth forever. The phrase "in the days of" is roughly equivalent to our "during the reign of." The reigns of Uzziah, Jotham, Ahaz and Hezekiah[12] covered a total of 81 years (767-686 B.C.). Isaiah's ministry began in the year of the death of Uzziah, 739 B.C., and continued until some time in the reign of Hezekiah, his last public act possibly being in the year of the visit of the Babylonian envoys.[13]

After this time the prophet may have gone into retirement and composed the last 27 chapters of his book. If during this period he engaged in some public preaching, there is no record of the fact. It may be that during the co-regency between Manasseh and Hezekiah the close relationship which had existed and con-

---

usually mentioned before Jerusalem, but cf. 37:22 with 52:2. In 52:1, however, the order Zion-Jerusalem is found. Hence, the order Judah-Jerusalem is no argument against Isaianic authorship.

[11] Jerusalem is mentioned 47 times whereas Judah is mentioned only 25 times. In chaps. 1-39 Jerusalem is mentioned 29 times, in chaps. 49-55, 9 times and in chaps. 56-66, 9 times. Judah appears 22 times in chaps. 1-39 and elsewhere only in 40:9; 44:26 and 48:1.

[12] The proper names are unconnected (cf. Hos. 1:1; Mic. 1:1). When the language bears the character of enumeration (as here), a list of proper names may be used without the conjunction (e.g., 1 Chron. 1:1-4). In Gen. 14:9 the conjunction appears three times. In 14:1 with the same names it is found but once. In 14:8 it appears four times, but in 14:2 three times.

[13] According to 2 Chron. 26:22 Isaiah wrote a history of the reign of Uzziah, but this does not imply that he carried on his ministry during the entire reign of that king.

tinued between Hezekiah and Isaiah became a source of irritation to Manasseh, with the result that after Hezekiah's death, this irritation may have found expression in Isaiah's martyrdom.[14]

kings of Judah — This phrase identifies the four kings for future readers.[15] The practice of identifying the country over which one ruled was common. For example, Sennacherib designated himself "king of Assyria." This practice was followed not only by the kings of Assyria, Babylon, Egypt and the Hittites, but even today is employed by rulers in their official documents and pronouncements.

2 *Hear, O heavens, and give ear, O earth* — Isaiah begins with a majestic appeal with striking force which Rosenmüller has aptly called, *Magnificum et grave exordium!* The first two words in Hebrew begin with *sh* and *m*, and between the two there is a similarity of sound: *shim'u shamayim.* The next two (at least as far as the root is concerned) also exhibit alliteration: *haazini eretz.*[16]

---

14 2 Chron. 32:32 suggests that Isaiah may have outlived Hezekiah. If so, his ministry would have lasted 53 years at least. The last dated event is the 14th year of Hezekiah (701 B.C.) in 36:1, but Sennacherib's successor, Esarhaddon, is also mentioned. Jewish tradition asserts that Isaiah was put to death during the reign of Manasseh (*Yebamoth* 49b, *Sanhedrin,* 103b.; cf. also 2 Kings 21:16). Some of the church fathers thought that there was an allusion to this in Heb. 11:37.

In the light of 37:38 it may be that Isaiah's ministry did continue into the reign of Manasseh. This would not necessitate the name of Manasseh in the title (1:1) for Isaiah had retired from public life and may have been engaged in writing, and also for nine years Manasseh was a co-regent with Hezekiah.

15 עֻזִּיָּהוּ occurs both in 1:1 and 6:1. The shorter form is found in the headings of Hosea and Amos. This shows that the headings were not stereotyped in nature. יְחִזְקִיָּהוּ occurs frequently in Chronicles, but also in 2 Kings 20:10 and Jer. 15:4. This fuller name well befits the solemn and diplomatic character of the title (cf. Introduction). König objects that the phrase "kings of Judah" would not have been necessary after the fall of Judah. If, however, Isaiah as a prophet was writing with the expectation that his message would be preserved, it is natural that he would insert this explanatory word for the benefit of future generations. In the excavations at Elath a signet ring was discovered, bearing the inscription, "To Jotham." Cf. *BASOR,* No. 163, Oct. 1961, pp. 18-22.

16 An imper. with *waw* conjunctive may follow another imper. as here, for the sake of giving greater emphasis to the command by the introduction of a parallel thought (cf. also Deut. 4:9; Amos 5:15). In 1Q and in some Greek mss. the article appears with the word earth. In Heb., however, the article is not necessary to express the vocative (cf. *GKC,* # 126e and Isa. 23:16; 49:13 where it is also omitted in 1Q).

The address begins in the style of Deuteronomy 32:1, "Give ear, ye heavens, and I will speak, and hear, O earth, the words of my mouth." Moses had already summoned the nation ". . . that I might cause to witness against them the heaven and the earth" (Deut. 31:28, 29). Moses was soon to die, and the time would come when the people would turn aside from the way which he had caused them to see. Heaven and earth would long outlast the sinful people, however, and for that reason they are invoked to bear witness against it.

The book of Deuteronomy is a summary of the previous Mosaic legislation, and Moses' song is a summary of Moses' last discourse in Deuteronomy.[17] Delitzsch asserted that with respect to other prophecy it sustained that position which the Ten Commandments occupy to other laws, and the Lord's Prayer to other prayers. The song deals with the greatness of God and His choosing Israel to be His people, Israel's faithlessness and rebellion, and God's sovereignty over Israel and all nations.[18] Thus, in summary fashion, it contains the theme of Old Testament prophecy generally.

When in such conscious dependence upon Moses' song Isaiah thus begins his prophecy, he serves to call attention to the exalted position which Moses held as the human founder of the Old Testament economy (Num. 12:1-8). Moses was a servant, faithful in all God's house, and one who stood above the prophets in the Old Testament dispensation. His true antitype was Christ (Heb. 3:1-6). Midway between them stood the evangelical prophet, Isaiah, who pointed forward to the Messianic office of Jesus and yet began his work with deliberate reflection upon the discourse of Moses. Isaiah is thus a prophet under Moses, belonging to that Mosaic age or dispensation which was a witness of "things to be spoken of," even Jesus.

Isaiah faced a rebellious and apostate nation. Since the time of the schism under Jeroboam calamity and defeat had befallen the people, but neither these nor yet the prosperity of Uzziah's

---

[17] A recent and valuable introduction to Deuteronomy is G. T. Manley, *The Book of the Law* (Grand Rapids: 1957).

[18] The song may be analyzed as follows: Moses appeals to heaven and earth, for he will speak words of truth and glorify God (vv. 1-6); he appeals to the great acts of God in former times, particularly to the election and exaltation of Jacob (vv. 7-14); despite all that God had done for her, Israel rebelled, and became idolatrous (vv. 15-52). The remainder of the song deals with a further statement of Israel's sin and of the sureness of God's punishing judgment.

reign had led to repentance. Inasmuch as men are "bereft of their senses" (Calvin), the prophet invokes elements of the creation which are without feeling, namely, heaven and earth.[19] When insensate objects are commanded to witness a condemnation of sensible creatures, the guilt of the latter must truly be great.

To these elements the prophet appeals, not merely as hearers, but as actual witnesses.[20] Inasmuch as Isaiah is so deliberately reflecting upon the language of Deuteronomy, the same reason for the appeal is to be expected in the present passage. The two words, heaven and earth, call to mind Genesis 1:1, and point to the entire creation. Such an appeal shows the significance and importance of the message, and also shows that the LORD who speaks, namely, Yahweh, the covenant God of Israel, was no mere local, tribal deity, but the God who could command attention from all creation. He alone, the God of Israel, had the right to order all creation, for He Himself had brought it into existence.

In Deuteronomy 4:36 God spoke from *heaven* to instruct the nation, and on *earth* Israel had seen the fire from which His words had been heard. When in grace He formed Israel into a nation, the heavens and earth had been present as witnesses. They were also summoned to be witnesses of the fact that God will remove the nation from its land (Deut. 4:26). They were again called upon to witness that a choice of blessing and cursing had been set before the people (Deut. 30:19). These were witnesses that had been present throughout Israel's history; to them the LORD appeals now that the corruption of the nation must be brought to light and her punishment meted out.

Ewald had entitled this chapter "The Great Arraignment," and G. A. Smith described it as a trial at law, a crown case in which God appears as judge and plaintiff with Judah the defendant, and the heaven and earth as assessors. This does not do justice to the Scriptural data, however, for Judah and God are not presented as equals appearing in court, nor does the passage teach that God will abide by whatever verdict heaven and earth may render. For that matter it does not teach that

---

19 For the conjunction of the two verbal roots in Isaiah, cf. 1:2, 10; 28:23; 32:9; 64:3 (cf. also 42:23).

20 Cf. Virgil, *Aeneid*, xii. 176: *esto nunc sol testis et haec mihi terra vocanti;* and Livy, i.32; iii.25. König thinks that the elements are intended to serve merely as an audience (cf. 1 Kings 22:28).

these bodies are to render a verdict at all. The appeal to them is simply for the sake of man. If the insensate planets can be appealed to as witnesses of the sinfulness of men, how great is that sinfulness! It may also be that the unfeeling elements are thus indirectly regarded as more faithful than Israel.

We cannot accept that interpretation which assumes that behind the appeal lay an old polytheistic background, as though there were a god of heaven and one of the abyss. This is opposed among other things by the Biblical representation of the created universe as being in sympathy with the welfare of mankind (e.g., Job 16:18, 19; Jer. 2:12 and Amos 8:8). Furthermore, the prophet does not summon any inhabitants (gods or angels) of heaven and earth, but merely the creation itself as personified.[21]

for the Lord — These words give the reason for the command: the message is not of human origination, but comes from God.[22] Isaiah uses the covenant name, rather than the more general name Elohim (cf. Gen. 1:1) and thus shows that the LORD who at Sinai had formed Israel into the theocracy is the God of creation and can command the heaven and earth to do His bidding.

It is a solemn command, and since the LORD speaks, heaven and earth must reverently listen. "Be astonished, O ye heavens, at this, and be horribly afraid, be ye very desolate, saith the LORD" (Jer. 2:12). This verse contains a command which was also uttered because of the sinful condition of the nation. For

---

[21] Cf. *KUB*, 120. This is a Hittite text which begins with an appeal to the gods in heaven and those in the dark earth to listen. Appeal is then made to individual gods. Then the narrative suddenly begins, "Once in the days of old Alalus was king in heaven" (cf. *ANET*, p. 120a). There are no traces of a polytheistic conception of nature in Isaiah's appeal (Wright, *Biblical Archaeology*, p. 105). It may be that the appeal to heaven and earth was intended to set the framework of the covenant. The Hittite suzerainty treaties began with an appeal to the elements. This same framework is found in Deut. when the sovereign God approaches the people to give to them His covenant. The value of these formal similarities with Scripture is that they tend to support the early date of Deut. Also, if Isaiah is consciously reflecting upon Deut. 31:28, we have a good argument for the priority of Deuteronomy (cf. Huffmon, "The Covenant Lawsuit in the Prophets," *JBL*, December, 1959, Part IV, pp. 285-95; Kline, *Treaty of the Great King*, Grand Rapids, 1963).

[22] Each of the four sections of chapter 1 begins with the LORD speaking (vv. 2, 10, 18, 24) and in the first two sections the prophet uses the imperative "hear," to call attention to the Lord's speaking.

that reason, it offers a clue as to how heaven and earth are to listen.[23]

speaketh — The introductory word *ki*, "for," calls attention to the dignity of the speech of the LORD. The insertion of the subject before the verb lends a certain emphasis: It is the LORD who speaks. In the common English versions the verb is rendered by the past, "hath spoken"; but although God had already spoken to the prophet by means of vision, He also is speaking through Isaiah as the prophet summons heaven and earth to witness.[24] The choice of *dibber* (to speak) instead of *amar* (to say) was doubtless deliberate for the sake of avoiding a familiar word in a somewhat stereotyped expression. *Dibber* probably therefore has a certain amount of emphasis which would have been lost had *amar* been used.

To listen to Isaiah in his capacity of prophet is to listen to God, for the words which he utters have been received supernaturally and are of supernatural origin. We must reject as untrue to the Scriptural phenomena the view of Duhm and others wherein distinction is made between what the prophet in ecstasy supposedly received from God and what he presented as his own.

What a remarkable announcement the prophet makes! The LORD, who has identified Himself as the God of His people Israel, is speaking. The reference is not to general revelation but to the actual words which follow. The revelation is propositional, for it consists of information which God is communicating. The words are themselves revelation; they are the Word which God gives to His people.

Sons — With this word the divine message begins. Verses 2b and 3 are a summary of the first chapter. Not only is God the creator of heaven and earth but He is also the "creator" of His people (cf. Isa. 43:1, 15). Isaiah immediately introduces the concept of the LORD's fatherhood over His chosen people.[25] To assume that the concept of God's fatherhood is restricted to the New Testament is to betray an ignorance of the facts. Duhm claims that the concept of fatherhood was common to nearly

---

[23] This verse seems to be a conscious reflection upon Isaiah's command. Note the alliteration: שְׁמוּ שָׁמַיִם *šommû šāmayim*.

[24] We may paraphrase: "The Lord has once spoken to me and now speaks through me."

[25] The first explicit occurrence of this concept in the Bible is in Exod. 4:22. Cf. also Deut. 1:31; 8:5; 32:6 (upon which the present passage may reflect); Isa. 63:16; Jer. 3:19; Hos. 11:1 and Mal. 1:6.

all the ancient religions and makes appeal to Numbers 21:29 and Jeremiah 2:27. Between the common view of the ancient world and the present passage, however, there exists not even a formal similarity, for the sonship herein mentioned is based upon the covenant between the LORD and Israel which was formed at Sinai, and to this covenant idea there is no real parallel in the ancient world, although there are examples of covenants.[26] Upon the basis of the covenant made with the patriarchs, "I am the God of thy father" (Exod. 3:6), God established Israel into a nation at Sinai. Israel was to be a peculiar nation in that it stood in relation to the LORD as sons to a father, a relationship which applied to the individual as well as to the nation as a whole. In this unique relationship we see the tender affection of the LORD to His people which is a preparation for the New Testament doctrine of the love of God. The act of adoption was one of God's free grace (cf. Jer. 2:2; Ezek. 16:4ff.; Hos. 9:10).

The word *sons* is placed in an emphatic position before the verb because it expresses the grace of God manifested at its highest point. It may therefore be rendered children as in Genesis 3:16 and Joshua 17:2. The nation's rebellion thus appears in a more striking light and in more hateful colors. How base is the sin of ingratitude shown to be! Lycurgus is said to have been unwilling to make any law against ingratitude, because he thought that no one would be base enough to be guilty of it. The inspired Scripture paints a more accurate picture of human nature.

reared and brought up — The first act in which God manifested His grace toward the people as a whole was the adoption by which Israel was constituted a nation of sons. The second act was the bringing up of these sons. Although they have practically the same meaning, the two words *giddalti* and *romamti* need not be regarded as precise synonyms.[27] The second is possibly a bit stronger than the first. With the first verb we recall the promise made to Abram, Genesis 12:2 (*goi gadol*); whereas the second stresses Israel's peculiar position in history.[28] Thus far, Isaiah

---

[26] Cf. Young, *The Study of Old Testament Theology Today* (London: 1958), pp. 61ff.

[27] The pret. with conjunctive *waw* here gives distinctness to almost equivalent expressions (cf. also 9:7; 41:4 and 44:8).

[28] גדל is "making great" with respect to natural growth (cf. 2 Kings 10:6; Isa. 23:4; 49:21; 51:18). רוממתי points to that high position toward which the tender and loving father gradually leads his child (cf. Isa. 23:4).

has used three verbs to designate the LORD's activity, and each of these is in the intensive stem.

When God chose Israel she was a small and insignificant people. From small beginnings He reared her and brought her to a position of eminence and exaltation, not merely by enlarging her numbers, but also by the special gifts which He gave to her, the law and the prophets, together with the whole course of special revelation which the theocracy received.

and they — The words are in the emphatic position in order to stress the contrast between the LORD's faithfulness and Judah's unfaithfulness. One might have expected an adversative particle, yet even the conjunctive *waw* (and) serves to render the pronoun prominent and emphatic, and thus to bring to the fore the distinction between the nation and God: "*I* have reared . . . and *they* have rebelled." The *waw* is thus not to be construed as adversative, but energetically as in Isaiah 6:7. The word *wehem* serves as a *casus pendens*, the force of which is as follows, "*and they* . . . they have transgressed." When thus set in contrast with the free grace of God in adopting the nation and bringing it to maturity, the transgression of the people stands out in bolder relief as the more heinous.

have transgressed — The word *pesha* belongs originally to the political sphere and signifies rebellion, the breaking of a legal relationship.[29] That legal reference is not absent here, for the break with God has been occasioned by transgression of His commandments. Israel constantly despised His salvation and broke His covenant. It is not a specific act but rather the general state of the people which is in view. The nation, having transgressed, is now in that state in which it must be denominated "transgressors." This inward departure manifested itself in outward acts of rebellion, apostasy and idolatry. The heinousness of the ingratitude lies not merely in the fact that a nation rejects God, but that a nation of *sons* (i.e., a nation which is made up of individuals who are sons) casts aside a loving father. Those who think that Israel had a genius for religion would do well to remember this verse.

against me — He who should have been the object of their filial love and devotion was rather the One against whom they rebelled. All sin, whether the sinner realizes it or no, is ultimately against God. "Against thee, thee only, have I sinned and

29 Cf. von Rad: *Theologie des Alten Testaments* (München: 1957), p. 262.

done this evil in thy sight" (Ps. 51:4a). Here shines through the tender love of God toward sinners. *"Against me"*: not against her rulers, not against enemy oppressors, but against Me, the One that has given her all she has, Israel has rebelled. The frightening contrast stands out: God has done everything necessary to make Israel a unique nation; Israel, however, has chosen to act like a nation which did not even know God.

3 In verse 2 the prophet has tacitly made a comparison between Israel and the inanimate creation, inasmuch as the appeal to heaven and earth implies that these are not transgressors like the nation. In the third verse the people's attitude is set over against that of dumb brutes. First there is a contrast between man and animals. At the creation man was placed over the animals (Gen. 1:28-30), a fact which is seen in Adam's naming them (Gen. 2:19, 20). In this act of classifying and categorizing Adam displayed an intelligence not possessed by the animals. Now, however, men who were endowed by God with intelligence do not exercise it, whereas the animals, not endowed with such an intelligence as man possesses, nevertheless act more intelligently than man. Next there is a contrast between the most enlightened of men, Israel, and two animals noted for their dullness (Prov. 7:22). Israel was most enlightened, not because she possessed greater intelligence than other peoples, but for the reason that unto her God's special revelation had been committed. If the ox and the ass act more wisely than Israel, Israel must be dull indeed. Thirdly, there is a contrast between animals that belong to a master, who uses them solely for his own advantage and is not primarily concerned over their welfare, and *sons* who have a tender and loving Father who has done everything for them, having adopted them when they were no people, and having blessed them with spiritual gifts throughout their entire history. Israel's guilt therefore is completely inexcusable.

The ox — The indefinite word (note omission of the definite article in the Hebrew) determines the category. We might paraphrase: "every ox, every ass knows." Neither the ox nor the ass was a particularly sagacious animal, but, on the contrary, dull and plodding, a fact brought out in an interesting manner in the "Tale of the Ox and the Ass" in the *Thousand and One Nights*.

knoweth — Here the thought is merely that the ox knows who it is that feeds and sustains him.[30] The perfect is employed because it expresses a general truth derived from experience and observation. "To know" (*yada*) is often used to express the relationship of the LORD to His people (cf. Amos 3:1ff.). God has known Israel in that He has set His affection upon her by choosing her to be His own.

its owner — The one who possesses it, having acquired it through purchase.

the ass — The common beast of burden of the Near East.

the crib — The place where its food is set. The context and not etymology must determine the meaning.

his master (lit., "his masters") — The plural does not designate a plurality of masters, but indicates ownership. It is a plural of intensity, and inasmuch as it is used of the master of possessions, may also be regarded as a plural of majesty. The animals return to the crib which belongs to their master.

Israel doth not know — It is not necessary to supply an object after the verb, the object being understood and corresponding to the words "owner" and "master's crib" of the preceding. The animals, which in antiquity were thought to belong to the household, (cf. Exod. 20:10, 17) possessed a knowledge which sons did not have (cf. Jer. 8:7). Israel does not know who her Creator and Preserver is. God manifested knowledge toward Israel when He set upon her His particular, discriminating, sovereign, electing love. In return Israel did not even have a knowledge comparable to that of the ox or ass. If the chosen people know so little, how great must be the ignorance of those who are not chosen. And how obvious it now is that all that Israel received in the way of spiritual blessing was a gift from God. Israel was the name given to Jacob when he wrestled with the angel and prevailed. In deep faith he had commanded, "Tell *me,* I pray thee, thy name" (Gen. 32:29a). That nation which now bears Israel's name does not know the God with whom he had once wrestled.

Israel's ignorance of the source of her life and sustenance was due to the fact that the individuals who had composed the nation had had their understanding darkened and consequently were alienated from the life of God (Eph. 4:18). The nation Israel, still acknowledged by God as His own, was like the unregenerated

---

30 Some objects of the word *knoweth* which have been suggested are: me (B), it (Luther, Duhm), him (Maurer), that (Nägelsbach). M is straightforward and forceful; the various deviations do not improve it.

Gentiles, in that she too was ignorant of God. The implication is that knowledge comes from God alone, and when an individual or nation is without God he has no knowledge but is in darkness and ignorance.

my people — Note the structure and arrangement of the verse. In the first line in Hebrew, the verbs are placed first, for Isaiah merely expresses a truism. In the second line, however, the subjects Israel and my people receive the emphasis by their position before the verbs. We may paraphrase: "As may be expected, the animals know their owner, but as for Israel, even my people, they do not know."

As at the beginning of chapter 40 so here the LORD exhibits a concern for His people. The designation my people (*ammi*) is a favorite with Isaiah, occurring some 23 times, 11 in chapters 1-39 and 12 in chapters 40-66.[31] God still calls the nation *my people* and *sons* to show that He has not cast it off. He is faithful to His covenant promises and is deeply concerned for the welfare of those whom He has chosen. In this expression and in the designation *banim* (sons) we have the first appearance of the "comfort ye my people" of chapter 40.

doth not consider — Does not engage in conscious reflection either upon its own true interests or upon its immense obligations. The animals which did not have the ability to consider, did at least know whence came their sustenance. Although endowed with capacities not possessed by the animals, Israel did not employ these divinely given capacities and so appears as less understanding than the beasts.

If it be asked how Israel could be the people of God and yet be so spiritually brutish, the answer is that election is of grace and not of works. Israel's sin would lead to separation from God; His grace would preserve her until His saving purposes had been accomplished.

b. The condition of the nation (1:4-9)

4 Alas! sinning nation, a people heavy with iniquity, a seed of evil-doers, children that are corrupters: they have forsaken the LORD; they have spurned the Holy One of Israel; they are estranged backward.

---

[31] It also occurs frequently in Jer. (28 times) and in Ezek. (20 times); in Hos. 8 times, in Joel 4, Amos 5, Mic. 9, Zeph. twice, Zech. twice, and Obad. once.

5 Why will ye be stricken any more, ye continue to revolt; the
  whole head is sick and the whole heart faint.
6 From the sole of the foot even unto the head there is no soundness in it; but wounds and stripes and fresh sores; they have not
  been pressed out neither bound up, nor mollified with oil.
7 Your land is desolate, your cities are burned with fire; as for
  your land, before you strangers are devouring it, and it is desolate, as an overthrow of strangers.
8 And the daughter of Zion is left like a booth in a vineyard, like a
  hut in a garden of cucumbers, like a blockaded city.
9 Except the LORD of Hosts had left us a very small remnant, we
  should have been as Sodom, we should have been like unto
  Gomorrah.

4 The prophecy began with an announcement of God's judgment over His people, expressed in words spoken by the LORD
Himself. In the present verse the prophet utters a cry of anguish
over the tragic moral condition of the nation. It must not be
thought, however, that whereas in verses 2b and 3 we have the
word of God, in verse 4 we have only the prophetic word of
Isaiah.[32] What Isaiah proclaims in verse 4 is as much the word
of God as are the words which appear in verses 2b and 3. Both
have been revealed to Isaiah: verses 2b and 3 in the form of quotation, and verses 4ff. in the form of normal prophetic utterance.
We must not, therefore, make too sharp a distinction between the
introductory words of God and the speech of the prophet. It
would be a mistake to assume that verses 4ff. merely represent
the convictions of the prophet which he speaks in his own right,
for these are also revealed words. Herein lies the wondrous mystery of prophetic inspiration; all the prophetic utterances were
divinely revealed, and yet, in the deliverance of the message the
personality of the prophet was preserved. It is in this light that
the following utterance is to be understood.

Alas — It is somewhat difficult to determine the precise force
of this exclamatory word. Many commentators (e.g., Marti,
Drechsler, Barnes) think that it expresses threat, lamentation or
execration as in 5:8, 11; 10:1; 31:1. In all probability, however,
it includes also the thought of pain, pity, wonder and deep abhorrence at the unbelievable ingratitude of the nation. The
verse introduces a general picture of the sad moral condition of

32 When Herntrich claims that the word before us is always witness (*Bezeug-
ung*) we cannot agree. The words uttered by the prophet are not witnesses
to God's Word; they are themselves His Word.

the nation which has resulted from the alienation from God mentioned in verse 2. Isaiah is a true evangelist, for a true evangelist must ever be grieved by sin and by the lost condition of the sinner to whom he speaks. Such grief flows from a true love for those who need his message. The condition of the nation brings forth upon Isaiah's part a cry of pity that things are as they are, a cry mixed with indignation against those who could so sin, together with wonder that men who had received so much from God could so easily turn against Him in forgetfulness. Words are not sufficient to express Isaiah's feelings; he must break forth into an agonizing cry.

The particle *hoi* (alas!) is found 21 times in the prophecy and only 28 times in the other prophets. Together with the following word *goi* (nation), it forms a paronomasia, although it is also to be construed grammatically with the following three nouns. This cry thus continues the complaint of the LORD which had been expressed in verses 2b and 3. Duhm thinks that Isaiah's words are more passionately spoken than are those of the LORD, whose words, he says, always possess a certain majestic calm. Such a distinction, however, is questionable, and it should be noted that even verses 2b and 3 reveal God as a loving Father who is deeply grieved over the base ingratitude of His people.

sinning nation — The active participle indicates constant and habitual sinning, and so presents a remarkable contrast between what Israel's destiny was intended to be and what the nation had actually become. The corruption pertains to the nation as such, and not merely to a part thereof. Each one of the appellations is accompanied by a statement of guilt.[33] The epithets show what Israel had actually become, and yet also point indirectly to what she had been intended by God to be. The moral state herein described was not only a result of the alienation mentioned in verses 2 and 3, but was also inseparable from that alienation. A frightening gradation appears in the epithets. Side by side with the first list: nation, people, seed, children; there is another: sinning, heavy with iniquity, evildoers, corrupters. Some commentators find in the word *goi* a touch of disdain or a designation of reproach. But probably no such reproach

---

[33] Keizer's pithy comment is to the point: "as many designations of guilt as there are names" (*zoovele benamingen, zoovele beschuldigingen*). חמא — a part. (cf. Amos 9:8). For a recent discussion of paronomasia in Hebrew see H. S. Nyberg, *Hebreisk Grammatik* (Uppsala: 1952), pp. 301ff.

is intended. The thought expressed is that of the Israelites brought together as a nation by a common descent and ancestry, a common language and country. It is a nation, looking back to Israel as its forefather, speaking the Hebrew language, living in Palestine and sharing a common heritage. Formally it gave expression to its religious belief in the worship of the LORD, who had formed it into a nation at Sinai. He had intended it to be a holy nation (Exod. 19:6).[34] Israel now constantly engages in the practice of sin; she regularly misses the mark intended for her by God. Calvin is correct in asserting that Isaiah charges the nation with abandoned wickedness.

a people heavy with iniquity — Iniquity is here regarded as a burden which the people must bear.[35] In accordance with the idea that the one who carries a burden is that much heavier himself, the weight which is carried is attributed to the people who carry the burden. Under the crushing weight of accumulated iniquities the whole nation is pictured as bowed and weighted down. The idea expressed in the word "heavy" (*kabed*) may be illustrated by the following passages which, although not all referring to iniquity, nevertheless show how the thought is to be understood (cf. Gen. 4:13; 12:10; Exod. 4:10; 18:18; Num. 11:14). Here the word *kabed* is used of the weight of guilt (cf. also Exod. 28:38, 43; Lev. 10:17).

How can iniquity rest heavily upon a person or nation? Iniquity itself is something intangible, and hence cannot be a burden in a physical sense. But iniquity brings evil results with it. The people had dealt iniquitously, and the fruits of their actions were now with them. More than that, iniquity involves guilt; indeed, the word signifies the perversity and crookedness of sin. Thus, it is not a sense of iniquity that weighs the nation down — would that it were — then there might be some desire for repentance. It is rather the bondage and guilt of their iniquity that lies upon the people like a pressing burden. From that guilt and bondage they cannot free themselves. They have not the strength — they are slaves.

a seed of evildoers — Is the word *zera* (seed) construct or absolute? According to Duhm, it is absolute, and stands as a

---

34 For a discussion of the significance of "holy" and "holiness," see chap. 6, n. 18.

35 The basic idea is, "a people, heavy (is) its iniquity." From this it would be a step to "heavy of iniquity."

parallel to *banim* (sons). He takes it as signifying seed, and not descendants. Gesenius likewise takes it in the sense of brood (as in Matt. 3:7), a brood consisting of evildoers (cf. Isa. 14:20; 31:2 and 65:23). It is, thinks Marti, the entire present generation, which, although not sinful in itself, has become so. On this construction *zera* stands in opposition to *mere°im*, (evildoers), a seed consisting of evildoers. It is true that *zera* designates the people as a unit, but it is also true that the word bears within itself the character of its origin, and this consideration would support the view that it is to be taken as a construct.

If, however, it is a construct, what is its force? It has been taken to mean a seed produced by evildoers. These evildoers could then be contemporaries, and the phrase would in that case mean a seed which was produced by the evil men who constitute it. It could also mean that the seed was descended from evildoers. This would not necessarily suggest that it was an illegitimate seed, descended from an evil line, but simply that the ancestors of the seed had themselves been evildoers. Nor would there necessarily be, as Herntrich suggests, an emphasis upon inherited guilt.

If *zera* is a construct, the phrase need not, however, necessarily designate a seed produced by evildoers. The thought seems to be merely that this was a seed (the word *zera* is stronger than *anashim*, "men," consisting of evildoers,[36] but it is also a group which had a heritage. Whether this heritage was good or bad is not explicitly stated, but the parallelism with *banim* would seem to refer to the patriarchal promises and the adoption at Sinai. Both the words *zera* and *banim*, then, point to the basic character of the nation. It should have been the seed of blessing or of holiness, for so much had been given to it by God; it was rather a seed consisting of evildoers.

children that are corrupters — Like *zera*, *banim* contains a reminder of the true identity of the people. Although they are corrupters, they are still sons (cf. 2 Chron. 27:2; Isa. 30:1, 9 and Jer. 4:22). *Banim* is not dependent upon *zera*, but is coordinate with it. The paradoxes, as Herntrich correctly indicates, reach their height in this phrase. The sons, that is, those who should have been sons of God, are acting in such a way as to be destructive both to themselves and to others. The idea

---

[36] Calvin aptly appeals to the Greek usage, ῥητόρων, ἰατρῶν, φιλοσόφων, γραφίων παῖδες which may be rendered "orators, doctors, philosophers, writers."

contained in the word "corrupters" is that of destruction such as would be caused by an invading army.[37]

These four epithets do not represent the opinion which the nation held of itself, but rather the divine judgment as pronounced by the word of Isaiah. As the practical Calvin emphasizes, this is the only means of arousing hypocrites to a consciousness of their sin. They must be told precisely what they are. There can be no greater mistake than to minimize the sinful condition of mankind in our Christian preaching and activity.

they have forsaken the Lord — Isaiah, like Hosea, emphasizes the fact that Israel's sin consists in apostasy from God. The word "forsaken" serves as a comprehensive term for apostasy, including, of course, apostasy of the heart; hence, a complete, whole-souled revolt from God. With this phrase Isaiah makes clear that the nation is not merely guilty of a single crime but it has also given itself up to sinful practices.

they have spurned the Holy One of Israel — Not merely had they depreciated God's power or His ability to carry out His threats. No doubt they did hold a contemptuous view of God, for whenever men sin, they prefer sin to God and despise Him, but they also consciously manifested their contempt in overt acts of transgression. This they did to such an extent that His indignation was aroused (cf. Prov. 1:30; 5:12; 15:5). It is a sin to mock at anything good; it is a far greater sin to mock at God, the Holy One. But the sin is still greater when Israel, the nation upon which God had fixed His love, mocks at Him (Delitzsch); inasmuch as God is holy, Israel should also have been holy. "Ye shall be holy: for I the LORD your God *am* holy" (Lev. 19:2b).

The designation of the LORD as the Holy One of Israel is a keynote to Isaiah's prophecies, occurring all told 26 times, 12 in chapters 1-39 and 14 in 40-66. It was the Holy God whom Isaiah saw in vision in the Temple (chap. 6), and with this designation he delighted to refer to Him. This Holy One, who had appeared to Isaiah and whose prophet Isaiah was, was the One whom the nation had spurned.

The force of the phrase is "the Holy One who is Israel's God," rather than "the God who is Israel's holiness." The word *qadosh*, "holy," denotes God's complete separateness from His creation

---

37 משחיתים is "those that corrupt" their way; used as an absolute (cf. Gen. 6:12; Deut. 4:16; 31:29; Judg. 2:19).

47

and so His own self-sufficiency as well as His own separateness from all that is sinful.

They are estranged backward — Seven statements occur altogether; four of these are nominal clauses and contain no verb. They describe the sinful condition of the people; three are verbal clauses, each one being introduced by a finite verb and picturing the nation's apostasy. The adverb signifies retrogression into a former state. It is a general estrangement and should not be restricted to idolatry (*Kissane*). The nation is estranged from God, and the direction in which it is estranged is backwards.

SPECIAL NOTE

Marti thinks that the last half of this verse, both in its form and contents, disturbs the progress of the prophetic speech and is to be regarded as a gloss. Verse 4a is said to presuppose the second person and v. 5 employs the second person, but v. 4b uses the third person. The accusations also are said to be general and do not meet the condition of the accused. The vocabulary is thought not to be Isaianic; עזב is Deuteronomic and means "to serve other gods," a thought which Isaiah would not have been able to express (cf. 1:10-17). נאץ is not Isaianic, nor is קדוש necessarily an Isaianic expression. The double occurrence of the prosaic את is suspicious, as is the fact that the last two words are missing in B.

In reply it may be stated that v. 4a does not necessarily imply the second person. Verse 3 had used the third person, and this may possibly be carried over in 4a, "Alas, (it is) a nation sinning, etc." Isaiah is not, therefore, necessarily addressing the nation in the second person. Even if he had done this, however, changes of person are frequent in Isaiah. As to the charge that the accusations are general, this is true, but these general accusations do meet the need of the nation. The basic difficulty with Israel was its apostasy from God, and this fact must be established before there is any detailed discussion of particular sins or maladies. The vocabulary in no sense militates against Isaianic authorship. It is furthermore more and more being maintained by modern scholarship that in this chapter Isaiah does condemn idolatry. At this point Marti's objections are based upon a view of Israel's religious development which must be rejected. That the verb עזב need not necessarily refer to idolatry is shown by the following passages: Isa. 58:2; 2 Chron. 12:1; 2 Chron. 21:10, 11 (note that here idolatry is mentioned in addition to forsaking the LORD). In Jer. 2:13 the forsaking is mentioned as a distinct evil from hewing out cisterns. As for נאץ the root occurs in Isa. 1:4; 5:24; 37:3; 52:5 and 60:14. It is found 5 times in the Psalms, 3 times in Jeremiah and once in Ezekiel. To say that קדוש is not necessarily an Isaianic expression is to betray an ignorance of the facts. The singular form occurs 43 times in Isaiah, 13 in Leviticus, 2 in Exodus, 4 in Numbers, 6 in Deuteronomy, 2 in 1 Samuel, 2 in 2 Kings, 2 in Job, 11 in the Psalms, 2 in Jeremiah, 2 in Ezekiel, once in Hosea, once in Habakkuk, once in Ecclesiastes, once in Daniel and 3 times in Nehemiah. Mere statistics, however, are not enough. The emphasis upon God's holiness which is embedded in Isaiah's prophecy is in itself sufficient to refute Marti's comment. Nor is there anything suspicious about the twofold occurrence of את. Poetry and prose intermingle in Isaiah. Lastly, we may note that the text is preserved entire in 1Q.

5 *why will ye be stricken?* — Turning to the nation the prophet addresses it directly. The Vulgate renders *super quo,* i.e., either, "upon what part of the body will ye be further stricken?" (so, e.g., Alexander) or "where can ye be smitten with effect?" This last is in effect adopted by Fischer who remarks that if Israel sins any more, He (God) will hardly know where He should strike. On this construction, namely, that 'al-meh is to be rendered "upon what place?" the prophet sees the nation as a body so wounded that there is no place remaining upon which it can be smitten.[38]

Condamin, however, observes that the one who inflicts blows or plagues does not take pains to discover a part not yet smitten. For that reason he and others prefer to render the Hebrew words by "wherefore" or "why." In support of this Wade points out that the people are still addressed in the plural and that the corporate body is not spoken of as an individual until the next clause. On this construction the meaning is, to what purpose will ye further be stricken? Your continued state of apostasy and rebellion simply brings additional chastisements; why then are ye so foolish as to continue therein? If you would repent the punishment would cease.[39]

Of the two interpretations the latter seems to have the most in its favor. The meaning then is not, why should God punish you further, inasmuch as further punishment will not bring about repentance, and God's labor would then be lost. The thought

---

38 Cf. Ovid, *Ex Ponto* ii. 7, 42; Cicero, *De finibus* iv.14; *Tusculam Disputations* iii.22; *Ad Quintem Fratrem* ii.25; Sallust, *Cataline* x.

מה is pointed with Seghol possibly because it stands at some distance from the principal tone of the sentence. The two words may be rendered as "whereupon, for what reason?"

39 It is also possible that the words are to be taken as an expression of dismay upon the prophet's part, as though he were saying, "There is no point in your being smitten further; it will not lead to repentance."

that God's labor is in vain is foreign to the teaching of Isaiah, in fact of the entire Bible. Isaiah's concern is that the people, by not turning to God, are bringing upon themselves more chastisement. He is thus pointing out the folly of sin.

any more — It is best to construe *'od,* "yet," with what precedes and to render the text, "why will ye yet be stricken," and not "ye still add rebellion."

ye continue to revolt — This clause serves to express a particular reaction to the general condition set forth in the question, "whereupon will ye be stricken more?"[40] One result of the chastisement is a continued condition of rebellion. Thus appears the true condition of the nation. If the heart is right with God, the tendency of affliction and chastisement is to humble it. The people of Judah, however, did not become humble, but continued to rebel. The punishing hand of God did not bring true submission.

the whole head is sick and the whole heart faint — Should *kol* be rendered "every" or "the whole?"[41] Drechsler favors "every," as though each individual in the nation were so overcome with misfortune that his head and .heart were quite sick. On the other hand, the language has a poetical flavoring which would explain the omission of the definite article (as in Ps. 111:1). Furthermore, the word *kol* is here in the construct, meaning the entirety of, the whole. More important is the fact that the context requires this interpretation, for it is the body politic itself which is in view, and not primarily the individual members of that body. In the preceding context the body has been designated with the words "nation," "people," "seed," and "sons."

This sickness is present in the most important parts of the body, the head and the heart. Note the *lamed,* "the whole head is for sickness"; it is in the state or condition of sickness. The *lamed* here serves to denote a condition as in Psalm 45:15; 69: 22 and 2 Chronicles 21:18.[42] Outwardly (the head) and inwardly (the heart) the nation has been so smitten by God's punishments that it is personified as a man whose head is sick and

---

[40] The circumstantial clause is introduced without *waw: "ye add rebellion,"* i.e., continue to revolt (cf. also Isa. 5:11).

[41] When followed by a definite noun, כל means "all" or "the whole." Cf. *HG,* p. 268. In a circumstantial clause such as this the pred. adj. generally follows the noun.

[42] Possibly the prep. has the same force as the Egy. m. of predication: *iw.t m b'k.t* (thou [f.] art in the place of a slave).

whose heart is faint. Procksch suggests that the nation is pictured as a slave beaten by its master, but this is not necessarily
the case. It is true that Israel had been freed from bondage,
but she is not now God's slave. He regards her as a nation of
sons and punishes her as a loving father in order that she may
repent. As the following shows, this chastisement was actually
wrought through the ravages of war.

6 *From the sole of the foot* — The article is omitted before
regel, "foot," as is often the case in familiar and frequently repeated expressions (cf. Gen. 24:11 and Deut. 4:47; 11:12). The
language is somewhat similar to Deuteronomy 28:35.[43] The description begun in the preceding verse is now continued in more
detail. The verse begins with a common description of the body
of the nation in its entire extent. The purpose of the verse is
to show that the sad condition has spread throughout the whole
nation, and this is done by continuing the figure previously introduced. The sole of the foot, is, of course, the lowest part of
the body. In contrast, however, merely the head is mentioned.
There is no need to mention the top of the head, for if the head
itself is not sound, the whole being is affected.

soundness — The noun actually signifies a place of soundness.
A striking contrast is introduced. The body has wounds, stripes
and fresh sores; the one thing that it does not possess is a place
of soundness.

wounds — Wounds which have cut into the flesh, such as those
made by a sword.

bruises — The wound or sore made by the stripes (Prov. 20:30).

fresh sores — Literally, a fresh smiting. The word has collective force, and would designate raw and untreated wounds, which
needed to be softened and cleansed. The language shows that
God's punishment was a bitter, cutting one, and that by it the
nation had almost been destroyed. As long as such blows fall,
there can be no cure. The chastisement is not necessarily that
of the exile (Kissane), but every punishment which had come from
the hand of God including also the low moral condition brought
on by the nation's sin.

they have not been pressed out — The nation has been so
plagued that there is no part free, and yet the wounds have been
completely neglected. The moral condition of Judah had been

---

43 The character of פָּרוֹן as a construct is so lost sight of that a word may
be inserted between it and its noun.

set forth under the figure of a wounded body; the remedies mentioned are the practices of the ancient world in the healing of diseases. The festering pus has been allowed to remain in the wounds and has not been pressed out[44] to cleanse the wound and to free it of impurities.

neither bound up — So that they would quickly heal. The picture is that of a body which has been neglected as far as healing measures are concerned, but not neglected with respect to continuing chastisement.

nor mollified with oil — Michaelis refers this to each of the preceding, "none of them is mollified with ointment." It would seem more suitable, however, to take the phrase independently. Thus, three characteristics of the body were mentioned: wounds, bruises, and fresh sores, and three methods of healing are likewise given: pressed out, bound up, mollification by oil.[45] The only remedy for such God-inflicted wounds is God Himself. Judah is a nation punished by God, and unless He intervenes there is no hope for her.

Isaiah first mentions Judah's sufferings in order that she may then hear a statement of the cause of those sufferings, namely, her guilt. Thus he seeks to gain Judah's ear. She has had no alleviation from her tragic condition and, in speaking of this condition, Isaiah seeks for a sympathetic response. The picture is that of a people completely under the rod of punishment, yet receiving no relief from that punishment. The reference therefore is not primarily to the moral character of the nation, although that moral character is reflected upon, inasmuch as it was the basic reason for the chastisement. The emphasis, however, falls upon the chastisement which, because of that moral character, has come upon Judah.

7 Isaiah abandons the figure of a man beaten with stripes and directs his hearers' consideration to the present condition of their own land. The effects of the divine chastisement are described without the use of figures. In the first three statements there are no finite verbs, and this, as Alexander says, ". . . gives great rapidity and life to the description."

---

[44] זרו is usually identified as a *Qal* passive. The *u* of the penult naturally appears as *Holem*.

[45] The definite article occurs with שמן to indicate that it was the well-known medicine, namely, oil (cf. Luke 10:34) which was highly esteemed for its healing properties (cf. Jer. 8:22; 46:11 and Pliny, *Natural History* 31.47).

Your land — It is your land, the land which you inhabit, promised to you as the holy land, flowing with milk and honey; it is now desolate, and the cities of that land are now burned with fire.

desolate — Literally, a waste or desolation. The concrete word "desert" for the abstract "desolation" lends a particular vividness and emphasis. The contrast is strong — the promised land has become a desert. What ingratitude is manifested when one perverts or destroys the gifts of God!

burned with fire — By means of, or because of fire.

As for your land — The word forms a *casus pendens*, and is emphasized by being placed first. A particular fact concerning this *casus pendens* is then stated: "As for your land, before you strangers are devouring it." Isaiah does not here state what had made the land desolate. The land is the earth considered as an element, the land which provides nourishment and sustenance.[46] Possibly the word actually signifies "the fruit of the land."

After the description of verse 6 this expression is particularly apt to arrest the attention. First a body covered with cutting sores and then a land utterly desolate. There is also a remarkable correspondence with the curses of Leviticus 26 and Deuteronomy 28. Indeed, from now on until the downfall of Jerusalem, the condition of Judah was actually a manifestation or realization of the curses promised in the law of Moses.

before you — As though to increase your grief (Deut. 28:31, 32). Here was an indignity which the nation was compelled to witness, and which it was important to halt. It was a chastisement accompanied by embarrassment.

strangers — The instrument of punishment was the invasion of foreigners. The strangers were aliens, belonging to another race. Who they were we are not expressly told. The land was not theirs, nor did they belong there. Hence, the term could be applicable to any who were not natives of Judah. Calvin thinks that the statements have reference to past occurrences, and others have sought to make particular identification of the foreigners.[47]

---

46 The passive part. is employed in the const. before a gen. of cause. 40 mss. add the conj., but the language is stronger without it.

47 Kissane applies the verse to the exile; others to the time of Ahaz or to the hordes of Syrians or Philistines mentioned in 2 Chron. 28:18. Gray takes it as a literal description of Judah in 701 B.C.

are devouring it — The passage presents a picture of devastation such as might have occurred at several points in Judah's history. The strangers are constantly devouring the land; it is a continuous action (cf. Isa. 9:11; Hos. 7:9). Isaiah personifies the nation, and in this one description sums up and brings together its entire past history. In devouring the land, the strangers are devouring the produce or fruit of that land (cf. Gen. 3:17; Jer. 5:17; 8:16). Those to whom the land was promised suffer hunger and deprivation. Judah had refused to serve God, the Owner; she now must serve unjust and usurping strangers who have no right to the land.

and desolate — The noun stands for an entire sentence, as though the prophet had said, "desolation is present." It is a short, forceful expression. The repetition of the word "desolate" (*shemamah*) is an example of anaphora, so common to Isaiah's prophecies.

as an overthrow of strangers — Is *zarim*, "strangers," a subjective or an objective genitive? Is the thought, "an overthrow such as comes upon strangers" (objective) or "an overthrow such as strangers cause" (subjective)? Those who adopt the former view, generally substitute Sodom for strangers, thus, "as the overthrow of Sodom." The reference, however, is not to the overthrow of Sodom, and the substitution of that word is arbitrary. Hence, it is best to take the word "strangers" as a subjective genitive: it is a destruction such as wandering strangers would accomplish. It is what one would expect from strangers who have no compassion and hence destroy all before them since it is not their own. The thought is illustrated by Jeremiah 8:16, "The snorting of his horses was heard from Dan: the whole land trembled at the sound of the neighing of his strong ones; for they are come, and have devoured the land, and all that is in it; the city and those that dwell therein." It is a vivid and forceful picture of utter desolation and destruction. In the repetition of "strangers," we have in this verse a second example of anaphora.

8 *And is left* — From a consideration of the land the prophet now turns specifically to the city itself, following the same order that he had employed in the title, namely "Judah and Jerusalem." The conjunction serves as a loose copula. The thought is either that the daughter of Zion is left as a remnant, namely, in a weakened and divided condition, or simply that she is left behind as a survivor. Possibly the latter is better. Whereas the other cities

of the land are burned with fire, the daughter of Zion remains as a survivor. In these words Isaiah introduces the doctrine of the remnant for the first time. Even this remnant, as Herntrich well points out, is itself a witness to the frightful character of the destruction.

the daughter of Zion — The word *bath*, "daughter," is a feminine singular collective noun with neuter force, signifying the aggregate of the inhabitants of a city or country personified as a female.[48] This phrase means not Zion's daughter, but the daughter who is in Zion. Zion refers to the entire city rather than to the hill Ophel alone, and is thus a synonym for Jerusalem. In the Old Testament cities are generally designated in poetical fashion as women (cf. 2 Sam. 20:19; Ps. 87:5; Isa. 47:1; and Amos 5:2). The verb is best considered as contemporary with the action expressed in verse 7, "Your cities are burned with fire, and Jerusalem remains." Perhaps the expression "daughter of Zion" is one of tenderness, and characterizes Jerusalem as the beautiful city which was a delight to the Israelites. That city remains, but it remains alone, a witness to the fearfulness of the judgment.

like a booth in a vineyard — Note the threefold use of "like"; in two instances the following word begins with *in*. The evils depicted will reach unto the city itself, until it has the aspect of a mere cottage. The booth was a temporary shelter made of branches and leaves, and is the word employed for a booth in the Feast of Tabernacles. It was erected in the vineyard, for the protection of the one who watched over and guarded the vineyard. Zion, the city in which the temple stands, is now but a booth. Amos 9:12 describes it as a booth which is fallen which God will raise up again in the Messianic times. Just as the booth stands solitary, the only object remaining in the field, so the city of Jerusalem is left standing alone. "How doth the city sit solitary" (Lam. 1:1a).

like a hut in a garden of cucumbers — The word *melunah*[49] here designates the place where one spends the night, and may

---

48 See Brockelmann, *Hebräische Syntax*, p. 70. He takes the general conception, i.e., Zion, as more closely defined by a particular or individual which designates origin of possession, i.e., the daughter which came from Zion, namely, the people. Others take the words in apposition, the daughter which is Zion, and others take the words as expressing a personification of the city (Van Hoonacker).

49 In Isa. 24:20 *melûnāh* seems to designate a kind of hammock.

be a synonym of *sukkah*. The cucumbers[50] are probably the Egyptian cucumbers which were sweet and green and easily digested (cf. Num. 11:5). That the land is compared with a cucumber field and Jerusalem with a lodging shows how great a devastation has come. The abundant land, flowing with milk and honey, is now but a cucumber field, and the *melunah,* far from being a strong, fortified building, is but a mere hut, alone, unprotected, a picture of misery.

like a blockaded city — Like a city undergoing siege and so stands alone.[51] The phrase simply adds vividness to the description of the condition which has come upon Jerusalem. After the invasion of the enemies, the city remains alone, a tragic testimony of the destruction that has taken place. That the city still stands, however, is due to the gracious work of the LORD.

The threefold comparison presented in this verse is characteristic of Isaiah, who often states truth in a threefold manner.[52] In the present chapter note verses 4, 6 (two examples), 7, 11b, 13b, and 14.

9 Attention is now directed to the part which the LORD has played. He has kept a remnant in existence, otherwise total destruction would have resulted, and the Christ would not have come. For it was through that remnant, in the fullness of time, that He purposed to bring the Redeemer into the world. The deliverance is thus seen to be due to God, and the doctrine of salvation by grace is for the first time introduced in the prophecy.

except — The word introduces a conditional sentence, the protasis of which is true to fact, but the apodosis hypothetical.[53] By this use of a conditional sentence an element of pathos is brought into the discourse. Out of the general ruin of the whole nation the LORD of hosts by His special grace has rescued His people,

---

50 מקשה is literally a place, field of cucumbers (cf. Ar. *maqṭa' tun*).

51 The language is difficult. The word נצורה is best taken as a *Qal* part. of *ntzr*. In Jer. 4:16, possibly with reference to this passage, the enemy is designated *nô-tze-rîm*. Marti translates, "like a watchtower" (*wie ein Turm der Wacht*), taking the form as an infinitival noun like *gᵉbûrāh*. Procksch and BH suggest *netzôrāh*, which would be a *nifal* part. of *tzûr*.

52 The *kaf* is sometimes taken as *kaf veritatis*, so that the rendering may be obtained, "is left a booth, a hut, etc." But the threefold occurrence suggests comparison, like a booth, etc.

53 The perf. in a conditional mood expresses the past, i.e., "we should already have been, etc."

and from this group which has escaped the Redeemer will one day come.

the Lord — The covenant name of God is placed first for emphasis. The Targum renders: "Except the exceeding goodness of the Lord of hosts had left us a remnant in mercy." The Hebrew, however, directs the thought to the LORD Himself who is the source of grace and goodness.

of hosts — The LORD, the God of hosts. The name designates the LORD as omnipotent, and this specific form *yahweh tzebaoth* is used by all the writing prophets except Ezekiel, Joel, Obadiah, and Jonah. The term "hosts" designated the armies of Israel (cf. 1 Sam. 17:45). It could also refer to the angels, the heavenly messengers of the LORD (cf. Isa. 6:5; 31:4; 37:16), and to the stars as God's hosts (cf. Isa. 40:26; 45:12; Ps. 33:6; Neh. 9:6). When, as here, it appears without further qualification, it designates the LORD as the God of all hosts, and is thus an equivalent expression for "the all-powerful God."[54]

By its religious practices that nation had deceived itself into thinking that all was well. Far from all being well, however, it was so far gone that the only One who could save it was He who possessed all power, the LORD of hosts. Since He is the God of hosts, He has power over them and can use them as He will, either to create or to destroy. The enemy armies, therefore, could destroy only as much as God permitted.

had left for us — Isaiah associates himself with the nation. That a remnant had been left is for the blessing of the people. Since God had determined to save His people and since He would ever have a people to call upon Him in consonance with His commands, He had caused a remnant to be left.

a remnant — Literally, "a survivor" (cf. Rom. 9:29). The survivor has escaped the general destruction.

very small — Duhm would construe these words with what follows, "almost like Sodom, etc." He interprets this to mean that the nation was almost but not completely like Sodom, because the Assyrians had not succeeded in killing all. As is shown by the Hebrew punctuation, however, the Masoretes construed the word with the preceding, and this yields a good sense. On this construction the word describes the remnant as very little, "a survivor almost," and so stresses the severity of the judgment.

we should have been as Sodom, we should have been like unto

54 Note the causative form of the verb (cf. Isa. 4:3).

Gomorrah — The name is emphasized by being placed first. The Hebrew is very forceful, "like Sodom we were, to Gomorrah we were like." The reference is not so much to the character as to the destiny of Sodom. We, so the argument runs, should have been like Sodom in that the overthrow of Jerusalem, had God not spared a remnant, would have been like that of Sodom. The destruction of Sodom and Gomorrah is a type of judgment meted out upon great wickedness.[55]

With the close of this verse we reach the first major break in the thought. We have been introduced to the theme which is to be developed in the latter portion of Isaiah's prophecies, namely, the glorious declaration that only the grace of God has averted complete destruction and has preserved alive the people of His good pleasure. Having announced this theme, Isaiah, before breaking forth in an accusation against the sinful nation, brings his first section to a close.

SPECIAL NOTE

In Sodom and Gomorrah there had been no remnant; therefore the destruction which came upon them had been complete. A remnant has been preserved from Israel and hence Israel's destruction will not be complete. For the sake of the righteous remnant, itself not deserving to be spared, the nation is spared a full overthrow. Consequently, the attitude of the nation toward the righteous should ever be one of deep gratitude. Instead, the righteous are hated by the world, even though for the sake of the righteous the destruction of the wicked is postponed.

On the other hand, the deferring of punishment also involves a deferring of the fulfillment of the promise. God is long-suffering and truly a God of all the world, not desiring that any should perish. Whereas, however, the delay of judgment also involves postponement of blessing, nevertheless the fact of the choice of the remnant is evidence that God is fulfilling His purposes in history. Here, then, is the true philosophy of history. It is because of the elect that the world remains. The wickedness of the world is permitted to continue until the time of punishment has come. That time is delayed for God is truly the God of the heathen also, a God of long-suffering and mercy. At the same time, in that delay, the delay of the full accomplishment of the blessing is also involved. The preserving of a remnant, however, is a step toward the fulfillment of the promise of blessing.

[55] Sodom and Gomorrah were cities of the Pentapolis, the other three cities being Admah, Zeboiim and Bela or Zoar (cf. *BA*, V, No. 2, May 1942, 17-32; VI, No. 3, Sept. 1943, 41-54).

2. God's Judgment upon Judah (1:10-31)

a. *Judah's hypocritical worship* (1:10-17)

10 Hear the word of the LORD, ye rulers of Sodom; give ear to the law of our God, ye people of Gomorrah.

11 Of what use to me is the multitude of your sacrifices, saith the LORD, I am full of the burnt offerings of rams and the fat of fatlings; and the blood of bullocks and of lambs and he-goats I do not desire.

12 When ye come to appear before me, who hath required this from your hand, the trampling of my courts?

13 Bring no more vain oblations; it is an incense of abomination to me, the new moons and sabbaths, the calling of assemblies, I cannot bear iniquity and the solemn assembly.

14 Your new moons and your appointed feasts my soul hateth; they have become a burden upon me, I am weary of bearing them.

15 And when ye spread forth your hands, I will hide mine eyes from you; also, though ye multiply prayer, I am not hearing; your hands are full of blood.

16 Wash you, make you clean; turn aside the evil of your doings from before mine eyes; cease to do evil.

17 Learn to do well; seek judgment, set right the oppressor, judge the fatherless, plead for the widow.

10 This verse, which introduces the second section of the chapter, begins with a command to hear the LORD speaking. The same imperatives which in verse 2 were addressed to heaven and earth are here directed to the sinful people themselves. Although a new section is introduced, nevertheless the references to Sodom and Gomorrah connect the verse with what has preceded. A remnant has been spared, and consequently the fate of Judah was not that of Sodom; nevertheless, in respect to iniquity, Jerusalem has become a spiritual Sodom, and her inhabitants a people of Gomorrah (Rev. 11:8). This comparison is introduced by the form of address itself, "ye rulers of Sodom." If a milder outcome has been granted to Jerusalem than to the cities of the plain, it is not due to any merit found in Jerusalem, for she was

59

a city of hypocrites, but only to the wholly unmerited favor of the sovereign God in whose hands lie the destinies of cities and nations. In His own good pleasure God had chosen not to destroy Jerusalem utterly.

Hear — The imperatives focus attention upon the message and introduce it with a certain measure of grandeur. At the same time, they place a responsibility upon those addressed. There is no option: men must hear.

the word of the Lord — Isaiah does not call attention to his own words, but to what God has spoken. *Dabar* (word) is a technical term for the prophetic revelation considered as absolutely authoritative, a rule of faith and practice. It here refers to the content of the following verses. The *dabar* therefore is not an event or an encounter, but a spoken word or message. Judah is not commanded to experience, but to hear. The imperative implies more than the mere physical act of hearing; it implies a hearing that results in obedience to the thing heard. The force of the verb is well illustrated in 1:19. A mere hearing of the word is of no profit. "But be ye doers of the word, and not hearers only" (Jas. 1:22). One does not truly hear God's Word unless he obeys that word. If one does not obey, it is as though he had not even heard.

rulers — These princes may have been judges who were responsible for the conditions of iniquity that prevailed. The rulers are thus first addressed, rather than the people themselves, for the rulers are the people's representatives. The phrase "judge of Sodom" came to be proverbial for unjust judicial decisions.[1]

Sodom — The word connects this verse with the preceding. In verse 9 a comparison had been made. In this present verse a further step is taken, and the people are themselves equated with Sodom. In destruction Judah was almost like Sodom; in wickedness she is identical therewith.

the law of our God — Calvin regards this as the law of Moses. An appeal to the law of Moses at this juncture, however, would not be as pertinent nor immediately relevant as an appeal to a

---

[1] "judges of Sodom" — Judges that are like Sodom. The gen. serves for comparison. Cf. Sophocles, *Antigone* 114, "a wing of white snow," i.e., a wing like white snow. Cf. Meidani, No. 230: "more unjust than a judge of Sodom" (*ajwar min qāḍi sudūm*). Note also the *u* in the penult of *sudūm*, which appears as *Shewa* in Heb.

message which God was then and there revealing, a message which had direct relevance to the then present situation.[2]

In the present instance the word *torah* is clearly parallel to *dabar*, and hence denotes the law which is to be immediately set forth in the following verses. Note that whereas the rulers were first addressed, the people are now also included. No distinction in wickedness is intended between Sodom and Gomorrah. The phrase "princes of Sodom, . . . people of Gomorrah" means "princes and people of Sodom and Gomorrah."

SPECIAL NOTE

The following verses have been greatly misunderstood. Gray, for example, says that the rejection of sacrifice is that which distinguished the religion of Israel. Marti claims that Yahweh demanded justice and righteousness, not sacrifice. According to Marti this section shows that *torah* should not be confined to cultic prescriptions, and that the ethical requirements stood in the foreground for Isaiah. Marti does not claim that Isaiah actually demanded the abolition of sacrifice, but thinks that such a consequence would follow from his opposition thereto. Inasmuch, he claims, as sacrifice had no sure foundation in prophetic religion, Isaiah's opposition was of principial significance. Marti thinks that Isaiah's viewpoint was the same as that of Amos, Hosea, Micah, etc., and so concludes that the Priestly code (so-called) was not known at this time.

This position, however, which so largely characterized the Wellhausen school, fails to understand the true character of the prophetic teaching. What Isaiah opposes is not sacrifice in itself, but the misuse thereof. For a thorough refutation of this erroneous viewpoint, cf. Oswald T. Allis, *The Five Books of Moses* (1943).

11 In answer to the prophet's condemnation the people might have pointed to their religious activities. Did they not bring sacrifices as the law had commanded? Did they not stretch out their arms in prayer? How then could Isaiah speak so harshly of them? Whether these questions were actually ever formulated by the nation, we may not know, but Isaiah proceeds to take away any such refuge, and clearly condemns mere formalism in religion.

Of what use to me is the multitude of your sacrifices — Note

---

2 "law" — Not merely direction (*veiledning*), HTC, p. 218. The word involved rebuke, reproach, condemnation, command, statement. It was, in short, the communication of information by means of words, divine instruction in general.

the alliteration in *lammah li*.[3] Isaiah's question is intended to express the thought, "What pleasure can I have in sacrifices unless they are offered from the heart?" The same idea appears also in 1 Samuel 15:22, "And Samuel said, Hath the LORD *as great* delight in burnt offerings and sacrifices, as in obeying the voice of the LORD? Behold, to obey *is* better than sacrifice, *and* to hearken than the fat of rams." Likewise Jeremiah 6:20, "To what purpose cometh there to me incense from Sheba, and the sweet cane from a far country? your burnt offerings *are* not acceptable, nor your sacrifices sweet unto me." (Note also Hos. 6:6 and Amos 5:21-24.) "Hypocrites abound in outward religious observances just in proportion to their neglect of the spiritual requirements of God's word" (Barnes; cf. Matt. 23:23). Although these sacrifices had been commanded by God and although the sacrificial system as such had been instituted by Him, they were no delight to Him because the heart of the offerer was far from Him. Bentzen is correct in pointing out that Isaiah does not actually reject the cult as such inasmuch as He also rejects the people's prayers.

The sacrifices were those of animals, and these are here further subdivided into burnt offerings and fat. In these sacrifices the male animals were principally used; compare the Iliad wherein is given a description of sacrificing among the Greeks. We may render the passage as follows: "They first drew up their heads and slaughtered and flayed them, the thighs they cut out and with the fat they covered them. Having done this twice, they placed raw meat upon them" (1:459). The sacrifices themselves had been prescribed by God. When, however, the offerer's attention was directed only to the sacrifice and not to the proper object of that sacrifice, the offering became no different from those brought by the heathen. Having abandoned a true view of the One to whom they were sacrificing, men placed their emphasis upon the sacrifice itself, and thus came to the belief that such an offering was necessary for God. They thus bring the offerings of their hands, but at the same time withhold the integrity of their hearts. Without faith it is impossible to please God in worship or in any other aspect of life. Worship in contravention of God's commandments is no true worship, and a sacrifice offered

---

[3] רב — It is difficult to explain the *Holem* in a closed, unaccented syllable (note Job 23:6; 2 Kings 19:23). The *Metheg* may simply direct attention to the irregularity.

without faith is a hollow mockery. God had commanded sacrifice, but He had not commanded it from a people of Gomorrah.

saith — The verb is frequentative and sets forth God's incessant appeal. It is not a single cry but a constant complaint of God. The form *yomar*, occurring in the middle or end of a sentence is characteristic of Isaiah. The pointing with *Pathach* is striking and for the most part is found in Isaiah. Elsewhere it occurs only four times, and two of these are in Jeremiah 51:35, a passage which shows Isaiah's influence. In Isaiah it appears in 1:11, 18; 33:10; 40:1, 25; 41:21; 58:9; 66:9. This form indicates a unique pronunciation which probably goes back to the prophet himself. The occurrence of the form strengthens the view that the book is a unity.

I am full — The expression is of course anthropomorphic. The whole clause may be rendered, "I am satisfied in respect to the burnt offerings of rams and the fat of fatlings." Bentzen thinks that the expression is somewhat ironical, but this is ruled out by the deep earnestness of the LORD's language. The LORD is a spiritual being, and has no need of carnal oblations.[4] It is as though He had said, "I am glutted with these sacrifices." Trapp comments, "Your devotions are placed more in the massy materiality than inward purity and therefore rejected." The verb expresses weariness, tiredness, disgust (cf. Job 7:4). Both verbs express a state which was complete in the past; yet which extends its influence into the present: "I did not desire and, hence, do not now desire." The prophet then proceeds to enumerate the offerings in order to show that God has no pleasure therein.

burnt offerings — The *olah*, apart from the skin and bones, was brought in its entirety, neither the priest nor the offerer partaking thereof. The choice of the animal was voluntary, although only the male was acceptable. In this case the animals were rams.

the fat — The best part of the animals, which constituted an admission that the people had at least made an external compliance with the law (cf. Amos 5:21-24; Ps. 51:16-19). The fat was burned on the altar, and the blood sprinkled thereon.

fatlings — The beasts which were fattened expressly for sacrifice upon the altar.

the blood — Together with the fat, the blood constituted the

4 For a discussion of the sacrifices, see *Vos, BT* (1948), pp. 172-90.

elements in which the essence of the sacrifice consisted. The
mention of fatlings suggests that the sacrifices were carefully
prepared for the altar. The blood was reserved for God (cf.
Lev. 3:15, 16; 17:11).

bullocks — Young bulls or steers.

lambs — Male animals from the first to the third year.[5] The
form of the sentence is striking, beginning with "I am satiated,"
it concludes with "I do not desire."

12 "This is God's voice to all superstitions and will-worship-
ers and carnal-gospellers" (Trapp). The thought may be thus
paraphrased. "Whenever ye come to the Temple in order to
appear before Me, who hath required of you that by means of
trampling ye profane My courts?"[6] The purpose of the people
in coming to the Temple (My courts) was supposedly to worship
the LORD their God. It is even possible that in so coming some
of the worshipers were sincere. Sincerity, however, is not sufficient; it is no substitute for obedience to God's commands. Unless one worships God in the manner, and only in the manner,
which God Himself has prescribed, he will profane the LORD's
courts.

who hath required — The question is to be construed with
what follows and not with what precedes. The question is not,
"Who hath required the appearance before My face," but "Who
hath required the trampling of My courts?" When men approach
God with a heart devoid of faith, they consider as obedience what
God has not commanded and which consequently is vain, useless, and to no point.

Bentzen suggests that the people might have employed the language of Exodus 34:20 as an answer to the question. They
might, in other words, have replied that none was to appear before God empty. But Exodus 34:20 does not merely teach that
any offerer whatever is not to come with empty hands before
God, but that the true worshiper who comes to God in faith
must not come with empty hands. To trample the courts of the

---

[5] אילים — Cf. Akk. *ailu*. The penult represents the normal pointing of a
diphthong in an unaccented syllable.

[6] תבאו appears to violate Barth's law that an *a* vowel in the preformative
should be followed either by a *u* or *i* as the thematic vowel. Gordon (UH)
suggests an original *tabu*. לראות — the same consonants are found in 1Q
(cf. Exod. 23:17; 10:3; 34:24; Deut. 31:11). Is Isaiah here deliberately following Deuteronomy? (Rignell).

LORD is to profane them. Whether the trampling was done by the animals or the worshipers may be difficult to determine. The responsibility for this trampling, however, lay in the hands of the worshipers who brought the animals into the courts.

At this point there is something similar to Paul in Isaiah's style. The conditional sentence is broken off, and a question forms the apodosis. This question implies a negative answer. No one has required the profaning of God's courts. Isaiah's question is therefore completely justified.

13 *Bring no more* — The prophet begins with a direct emphatic prohibition which takes the place of the interrogative. The infinitive appears without the preposition; it is to be taken in an objectival sense, "ye shall not add the bringing." The thought is that enough has already been brought, ye shall not add to it by bringing more. The words constitute an utter repudiation and condemnation of what the inhabitants of Jerusalem had been practicing. The phrase harks back to the idea to which expression was given in verse 5, "ye add rebellion." In the very worship of God the nation was continuing its rebellion. By thus combining rebellion and worship, it was seeking to join what God had separated.

vain oblations — Literally, an "oblation of vanity." The word *minchah* may be employed as a general designation for sacrifice. As used here, it designates an offering or sacrifice, which from the formal and outward standpoint fulfilled the prescriptions of the Mosaic ritual, but which, inasmuch as the heart that offered it was estranged from God, was in reality nothing more than a dead work of hypocrisy. It was a *minchah* in name, but not in fact, for it did not represent what the true *minchah* should represent, in that it was not backed by the heart of faith which would have found expression in a true *minchah*. For this reason it was a *minchah* of vanity or nothingness. This vanity is seen in the fact that the offering was not acceptable to God, and that it was not offered in faith. It was an unsubstantial *minchah*, and so ineffectual. It was vain.

incense — The word here indicates the smell of the flesh which is burned in the sacrifice.[7] The sacrifice rises in the smoke to the LORD who smells a smell of a sweet savor (cf. Gen. 8:21).

---

[7] קְטֹרֶת may be either absolute or construct. The conjunctive *Darga* shows that the Masoretes apparently took it as const.

an abomination — That which was loathsome. Isaiah is not repudiating a conception of God's attitude to sacrifice such as is expressed in Genesis 8:21. If these sacrifices had been offered by men whose hearts were submissive to Him, He would also have smelled in them a sweet savor. Inasmuch as the sacrifices are what they are, however, they are an abomination.

the new moons — Celebrated on the first of the month. "Also in the day of your gladness, and in your solemn days, and in the beginnings of your months, ye shall blow with the trumpets over your burnt offerings, and over the sacrifices of your peace offerings; that they may be to you for a memorial before your God: I *am* the LORD your God" (Num. 10:10; cf. also 1 Sam. 20:5ff.). When construed with the phrase "new moons," *shabbat* designates the weekly sabbath.

the calling of assemblies — These were solemn assemblies for worship (cf. Lev. 23:2; Jer. 44:22).[8] They belonged unto the LORD, and hence any misuse of them was a usurpation of what did not belong unto the worshiper. The last clause may be rendered, "I cannot bear iniquity and the solemn meeting." Iniquity and the solemn meeting do not belong together. The last two words thus bring out the heart of the entire matter: the religious exercises of Judah were mixed with iniquity. The people worshiped God with their lips, but their hearts were far from Him. They divorced doctrines and practice, a procedure always attended with disastrous results. Hence, their worship had become mere idolatry.

14 An impressive repetition of the preceding, emphasizing the abhorrence in which the nation's religious practices were held by the LORD. At the same time it carries the thought a step farther.

Your new moons — It is as though God had said, "These feasts of the new moon are not Mine; they are yours. Their celebration has not become what I have wanted, but what you have wanted. They are yours, celebrated in your own fashion, and you are responsible for them." The LORD's new moon festivals would have been observed in true devotion to Him; *your* new moon festivals on the other hand are something quite different.

appointed feasts — Those which were convened at regular set times. The word *moed* signifies "appointed time or place," and

8 Cf. Driver, *TT*, p. 267.

so would include all the feasts and feast days which were prescribed by God to be observed. Actually, however, the designation is restricted in the Scriptures to the sabbath, passover, pentecost, day of atonement, and the feast of tabernacles. Herntrich, however, says that *moed* is the most all-embracing designation of the cultic festivals, and includes every form of gathering. If so, the entire worship is condemned.

my soul hateth — Through its worship the nation thought that it was drawing forth the favor of God; instead, it merely succeeded in drawing forth His anger. This was not because God had not commanded the sacrifices and other elements of the worship, but because the worship was conducted without the proper attitude upon the worshiper's part. "My soul" is not merely a substitute for the personal pronoun, but, as Delitzsch says, ". . . the center of His being, regarded as encircled and pervaded by self-consciousness." It is thus a hatred that is found in the inmost depth and to the utmost bounds of God's being. We may paraphrase, "All that is in Me hates." The language is anthropomorphic, and serves to express the opposition which the Holy One of Israel entertains toward such superstitious worship. It is a graphic picture. That very worship which this same God had commanded is now declared to be the object of His deepest hatred, for it has been debased by the Judahites into mere formalism. Even though the formal prescriptions of the Mosaic law are fulfilled, the service is but superstition. This is seen in two ways. First, men worship God in a manner that He has not commanded (e.g., as seen in the trampling of His courts) and so are guilty of what the apostle calls will-worship (Col. 2:23). Secondly, in the attitude of the worshiper's heart and mind there is no living faith in God.

The word *naphshi,* "my soul" emphasizes the fact that God Himself is not worshipped when men engage in formalism. Although they have brought their sacrifices and so exhibited an outward conformity to the law, yet God Himself is not the proper object of their devotion, and they have not succeeded in worshiping Him. Only that worship is acceptable to Him which is in exact conformity to His will, which neither adds thereto nor detracts therefrom.

they have become — Literally, "they were upon Me for a burden." The implication is that they were not always so. The formal worship has continued so long, however, that it has now become a burden, and rests heavily upon the LORD (cf. Deut. 1:12).[9] The picture is forceful; the sinful worship of the unbelieving nation has become a burden upon the back of the LORD, which weighs Him down so that He is weary from bearing it. The second half of the verse is shorter than the first, thus yielding a certain vigorous effect.

The number of religious practices condemned would suggest that there was a corresponding law containing a rich variety of cultic prescriptions. If there was at this time no written law, it is surely difficult to explain how the nation ever came to the conclusion that it was pleasing the LORD by means of such detailed ceremonies.

15 Not only are sacrifices and offerings rejected, but prayer likewise. Sacrifices belonged to the Old Testament dispensation which had an end, but prayer is also enjoined in the worship of the New Covenant.

when ye spread forth — Literally, "and in your spreading forth your palms."[10] The reference is to the worshiper's attitude in prayer, an attitude which indicates supplication (cf. Exod. 9:29; 17:11, 12; 1 Kings 8:22). The condemnation of the nation's prayer — it should be noted that not all prayer, not prayer in itself, but simply "your" prayers are rejected — is clear evidence that Isaiah is not denouncing sacrifice as such. When men spread forth their hands in prayer, they are acting in accordance with the dictates of human personality. They are so constituted that they must thus betake themselves to God. If, however, they do not approach God in faith, they are offering their words and desires unto idols (cf. Heb. 11:6). As Calvin has beautifully expressed it, "Faith is the mother of calling on God."

---

[9] "upon me" — It rests upon me. Note omission of the prep. as in Jer. 6:11.

[10] ‏ובפרשכם‏ — *Qametz* stands in a distant opened (in distinction from open) syllable, and should be accompanied by *Metheg*. That *Tzere* should shift to *Seghol* in a closed, unaccented syllable is natural; it is the shift from *Seghol* to *Hireq* that is difficult to explain. There are several examples of such a shift before the heavy suffix of the 2nd pl. (cf. Exod. 31:13; Job 16:5; Isa. 52: 12). In the *Polel* the same shift occurs before the s. suffix; cf. Isa. 25:1; Ps. 30: 2; 37:34; 145:1 — all with the root *rûm*, and three are the same form. "I shall conceal" — The thought, introduced by an inf. is concluded by an imp., which expresses an action belonging to a specified future time: "at the time when ye spread out . . . then I shall conceal." "bloods" — An acc. of specification, preceding the verb for emphasis. The pl. denotes blood usually shed in violence; it then comes to have the significance of a bloody deed.

I will hide mine eyes — It had been made clear to the nation what the LORD required of it as to offerings and approach unto God. Despite this fact the nation had chosen to draw near to Him with a heart of unbelief and to rely upon some supposed intrinsic merit in the sacrifices rather than upon the LORD's promises. Thus it had become guilty of idolatry, seeking to worship Him as though approaching an idol. He would therefore be to Judah as an idol. The idol could not open its eyes, so He would not open His eyes. The idol could not hear, so He would not hear the multiplied prayer. People who thus sin deserve only an idol. But there was a difference. In reality God was not acting as an idol. He closed His eyes and ears, it is true, but in so doing, rejected the worship and prepared to bring judgment upon the worshiper.

ye multiply — These words may mean either that the people were guilty of vain repetitions in prayer or, what is more likely, that in a time of danger and difficulty, when they prayed fervently and continually to Him, He would not hearken. Fervor and zeal in prayer are not substitutes for obedience. As in the preceding verse, so here, the second half is shorter than the first, a device which procures emphasis.

your hands are filled with blood — The words "your hands" serve as a *casus pendens*. The force is, "As for your hands, with blood they are full."[11] The hands stretched out to God in the hope of obtaining His favor had committed violent deeds. The word *damim*, meaning violently shed blood, is placed before the verb in order that it may be made prominent. Two principal views are held. Calvin, Alexander, Herntrich, Duhm, and others think that the language refers to the blood of the animals which had been slain in the sacrifices. Such blood is thought to be symbolical of unjust deeds. The people were not murderers, says Calvin, but those who wished to be thought good and who kept

---

11 Cf. Virgil, *Aeneid* 12.196, *tenditque ad sedera palmas*, 1.93 (*tendens*); Horace, *Odes* 3.23.1; *Hesiod* 724ff; and Homer *Iliad* 6.267 which we may render, "Nor in any way to Cronos' son, ruler of the dark clouds, With blood and filth besprinkled, should one make prayer." If even the superstitious Greeks can speak as Homer has done, how much more should God's people depart from iniquity? Quite the opposite picture is given by a Hittite text (*KUB*, xxxiii, 100) when Ea, the king of wisdom, warns the gods that if they destroy mankind, no one will any longer care for the gods and sacrifice loaves and libations to them. The gods would then even have to do the work of man. Ishtar and Hebat, for example, would have to work at the grinding stones (See *ANET*, p. 124a).

up some kind of a reputation. The blood was from sacrifices which they had offered in hypocrisy. On the other hand, Drechsler, Delitzsch, and others think that the reference is to actual deeds of violence. Drechsler calls attention to the word "murderers" in verse 21 and cites 2 Chronicles 24:21 as a historical example of what the prophet intends (cf. also Matt. 23:34, 35). The word *damim* points to crime and guilt of a high order (Barnes). If the reference were simply to the blood of sacrifices, we should expect the singular *dam*.

It is difficult to understand why such a strong form is employed if the reference is merely to the blood of sacrifices. In offering such sacrifices blood would of course be shed, and the hand of the offerer would thus become bloody. The emphatic position of the word before the verb would lead one to expect a stronger reference than to the blood of sacrifices. The language calls attention to the hands. If the blood which fills these hands was merely that of the sacrifices, it would be unlikely that the hands would be so emphasized. The hands, being outstretched in prayer would go through the motions of worship, but they were hands which had committed deeds of violence. This interpretation is borne out by the following command to wash and the parallel "turn aside the evil of your doings." The command to wash would certainly be strange if the blood was merely that of sacrifice. Note that the hands are not merely stained with blood; they are filled therewith as though they had actually been dipped in blood and had scooped it up.

16 The divine accusation is now fully established by means of nine admonitions in which the difference between a true and a false righteousness is pointed out.

wash ye[12] — If there is to be a true service and worship of God, there must be a genuine repentance. The command of course must be understood in a moral sense, for the reference is not to ceremonial washings, but to a cleansing of the heart and flesh from all defilement and filthiness (cf. Jas. 4:8). Only if the blood of violence is washed away will the nation's prayers be heard. Duhm says that the command to wash would not be imposed upon murderers. But they are the very ones who do need

---

[12] הזכו is usually explained as a *Hithpael* imper. Probably, however, it is a *Nifal* imper. of *zkk* (*hin-zak-kú*). Cf. Honeyman, *VT*, I, 1, Jan. 1951, 63-65. "the evil of your doings" — Cf. Deut. 28:20.

such a command. There is hope even for one who has shed blood, if only he washes. Delitzsch rightly declares, "the love which is hidden behind the wrath, and would gladly break through, already begins to disclose itself."

This command, like similar commands addressed to sinners has been greatly misunderstood. Kissane, who writes from the Roman Catholic point of view, maintains that if prayer is to be heard, men must do penance for their sins. The present verse does not prescribe acts of penance, however, but a thorough reformation of the heart, a reformation such as God alone can produce. Can we imagine God demanding a cleansing that is anything less than He Himself can give? Such a cleansing would be no cleansing at all. Barnes says that Isaiah addresses the nation as "moral agents, and as having ability to do it. This is the uniform manner in which God addresses sinners in the Bible, requiring them to put away their sins, and to make themselves a new heart." Here is really the ancient error of Pelagianism. For nowhere is it implied or taught in the Bible that fallen man has the ability to do what God has commanded him. Calvin has gone to the heart of the matter: "Now we know that the sacred writers attribute to men what is wrought in them by the Spirit of God, whom Ezekiel calls *clean water,* because to him alone belongs the work of repentance" (cf. Ezek. 36:25). Drechsler also points out that man cannot wash himself, only God can do so. Alexander rightly says that the washing is not the *causa qua* but the *causa sine qua non* of restoration of God's favor. It is thus not the act of repentance itself, God-wrought as that act is, which brings upon a sinner the favor of God, although without repentance God's favor will not come to the sinner.

How, then, was the inhabitant of Judah expected to act when he heard God's command uttered by Isaiah? He was to cease his evil doings and to turn to God, trusting God's promises and seeking to live in accordance with them. Inasmuch as in himself he did not have the power to do this, when he did repent, it was an evidence that God had worked in his heart. True washing was the work of God. In the last analysis, the only thing that could wash away the blood of violence was the blood of Christ.

make you clean — The two imperatives may be construed as a hendiadys, "wash yourselves completely clean." The act of cleansing is thus the result of washing. The thought is: "Wash yourselves, and having once washed yourselves, make you clean."

turn aside — The true service of God is based upon genuine repentance. When once the heart has been cleansed that fact must be manifested in an abhorrence of evil. One who has repented must turn away from his evil doings.

the evil of your doings — A most emphatic way of saying, "your evil doings." "That which characterizes your doings (i.e., your actions)," the prophet is saying, "is *evil*."

from before mine eyes — Out of My sight, so that I shall no longer see them. Put an end to them. Like verse 15b, so 16b is short for emphasis.

cease to do evil — Herein consists the true nature of repentance; it is both a cessation of the doing of evil together with a whole-souled turning unto God. An entirely new manner of life is demanded.

The verse contains four imperatives, uttered with absolute authority: wash, make you clean, put away, cease. Why are these commands given if the men of Judah did not have within themselves the power to obey them? The answer is that they serve to bring men to a conviction of their need for washing and cleansing. Like men of today the inhabitants of Judah thought that they had no such need. They brought sacrifices; was that not satisfactory? These commands also serve to convince men of their inability to obey. What man in his own strength has ever been able to wash and to cleanse himself from the stain of sin? They also serve the purpose of causing a man to seek after the true and proper source of cleansing, even the grace of God Himself.

17 *Learn to do well*[13] — After the negative exhortation of the preceding verse, Isaiah now gives five positive exhortations, the first of which lays the foundation or groundwork for all the remainder. These commands are addressed to the state officials, the princes of Sodom, and also to the people themselves, the people of Gomorrah, and they are addressed to these people as individuals. A nation cannot repent unless the individuals which compose that nation repent. There can be no reformation in the church unless the individuals who compose the church reform themselves individually. It is true that Isaiah has a deep con-

---

[13] "to do well" — Learn in respect to doing well. The inf. is probably an adverb of manner, stating how the nation is to learn. The word "oppressor" is possibly an inf. abs. I see no warrant for taking it as a passive.

cern for the welfare of the government and for its judicial proceedings, but he is not commanding some abstract body to repent. It is rather the individuals who are members of the state whom he orders to cease their evil ways.

The first command implies that the people needed to be taught. To do well was something new to them, something that had to be learned. As Calvin puts it, the people are like scholars who had not even learned their first lesson. The nation is to become skilled in doing well, just as at present it is skilled in doing evil. From whom were the people to learn this lesson? Certainly not from themselves, but from God, who is the only true Teacher of welldoing. The content of the concept "welldoing" is expressed in the following commands.

seek judgment — With this command there begin several specifications which show how the nation was to do good. It was to seek to devote itself with zeal to the pursuance of, or to make the object of, intense interest, the pursuance of justice. This they were to do not merely to be pure as far as the cult was concerned (Herntrich), but because it was the command of God. This justice was not merely civil righteousness, but right judgment in every sphere of life. The *mishpat* is the judgment which has been pronounced in accordance with the absolute will of the LORD and is, therefore, right judgment, judgment in accordance with strict justice and truth.

The judgment is from God, the Author of absolute justice. The term has a connection with the covenant, so that the practice of judgment is the fulfilling of all the duties and responsibilities which a holy God has placed upon His covenant people. Three specific examples of the manner in which judgment is to be pursued are now given.

set right the oppressor — The imperative means, "to cause a person to take a right or straight way." This end may be accomplished either by bonds or by other punishment, and the idea of constraint is present in the imperative. Wrongdoing has hitherto been allowed free course, a situation which should not be. When it is not checked, justice cannot flourish; it must, therefore, be confined. The first step in pursuing judgment is the restraining of oppression, so that it must go the straight way. Inasmuch as the command is addressed to the people, it would seem that the oppression is not to be thought of as the work of a foreign foe, but rather as wrongdoing among the people. Whoever oppresses the poor and the helpless may be classed as an oppressor. Justice cannot triumph as long as oppression may be practiced by one group or one individual against other members of the nation. If the strong oppress the weak, there can be no justice. This condition must be righted, and wrongdoing must be restrained.

judge the fatherless — Give the orphan the right of a just judgment, in order that he may present his case and receive a thoroughly just treatment.[14] The language need not, however, have specific reference to trials or cases at courts; it may simply be a command or injunction that the orphan should be always treated justly.

plead for the widow — The widow and orphan are mentioned together because of their helplessness, and they thus become a symbol of those that are weak and without help. They have no one to plead their cause or to defend them. Hence, in a true theocracy, the weakest members should receive a just treatment. Inasmuch as an unjust judge realizes that he will receive no bribe or reward from the widow or orphan, he has no concern to defend them; compare Luke 18:2-5: "Yet because this widow troubleth me, I will avenge her, lest by her continual coming she weary me." It is the more necessary, therefore, that such helpless ones receive just treatment.

The passage clearly reveals a concern over the social injustices of the time. Such social injustices, however, could only be corrected by a change of heart upon the part of individuals. The officials are mentioned (v. 10), for if they are corrupt, their influence may affect the entire nation. In this instance, such was the case (cf. "people of Gomorrah," v. 10). If then the nation is to improve, there must be a change upon the part of the leaders. The greatest problem which any nation has to face is that of righteousness in its officials. Christians should not only pray for their rulers, they should also pray that God will give them righteous magistrates. They should also remember that they themselves are the salt of the earth, and that the best thing they can do with respect to social conditions is to live as Christians and to seek to apply the principles of Christianity to every aspect of life.

---

14 One duty of the covenant was the care of widows and orphans (cf. Deut. 10:18; 24:17; Jer. 7:6 and Aqhat 11:5:7). It is said of Dan'el that he "judged the cause of the widow and tried the case of the orphan" (*dn. 'almnt. ytpt. tpt. ytm*).

b. *An appeal to repentance* (1:18-23)

18 Come now, and let us reason together, saith the LORD; though your sins be as scarlet, they shall be as white as snow; though they be red like crimson, they shall be as wool.
19 If ye are willing and hearken, the good of the land ye shall eat.
20 But if ye refuse and rebel, ye shall be devoured with the sword; for the mouth of the LORD hath spoken.
21 How is the faithful city become a harlot; it was full of judgment, righteousness used to lodge in it, but now murderers.
22 Thy silver is become dross; thy choice wine weakened with water.
23 Thy princes are rebellious, and the companions of thieves; every one loveth gifts, and pursueth rewards; they judge not the fatherless, and the cause of the widow doth not come unto them.

18 *Come now* — The imperative is used, for it is God who speaks. The verb generally serves to introduce a proposition which is intended to benefit the ones addressed, and sometimes for the benefit of both parties, for it may also be used of equals. (For other examples, cf. Gen. 19:32; Judg. 19:11 and 1 Sam. 9:10.) This general usage of the verb supports the view that the proposal about to be made is one that is of benefit to those addressed. This is a command which cannot be evaded; it must be obeyed. God alone can lay down the conditions which must be followed. It is not a meeting of equals, but of God with His sinful people. The command, however, is softened by the precatory particle *na*, "now," and so takes the form of a gracious and loving invitation, and reveals the tender manner in which God always invites the sinner (cf. Matt. 11:28).

and let us reason together — The verb contains the idea of reciprocity. At the same time, it is cohortative, and so constitutes an invitation to discuss together the accusation which the LORD has made against Israel. In the light of the preceding imperative this amounts to a command to appear in a discussion in which it will be shown that Israel is precisely that sinful nation which God has accused her of being, and also that He is a God willing to forgive. "This verse contains an invitation to discuss the question whether God was willing or unwilling to show mercy, implying that reason as well as justice was on His side, and asserting His power and His willingness to pardon the most aggravated sins" (Alexander). Inasmuch as God is thus willing to reason with the nation, the blame for its destruction falls back on itself.

Reason is not here conceived as a certain *tertium quid* to which both God and the nation must submit in order that God's claim may be seen to be reasonable. "To reason together" is to sub-mit absolutely to the dictates which God Himself lays down. That which is reasonable is reasonable only because God Him-self has declared it to be so. Reason is derived from God; it is not a standard independent of Him to which He like man must submit, and man can be reasonable only when he thinks and acts in accordance with the revealed will of God. Man must think God's thoughts after Him. In the present instance, there-fore, to be reasonable is to obey the commands which God has given and to believe the revealed fact that, although one's sins were heinous, they would nevertheless become white as snow. While the terminology employed is probably legal, nevertheless, it is not a legal trial which is here described. It is rather a com-mand to be judged in the light of God's law (i.e., to reason to-gether) and to repent. As Drechsler points out, throughout the chapter God has been reasoning with the nation. The first step in a genuine repentance would be to realize that one's actions have not been in accord with reason (God's commands). All sin, whether of thought, word, or deed, is unreasonable.

saith the Lord — Isaiah inserts these words to emphasize the fact that the message was from God. It is not merely the prophet, but God, who addresses the nation. The offer of pardon and justification was genuine because the LORD had made it.

though your sins be like scarlet[15] — The particle *im* introduces a concessive clause, and takes the imperfect in both protasis and apodosis, since the clause refers to a contingent event, one that is actual at the time the clause is uttered. The thought is, "even though your sins were — and as a matter of fact they actually are — like scarlet." The plural *shanim*, "scarlet," may be used because the word refers to the color and to the material which has been colored by it. The chiastic structure of the clause should be noted:

though they are as scarlet . . . as snow they shall be white.

---

[15] "like the snow" — The definite article is employed with this and with other objects of comparison in the verse, for the object to be compared is looked upon not individually but generically. אם — In a conditional sen-tence, when the apodosis differs from what one might expect, the particle is equivalent to "although." Many have denied that this verse contains a dec-laration of forgiveness, assuming that the protasis is a summons to judgment. But it is questionable that "let us reason together" is a summons to judgment or designates a legal process. Also, it is held that forgiveness is not offered unconditionally. But cf. v. 19. Gray's discussion is excellent.

The denominative *Hiphil* form may best be rendered, "they may become white."

though they be red — Red is the color of the unjustly shed blood. Herntrich compares red to the fire which seeks only itself and devours and destroys. Delitzsch also states that red is the color of the fire which leaps out of the darkness and returns to it, whereas the white, without any admixture of darkness, represents the triumph of light. But the red seems to remind one of the blood of violence. If sin is this red, as red as possible, it may become the purest white.

like crimson — *Tola* signifies first of all the worm which gives the crimson its color, and then comes to be used of the color itself, thus having essentially the same force as *shanim*. The chiastic order is again employed, giving a peculiar force to the verse:

if your sins are *as scarlet . . . as snow* they shall be white
if they are red *as crimson . . . as wool* they shall be.

Note further the chiastic use of *yihyu,* "will be," with respect to the other verbs.

There is gracious condescension in the language, and Isaiah, who has been commanding repentance, shows himself as a prophet of grace. Even if the nation's sins are the deepest red, they may yet become the purest white: the very opposite of what they now are, in other words, non-existent. The doctrine of a forensic justification is found in these words. God now regards the sins of the people of Judah as blood-red; He will, however, regard them as snow-white. How can such a blessing be wrought? Only through God's mercy in which forgiveness, pardon, and life are offered to men who are required to repent of their sins. If, however, the people's sins are regarded as white, as non-existent, by God; this is tantamount to saying that God has justified the people. "I now regard your sins as blood-red," we may paraphrase, "but I shall regard them as white." Lest anyone should think, however, that this was a straightforward offer of pardon irrespective of whether or not there was repentance on the part of those addressed, the LORD immediately calls the attention of the nation to the need for repentance.

19 *if ye are willing and hearken* — After the announcement that there may be forgiveness of sins, the LORD still places before the nation the choice between blessing and curse, a choice which had been set before it under Moses (cf. Deut. 28). Will God accept a mere willingness in place of obedience? The two verbs willing and hearken belong together,[16] for the hearing is one that is to be accompanied by obedience. It would be a great mistake to assume that Isaiah was here teaching that Israel possessed within itself the ability to will and to hearken. Such an idea is refuted by the entire context. The nation is represented as completely permeated by sin and corruption, and in need of a healing hand applied from without. Inasmuch as there is no soundness in the body, how can one expect soundness to come forth from that body? If there is to be soundness, it must come from without the body, namely, from God. It is only by the path of willingness and hearkening that there can be true blessing; nevertheless, this is a path which the nation in its own strength cannot follow. These are gifts — the ability to will and to hearken — which God bestows only upon those of His favor and choice. At the same time the responsibility of the nation to obey is not lessened. It is the mystery of the free offer of the gospel which here confronts us. If the people would be willing and consequently obey, they would not only escape punishment, but would also be the recipients of positive good and blessing. Note that whereas the conditional sentences of verse 8 were synonymous in parallelism, this one and the one in verse 20 represent antithetical parallelism.

the good — The best (cf. Gen. 45:18, 20, 23). The people are to eat, that is, live from the best that the land has to offer. It is a picture of tranquillity and peace, the full and complete enjoyment of domestic boons.

the land — This is the promised land, Canaan, the land "in which you now dwell and which is your home." If you are willing and as a result of your willingness manifest obedient hearing, you will enjoy the best that the land can produce. The promise offers a material blessing and it is true that such material favor would have followed obedience. At the same time, the reference is not entirely to material gifts (Gill) but stands for the greater benisons which God will provide, namely, the for-

---

[16] "ye will and ye hearken" — The co-ordinate verbal forms usually correspond to one another; if the first is imp. the second will be also, connected by the simple conjunction. In a few cases, however, the imp. is followed by the perf. with *waw* cons. (cf. Deut. 31:12; Esth. 8:6; Dan. 9:25b). The form evidently represents *ta-bû*. Long *a* appears in Heb. as *ô*; in the modern Ar. of South Palestine *ya'kul* is pronounced *yôkul* (*GKC*, p. 184, n. 1; cf. Honeyman, *JAOS*, LXIV, 81ff.).

giveness of sins and the consequent benediction of God's presence. Note that the conditions for obtaining this mercy are spiritual in nature, namely, to be willing and to be obedient. Hence, the blessings promised must also be spiritual. This interpretation is supported by the previous verse, where the benison is equated with complete forgiveness of sins.

SPECIAL NOTE

At this point a word must be said about H. Bultema's strange interpretation.* To talk with a Jew about heaven, he says, produces no interest, but describe to him the glories of Canaan and his face will light up. This, says Bultema, is to be explained by the fact that Israel is the people of the earth whose citizenship, unlike that of the Gentile believer, is not in heaven, but on earth. The blessings set forth therefore are to be enjoyed *in the land.* This view of Bultema overlooks the fact that the promise is conditional, dependent upon spiritual qualifications, and that it is practically equated with the forgiveness described in the preceding verse. At the same time the verse does teach the truth that there is a connection between true obedience and material prosperity. One of the favors which God sometimes bestows upon His people is that of material prosperity.

20 This verse sets forth the converse of the preceding, and no more than the preceding may it be used to support the doctrine of free will. It teaches rather that persistence in a wicked way must bring with it the consuming punishment of the LORD. When men cease from their evil ways and turn to God, He is ready to receive them, but those who persist in sin without repentance will meet only punishment (cf. Lev. 26:14-46). The opposite of to be willing and to hearken is *to refuse* and *to rebel.* Disobedience to God's commands is the equivalent of rebellion.

ye shall be devoured with the sword — The word "sword"[17] is an adverbial accusative, "with respect to the sword." It is placed first for emphasis. In the two conditional clauses, the futures are followed by two verbs with *waw* consecutive, for both obeying and rebelling are the consequences of an act of the will.

---

* See H. Bultema, *Commentaar op Jesaja* (Muskegon: 1933).

17 "sword" — If a verb in the active takes two objects and the verb is placed in the passive, the remoter object (you) is made its subject, and the nearer object (sword) is retained (*GKC*, p. 388). The passive is *Qal,* although the analogy of Ar. would lead us to expect *tu-ka-lû.* Rignell thinks that Isaiah may have had in mind the words of Deut. 28.

Hence, we may paraphrase, "If ye are willing and consequently will obey; if ye refuse and consequently will rebel."

for the mouth of the Lord — Since it has been spoken by God Himself. He, as it were, has declared this condition with His own mouth, and this assures the certainty of the message. The language is anthropomorphic, but it clearly teaches us that God has given to man a revelation in words. He has spoken a message with His mouth.

21 Verses 21-23 form a subdivision of the main section, verses 18-23, and serve to introduce a lament over the tragic situation that has come upon Jerusalem. Note the prominence of the *a* sound in the first line, each final and accented syllable containing this vowel, *eykah, hayethah, lezonah, qiryah, neemanah.*

how — The word *eykah*[18] is the keynote of a lamentation, giving expression both to complaint and amazement. How is it possible that a faithful city could become what she now is, a harlot?

an harlot — Like the harlot, Jerusalem, which once was faithful, no longer has faithfulness. Her infidelity is basically one of the heart and can express itself in various ways. Barnes thinks that the reference is primarily to idolatry, and Gesenius takes the word *zonah* as the equivalent of idolatress (cf. Ezek. 16:22). On the other hand Marti thinks the infidelity consists in the thwarting of justice and the failure to fulfill the ethical demands of the Lord. Possibly both of these are included, although the latter is stressed in the text. When infidelity reigns in the heart in which righteousness once lodged, it will express itself in many ways. One of these may have been idolatry, but since the following words seem to be explanatory, we may say that the presence of murderers and the general corruption of the state which has been described were also manifestations of this unfaithfulness. The word "harlot" is emphatic; "how has become a harlot . . . the faithful city!"

---

[18] The ejaculation expresses lament (cf. Lam. 1:1 and 2:1 and Ug. *'k*). מלאתי — *Tzere* is retained before the f. termination *at*. Apparently there were two f. constructs, *qiṭ-laṭ* and *qe-ṭē-laṭ*. Gesenius holds that the final *yod* was a type of old case ending. If so, it would have been a termination of relationship similar to the construct ending אבי for it is long, whereas in both Ar. and Akk. the normal case endings are short (cf. *GKC*, p. 252). "used to dwell" — the imp. may express an action which continued in the past for a longer or shorter time.

full of judgment — These words serve to characterize the condition of the city at the time when she was faithful. At that time, probably under David, Jerusalem was filled with judgment. At the time of Jehoshaphat also there was judgment in the city. "And said to the judges, Take heed what ye do: for ye judge not for man, but for the LORD, who *is* with you in judgment" (2 Chron. 19:6). By judgment[19] we are to understand a condition of things in which the revealed will of God was positively realized. Calvin equates it with the word uprightness, and Bewer with justice. Included is the idea of the righteous administration of the righteous and just will of God.

righteousness used to lodge in it — Jerusalem used to be the home or the dwelling place of righteousness,[20] in which it was accustomed to find not a transient but permanent dwelling place. As used here *zedek* is the administration of law which is in perfect conformity with the will of God, and therefore is a righteous administration. Judgment such as God would approve together with a righteous condition of things and the resulting blessedness were the former characteristics of the city.

but now murderers — These words bring out the contrast between the former and the present conditions of the city, and they also serve to point out wherein the city had become a harlot. *Then,* righteousness; *now,* murderers. The word "murderers" indicates those who are habitual or professional murderers, the lowest and worst class of men engaged in violent crimes. Furthermore, as Pool has pointed out, murder is mentioned in order to assure us that other crimes of a lesser nature were not only not punished, but were apparently even encouraged. If

---

19 Cf. *TWNT*, Band II, pp. 194-214.

20 The basic meaning of the root *tsdq* is "a state which corresponds to a norm." Thus, for example, just balances and weights are those which correspond to standard (Lev. 19:36). When God acts righteously, He acts as God. Not that there is some norm apart from Himself to which He must conform —He is Himself the Standard; the Law is a manifestation of His nature and He always acts accordingly. He is God that cannot lie (Heb. 6:18). A righteous man is one who stands in a right relationship to the divine law. When Isaiah says that righteousness used to dwell in Jerusalem, he means that men who were themselves righteous and therefore acted righteously dwelt therein. Cf. R. Haldane, *Commentary on Romans* (1957); Kautzsch, *Die Derivate des Stammes tsdq im alttestamentlichen Sprachgebrauch*, (Tübingen: 1881); K. H. Fahlgren, *Sedaka. Nahestehende und entgegengesetzte Begriffe im Alten Testament* (Uppsala: 1932); Von Rad, *Theologie des Alten Testaments* (1957). Further literature will be found in these volumes.

the city could now be the lodging place of murderers, it would follow that it could also be the lodging place of those whose crimes were less serious.   It is a telling contrast: the lodging place of righteousness and the lodging place of murderers.   Once righteousness found Jerusalem a safe and secure place in which to dwell; now murderers do.   Hierapolis, as Trapp cleverly puts it, has become Ponerapolis.   Even the purest churches on earth may degenerate into a synagogue of Satan.   How all-important that we who are members of Christ's church be always vigilant, and cherish and love that church that she may ever be found faithful before Him.

Does Isaiah here simply present an ideal picture of Jerusalem's past (von Rad)?   We would answer this question in the negative. We are not to understand the reign of David as one in which no unrighteousness is to be found.   Essentially, however, David was a man after God's own heart and so a type of the coming Messiah.   In contrast with the present evil condition, the city, at that time, because of David's basic devotion to God, could be called a city filled with righteousness.

22 In the preceding verse the change which had come over the city was represented as adultery; now, as Alexander suggests, it appears as adulteration.   Silver represents all that is noble and pure; how valuable to the city were virtuous princes and rulers! This silver has now become something else; it has not become gold, but dross.   The thought is not that here and there specks appear upon the metal but that the metal itself has turned into dross.   It is no longer silver, but its opposite.   The word *sigim,* which is plural, perhaps for the sake of indicating intensity, denotes what is removed from metal.   It is the baser material which is separated from the purer metal by means of smelting.

weakened — Literally, "cut." By means of cutting, the strength of the wine is impaired. *sobek* is fine wine, used here in parallelism with *kaspek,* "thy silver."   The metal that was so pure that light could find in it a clear reflection, as well as the fine wine of the land, was destroyed, the wine having been weakened (lit., cut, mutilated, circumcised, castrated) by water.

the water — The reference is not to the Arabic *muhl,* "fruit juice," but to choice wine to which so much water had been added that its unique character had been lost.[21]   The expression "to cut

<hr/>

21 Smith, "The Messianic Ideal of Isaiah," *JBL,* XXXVI, 162. He suggests that the reference is to olive juice and compares Ar. *mahl.*

wine" may be paralleled from other sources, for example, Latin, *castrare vinum* and *scelus est iugulare Falernum* (Martial); Arabic, *udah maqtu'ah*, i.e., the cut oil of aloes; French, *couper du vin, du lait;* and Spanish, *trasegar.* The verse, although employing a different figure to depict the change which had come over Jerusalem, nevertheless continues the element of pathos and sadness which had already been introduced. Jerusalem once possessed something desirable, represented by silver and choice wine. A great change, however, has come over the city; the silver and choice wine are gone, and in their place are dross and wine mixed with water.

23 *Thy princes are rebellious* — A step in advance is now taken in that Isaiah gives an explanation of the figures of speech just employed. Since the corruption of a nation generally begins with its rulers, Isaiah singles these out for denunciation. The thought is: "thy princes who should have been faithful to God have become rebellious." This rebellion did not necessarily manifest itself in Judah's dependence upon Assyria (Knobel) but rather in a general rebellion of heart and life against God. Many have sought to bring out the paronomasia in their translations; thus, Calvin, *primi pravi;* Van Hoonacker, *tegenworstelen doen vorsten;* Herntrich, *deine Führer sind Aufrührer.* The verse harks back to the words, "ye multiply rebellion" in verse 5.

and the companions of thieves — This was because of their rebellion against God. Thus is exemplified the truth that the inward disposition of the heart governs the outward conduct. If that inward disposition consists in rebellion towards God, one example of the outward manifestation of the fact may be found in one's becoming the companion of thieves. Duhm remarks that Isaiah complains, but never thinks of proposing measures that would have healed the terrible situation. This statement hardly needs refutation. Throughout his entire prophecy Isaiah sets forth the LORD as the only hope of man. Only through being willing and hearkening will a reversal of the present condition come about. The fallacy of that modern phenomenon, sometimes known as the "social gospel," is found in its low estimate of the nature of sin. A mere program of amelioration will not suffice for the heart that is rebellious against God. What is needed is a new heart, and only from the LORD Himself may such a heart be obtained.

Through their unjust judgment these base rulers aided the lot of the thief, and furthered the cause of unrighteousness. The *gannab* was a professional, habitual thief.

every one — Literally, "all of it, its totality."

loves — The participle expresses both present and habitual action.

pursueth rewards — This they do instead of pursuing peace, as commanded in Psalm 34:14, "Depart from evil, and do good; seek peace and pursue it." It is a vivid picture. Everyone has set his deepest affection upon bribes, and pursues rewards as one would pursue something he wished to catch. Where such a condition obtained, there is little likelihood that any attention would be paid to the gracious declaration made in verse 18; hence the LORD announces the destruction of the nation. Such selfish leaders have no time for those who should be protected by a true justice.

Very possibly Isaiah is reflecting consciously upon Deuteronomy 10:17. "For the LORD your God *is* God of gods, and Lord of lords, a great God, the mighty, and the terrible, which regardeth not persons, nor taketh reward." How different the people. In this contrast between the actions of the Lord and those of the nation, the depth to which the latter had fallen becomes apparent.

the cause of the widow — Literally, "the quarrel." The plight and claims of those that are weak do not even come before the rulers, for there is corruption in high places. Isaiah truly "waxes bold" when he dares to paint such a picture of Jerusalem. Gesenius refers to a Turkish poet to show that a prophet could freely denounce corruption in the court. But we do not have in Isaiah the mere picture of a professional prophet. He is a spokesman of the LORD, and preaches with deep earnestness and with the conviction that the present state of affairs must be changed.

c. The announcement of coming judgment (1:24-31)

24 Therefore, saith the Lord, the LORD of hosts, the mighty One of Israel, Alas, I will ease me of mine adversaries and will avenge me of mine enemies.

25 And I will turn my hand upon thee, and purge thy dross as the lye, and I will take away all thy alloy.

26 And I will restore thy judges as at the first, and thy counsellors as at the beginning; afterward thou shalt be called the city of righteousness, and the faithful city.

84

27 Zion shall be redeemed with judgment, and her converts with righteousness.

28 And the breaking of transgressors and sinners shall be together, and they that forsake the LORD shall be consumed.

29 For they shall be ashamed of the mighty trees which ye have desired, and ye shall be ashamed because of the gardens which ye have chosen.

30 For ye shall be as a mighty tree whose leaf fadeth, and as a garden that hath no water,

31 And the strong shall become tow, and his work a spark, and they shall both burn together, and none shall quench them.

24 *Therefore* — The word refers to all that has preceded, and principally to the description of the nation's condition. The description is true; there is no justice in the land, the LORD therefore will act. Judgments will come even more severe than those which have already appeared, and in these coming judgments there will be a purifying or purgation. The salvation of Judah can only come through sore judgment.

saith — It is not often that the word *neum*, "utterance," occurs at the beginning of a sentence. Whatever its etymology may be, in its very sound, it ". . . corresponds to the deep earnest pathos of the words" (Delitzsch); (cf. 1 Sam. 2:30; Ps. 110:1).

the Lord — There are probably more designations of God given in this passage than in any other one verse of Isaiah. The first of them, *adhon*, means lord or master.[22] The definite article shows that it is the Lord of lords, or the Lord *par excellence*. In Isaiah the designation is often followed by the phrase, "the LORD of hosts" (cf. 3:1; 10:16, 33; 19:4). The etymology of *adhon* is uncertain. In the present passage it serves to point out that the LORD is the absolute master of all, and that at will He can ease Himself of His enemies. Herntrich suggests that it also indicates the relation of a master to a slave. If so, it simply lends force to the present usage: God, who is the Master of all, will ease Himself of His enemies.

the mighty One of Israel — These words lend great force to

---

[22] הָאָדוֹן is also found in Ug. (B iii* b 15, 32, etc.). We find *Aduni-baal* and *Aduni-apla-iddin* (*KAT* 398) and in Plautus, *Poenulus* 998, *donni*, "my master." Cf. also *Adonis*. As used in Isaiah the word designates the true God as Lord over all. δεσπότης (B) is not unsatisfactory. "hosts" — In Ug. the primary meaning is star , or heavenly bodies. Cf. Egy., *sb'*, "star." In the present phrase it has reference to all hosts without distinction. Note that this verse is reminiscent of Deut. 32:41.

the passage: "God is the mighty One who belongs to Israel!" *abir* signifies a steer, and is used here in a metaphorical sense. Or, it may be that the original force of the word is so weakened that it is simply to be rendered, "mighty." The word does not show that Israel worshipped the LORD in the form of a steer, nor is there any reflection upon Egyptian steer worship. In the official Israelitish religion such worship had been proscribed. The word here signifies that the LORD is powerful, and calls to mind the patriarchal period, when God showed Himself as the Strong One who protected the patriarchs (cf. Gen. 49:24). Now this same Strong One will manifest His strength in judgment instead of protection. The heaping together of names lends a tremendous force to the announcement. There can now be no averting of the threatened judgment, for the omnipotent Lord has announced that this judgment will certainly come.

alas, I will ease me — The particle may be rendered "alas," although its purpose at this point is to indicate the fact that the judgment will surely come. We are reminded of the burden mentioned in verse 14. Through their sins the people of Jerusalem and Judah had become a burden upon the LORD. It was a grievous, annoying burden, and one which He was not called upon to bear. Therefore He would ease Himself of this burden, and in so doing would thereby avenge Himself of His adversaries. Those who caused this burden to rest upon the LORD were His enemies and adversaries. These enemies were the Israelites themselves and not outsiders or foreigners. The language is again anthropomorphic, and there is no danger that it will lead one to entertain a low view of God. His utter omnipotence is clearly shown by the designations herein given to Him. It is clearly taught, however, that the one who persists in his sin is an enemy and adversary of God (cf. Ezek. 5:13), and God must be rid of him. God is truly the master, and when He decides to punish sinners, He is fully able to do so. The sinner, and not merely the sin, is like a wearisome burden to God, a burden from which He will seek easement.

25 *And I will turn my hand* — The hand of God has been at rest but now it is to be turned. *Shub* indicates a movement of the hand, either for the purpose of inflicting punishment (as in Amos 1:8; Jer. 6:9; Ezek. 38:12; Ps. 81:15) or of bringing blessing (Zech. 13:7). It is here employed in this latter sense; the hand is to be turned in order that it may perform a work of purifying judgment and so restore the church. The judgment to come, then, is not for the purpose of complete destruction, but of purification.

thee — The word, which is feminine, has primary reference to the city itself. Upon the city this hand will be placed so that its weight will be felt.

and purge out thy dross as lye — This dross is the unjust rulers and leaders and their sinful practices as well as the general hypocrisy and sinfulness of the people themselves. These must be subjected to a thorough and drastic judgment in order that the city herself may continue in existence. Refining silver is a radical process, and the refining which must take place if the nation is to be saved is also radical. Those whom the LORD loves He chastens. The process of purgation cannot be wrought by man but by God alone. If sinners are to be saved, they must be cleansed and purged.

and I will take away — Literally, "and I shall turn aside thy alloy." The alloy is probably some metal found in combination with the more precious metals.[23] That which had caused the pure silver to become mere dross must be turned aside so that the silver would be as before. This can be accomplished only by means of drastic purgation such as a judgment.

26 *And I will restore thy judges* — The *Hiphil* of the word *shub* means to bring again, to cause to return. In what sense, however, is this to be understood? Duhm says that Isaiah simply wanted to restore the Davidic age, and that at a later time he thought the Messianic age would surpass that of David. Gesenius, on the other hand, points out that what is intended is not a mere improvement of the present judges, but rather the raising up of new ones. Vitringa refers verses 25, 26 to the exile and thinks that, inasmuch as there is no mention of a king, the fulfillment first occurred in the post-exilic period and then in greater measure in Christ. Barnes likewise maintains that the blessing would come immediately after the Jewish captivity.

The Scofield Bible applies the present verse to the millennium which it identifies as the "kingdom," and then maintains that during this kingdom the ancient method of administering the government over Israel will be restored. On this view the return to the city's pristine faithfulness will be accomplished not im-

[23] "thy alloy" — *GKC* points out (p. 400) that the pl. is employed to indicate "particles of *alloy* to be separated by smelting."

mediately after the judgment of purgation, but only after the intervening of the exile, the first advent and the entire age of the church. Then, when Christ has come for His saints, and the seventieth seven of Daniel has run its course, Christ will return with His saints to set up a kingdom of a thousand years' duration. It is during this time, according to Scofield, that God is to restore the nation's judges. Such an interpretation, however, divests the passage of its force and renders it almost pointless. Of what comfort could such a promise have been to the sinful Judah of Isaiah's day?

as at the first — It is true that the phrase has reference to the early history of the nation, possibly the Davidic age and even earlier. This age is used as a type of the purity and faithfulness of the city. The promise given in the present verse is not that of a mere restoration of conditions, but the introduction of conditions that are the opposite of those now prevailing. It is thus a picture of the ideal or Messianic future. Possibly there is some reference to the exile, but the fundamental meaning of the prophecy is that there will come a time, typified by the reign of David, in which true righteousness and justice will be found, namely, the Messianic Age. In answer to the objection that the king is not mentioned, we may note that in this first chapter the Messianic age is always described in general terms, with no mention of a king. It is clear, however, that this period of blessedness is not to be brought about by the remnant itself, but is wholly the work of the LORD and hence of grace. We are thus face to face with an omnipotent declaration of grace, "*I will restore.*" This is the grand announcement which forms the background against which the Messiah's work is to be performed.

The charges which the LORD has raised are leveled primarily against the judges and counselors, who by their perfidy and lack of justice had corrupted the nation. They, therefore, must be removed, and in their stead perfect justice introduced. There is thus a twofold allusion to verse 21. After justice has been restored, then the city may be called faithful. When there are just rulers in the city, then she may be called the city of righteousness, in which perfect justice is administered and each one deals justly and equitably with his neighbor. Only after a work of sovereign grace has been performed, however, may the city be called righteous and faithful. God first acts, then follow righteousness and faithfulness.

27 This verse amplifies the preceding, and is probably to be regarded as the prophet's utterance rather than a direct quotation of the LORD's words, like the preceding verse.

Zion — Originally Zion was a designation of the hill Ophel, but came to be applied to the entire city as well. It thus serves as a synonym for Jerusalem and is so employed throughout Isaiah. Zion was also a designation of the locality on which the Temple of God was erected.

shall be redeemed[24] — The verb *padah* denotes a deliverance that is obtained by means of payment of a price (e.g., Exod. 13: 13; Num. 18:15, 16, 17; etc.). The means by which this deliverance is to be accomplished are mentioned, namely, judgment and righteousness. The two words occur in parallel construction also in 9:6; 28:17; 32:16 and 33:5.

There would, however, be little comfort to the inhabitants of Judah in the thought that they were to be redeemed through their own righteousness, for the truly devout among them would realize that they had no righteousness.[25] Furthermore, it is the consistent representation of the Scriptures that these qualities are gifts of God and cannot be received by men except from Him. Hence, the *mishpat* and *tzedaqah* here mentioned belong to God and not man, and the purpose of the promise is that the godly may be comforted. Through God's justice and righteousness Jerusalem and her converts will be redeemed.

Mishpat is the exercise of justice upon the part of God (cf. 4:4; 5:16; 28:17), and *tzedaqah* that which is manifested in His exercise of justice. If Zion is to be redeemed, God's righteous justice must appear in judgment. In the deliverance of Zion all the claims which absolute justice might have advanced against

---

[24] "redeemed" — The basic thought is that of redemption by the payment of a price (cf. Exod. 13:13, 15). The first-born was to be offered to God, but satisfaction might be obtained by the offering of a ransom. A slave could also be redeemed (Exod. 21:8), and the Levites were a redemption for the first-born (Num. 3:40ff.). Cf. Leon Morris, *The Apostolic Preaching of the Cross* (1955), p. 16. He points out that in this and in similar passages there is the "underlying thought that Yahweh is bestirring Himself on His people's behalf; it is no ordinary activity that is thought of." "Even more impressive than specific quotation is the general implication of many passages that Yahweh was putting forth His mighty power on behalf of those He loved when He redeemed them" (p. 17).

[25] Von Orelli correctly remarks, "Not indeed by acts of their own of this kind, but by divine Messianic acts, as ix. 6 shows."

Zion will be satisfied, and a righteous gift of grace will also be seen (cf. Dan. 9:24; Isa. 53:11; Ps. 143:2).

and her converts — Literally, they that return of her, those belonging to Zion who return to God through true repentance. Calvin justly observes that God is righteous and so will not permit His entire church to be destroyed. Zion will be redeemed together with those of her who turn — not the sinners or transgressors — but those only who turn to God (cf. Isa. 59:20). "And the Redeemer shall come from Zion, and unto them that turn from transgression in Jacob, saith the LORD." Note the emphatic position of Zion in the sentence.

28 Here is the converse of the preceding. The verse begins with an exclamatory clause, the predicate of which is omitted, possibly because of the vigor and excitement of the speaker. On the other hand, verse 28b is a declarative verbal sentence.

their breaking — Dörderlein thinks that the verb should be used instead of the noun, but Drechsler rightly points out that the noun stands as a substitute for the verb. (Similar elipses are found in 13:4; 52:8; 66:6. For the idea of breaking, cf. Lam. 2:11; 3:4; Prov. 16:18). The reference is to those who are not the converts of Zion, who have rebelled against God and will therefore be destroyed together. If there is to be purity and prosperity for the true church, the wicked and apostates must be broken. If the silver is to be refined, the dross must be purged out.

shall be consumed — They will perish, come to an end. The reference is to complete extinction (cf. Job 7:9; Ps. 37:20). The verse is a solemn announcement that those who forsake the LORD, the class that has been addressed throughout the chapter, must be destroyed if Zion is to be redeemed.

29 Verses 29-31 serve to justify the threatening given in verse 28. The thought is, "Those who forsake the Lord will be consumed, and this is seen in the fact that *(ki)* they will be ashamed." *Ki* is thus to be translated "for."

they shall be ashamed — The first verb may be taken in an impersonal sense: "they, the people, will be ashamed."[26] When the punishment comes upon the transgressors, they will be ashamed of the things in which they had delighted. One result of the

---

[26] "they shall be ashamed" — *BH*, Gray, Targ., 3 mss. read 2nd person. But cf. Krt I:38, 39 *m'at krt kybky* (what ails thee Keret, that he weeps?) Rignell observes that such a change of persons is normal in Heb.

punishing hand of God is that the sinner looks with shame upon what was once his confidence and delight.

the mighty trees — Why should anyone be ashamed of great trees which he had planted? Had the inhabitants of Judah committed a sin in planting great and mighty trees? Some of the best expositors of Isaiah have thought that such was the case. Drechsler, for example, thinks that the prophet is inveighing against the planting of trees and gardens which were mere luxuries, and in which the Judahites reveled and to which they pointed with pride. Caspari, likewise, one of the most penetrating interpreters of the book, adopts a similar position. Men such as Paulus and Hitzig agree with them. It is of course true that even the best of God's gifts may be misused, but the question is whether Isaiah did not intend something more in his condemnation.

It is quite possible that the people did point with pride to the mighty trees which they had planted. It would, however, be but a step from this to the worship of the LORD on the high places and then to the idea that in the trees themselves a divinity resided. Hence, it would seem that the prophet was here actually condemning a form of idolatry whether that idolatry was carried on in the name of the LORD or not. In all probability these were green trees in which the numina were thought to dwell (cf. Deut. 16:21; 1 Kings 16:33; 2 Kings 16:4; Ezek. 6:13). There is a tree cult in Palestine even today. In ancient Canaan idolatry found expression in that divinity was attributed to the powers of nature and worship was held under the trees. God has chosen Judah, but Judah had chosen a tree, the symbol of man's fall into sin. Yet man cannot find in nature or nature worship an answer to the deepest needs of the soul.

ye have desired — The word *bacher* signifies choice from a number of objects that are before one. Of all the people of the earth which were before Him, God chose Israel, and of all that Israel had before her, she chose trees and gardens. Foolish choices of an object of worship betray a mind beclouded by sin. The desire of the people has been for the mighty trees; the time would come, however, when they would be ashamed of what they had desired. The two verbs found in this verse are employed elsewhere in Isaiah of the choice of false gods: 41:24; 44:9; 66:3.

gardens — The first word, *elim,* is without the article, but the second word has the article. Here the reference seems clearly to be to unlawful places of worship (cf. 57:5; 65:3; 66:17). In themselves these gardens may have been innocent delights, but when they were devoted to the exercise of idolatry, as seems to have been the case, they became objects of which one would be ashamed.

ye have chosen — God had chosen Israel to be His people, but Israel had chosen gardens. The contrast is striking (cf. Deut. 7:6 and 1 Kings 21:2). The desires, the inward disposition of the heart, and the choice, the act in which these desires come to expression, can lead only to shame. Both verbs in the sentence may be rendered "to be ashamed."

30 *For ye shall be* — After the exclamation of the preceding verse in which the shame of the nation is predicted, the prophet, apparently overcome with excitement and emotion, turns to a direct address. Like the previous verse, this one also begins with *ki* and serves to justify the assertion which was expressed in the words "they shall be ashamed." The people have planted mighty trees, but when the judgment comes they will be ashamed of those mighty trees.

a mighty tree — The feminine is probably deliberately chosen. The Hebrew word simply means "a mighty tree," without specifying what kind of tree is intended.[27]

whose leaf fadeth — It was a mighty tree which the nation had delighted in and chosen; now the nation itself would be like a mighty tree, not however, when that tree stood forth in all the glory and beauty of its foliage, but when it was fading, with respect to its leaves. The Hebrew may either be rendered, "fading is its leaf," or possibly, "fading with respect to its leaf."

as a garden — The people would also be like a garden; not, however, one of the luxuriant gardens which they had chosen, but a garden which would be without water. A tree whose leaf fadeth is one which can easily catch fire and be destroyed, or one which might die. A garden without water has lost all its delight and attractiveness. Whatever is in it will die. The shortness of the second half of the verse lends force to the description. In this chapter it has been Isaiah's practice to make the second half of a verse short and forceful.

no water — The word order is strong: literally, "like a garden — water is not in it." This order renders emphatic and prominent

---

[27] אילים are terebinths (*pistacia Palestina*) which drop their leaves in winter. Modern scholars usually assume that the word simply denotes big trees.

the thought of water. That which is essential to sustain life and to render the garden pleasant to man will be lacking in this garden. By the use of such striking figures Isaiah shows what must be the nature of the end that awaits those who forsake the LORD.

31 *the strong* — Those who are strong among the people, and hence, like the mighty tree, are those who will perish.[28] A mighty tree can have leaves that will fade, and so the strongest among Judah will one day lose their strength. Perhaps they themselves thought of themselves as the strongest; perhaps they were so regarded by others. It is difficult to say, but those who actually were the strongest would perish.

tow — The coarse part of flax or hemp, shaken off from the flax when it is beaten.

and his work — All that those do who are strong among the people. The reference includes idolatry, but it includes more than that. The work of the strong is all his conduct which flows from his proud heart.

spark — Such work, as Delitzsch pointed out, carries within itself the spark or fire of destruction. Thus, man's work is here set forth as the cause or the occasion of his destruction. What he has performed becomes the spark that sets on fire the tow itself (cf. 33:11 and 50:11).

burn together — The work which sinful man has performed together with the man himself will perish. Together they will be destroyed, the man and his work.

and none shall . . . quench — Literally, "and none is quenching them." The phrase lends emphasis to the absoluteness of the destruction and forms a terrifying climax to the entire chapter. Since the causes for which the judgment is to come are spiritual in nature, namely, the sins of the nation, it follows that the punishment will have a relation to those sins. It will not be a mere carrying away of the nation into exile nor merely the death of the present generation, but will itself be spiritual. Even in this first chapter there is a note of hope. We are not told what is the basis upon which that hope may rest other than that it is the decision of God to save a remnant. From other portions of Scripture we learn that this hope is based upon the work of Christ Himself.

---

28 An the basis of comparison with Akk. *ḥasânu*, "to enclose," Rignell refers *ḥsn* to the image, enclosed in the sacrificial grove. Cf. Deut. 7:25; 12:2.

B. EARLY MESSAGES OF ISAIAH (2:1–5:30)

1. GOD'S BLESSING AND JUDGMENT (2:1-22)

a. *A glorious future for God's people* (2:1-4)

1 The word which Isaiah the son of Amoz saw concerning Judah and Jerusalem.

2 And it shall come to pass in the latter days that established shall be the mountain of the house of the LORD at the top of the mountains and shall be lifted up above the hills and all the nations will flow unto it.

3 And many peoples will flow and they will say, Come ye, and let us go up to the mountain of the LORD, unto the house of the God of Jacob; and he will teach us of his ways, and we will walk in his paths, for out of Zion shall go forth the law, and the word of the LORD from Jerusalem.

4 And he shall judge among the nations, and shall reprove many peoples, and they shall beat their swords into mattocks, and their spears into pruning knives: nation shall not lift up sword against nation, neither shall they learn war any more.

1 This verse constitutes the title or heading of the second prophecy. Inasmuch as there is no clear connection with the preceding chapter it stands where we might expect to find it, for in the book of Isaiah a new title is inserted when there is no continuous development of thought or steady progress in the presentation of an argument. Chapter 1 is an introduction to the entire prophecy, whereas with chapter 2 the prophetic messages proper begin. Hence, it is to be expected that the second chapter should commence with a heading. As Trapp points out, it is an august title or inscription.[1]

---

[1] The title is supported by IQ and ASTh. The title in B varies slightly. Duhm thinks that at one time this little book (vv. 2-4) probably had an independent existence, and that the redactor regarded it as a genuine book of Isaiah, as seen by the contents of the title which the redactor composed. This

the word — The thing or matter, the prophecy itself which follows. *Dabar* is a synonym of *hazon,* which appeared in 1:1. Prophecies are designated "word" in 1 Samuel 3:1 and Jeremiah 18:18. The article lends a certain force; it is the specific word or the well-known word which Isaiah saw. A strange expression! "to see a word!" — yet it makes clear that words formed an essential element in the divine revelation. Isaiah saw this word or revelation not with the physical eyes, but with the inner eyes. In the dim mystery of a divinely imposed vision, when the outer eyes were closed to the world round about, the inner eye or eye of the mind saw what the sovereign God revealed. Isaiah does not hear; he sees the word. The phrase simply refers to a revelation in vision, which was communicated in words. It is the fact of its "spokenness" that is paramount. Somewhat flippant is the remark of Duhm that the *dabar* was ". . . part of the treasury of mysteries which were kept in heaven and piecemeal revealed to the individual prophets."

Judah and Jerusalem — The prophecy to follow, therefore, as Calvin points out, is a confirmation of the doctrine of the church which had been presented in the previous chapter, particularly in verses 26 and 27.[2] The order, Judah and Jerusalem, is again used, and this tends to confirm the genuineness of the title. Whatever deviations from this order or manner of statement may follow, the great subject matter of the prophecy is Judah, but more particularly it is Jerusalem, the city of David, the city of the great king.

2 Verses 2-4 form the text or introduction to the first great section of the prophecy, namely, chapters 2-4. This introduction may be the work of the prophet himself, or it may have been incorporated by him from some other work. With respect to

---

implies, thinks Duhm, that neither chap. 1 nor any other Isaianic piece preceded. Herntrich regards 2:1 as the heading of a section that extended from 2:6-4:6. Verses 2-4, inasmuch as they include the whole world, were probably not original (in distinction from v. 1 which mentions only Judah and Jerusalem).

2 To this Bultema objects that the title speaks only of Judah and Jerusalem. But this statement is made on the background of the dispensational position which influences Bultema's interpretation. Bentzen believes that a definite scheme was employed in which prophecies of fortune followed those of misfortune. Hence, he argues, 2:2-4 was originally a conclusion of chap. 1 (*Muligvis har saa 2,2-4 oprindelig dannet afslutningen paa kap. 1, —*).

verses 2-4 of the present chapter, there is question as to whether it is original with Isaiah, or whether Isaiah took it from Micah or elsewhere and employed it as a suitable introduction for his message, just as the Arabian writer Ibn Doreid in his *Makzura* uses as a heading a verse which he has taken from Motanabbi. Whether then the section be originally from Isaiah or not, it is in a fitting and proper place and is genuine. Had this introduction been interpolated in a purely mechanical fashion, it would have been copied in a slavish manner and would agree word for word with the original. It would seem that if this introduction had been adopted from elsewhere, it was written down from memory, and expressed not a slavish *verbatim* repetition of the original, but rather the essential thought of that original.

And it shall come to pass — With sudden abruptness he begins; the first word is the surprising *and*. In Micah this "and" joins well with what has preceded, but here in Isaiah it is abrupt, which may indicate that the prophecy was original with Micah. The conjunction seems to connect with something which has gone before, but with what? It may be that the very abruptness of the conjunction suited the purposes of Isaiah, enabling him to bring us immediately and in a startling manner face to face with the fact that there will be a glorious future for Zion. The perfect sets the time sphere, placing it in the future, for it is introduced with a consecutive *waw*, and the narrative is then carried on in the imperfect.[3] Thus, the introductory phrase lends great force to the fact that the vision is something that will take place in the future. The phrase stands by itself, and should be followed by a pause, the following message being a self-contained unit. Thus: "And it shall be — in the last days, ..."

Isaiah was no mere dreamer, presenting, as George Adam Smith erroneously maintained, a vision of Utopia, which would be impossible of realization, and which Isaiah at first thought his countrymen would immediately receive.[4] Not at all; he speaks with

---

[3] וחיה serves to emphasize a concept that belongs to the future. Rosenmüller compares Deut. 12:11, but the *Legarmeh* shows that there is to be a separation from what follows.

[4] Kroeker asserts that if Isaiah had not been close to God (*nicht im Umgang mit Gott gestanden hätte*), he would never have had such a vision. Only those who have seen God, he says, can behold a future that belongs to God alone. But the prophets who received this vision, were, to judge by their own statements (cf. Isa. 6:5) unworthy men. They were honored by God in being chosen to serve Him, and their choice was a matter of grace.

the certainty of one who has received a message from God, who is His true prophet. "It shall be," he declares with a blessed dogmatism, for the promises of God are sure of fulfillment, whether the present Israel would believe the promises or not. If there is anything that is sure, it is that Zion will one day be exalted, for God has so decreed and made known His decree to the prophet.

in the last days — The word *aharit* denotes what is hindmost or farthermost. For the most part, it has a temporal significance, as may be seen from Deuteronomy 11:12, "from the beginning of the year even unto the end of the year." The phrase in itself simply indicates the last part of the days.[5] The prophet employs

5 In the Old Testament אחרית is used both spatially and temporally. In Ps. 139:9 it signifies the farthest, uttermost, most distant parts of the sea. Temporally, it designates the "farthermost, most distant parts of the days" (Vos). Thus, we may render, "the final, last parts of the days." We cannot agree with Munch (in Bentzen) that the phrase is merely equivalent to "at last" (*til sidst*). Rosenmüller seems to weaken the force when he renders, "*in posteritate dierum, i.e., futuro aliquo tempore.*" Cheyne renders, "the sequel of the days," and Edelkoort, "*na verloop van tijd.*" Mowinckel's "at the end of the days" (*ved dagenes ende*) is not precise, for the phrase does not designate a period when the days have terminated, but the last parts of those days.

Is the phrase merely chronological, or does it also suggest that a foregoing process will eventuate in full fruition when the last days have come? Passages such as Job 8:7; 42:12; Prov. 5:4, 11; 23:31, 32 suggest the latter. The phrase, therefore, is eschatological; when the latter days appear they will reveal the Messiah, who is the fulfillment and goal toward which all previous history has been pointing. (See Vos, *The Pauline Eschatology*, pp. 2ff.).

Mowinckel thinks that the phrase occurs only in late passages, and that it is probably influenced by Persian usage. In the early, pre-prophetic age, he claims, there was no eschatology in the strict sense. The earlier prophets of doom also had no eschatology; the future which they foretold was the immediate future (but cf. Watts, *VPA*, pp. 68ff.). In answer to Mowinckel we must first note the antiquity of the phrase itself (cf. von Gall, *Basileia tou Theou*, pp. 91ff.) which appears in Akk., *ina ahrat umi* (in future days). Secondly, even early occurrences of the phrase, e.g., Gen. 49:1, may have eschatological significance. Thirdly, the messages of the early prophets cannot be reduced to judgment alone. This point we shall seek to establish in the exposition.

Vos contends (rightly, we believe) that the phrase belongs strictly to the field of eschatology; it relates to the collective aspect of eschatology, and is both elastic in extent and movable as to its position. The New Testament teaches that this period, "the last parts of the days," began to run its course with the first advent of Christ. It is the "consummation of the ages" (Heb. 9:26) and "the ends of the ages" (1 Cor. 10:11). The "last parts" will come to a close, when the Lord returns in glory.

the definite article, *the* days, regarding them as a totality or whole. It is, then, the last part of *the* days, the days which were then and there running their course, that forms the period of time in which the events of this prophecy were to be fulfilled.[6] According to the Hebrew method of designating history, human history was called "the days." Thus, the Hebrew title of the books of Chronicles is "words of the days." The days are those of our human lives here upon this earth. These days will at one time come to an end, and in their last part, the last part of human history, the prophecy will be fulfilled.[7]

There are two considerations which show that this phrase comes to have a technical eschatological significance. In the first place, it is thus often employed in the Old Testament of the time when the Messianic salvation will be accomplished. In the second place the New Testament definitely and clearly applies the phrase in this eschatological sense to that period of time which began to run its course with the first advent of Jesus Christ (see Acts 2:17; Heb. 1:2; Jas. 5:3; 1 Pet. 1:5, 20; 2 Pet. 3:3 and 1 John 2:

---

[6] The article of totality should be noted, for some refer this passage to a millennium which would begin after the church age. But the blessings depicted here take place in the period of the latter days. The distinction between "last days" for Israel — her kingdom glory in the earth (Isa. 2:1-5), and the "last days" for the church, is arbitrary and without exegetical foundation. Cf. Pentecost, *TTC*, p. 154. If the millennium is regarded as a part of the eternal state it cannot then be considered a part of the last days, and hence this prophecy cannot refer to it.

[7] We are compelled to reject the view of Herntrich that the reference is to a completely different time (*die ganz andere Zeit*), not human history, but God's time. Hertzberg also comments that when human time ceases, God's time begins and that time and space mean nothing when the Lord takes over the rule of the world. Nor does Bewer's comment help, "when the ideal shall be real." It must be stressed that the prophecy refers to a period of human history, when the Messiah, laden with spiritual blessings, will come to this earth.

Herntrich also claims that the beginning and end of the days is the return to Paradise. And Mowinckel (*Han Som Kommer*, København, 1951, p. 175) says that "in the latter days" all things return to their original state (*da tingene vender tilbake til begynnelsen*). This "wholly other" character of the *eschaton* can only be expressed in "mythical terms, metaphors, and colours" (*er de mystiske uttrykk, billeder og farger en nodvendig uttrykksform*). But this lifts the future state into the mythical sphere. It is the application of a modern "theology" to the Bible. In this passage there is no talk of a return to Paradise. The end-time is not a simple return to Paradise, but the redemption and completion of the creation.

18). On the basis of the Old Testament alone we may represent human history as follows:

THE DAYS

THE OLD TESTAMENT AGE   THE MESSIAH   THE LAST DAYS

*   *   *   *

In the light of both the Old and New Testaments we may represent human history as follows:

THE LAST DAYS

THE OLD TESTAMENT AGE	CHRIST'S FIRST ADVENT	THE AGE OF THE CHRISTIAN CHURCH	CHRIST'S SECOND ADVENT

The period which is intended by the phrase "the last days," is the age of the Christian church which began its course with the first advent of Christ. It is true that from the Old Testament alone so much is not apparent, but in the Old Testament the phrase does signify the age or time of the Messiah, the period of deliverance and salvation.

It is not the present upon which the eyes of the Israelites are to be directed, but a time which is the end of the contemporary course of events, when the Messiah will have come and the breach which sin had introduced between man and God will be healed.

In speaking of the future or Messianic age, Isaiah, as a prophet of the Old Testament, uses the thought forms and the figures which were current in that age. It is obvious that the language of the prophet cannot be interpreted in a consistently literal sense. Rather, Isaiah takes the figures which were the property of the Old Testament economy and makes them the vehicles of expression for the truths of salvation and blessing which were the characteristics of the age of grace. Calvin remarks with justice, "We must also observe the harmony between the figures of the law and that spiritual worship which began to be introduced at the coming of Christ."

The figure of the exaltation of Zion is impressive. At the time when Isaiah spoke, the very reverse was the case. "Why leap ye, ye high hills? this is the hill which God desireth to dwell in; yea, the LORD will dwell in it for ever" (Ps. 67:16). The Temple in

Isaiah's day was situated upon Zion, but the false gods had their mountains as well: the Capitol, Olympus, Albordash, Meru, and Zaphon. The mount which now is comparatively insignificant will one day surpass all others. Even Sinai, the mount of the law, will recede into the background, for the new covenant is superior to the old.

established — It is essential for a right understanding of the passage that the force of these words be clearly seen. The phrase which begins "in the latter days, . . ." constitutes a unit in itself, which is to be separated in thought from the previous "and it shall be." After the introductory "in the latter days," the word established is placed first in order that it may receive the emphasis which is its due. The word established expresses the idea of permanent duration, which idea is strengthened by the auxiliary "shall be." The force of this may be more clearly seen if we recognize that the words are not to be translated as a future passive, "will be established."[8] Thus, this passage does not describe something that will take place or materialize during the latter days. It describes rather a condition that will already be in existence when the latter days begin to run their course. "The world also is established, that it cannot be moved. Thy throne *is* established of old, thou art from everlasting" (Ps. 93:1b, 2).

shall be the mountain of the house of the Lord — The language of the prophecy draws its symbolism from the Old Testament economy, and for that reason we are to understand the mountain as having reference to Moriah, on which the Temple had been built. This was actually separated from Ophel or David's city, (Zion) but in the Scriptures the one word Zion designates both without necessarily making a distinction (cf. Ps. 76:2; 78:68).

at the top of the mountains — The mountain upon which the house of the LORD is now situated will in the last days be in the lead, or the leader of all the mountains.[9] It will be at the head

---

8 With a form of הוה the passive participle serves to indicate "a condition as existing rather than an act as performed at the time referred to" (Green, *HG*, 278: 4:a). Green calls attention to the German *sie waren beschnitten*, and not *sie wurden beschnitten*. Luther renders *gewiss* (certain); and Lowth seems to base his interpretation upon B, " . . . will be eminently conspicuous, so as to be the light of the world . . . . "

9 Some regard the prep. as *beth essentiae* and translate "on the top of the mountains," the chief of the mountains. This may be possible, but would not apply in the analogous passage, Deut. 20:9. Furthermore, the same sense is obtained without thus construing the prep. Marti interprets, "on the highest of the mountains," and claims that the mountains must be lifted up physically.

of all other mountains, just as in Deuteronomy 20:9 the captains are to be at the head of the people, to lead the people. Zion, therefore, which in Isaiah's day was by no means a great and imposing mountain, would in the latter days take first rank among all mountains.

and shall be lifted up above the hills — Isaiah is not content with expressing the truth of Zion's exaltation once only. He is a true Hebrew poet, and although he writes in a beautiful elevated poetic prose rather than in poetry in the strict sense, he gives utterance to his thought a second time in parallel fashion. In mentioning the hills, he has exhausted the category. Mountains and hills, all that is high will sink in importance before Zion. Again, the prophet does not use the future passive, "it will be lifted up," but simply expresses the condition of Zion with respect to the hills, namely, that it is "lifted up." The word is not an exact parallel of "established." The first participle, established, expresses the thought that Zion is so fixed that she cannot be moved; the second sets forth her position as elevated and higher than the hills.

and all nations shall flow unto it — The strange picture is that of all the nations, even the two great nations of Isaiah's day, Assyria and Egypt, flowing in a mighty confluence unto the mountain upon which the Lord's house is builded. The peoples of the world are actually likened to rivers. It is strange, particularly as it seems to involve the thought of flowing up to a mountain.[10] Vergil uses a somewhat similar idea with respect to the bees when he remarks, "*apes confluere arbore summa.*"[11] The same thought is expressed also by Jeremiah, who has probably based his language upon this present passage, "Therefore they shall come and sing in the height of Zion, and shall flow together to the goodness of the LORD" (31:12a; cf. also 51:44). This last clause must be construed as one which expresses result. As a result of the establishment and exaltation of Zion, all nations will flow unto her.

By means of this picture Isaiah wishes to teach the truth that the worship of the LORD, expressed by metonymy as the mountain of the house of the LORD, will triumph over all other religions and forms of worship. Corresponding to the rank in which the superiority of the worship of the LORD is revealed is that of its recogni-

---

[10] A note in the Berkeley version states that in God's spiritual world water will flow upward. This misses the import of the passage. The Hebrew root means to flow. Cf. Jer. 3:17; Zech. 8:20-22; Jer. 31:12; 51:44.

[11] *Georgics* IV, 558.

tion outside of Israel. In Isaiah's day this worship was comparatively obscure and was practically confined to Israel. The nations regarded the LORD as the God merely of Israel, a local deity,
like Chemosh of the Moabites. In the latter days, however, inasmuch as Zion would be exalted, this religion of Israel would be
known throughout the world. As during the old covenant Jerusalem had been a pilgrimage center for the three annual festivals,
so during the last days it is to become a center for the entire world.
The mount is thus to serve as a unifying force for the whole
world. It is to be a reversal of the dispersion (Babel). At the
city of confusion, Babel, mankind was dispersed; so at the city of
peace (Jerusalem) mankind is to be united. In the place of the
city of confusion stands the city of peace. In place of great human activity there is the reign of God alone.

In the light of the New Testament we may say that the reference of this prophecy is to the church which Jesus Christ founded.
Beginning at Jerusalem the disciples went throughout the world
proclaiming the true salvation. This church is the pillar and
ground of the truth. By it the truth is to be preached to every
creature (cf. John 4:22b; Luke 2:32).[12]

3 *And many peoples will flow* — The first thought is parallel
to the last thought of the preceding verse. The words "many
people" parallel "many nations," and the verb "will flow," (lit.,

---

[12] By a number of modern writers this passage is said to be fulfilled during
the millennium to follow the return of Christ. Cf. Chafer, *Systematic Theology*,
IV, 374-75. He makes a distinction between the "last days" for Israel and the
"last days" for the church. For Israel the "last days" are the days of her kingdom glory in the earth. Despite Heb. 12:22, Isa. 2 is said to have "nothing
whatever to do with the church," according to Arno C. Gaebelein, *The Annotated Bible* (IV, 172), New York, 1921. The argument seems to be that inasmuch as we do not now see the fulfillment of the prophecy, it must be reserved
for the millennium.

In reply we must note that this prophecy is attributed to the latter days,
which is the Messianic age. Furthermore, the blessings herein depicted
are spiritual. Men will seek the Lord that they may walk in His ways. But
men seek the Lord only when the Lord causes them to do so (Isa. 53:1). It
is the work of the Holy Spirit in connection with the preaching of the Gospel.
For an introduction to the subject, see Oswald T. Allis, *Prophecy and the
Church* (1943); J. Dwight Pentecost, *TTC* (1958); L. S. Chafer, *Systematic
Theology*, Vol. IV (1948); Alva J. McClain, *The Greatness of the Kingdom*
(1959); Loraine Boettner, *The Millennium* (1958).

"will go",[13] parallels the "will flow" of the preceding verse. The reason for this great confluence is that those who come to Zion know that in Zion they will learn from the true God. This confluence at the same time evinces a dissatisfaction on the part of the people with their present condition. Many will abandon their idolatry and their false belief and will flow unto Zion.

Note how clearly the doctrine of grace is present in this passage. It is not in their own strength that peoples resolve to flow unto Zion.[14] They act only because God has worked in their hearts, making them dissatisfied with their present condition and inclining them to seek Him. This confluence is a result of the establishment of Zion.

No longer does merely one nation know the LORD, but all nations know Him. When Isaiah says many people, he does not mean all people, but simply a great multitude. Those who formerly were but "strangers and foreigners" are now "fellow citizens with the saints." During the Old Testament dispensation the glory of the gospel was hid with the nation; in the latter days, however, the church stands out, and to it men of all nations will come. The people are now scattered nations, whereas in returning to the LORD they will become one. All nations will flow unto Zion, and no nation will be excluded. Out of all these nations there will be many people.

Zion is the center of truth. If a man wishes to hear the truth he must go to the place where the truth is to be found, namely the church of the living God, where the truth of the gospel is taught.

and they shall say — Those who go to Zion mutually encourage

---

13 וְהָלְכוּ — Alexander renders "they shall set out or put themselves in motion." Fischer, *"sich aufmachen"*; Van Hoonacker, *"zullen gaan."* These renderings may be correct but I am inclined to regard this verb as at times a practical synonym of וְנָהֲרוּ (v. 2). It is used in the sense of flow in Isa. 8: 6, 7 and this is supported by one of the Mari texts: "half of the waters were flowing continually into the midst of this suripum" (*mu-u ka-a ia-an-tam i-na li-ib-bi šu-ri-pi-im še-ti i-la-ku*). Note also the Ug., "the valleys flowed with honey" (*nḫlm. tlk.nbtm*, Baal 3:3:7). Cf. Ezek. 32:14; Job 20:17, and "I shall cause to flow" (*ašhlk, Aqhat*, 3:6:8 and *Baal* 5:5:25). The sentence seems to have been, "As for thy head, I shall cause thy gray hairs to run with blood."

14 God's throne is in Zion, but this does not involve any earthly limitation of His presence. He, the Creator of all, dwells in the midst of His people to bring them redemption.

and exhort.[15] They are truly seekers after the LORD, for they exhibit the genuineness of their conversion in their desire to persuade others also to go to Zion. Those who thus speak are filled with such a burning desire to make known the doctrines of true religion that they would also persuade others to go with them. That faith which keeps silent about the gospel is a dead faith. As Calvin remarks, "And indeed nothing could be more inconsistent with the nature of faith than that deadness which would lead a man to disregard his brethren, and to keep the light of knowledge choked up within his own breast."

This passage furthermore teaches the manner in which the true doctrines of the gospel are to be made known, namely, by the voice of man, or as the New Testament calls it, by the foolishness of preaching (1 Cor. 1:21). Such activity not only imparts concern for the salvation of one another, but also encourages and strengthens us in our own belief. Whenever and wherever in the church preaching the truth has been relegated to a secondary position, in that measure the church has been unfaithful to the will of God as expressed in this prophecy.

come ye and let us go up — The desire of the people is not to ascend the mount, but simply to go up to the mount where the Temple is.[16] Those who ask others to come will show by their example that they are in earnest in desiring to be instructed in the ways of the God of Jacob. Here is a beautiful example of true evangelism.

unto the house of the God of Jacob — The God whom Jacob adored is the same God whom the nations wish to revere. Thus the worship of Israel is tied in with the time of Jacob, and so its continuity is shown. The true saving religion was not first revealed to Jacob but rather to Adam immediately after the fall. Jacob, however, is mentioned, because he was the great ancestor whose name the nation bore.[17]

and he will teach us of his ways — Is this the purpose why people

15 According to Marti these words are a gloss after Zech. 8:21. But may not Zechariah have depended upon Isaiah? The text in Zechariah is more expanded than that in Isaiah which would point to Isaiah as the original.

16 Barnes places a somewhat literal interpretation upon this figure in that he points out how often heathen people have journeyed to reach a mission station and to be taught God's Word.

17 In Micah the term Jacob appears as a name of affection for the chosen people. Frequent also is the phrase "many peoples" which would argue for the originality of the Micah passage.

go to Zion?[18] Possibly so, but more likely these words of the people simply stand in correlation with their first thoughts. "We shall go, and He will teach." If the words be so understood they express an element of hope on the part of the people. They also set forth a certainty that if one goes to Zion, God Himself will teach him. Those who come to Zion do not know God's ways; they must be taught what these ways are in order that they may walk therein. To them no instruction had previously been given, whereas Israel, who had received instruction from the LORD, does not know Him ("Israel doth not know," Isa. 1:3a).

SPECIAL NOTE

Two points must be stressed. First, God and God alone can teach the truth, for He only is the source and foundation of truth. Hence, those who proclaim the Word of God must exercise supreme care that what they preach is the Word of God. This can be accomplished only when the messenger bases his message squarely upon and makes it consonant with the written Word of God, the Bible. When the minister preaches, God must be heard. Secondly, this passage teaches that what unbelievers need above all else is teaching or doctrine. What blinds the understanding of men is ignorance, and ignorance can only be dispelled by truth. Hence, the missionary and evangelistic activity of the church must be doctrinal in character.

When the prophet asserts that God will teach of His ways, He is probably indicating the source of the teaching, namely, the ways of God. It is as though Isaiah had said that God would teach from the abundance of the ways which are His. They are His very own, and they are ways that men must learn. They are the paths in which the walk of the learner is to be conducted. This walk is the entire course of a man's life, what he thinks and says as well as how he lives. A way naturally involves a certain amount of restriction and confinement; one who would walk in God's ways must not transgress their bounds. If it be objected that the ways of God are narrow and confining, the reply must

---

18 מִן may be rendered "concerning," or it may have a partitive sense, "some," or it may express the source of the teaching " . . . make us know from the fullness, the treasure of his wise ways" (Orelli). The "ways" are "the plan of worshipping him and of seeking bliss through that worship" (*rationem ipsum colendi et per eum cultum felicitatem consequendi* — Rosenmüller). Gesenius takes the word in the sense of religion and appeals to the Koranic phrase, *sabíl 'illah* (*Koran* 4:76, 77, 78, etc.). Calvin takes it of the limits beyond which we must not go.

be that they are truth. Of what use is a broad way which leads only to destruction and eternal ruin?

and we shall walk in his paths — As a consequence of being taught, men want to walk in God's ways. True doctrine places within one's heart the desire to walk in the law of God. Truth leads to godliness, and when one has been truly instructed, he will want to do God's will. Furthermore, we learn at this point that one must first be instructed before he can walk aright. Doctrine and ethics must go hand in hand. There can be no right obedience, nor can there be any right worship, until first one has learned of God.

It should further be remarked that this teaching is not of a speculative or theoretical character, but rather is eminently practical. It produces righteousness. From this the church must learn to teach in such a manner that her hearers will be edified and will have their thoughts turned to godliness. The Bible is through and through a practical book, and nowhere does its practical character appear more clearly than at this particular point.

for out of Zion — The reason why the many go to Zion is that from Zion God's Word goes forth. It is from Zion that there issues whatever promotes the true welfare of the nations. By means of proclamation the truth goes forth from Zion.

the law — The true instruction which God has given to mankind. It is the true religion considered in its aspect as a rule of duty, which is primarily in view.[19]

the word of the Lord — The word which belongs to and which comes from God. It is an expression of the will of God, and hence serves to designate the true religion as a revelation. True religion, therefore, is supernatural in its origin and character.

For the ancient world Zion was the source of religious truth, but in the new dispensation that source is the preaching of the church. Thus the heathen world is dependent upon the faithful preaching of the church. This passage clearly teaches that the great need of the world is the preaching of the gospel, preaching that is of such a nature that it may be characterized as the very teaching of God.

---

[19] "the law" — Absolute and not construct. Bentzen makes an unnecessary distinction between the written law and the living revelation (*ikke den skrevne lov, men den levende aabenbaring*). The word simply means divine instruction as such. Why may not such instruction be written?

4 *And he shall judge among the nations* — God is now represented as one who in a peaceful manner intervenes in the disputes of nations, and settles them so that the nations change the implements of war into utensils of peace, with the result that the very knowledge of war is lost.[20] When contending nations wish to settle their disputes, they no longer engage in war, but go to God. In so doing they are assured of a judgment which is absolutely just.[21] It is through the Messiah that God makes such judgment, although that fact is not explicitly stated in this passage. Inasmuch, however, as in the broader sense, this passage does speak of the coming salvation, it is to be regarded as messianic. It is a picture of universal peace that Isaiah gives, but it is a religiously founded peace. Isaiah makes clear elsewhere (e.g., chaps. 9, 11) that peace is the work of the Messiah. Here then we have a picture of the wondrous period of peace which Messiah's coming will introduce.

and shall reprove — The verb is a practical synonym of the "shall judge" of the preceding clause, and pictures the LORD in the position of Judge and Arbiter who pronounces decisions concerning the nations and their disagreements.

and they shall beat — Lit., "they shall cut." These words begin a description of the blessed results which flow from the just rule and judgment of the LORD. This peace is genuine and hence all the prerequisites of true peace are to be found. There can only be a true peace when the hearts of men have been regenerated by the Spirit of God, the Third Person of the ever-blessed Trinity, and a new nature given to them. Consequently, when the hearts of men have been regenerated, we are to understand that the barriers which separated God from man have been removed. The peace of which Isaiah speaks is not so much a peaceful attitude or disposition which man maintains toward God, as it is a peaceful disposition which God entertains toward man. What had caused God to look upon man in wrath and judgment was man's

20 "and he will judge" — The perf. with *wāw* cons. has the same tense as the preceding imperf. used in the future. Calvin takes the verb in the sense of ruling or reigning. Drechsler refers it to God's ruling over the divisions of men which have existed since Gen. 11. Herntrich says that this rule means the return to Paradise. But the verb is really a synonym of הוכיח, to decide, arbitrate. Le Clerc has correctly interpreted, "*dissidia eorum componet, easque ad pacem adducet.*"

21 Cf. 11:4 with the acc. as in Prov. 9:7. Keizer interprets this of the work of convincing the nations of their sins.

sin. This sin has now been removed, and so God regards man with favor. He therefore approaches man with the gracious offer of salvation and brings man to Himself, giving to him a new heart and declaring that man stands in a right relation to Himself.

Man, therefore, born again from the dead, now seeks peace and pursues it. In so far as he is now true to the new principle of life within him — for sin still remains and prevents him from acting in perfect consistency with his new nature — he seeks peace. Isaiah represents this spiritual blessing by a picture of man ceasing to learn the arts of war and turning rather to those of peace. The peace herein described is not one which can be obtained by the means of what is today called pacifism, nor, for that matter, by any human efforts. Man unaided cannot establish on this earth a condition of peace. Only God can bring peace. The fulfillment of the present prophecy began with the angels' "peace on earth," and more specifically with the first preaching of the gospel. As Keizer well puts it, what is herein described is the "blessed result" of the preaching of the gospel, peace on earth through the common faith in God the Lord. The reference of the prophecy, therefore, is not to the peace which prevailed on earth at the time of Christ's birth, for while at that time there was a cessation of war, the law (in the sense intended by this passage) had not gone forth from Zion.[22]

SPECIAL NOTE

There are two prevalent types of answer to the interpretation given in this commentary.[23] On the one hand, there are those who teach

[22] *Pax Romana* is the designation of the period of peace found on earth at the time of Christ's birth. It began with the reign of Augustus Caesar. Both the civil wars of Rome and external wars had come to an end. Romans, Greeks and Jews found themselves united under one nation, and the world was prepared for the reception of Christianity. For the first time the world was united, and into this united world the Saviour was born.

[23] Some, like Pool, think that war may cease entirely before the end of the present age. Barnes claimed that wars were less barbarous than formerly, and that the tendency was toward peace. He wrote in 1838. Alexander says that the prophecy will not be fulfilled until the nations flow to the church. Cf. Boettner, *op. cit.*, p. 120.

This passage is difficult to interpret. It teaches that the blessings described will take place within the latter days, and it is this fact which supports the postmillennial interpretation of Boettner and others. Cf. Roderick Campbell, *Israel and the New Covenant* (Philadelphia: 1954). At the same time other passages speak of wars continuing until the end. Some, therefore, like Boettner

that it is possible that war may cease entirely during this present age before the return of Christ from heaven. On the other, those who are known as dispensationalists maintain that the prophecy is not fulfilled during the present age but will be fulfilled during the millennium which follows the return of Christ. This latter type of interpretation does violence of a serious kind to the general structure of Biblical eschatology. We may answer both these positions as follows: In so far as men learn of the LORD and are taught of Him they will seek to apply in their lives the principles of His government. Consequently, even at the present day, in so far as men believe the gospel and seek to practice it in their lives this prophecy finds fulfillment. At the same time it must be remembered that sin is still present, and it will not be until the complete removal of sin at the second advent of the LORD that this prophecy will be realized in its completeness. Whereas, therefore, the latter days continue until the second coming of the LORD, the blessed conditions which are introduced by these "last days" will abide forever. This prophecy, therefore, can only be understood in the general light of the structure of Biblical eschatology.

they shall beat their swords into mattocks, and their spears into pruning knives — These swords, made of iron, will be refashioned for a different usage. The word *ittim* probably denotes a sharp-edged instrument such as a mattock.[24] Possibly it is the plough knife which cuts the furrows for the ploughshare to turn up. This domestic instrument is made of the same material as the sword. The *masmeroth* are the sharp knives which were used for pruning the vines in order to increase their power to bear fruit.[25] Such instruments are mentioned only as symbols. The prophecy does not mean that men will, at the time of fulfillment, revert to the use of these weapons of war or to these particular implements of

---

(whose book is admirable) believe that the world will become relatively better, merely a foretaste of heaven. But the present passage does not speak of relative improvement but of an absolute change.

It is necessary then to maintain that the prophecy will be absolutely fulfilled in principle during the latter days. When at the second advent sin is removed, we shall realize all the blessings which are promised. This interpretation has difficulties, but it is all that one can do if he would be faithful to the language of the Bible. The postmillennial interpretation does not do adequate justice to those passages which emphasize the evil character of this present world (e.g., Joel 3:9ff.), an evil that continues to the end.

[24] אטים cf. Akk. *ittu.* spear — cf. Egy. hnj.t.

[25] מזמרות — The retention of the *Tzere* is unusual. In a near open syllable, when preceded by a long syllable, *u* and *i* generally drop to *Shewa.*

domesticity. The thought rather is that the instruments of war, whatever they may be, will be given over and refashioned to domestic uses. The result of this refashioning is that the nations will no longer be against one another as in Genesis 11, nor will individual man be against individual man as in Genesis 4.[26] There will no longer be any swords remaining for one nation to lift up in war against another.

neither shall they learn war any more — Not merely will the nations no longer practice war, they will not even know how to practice it; they will not learn war.[27] The picture herein described differs from the utopias presented by the secular poets, for this peace is the result of the instruction of the LORD. We may well give utterance to Calvin's prayer, "Would that Christ reigned entirely in us! for then would peace also have its perfect utterance."[28] The basis of the present prophecy rests upon the covenant which God made with the fathers, notably with Abraham, and enlarged by Moses. (For parallel expressions compare Isa. 9:6; 11:6-10; 19:23-25; 54:13; Jer. 3:18; Ezek. 17:22-24; Hosea 2:20; Zech. 9:10; 14:16; Ps. 72:3; 85:11. The opposite picture is given in Joel 3:10 and cf. Deut. 28:25, 36, 43, 44, 49ff.)

THE ORIGIN OF ISAIAH 2:2-4

Concerning the origin of this section much has been written. Generally speaking, we may say that there are three basic positions. (1)

[26] War as such is not condemned in this passage nor is pacifism defended. It does not necessarily follow, however, that the Messiah uses war as a means of judging ("*dat God tusschen vele volken zal richten en vele natiën zal tuchtigen* [vs. 4], *dan is ongetwijfeld de oorlog als middel daarbij gedacht*" — Edelkoort, p. 198). But the martial figure is frequently used in Scripture of the Messiah (cf. Isa. 11:4 and Rev. 17:14). Scripture makes it clear that, even though war is a result of sin, participation in war in itself is not necessarily sinful. There is only one way to proceed toward abolition of war; it is not pacifism, but individual learning the law of the Lord.

[27] Cf. Song of Sol. 3:8. Bentzen thinks that the picture of peace given in these verses stems from the old *Thronbesteigung* Psalms (46:10-11) behind which lay the whole myth of the condition of Paradise. Secular poets have often pointed to a picture of peace. Thus, Martial, *Falx ex ense: Pax me certa ducis placidos curvavit in usus; / Agricolae nunc sum, militis ante fui.* But Vergil, *Georgics* i.506ff., gives the opposite picture: *non ullus aratro / dignus honor, squalent abductis arva colonis / et curvae rigidum faces conflantur in ensem.* Also Ovid, *Fasti* 1. 699.

[28] The passage does not teach that Isaiah developed from a militarist to a pacifist; cf. Edelkoort, *De Christusverwachting in het Oude Testament* (Wageningen, 1941), p. 197.

Isaiah is thought to be the original author. Cf. Schmidt, *SAT*, II, 2, 112. He maintains that the passage agrees with 9:1 and 11:1 and that Isaiah was a more important prophet than Micah. Duhm thinks that no sufficient arguments have been raised against Isaianic authorship, and he believes the prophecy is related to 11:6ff. and 32:1-4. Fischer leans mildly toward this view, also Procksch and Steinmann, and among older writers, Lowth, Vitringa and Umbreit.

(2) The prophecy is not original either with Micah or Isaiah. Bleeker (*Kleine Profeten*, II, 104) holds that there was an old oracle which stood in a twofold tradition. One redactor ascribed it to Micah, another to Isaiah. Van der Flier (*Jesaja*, I, 86) denies the passage to either, but does not know from what period it came. Marti believes that the passage comes from a disciple of "2nd Isaiah," because of its phraseology and concepts. Weiser attributes it to the work of the editor of both writings and hence regards it as anonymous (*Einleitung*, p. 150). Möller thinks that both passages go back to an older prophecy which both Micah and Isaiah used. Many older writers held essentially this view, Eichhorn, Hitzig, Ewald, Koppe, Rosenmüller, Maurer. Two objections are raised against it. It is said to conflict with the heading. But if Isaiah used the prophecy under divine inspiration this objection would be removed. Also, Isaiah is then said to be reduced to a man who flaunted other men's prophecies (Edelkoort). But Isaiah is doing no such thing. He simply adapts the prophecy to his uses.

(3) Micah is the original author. This position is not without difficulty, but on the whole it probably has most to commend it. It has been held by Gesenius, Ryssel, Van Hoonacker, Keil, Delitzsch, etc. Marti thinks that Jer. 26:18 is a decisive veto of this view, in that it shows that at Jeremiah's time people knew only of Micah's prophecy of Zion's destruction and not of its glorification. But the fact that Jeremiah mentions one of Micah's prophecies does not mean that he did not know of others. Furthermore, the prophets spoke both of blessing and judgment. Jeremiah quoted the one prophecy merely because it was applicable and pertinent.

Kroeker states that we do not know the occasion which caused Isaiah to utter these words. Steinmann thinks that the presence of the passage in the two great eighth-century prophets shows that it comes from that time. Against the view that the universalism points to the exilic or postexilic periods is the consideration that universalism characterized the Old Testament revelation almost from its beginning (cf. Gen. 12:1-3; 18:18, etc.).

According to Herntrich, the present passage is an interpolation. He thinks that originally there must have been another introduction to verses 2-4. Bentzen also remarks that the prophecy is to be regarded as an anonymous utterance. The thoughts of these verses, he maintains, would not have been known in the days of Isaiah or of his disciples. On the other hand, the description of Zion herein given does not agree with that of the so-called "second Isaiah," consequently, we are not to look to postexilic times for the period of authorship. Rather, the passage rests upon the idea of the enthronement of the king. It is, he says, a typical example of the eschatologizing of the Enthronement Psalms (*Digtet er et typisk exempel paa tronbestigelsesalmernes eskatologisering*). This view is of course based upon the assumption of certain modern scholars that in ancient Israel there was an annual festival of the enthronement of the king. (See Appendix III.) Bentzen remarks that in former times it was generally assumed that either Isaiah or Micah had taken this passage from one another, for, as is well known, this prophecy occurs with minor variations in Mic. 4:1-5. Jer. 23:30, however, Bentzen thinks, sufficiently refutes this conception.

We cannot dismiss this old view so easily, however. This is the only prophecy in Isaiah which begins with *wehayah*, which in the context must have a future force. The abruptness of the prophecy is used as an argument to support the position that it was taken from another source and is not original with Isaiah. At the same time, even if this were the case, it forms a suitable introduction to the message which follows, in which the prophet proclaims the judgment of the Lord and returns to a conclusion which consists of promises of the same nature as those found in this present section.

It has also been held that the passage is original with Isaiah, and in support of this position appeal may be made to the first verse, which explicitly speaks of the word that Isaiah saw. Bultema holds the rather strange position that the same prophecy was revealed twice to different persons upon two different occasions. Gesenius, on the other hand, in his commentary, considered the prophecy to be one that was well known in those days, and which each prophet adopted for his own uses.

If we examine the form of the prophecy in Micah we discover that it there constitutes an integral portion of the book. In the first place, it forms a striking and cogent contrast to the picture of desolation previously given in Mic. 3:12. One passes from 3:12 to the present prophecy very naturally. It should also be noted how naturally Mic. 4:4 follows this promise. This strongly supports the position that the original form of the prophecy is found in Micah. The variations which appear in Isaiah are such as we might expect from a writer who has adapted another prophecy or passage to his own uses.

Isaiah	*Micah*
2. and all nations shall flow into it	1. and people shall flow into it
3. and many people shall go and say	2. and many nations shall come and say
4. and he shall judge among the nations	3. and he shall judge among many people
and shall rebuke many people	and shall rebuke strong nations afar off.

Duhm thinks that this is the language of a poet, since it is not introduced with a "Thus saith the Lord." He thinks that 11:1ff. could once have preceded this strophe, and on the whole he prefers the Septuagint text (B), which we may translate as follows; "For there shall be in the last day visible (ἐμφανές) the amount of the Lord and the house of God upon the tops of the mountains and it shall be lifted up above the hills. And there shall come upon it all the nations, and many nations shall go and they shall say, Come, and let us go up into the mount of the Lord and unto the house of the God of Jacob, and he will announce to us his way, and we shall walk in it." Duhm favors the LXX, " —because of verse three, because of the metre, and especially because of the better sense."

In spite of Duhm the Hebrew text does yield a good sense. To be sure, it is difficult, but that is in favor of its originality. B seems to represent an attempt to smooth out the difficulties found in the Hebrew. In B the ὅτι ἔσται after a preceding λόγος has a recitative effect.

b. *Judah's present corruption* (2:5-11)

5 O house of Jacob, come ye and let us walk in the light of the Lord.

6 For thou hast forsaken thy people the house of Jacob, because they are filled from the east, and are soothsayers like the Philistines, and with the children of strangers they associate.

7 And his land is filled with silver and gold, neither is there any end to his treasures; and his land is filled with horses, neither is there any end to his chariots.

8 And his land is filled with idols; to the work of their hands they bow down, to that which their own fingers have made.

9 And the mean man is bowed down, and the great man is humbled; and forgive them not.

10 Enter into the rock, and hide thee in the dust, from before the fear of the Lord, and from the glory of his majesty.

11 The haughty eyes of man shall be humbled, and the haughtiness of men shall be bowed down, and the Lord alone shall be exalted in that day.

5 This impassioned cry forms a suitable connection between what precedes and what follows.[29] From the wondrous picture of the future, from the contemplation of the blessing that is one day to come, Isaiah turns to the actual city of Jerusalem and the actual people of Judah in whose midst he lives. The house of Jacob, those who are descended from Jacob, the inhabitants of eighth-century Jerusalem and Judah, is quite different from the Zion of the future. The Temple stands there in all its Solomonic beauty; the sacrifices are performed, but the nation does not delight in the law of God. All about is oppression and wickedness. Does not this people, the house of Jacob, know that Zion will one day be the center of salvation? As though echoing the words of the nations, "Come, and let us go unto the mount of the LORD," the prophet breaks forth in this mighty command. Once before Isaiah had so commanded the sinful nation, when he had said, "Come, and let us reason together." In each instance the imperative is followed by a cohortative, "Come, and let us. . . ." It is as though Isaiah had said, "Leave the place where you are, the place of your sin, and come, together let us walk."

What the foreign nations will do in the latter days thus forms an occasion for the prophet to incite his own people, to whom the promises of future blessing had been made, to imitate the practice of these nations. The accents of an appealing tenderness are found in this exhortation, as the prophet is mindful of the gracious purposes of God toward His people. We are to understand the force of the word "light" in connection with the "he

[29] Marti considers v. 5 a later addition, too similar to Mic. to be connected with the following. Bentzen, however, says that the verse has no parallel in Micah and its insertion is to be explained as the work of a reader who wanted his people to follow the example of the heathen (this is a tacit acknowledgment of the propriety of the verse's present position).

The verse is not a call to repentance but an exhortation to enjoy privileges, claims Fullerton. Inasmuch as it lies outside the strophical scheme (3 stanzas of 6 lines each) it is probably a later comment upon the poem. The final editor found it attached to vv. 2-4 upon which it is based. Who inserted it we do not know. The condition for which v. 5 pleads is affirmed by Mic. 4:5 as already existing. Mic. 4:5 is therefore a corrective of Isa. 2:5 (cf. *JBL*, XXXV (1916), 134ff.).

But Isaiah did not bind his utterances in a mechanical strophic arrangement. How much more satisfactory than the above suggestions is the natural interpretation that, overcome with the grandeur of the majestic prediction he is uttering, Isaiah, seeing the terrible reality at hand of a sinful people, pleads with them here and now to walk in the light of the Lord!

will teach" of verse 3. The word does not, therefore, primarily designate salvation, but rather saving teaching or doctrine. In the broadest sense, it may be taken as a synonym for "revelation," and specifically, God's revelation concerning His will and the duty which He requires of His people. To walk in such a light is to order the course of one's entire life so that it will be in conformity with that light.[30] It will not be a walking in darkness, but in the open clear light where it may be plainly seen and where the course upon which one is to walk is also lucent and is not obscured by the darkness or ignorance of sin.

6 *For thou hast forsaken thy people the house of Jacob* — The change in subject is surprising, but Isaiah was full of his message.[31] The reason for the rejection is stated in a prayer of agony addressed directly to God. The people are not walking in the light of the LORD, and the prophet, reminded of that tragic fact, turns to God, conscious that God has rejected His people.

In thus speaking Isaiah does not mean that God has abandoned His promises of mercy, but rather that God has cast the people off, left them to their own devices. For His name's sake, He will not abandon them utterly (1 Sam. 12:22 and Ps. 94:14). Twice in this verse Isaiah uses the word "for" (*ki*). The first *ki* is a reminder, a warning, which is substantiated and vindicated by the second.

Isaiah now proceeds to state the consequences of the divine rejection, which consequences at the same time constitute the grounds or reason for the rejection.[32] It is difficult to tell which emphasis is the more prominent, but it is probable that the phrase,

---

30 Cf. Vos: " . . . to be open always to the influx of divine truth (2:5). The ideal in the prophet's mind is that Israel as a whole shall live in such unbroken communication with Jehovah as he was aware of possessing for himself (note the plural 'let us walk')," (*BT*, p. 300).

31 "thou hast forsaken" — B has the 3rd person, but IQ, ASTh have the 2nd person. Cf. also Jer. 15:6 and Deut. 32:15. Calvin takes the introductory particle as surely (*certe*). Perhaps it is better to treat *ki* here as a causal particle *because*, which grounds the appeal made in verse 5.

32 Cf. Ps. 94:14; 1 Sam. 12:22. König interprets "for thou house of Jacob, hast given up thy people." "Thy people," he says, can indicate the nation at it should be in God's sight. In reply, we would point out that "thy people" can only refer to God's people. How could the Israelites abandon the Israelites? The text does not say that Israel has abandoned her ideal as people of God. The Targ., "for ye have forsaken the fear of the Mighty One, who was delivering you, O ye that are of the house of Jacob."

"they are filled" stresses primarily the ground for God's rejection of His people. The fourfold recurrence of this thought is striking; 6b, 7a, 7b and 8.

they are filled from the east — The picture is that of a vessel that is filled, and hence has no room to hold anything further.[33] The nation is filled with what comes from the east which is always represented as the source from whence these superstitions have filled the nation.[34] To state the case in a slightly different fashion, we may say that the nation is filled with the east. By means of caravans crossing the desert east and northeast of Palestine there had actually been an influx of soothsayers and an introduction to eastern ways of life. The east is probably the Syrian desert and the lands beyond.[35]

What a contrast! In the latter days other nations will come to Zion to learn the ways of the God of truth. Now, other nations come to Zion and influence it to follow the superstitions of their gods. Zion is now satiated with these things from the east. Once the nation was full of judgment and the knowledge of God. They are no longer filled with that knowledge but rather with what the east provides (cf. 1:21b).

soothsayers like the Philistines — Not only are the people filled from the east, but there are present soothsayers like the Philistines as well. The two clauses are correlative, and the second is not to be taken as the object of the first. The soothsayers, who

---

[33] "they are filled" — The prophet indicates an action performed or a condition brought about in the past whose effects still continue. Those who deny the unity of the passage divide it differently. Procksch, dating the passage after the inaugural vision, divides it into three sections: vv. 6-10; 11-17 and 18-22, and finds additions in the later section. Bentzen entitles the whole "the day of Yahweh," regarding vv. 6ff., as an oracle of punishment, vv. 12ff. as an oracle of judgment (also vv. 19ff.). These denials of the unity of the chapter rest largely upon the assumption that vs. 6 is not to be connected with what precedes. Thus, Herntrich says that *ki* could refer to a lost beginning but is not completely persuaded of this, for he compares the similar construction in 3:1; 15:1 and 29:30. He acknowledges that *ki* may be translated "certainly."

[34] מן — here seems to indicate the material with which one is filled. Parallels are Gen. 28:11; Exod. 17:5. Trapp comments, " . . . more superstitious than the Syrians and Mesopotamians." He compares the influx of heathenism before the time of Christ. Brenz (see Gesenius) seems first to have conjectured reading קסם for קדם. This is favorably regarded by Vos, but the textual evidence is against it.

[35] Drechsler points out that some of the articles mentioned in chap. 3 are of eastern origin.

are observers of omens of some sort, do not come from Philistia, but are to be compared with Philistia. The nation of sons has now become like the uncircumcised Philistines in that, just as the Philistines are filled with the soothsayers, so also is the nation filled. The written law of God had expressly forbidden the existence of soothsayers in the land, and their widespread presence at this time shows how far the nation had departed from the LORD (cf. Lev. 19:26; Deut. 18:10).

they associate — The Israelites were forming their constant associations with men of foreign descent.[36] Their own background and history they are ready to reject. They do not glory in the mighty acts of the God of their fathers, but instead fraternize with those who do not know God's wondrous deeds. In itself the association with foreigners is not to be condemned, but in this context it is tantamount to a rejection of Israel's own history and a preference for those who by birth are not heirs of the promise. Abraham longed for a seed, but the Judah of Isaiah's day would reject that seed and the promises which had been made to it.

7 And his land is filled — A second evidence of filling from the east. The land of the people; the suffix "his" probably refers to the word "people" of the preceding verse. The verb employed has a descriptive rather than narrative force, and so pictures the condition of the land as filled. The thought is that the land once was full and now as a consequence is still filled.

silver and gold — In the law (Deut. 17:17) the king was forbidden to multiply silver and gold, for these would tend toward an effeminate manner of life and to the destruction of religion and morality, inasmuch as those who possess much silver and gold are never satisfied with what they have but always seek to procure more.[37] There was also the danger that the accumulation

---

36 וישפיקו — The imp. may express customary action in present time. This verb is difficult to interpret. Barnes renders, "they please themselves"; Delitzsch, "they make common cause with"; Alexander, "they abound in"; Calvin, "they acquiesce in" (*acquierint*). Cf. the Ug., "he satisfied [?] the sheep gods with wine," *špq. élm krm. y[n]*, Baal VI:47. Here the verb is transitive; Cf. Ar. *shafaqa*, "to be niggardly." In Hebrew the root means *"to clap hands with a person,"* to associate with someone.

37 "is filled" — When the active verb can govern a double object, the passive, here a verb of plenty, may govern the more remote object. "silver and gold" — Like Tyre (cf. Zech. 9:3), Deut. 17:17 forbade the accumulation of silver and gold (cf. 1 Chron. 29:4; 2 Chron. 8:18; 9:10). Rosenmüller

of great wealth would tend to draw the interest of other powers, a danger which was actually realized when the Babylonian envoys came (Isa. 39).

Whether the silver and gold were ill-gotten gain or not cannot be proved. It is not silver and gold in themselves which are condemned, but the filling of the land with these things. An overabundance even of good things can turn the heart away from God. When God's people are filled with the fullness which the world offers, they are empty toward God. What should be emptiness for them is fullness for the nations. Having given up the richness of the promises of God, the nation falsely appraised the treasures of the world and then the world's ideals and finally its idols.

any end — These words signify the eager and insatiable desire for the pursuit after money. The people have literally become money mad.[38]

treasures — As just described these were chiefly of silver and gold.

horses — Deuteronomy also forbade the multiplying of horses (17:16), for this would tend to remind the nation of Egypt and its power, and would also lead towards war and confidence in human ability and so toward idolatry. From Egypt Israel had learned the art of war with horses. The multiplication of horses would suggest a standing army, and a standing army can at times be dangerous. In case of defense a standing army may have been legitimate, although even in such a case the nation was to rely upon the LORD. The tendency, however, would be to increase the size of the army and in times of emergency and danger to trust in it. Such an army would lead to reliance upon human power

---

calls attention to Horace, *Epistles* 1. 2, 56: *"semper avarus eget,"* and comments, *"possidentium animus non impleatur."* Luxurious living produces forgetfulness of God, so that men do not discern His work in history; "every truly religious man ought to have his eyes and ears open to what the course of history portends. Isaiah has here distinctly formulated the thought that history is a revelation of Jehovah, in which there is no place for accident or confusion" (Vos). The multiplication of riches is thus a symptom of religious apostasy (Verhoef). God's people should be filled with those things in which the world is empty.

38 Calvin refers these words to the insatiable appetite of those who seek for money and wealth. Alexander thinks that they simply indicate the great extent of the treasures already acquired.

rather than upon God and so was contrary to the true spirit of the theocracy.[39]

8 *And his land is filled with idols* — The most heinous and offensive of those objects with which the land was filled were the idols, for they formed a ghastly caricature of the true destiny of the nation. The existing glory was but a parody of the true glory which had been promised to the people. To it God had given His law and prophets. He made His ways known unto Moses, and His acts to the children of Israel. But Israel would not have Him. Instead of the land being filled with the glory of *El*, the true God, it was filled with *elim*, nothingnesses. These were not merely private idols, but idols which formed the worship of the entire land. Through traffic and commerce with other countries, idolatry was introduced into Judah. The folly of idolatry, a favorite theme with Isaiah, is now introduced. To bow down to what the hand of man has made is the height of folly.

In the broadest sense we may understand as idolatrous all that is created by man and then worshiped by him. In such a category belong all false philosophies and all the theories of unbelief. These are human products, and to regard them as in any sense regulative of the life and conduct of man is to engage in idolatry.[40]

---

[39] Solomon broke the command of Deuteronomy (cf. 1 Kings 10:26). Alexander, however, thinks the verse teaches that the nation had undue dependence upon the power of other nations. That is possible, but does not exhaust the verse's meaning.

[40] The enallage of the numbers is due to the fact that the subject is considered in a distributive sense, whereas the verb is collective. *BH* would take the verb in the singular, but manuscript evidence opposes this and interchange in the number of the suffixes is common in Semitic. The use of the imp. is striking, expressing action in what would otherwise have been a colorless description. "and the land is filled with idols, to the work of their own hands . . . they bow down." As to the verb I incline to derive it from חוה. It would then be an *Istaf'al* (the tenth stem of Ar.) "to ask for life," and so, "to bow down, to prostrate oneself." In Ug. *hwy*, (to bow down) in the *'st* stem: *lp'n. il. tḥbr. wtql tštḥwy. wtkbdh.* "at the feet of Il she bows and bends, she prostrates herself and honors him" (Gordon, *UH*, i, pp. 72, 73).

אלילים is really a disdainful term, "little gods," or "godlets." Probably the basic meaning is "worthless," "insufficient." Cf. Akk. *ul*, "not"; Syr. *'alil* ("weak", "miserable"). There is possibly a relation with South Ar. *'l'lt̲*. These worthless gods fail to measure up to the conception of true deity. We are not to think of the beautiful statues of the Greek gods and goddesses, but of the repugnant amulets which archaeology has made known. These may have been figurines of gods in the form of animals, demons, placques of Astarte, etc. Cf. Steinmann, p. 61; H. Vincent, *Canaan*, pp. 158ff.

The condition of the nation at that time was a living violation of the first commandment.

9 Isaiah now passes from a description of the sins to their consequences.[41] He is not, therefore, simply continuing the description of those sins. In Isaiah's day, however, this humbling had not yet taken place, and so the prophet uses the phenomenon of the prophetic perfect in order to express the certainty with which this humbling will come. The thought is that as a result of the conditions described in verse 8, the mean man is bowed down, or will be bowed down.

Two words, *adam* and *ish* are employed, the first of which signifies mankind as such, and the second the man of importance. All men, therefore, whatever their station in life may be, whether low or high, will be bowed down. This is not a bowing performed out of adoration, but one which is brought about by compulsion. The people have lived in worldly glory and in utter contempt of the glory of the true God; they will, therefore, one day feel the weight of His punishment, and will be bowed down under it.

forgive them not — The verse closes with a command, whereas we might expect a simple indicative.[42] The prophet, however, describes the occurrence under the force of an imperative. There can be no pardon; "thou canst not possibly pardon them." We are reminded of the passage upon which this verse is based, ". . . and that will by no means clear the guilty . . ." (Exod. 34:7). By his direct address to God Isaiah thus intrudes himself into the midst of the condemnation. Because of the sinful practices described in the preceding verse, the humbling judgment of God

41 Trapp, for example, thinks that this verse simply describes how all kinds of men bow down to idols, "lords and losels, kings and caitiffs; all sorts were idolaters." The *wāw* cons. expresses result, as in Ps. 33:9; Isa. 40:14; 51:15. Here the verb is the equivalent of the prophetic perfect. It is connected with the historical statements of vv. 6-8 as though it were actually accomplished, "and, as a result, man will be bowed down" (lit., "and man was bowed down"). Fullerton offers a somewhat subjective analysis of 2:9-21 in *JBL*, 38 (1919).

Luther distinguishes between אדם and איש in *der Pöbel und die Junker*. Note the distinction between *vir* and *homo*, and ἀνήρ and ἄνθρωπος. Cf. also Isa. 52:14. Verhoef remarks, *"gewone mense wat in die massa verdwyn, en mense wat daarbo uitsteek"* (p. 14).

42 אל with the jussive may stand in the graphic language of poetry for a prediction, which in prose would have been expressed by לא with the indicative. In a common formula such as this the definite object may be omitted (cf. Gen. 18:24, 25).

will come upon all men, and then it will be too late for forgiveness. Then God cannot forgive them, and this act will vindicate the word of the prophet.

10 The judgment is surely coming, a terrible judgment, and if anyone would seek to escape it, supposing that were possible, he should hide himself in the rock.[43] Isaiah is not pleading for repentance but he is trying to impress upon his people the awfulness of the punishment to come. The Hebrew word *bo,* which we have translated "enter," is more literally rendered, "come." It is as though the prophet had commanded, "Come, you nation which sought to exalt yourself through your idolatry and sinful practices — your utter confidence in man alone — come now into the lowest of places, the rocks and the dust, for God, whom ye neglected, is now coming in judgment."

There need not necessarily be irony in these words. There is, however, a terrible earnestness. It is of course impossible for man to obey the prophet's command, for it is impossible to hide from God. A time for repentance had passed and Isaiah would have the nation realize its terrible predicament.

the rock — The land of Judah was mountainous, and there were many caverns and caves which would have provided suitable hiding places for escape from an enemy. From the glory of the Lord, however, they will provide no refuge.

the dust — The clefts in the earth. The word "dust" is sometimes used of the grave, but that is not necessarily its sense here. If even a hole in the ground may be found, that is to be chosen for refuge. This coming judgment, as Calvin puts it, is more to be dreaded than a thousand deaths.

the fear of the Lord — Isaiah's thought is not so much that the very presence of Yahweh inspires fear as that His appearance itself is fearful and terrible. People are to seek refuge from the fearful appearance of Yahweh.

and the glory of his majesty — His glorious majesty. The appearance of Yahweh in judgment is thus depicted as something that is most glorious and terrible. Not only is God's glory manifested in His grace, but in His judgment as well. It is from such an appearance that men are commanded to flee, the very command in itself making clear how impossible this is: men cannot flee from

---

[43] This entire verse is omitted in 1Q. B adds the refrain to make this verse conform with v. 19 (Gesenius).

God and hide themselves from Him. In preaching as he does here, Isaiah is going contrary to modern psychological theories which assert that it is unwise and even wrong to use fear as a motif in preaching and teaching. How different God's appraisal of preaching! The judgment, and it is primarily the last judgment that is here in view, is set before sinful men as a terrible reality. They must turn from their sins, if they would escape such judgment. This is the only motif in preaching that will prevail with sinners. Then men might begin somewhat to understand the hatred that God has for sin and to turn from their evil ways to flee to Christ for refuge. The only way to run from God is to run to Him.

11 This verse forms a summary of what has previously been said; man is to be brought low, and God alone will be exalted.

the haughty eyes — Man's haughtiness is personified; its eyes with which it has looked are to be humbled.[44] Haughty looks and proud eyes must be abased (cf. Ps. 18:27; Prov. 21:4; Isa. 10:12).

shall be humbled — Isaiah uses the verb in the singular, and apparently takes the subject in a collective sense. The thought of the language is not so much that man himself will be brought low as that the haughtiness expressed in his looks will be humbled. This has not yet occurred, although the prophet uses a verb in the perfect to express the certainty that it will take place.

shall be bowed down — The thought is, "The eyes of the haugh-

---

[44] שפל — The simple perf. expresses the certain and inevitable fu. With what is the verb to be construed? Maurer maintains that it refers to the last proper name mentioned, and Drechsler also. Logically this would seem to be correct, but the thought is not so much that man himself will be brought low, as the haughtiness expressed in his looks. Gesenius therefore construes the verb with "eyes." Possibly, the whole complex idea serves as subject. *BH* suggests emending the verb to the pl., but in a compound subj. the pred. may sometimes agree with a gen., rather than with the cons.

ונשגב — After a perf. expressing definite assurance, the perf. with *wāw* cons. may be used to express a fut. action which is the consequence of the action set forth by the previous verb. Driver takes the *wāw* as weak, expressing co-ordination with the preceding verb.

Barnes finds the reference to the exile. Primarily, however, it refers to the time of exaltation par excellence, when the Lord will be exalted not only in fact but also in the estimation of His creatures, namely, the final judgment. It may well be that there are certain proximate fulfillments of the prophecy, as appear, for example, in chap. 3, but the ultimate reference is to the last judgment.

tiness of man shall be humbled, and consequently the haughtiness of men shall be bowed down."

and the Lord alone shall be exalted — At the time when men shall be abased, Yahweh will be exalted and He alone. The primary reference is to the time when Yahweh will be exalted, not only in fact, but also in the estimation of all His creatures, and that is the time of the final judgment.[45] All previous judgments and exaltations are but precursors of the final judgment and exaltation.

c. *The Day of the Lord* (2:12-22)

12 For the Lord of hosts hath a day upon everything haughty and lofty, and upon everything that is lifted up and it shall be brought low.

13 And upon all the cedars of Lebanon, that are high and lifted up, and upon all the mighty trees of Bashan.

---

45 Involved in the exaltation of God is the abasing of man. This exaltation in which judgment falls upon man consists in a purification by destroying all that is evil in the creation, and in preserving the remnant. According to von Rad (*JSS*, IV, No. 2, 97-108), the concept derived from the ancient idea of the "wars of the Lord." Watts (*VPA*, pp. 70ff.) thinks that the term "day of the Lord" was a suitable description for the high point of the autumnal festival of the New Year, and at the fulfillment or realization in history of what the cult pictured the "day of the Lord" as being. Smith thinks that it is a mere recoil from the exalted message of 2:2-4 that leads Isaiah now to speak of an exaltation of Yahweh and an abasement of man. Mowinckel asserts that the day was originally the festal day of Yahweh's enthronement.

Whether or not God used historical antecedents in His revelation of "the day" to the prophets, one cannot always say. In Isaiah the characteristic of that "day" is the " . . . sweeping away of all that is a caricature of divinity" (Vos, p. 313). It will be an appearance of the Lord, so that as Isaiah once was dismayed, the seraphim hid their faces, Moses and Elijah hid in caves, the whole earth will be shaken.

The expression has already occurred in Amos 5:18; Joel 1:15 and Zephaniah 1:14, and has eschatological significance.

MODERN LITERATURE ON "THE DAY OF THE LORD": W. O. E. Oesterley, *The Doctrine of the Last Things* (London: 1909); S. Mowinckel, *He That Cometh* (Nashville: 1954); P. A. Munch, *The Expression bajjōm hāhū* (Oslo: 1936); G. Hölscher, *Die Ursprünge der jüdischen Eschatologie* (Giessen: 1925); E. Sellin, *Israelitische-jüdische Religionsgeschichte* (Leipzig; 1933): L. Köhler, *Theologie des Alten Testaments;* J. Pedersen, *Israel* I, II (London: 1926-1947), I, 547ff.; P. Volz, *Die Eschatologie der jüdischen Gemeinde im neutestamentlichen Zeitalter* (Tübingen: 1934); W. A. Heidel, *The Day of Jahweh* (New York: 1929); L. I. Pap, *Das israelitische Neujahrsfest* (Kampen: 1933); P. Verhoef, *Die Dag van die Here* (Den Haag: 1956); Van Imschoot, *Theologie de l' Ancien Testament,* I (Tournai: 1954); Pentecost, *TTC*, pp. 230, 231.

14 And upon all the high mountains and upon all the hills that are lifted up.

15 And upon every high tower, and upon every inaccessible wall.

16 And upon all the ships of Tarshish, and upon all the ships of pleasure.

17 And the loftiness of man shall be bowed down, and the haughtiness of men shall be made low, and the LORD alone shall be exalted in that day.

18 And as for the idols, the whole of them shall pass away.

19 And they shall go into the caves of the rocks and into the holes of the dust, from before the fear of the LORD and from the glory of his majesty, when he ariseth to cause the earth to tremble.

20 In that day a man shall cast his idols of silver and his idols of gold, which they made each one for himself to worship, to the moles and to the bats.

21 To go into the crevices of the rocks and the clefts of the crags from before the fear of the LORD and from the glory of his majesty when he ariseth to cause the earth to tremble.

22 Cease ye from man, whose breath is in his nostrils: for wherein is he to be accounted?

12 Isaiah now announces the judgment with particular reference to a number of objects in which man had placed his confidence. We may paraphrase the thought: "In that day Yahweh alone will be exalted, for, as a matter of fact, there is a day which belongs alone to Yahweh of hosts. Man has had his day, a day in which he has chosen the idols to be his supports. Now, Yahweh is to have His day, and that day of His will affect all that in the sight of man is high and lifted up."

a day — The word is prominent. A day is coming, and so the present order will be overthrown. But does not a day, in distinction from night, bring the light of blessing? This day, however, belongs to the Lord of hosts. It is the time of world judgment, adumbrations or foreshadowings of which are to be found in the earlier judgments of Yahweh, such as the exile and the first advent. Other prophets had already mentioned the day, but it is in Isaiah that the concept obtains a force not found previously. It is pictured as a storm which sweeps over everything that in the opinion of man was lifted up and exalted.[46] It is going too far,

---

[46] This seems to be implied in the rendering of the Targ., "for a day is about to come from before the Lord of hosts." Kissane and Gray even indicate the direction which the storm is supposed to take, coming from the northeast and sweeping across the country to the southwest.

however, to maintain that we can actually trace the directions that this storm will take. What is important is that just as a storm of wind blows in force over the land so also will the day come. As the approaching storm sweeps over the entire land and devastates it, so the storm of judgment will utterly bring the whole earth to ruin and destruction, and particularly all that man used as an object of confidence.

over everything haughty and lofty, and on everything that is lifted up — The judgment to come will be over everything; it will be on them in the sense of being against them. These three designations sum up the entirety of that upon which God's wrath will fall in punitive judgment; thus, the objects of judgment and the judgment itself are comprehended briefly in one phrase or sentence.

In the Fall the inanimate creation was also affected and cursed. Instead of developing the creation to the fullest that the name of God might be glorified, man has misused it by idolatry, worshiping the creature rather than the Creator. He has taken of this creation and from it has made for himself gods to which he has bowed down. Therefore, the creation itself, which has been so misused, is to feel the effect of the divine judgment, not because it is evil in itself, but because it has been abused and perverted by man. The day will show that the creation, which man had

---

The expression occurs in Akk., "May they reach to thy fearful day" (i.e., the day of the fire god). (Tallqvist, *Die assyrische Beschwörungsserie, Maqlu*, I, 117; Hölscher, *Geschichte der israelitischen und jüdischen Religion* [1922], p. 105). Hölscher thinks (in opposition to Gressmann) that the phrase has nothing to do with eschatology, but merely refers to an epiphany of God in storm and thunder against His foes. The same thought, he tells us, appears in Greek literature, where Poseidon helps Scipio to take Carthage by means of a flood (Polybius x.11.14). But such comparisons are superficial. In Isa. 2, the "day" is one in which all that in which man exults and even man's haughtiness will be abased, and God alone will be exalted. There were doubtless foreshadowings of this fact in earlier judgments such as the exile or the first advent of Christ, but if we take the language of Isaiah seriously, how can we fail to see that the prophet is speaking of an absolute exaltation of Yahweh in which all else will be completely suppressed? That is the last judgment, and to speak of the last judgment is to speak of eschatology.

In the Koran the expression occurs based on the Old Testament (cf. Sura 2:8). In itself the word *yawm* in the Koran refers to the day of judgment. Thomas of Celano has rightly interpreted the Scripture in his hymn:

> *That day of wrath, that dreadful day*
> *When heaven and earth shall pass away!*
> *What power shall be the sinner's stay?*
> *How shall he meet that dreadful day?*

regarded as high and lofty, is in reality only something created, and that Yahweh alone is to be truly exalted.

and it shall be brought low — This thought is expressed in the Hebrew by one word; one word suffices to state the outcome of judgment. The day not only exalts the Lord, but it brings all else low.

The verse clearly states the fact that there is a day, a particular period which belongs to Yahweh of hosts. We are not, however, to conclude that only this one special period belongs to Him, for He is the Lord of all and is sovereign over time as well as over all else. This one day, however, is singled out for mention, inasmuch as therein His sovereignty will be manifested in the judgment, and will also be recognized universally.

13 Isaiah now begins to enumerate the objects which will be affected by the divine judgment. In so doing he seeks to give specimens of those things upon which the judgment will fall, and does not merely mention them as symbols of the type of object that will perish. Nor does he use these terms in a metaphorical sense to designate or to signify the leaders of the nation.[47] The things mentioned will themselves feel the punishing hand of God. All nature is bound up with man in one common history; in every sense of the word this is a fallen creation, and because of man's sin, nature must suffer.

cedars of Lebanon — These cedars were particularly admired by the Jews of Old Testament times (cf. Ps. 92:12; 104:16; Ezek. 31:3).[49] The cedar was used by Solomon in the building of the Temple at Jerusalem (1 Kings 5:6); it was also used in the building of the second Temple (Ezra 3:7). The trunk of the cedar was employed for masts of ships (Ezek. 27:5). The cedar is a conifer, having large cones, and also evergreen leaves which do not fall off in the wintertime. Lebanon is used in the Bible as a symbol of beauty (Jer. 22:6, Zech. 11:1ff.).

---

[47] Kroeker maintains that what the people possessed will now become its curse and downfall, and quotes the Russian by way of example, *"mwee vahs oobyawm vahsheem rooblyawm,"* i.e., "we shall kill you with your own rubles." Spiritual and moral subjects, maintains Barnes, are represented by the beautiful imagery taken from objects of nature, so that here the reference is to princes and nobles.

[48] ארז — Cedars (*cedrus Libani Barrell*), see Löw, I, *Die Flora der Juden*, I-IV (1924-1934). But this tree does not have sufficiently long trunks for building purposes. BK therefore suggests *abies cilicica* or some other conifer of tall growth (cf. *Baal*, ii:vi:18ff.). "They went to Lebanon and its trees, to Siryon for the choicest of its cedars" (*arzh*) (cf. 2 Chron. 2:7ff.).

mighty trees of Bashan — Bashan is the region south of Damascus, east of the Jordan River, the modern Hauran. The oaks of this district were apparently quite famous (Ezek. 27:6), as were also the pastures and flocks (Ezek. 39:18). The cedars and oaks were notable specimens of trees, and the point of the verse is that these things, which to men seemed to be high and lifted up, would in the judgment of God become low.[49] Because of man's sin, even the great and beautiful things of creation were to be destroyed.

Man does not have the right to destroy the creation in a wanton manner. Wanton demolition of nature may often bring with it the recompense of its reward. The destruction of forests, for example, may sometimes cause serious floods. God, however, is the Creator, and He alone has the right and prerogative to create and to destroy.

14 By a general mention of mountains Isaiah completes the picture. The mountains are specimens of what is grandest and highest.[50] "Before the mountains were brought forth, or ever thou hadst formed the earth and the world, even from everlasting to everlasting, thou *art* God" (Ps. 90:2). The implication of this verse is that the mountains stood forth even before man himself was created and so are enduring. Yet even over such majestic and high mountains will the sovereignty of Yahweh be displayed.

15 The prophet now leaves the objects of nature, grand and majestic as they are, and turns to those things which were the creation of men's hands and on which men depended for protection.

every high tower — In the world of men the tower is lofty and glorious, "And there shall be upon every high mountain, and upon every high hill, rivers *and* streams of waters in the day of the great slaughter, when the towers fall" (Isa. 30:25). Such towers were not necessarily objects of false confidence.[51] In a day

---

49 אַלּוֹן Akk. *allanu*, possibly the *quercus aegilops;* cf. BK; Löw, I, 621; Hadad, 1:20, "by an *aln* do thou rest."

50 Knobel finds here a reference to the fortresses built by Jotham upon mountains, Lowth to kingdoms and Trapp to "the grandees and magnificoes, and all that are puffed up with an opinion of their own power and policy." Kissane limits the reference to mountains west of the Jordan which the invader would attack.

51 The Targ. apparently conceives of the towers as dwelling places, "and upon all that dwell in lofty towers." Gray interprets of towers and fortifications built by Uzziah (2 Chron. 26:9; 27:8). But this limits the reference unwarrantably.

127

of attack they doubtless would have served well, yet when Yahweh comes, they, like everything else in which man placed his confidence, would perish. They would be no protection against the judgment of Yahweh. In some instances, it may be that men regarded these towers as invincible. If so, they would be greatly deceived in the day of Yahweh.

every inaccessible wall — These were objects of protection. Isaiah describes them by a word which can possibly best be rendered in English, "inaccessible." Man could not scale nor climb these walls, but before the storm of judgment, they would go down in ruin.

16 *ships of Tarshish* — Isaiah mentions in conclusion those objects which bring to man the necessities and luxuries of life. Tarshish was the name of an ancient city to the west (Gen. 10:4), and was probably located in northern Africa, near present-day Tunis.[52] It may be that the term came to serve as a general designation for ships which plied their long-distance trade on the Mediterranean Sea, and some of the German commentators rightly compare such modern designations as *Indienfahrer* (India merchantmen) and *Grünlandfahrer* (Greenland ships). We speak of transatlantic liners. Such ships of Tarshish were engaged in foreign trade, and hence constituted an essential element in the life of the nation. Their condemnation by the prophet is not as something evil, but rather as something which man highly prizes, which nevertheless must fall under the oncoming tide of the Day of the Lord.

ships of pleasure — Only recently has the true force of the word *sekiyyoth* been discovered.[53] In his ninth campaign Thuthmosis

---

[52] B ἐπὶ πᾶν πλοῖον θαλάσσης. Saadia, likewise. Cocceius, apparently following this reading, renders, *naves oceani;* Targum, "and upon all that go down in ships of the sea." Generally, commentators have considered Tarshish to be the name of a city and have offered various identifications. Cilicia (Josephus); Carthage (B); India (Jerome). From Gen. 10:4 we learn that Tarshish was in the west. It has often been equated with Tartessus at the mouth of the Guadalquivir (Baetis) River in Spain. It is now often equated with a district near Tunis in northern Africa (cf. Köhler's *Lexicon* and Aalders, *Obadja, Jona;* Kampen: 1958). C. S. De Ausejo, *El Problema de Tartesos*, "Sefarad," 2 (1942), pp. 171-91.

[53] Lambdin (*JAOS*, LXXIII, No. 3, 1953, 154-55) suggests that Hebrew *ś* equals Egyptian *s̀*, and that the original text was *škyt*. Albright ("Baal-Zephon" in *FAB*, Tübingen, 1950, p. 4) has shown that the Hebrew word is a loan from Egyptian *s̀k.ty*, a ship, and equivalent of Ug. *ṯkt*. Cf. also Driver, *SOTP*, p. 52. and Alt: "Ägyptischugaritisches," *AfO*, 1951, 69-74. Perhaps B had an understanding of the word as is shown by its rendering ἐπὶ πᾶσαν θέαν

III mentions *skt*, "ships," and the same word appears as *tkt* in Ugaritic. It is a loan word from the Egyptian, and so fits in well here in the parallelism. The judgment, we are taught, will come not only upon those ships which are employed for commerce, but also upon ships of pleasure. All ships, of whatever kind, will be affected.

17 The exaltation of Yahweh, already expressed in verse 11, is here repeated, a fact which emphasizes and renders graphic the thought.[54] Both these verses make the beginning and the ending the central fact or theme of the judgment. "The Prophet," says Calvin, "declares that he had his eye on *men*, when he described the various kinds of *loftiness;* for God is not displeased with the steep mountains or tall cedars, which He created, but informs us that the whole evil lies in *men*, who vainly trust to what is high and lofty." It is possible to translate, "so the loftiness of man, etc.," and thus the thought is expressed that the judgment will come upon man as well as upon the inanimate creation.

that day — What words of terror for the unrepentant wicked![55] That day shall come, and the Lord alone will therein be exalted.

18 *idols* — How strange that men should worship idols.[56] In verses 6-8 they were mentioned last in the list of those things with which the land was filled. Now again, in the list of those things that will be overcome by the judgment, the idols appear last. The reason is that idols are the root from whence the other

---

πλοίων κάλλους. It is not necessary, however, to assume with Driver that חמדה must designate a land. Procksch had suggested that the word itself could be the name of a country, and Driver adds the definite article, referring the word to Arabia Felix.

54 ושח — When the predicate precedes the subject, it may be m. and the subj. f. If the f. denotes an inanimate object, it is almost a rule that the pred. should be m.

55 Duhm suggests that the earthquake under Uzziah which Isaiah had experienced as a child impressed him with the sublimity of the Lord, and the nothingness of man.

56 The verse is short, and so *Tiphcha* instead of *Athnach* marks the principal break; "as for the idols [a *casus pendens*] the entirety of them will pass away." יחלף — The pl. occurs in B and 1Q, but is not necessary. Barnes renders, "shall cause to pass away," and Calvin, "*abolebit*," but the verb is *Qal.* "the whole" — On the basis of Judg. 20:40 Delitzsch renders "all" or "utterly." Drechsler also takes the word as an adverb. But it is ordinarily a noun, and the omission of the article may be explained by the poetic nature of the language.

evils flow. When men turn to idolatry they pervert everything else. The root, therefore, must be done away.

At the same time, despite the prominence of the idols as the source of other evils, Isaiah mentions them almost in one breath, thereby indicating his utter disdain of them, as though they were but an afterthought with him. It is as though he had said, "As for the idols, those idols which have caused the nation's decline — they shall pass away." The abruptness of this verse is not without purpose, for it emphatically states the complete abolition of these idols. "In that day shall a man look to his Maker, and his eyes shall have respect to the Holy One of Israel. And he shall not look to the altars, the work of his hands, neither shall respect *that* which the fingers have made, either the groves, or the images" (Isa. 17:7, 8).

19 Instead of uttering a direct warning to men to flee the wrath to come, Isaiah predicts the terror that will overtake men in their vain efforts to flee from that terror when the final judgment does come.[57] By such a means he is warning the men of his own generation to flee the coming wrath. When Yahweh arises to cause the earth to tremble and comes with a sword to take vengeance upon the ungodly, men will endeavor by every conceivable means to escape His presence.

Isaiah expresses this truth by means of figures which would be filled with meaning for the men of Judah of his own day. Palestine is a land of hills and crags. Men will go into the caves of the rocks and into the holes of the dust; they will also seek refuge in natural and in man-made shelters; all of which will prove to be ineffectual.

caves — These would be natural caves of the earth with which the Judean hills are honeycombed (cf. Judg. 6:2 and 1 Sam. 13:6).

holes — Perhaps caverns or subterranean excavations of some sort. Man, who is created from the dust of the ground, now returns to that dust in search of refuge from ultimate destruction. The presence of the Lord is dreadful, and His majesty brings glory; from these, like Adam in the garden, man will seek to flee.

ariseth to cause the earth to tremble — When God sets Himself to action, the Scriptures speak of Him as arising, as though for a

---

[57] This verse certifies what had been commanded in v. 10. The indicative is carried out in more detail than the imper. It would weaken the strength of the verse to substitute the pl. imper. (*BH*) for the indicative. B has a part. 1Q supports M.

long time He had been inactive (cf. Judg. 5:4; 2 Sam. 22:8-16; Hab. 3:6-10; Heb. 12:26). It is a graphic figure for expressing the truth that the time appointed for the judgment has now come. The day of man was a day in which man worshiped the work of his own hands and that day is past; Yahweh, who has remained apparently inactive, now arises to come and perform His work of judgment. Herntrich's suggestion that the figure is that of a king arising from his throne is interesting and possible. In the last two words in the Hebrew, *Laarotz haaretz*, there is an interesting paronomasia, which some of the commentators have sought to preserve in their translations. We may note: *ad terram terrendam* (Calvin); *wenn er sich erhebt und die Erde bebt* (Gesenius); *ut terreat terram* (Delitzsch). In causing the earth to tremble the Lord does not shake the physical earth, but rather the wicked inhabitants of earth, who will feel the effect of His judgment.

20 "This is an amplification of verse 18, explaining how the idols were to disappear, viz., by being thrown away in haste, terror, and shame, and desperate contempt, by those who had worshiped them and trusted in them as a means of facilitating their escape from the avenging presence of Jehovah" (Alexander). This casting away of the idols will take place in that day, at the time of God's judgment. When God thus appears, man will be ashamed of his idols and will seek to cast them away.[58]

---

[58] "shall cast" — The imp. expresses an action belonging to some particular unspecified time in the future. "the idols of his silver" — His silver idols. The suffix is not attached to the const. but to the governed noun. אֲשֶׁר עָשׂוּ — The s. suffix with the preposition is used distributively with reference to the pl., "which they made [each one] for himself." "to worship" — The inf. is to be construed grammatically with "they made," even though B, Vulg., and Targ. construe with the following. Jerome, e.g., "to worship images as blind as moles"; Luzzatto, "to bow down to moles and bats." I can find no warrant for the view that Isaiah conceives of idolatry as fetishism. Possibly in some instances men may have thought of their expensive images as containing magic power (cf. Y. Kaufmann, "Bible and Mythological Polytheism," *JBL*, Sept. 1951, p. 190).

לַחְפֹּר פֵּרוֹת — B, τοῖς ματαίοις; A, ορυκταις; S, ακαρμοις. In M the first word is an inf. const., probably "to dig" holes. Th., however, transliterates φαρφαρωθ and 1Q has לחפרפרים. Hence, even though the accentuation favors a division, the above considerations together with the parallelism favor one word. 5 mss. also read as one word. Possibly the word is the name of an animal (the shrewmouse?) which eats insects and which was worshiped in Egypt and frequently mummified.

silver — Evidently the idols were of some value and had been expensive, hence the act of casting them away becomes the more significant. The coming of God will reveal to men how foolish was trust in those things which human hands have made. Even today we find educated men defending the practice of idolatry. Pratt says, "Much more may thus be said in defense of the practice of 'idolatry' than most of us have been brought up to suppose. It is based upon a perfectly sound psychological principle, and it appeals to a widely felt human need."[59] The present verse, however, stands as a most wholesome corrective to such a false opinion. The Lord arises that He may cause the earth to tremble, and those who until this time have placed their confidence in the work of human hands, now in utter disgust and anger at their folly cast away their valuable idols. Valuable idols — they are for mice and bats, and the dark and unattractive places where mice and bats live.

21 Men cast away their idols, because these idols, although expensive and valuable, are nevertheless hindrances and encumbrances. If men wish to escape the coming of the avenging and judging Yahweh, they must disburden themselves of the idols. This they must do in order to find refuge in the crags and clefts. When men worshiped them, the idols were hindrances in that they precluded worship of the true God. Now, when men seek to flee from God, the idols are again in their way, and must be cast aside.[60]

crevices — In the rocky mountain country of Judea there are many such crevices or holes in which a man may hide and disappear from the sight of his pursuers. Whereas, however, such a hiding place might enable one to elude the eye of a human foe or pursuer, it will prove to be vain when he seeks to take refuge there from God.

clefts — The fissures of the rocks. For the third time in this discourse Isaiah sees men fleeing from the LORD. "And the kings of the earth, and the great men, and the rich men, and the chief captains, and the mighty men, and every bondman, and every free man, hid themselves in the dens and in the rocks of the moun-

---

59 *The Religious Consciousness*, p. 276.

60 The inf. expresses purpose and hence is not to be translated by the future. Bentzen thinks that the subj. is mankind of v. 20. The thought may be paraphrased, "In that day man (mankind — note the definite article) will cast away his expensive idols, that he may go. . . . "

tains; And said to the mountains and rocks, Fall on us, and hide us from the face of him that sitteth on the throne, and from the wrath of the Lamb; For the great day of his wrath is come; and who shall be able to stand?" (Rev. 6:15-17).

22 The command is to cease and desist from placing confidence in man.[61] Trust in idolatry might in a sense be regarded as trust in man himself, for the idols were the products of his ingenuity and creative powers. But not only when man makes idols must one place no confidence in him, but at all times. Man is set forth in opposition to God, and the point of this verse is to show the folly of trust in man instead of in God. The life of Judah represented a confidence reposed in man and in human wisdom, and from such vain confidence Judah is now commanded to desist. Isaiah's language may be rendered, "Cease for yourselves, for your own benefit and welfare."[62] It is for one's own advantage and benefit that he cease to place his confidence in man.

whose breath — Literally, "who, breath is in his nostrils." Here is the reason why it is folly to trust in man; in his nostrils there is a breath. Man's life is transitory. God had breathed into man the breath that brings life (Gen. 2:7; 7:22). Man therefore does not exist through his own strength. As that breath was breathed into him, so also it may be taken away and depart from him (Ps. 146:4).

for wherein is he to be accounted? — The answer implied is, "Nothing."[63] What estimate is to be placed upon man in whom ye trust? None whatever, for he is transitory, and his breath de-

[61] This verse is omitted in B but not in ASTh nor in 1Q, but Penna acknowledges that its thought sums up the content of the chapter (cf. A. E. Osborn: "Divine Destiny and Human Failure, Isaiah 2" *Biblical Review*, XVII, 1932, 244-48). Herntrich thinks that the verse may express an approving refrain of the congregation. If this verse expresses the impression made by the foregoing upon a reader, that fact amounts to a tacit acknowledgement of its relevancy. The arguments for its omission are not sufficiently strong. breath — For the sake of emphasis the pred. noun is placed first, "who . . . breath is in his nostrils."

[62] "cease ye" — Lit., "for yourselves." The ethical dative of advantage introduced by the prep. after a verb of motion.

[63] wherein — Jerome, *"excelsus";* Drechsler, "how much?" The *beth* may be regarded as precative, "what is he to be thought of?" reckoned — *aestimandus.* The passive part. not only denotes a constant expression of the verbal idea but also a permanent quality which is the ground of that constant expression, "worthy to be thought of."

parts from him. The verse therefore does not depreciate a proper estimate of man but does depreciate an improper estimate of him.

What an accurate description of the condition of mankind apart from God! Fallen mankind places all its confidence and hope in man. In its crudest form this confidence may appear as idolatry, such as existed when Isaiah wrote. The greatest need of man is to reject man, and, as children, to seek the heavenly Father. The verse thus forms a fitting conclusion to the chapter, and at the same time it also serves as a bridge between the proclamation of universal judgment made in chapter 2 and the more specific judgment to be introduced in chapter 3.

SPECIAL NOTES

Certain phrases appear as refrains in vv. 9, 11, and 12:

v. 9:
and there is bowed down the mean man ... and there is humbled the great men

v. 11:
man shall be humbled ... and there is bowed down the haughtiness of men

v. 17:
and there is bowed down the loftiness of *man* ...
and there is humbled the haughtiness of men
The same is true of vv. 10, 19, and 21:

v. 10:
Enter into the rock, and hide in the dust
from before the fear of the Lord
and from the glory of his majesty

v. 19:
And they shall enter into the caves of the rocks and into the holes of
the dust
from before the fear of the LORD and from the glory of his majesty,
when he ariseth to cause the earth to tremble.

v. 21:
To enter into the crevices of the rocks and the clefts of the crags
from before the fear of the LORD and from the glory of his majesty
when he ariseth to cause the earth to tremble.

2. JUDAH'S PUNISHMENT AND GLORY (3:1—4:6)

a. *The removal of order* (3:1-7)

1 For behold! the Sovereign, the LORD of hosts, is about to turn aside from Jerusalem and Judah the stay and the staff, the whole stay of bread and the whole stay of water.

2 The warrior and the man of war, the judge and the prophet and the diviner and the elder.

3 The captain of fifty, and the favored person, the counselor and the skillful artificer and the expert enchanter.

4 And I shall give youths as their princes, and caprice will rule over them.

5 And the people shall oppress themselves, one with another, and everyone against his neighbor; the youth will storm against the ancient and the despised one against the honored.

6 When a man shall take hold of his brother at the house of his father, saying, Thou hast raiment, a ruler thou shalt be for us, and this overthrown mass will be under thy hands.

7 In that day he will lift up (his voice) saying, I will not be a healer, while in my house there is neither bread nor garment, ye shall not appoint me as a ruler of the people.

1 This chapter is intimately connected with the preceding, whose last verse constitutes an appropriate transition between the two. Not only does the present chapter continue to show the folly of trusting in men, but it also gives a reason for the admonition contained in verse 22.[1] That reason is that inasmuch as God will soon take away the princes and rulers, it is mere folly to continue relying upon man. In the second chapter there had

---

1 As forming a bridge between the universal judgment of chap. 2 and the more specific one of chap. 3 Kissane thinks that 2:22 explains the *ki* of 3:1. Duhm, however, believes that 3:1-12 has connections with 9:13ff., and probably belongs to a time before the Syrian invasion. If *ki* is original, he says, the connection with the preceding is lost. Marti suggests that *ki* links the passage with 2:6ff., and Dillmann with 2:22, which is correct, for through 2:22 *ki* also refers to the entire preceding discourse. "Inasmuch as world judgment will come and man is not to be trusted in, the Lord will remove, etc."

been a picture of universal judgment, whereas in the third the application of judgment is more specific, being limited to the nation itself which is to be deprived of the indispensable support of a stable government. The fulfillment is not to be sought in the Babylonian exile but in all the judgments which from that time on came over Israel and that still rest on that unfortunate people (cf. comments on v. 12). Israel's whole history is seen at a glance, as though the entire drama were completed in the first act. The exile only began the fulfillment (there were still prophets in the exile); it did not complete it.

behold! — A favorite word of introduction in Isaiah, which he often employs to strengthen a following participle when the latter expresses time in the future. Hence, the thought is, "Behold, the LORD — is about to turn aside." Isaiah does not explicitly state how this removal is to take place, but from later passages (e.g., 5:8ff.) we learn that it was brought about by means of the Assyrians. The Assyrians and the Babylonians usually took as their first captives the leaders of the nations which they conquered. "And he (the king of Babylon) carried away all Jerusalem, and all the princes, and all the mighty men of valour, even ten thousand captives, and all the craftsmen and smiths: none remained, save the poorest sort of the people of the land" (2 Kings 24:14). The result of such a deportation would work great cruelty and hardship upon those who remained in the land and would result in an anarchy such as that described here.

the Lord — The sovereign master.[2] The word is often employed in Isaiah to indicate God's sovereignty. He is further identified as the LORD (Yahweh) of hosts. Again there is a heaping up of titles such as was found in 1:24. God certainly has no need of a multiplicity of titles; however, these various designations serve to impress upon us the seriousness of the condition which is to come. *Adhon* signifies God's supreme power and authority; Yahweh designates Him as self-existent and eternal, yet as the one who at the same time is the God of revelation and the God who stands in peculiar relationship to His people. The qualifying words, "of hosts," serve to call attention to the fact that God is the ruler of all things. Because of the utmost seri-

---

[2] Notice the many titles of God and contrast with 2:18, 22. These solemn titles serve to induce a sense of fear and reverence, and are used when Isaiah wishes to announce the judgments of God; cf. 1:24; 10:16, 33; 19:4.

ousness of the calamity which is to come upon the people of God these many designations are employed. Perhaps when the people hear these solemn titles, they may give heed to the message which is to be proclaimed unto them. At the same time, these names make clear to the nation that the calamities which will befall them are not the result of chance, but come from the Lord Himself. When judicial acts of God are to be introduced, Isaiah employs the divine names in compound form (cf. 1:24; 10:16, 33; 19:4). Hence, this compound divine name shows that a new announcement of judgment is to be made.

Jerusalem — The city is mentioned first, because it was the seat of the kingdom, and would be the first to suffer through the removal of the officers of government. From Jerusalem the anarchy would then spread out over all the land.[3]

the stay and the staff — Two Hebrew words are employed, one masculine and the other feminine, and thus the thought of totality is presented.[4] Every kind of stay and staff will be removed. A

---

3 "is about to turn aside" — This is to be done, thinks Fischer, not so much by an external foe as by means of a revolution (cf. 5:4, 5). Penna says that it may be an *eccidio*, especially if a great *chiarrezza* should accompany it. Dillmann states that it will probably be accomplished by means of foreign foes. Hertzberg sees the fulfillment in the political conditions existing during the Assyrian and Babylonian period. These nations took the leaders first into captivity (cf. 2 Kings 24:14). Note the reappearance of this root in v. 18 and cf. Exod. 11:5. The active part. expresses something that will be done in the proximate future.

4 The forms מַשְׁעֵן and וּמַשְׁעֵנָה appear only here. Otherwise *mish'an* and *mish-'e-neth* are employed. It may be that the choice is deliberate to accomplish a rhetorical effect. As to the more usual words, *mish'an* appears in 2 Sam. 22:19; Ps. 18:19, whereas *mish-'e-neth* is found in Num. 21:18; Ps. 23:4; Isa. 36:6; etc. Other examples of m. and f. to denote totality appear in Isa. 11:12; 22:24; etc.

It is difficult to distinguish the precise force of each of these words. Delitzsch rather aptly compares the Latin, *fulcrum, fultura* and *fulcimen*. *Mish'ēn* may be "supporter" and *mash-'ē-nāh*, "means of support." The mention of the three similarly sounding words lends a dignity and force to the discourse; thus, "all kinds of support, and first of all the whole stay of bread, etc."

Inasmuch as the following description has reference to the officers of government, many critics regard 1b, with its mention of bread and water, as a gloss. Yet the presence of these words is supported by textual evidence.

The language of 1b, together with the enumeration in the following verses, yields a heightening effect. The stays include all that forms the basis for the people's common life. Rulers are included, but they do not exhaust the

similar phenomenon appears in the Arabic language: "he has not either male or female lamb," meaning he has nothing (Hariri) and "male and female wild beasts," every kind of wild beast.

By using both masculine and feminine the prophet exhausts the category; the thought is that every kind of support — all support whatever — will be removed. Isaiah employs three words of similar sound, thus lending dignity and force to the discourse, *mishen, meshenah* and *mishan*. Eight words in this verse begin with the consonant *mem* (m).

the whole stay — All kinds of support will be removed, and first of all that which is found in bread. Bread and water are the indispensable conditions for existence. The whole stay, however, even bread and water, will be removed, and thus the nation will be deprived by God of its most necessary means of life. It is easy to take for granted these ordinary necessities and to forget that God can withdraw them as He wills. Luther remarks that "daily bread is everything that belongs to the support and wants of the body, such as food, drink, clothing, shoes, house, home, field, money, goods, a pious spouse, pious and faithful rulers, good government, good weather, peace, health, discipline, honor, good friends, faithful neighbors, and the like." It is interesting to note that under the category "bread" Luther includes "pious and faithful rulers, good government." Compare 19:10, where *shātot*, "stays," designates "princes." Luther had a deeper understanding of the Scriptures than those critics who insist that this portion of the verse is to be rejected as a gloss because it has no connection with what follows. The destruction of Judah, therefore, was to begin, and as a matter of fact did begin with the removal of the basic necessities of life.

---

category. Likewise those of superior talents, abilities and gifts are mentioned, those who represent the higher cultural life of a country. The removal of these stays amounts to a descent from organized life to anarchy and dispersion.

If the staff of bread be removed, destruction results (cf. Lev. 26:26; Gen. 18:5; Judg. 19:5, 8; Ps. 105:16; Ezek. 4:16; 14:13). Water is not elsewhere mentioned as a staff, but its use here may be due to *zeugma*. Cf. Horace, *Satires*, II:3:153, *Deficient inopem venat te, ne cibus atque Ingens accedat stomacho fultura ruenti*. Cf. also Lam. 2:20; Josephus, *Wars*, 6:3:3:4. The genitives are appositional; thus, "the whole stay, even bread and water."

Mish'an is const. of *mish'ān*. In the closed unaccented syllable *a* has shifted to *i* to avoid two *a* vowels together (dissimilation). The original form was probably *mash'ān*.

2 Now follows an enumeration of the stays of Judah's life. This and the following verse begin by mentioning warriors, one of the principal supports of the nation. The warrior was a hero or mighty man of war and valor who was possibly of greater military rank than the man of war.[5] He was probably a man of valor whose valor had already been tried and put to the test. On the other hand the appellation "man of war" may simply designate the common soldier. Probably the unbelieving portion of the nation had placed its hope in the military.

From the mention of the two categories of warrior, if such they actually be, Isaiah next names the judges. The verse thus divides itself between the military and the civil. As Drechsler cleverly expressed it, *"der Wehrstand und der Lehrstand."* The judge was a civil officer who not only had the task of making decisions, but whose functions were also of governmental nature. In the order of enumeration in the second part of the verse, there does not appear to be any particular scheme. Isaiah's purpose is not to show that there was lack of order and actual anarchy in the state. On the other hand, it is difficult, if not impossible, to state why he does follow the order that he does.

With the mention of prophet Isaiah shows how serious the deprivation will be that is to come upon the nation. It was through the prophet that the will of God was made known, and when the people are left in ignorance of divine revelation their plight is tragic indeed. A famine of hearing the words of the Lord is more serious than a famine caused by lack of food. A contemporary of Isaiah had said, "Behold, the days come, saith the Lord GOD, that I will send a famine in the land, not a famine of bread, nor a thirst for water, but of hearing the words of the LORD" (Amos 8:11).

The diviner was no legitimate support of the nation, even though Judah did depend upon diviners. In ancient times the

---

[5] "Warrior" — I have so translated inasmuch as the word stands in conjunction with "man of war"; cf. 2 Sam. 23:8 and 2 Chron. 13:3. The form represents original *gab-bâr*, the short *a* having shifted to *i* in a closed unaccented syllable. Cf. Ar. *gab-bâr*.

Note the threefold appearance of *wāw* conjunctive in 2b. For a discussion of the terms "prophet" and "diviner" cf. *MSTP* (1952). Penna thinks that here *qesem* may have a good sense in that it would refer to him who makes decisions irrespective of the means employed. But the regular usage of the word supports Drechsler's assertion that it has a secondary unfavorable connotation. Nothing in this verse supports the view that the prophet held a political office.

diviners had been severely condemned. The nation therefore is to be deprived not only of its legitimate but also of its illegitimate supports. Hosea also had proclaimed (3:4), "For the children of Israel shall abide many days without a king, and without a prince, and without a sacrifice, and without an image, and without an ephod, and *without* teraphim." The entire present order of things, "the Judean way of life," was to be changed radically.

At the very foundation of the government were the elders, men who by reason of their experience were particularly qualified and fitted to give the advice that was necessary for the good administration of government. Rehoboam, for example, blundered badly when he did not heed the advice of the elders. For the government to pass from the hands of experienced men would be a serious blow indeed.

3 Isaiah continues with an enumeration of stays of second rank which will be taken from the nation.

captain of fifty — A designation of a particular officer, a leader over fifty men.[6] In 2 Kings 1:9 we read, "Then the king sent unto him a captain of fifty with his fifty." The phrase also appears on the cuneiform inscriptions as *rab hamsa*. In the Bible the usage seems to be derived from the decimal arrangement of the nation in the wilderness, as described in Exodus 18:25, "And Moses chose able men out of all Israel, and made them heads over the people, rulers of thousands, rulers of hundreds, rulers of fifties, and rulers of tens." In the Old Testament at least this seems to be the basic meaning of the phrase. We may compare this with the titles in classical literature such as centurions and chiliarchs. Samuel says that the future king will ". . . appoint him captains over thousands, and captains over fifties; and *will set them* to ear his ground, and to reap his harvest, and to make his instruments of war, and instruments of his chariots" (1 Sam. 8:12),

---

[6] For examples of grouping companies into fifties, cf. 2 Kings 2:16, 17, *Odyssey* 20:49 and *Iliad* 8:563. See the discussion in Gordon, *The World of the Old Testament*, 1958, p. 109. Rosenmüller compares this title with the centurions, who had charge of one hundred soldiers, and the chiliarchs who were over a thousand. In the order of enumeration the offices are mixed, hence we need not maintain that they all refer to civil offices (Rosenmüller). פנים expresses specification; lit., "lifted up of . . . in respect to faces." Delitzsch refers this to persons of influence. Bentzen to those favored by the king (*den, der har kongens naade*). This construction is favored by Heb. usage; Deut. 10:17; 2 Kings 5:1; etc. He who is lifted up with respect to the face is he who is favored.

from which it would appear that these men were equiped to serve the king in a military way. It is interesting to note that the division into fifty is found also in the Homeric poems. Thus, in the *Odyssey* (20:49) Athene says, "even though fifty groups of mortal men should stand about us."

and the favored person — The favored persons were those who had the favor of the king. Inasmuch as they enjoyed such backing, they probably occupied positions of responsibility and authority.

the counselor — It would seem that the counselor was not one engaged in private business, but rather one who served the public generally. The importance of the position appears from the consideration that one of the titles in Isaiah 9:6 is "Wonderful Counsellor."

the skillful artificer — This is one who is wise or skillful with respect to arts.[7] What, however, were these arts? The following phrase clearly refers to enchanters; does this present phrase have a similar reference? Some think so, but it must be remembered that the thought of a man being skilled and clever in mechanical arts was a widespread one in the ancient Near East. Thus, for example, we note that the "divine" artisan of ancient Ugarit bore the name *Ktr wHss,* meaning cunning and skillful. Likewise in the *Iliad* (18:380) Hephaistos, the god of crafts, is described as working with "cunning skill." In addition to this, we may note that the words then form a striking contrast to the following phrase, and do not merely state what is found in that

---

7 "artificer." Gesenius refers the word to those who practice magic (*peritus praestigiarum*) and this interpretation has found many supporters, most recently Penna, who says, "*personaggi dediti alla magia* (Gen. 41:33, 39; Deut. 1:13; 4:6; 1 Re 3, 12) *e agli incantesimi, specialmente incantatori di serpenti* (Sal. 41, 8; Eccl. 10, 11) ." König, Kissane, Ewald, Marti, etc., held similar views. Vulg. renders *eloqui mystici.* For a discussion of this position cf. A. D'Alpe: "*Quis sit prudens eloquo mystici*" in *V.D.* 23, 1943, pp. 133-37.

Bentzen, however, rightly points out that the oldest tradition, in the old translations, favors the rendering, "skilled artificer." *BDB* gives חרשים as the pl. of חרש. At the same time this form must be distinguished from the pl. with long *a* in the antepenult. May not there have been two developments of the pl., namely, (1) *hārāš, const.* pl. *hárāsim;* (2) *hārās;* pl. *harāsim?* Orelli points out how the land was weakened by the removal of skillful artificers from its midst; cf. 2 Kings 24:14, 16.

"expert enchanter" — the AV, "eloquent orator," an interpretation really going back to the Targum and essentially supported by Luther, Calvin, etc., (see Barnes for its defense) is without solid foundation.

phrase. At the time of the exile, the craftsmen were carried out of the land (2 Kings 24:14ff.; Jer. 24:1 and 29:2).

the expert enchanter — This was the man who could whisper or mutter magical formulas. This profession was evidently rather widespread, and there were many who in defiance of the divine prohibition resorted to enchanters. The Lord's purpose was to remove from Judah every stay, whether good or bad, whether divinely ordained or not. The present culture would be radically altered, and all those things which the people were accustomed to depend upon would be removed by way of punishment. In that day of judgment there would be no stay whatever; all that the nation now trusted in and leaned upon would at that time be taken away.

4 When competent and capable men are removed from positions of authority in government, it is to be expected that incompetent and capricious rulers will take their place, and it is precisely that change which is here pictured.

And I shall give — By an abrupt change of the person, such as sometimes occurs in the prophetical books, Isaiah continues the description of the Lord's activity which he had begun in the first verse of this chapter.[8] The Lord is introduced here as speaking in a sudden manner, a device which lends force to the description. The terrible change which is to take place in the land is not the result of chance, but is due to the Lord's deliberate design and determination.

youths — How great a calamity it is when those who rule are inexperienced. Such inexperience of course characterizes a youth.[9] Rehoboam forsook the judgment of the experienced elders and listened to the impetuous and inexperienced youths with disastrous consequences as a result. After the time of Jeroboam II there were youthful rulers upon the throne of the northern kingdom, and their rule was not characterized or distinguished by wis-

---

[8] The imp. "they rule" here denotes a continuous action referring to some point in the future, "they shall be continuously ruling."

[9] "youths" — Many refer this to Ahaz, but as Van Hoonacker remarked, *"Waarom met 'de knapen' bepaald Achaz zou gemeend zijn, kunnen wij niet zeggen."* Some take the word as indicating those young years. Dillmann thinks that this was exemplified in Israel after the time of Jeroboam II; Kissane says that after the deportation only youths and the poorest remained, 2 Kings 24:14; 25:12. Duhm renders, *"junge Feuerköpfe, und halbreife Buben."* Lowth: "the weak and wicked princes that succeeded Isaiah."

dom. In all probability, however, Isaiah at this point does not have in mind those who with respect to years were youths, but those who with respect to experience and capabilities were so weak and incompetent that they were but youths. Solomon had thus spoken of himself, exhibiting a praiseworthy modesty, "And now, O LORD my God, thou hast made thy servant king instead of David my father: and I *am but* a little child: I know not *how* to go out or come in" (1 Kings 3:7). His words well describe the lack of knowledge of those who were but children in ability to govern. It is the hotheadedness, the confidence and the recklessness of youth that are prominent. The lack of maturity in judgment and decision could only work great harm to the state. The gifts which God has first offered are rejected by the nation, and so the Lord now gives other gifts. He gives rulers which are incompetent and hence harmful. "I gave thee a king in mine anger, and took him away in my wrath" (Hos. 13:11).

SPECIAL NOTE

Calvin thinks that the prophet has in mind particularly those who are so weak and effeminate that they are unable to wield the sword of government which is entrusted to them. His words are worthy of serious consideration, "But it must be laid down as a principle, that no man is qualified for governing a commonwealth unless he has been appointed to it by God, and be endued with uncommon excellence. Plato, too, understood this matter well: for though, being a heathen, he had no true knowledge of this kind, yet his quick sagacity enabled him to perceive that no man is fit and qualified for public government who has not been prepared for it by God in an extraordinary measure; for public government proceeds from God alone, and in like manner every part of it must be upheld by him. Besides, they whom the Lord does not govern have nothing left for them but to be *children,* or rather to be twice *children,* that is, destitute of all skill and of all wisdom."

as their princes — The word "prince" need not designate the king alone, but might also be employed of princes and other rulers. The nation was to be inflicted with a plethora of inept officials in general, rulers who quite possibly came from the very dregs of society. When men who in experience and ability have the capacity of children take over the reigns of the state, chaos is bound to follow.

and caprice — The word is plural and we may thus render,

143

"caprices, puerilities, childish things."[10] It is an abstract noun, used for the concrete; hence, we may render, "caprice will rule"; that is, capricious persons will rule.[11] When such a state of affairs has come, it is an evidence that God, who alone can raise up and depose rulers at will, has removed from the nation one of His greatest gifts. As an Arabian writer said, "A blow in the face by an axe is easier to take than the rule of a boy" (Zamaschari). How good God is to give a nation worthy rulers. May we ever appreciate such and constantly render our gratitude to Him for them. May we pray that He will spare us from the calamity of unworthy and unable rulers. Prayer must always be made for the officers of state.

5 Anarchy follows as a consequence from the poor government predicted in the preceding verses.[12] Inasmuch as there no longer exists any government with power to restrain lawlessness, each one will oppress the other. It thus becomes clear that the principal function of government is to protect its people from unjust oppression. The oppression herein described is one which probably consisted in the issuance of unjust demands and exactions.

When respect for age goes, moral anarchy is at hand. Youths will storm against, that is, they will act insolently or will press on against the aged. Respect for old age had been coupled in the law with the fear of God, "Thou shalt rise up before the hoary head, and honour the face of the old man, and fear thy God: I am the LORD" (Lev. 19:32). When all authority passes, respect for age also passes. One evidence of the degeneration of a government and people is seen in the manner in which the aged are treated. What is here pictured is a war of all against all.

the despised one — The reference is to those who belonged to the lowest rank in society. Hence, it is not necessarily moral character which is in view. The usage of the definite article be-

---

10 "caprice" — This unusual word occurs only here and in 66:4. The noun designates these expressions of caprice, whether in jest or earnest, which bring harm to others; hence, puerilities, childish things, caprices. *Abstractum pro concreto.* Cf. Exod. 10:2; Num. 22:29; Judg. 19:25; 1 Sam. 6:6, for the root.

11 It would seem that the language of this verse is to be taken in a non-figurative sense, a view which is supported by the language of v. 5.

12 נגשׂ is a *Nifal* with reflexive force. When construed with בְּ , the verb refers to persons and signifies "to act as a tyrant"; cf. 9:3. In Exodus this root refers to the overseers (Exod. 3:7). In Amharic the word *negus* means "king," an interesting commentary on the character of rulers. "will storm" — Marti aptly describes the condition as a *bellum omnium contra omnes*.

fore the word "despised" seems to indicate something of a superlative character, as though the prophet had said, "The most despised." Disrespect for age and for those deserving of respect is a sign of pure barbarism. In such times, when the government itself is no longer responsible, the lowest classes gain the upper hand. It is a time when neither life nor property is safe, and when the decencies of life are constantly violated. Good government is one of God's best gifts to a sinful race. How great then is the sin of those who refuse to concern themselves with their responsibilities as citizens of the state!

6 The extremely critical condition of the nation appears from the fact that anyone who is found in the possession of a mere garment is regarded as capable of righting conditions and restoring a semblance of good government. The entire sixth verse forms a protasis, verse 7 serving as apodosis. At the same time, we have here more than a mere condition. It is not a mere hypothetical case that is mentioned, but an actual prophecy of what will take place when the government is removed. The thought is that in that time conditions will become so bad that whenever a man should ask his brother — and men in that day will thus ask their brothers — then certain results will follow.

shall take hold — Under ordinary conditions men strive earnestly for position in government; places of authority are eagerly coveted, and great is the price that men will sometimes pay in order to hold a position of influence and authority.[13] When, however, the punishing hand of God is felt, and stable government is removed, conditions have become so desperate that men not only do not strive for power, but rather even shun it. "Hence it follows," says Calvin, "that everything is in a deplorable condition, when that dignity is not only despised but obstinately rejected; for the mournful calamity has reached its lowest depth, when that which men naturally desire with the greatest ardour is universally disdained." To obtain rulers men will not seek to persuade, as in ordinary times, but will take hold by force of those whom they wish to rule in an effort to compel them to govern. They will actually grasp or lay hold of those whom they wish to rule over them.

---

13 The introductory particle has been variously translated; Targ. "for"; Vulg., *enim*; B, ὅτι; Lowth, "therefore"; König, *denn*; Rosenmüller, *tum, si*. I prefer rendering "when," taking v. 6 as a protasis and v. 7 as the apodosis.

his brother — The word is probably not used of actual blood relationship, for the situation is so serious that it is not likely that the question of which member of a family is to reign is the pressing question. Rather, brother here in all likelihood denotes a fellow citizen.[14] At this time all men will be brothers in that they will all be bound together by dire want.

at the house of his father — The ancestral or paternal home is the place where one would most naturally stay during such a time of anarchy and calamity. The honorable man holds back from public or common matters and seeks rather the solicitude of his paternal home. In that paternal home a man is approached by those who would compel him to be their ruler. We may understand the connection of this statement with what follows if we inject the word "saying," to introduce the language of those who speak.[15]

Thou hast a raiment — The *simlah* was a garment worn by the poor, and in itself was a sign of extreme poverty. When men speak to the possessor of a *simlah,* their language means, "Thou at least hast a garment." The condition of things is so serious, and the hunger and poverty so widespread, that one who possesses even a garment such as a *simlah* is considered to be suitable to take over the reigns of government. As Matthew Henry comments, "The government goes a begging"; and we thus see how an extreme condition can blind men's proper use of their judgment.

a ruler thou shalt be for us — This is no mere request; it is a command, as though the people said, "Thou must be our ruler." The ruler or *qazin* was the one whose function it was to pronounce decisions, and by so doing he was expected to bring order out of

---

[14] Delitzsch, however, takes this literally, holding that through hunger the population would have become so dispirited that within the circle of a family it would not be difficult to decide who was to be ruler. Kissane translates, "in thy father's house is a cloak," substituting "thy" for "his." "raiment" — A garment that even the poorest would possess, cf. Exod. 22:25; Deut. 24:13. It is therefore not a sign of wealth. Cf. H. H. Weil, *Revue Biblique* No. 49, 1940, pp. 76-85. The garment is not necessarily a sign of officialdom (Marti) nor did its owner necessarily belong to a family that supplied officials to the state.

[15] Similarly, 14:8; 22:16; 33:14; Jer. 51:19; Ps. 11:3. Cf. also Koran Sura 32:12, "When the guilty hang their heads before their lord (saying), Our Lord, . . . " (*rabbihum, rabbanä*). Marti takes לכה as the emphatic imper. *Auf!* Also Kissane, "Come, thou shalt be our chief." These renderings disregard the Masoretic punctuation. The *He* is paragogic as in Gen. 27:37.

chaos. It was not the function of king which the people necessarily demanded, but simply that the man who possessed a garment should be a leader immediately over them, a leader whose decisions would have a beneficent effect on their own welfare. They demanded that he be a *qazin,* but that he be a *qazin* for their own benefit. The demand, then, was not basically one for the right kind of government, but merely for a leader who would bring benefit to the people. In times of chaos and calamity, the evil ruler can obtain a following by promising the people what they think is for their own benefit. In such a time, men are little concerned over what is right, but much concerned over what is expedient.

and this overthrown mass — Jerusalem had stumbled and Judah had fallen (cf. 3:8), and the result was simply a mass that had been overthrown. This graphic figure shows that the state has tottered and stumbled; the weight which it had to bear was too great, so it has now crumbled and is but a ruin. This overthrown mass of the state is under the hand (i.e., the responsibility) of the conscripted person.[16]

Those who seek to conscript a ruler recognize well enough that a sad condition of things has arrived, but they do not recognize the basic reason for the condition, namely, their own sin. Even now, when in desperation men seek for a ruler to help them, they will not confess their wickedness and turn in repentance to God.

7 There now follows the response of the one who is conscripted into service against his will. This verse thus forms an apodosis to the preceding, and the thought of the entire expression is, "When a man seizes his brother . . . then at that time, he [the brother] will say, 'I will not be a healer,' " etc.

he will lift up — As may be seen by a comparison with the Hebrew, no object is supplied to the verb.[17] What is it, then,

---

16 "under thy hand" — Cf. Gen. 16:9. Some mss. have the dual, but in the light of Gen. 16:9 the s. is probably preferable. 16b may be taken as a circumstantial clause, "this overthrown mass being under thy hand," cf. Song of Sol. 2:6.

17 It may be, however, that the second verb is to be taken pleonastically, "he will answer, saying." If an object is to be understood, some would prefer "hand," as in Gen. 14:22. Calvin, *se iurabit,* and Luther also. But the one who is approached does not issue a solemn oath. He rather responds vigorously, and hence many prefer to understand "voice" as the object. As in 24:14 there appears to be a certain intensification in the words. For the ellipsis, cf. also

that the conscripted person lifts up? In the light of other passages of Scripture, we are probably to understand the words "his voice" as the object. Hence, it is more than a mere reply that is in view here; it is a solemn protest. In no uncertain tones he raises his voice to declare that he refuses to serve. The omission of the object lends a certain intensity and force to the description.

In that day — At the time when men seize him and seek to compel him to be a ruler.

I will not be — A definite and positive refusal.[18] No mere shrinking back from lack of ability causes the speaker to decline, but a positive refusal to consider the proposal. This declination is based upon the fact that the speaker does not begin to have the means necessary to alleviate the existing condition. How great an evil it is when citizens seek to compel a man to run for office who is not qualified therefor!

a healer — One who binds up wounds, a surgeon. The speaker does not wish to be such, for he realizes how great are the wounds of the state. In this he agrees with the estimate which had already been placed upon Judah, "From the sole of the foot, even unto the head, *there is* no soundness in it; *but* wounds, and bruises, and putrifying sores: they have not been closed, neither bound up, neither mollified with ointment" (1:6).

while in my house — Not merely do not I myself possess bread or garment, but in my house itself these things are also lacking.[19]

neither bread nor garment — In Homer even the possession of a garment was regarded as a sign of wealth, and in Persia the ruler was supposed to provide clothing for his people. The speaker, however, does not possess such clothing, nor does he have the food necessary to nourish his people. He does not, in other

---

42:2. Bewer is probably reading too much into the words with his rendering, "he frantically declares that he is unable to heal the situation."

[18] חבש may lose its participial force, and be rendered by a noun. Hence "a healer," rather than "I will be healing." Steinmann therefore renders, *je ne suis pas médecin,* and Vulg. *medicus.* Ug. *ḥbš,* sheath. B also takes the word as a noun and renders, "prince," "ruler"; cf. Job 34:17 and a Canaanite gloss in the Amarna texts; Saadia, "one who binds his head with a diadem," and Arias Montanus, an executioner.

תשׂימני — like other verbs expressing appointing, forming into, this one takes two objects, one direct and one expressing the product.

[19] Perhaps there is an emphasis on the suffix, in *my* house. The words introduced by *wāw* constitute a circumstantial clause. The thought is: "Not merely do *I* not have, but in my entire house there is not."

148

words, have those prerequisites which were essential to rulership. The assumption of those who sought to force him were incorrect; he had no garment such as they had assumed.

ye shall not appoint me — This is final. There is no question about it. He will not accept the office. How different from the wily refusals of politicians, whose one desire is to obtain the office, even though they are totally unqualified for such a position. This man, however, although he is poor, nevertheless realizes somewhat the responsibilities of the office, and his grounds for refusal are worthy ones. At times we may best serve our country by recognizing our inabilities and by refusing to accept public office. If a man cannot discharge the responsibilities of government, he does a great service to his country by refusing to accept office.

It is interesting to note that in this passage there is no mention of the king. We cannot say why he is not mentioned, but it may be that the conditions of anarchy were so great that the central government was ineffectual and powerless in checking it. Things were so bad that when even a man who supposedly had a cloak was approached to be a ruler, he refuses even that comparatively minor office. What is immediately needed is an arbiter who would settle disputes and render just decisions. This the king apparently could not do. To preserve order and the rights of the individual, a *qazin* was needed, but as a result of capricious government, even the *qazin* could accomplish nothing. It is indeed tragic that conditions can become so calamitous that a righteous man will refuse to undertake the responsibilities of public office.

b. God pleads with fallen Judah (3:8-15)

8 For Jerusalem has stumbled, and Judah has fallen; for their tongue and their doings are against the LORD, to show rebellion to the eyes of his glory.

9 The expression of their countenance doth witness against them; and they make known their sin like Sodom, they do not hide it. Woe unto their soul, for they have done evil to themselves.

10 Say of the righteous that it shall be well; for they shall eat the fruit of their doings.

11 Woe to the wicked, it shall be evil, for that which is done of his hands will be done to him.

12 As for my people, their oppressors act as children, and women rule over them. O my people, thy leaders cause thee to go astray, and the way of thy paths they destroy.

13 The LORD standeth to plead, and is standing to judge the peoples.
14 The LORD will enter into judgment with the elders of his people, and its princes; and ye have consumed the vineyard, the spoil of the poor is in your house.
15 What mean ye that ye crush my people and grind the faces of the poor, saith the Sovereign, the LORD of hosts.

8 Isaiah himself now speaks and points out the reason why the conscripted man refuses to accept the reins of public office.[20] In so speaking Isaiah justifies the dark picture which had been drawn in the earlier verses of the chapter.

has stumbled — This is the general fact which has occasioned the direful picture of misery described in verses 6 and 7. Jerusalem, the city of the great king, the city from which the law of the LORD and the word of God would go forth, the city in which the Temple was located; Jerusalem, the city set on a hill — even Jerusalem has stumbled. The people had called it a fallen mass, *machshelah,* and now Isaiah declares by way of corroboration that it has truly stumbled, *kashelah.* Burdened under her load of weakness and wounds, the state first stumbles and then falls. Morally, the city had already fallen, and consequently, the outward fall would soon follow in its wake. Jerusalem had turned against God, and pays no attention to His law.[21] Soon she will fall to a position of obscurity. The greatest act of self-preservation in which any nation can engage is that of hearkening unto the commandments of God.

their tongue and their doings — With word and deed the people are against the Lord.[22] The expression "tongue" is used somewhat

---

[20] "for" — The word is causal, hence not to be rendered "yea." Note the chiastic arrangement of 8a.

[21] כשלה obviously reflects upon the מכשלה of v. 6. With the subsequent verb it is to be taken as a prophetic perfect. Although the two verbs are parallel, yet they seem to preserve a certain progression of thought, "she will stumble, she will fall." Judah in M. is construed as m., but 1Q places both verbs in f.

[22] "to show rebellion" — In both *Qal* and *Hifil* this stem may take the acc. of the person as in Ps. 78:17, or the prep. ב or the acc. of the thing. Here the form is best taken as *Hifil.* The *He* of the Hifil inf. is often omitted after *Lamed.* "eyes" — His glorious eyes. 1Q and several Heb. mss. have a *plene* reading, and there is no need for emendation; cf. *BH.* The verb "to show rebellion" may be construed with "mouth" and even with "spirit" (Ps. 106:33).

picturesquely as a substitute for word; for it is the tongue which produces the word. In speaking and in acting the people are against the LORD. Hence, the entire being, within and without, is against God. It is a whole-souled condition of rebellion and antagonism toward Him. As Herntrich has suggested, the confessional statement of the nation could be expressed in the words, "Against God." "I will be your God," the LORD had said at the Exodus; "Against God" is the present cry and attitude of that people which had received so much in the way of blessing from His hand. Their state of mind is directed against the Lord in order that they may show disobedience and rebellion against Him.

the eyes of his glory — His glorious eyes. When someone does something before our eyes to provoke us to anger, he clearly manifests his brazenness. When a nation deliberately commits sins before the eyes of God's majesty, it likewise exhibits its depravity. The glory of God is pictured as having eyes which see all that mankind does. In mentioning this glory Isaiah has reference not to the essential glory of God, which God has in Himself, but to that glory which God has displayed in all His creation. God's majesty appears in His works, works which have been particularly glorious toward the sinning nation of Judah. Against the eyes of this glory Judah constantly sins. How great an affront to the divine majesty!

9 The very expression which appears on the faces of the inhabitants of Judah is such that it enables one to learn what sort of people they are.[23] The emotions of the heart often find ex-

---

[23] The opening words of this verse have been the subject of much debate and discussion.

There are two major interpretations. Targ., "their respecting of persons in judgment." So, also, Ridderbos, Gray, König, Kissane ("their partiality"), Marti (*ihr parteiisches Rechtsprechen*), Kimchi, Maurer, Rosenmüller, *De Bijbel* (*partijdigheid*), Penna, (*la loro parzialita*). Those who adopt this view appeal to the common Heb. idiom, *hikkîr pānîm*, as found in Deut. 1:17; 16:19; Prov. 24:23; 28:21. Cf. also Rom. 2:11; Eph. 6:9; Col. 3:25, and Jas. 2:1. In the idiom as used in the above passages the verb means "to respect persons."

The phrase may be rendered literally, "the regarding of their faces." Is it the regarding of the faces of others, or the regard (look) upon their own faces? The question cannot be decided on grammatical grounds alone. It should be noted that Isaiah is not speaking of specific sins but of general character.

pression on the countenance, a fact which should remind us of the importance of keeping the thoughts of the heart true and pure; and inasmuch as these emotions do find expression in the countenance, there is no need for outside witnesses. The very look which the inhabitants of Judah bore on their faces was sufficient to serve as a witness against themselves. Calvin expresses the thought correctly, when he says, ". . . they carry, as it were, in their forehead a mark of their deceit and hypocrisy." While it is true that we cannot always judge the character of a man by his countenance, it is also true that that character often comes to expression in the countenance. In a very true sense, we are what we think. What the Judahites were could be seen from the very look which they bore on their faces.

doth witness — Meaning, "has answered against." The look which was upon the countenance had, as it were, actually taken the witness stand and had uttered a testimony of condemnation. That look had spoken against the one who bore it. In answering the question, "Is this man guilty?" it had said, "He is guilty."

and they make known their sin like Sodom — These words carry out the thought of the preceding.[24] The proclamation of the sins is not accomplished by way of the voice but by means of the people's actions. Just as their expression betrays them, so also do their sins speak out and cause to be made known what man-

---

Also, the phrase "their sins as Sodom they make known" supports the view that the reference is to the expression of the countenance. Furthermore, the passage has reference to the entire nation and not to the judges or lawgivers specifically, and hence does not refer to the showing of partiality in judgment. It seems, then, that the reference is to the expression on the countenance. This, however, is to be taken in a general sense, and not as indicating some specific expression, as shame (B); steadfastness (Lowth); impudence, pride (Barnes). The Heb. is best rendered by words such as "expression" (Alexander), *probatio* (Calvin), *der Anblick* (Drechsler), *das Ansehen* (Herntrich), "the look" (Delitzsch).

We should expect *hak-ke-raṯ*, inasmuch as the penult is now a distant open syllable. Evidently, then, the absolute would be *hak-kâ-rāh*, which proves that the form is not *Nifal* but *Hifil*, a fact also borne out by the phrase פְּנֵים הכיר The form is identical with Ar. verbal noun IV stem, *'if-'al*, save that it has the f. termination, the vocalization of the antepenult follows the analogy of infinitives, like *hag-gîš, hag-gēš.* They do not hide it — A circumstantial verbal clause.

24 Ginsberg translates, "and their sins have told everything." ("Some Emendations in Isaiah," *JBL,* Vol. LXIX, Mar. 1950, p. 52.)

ner of people they were. In this respect they may be compared with the heathen nations who have not the knowledge of the law of God. The nation causes its sins to be made known in that it does not conceal those sins. It glories in them. They are something to be boasted of. There was no longer even the maintenance of external decency.

Woe unto their soul — In this agonized cry, the prophet gives expression to great abhorrence of the nation's sins. It is the cry of a true evangelist, for it expresses the painful truth that those who have thus sinned are in a direful condition. Only woe and grief can come to their soul.

they have done evil to themselves — Meaning, they have rewarded or requited evil to themselves. Sin truly has its reward, and the people of Judah by their actions have received a reward. They have reaped as they have sown. They have so demeaned themselves as to have earned evil. Joseph's brethren had so acted as to bring upon themselves the expectation of evil; hence, they implored forgiveness from Joseph. "Forgive, I pray thee now, the trespass of thy brethren, and their sin; for they did unto thee evil: and now, we pray thee, forgive the trespass of the servants of the God of thy father" (Gen. 50:17). They did not want to be requited with the evil which they had earned. What Judah has earned is also evil, and the verse reaches its tragic climax in this word "evil." The nation's actions have been for themselves, and their reward is . . . evil.

10 A ray of sunshine and brightness breaks into the otherwise totally dark picture. The judgment will not completely destroy all; it will not be indiscriminate. There are those who will be delivered, even the righteous inhabitants of Judah and Jerusalem. For them and for them alone there is comfort in these words. But who are these righteous of whom it may be said, "All is well"?[25]

---

[25] Isaiah recognizes gradations and distinctions in the moral condition of the people; there are wicked and there are righteous. Duhm, Marti, Bentzen, etc., however, hold that the doctrine of individual retribution first appeared at the time of Ezekiel, and Bewer thinks that vv. 10, 11 are interpolated general sayings on the subject of individual retribution. Herntrich well counters by saying that the doctrine of the remnant presupposes a distinction between righteous and wicked.

צדיק is best construed as an acc. of specification and not as a direct obj.

To answer this question we must understand that the historical entities Jerusalem and Judah in themselves are not to be equated with the elect people of God. At Sinai God chose the Israelites to be a royal priesthood, and later formed this nation into the theocracy. It was the historical nation as such which constituted the theocracy. At the same time it soon began to appear that in this nation there were both those who sought to obey the voice of God and those who had no intention of so doing. Consequently, the prophets make a distinction between the righteous and the wicked. The righteous are the remnant, the true believers. The doctrine of individual retribution found in this passage is in reality the common doctrine of the prophets and of the Psalms.

In all probability we are to understand the force of Isaiah's language as follows: "Say with respect to the righteous that it is well." The command thus becomes a message of encouragement and hope for the righteous. Although in the coming judgment others may perish, his lot is well. From this command we learn that even in the midst of the deepest degradation and the blackest sin about us God has not forgotten the righteous, those who have hearkened to His voice. The manner in which the blessing is to be realized is expressed in the latter part of the verse.

for the fruit of their doings they shall eat — It is well with the righteous because they (the righteous are evidently conceived as a collective) will enjoy the result of what they have done. It is a teaching of the Scripture that as a man soweth, so also shall he reap. And the righteous, who have sought to live in obedience to the commands of God, will enjoy the result of their doings. It would, however, be a grave mistake to find in these words some doctrine of salvation by works of righteousness, for such is not the verse's teaching. The destiny of men is clearly seen to be in the hands of the LORD. If they are obedient to Him and believe Him — for such is the work of righteousness — they will eat the fruit of their doings. If, however, on the other hand, they rebel and continue in their sins, there can await for them nothing but destruction. Hence, we learn here that the deepest ground of human salvation — indeed, the only ground — is not to be found in the work of men but in the grace of God and His promise which is received through faith. It is this faith which alone justifies and from which flow those fruits of righteousness the blessings of which are to be enjoyed by the righteous.

11 In this verse we have the converse of the foregoing proposi-

tion.[26] The introductory "Woe" corresponds to the "Say ye" of the preceding verse.

to the wicked it is evil — The cry is uttered in consideration of the tragic condition of the wicked. Their lot is one that is evil, the very opposite of the good promised to the righteous.

that which is done — The suggestion seems to be implied that sin brings its own wages. The evil which comes upon the wicked is that which he has earned and merited through his own works. This verse represents the attitude of a true evangelist, namely, a note of anguish that the evil who have refused to hearken to the voice of God are now to be requited with the result of their own doings. Salvation is purely of unmerited grace; destruction is brought upon us through the labors of our hands. Salvation is a gift of God; destruction is the reward of our own efforts.

12 Twice in this verse the Lord speaks of the nation as "my people,"[27] and this designation, being placed first, is emphasized. It is a vocative, and the people are addressed; but are they addressed as God's people or as those of the prophet? Is it God or the prophet who claims the people as his own? Perhaps this question cannot be answered with certainty, nor does it matter too greatly, for even if it be the prophet who speaks, he speaks in the name of the Lord and as His representative. It is therefore, in either case, the Lord's people who are in view.

their oppressors — Those who are oppressing the people are supposed to be its rulers.

children — The word suggests a playful boy, one who acts the part of a child.[28] The thought is: thy oppressors are each one as children.

---

[26] According to the Masoretic accents the words "wicked" and "evil" are to be joined. Some take רע as an adj. Drechsler even takes the word as a verb, *geht's übel*. But the symmetry is better preserved if both טוב and רע are taken as nouns.

[27] B simplifies with the 3rd person, "his people," but 1Q supports M. "their oppressors" — The pl. is numerical, although the pred. is s., in which each individual is represented as affected, "their oppressors are each one child-ish." Dillmann refers this to Ahaz who began his reign at the age of 25, and Penna renders, "*Il mio populo! un bambino lo governa.*" The pl. would then express majesty. "cause thee to go astray" — The paronomasia of some renderings does not reflect the Heb., e.g., "those who lead thee mislead thee"; *qui ducunt te seducunt te; deine Führer sind Irreführer.*

[28] מעולל — Penna suggests *'ôle-lû-lô, su cui governano usurai.* M is *me-'ô-lil* and seems to be similar to the III act. part., Ar. *mu-qâ'-til.* Hummel

women rule over them — The prophet probably does not intend to describe an actual situation in which women were ruling over the nation, but rather would suggest that the rulers were weak as women.   Those who are the rulers are weak men and have no more authority than a child.   They are possibly influenced by women who were members of the harem.   The Arabian proverb is here in place, "I fled to God from the rule of boys and the reign of women."

the leaders cause thee to go astray — Those who should lead the nation in the straight way have as a matter of fact caused the nation to go astray, so that it does not know where it is going. Isaiah uses a participial form, and thus describes this action of going astray as something contemporaneous.   Even as he speaks, the leaders, those who should lead straight, are engaged in causing the nation to go astray.

and the way of thy paths they destroy — The way in which thy path should lie, the way which should lead to blessedness, for it is the way laid down by God Himself, is destroyed by these leaders, so that the nation must of necessity go astray.   Job describes the horse (39:24), "He swalloweth the ground with fierceness and rage. . . ."   Just as the horse gallops over the road and throws behind piece after piece of the earth, so these rulers of Judah in their rough manner devour the path in which the nation is to walk.   The result is that the people do not know where to go.

13 The twelfth verse had served to bring again to mind the calamitous condition of the nation which had already been pictured in the first seven verses of the chapter, and also to show that the actual state of the nation (described in verses 8 and 9) was such as would bring the judgment of God.[29]   It is that

---

(*JBL,* June 1957, p. 100) suggests that the *mem* is enclitic.   He would read *ngsyw-m'wll*.

[29] The first part. is reflexive, "placing, presenting himself, taking his stand." עמים B has s. and this is favored by Gray, Kissane, etc.   The argument against retention of the pl. is that the word refers to the nations whereas the idea of world judgment was in vogue only after Isaiah's time.   Hence, the pl. is thought to be the work of someone who at a later date wished to change the idea of particular judgment into that of world judgment.   Duhm, let it be said to his credit, does not follow B, and Bentzen is cautious, arguing that the pl. may come from some older form of oracle.   Those who retain the pl. argue that the word may describe Israel herself; cf. Gen. 49:10; Deut. 32:8; 33:3, 19.   It is quite probable. however, that this verse is an announcement of universal judgment.   It stands in relation to v. 14; which describes a

judgment to which attention is drawn in the present verse. The prophet employs participles in order to depict the action as taking place while he is speaking. It is the act of taking His stand which is emphasized. We may render, "Taking His stand to plead is the LORD, and standing is He to judge the peoples." The concept of the LORD as taking His stand implies that He is an executor ready to conduct and to carry out the trial to its conclusion. In so standing He shows Himself to be in control of the entire situation. He is ready to plead and to prosecute His case, and so is represented as the accuser.

In the second half of the verse the LORD is seen to be already standing to judge the nations. The announcement is probably to be regarded as that of a universal judgment, and seems to stand in relation to the particular judgment mentioned in verse 14 somewhat as 2:12-22 does to 3:14.

14 Turning from his declaration of a universal and general judgment, Isaiah gives a particular instance of that judgment, as applied to the elders and princes of his own people. He first mentions the LORD in order to direct attention to the fact that it is the LORD who takes the initiative and brings this judgment upon His people.

will enter — Will enter into litigation. The coming of the LORD is to be characterized by a judgment which He Himself will bring. Before Him no man can stand. "And enter not into judgment with thy servant: for in thy sight shall no man living be justified" (Ps. 143:2).

with the elders of his people — The elders were the ones responsible for the welfare of the nation. These elders were the heads of the houses, families and tribes, and had been appointed in the wilderness to aid Moses (cf. Num. 11).

and its princes — Just as the word "elders" reflects upon verse 2, so the word "princes" refers to verse 3. The princes were officials of the government. It is thus those who were responsible for the welfare and administration of the government who were the objects of God's punitive judgment, for they should have

---

particular judgment, as 2:12-22 does to 3:14. The pl. is found in 1Q. Hummel takes the *mem* as enclitic (see n. 28), which may be correct. The word is acc. after the inf. which is not to be regarded as const. "for judgment" — Note the emphatic position of these words.

manifested this responsibility toward God's people. Probably we are not at this point to identify the "my people" with the entire nation, but rather with those who were in poor condition and helpless. It is the Israel of God, which belongs to God and is the object of His special love and care.

and ye — Ye, who ought not to have done so, have consumed the vineyard.[30] We may paraphrase the thought: "The Lord will enter into judgment with the elders, who should have led the people faithfully; and as for you who should have known better, you have consumed," etc.

have consumed — The word is better rendered, "ye have depastured." The people are thus compared with animals which spoil the pasture land. It is not that they have permitted their own beasts to do this, but they themselves have depastured the land. "You who ought to have protected the land," the prophet is saying, "so that it would not be destroyed, you yourselves have destroyed it."

the vineyard — This word serves as a figurative description of the nation. It is a thought which is developed more fully in chapter 5. The vineyard, or the people of God, needed to be protected and cultivated. Instead of that it was oppressed. From this figurative description Isaiah now passes over to the actual.

the spoil of the poor — This particular sin is singled out as an example of the manner in which the rulers and those in authority had despoiled the vineyard. The phrase is equivalent to, "the spoiling of the poor." That which had been obtained by means of despoiling the poor was to be found in the houses of those who had the responsibility for the well-being of these same poor. The objects of this spoiling were the oppressed, who could not plead their own cause. The poor had as much right and claim to justice and protection as did the rulers; the action of the elders and princes, therefore, was completely unjust.

---

[30] "and ye" — The *wāw* contains a tacit allusion to something preceding, which may or may not have been expressed. Vulg., *vos enim;* König, *und zwar; nämlich;* cf. Ps. 2:6. "have consumed" — The perf. here denotes an action completed in the past, the effects of which are still in existence. B, "ye have burned." In the *Qal* in Jer. 10:8 the root בער has the sense, "to act as a dumb brute"; in the *Piel* "to depasture" (*abweiden*) , and in the *Hifil* "to bring to pasture." Cf. Exod. 22:4. גזלת "the things taken away" from the poor. We should expect *giz-laṯ*, but *Tzere* is retained as in the pl. const. *kᵉ-bē-ḏēy*, and *re-ē-bēy*. The line of demarcation between e and ē (both represented by *Tzere*) seems here to be very fine.

This particular sin is singled out as an example of the lack of responsibility, the injustice and greediness of those who were in authority. It is a peculiar example of cruelty, and, for that reason, God will come to exact vengeance upon those who have been guilty of it.

15 Isaiah breaks forth in surprise and indignation that men who have been entrusted with great responsibility would act in so despicable a manner.[31] What do you mean? he asks. What is your idea? By what right are you doing this? What evil spirit is impelling you to act in this way? How can ye dare to do so? It is the language of high emotion. In the burning anger in which the prophet utters his indignation against the sinful rulers he breaks forth in somewhat disjointed phrases. "What mean ye? — ye crush My people."

ye crush my people — Your oppressing measures are so severe that they weigh down as a heavy load and actually crush those who belong to Me.

My people — Those whom ye crush are His, and God has a tender concern for them and a zeal that those who belong to Him be not oppressed nor unjustly treated.

and grind the faces of the poor — Just as men grind grain between two heavy millstones, so ye, with your callous oppression are grinding the faces of My people. You have placed them between the cruel millstones of your greed and ground them to powder. What right do you have to do this? The poor, as well as you rulers and officials, are also members of the nation. These poor cannot defend themselves, and so you grind them, squeezing out from them all that you can to satisfy your greedy desires.

---

31 The omission of *He* in מלכם is permissible; cf. Exod. 4:2. In Ug. the *h* in *mh* seems to be a strong consonant, hence, in the light of this fact and also of the compensation for *Hē* by *dageš*, we do not need the distinction between *Qere* and *Ketib*. The *Ketib* is a synaeresis for *mah la-ķem;* lit., "what to you?" i.e., "what is your idea?" Cf. Koran, Sura 57:8,10, "and what reason have you?" *(mâ' lakum)*. "ye crush my people" — Note the chiasm; verb-obj.; obj.-verb. Note also the asyndetic construction with the preceding, which can appear in general questions. In Isa. 22:1 there are two similarly constructed sentences, save that a *ki* is inserted. Here, however, the *ki* is not necessary; cf. Jon. 1:6 for a similar example of its omission. Alexander discovers the figure in the trampling upon the bodies that are lying on the earth so that the face is ground into the dust. The imp. represents action as taking place and likely to continue. It is action to which the speaker's attention has been directed.

It is God who speaks, and the prophet here designates Him as the LORD of hosts. The designation is reminiscent of Psalm 69:6, "Let not them that wait on thee, O Lord GOD of hosts, be ashamed for my sake." We may remember the words of Psalm 82:1, 2, "God standeth in the congregation of the mighty; he judgeth among the gods. How long will ye judge unjustly, and accept the persons of the wicked?" What a forceful climax is found in these words! The sovereign One, who is Judah's God, the LORD of hosts, is uttering the condemnation against the officials and consequently there can be no doubt as to the certainty of the judgment to come.

c. *The women and their tragedy* (3:16—4:1)

16 Moreover, saith the LORD, Because the daughters of Zion are haughty and walk with outstretched neck and ogling with their eyes, walking and mincing as they go, and making a tinkling with their feet,

17 And the Sovereign One will smite with a scab the crown of the daughters of Zion, and the LORD will discover their secret parts.

18 In that day the LORD will turn aside the finery of the anklets, and the front bands and the crescents,

19 The pendants, the bracelets, and the veils,

20 The head-dresses, and the armlets, and the sashes and the perfume boxes and the charms,

21 And the rings and the nose jewels,

22 And the plaits and the overtunics, and the cloaks and the purses,

23 And the hand mirrors, and the linen wrappers, and the turbans, and the large veils.

24 And it shall come to pass, that instead of balsam oil there shall be decay, and instead of a girdle an encircling rope, and instead of braided work baldness, and instead of rich robes a girding of sackcloth, burning instead of beauty.

25 Thy men shall fall by the sword, and thy strength in war.

26 And her gates shall lament and mourn, and she shall be cleaned out sitting on the ground.

4:1 And seven women will take hold of one man in that day, saying, Our bread we shall eat, and our clothing we shall wear, only let thy name be called upon us, take away our reproach.

16 It is Isaiah who prophesies, but he knows that he is proclaiming God's Word; it is therefore God who speaks through

Isaiah.[32] A new aspect of the message is now before us, and hence, the prophet gives strength to it by calling attention to the fact that it is God who speaks.

because — The verse is a protasis, the conclusion or apodosis following in the next verse. In this protasis Isaiah summarizes the contents of the message he is about to deliver. Haughtiness is again before us. Isaiah has already condemned the "proud, arrogant deeds" of the people and their haughty demeanor. But now he directs his attention to the women. When the women are wholly vain and self-centered, the cancer of moral decay is truly consuming the nation's heart. Proper adornment and true beauty in women should be a reflection of the glory of God. When women cultivate and cherish beauty only for itself, they are infringing upon and detracting from the glory and beauty that belong to Him. That ordinary women of the world should be vainglorious might be expected. But the daughters of Zion, women who live in the city of God, under the very shadow of the Temple, who should have set the example of the beauty of holiness, these are haughty and walk with outstretched neck.[33]

Is Isaiah, however, one who can see no place in life for the beauty of adornment? Does he condemn beauty and ornament as such? That is not the case. It is not the various articles of jewelry in themselves which are reached by his condemnation. Something more serious has gripped his attention and drawn down upon itself his condemnation. In Jerusalem there was an inner pride and corruption of the heart which manifested itself out-

---

32 The phrase has been taken in a figurative sense for the souls of men or the smaller cities about Jerusalem (Eichhorn) ; cf. Josh. 15:45, 47.

נטויות — It is a question whether to Q^ere is to be preferred, for in the passive part. of *Lamed-He* verbs, the 3rd radical sometimes appears as *wāw*. Cf. 2 Kings 23:4 (see notes in Ginsburg Bible) .

33 The word is probably denominative from *taf*, "child," and denotes the short, mincing or tripping steps which the women must take because of the ornamental chains which bind their legs. "and with their feet" — A m. suffix refers to a f. antecedent. Originally the m. form was probably common to both genders. So with reference to the 3rd pl., cf. Exod. 2:17, etc., and in the Nuzi texts. Note that the inf. abs. denoting continuous action actually precedes the finite verb, which being in the imp. itself expresses continuous action. In going and tripping, they are accustomed to go.

תעכסנה — In the accented syllable we should expect *Tzere*. Here and in Isa. 13:18 both in pause, there is a shift to *Patah* before a sibilant. We should expect *Qametz*, but cf. *yŏ'mer* > *yŏ'mar*, and *GKC*, #29q.

wardly. That it was which attracted the prophet's censure. "Wherever," says Calvin, "dress and splendour are carried to excess, there is evidence of ambition, and many vices are usually connected with it; for whence comes luxury in men and women but from pride?" And again he remarks, "First then, he justly declares pride to be the source of the evil, and points it out by the sign, that is, by their gait." Isaiah is in no conflict with Peter, who stated, "Whose adorning let it not be that outward *adorning* of plaiting the hair, and of wearing of gold, or of putting on of apparel; But *let it be* the hidden man of the heart, in that which is not corruptible, *even the ornament* of a meek and quiet spirit, which is in the sight of God of great price" (1 Pet. 3:3, 4).

Different climes and different cultural and social milieus produce different kinds of dress. What is regarded as immodest in one place may not be so regarded elsewhere. The problem is not basically one of dress; it is one of the heart. What thunders forth from the mouth of the prophet is the devastating accusation, "They have become haughty."

Haughtiness — In that word Isaiah expresses the true core of the problem. First let the heart be right with God, and other matters will then take care of themselves. To bring out the true situation Isaiah uses a verb whose force may be expressed, "They become haughty and now continue so to be." The action took place in the past and its results continue to the present. They have become haughty, and now continue in that state.

Inasmuch as they are haughty, they walk with a stretched-out neck. An affected position, to be sure, but in such a position they can hold their heads high, and thus call attention to themselves. "To stretch out the neck" served in the ancient world as a succinct expression for haughtiness. In the ancient Syriac language, for example, "to stretch out the neck" meant "to be haughty." In the Hamasa it is said, "by our noses and necks pride is shown," and in the Proverbs of Maidani (No. 30), we read, "Much money does nothing else than to make the neck long."

When haughtiness is thus displayed, it must not go unnoticed. With their eyes the women ogle or flirt, in a desire to attract attention.

walking and mincing as they go — Meaning, "going and tripping as they walk.[34] In order to set forth the thought of long continuance the prophet uses two infinitive absolutes before the main verb. Because of the ornamental chains about their legs, the women take mincing and tripping steps. With their feet they rattle their bangles, and so make a tinkling sound. Against this practice, apparently also widespread, Mohammed had warned in the Koran, "Let them not strike with their feet, so that those ornaments of theirs that be hidden be made known" (Sura 24:32). In the Moallaka (5:18) we find,

> two pillars of alabaster of marble
> on which the rings of beauty jangle.

These were women with concern. They were concerned about their appearance and with drawing attention to that appearance. About the utter lack of justice in the land and about the apostasy from God, however, they had no concern. In the work of the Lord women often take an active part. In Jerusalem, however, they were the leaders away from God. Little did it matter to them that the poor were the objects of abominable tyranny. So self-centered and puffed up were these women that they were only concerned to call attention to themselves. When the women of a nation have turned to such an extent away from God, the end of that nation cannot be far away.

---

34 *Wāw* cons. introduces the verb, and we may render "therefore." Calvin, however, reasons that the gentle words and advice have not succeeded in reforming the women, therefore the Lord will undertake harsher measures. "will smite with a scab" — From this action baldness may result. Some think that the verb means "to make bald," but they differ as to the precise significance. Rosenmüller, the act of mourning; Knobel, shaving the heads of prisoners; Gesenius, falling hair as a result of scab. The verb is spelled with *Sin* (cf. *mis-pāḥ* in Isa. 5:7), but a *Sameh* is found in *śappahat*, Lev. 14:56, and *mis-pa-hat*, Lev. 13:6-8, "the place from which the hair is fallen."

כתהן — The word is difficult. The pointing of the suffix with *Tzere* occurs only here. In 1 Kings 7:50 we have פהה "sockets of the lintel and threshhold in which the door pivots turned." Ar. *fu-tun*, the space between two fingers; from this it has been inferred that the word designates the *pudenda muliebra*. Vulg. *crinem earum;* Koppe. Hitzig, Stade, etc., take it as a shortened form of פאה, hair. Eitan similarly derives it, appealing to the parallelism of Num. 24:17 and Jer. 48:45. I incline toward Eitan's view, but as it stands the form is *pot-hēn*. The object immediately follows the subject, the two being separated by *Tifha*. The force is, "The Lord . . . their secret parts (?) He will lay bare."

163

17 No vain charge was Isaiah's accusation.[35] The women were haughty as he had accused. For that very reason, the Lord would punish them in the severe manner herein described. This verse is the apodosis; the women were haughty, the punishment would hence be sure. In place of their beauty there will be a scab, for the LORD will smite them. Walking about in their finery and ornamental head-dresses, the daughters of Zion will be stricken, so that their hair, which is their glory, will fall out. The One who will act is the LORD, the God of power. The proud women of Jerusalem have their day and walk in their utter lack of concern for the condition of the nation, but the One in whose hand their destinies lie will in the future assert Himself and punish with strong hand.

and the Lord — The covenant Name of God is now used. Israel was the chosen nation, and her own God will punish her. By means of exposing their shame the women will be humiliated. They themselves had already exhibited their shame by means of their conduct, but God's punishment will turn their pride and shame into something contemptible. Isaiah does not say how this will be done, but it is likely that it is to take place at the hands of rude and rough men when like a flood the enemy comes in upon Jerusalem and Judah. Those who delight in immodest exposure will be rewarded with immodest exposure at the hands of vile men.

18 The passage begins by stating the time when the judgment is to come. It is to be "in that day" (i.e., at the time when) the LORD will smite with a scab. With respect to this finery,[36] the LORD will turn it aside, and thus, with the thought "to turn aside," we are reminded of the first verse of the chapter.

[35] Jacob believes that the passage refers to eschatological realities. Several mss. have the Tetragrammaton. 1Q also, but writes אדני above the line as a correction. It is this word which Isaiah uses when he wishes to stress the sovereignty of God.

[36] The finery, *tipheret*, is followed by twenty-one nouns with the definite article. There is much difference of opinion with respect to the meaning of some of these articles of jewelry. In 1745 N. W. Schroeder issued his *Commentarius philologico-criticus de vestitu mulierum Hebraearum ad. Jesaie* 3:16-24 (Ludg. Batav.), which is an exhaustive discussion of these nouns and their meanings. A less exhaustive work is that of Anton Friedrich Hartmann, *Die Hebräerin am Putztische und als Braut*, 1809-10. In Rosenmüller's *Scholia* there is also a thorough discussion. The reader may also consult Gray's Commentary.

the anklets — *Akasim* is a word which calls to mind the language used in the description in the sixteenth verse, "they trip along."

the front bands — The word has generally been taken as signifying a caul or cap of network, "a net band" (Gray). In New Hebrew *shevis* designated a decorative band, which passed from ear to ear over a net-covering. Schroeder, however, considered the word to be related to *shemesh*, the sun, and took it as standing in opposition to the following noun, *moons*. König calls attention to the sunbarks which were used as amulets by the Egyptians. The word has now appeared in Ugarit and should be rendered *suns*. Evidently it was an amulet in the form of a sun or bearing an image of the sun.

the crescents — Probably these were metallic ornaments in the shape of moons. We read, "And Gideon arose, and slew Zebah and Zalmunna, and took away the ornaments [the crescents] which were on the camels' necks" (Judg. 8:21b). "And the weight of the golden earrings that he requested was a thousand and seven hundred shekels of gold; beside ornaments [crescents] and collars [*netiphoth*], and purple raiment that was on the kings of Midian, and beside the chains [*anaqoth*] that were about their camels' necks" (Judg. 8:26). In the Aramaic Zakir Inscription of the ninth century B.C. the word *shr* is found, and in Arabic *shahar* is the name of the moon god.

19 *the pendants* — Read again Judges 8:26. The root *ntf* means to drop. The Arabic word *nattafat* indicates a small pearl or earring. König is probably correct when he translates "drop-shaped ear-pendants" (*die Tropfenartigen Ohrgehänge*).

the bracelets — Whether these were bands for the arms or neck cannot be definitely decided. The word *semiru* occurs in Akkadian.

the veils — In the light of the Arabic word *rac-lun*, we are probably to render "veils," and these were probably veils which consisted of two pieces hooked together below the eyes.

20 *the head-dresses* — In Isaiah 61:3 and 10 the singular form *peer* is used.[37] The reference is probably to diadems, or circlets of gold or silver (cf. also Exod. 39:28 and Ezek. 24:17, 23).

the armlets — Either these were armlets or armbands, or else

---

37 Cf. Zech. 3:4. Note unusual pointing of the definite article. Cf. a similar pointing in Isa. 17:8.

they were ankle chains designed to make the steps short. Probably they were the latter. The corresponding word in Arabic, *assad*, denotes a large bracelet (cf. also Num. 31:50 and 2 Sam. 1:10).

the sashes — Girdles, ornaments of the bride (cf. Jer. 2:32).

the perfume boxes — Houses of breath, or houses of the soul (cf. Song of Sol. 1:13; Prov. 27:9; and the alabaster boxes of Luke 7:37; Matt. 26:7 and Mark 14:3).[38]

the charms — Amulets or charms which perhaps were inscribed with an incantation. Note the occurrence of the word in verse 3 (cf. Gen. 35:4).

21 *the rings and the nose jewels* — Either finger or nose rings (cf. Esth. 3:12; Gen. 41:42; 24:22, 47).

22 *the plaits* — The root implies that these were garments that were pulled or stripped off, and hence used only on special occasions.[39] Bewer translates, "festal robes"; Gray, "state gowns," and

---

[38] On the basis of Akk. *napištu*, "neck," Eitan suggests the rendering "collar" (*HUCA*, XII-XIII, 55-88).

[39] Those who hold that vv. 18-23 are an interpolation claim that this verse continues the thought of v. 17 (e.g., Bentzen). "decay" — Cf. Ps. 38:6; Zech. 14:12. "encircling robe" — The word seems to denote a cord or rope. Saadia has, however, "torn, rent garments." Others, "a plague"; Targ., "marks of smiting"; Calvin, *laceratio;* Cocceius, *lacerum.* A cord stands in contrast to a girdle more suitably than to wounds and this meaning also agrees with the root *nqf.* "braided work" — The word "work" should not be deleted (Duhm); it may have a technical sense, "care." The word is not const. but stands in apposition to the following noun: "work, even braided work." מקשה — Cf. the root in Exod. 25:18, 36, etc. *qšh* may also mean "to turn around," hence, *miq-šch* may indicate "plaided work." Perhaps the noun indicates a kind of artistic treatment of the hair. Whatever it is, it stands in contrast to baldness. Cf. Num. 8:4; Jer. 10:5. "rich robes" — B, "cloak of half purple," also Syr.; Targ., "their walking with pride"; Vulg., *"pro fascia pectorali."* Abravanel, "pectoral girdle." He claimed that this girdle was worn by the women on festive occasions. Others render, "fullness of joy," as opposed to sackcloth. Rich garments were a sign of rejoicing, cf. Isa. 52:1; 61:3, but the precise force of the word is not known (cf. Tur-Sinai, *VT*, 1, 1951, p. 307, for an emendation). "burning" — 1Q takes the word as a prep., making a contrast between beauty and shame, which is an easier reading, "for instead of beauty shame." But this gives a form to the comparison different from the preceding comparisons. It is defended, however, by Nottscher, in *VT*, 1951, p. 300, and J. T. Milik, *Biblica*, 31, 1950, p. 216. But cf. Driver in JTS, 1951, p. 25. The clause is inverted, and the word "instead" appears between the two nouns.

Alexander "holiday dresses" (cf. Zech. 3:4ff.).

the overtunics — Whether these were large flowing overgarments or whether they were undergarments is a matter of dispute. The corresponding Arabic word means a "mantle."

the cloaks — Gray renders "the shawls."

the purses — Drechsler translates "pockets," and some think that these were pockets in which the previously mentioned shawls were placed, or which belonged to those shawls. The corresponding Arabic word has the same meaning.

23 There is question as to the exact significance of *gilyonim*. Alexander, for example, takes it as indicating small metallic mirrors. Others, on the basis of B, think that transparent clothing is intended. The Akkadian word *gulenu* denotes an article of clothing, and the Arabic *jalwa* fine silk clothing. Bewer translates "garments of gauze." In Isaiah 8:1 the word definitely refers to an object upon which one may write.

the linen wrappers — Inner garments made of fine linen. The Akkadian word *sudinnu* designates a "garment" (cf. also Judg. 14: 12, 13; Prov. 31:24).

the turbans — The root *tzanaph* means "to wrap" (cf. Isa. 62:3; Zech. 3:5; Job 29:14 and Eccl. 11:5; 47:6).

SPECIAL NOTE

According to Duhm v. 24 should follow immediately upon v. 17, and vv. 18-23 should be considered as a gloss which breaks the connection. No one could seriously ascribe this inventory to Isaiah, he thinks; it would show that Isaiah was astonishingly well versed in this field. To which we may reply, "Of course he was." Why should that be an objection to the genuineness of the list? Duhm is proceeding upon subjective grounds. The list is found in both B and 1Q. Nor can it be legitimately objected that because this list is given in prose, it is therefore not Isaianic. It would be difficult to see how it could have been presented in any other manner.

Whether there is definite order in the list or not is difficult to de-

---

Others who have taken *ki* as a prep. are: Targ., "because they have gone astray in their beauty"; Syr. "because their beauty is corrupted." B and Vulg. do not render *ki* but connect this verse with the following. The word is best regarded as a noun, "burning," from a root *kwh*. Cf. רי Job 37:11 and אי from *'wh*, and Ar. kay, "cauterizing."

The usage of the verb in Isa. 43:2; Prov. 6:28 shows that the reference is to a mark obtained by fire.

termine. Condamin, for example, held that the jewels and adorn-
ments are first mentioned and then the articles of clothing. But a
close reading of the passage shows that this is not carried through
consistently. Kissane maintains that this is the main division, although he recognizes the difficulties, and he further asserts that the
second group is further divided into outer garments, inner garments
and headgear. The reader should study the discussion of each word
and then judge for himself. Condamin also points out that there are
twenty-one forms which are to be divided into groups of 8, 5 and 8.
Thus, we have:

> (1)   8 forms: 3 masculine plural
>   3 feminine plural
>   1 masculine
>   1 feminine
> (2)   5 forms; namely, verses 20b and 21
> (3)   8 forms: 3 feminine plural
>   3 masculine plural
>   1 feminine
>   1 masculine

Whereas in v. 24 the nouns are anarthrous, with these nouns the definite article does appear. This phenomenon, however, is no objection
to Isaianic authorship. Its purpose is to make the judgment more
explicit, and also to point out the extent to which the luxury of the
women was carried. Says Calvin: "It is enough if we understand the
general import and design of the prophet, namely, that he heaps up
and enumerates these trifles in order that the prodigious variety of
them may disclose their luxury and ambition, so as to leave them
without any excuse."

24 We are back again with the thought of verse 18, although
this present verse is not necessarily its continuation. It does, however, set forth clearly the conditions which will obtain when the
LORD acts. The key word of the verse would seem to be "instead"
which is found five times. The long list of articles simply serves
to stress the scorn with which the prophet points out those things
in which the women of that time found pleasure. The entire
order of things, however, is to be reversed. In the first four members of this verse "instead" appears first for the sake of emphasis.
In the fifth clause, however, the order is changed, which fact in
itself lends a peculiar force to the contrast.

instead of balsam oil there will be decay — Now it is aromatics
or ointment; then, in that day, it will be the stench which arises
from putrefaction. In the place of the balsam oil which now gives

a sweet smell and is a delight to the inhabitants of Judah there will come the reek and malodor of decay.

instead of a girdle an encircling robe — In ancient times there were many uses for the girdle. Here it was evidently considered as decorative, and it may also have been richly embroidered. This decorative cord will be removed, and in its place there will be a cord such as that with which the slaves and prisoners were wont to be led. Likewise, instead of the braided work of the head there is to be baldness. Rich garments also, the sign of satisfaction, delight and ease, will be replaced by that emblem of mourning and bitterness, sackcloth. The beauty which now belongs to the women will be replaced by burning, possibly the branding of captive slaves. The entire order will be reversed.

25 To the city Isaiah now speaks.[40] In this city there are men as well as women, and these men who belong to the city will perish in war. The men are mentioned here, as often in the Old Testament, in distinction from women and children. Hence, it is not the populace generally, nor the lower classes, of which the prophet is speaking, but the males. A catastrophe is certain to come, and it is now clear that that catastrophe is war. Inasmuch as the male population will be destroyed in war, the tragic condition described in verse 24 will set in, and this in turn gives an explanation for the conditions described in verse 25, which will continue even to the point depicted in 4:1. "The young and the old lie on the ground in the streets: my virgins and my young men are fallen by the sword; thou hast slain *them* in the day of thine anger; thou hast killed, *and* not pitied" (Lam. 2:21).

When the male population is destroyed, then the strength of the city will be gone, for a nation's strength consisted in her fighting army. Jeremiah uses a slightly different figure when he says, "Thus saith the LORD of hosts; Behold, I will break the bow of Elam, the chief of their might" (49:35).

26 When a great slaughter occurs, there will be sad effects, and those effects are now set before us.[41] At the gates of the city the

---

40 B connects the two verses. The person addressed is changed, as elsewhere in Isaiah; cf. 1:27; 8:19; 28:14; 31:6. These changes are good Semitic usage and do not warrant questioning the genuineness of the verses. "thy men" — Emphatic, a *casus pendens*. The word is used in contradistinction to women and children, "thy males."

41 "mourn" — The second verb expresses the principal idea, and the first

people often were wont to gather, but now those gates are themselves in mourning, for the people are no longer there. The gates mourn for them. The city itself is empty, for it has been cleaned out entirely of inhabitants. While she is sitting on the ground, the city herself is cleaned out. She sits alone in mourning. In Lamentations we are given a picture of such mourning, "The elders of the daughter of Zion sit upon the ground, and keep silence: they have cast up dust upon their heads; they have girded themselves with sackcloth: the virgins of Jerusalem hang down their heads to the ground" (2:10). There is extant a coin from Vespasian which pictures the conquered Jerusalem as a dejected woman sitting under a palm tree, a soldier standing before her, and which bears the inscription *Judaea capta,* or *devicta.* Jerusalem alone. The holy city, the city from which the law would go forth, alone, sitting on the ground, utterly cleaned out. Desolation reigns where once false security and material prosperity held sway.

4:1 Herein is set forth the conclusion of the matter.[42] Desolation reaches its high point in what this verse describes. Here, in vivid and concrete form, the coming misery is depicted. The verse continues the reference to the women of Judah by showing the desperate straits to which they will be reduced in order to protect themselves from reproach. Seven women are mentioned, by which we are simply to understand a large number. Because of the calamity which has befallen Jerusalem a great disproportion between the sexes has also appeared. In the ordinance of creation, man and woman were to stand in equal ratio, one woman to one man; the desolation caused by war has so changed this that now the ratio of seven to one may be used.

At the time when the calamity will come the women will sur-

---

qualifies it, "and they shall mourn lamenting"; cf. Isa. 19:8. As seen from Gen. 19:6 the *petah* differs from the *delet,* or "door," in that it is the opening in which the door is to be found, the doorway or gate. Cf. Isa. 14:31. "cleaned out" — The root נקה is associated with the Ar. which has the idea of purity, then of emptiness. So in Num. 5:19; 1 Kings 15:22. Here the form is *Nifal,* "being emptied, cleaned out." The following imp. has the force of a circumstantial clause.

42 "take away" — Lit., "gather," from us, so that it will no longer be with us. In Ug. *lhm* may signify either bread or food. Here bread seems to be a designation for food generally.

round the man eagerly and beseech him with these words in which they give expression to the heart of their request.

Our bread we shall eat — According to the law the husband must provide the support for his wife. "If he take him another *wife*, her food, her raiment, and her duty of marriage, shall he not diminish" (Exod. 21:10). When the calamity would strike Jerusalem, however, the situation would become so desperate that the women were ready to accept the conditions of marriage upon the most disadvantageous terms. The law entitled them to support, but now they were willing to provide for themselves. Scripture does not say whether they would provide this support through work or whether they had inherited it. If only they can be called the legal wife of a man, however, they are confident that they can provide their own living. What weighs most heavily in their minds is expressed in the word "only." If *only* they may be regarded as ligitimately married, they will provide for other matters. What really counts in their minds is that they should possess the married name.

The woman was named after the husband, as is the case among us. This name they desire to be placed upon them and in so speaking give tacit recognition of the fact that the husband is to be acknowledged as the head. He whose name is placed upon a person has a certain claim upon that person. "We are *thine;* thou never barest rule over them; they were not called by thy name" (Isa. 63:19). To this one man the women address a pathetic plea. "Take away," they cry, and their words signify literally, "gather from us, so that the reproach will no longer be with us." The reproach which rested upon these women was that of childlessness, and this was the case probably because they had become widowed. ". . . and shalt not remember the reproach of thy widowhood any more" (Isa. 54:4). It was the fear of a lack of seed that had led the daughters of Lot to act in the shameful manner described in Genesis 19:32ff. The noble and honorable women might of course have become the objects of insults on the part of the enemy and of those of the lowest classes who wandered about at this time of calamity and distress. More than that, however, it seems to be the reproach of widowhood and childlessness which was uppermost in the minds of these women. They could no longer live as normal women; an offspring is not to be theirs, and they greatly feel this reproach. For this reason they abandon their natural modesty and take the initiative in a bold way, openly

171

asking a man to marry them that they may have his name. As an illustration of their desire we may note the epigram of Lucian:

> Give me only the empty name of a wife,
> Let there be inscribed on the tomb,
> Marcia, the wife of Cato.

Thus the order instituted in Eden is reversed. No longer is man the head of the wife. He does not seek her, but she him. She has taken his place and is in the position of Eve who led Adam to hearken to Satan. Sin leads to worse sin. When sin reigns, the ordinances of God are trampled under foot.

With this verse we come to the conclusion of the announcement of judgment against the women of Jerusalem. This oracle has formed a companion piece to those directed against the wicked officers and rulers of the land. Together the two are but specific illustrations of the more general condemnation and judgment which was to come upon Jerusalem. Lastly this general judgment itself is set forth by the prophet merely as a specific application or illustration of the great day of judgment which would finally break over all the earth.

d. *The Sprout of the Lord* (4:2-6)

2 In that day will the Sprout of the LORD become beauty and honor, and the land pride and glory for the escaped of Israel.

3 And it shall be that he that is left in Zion and he that remains in Jerusalem shall be called holy, everyone that is written for life in Jerusalem,

4 When the LORD will have rinsed away the filth of the daughters of Zion and will have purged the blood of Jerusalem from her midst by the spirit of judgment and by the spirit of removing.

5 And the LORD will create over every place of mount Zion and over her assemblies a cloud by day and smoke and the brightness of a flaming fire by night, for over all the glory there shall be a covering.

6 And there will be a booth for a shadow by day from the heat, and for a covert and for a hiding place from the storm and the rain.

The present section, 4:2-6, forms a conclusion of the prophecy, 2:1-4:6. A blessing had also served as introduction, namely, 2:2-4, whereas the main body of the oracle or prophecy concerned itself with the theme of judgment. The entire section may be analyzed as follows:

2:1   The heading.
2:2-4   The future exaltation of Zion.
2:5-22 The coming general or universal judgment and the day of the LORD.
3:1-4:1 The specific application of the judgment to Judah.
4:2-6   Conclusion of the prophecy. The glory of the coming age which is to be brought about by the Branch of the LORD.

2 *in that day* — How great this concept looms in the mind of the prophet! Here is the seventh time that the phrase occurs in this particular section. In 3:18 and 4:1 these words were used to announce the time of punishment and the suffering which that punishment would bring. In the present passage the words have the same force. They plunge us at once into the midst of the judgment. "The people that walked in darkness have seen a great light" (Isa. 9:1). In the vision of the Old Testament prophet, at least at this point, the Day of the LORD is regarded as one, and we are not justified in treating it in atomistic fashion. Light and darkness, salvation and judgment go together and form the concept, the Day of the LORD. Hence, Isaiah can speak of judgment and punishment and in the next breath, as it were, of salvation also. All of these phrases (3:18; 4:1, 2) refer to the same period, the time when both judgment and salvation will come to the earth. God will manifest Himself as Judge and yet as Saviour.

the Sprout of the Lord — Isaiah apparently reflects upon the language of 2 Samuel 23:5, "Although my house be not so with God; yet he hath made with me an everlasting covenant, ordered in all things and sure: for this is all my salvation, and all my desire, although he make it not to grow." Taking up the thought found in the passage in Samuel, Isaiah now uses the same root to designate the Messiah.[43] Interpretations or enlargements of

---

[43] צמח — In Ezek. 17:9, 10 the word has the force of a verbal noun, and of a collective in Gen. 19:25; Ezek. 16:7. B and Ephraim Syrus interpret it of the rising of the sun, but the word is always used of the sprouting of a plant. In Keret (2 Kings 2:43:49; 2:1:10, 21, 23) we have *sph ltpn lyh*, "the shoot [progeny] of *Ltpn* will live." I Kings 1:3.48; 6:33 has *wld. sph. lkrt*, "a

the Isaianic passage are found in Jeremiah. "Behold the days come, saith the LORD, that I will raise unto David a righteous Branch, and a King shall reign and prosper, and shall execute judgment and justice in the earth" (Jer. 23:5). "In those days, and at that time, will I cause the Branch of righteousness to grow up unto David; and he shall execute judgment and righteousness in the land" (Jer. 33:15).[44]

In the present passage the Sprout is that shoot which comes from the tree of David which has been cut down, and which springs to life from its fallen trunk and brings the tree to more glorious and wondrous heights than before. We must note Isaiah 28:5, which sustains the same relation to Isaiah 28:1 as this passage does to the preceding (4:1). In 28:5 that is attributed to the Lord Himself which in the verse before us is spoken of the "Sprout." Indeed, it is difficult, in the light of this fact, to see how a general reference of the word can be acceptable. This parallelism with 28:5 would seem to refute the view that 4:2 contains simply a reference to the products of the land.

---

child [as] offspring to *Keret*." In late Phoenician the phrase *semah seḏek*, "the rightful shoot," designates the lawful heir of the throne. The Phoenician inscription was discovered in 1893 at Larnaka, Cyprus, and comes from the 3rd-2nd century B.C. Cf. G. A. Cooke, *A Textbook of North Semitic Inscriptions* (1903), p. 83. Both these occurrences show that in Ugarit and Phoenicia the word was understood in an individualistic sense (see Eissfeldt, *El im ugaritischen Pantheon*, p. 35).

Mowinckel takes v. 2 as part of a passage that is a secondary paraphrase of some of Isaiah's words applied to a later age, for he thinks it presupposes the Diaspora. Yet he seems to take the word *tzemah* Messianically in Isa. 2:4 although he regards the passage as apparently later than Zechariah (*HTC*, p. 164).

In "Religion och Bibel," (*Nathan Soderblom-Sällskapets Arsbok*, ii, 1943, p. 61). George Widengren holds that a prophecy such as the present was influenced by an ancient oriental myth which identified the king with the mythical tree of life. While there is no evidence to support Widengren's view, at least it buttresses the position that *tzemah* may have an individual reference. Procksch maintains the authenticity of vv. 2, 3 whereas Duhm, Marti, Cheyne, Gray deny 4:2-6 to Isaiah.

44 In Zech. 3:8; 6:12 the word is employed as a kind of proper name. The line of development may thus be set forth: 2 Sam. 23:5, a general picture. Isa. 4:2, the noun is used, and the personal element begins to appear, "an early dawning, in or to the mind of Isaiah himself, of the great idea of all prophecy" (Strachey). Jer. 23:5; 33:15, the picture element is dropped. Zech. 3:8; 6:12, the noun has become a proper name.

As far as form is concerned, it will be seen that 28:1-4 may be compared with 2:5-4:1. The thought of Isaiah 28 is that in place of false beauty there will be the true beauty which is the LORD Himself, and it is this comparison which shows that in the present verse a mere reference to the land and its produce is to be excluded. A further development of the thought appears in Isaiah 60:9, where the LORD is said to have beautified Israel. In 60:19 God is said to be the nation's glory. In Zechariah 2:9 also the LORD is identified as a glory. The predicates which in 4:2 are used to describe the Sprout are those which in other passages clearly are applied to the LORD Himself. Inasmuch as the blessing which God brings to the world does not come in some vague, undefined manner, but rather is mediated through the Messiah, we are warranted in discerning in 4:2 a reflection upon the coming Messiah.

What, however, is the grammatical relationship in which the members of the phrase, "the Sprout of the LORD," stand to one another? Many have taken the phrase to mean, "that which the LORD causes to sprout." Others take it, "He who is sprouted forth from the LORD." The Sprout of the LORD, on this interpretation, is the Sprout which the LORD gives.

Perhaps it is difficult if not impossible to decide dogmatically which of these two interpretations is correct. The genitive indicates the source or origin. The Branch is of the LORD; it is His, and comes from Him. Whether this means that He is a Branch which the LORD causes to grow up unto David or whether He is simply a Branch which the LORD gives may be difficult to decide with certainty, but we incline toward the first view, for passages such as 2 Samuel 23:5 and Psalm 132:17, which seem to lie behind and to form the basis of our passage, support it.

Then, too, when we compare the parallels Jeremiah 23:5; 33:15; Zechariah 3:8, which really form a commentary upon Isaiah 4:2, we find that they also buttress this position. In these passages we are told that the LORD will raise the Branch; He will cause it to grow unto David; He will bring forth His servant the Branch. It would seem then that the phrase "Sprout of the LORD" signifies "that which the LORD causes to sprout." In either case, however, what is clear is that in identifying the Sprout as of the LORD Isaiah is excluding a reference to the mere produce of the land. He places in the foreground what the LORD is doing. The

175

reference then is to the divine origin of the One whom the LORD causes to sprout forth.

become beauty — Beauty was already present, but it was a false beauty, a sham. Articles of beauty had been on all hands (cf. 3:18ff.), but in the judgment this false beauty would be taken away, and the LORD Himself would be the true beauty of His people.

and for honor — The glory of Israel, that in which she might truly glory, was the Sprout of the LORD. In two respects the Sprout will benefit Israel. He will be their honor and their beauty.

Another consideration calls for attention. In 3:12-15 Isaiah had shown that the poor government with its attendant and consequent evils was the result of incapable and evil rulers. In the verse before us wherein we are told of the blessings to come, we should most naturally expect these blessings to be the result of the work of an individual. The more one ponders the text and its context the more cogent does the Messianic interpretation become. It is no surprise, then, that the Targum translates, "At that time shall the Messiah of the LORD be for joy and glory. . . ."

and the fruit of the land — Just as the Sprout is of the LORD, belongs to Him, and finds its origin or source in Him, so the fruit is of the land, belongs to the land, and therein finds its origin.[45]

---

[45] The phrase doubtless alludes to Num. 13:26 and Deut. 1:25. Hence, we are to render "fruit of the land" and not "fruit of the earth." That it refers to the land of Canaan is in keeping with such references as Lev. 25:19; Num. 13:27, and Jer. 2:7. In passages based upon this one we see the limitation of the human origin of the Messiah; cf. Jer. 23:5; 33:15, "unto David"; Zech. 6:12, "out of his place." In Mic. 5:1 the Messiah is born in Bethlehem. Hengstenberg correctly points out that the ground for this limitation lies in the fact that the Messiah is represented as belonging to the covenant people; "salvation is of the Jews" (John 4:22b).

The word fruit generally refers to the fruit of the tree and of the ground, and in a metaphorical sense the fruit of the womb. Israel's natural fruit is a symbol of the spiritual fruit herein intended. Hence Vitringa: *"de terrestri enim proventu haec verba intellegere vetat magnificentia orationis."* "pride" — Cf. Isa. 60:15, for an interpretation. "and glory" — Exod. 28:2, 40, also Jer. 33:6-9; Deut. 26:19. The first of these passages speaks of the holy garments made for the priests. Note the language of v. 40. At the time of Isaiah Israel already had a glory (*tiferet*), cf. 3:18, and it is this *tiferet* which the Lord will remove in judgment. "to the remnant of Israel" — In Deut. 30:1-10 it had been prophesied that a remnant which had passed through judgment would return to the Lord and this conception of a remnant is carried on throughout the prophetical books. The expression "remnant of Israel is to be

Is it then going too far to say that the phrase "The Sprout of the LORD," points to the deity of the Messiah and the phrase, "fruit of the earth," points to His humanity? In the Old Testament, when both the divine and the human origin of the Messiah are mentioned, the human origin is more definitely limited and qualified. "The fruit of the land" may have been an expression chosen deliberately against the background of Numbers 13, and without doubt the writer of the Epistle to the Hebrews had this prophecy in mind when he wrote, "For *it is* evident that our LORD sprang out of Judah; of which tribe Moses spake nothing concerning priesthood" (7:14). He employs a verb[46] which is usually used of the shooting forth of plants and herbs. The reference to the humanity of the Messiah in the Old Testament is more definitely limited because He is presented to the covenant people as belonging unto them. Thus, for example, Isaiah in another place (9:6) says, "For unto us a child is born." We may then paraphrase the thought of the present verse, "He whom the LORD will cause to sprout forth from Israel."

Are we, however, really justified in giving a Messianic interpretation to the words, "fruit of the land?" That the phrase does refer to the Messiah is seen from the following considerations. (1) The parallelism between branch and fruit. Both these expressions are from the realm of botany, and consequently place in a definite contrast *the Lord* and *the land*. The Sprout is from the LORD, and the fruit is from the land. The LORD indicates the divine nature of the Sprout, and the earth His human nature. He is the Sprout who comes forth from the LORD, and the fruit who comes out of the land. (2) In many passages of Scripture there is reference to the fruitfulness of the Messianic age. Only here, however, is it stated that the fruit is for the dispersed of Israel. Can we really think that the prophet has lowered himself to the point where all he is saying is that the dispersed, those whose desperate need is God, will have fruitful land in the Messianic age? (3) The text provides no contrast between fruitfulness and barrenness. If all Isaiah is teaching is that in the Messianic age the land will be fruitful, to what does this stand in contrast? In

---

construed equally with both members of the verse. This verse and the following, together with vv. 4-6, find their summary in Zech. 2:9. Cf. W. E. Müller: *Die Vorstellung vom Rest im Alten Testament* (Leipzig: 1939).

46 ἀνατέταλκεν

2:6, 7 the prophet has accused the people of leaning on the arm of flesh and seeking the wisdom of the east. In what sense does fruit set forth a contrast? We cannot really come to grips with this verse unless we take it in its general context, and in this general context a mighty contrast is intended. The actual Israel looked for her glory and ornament among foreigners and strangers; she neglected her true inheritance. The Israel of the future, however, will not judge with the eyes of flesh, but will understand that her true glory and ornament are found in her real inheritance, the long promised seed of Abraham through whom the blessing was to come. Isaiah says, "The LORD shall be unto thee an everlasting light, and thy God thy glory" (60:19). In place of the false glory and ornament (2:5-4:1) the genuine and real glory and ornament, namely, the LORD Himself, will appear (4:2). This is proved by the equation with 28:5.

(4) Lastly, it should be clearly noted that only when the phrase "fruit of the land" refers to the Messiah is there a satisfactory connection with what follows. On other views, this connection is broken. If Isaiah is speaking only of the productivity of the land, the thought is immediately dropped, and not introduced again. In fact, it is an abrupt thought, and the reason for its introduction is difficult to discover. If, on the other hand, he is speaking of the Messiah, then he has given a general statement, the details of which he introduces in the following verses.

pride and glory — The future glory of Israel is not to be discovered in contentment with mere material ornaments and decorations; her true beauty and glory as the people of God will be found in God Himself. Blessed is that nation whose God is the LORD!

to the remnant of Israel — The phrase is to be construed with both members of the verse. The thought is: "For the escaped remnant of Israel the Sprout of the LORD will become beauty and honor and for the escaped remnant of Israel the fruit of the land will be pride and glory." In the mention of the remnant we are brought again face to face with God's faithfulness to what He had promised. A remnant will be saved.

3 *And it shall be* — Words which he often employs when the following clause may begin with "whoever." The thought is, "And this shall be the consequence." Thus the mind of the reader is prepared for the mention of an event of unusual moment. Having spoken of the Messiah, the prophet now turns to His people,

those who will be called holy.[47] In the previous verse they were designated a remnant; they are those who have been preserved alive and have escaped the judgments of God. Here they are those who are holy, and their eternal destination is also stated.

he that is left — We have already been introduced to the remnant; now Isaiah gives a more detailed description of that remnant. Both the expressions "he that is left in Zion" and "he that remains in Jerusalem" are of equal compass with the "remnant" mentioned in the preceding verse. Isaiah uses two interesting words. *Notar,* "he that is left," may indicate the actual fact that one does remain; *nishar,* "he that remains," may point rather to the intention. It may be, however, that, legitimate as this distinction is, the prophet was not deliberately intending to employ

---

47 וחיה — Followed by *Legarmeh* as in 2:2, possibly to separate two *Hē-s.* This same phenomenon thus appears both in the beginning and in the conclusion of the section. "holy" — The reference is not primarily to cultic purity. Rather, it is particularly with respect to their destiny that the inhabitants of the new Zion will be called holy. "They become holy because they are partakers of the beauty of the exaltation and ornament which are to be bestowed upon the escaped by the Sprout of the Lord" (Hengstenberg). The holiness, therefore, is not the loyalty of the remnant.

This verse sets the ultimate ground of the preservation in the doctrine of election, and not in any merit to be discovered in the remnant. At the same time, Hengstenberg may be correct in asserting that the remnant was already holy in a moral sense. If such were the case, however, that holiness would have been a fruit of the election. It is true that without holiness no man shall see the Lord, but that holiness is not the ground of deliverance. The remnant must have clean hands and a pure heart, and doubtless the remnant did have. In that sense we may speak of it as ethically holy, and so as escaping the wrath of judgment.

The word bears the disjunctive which, following immediately after *Zaqef qaton* gives it a distinct emphasis, making it the most prominent word in 3a. Note that v. 3 forms the apodosis, the conditional element (protasis) being reserved for v. 4.

"book of life — Cf. also Ezek. 13:9 and Exod. 32:32, 33, to be blotted out of the book which God has written; Ps. 69:29, blotted out of the book of the living; Ps. 139:16; 1 Sam. 25:29, the bundle of life. The phrase probably goes back to the recording of genealogical records (cf. Neh. 7:5, 64). The word life may be taken as "the living ones" or as a pl. of intensity. The prep. would then express purpose, "written down for the purpose of life." The One who writes down is God, and hence, this phrase serves as a picturesque expression for election. Cf. Isa. 49:16.

For extra-biblical parallels to the process of enrollment we may note the catalog of ships, *Iliad* II; the rosters of captive towns, initiated by Thothmes III; the recording in Egypt of those who performed rebellious deeds, and the names of the Pharaoh's enemies.

it at this point. It may be that he was simply choosing two synonyms for the purpose of strengthening his description.

At any rate Isaiah uses a striking sentence. He emphasizes the concept of the remnant and that of "holy." The emphasis may be brought out as follows: "As for the one that is left and the one that remains — HOLY shall he be called." The striking force of this arrangement of the sentence will be apparent to anyone who will read the Hebrew aloud slowly several times.

holy — Israel was called to be a holy nation (Exod. 19:6). "The LORD shall establish thee an holy people unto himself, as he hath sworn unto thee, if thou shalt keep the commandments of the LORD thy God, and walk in his ways" (Deut. 28:9). Those who remain in Jerusalem and have survived the judgment will be separate from what has brought on the judgment, namely, sin. At one time men had been set apart by their walk and position in life; now, however, such distinctions of rank and condition will be removed, and all will be distinguished by the fact that they are designated as holy. The ideal which had previously been set forth will then be fully realized. To bring that ideal to realization, however, it will be necessary for the nation to be purged by means of a great judgment.

shall be called — When the remnant is addressed, they will be addressed as holy. Whereas it is not actually so asserted, the implication is that those who are called holy are as a matter of fact holy. They are not addressed in vain. Indeed, not only are they holy, but they are recognized as such. In the New Testament this designation is applied to those who are redeemed. In so far as there are saints in the church, there is a fulfillment to this prophecy.

all who are written — In a city the inhabitants are registered or enrolled. Likewise in Jerusalem those who are called holy are to be registered or written down. Thus Ezekiel says, "They shall not be in the assembly of my people, neither shall they be written in the writing of the house of Israel" (13:9; cf. also Jer. 22:30). What the prophet here envisions is not a mere writing down for a temporary period but a writing down for life. Even among the Babylonians there was a book of life, but here the thought is that of eternal life. Thus the remnant is traced to its true and ultimate foundation in the doctrine of election. Those who are called holy are written down either as living ones or else for

180

life — the word can be taken in either sense — and thereby their destiny is declared. The destiny for which they are to be written down is life. This life is the opposite of the condemnation which the judgment will bring. It is the life mentioned in verse 2 when the Sprout of the LORD will become beauty and honor for the escaped of Israel, and the fruit of the land will be their pride and glory. In other words, it is the life of eternity, which will come to the people because the Sprout of the LORD is their beauty, life which they have because of the work of the Messiah. It is, therefore, everlasting life, the destination which awaits those who remain after God's judgment.

In these words the doctrine of predestination is stated in figurative language. Those who have been written down — and the singular form would point to the fact that men are individually written down — are those who have been predestinated unto life, the life which comes from God. In the New Testament we find the same thought expressed in Acts 13:48, "And when the Gentiles heard this, they were glad, and glorified the word of the LORD: and as many as were ordained to eternal life believed." The ground of this writing is not to be found within men but within God. Hence, Delitzsch is not correct nor true to Scripture when he says that this takes place "on account of the good kernel of faith within them." Such an idea is introduced into the Bible from without; it is not a Biblical thought. It is true that those who are written unto life will have this kernel of faith within them, but this kernel of faith is a gift of God, given to those who are predestined unto life. The ground of this predestination is the sovereign good pleasure of God, and it is only of His good pleasure that any are written down for life.

4 Isaiah now introduces an element of judgment.[48] In the second verse he had depicted the Messianic reign and in the third the blessed condition of those who are the subjects of that reign. Now he carries on the thought found in the "in that day" of

---

[48] The Heb. perf. may be rendered by the English fut. perf., for it expresses a fact which will be in a completed state in the future (*futurum exactum*). The verb in the co-ordinate clause, however, although it has the same force, is in the imp. This substitution of the imp. generally occurs when the relation of priority need not be expressed; cf. Job 19:27; Isa. 6:11.

Commentators differ as to whether this verse is the continuation of v. 3 or the introduction to v. 5. Bentzen takes v. 4 as a continuation of v. 3, for

verse 2, and by way of summing up the entire argument of 3:1-4:1, introduces the element of judgment by way of preparation for verse 5. This judgment is essential in order that the filth of those who boasted in their glory and the violence of those who shed innocent blood might be washed. When this work of judgment has been completed, the LORD will then build a protection from the heat, the storm and the rain.

By way of summary we may say that verses 2 and 3 deal with the Messiah and the positive blessings which He brings to the elect. Verses 4-6 treat of the judgment and also of the blessings which follow thereafter.

This judgment occurs when God will have acted. Isaiah does not employ the covenant name of God, but speaks of Him as *Adhonai,* a favorite designation of God with him, and one which suggests that the work to be accomplished is of great moment and difficulty, such as could be performed by God alone.

will have washed away — The word intimates bodily washing as well as legal ablutions. Earlier Isaiah had commanded the people to wash themselves and to make themselves clean. But only a washing which the Lord performs is efficacious. In that day the LORD will have carried out those necessary actions of washing which will render clean (i.e., from sin) the truly sinful nation. The people of Isaiah's time saw no need for washing; it

---

in v. 5 a new subject is begun. Drechsler, however, construes v. 4 with v. 5.

"the filth" — Some of the older commentators derived this word from יצא and translated "excrements." Michaelis connected it with the Syriac *tzotho, foeditas,* and translated "filth." It is from a root צוא , which is found also in Ar., Eth., Syr. BDB compares Akk. *ṣi'* "destroy, ruin." The word is used of a drunkard's vomit, Isa. 28:8; of human excrement, Isa. 36:12. "daughters of Zion" — The parallelism is between daughters of Zion on the one hand and bloods of Jerusalem on the other. The word is purposely chosen because of its reflection upon 3:16ff. It does not denote, however, as Hengstenberg suggested, the towns surrounding Jerusalem. "will have rinsed" — In Jer. 51:34, דוח means to drive, cast out, but in Ezek. 40:38; 2 Chron. 4:6 it is used in the sense of rinsing parts of the burnt offering. In Akk. *dihu* and *rihsu* are synonymous. An interesting example of ritual purification is given in *Iliad* I:312ff. "The son of Atreus commanded the people to purify itself, so they purified themselves and cast the filth (λύμα) into the sea." They then sacrificed. In a Hittite text, "blasphemy and uncleanness" are regarded almost as material objects to be purged out, *ANET,* p. 346; cf. p. 348. "removing" — Better than "burning." It is more in keeping with the cultic emphasis to take the word in its technical sense as in 1 Kings 22:47; Deut. 13:6; Num. 24:22; Judg. 20:13. 1Q has סער.

regarded itself as pure. *"There is* a generation *that are* pure in their own eyes, and *yet* is not washed from their filthiness" (Prov. 30:12). As a matter of fact, Isaiah's generation was filthy and the only washing that could be efficacious must come from God Himself.

the filth — What a contrast this word offers to the opinion which the daughters of Jerusalem entertained of themselves! It characterizes the idolatry and superstition of the time and in addition the moral corruption of the women. With deliberate reflection upon 3:16ff., Isaiah identifies the possessors of filth as the daughters of Zion. It is a ghastly contrast. The daughters of Zion possess not holiness but filth. In this verse Isaiah takes up two important points which he had introduced in his third chapter. There he had mentioned first the violent deeds of the citizens of Jerusalem and then the supposed finery of the women. Now, in the present verse and in a chiastic order he makes mention of precisely these two points. First of all he calls attention to the women of Zion as though to say that their glory is actually not glory at all but filth, and then he discusses the question of the violent deeds of Jerusalem's inhabitants.

So it is with all that in which, apart from God, we find our glory. Our wealth, our activity, our philosophy, our good works, all apart from God are filth. But all these the gracious LORD will wash away. "In that day there shall be a fountain opened to the house of David and to the inhabitants of Jerusalem for sin and for uncleanness (Zech. 13:1). This wondrous act of God was accomplished when His eternal Son, the LORD Jesus Christ, shed His precious blood upon the cross of Calvary. Then was washed away all the guilt and power of sin of those for whom He died.

and the bloods of Jerusalem — The reference is to the blood guiltiness of the people generally. By using the plural Isaiah indicates blood spilled in violence, and it may well be that this was the innocent shed blood which led to the coming of the exile.

he will have purged out from her midst — Just as parts of the burnt offering were to be rinsed out so that filth should be removed from them, so God will perform a cleansing work to remove filth from the midst of His people. The inward part must be washed so that the Holy One may dwell in the midst of His people.

from her midst — These violent deeds remained in the city, and until they were rinsed or purged there could not be any true

183

cleansing. This work is to be wrought by the Spirit who brings judgment. Through His agency God will bring about these ends.

The language of this verse is reflected upon in chapter 11 in which Isaiah again speaks of the Spirit of the LORD. In Isaiah 28:6, also, the prophet speaks of a spirit of judgment. Inasmuch as Isaiah later uses this same language and also for the reason that the effects here to be accomplished must be wrought by a per-sonal agency, we must assume that the reference is to the Spirit as a Person. It is the Spirit who also is mentioned in Genesis 1:2, Psalm 33:6 and 104:30.

From the standpoint of the creature this Spirit is viewed from different aspects. He is here seen as the Spirit which brings judg-ment and also extermination, but the verse is not speaking of two different spirits. The Spirit brings judgment in that He discerns between the evil and the good and renders decisions in accordance with the principles of strict justice. It is not that He simply ex-ercises ordinary judgments in the course of God's providential dealings. Schelling had said, "*Die Weltgeschichte ist das Weltge-richt*," but, true as that may be, in this verse the Spirit is set forth as performing a special, particular work of judgment, one not to be equated with the ordinary work of God's providence. Whereas there was a judgment in the exile, and also in the first advent of Christ, in the fullest sense the judgment is that which we call the last judgment. For the establishment of Messiah's kingdom there is needed the positive work of the Messiah, the redemption of His people, but there is also needed the work of the Spirit in convincing the world of sin and judgment.

5 When the LORD will wash away, then He will create.[49] First, however, the filth must be washed away. The coming glory is

---

[49] Marti says that ברא is impossible, and Bentzen says that it was a frequent word in "2nd" Isaiah, and hence later than Isaiah's time. But must we remove from Isaiah all those words which do not fit in with certain critical attitudes? ברא is used in the Qal of the production of something fundamentally new, always with God as the subject, the material of which something is made never being mentioned.

"mount Zion" — Some take it in a distributive sense, over the cities. מכון is not employed of human dwellings; cf. Exod. 15:17; "over the whole (divine) habitation of Mt. Zion" (Skinner). "assemblies" — Also in Isa. 1:17 and Neh. 8:8, elsewhere only in the Pentateuch. In Num. 10:2 the word seems to have the force of a verbal noun; it then comes to designate those who are called out for the purpose of celebrating an assembly; (cf. Exod. 12:16; Lev. 23:3, 7, 8, 24).

comparable only with the creation. It is pictured as a return to the beginning, the absolute beginning. So great is the majesty and glory of that salvation that the most suitable comparison for it is that of the creation. To emphasize this fact, Isaiah employs a word which Moses had used in the first verse of Genesis. To create! What an appropriate word for the description of the work of God in introducing salvation! The verb *bara* is the most suitable for expressing the doctrine of absolute creation and is also the ideal word to picture that work of salvation which is attributable to the immediate activity and agency of God. It makes crystal clear the fact that the work is solely of God. As in creation God alone is active (indeed, only God could have been active, inasmuch as nothing had yet been created) so also in the work of salvation God exclusively is active (nor can any other be active, inasmuch as those to be saved are spiritually dead). It should further be noted that whereas in the protasis (v. 4) the word *Adhonai* was employed, in the apodosis we have the Tetragrammaton, the Covenant Name, which is used when the prophet is speaking of redemption. The creation of the new heavens and earth is the work of the LORD, the covenant God of Israel, and He is the second Person of the ever blessed Trinity.

over every place of mount Zion — "All of the place of the mount of Zion." We may render, "the whole place of Mount Zion." The word is not used of human dwellings, and so designates a divine place of abode, the divine dwelling of Mount Zion. Zion is thus

---

It is a forerunner of the NT *ecclesia*. Duhm would connect "smoke" and "night," but this does violence to the Masoretic accentuation, which has *Zaqef-qaton* over "smoke." "cloud" — Cf. Isa. 44:22. "smoke" — Isa. 6:4, 9:17; 14:31; 34:10; 51:6; 65:5. The two words may be construed as a kind of hendiadys, the cloud of smoke (cf. Exod. 13:21, 22).

Duhm argues that Isaiah would not have represented God by visible symbols and dates this section about the time of Ezekiel or the so-called Deutero-Isaiah. The later writers liked to compare the future salvation with the period of the Exodus, for they had read the Pentateuch. For Isaiah's time, however, the period of David is the classic type. The author of chap. 4, thinks Duhm, employed the developed eschatology of legalized Judaism of the second century. In answer to all of this we may point to its arbitrary character. Isaiah can at times, e.g., chap. 1, refer to the Davidic age as the time of glory, but there is no reason why he should be confined to such a type.

This passage serves as a basis for the description in Rev. 21:3ff., where the tabernacle and the temple become coextensive with the New Jerusalem (Vos).

conceived as a unit. No longer is it necessary for access to the presence of God to be confined to the high priest, for the Holy of Holies is here done away and the entirety of Mount Zion is now the recipient of the blessing of God's presence. There is an interesting assonance between this word *mekon* and the *nakon* of 2:2.

and over her assemblies — These were assemblies for worship, and the word is actually a forerunner of the New Testament *ekklesia*. The close connection between Zion and the assemblies would indicate that the true places of worship are to be found at Zion, and that over them all is the protecting cover of God.

a cloud by day and smoke — In the description of the coming salvation Isaiah uses language descriptive of the time of the wilderness wandering. This cloud of smoke had served as a protection for God's people. From it, however, there fell that fire which devoured the wicked. The cloud was first a guide to the people. "And the LORD went before them by day in a pillar of a cloud, to lead them in the way" (Exod. 13:21a). It was also a protection. "And it came between the camp of the Egyptians and the camp of Israel; and it was a cloud and darkness *to them,* but it gave light by night to *these;* so that the one came not near the other all the night" (Exod. 14:20). It was also an approach to the LORD. "Then a cloud covered the tent of the congregation, and the glory of the LORD filled the tabernacle" (Exod. 40:34). In the old dispensation the cloud was confined to the Holy of Holies; its use was restricted. The time is to come, however, when it will appear over all of Mount Zion.

the brightness of a flaming fire by night — "The brightness — fire of flame by night." When the flames of the fire shoot out at night they cause a brightness, and it is that brightness to which Isaiah adverts here.

for over all the glory a covering — A canopy, sometimes used for the wedding ceremony. Just as over the wedding ceremony there was a protective canopy, so here there will also be one which will be over all the glory. All Mount Zion will thus be glorious. Again in 6:3 Isaiah takes up this thought when he speaks of the fullness of all the earth being God's glory. In chapter 6 also the entire earth is in view. In the passage before us Zion seems to have supplanted the known earth and occupies the center of attention.

6 By using a different figure Isaiah continues the promise of protection.[50] He begins with emphasizing the word "booth." It is such a booth that men may find protection therein. In tender and loving tones the prophet introduces a simple figure from everyday life, one that would be well understood. There is to be a protection from all the misfortunes and enemies which might afflict God's people, even God Himself. Over all the glory of the new Zion there will be a covering. Now, however, the prophet brings the scene down to terms of everyday life. As in the fields there is a booth in which the shepherd may find refuge, so in the new age will there also be such protection. To an Oriental this would be a beautiful picture of the blessing and protection that was so much needed.

a shadow by day — One who has traveled in the deserts of Arabia and Sinai can appreciate this figure. It is during the day that the heat of the sun is burning, and a shadow becomes a wel-

---

[50] Skinner thinks that it is difficult to believe that Isaiah would have written "so weak a conclusion to an important article." Procksch also asserts that Isaiah could never have written such unclear verses as this one. The style and ideas are not Isaiah's, maintains Bewer, but probably come from a post-exilic writer. If, however, vv. 5 and 6 are late, so are vv. 2-4, for all form a unit. And this is the problem, for if the last verses or verse are to be denied to Isaiah, so must the entire section be denied to him. The chiastic reference to chap. 3, however, shows that these verses are indeed Isaianic; consequently, the entire section, which must be treated as a unit, comes from him.

As the text stands, it is forceful, emphasizing the first word; "and a booth, it shall become a shadow." Delitzsch translates, "and it will be a booth," finding the subject either in the verb itself (the verb having a pregnant sense, as in 15:6; 23:13) , i.e., there will be a booth, or else taking "Zion" of v. 5 as the subject. This latter is possible, but inasmuch as "Zion" is so far removed, and at the same time is in a secondary position, it is unlikely. It is better to make a new beginning, "and a booth" (thus the word is emphasized) , "it shall become," etc. *Sukkah* had already been used by Isaiah in 1:8, and possibly a contrast is intended. There, the nation had become a mere booth; here the booth is such that protection may be found in it. The picture may be taken from the booths of the shepherds. The booth was a small, protective structure, such as was used by Israel in the wilderness, at the Feast of Booths. סכה is the heat caused by the burning sun, cf. 25:5; 61:4; Matt. 13:6, 21. "and a covert and a hiding place" — מחסה "a place of refuge, shelter"; מסתור "place of shelter." Duhm thinks that this word is additional evidence that the passage is not genuine, for he says, Isaiah writes סתר , cf. 28:17; 32:2. Isaiah also uses the word in the sense "in secret" in 45:19 and 48:16. In 45:3 he uses the pl. It should be noted that this is the only passage in the Bible in which the word is used in the singular. Conceivably it is more forceful than סתר. The one designates a shelter; the other a place of shelter.

come relief. The writer recalls a great rock in the desert of Sinai, a rock which cast a long shadow, and in that shadow there was some relief from the broiling sun. The addition of these words "by day" lends a force and vividness to the description. Isaiah knew the blessedness of shadow in the day.

and a covert and hiding place — The booth will serve both as a place of shelter in which one may be protected from the elements and also as a place of secret in which one may be hidden from the enemy.

the storm and rain — Isaiah has in mind the inundation or driving rain which often accompanies thunder. The second word is a general term for rain, and in this particular context indicates driving, harmful, unwelcome rain.

The language is obviously figurative and not to be taken literally. Therefore the chapter closes with a note of comfort. In the new age, when the Messiah and His reign shall prosper, when God Himself through His grace will provide a covering over all the glory of Zion, there will be protection from evil and trouble. The thought is precisely the same, although expressed under a different figure, as that found in Isaiah 43:2, "When thou passest through the waters, I *will be* with thee; and through the rivers, they shall not overflow thee; when thou walkest through the fire, thou shalt not be burned; neither shall the flame kindle upon thee."

SPECIAL NOTE

Some of the principal views of this passage which have been held are the following:

(1) Among some expositors these verses have been thought to designate the pious remnant or outgrowth of the nation itself. To this view Michaelis, Koppe, Gesenius, Eichhorn, Knobel and Grotius have lent their support.[51] A strong objection, however, is that in these verses the remnant of Israel is definitely distinguished from the Sprout and the Fruit of the land. Both the Sprout and the Fruit are said to be *for* the remnant of Israel. Inasmuch as the text thus clearly dif-

---

[51] According to Hengstenberg this view was a product of rationalism. Targ.: "In that time the Messiah of the Lord will be for glory and honor." Kimchi: "By the seed of Jehovah must be understood the Messiah, the son of David, as Jer. 23:5 says." This is also the view of Vitringa and Rosenmüller, who even goes so far as to say, "*Quare nobis certum est, cogitasse et Jesajam h.l. de rege illo magno, sub quo reipublicae suae, auream aetatem reditturam esse, Israelitae sperabant.*"

ferentiates the two, it is difficult to see how they can be identified. If the word "Sprout" designates the pious outgrowth of the nation, such usage is without parallel. Not only is it without parallel, but the term is actually employed elsewhere to designate the Messiah. Gesenius seeks to refer the phrase "for the remnant of Israel" only to v. 2a and not to 2b. By this means he attempts to avoid an explicit reference to the escaped of Israel, but in so doing breaks the symmetry of the verse. He himself later recognized the weakness of this attempt and abandoned it. In Gen. 19:25, according to Gesenius, the word *tzemach* is used in a collective sense. But that fact in itself does not affect the force of the contention that the word may also be applied to an individual. If it did, it would also rule out a Messianic application of the word *tzemach* in a passage such as Jer. 23:5.

(2) A second interpretation is to the effect that the verse describes the wonderful fertility that will one day come upon the land.[52] Such fertility is thought by some to be a characteristic of the Messianic age. Kissane, for example, speaks of the "marvelous fertility of the soil in the Messianic age." Bentzen, Dillmann, Von Orelli, Edelkoort, maintain a similar position. To defend it appeal is made to the parallel expression, "the fruit of the land," which is said to preclude a Messianic reference.

(3) Duhm complains that the style of this section is more tedious and clumsy than in any other pre-exilic prophecy. For that reason he denies its authorship to Isaiah. Rather, he thinks, the passage reflects or mirrors the eschatological ideas of the second century B.C. It should be attributed to the collector of chaps. 2-4, a man who wanted this section to close on a note of comfort. Like other late sections this one also sets forth a period of productivity. The fruit of the land, according to such late eschatological passages, consists of pome-

---

[52] Maurer says, *"de proventu agri terrae sanctae intelligere."* Maurer so interprets to preserve the parallelism. Perhaps the best modern presentation of this portion is by Edelkoort, who even translates, *wat de HEERE laat uitspruiten.* His argument against the individualistic interpretation is that it is excluded by the parallelism, for 2b speaks of the fruit of the land, and the prophets have never presented the Messiah as "fruit of the land," but as a divine being who will appear in a wonderful way at the end time. The parallelism therefore shows that *tzemah* must indicate what the earth produces, which is not a natural process, but the work of God whose Spirit controls the life of nature (Ps. 104:30).

If this were correct we should expect the text to read *"tzemach* of the land of the Lord." Furthermore, the magnificence of the whole context opposes this interpretation (Rosenmüller). It is true that the blessings of nature are regarded as gifts of God (cf. Amos 9:13ff., Hos. 2:17ff., etc.), but a comparison of Isa. 4:2-6 with these passages shows that if it merely refers to the fertility of nature, the passage is really without analogy, for, on the face of it, the language of Isa. 4:2-6 appears to refer to far more than nature's productivity.

THE BOOK OF ISAIAH

granates, figs, balm, honey, wine, etc. These are a proof of the piety of the people and the triumph of their religion. If, apart from the *ipse dixit* of Duhm there is any evidence for this theory, I do not know what it is.

(4) Calvin maintained that the passage was not primarily individualistic, but that the figures employed had reference to an unusual and abundant supply of grace which would relieve the hungry.[53] His view is somewhat similar to the second view mentioned above.

(5) The prophecy has also been applied to Hezekiah,[54] which at least has the advantage of taking it in an individualistic sense.

(6) The view adopted in this commentary interprets these verses in a Messianic sense.[55] According to this view the Sprout and the Fruit of the land are to be identified, both being taken as designations of a personal Messiah. In order the better to understand this position, we must consider some of the more cogent objections that have been raised against it.

(i) If the expression *tzemach*, "sprout," actually designated a person, it is objected, it would not be asserted that he was for beauty and glory. König, who makes this objection, apparently thinks that this description is therefore not applicable to a person, although he does not enlarge upon the matter. In reply, it may be noted that this very language is used in Isa. 28:5 of a person. "In that day Yahweh of hosts will become a crown of glory and a diadem of beauty for the remainder of his people." Note also Isa. 24:16 and 2 Sam. 1:19 where the designation צְבִי is applied to both Saul and Jonathan. It should also be borne in mind that the language of Isa. 28:5 is obviously based upon the present verse.

(ii) It is further maintained that inasmuch as the parallel expression "the fruit of the land" has a collective force, the words "Sprout of the LORD" cannot be taken in a personal sense. The two expressions, however, as the exegesis will seek to maintain, are parallel, and if it can be shown that the first term is employed as a designation of the Messiah, so also must the second be.

---

53 Von Orelli: "It is the Messianic salvation, which the Lord makes wondrously to spring up after the judgment, and which the purified land will present as a divinely produced fruit. Outward and inward glory are here combined." Edelkoort's view possibly applies here also, for he takes the prophecy as a reversal of the curse uttered in Genesis. *"De verandering der natuur behoort tot de teekening van den messiaanschen tijd, d.i., zij is religieus gefundeerd en gewaarborgd."* Penna's view is somewhat similar, *"La solennita dell' inizio (in quel giorno) insieme all' abbondanza dei frutti della terra sembra legittimare invece un interpretazione messianica, non personale bensi indiretta."*

54 Rosenmüller mentions the view (without naming its advocates) that this passage refers to Hezekiah. Steinmann also holds this view.

55 The classic defense of this position is found in Hengstenberg. It is also adopted by Drechsler, Delitzsch, Möller, Fitch.

(iii) It is contended that in Isa. 11:1 the Messiah is designated the "Shoot of Jesse," and in Jer. 23:5; 33:15 the "Shoot of David." The present passage, however, is said to be earlier than these, and hence we must not look for the content and connotations which are to be found in later passages. This objection, however, can best be answered by means of a study of the word צמח.

3. GOD AND JUDAH (5:1-30)

a. *The parable of the vineyard* (5:1-7)

1 I will sing indeed of my beloved a song of my beloved concerning his vineyard; my beloved had a vineyard in a very fruitful hill.

2 And he dug it carefully about and he gathered out the stones thereof, and he planted it with choice vines, and built a tower in the midst of it, and also he hewed a wine vat in it, and he awaited that it should bring forth grapes and it brought forth rotten grapes.

3 And now, O inhabitant of Jerusalem, and men of Judah, judge, I pray you, between me and my vineyard.

4 What more could I have done to my vineyard that I have not done in it, why when I looked for it to bring forth grapes did it bring forth rotten grapes?

5 And now I would indeed have you to know what I am about to do to my vineyard; I shall turn aside its hedge and it shall become a consuming, and I shall break through its wall and it shall become a trampling place.

6 And I shall make an end of it; it will not be pruned nor will it be hoed, but there shall come up briers and thorns: and I shall command the clouds that they rain no rain upon it.

7 For the vineyard of the LORD of hosts is the house of Israel, and the men of Judah the plant of his delight; and he looked for judgment and behold! bloodshed, for righteousness and behold! a cry.

1 The prophet is determined to sing his song. His language is that of emphatic determination, *I will sing indeed.*[1] In order to

---

[1] This chapter presents a striking example of the variety that might be employed by the prophets in the presentation of their messages. There is the parable which Nathan told of the ewe lamb, and Amos upon occasion came forth with a dirge. Our Lord's parables concerning the vineyard are based upon this passage; cf. Matt. 20:1ff.; 21:28, 33-41; Mark 12:1; Luke 20:9-16; 13: 6ff.; John 15:1ff.

One is immediately struck with the richness of imagery and the beauty of the language, and can agree with Skinner that this is " . . . one of the finest

present his theme and to gain a hearing he assumes the role of a folk singer. We are not necessarily to assume, however, that this was a song to be accompanied by musical instruments or, for that matter, that it was a popular, well-known folk song. In all likelihood the prophet simply indulges in a rhythmical composition which he proclaims to his hearers. His words commence as a true song, but they soon pass over into a lamentation and an ex-

---

exhibitions of rhetorical skill and power which the book contains." Delitzsch gives expression to the beauty of the language when he says, "The winged rhythm, the euphonic music, the sweet assonances of this appeal cannot be reproduced." And indeed one cannot but be struck by the musical assonance of this passage. The reader should take his Hebrew Bible and read the entire parable (vv.1-7) aloud slowly and thoughtfully several times.

In the first verse alone the following assonances should be noted:

ashirah	shirath
lididi	dodi
lekarmo	kerem
na lididi	na lididi
kerem	qeren
qeren	ben .... shamen.

At the beginning of a poetic work in which God is praised the verb "to sing" is often used: Exod. 15:1; Judg. 5:3. In longer, extra-biblical works of antiquity we may also note its usage; e.g., the *Marriage of Nikkal and Ib* (*ashr*); the beginning of Hattussilis' *Apology* (*ša Ištar pa-ra-a ḫa-an-da-an-da-tar me-ma-aḫ-ḫi*), the *Iliad*, the *Odyssey*, *Aeneid*, (*arma virumque cano*). Note also Milton's *Paradise Lost* ("Sing, heavenly Muse"). Cf. also Isa. 26:1 and 42:10. In the Nikkal text there is also mention of vineyards (*krmm*) as "the fields of her love" (*ddh*) (lines 22, 23).

The *lamed* is taken in the sense of authorship (Fischer). Better, however, inasmuch as the song speaks concerning the friend, to translate "concerning."

"of my beloved" — Vulg. translated "uncle" (*patruelis mei*) and was followed by Luther. Ewald said that God represents Himself as the prophet's uncle. The word may also mean friend, or beloved one; and inasmuch as the possession of the vineyard is ascribed both to the *dodi* and the *yedidi*, they must be the same person. Cf. Ug. *dd*, "love." The word is a subjective gen., song of my beloved, i.e., my beloved's song.

"my beloved had a vineyard" — *Yadid* is a passive substantival, used in the sense of friend; cf. Deut. 33:12; Jer. 11:15; Ps. 127:2. "had" — Lit., there was to, i.e., had become his property. כרם stands first for emphasis. It is the theme of the parable.

"in a very fruitful hill" — Lit., "on a hill," the son of oil. In Ar. *qarn* refers to an exposed, detached hill. Firdawzi employs it in the sense of a mountain point, '*ala al-gabal*. The Greek *keras* designated mountains and promontories, and the Turkish *butun*, "nose," the same. Cf. *Georgics*: 2:112; Ovid, *Fasti*, 4:480. It may be that the imagery was suggested by Mt. Tabor.

193

planation. The chief characteristic of this song is lament and this soon gives way to denunciation. In a certain sense we may say that as the vineyard disappointed the Lord, so the song disappoints us. It is not entertainment to which we are introduced, but teaching.

The song has to do with one who was beloved by the prophet. It concerned the beloved, yet was also a song which belonged to that beloved and which had to do with his vineyard. As the prophet soon makes apparent, this friend is the LORD Himself. At the same time Isaiah wishes to bring the vineyard to the fore, and immediately draws the attention to it. With that word "vineyard" Isaiah plunges us into the parable. He uses an appropriate figure. In the land of Canaan, where she would be open to the influence of the surrounding heathenism, the nation Israel, like a vineyard, was in need of particular care. Using figurative language Isaiah says that the vineyard was upon a hill, and the hill he designates a horn. To picture a mountain as a horn is not uncommon; we speak for example, of the Matterhorn and the Schreckhorn; but such designations may lead us astray here, inasmuch as they are the names of high, snow-capped mountains. In Palestine the mountains are not so high, nor does Isaiah have snow-capped peaks in mind. Palestine was, however, a hilly country, and we may well imagine that this particular vineyard was located on the slope of a hill where it would have been exposed to the rays of the sun and thus would have every advantage.

The hill is very fruitful. In vivid language Isaiah calls it the son of oil or of fatness, as though it consisted of fatness. This is but a strong way of saying that it was very fat or fruitful. The location of the vineyard was all that could be desired, and the owner who had chosen such a select site had every right to expect that the vines planted in this choice location would produce only the best of grapes. What called forth such imagery in Isaiah's mind is difficult to determine. It may have been the thought of Tabor, but on the other hand, Palestine is full of such sites, and the prophet would have known them well.

Isaiah speaks of his friend, and later this friend is identified as God. The language is striking, but it is in keeping with Scripture. Abraham was the friend of God, and the Bible also speaks of the friend of the bridegroom. He who, like Isaiah, jealous for God's cause, can look upon God as his friend.

194

2 The assonances which lend such force and strength to the first verse appear here also. Note:

the ending *eyhu* of the first three verbs,

bo .... *betoko*
yeqeb .... *hatzeb*
anavim .... *beushim*

and he dug it carefully about[2] — What loving and tender care the Owner expended upon His vineyard! The ground of Palestine is unusually stony, and the Owner devoted all the care necessary to prepare the ground. Where the ground was hard, He dug

---

[2] עזק *hapax legomenon*. It has been incorrectly rendered by B, φραγμὸν περιέθηκα. Vulg. *sepsit eam;* Ibn Ezra, Jarchi and Luther. These latter interpret, possibly upon the basis of the Ar. *'izqa* (ring, circle) of the placing of a fence about the vineyard; AV, "and he fenced it"; Eng. RV, "and he made a trench about it." Kimchi, however, in his lexicon, but not in his commentary, rendered *chafar*, "to dig." The Talmud (Menach. fol. 83) "and he went to the field and he found him sitting and digging (*'ōzēq*) under the olive tree." Ar. *'zq* means to dig or hack, and the noun of instrument *mi'zaq* or *mi'zaqah* denotes the instrument wherewith one digs. The *mi'zaq* was employed where the plough could not be used. Hence the verb probably has reference to digging or turning over the ground. The *piēl* should also be represented in translation.

"and he gathered out" — The *piēl* has a privative force; cf. *GKC*, #52h. In English also we speak of stoning a field; cf. Isa. 62:10; 2 Kings 3:19.

"and he planted it" — נטע takes two accusatives; the first of which is the direct object, and the second an acc. of specification or *ḥal.* Jer. 2:21 forms a commentary upon this passage. The *sôrēq*, whatever its precise signification, was the choicest kind of vine. Cf. Gen. 49:11 for the f. form.

"wine vat" — Cf. Matt. 21:33, ληνός, and Mark 12:1, ὑπὸ λήνιου. Cf. also Job 24:11. The verb חצב is stative in form, although the context shows that it must be taken as transitive. Drechsler makes the interesting suggestion that it indicates an emotion, the difficulty of working, and compares with the verb *'ā-hēb*, which indicates a passion.

One cannot interpret symbolically each feature of the description. Kay sees in the erection of a fence (an erroneous translation) a reference to the law and to the physical geography of Palestine; the stones are the idolatrous tribes of Canaan, the tower is Jerusalem, the planting shows that Israel was to have been planted in Paradise to bless the whole world, and the wine vat is a reference to the temple as the repository of gifts and offerings.

"that it should bring forth" — The idea of patience and long-suffering is prominent in the verb. The inf. in Heb. is "to make grapes," and *'āsāh* is employed in the sense "to produce"; cf. 7:22. The sub. of the inf. differs from that of the main verb; "and he waited to (its) making grapes." Cf. Num. 6:4.

"rotten grapes" — Vulg. *labruscae*, i.e., unwholesome, acrid, wild-growing grapes. Sedulius 1:29, *"labruscam placidis quid adhuc praeponitis uvis?"* The designation "wild grapes" is probably as accurate as any. Cf. Job 31:40.

it about, so that it would be broken up for the vines which He was going to plant. He harrowed the soil, turning it over so carefully that it would be truly prepared ground.

and he gathered out the stones thereof — This was laborious and difficult work. The Arabs have a proverb to the effect that when God created the world an angel flew over it carrying a bag of stones under each arm. As he flew over Palestine, one bag broke so that half of all the stones in the world are in Palestine. He who has traveled in this land will appreciate the enormity of the labor involved in clearing a field of stones. The Owner labored assiduously in order that His vineyard might be free from stones.

and he planted it with choice vines — So the Lord remarks through His prophet Jeremiah (2:21), "Yet I had planted thee a noble vine, wholly a right seed; how then art thou turned into the degenerate plant of a strange vine unto me?" God planted the elite of the vines, indeed, they were so choice that a vale in Palestine which was noted for its excellent grapes became known as the vale of Soreq. We may not know the precise signification of the word *soreq*, but it quite evidently designated the best and most choice grapes. The grapes of Palestine are remarkable, both for their size and quality. It would seem, therefore, that Isaiah's purpose was simply to state that the best quality of grape had been planted.

and built a tower in the midst of it — For this vineyard the Owner builds not a mere booth, as was the case in 1:8, but an actual tower of stones which had been cleared from the field. The watchmen would thus have a place of protection from which they might oversee the well-being of the vineyard (cf. Matt. 21:33).

and also he hewed a wine vat in it — Not only did the Owner do everything possible to make the growing of good grapes easy, He also made preparations for the usage of those grapes. The *yeqeb*, "wine vat," was the lower part of the trough, often carved out of the solid stone, and served to receive the juice of the grapes which had been pressed down or trampled on in the upper trough or wine press (the *gath*). From this wine press the juice flowed down into the *yeqeb*. Isaiah, however, may be employing the word to designate the whole, for there would be no point in merely mentioning the digging out of one part of the trough.

It may be that the very verb which Isaiah uses in itself suggests the difficulty of this undertaking, and we are also reminded of that difficulty by the order of the words, "and also — a wine vat did he dig." It is the word *yeqeb* which receives the stress. That which was so difficult to make, the *yeqeb*, this Owner had provided. To hew such a vat from the stone was an unusually arduous task, yet even this was done in order that everything necessary for the vineyard to bring forth good grapes might be accomplished.

Up to this point the stress has been upon the activity of the Owner. In the choosing of Israel God did a gracious thing. Upon this people He showered abundant blessings, such as the Law and the Prophets. To it He clearly made known His ways. The first part of the verse is a living picture of the goodness of God. It is also something else. It is a clear refutation of the notion that Israel chose the LORD. The choice of Israel was a matter of pure grace on the part of a merciful God. What was the result of such a choice?

and He awaited that it should bring forth grapes — In calm, hopeful and patient contemplation the Owner awaits, anticipating as He watched the vines grow, that they would yield a crop of good grapes. After all the labor He had expended, such an expectation was most justified.

and it brought forth rotten grapes — In these words we have the climax, the sad and calamitous result of the Owner's labors. The grapes produced were not usable; they were bad and offensive. The Arabs speak of grapes that are unfit to be eaten as wolf grapes. Perhaps it was such that appeared on these vines. If we designate them wild grapes, we may not be too far from the truth.

Here is a pithy philosophy of the history of Israel. Israel was chosen and blessed of God through His wondrous grace, but despite God's blessings she was worthless and fit only to be cast out, as at last, when the exile came, she was finally cast out.

3 Isaiah has concluded his role of singer, and with the second verse has brought his story to an end.[3] The speaker is now seen to be the Owner of the vineyard, and He proceeds to set the case before the hearers for judgment and indeed commands them to pass judgment upon it. When even the guilty — for Isaiah's audience is the guilty people of Judah — are called upon to pass

---

3 "inhabitant" — The word is collective in force. 1Q has pl., as does B which also reverses the order. Cf. Jer. 4:4; Isa. 20:6; Zech. 12:7, 8, 10; Acts 2:14.

judgment, we surely find a strong proof of the righteousness of the case to be decided. There is a striking earnestness and directness in the manner in which the hearers are addressed.

And now — Inasmuch as what has been related is a true picture of the situation, the logical thing is that you yourselves pass judgment. At the same time, the introductory words "And now" also prepare for a second "And now" in verse 5. Those addressed are the inhabitants of Jerusalem and the men of Judah, the Hebrew in each instance employing a singular word which has the force of a collective. Those who dwell at Jerusalem are to be distinguished from the men of Judah, whose home is in various parts of Judah other than Jerusalem. The inhabitants of Jerusalem are mentioned first, it would seem, because they were at the capital city where the wickedness of which Isaiah complains was concentrated. The men of Judah, however, were also at fault, inasmuch as they acquiesced in the sins of the capital.

judge, I pray you — The hearers are placed in a position where they must obey the one who speaks. He commands them as though he has every right so to do. At the same time the command is softened by the precatory particle *na*. The owner of the vineyard is thus One who has the power to command the hearers to judge the rightness of His cause. This is a duty from which they cannot escape; yet at the same time they are approached courteously, for the Owner of the vineyard is One who has naught but good-will for men. What He commands His hearers to do is to act as arbiters, to pass a decision or to pronounce such a decision upon the rightness of His cause. How would the hearers pronounce such a verdict? The question may be answered by a consideration of the example of David after his sin with Bathsheba. Nathan came to him and recited a parable which brought his sin to light. David, therefore, in passing judgment upon the man in the parable, at the same time pronounced condemnation upon himself. When the inhabitants of Jerusalem and Judah pass judgment upon the two questions: first, Has the Lord done all that He should for the vineyard? and second, Did the vineyard bring forth wild grapes? they will have pronounced a verdict, and in so passing judgment will have condemned themselves. In other words, they will have acknowledged that the Owner did all that was necessary for the well-being of the vineyard, and also that the vineyard did indeed bring forth wild grapes. In making this judgment they will also have ac-

knowledged that the Lord had dealt with them in abundant grace
and mercy and that they themselves had rebelled against Him and
were worthless sinners.

4 Does Isaiah pause for a moment or so to give the hearers a
chance to respond? If he does, it is likely that he is greeted with
complete silence; the people know not what to say, yet their
very silence is an admission of guilt. David had cried out, "I
have sinned against the Lord." Those to whom this parable is
addressed, however, say nothing at all, for there is nothing to
say. Thereby they simply manifest most clearly their own guilt.
Isaiah then addresses a specific question to his hearers, a question
which merely brings to the fore one of the considerations already
mentioned, namely, had the Owner done all that He needed to
in order that the vineyard might bring forth good grapes?

What more could I have done? — If there was anything more
that needed to be done to the vineyard, the hearers can now point
it out.[4]

Why? — Isaiah's thought is, "Why — inasmuch as I looked for
grapes — did it bring forth rotten grapes?" Was there yet remaining anything to be done? Drechsler remarks that God had
done everything except to use force, for, thinks Drechsler, man
must choose his salvation without compulsion. It is true that in
the parable the Owner of the vineyard has done everything to
cause good grapes to grow. Likewise God in dealing with Israel
did everything to bless His people. He did not use force of a
physical kind, for force could never convert the soul or bring it
unto God. At the same time, the grace of God is sovereign and
efficacious; it breaks down all walls of resistance, accomplishing
that end for which it is designed. It is an irresistible grace, but
although it is irresistible, it is yet grace, and so makes the stubborn, recalcitrant heart willing.

It would also be a grave misunderstanding of the passage to
assume that it suggests that God is limited in His ability, and that
He had merely done the best He could under the circumstances.
Isaiah constantly sets forth God as sovereign, a fact which appears

---

4 "what more?" — Lit., what (is there) to do? The interrogative pronoun
followed by the inf. has gerundive force, *"quid faciendum est?"* what is there
yet to be done? This inf. appeared in v. 2.

"Why?" — The interrogative governs two co-ordinate clauses, but strictly
affects only the second. Logically considered, the first clause is really in sub-
ordination to the second.

even in this present parable where the rainfall is at God's disposal and command. The language of the question which Isaiah here asks is intended simply to manifest the abundant and overwhelming grace of God. No fault or blame can attach to what He has done for Israel. He has been faithful to His promises, and those who heard Isaiah's words must acknowledge this fact.

The verse closes with the sad refrain that had been used earlier. Despite the loving care of the Owner, a direful result had occurred: "it brought forth rotten grapes."

5 The tone changes. Threatening is announced. Judgment has come. Again the Lord says, "And now." This time, however, He is not commanding men to judge; He is rather declaring that He will Himself judge. As a result of the condition of things, He declares what His intentions are with respect to the vineyard. The voice that speaks is not that of a complainant but of a judge. Inasmuch as God has done all that was necessary for His vineyard, there remains but one expedient — the vineyard must be destroyed.

I would indeed have you to know — To render and bring out the full force of the Hebrew is difficult.[5] The verb is a causative, "I shall cause you to know"; it has the cohortative ending, "let me cause you to know"; it is followed by the precative particle *na*, "let me, I pray you, cause you to know." The people, apparently, have stood silent; they have said not a word; the Lord therefore will speak and indicate to the hearers what His intentions are. The vineyard belongs to the LORD and He may do with it whatever He desires.

With unusually forceful language the LORD states what He will do. He uses two infinitives absolute, "turn aside" and "break through." The thought may be paraphrased; "in turning aside and breaking through, I shall turn aside and break through."

---

[5] הסר — The inf. abs. is often employed adverbially. In Akk. it has the adverbial -u ending. Here also, the inf. has adverbial force, and we are to understand it as modifying an understood finite verb in the imp., "in turning aside, I shall turn aside." Cf. Young: "Adverbial -u in Semitic," *WThJ*, Vol. XIII, No. 2, (May 1951), pp. 151-54. משוכתו . . . either the form is *me-suk-kā-t̠ô*, in which case it is from *skk* (the sin being an equivalent of *śamech;* cf. *śukkāh*, 1:8; 4:6) or *me-sû-kā-t̠ô*, from *sûk̠*. Cf. Job 1:10; Hos. 2:8. I incline toward this latter derivation. Delitzsch, "the green thorn-hedge surrounding the vineyard." Drechsler, "the hedge which raises itself above the lower wall of stones" (Prov. 24:31).

About the vineyard there was a protecting hedge, probably like those hedges of prickly pears which today are found in Palestine. In fact there was often a double enclosure, one of stones and the other of hedge. Whether this latter always actually paralleled the former, or whether it may also have grown on top of the wall cannot positively be stated. When these protections are removed the cattle can enter the vineyard and so trample it that nothing can grow. Thus the nation is to be deprived of the very gifts which it has despised. The vineyard will be "for the sending forth of oxen, and for the treading of lesser cattle" (Isa. 7:25b), and the nation will become like a barren wilderness. It will no longer exist as the theocracy. When once the animals come into the vineyard it is unable to produce grapes, for it will be completely trampled under foot. The result of turning aside the hedge is that the vineyard is consumed, not by fire, but by the trampling beasts.

and I shall break through its walls — The stones of Palestine are used even today to construct fences and walls. After the tedious labor of erecting this strong protection of stone, the Owner will now break it down so that His vineyard upon which He had expended so much toil might lie open and accessible to any beast, wild or domestic, which wished to enter it. Israel then will also lie open and accessible to any nation which wishes to invade her. The vineyard will simply become a place of trampling; likewise, when the theocracy was brought to an end, Israel became and has remained ever since a place of trampling for the nation.

6 "Thorns also and thistles shall it bring forth to thee; and thou shalt eat the herb of the field" (Gen. 3:18). Like an echo from the original curse is the verse before us. God will now make of His vineyard a desolation.[6] Through neglect of the vineyard

---

6 "an end" — Lit., "and I shall constitute it (make it) an end (a destruction)." The verb is construed with two accusatives. A satisfactory explanation of בתה is not at hand. Possibly *bā-ṭāh* stands for *bat-ṭāh*, on the analogy of *kā-lāh*, or to distinguish it from *bat-ṭāh* with a different meaning. In Ar. we have *batta*, to bring to an end, and in Isa. 7:19, *battôt*. Gray is probably correct in suggesting that we follow the context and give the word a meaning such as "waste-land."

"pruned" — For the root cf. Ug. *zbr. yzbrnn. sbrm gpn* (they prune him with the prunings of the vine).

"hoed" — עדר has reference to the act of digging about the roots of the

201

there will abruptly come a total ruin. It has already been cultivated as much as it is going to be. No longer will the vines be pruned, nor will anything else that is necessary for their proper growth be done for them. Even the ground itself will no more be hoed.

The condition of the ground, rather, will be briers and thorns. Isaiah introduces a striking assonance, *shamir washayit* (cf. 7:23-25; 9:18; 10:17; 27:4). The vineyard is to grow, to come up from the ground, but to come up as thorns and briers. In a land where there is no rain, thorns and brier bushes grow. For this threat Isaiah has prepared us, for he has stated that God will withhold the rain from His vineyard. How great a punishment it is when God withholds from us the blessings of the rain! Chapter 4 presents a picture of abundance and blessing; here, however, a sharp contrast is found: thorns and brier bushes.

and I shall command the clouds — Who can utter such a command? Who can command the clouds? At one time David had said, "Ye mountains of Gilboa, let there be no dew, neither let there be rain upon you, nor fields of offerings" (2 Sam. 1:21). David, however, was uttering a mere wish; he was not attempting to tell the clouds what to do. Here, however, the speaker tells us what He intends to do. He intends to command the clouds to withhold their rain. God is the Owner of the vineyard, and He alone can control the elements which affect that vineyard. We may render: "And upon the clouds I shall command from raining upon it rain." The verse begins with the mention of clouds and concludes with the mention of rain. So Calvin remarks ". . . how manifold are the weapons with which God is supplied for punishing our ingratitude when he sees that we despise his kindness."[7]

---

plant to loosen the soil so that nourishment and growth will be facilitated.

"briers" — These words form a circumstantial acc., "it shall come up (with) briers and thorns"; cf. Ibn Hisham, *kutibat fi qalbi kitaban* (and it was written in my heart [as a] book). Note the striking assonance of the two words. Apart from Isaiah a different expression occurs in Gen. 3:18; Hos. 10:8. The Construction seems to be, "and the vineyard will come up . . . . "; cf. Isa. 34:13. Note the contrast between 5:1-6 and 4:2-6. Bentzen, appealing to 2 Sam. 1:21, held that God was not the owner. With this verse, however, Isaiah leaves fiction and turns to explanation. He had anticipated this explanation, in allowing the owner to command the clouds. Once we regard the owner throughout as God, the difficulty disappears.

7 *Commentary on Isaiah*, I, 168, 169.

7 The time for poetry and song is past.[8] The time for interpretation and application has come. The parable is one to which men must pay heed, because the vineyard belongs to the LORD. Again Isaiah thrusts that word "vineyard" into the fore. *Kerem;* it is the first word, the emphatic word. We have been listening to more than a parable: there is truly a vineyard; not any vineyard upon a Palestinian hill, but a vineyard which belonged to the LORD, even the entire house of Israel, which God Himself had formed. With remarkable ease the language shifts between speakers. Isaiah had begun; then the LORD had taken over the speech; now the prophet continues.

As he continues Isaiah becomes more specific and mentions the southern kingdom of Judah as the plant of the Lord's pleasantness. The vineyard was the object of the Lord's delight, and His pleasure was found in tending and caring for it. We may note the strength that is lent to the description by the chiastic arrangement.

for the vineyard of the .... the house of Israel
Lord of hosts
And the men of Judah .... the plant of His pleasantness.

"Vineyard" and "plant" are seen to be the same, and whereas the "men of Judah" and the "house of Israel" are not precise synonyms, the men of Judah were a part of the house of Israel.

This is election. There were nations other than Israel, but on Israel alone did God set His affection. She was His vineyard, and in her He found His delight. He did not choose her because she was greater than other nations, and certainly not because she was better. In her, however, He might show forth His glory, and for the sake of His glory He chose her. She was a vineyard that

---

8 "for — Non-causal (Rosenmüller); *judgment . . .* the striking assonance is an example of Isaiah's elegance of language (*tzehut hallashon,* as the rabbis called it). Cf. 13:6; 24:17; 33:1; 57:6; 61:3. Attempts have been made to bring out the paronomasia in translation: *richtige Wage, immer Klage; gerechtes Wort, blutiges Mort; Milde, Unbilde, gut Regiment, Blutregiment; Rechtsprechung, Rechtsbrechung; Gerechtigkeit, Schlechtigkeit; Beglückung, Bedrückung.* Cf. *sippēah* in 3:17, 1:15 and 4:4. Ar. *sph,* "to pour out," *suffah* is a tyrant who sheds blood. Cf. Koran, 6:146, *damman masfoûhan,* "blood poured out."

Delitzsch translates "grasping," appealing to *sph* with the connotation "sweep." It is probably impossible to prove the case one way or another, but the common rendering fits in well and is philologically possible. As in the case here, so in Matt. 23:13-29 the parable is followed by woes and denunciations.

needed to be tended and cultivated, that she might bring forth the fruit which her Owner desired.

and he looked for judgment — With eager expectation He waited in the hope that the nation which had received His law and oracles would bring forth righteousness in its life. Those who have been taught of God and have received His righteousness should be expected in their lives to exhibit judgment and justice. It was not judgment, however, that Israel brought forth, but bloodshed, not *mishpat* but *mispach*. The verse contains two striking examples of paronomasia; *mishpat* and *mispach*, and *tzedaqah* and *tzeaqah*. Paronomasia is a favorite literary device of Isaiah, but it is very difficult to render in translation. There should have been an external manifestation on the people's part; they should have exhibited practical justice. There was an external manifestation; they exhibited bloodshed. There should have been an internal condition, namely righteousness. And an internal condition there was indeed, namely a cry. What the LORD beheld is expressed in the phrases, "Behold! bloodshed"; "behold! a cry."

The second pair of words is probably to be regarded as subjective. *Tzedaqah* here indicates a condition of rightness with God which expresses itself in the doing of those things which are themselves righteous. It is a gift of God, as Jeremiah says, "the LORD our righteousness." Instead of righteousness, there was a cry, a cry from those who had been wrongfully oppressed.

The assonance would seem to point to the fact that the worthless grapes bore at least an outward resemblance to the good ones. In appearance at least the nation seemed to be the people of God. Outwardly they were the elect, and this resulted in a great deception. Inwardly there was a profound difference, and hence Israel was a deceiving nation. It was an empty people, an example of "living hypocrisy." Insincerity can merit only such severe condemnation as that herein described. May we who belong to the church ever examine our hearts that there be no such hypocrisy within us, but rather may our lives bring forth the fruits of that righteousness which comes from God alone!

b. *Analysis of Judah's sins* (5:8-23)

8 Woe to them that cause house to touch house and lay field to field, until there is no place, and ye be caused to dwell alone in the midst of the land.

9   In mine ears is the LORD of hosts, many houses shall surely become a desolation, even great and fair, without inhabitant.

10 For ten yokes of vineyard shall yield one bath and the seed of a homer shall yield an ephah.

11 Woe unto them that rise up early in the morning, that they may pursue strong drink, that delay in the twilight while wine inflames them.

12 And the zither and the harp and the timbrel and the flute and wine are in their feast; but they regard not the work of the LORD, neither consider the operation of his hands.

13 Therefore my people are gone into captivity for want of knowledge, and their glory is famished men and their multitude dried up with thirst.

14 Therefore sheol enlargeth herself and opens wide her mouth without measure, and their glory and their multitude and their pomp and he that rejoiceth in it shall descend.

15 And the mean man is bowed down and the great man is humbled, and the eyes of the lofty are cast down.

16 And the LORD of hosts shall be exalted in judgment and the holy God shall be sanctified in righteousness.

17 Then shall the lambs feed as in their pasture, and the waste places of the fat ones strangers will eat.

18 Woe unto them that draw iniquity with cords of vanity, and sin with a cart rope.

19 That say, Let his work speed and hasten that we may see it; and let the counsel of the Holy One of Israel draw near and come that we may know it.

20 Woe to those that say to the evil, good, and to the good, evil; that put darkness for light and light for darkness; that put bitterness for sweet, and sweet for bitterness.

21 Woe to those who are wise in their own eyes, and prudent in their own sight.

22 Woe to those that are mighty to drink wine and valiant men to mix strong drink.

23 Who justify the wicked for the sake of reward, and turn aside the righteousness of the righteous from him.

The expectation of the LORD is applied to the actual situation. The entire section falls into six sub-sections of varying length, each beginning with a woe.

(i)   vv.   8-10.   A covetous people.

(ii)   vv.   11-17. A debauching people.

(iii)   vv.   18-19. An unbelieving people.

(iv)   v. 20.   A truth-perverting people.

(v)   v. 21.   A people wise in its own eyes.
(vi) vv. 22,23. A justice-perverting people.

8 Having stated his theme in verse 7, Isaiah now begins to develop it. This he does by the presentation of six "woes" (vv. 8, 11, 18, 20, 21, and 22) and in response to these woes he utters three clauses introduced by "therefore" (vv. 13, 14 and 24). Thus we have a vivid denunciation of the living and bold sins of the nation.

Who are the people upon whom these woes are to fall? The first class consists of wealthy landowners who buy up all the property that they can until their houses touch one another.[9] In causing one house to touch against another they increase their own possessions, and so acquire for themselves as much property as possible. Whenever they buy a new house, that house touches the one which they already possess. The condemnation is not of the purchase of property as such, but of monopoly and the acqui- sition of what belongs to a poor owner. Although not stated in so many words the implication seems to be that this was an un- just acquiring on the part of the wealthy. Against such proce- dures the law had provided checks, but there were unscrupulous men in Israel who circumvented the law and were not content until they had obtained all the property which they could. Their actions revealed an ungodly disposition, one involving covetous- ness and selfish ambition. Calvin quotes John Chrysostom to the effect that "covetous men, if they could, would willingly take the sun from the poor."

---

[9] "cause to touch" — The verse begins with a part. and is continued by an imp. without *waw*, expressing customary, present action. The law had pro- vided checks against this kind of procedure: Lev. 25:8ff., Num. 27:5-11; Deut. 27:17. Cf. 1 Kings 21:3-19; Job 22:8. According to the discoveries made at Yorgan Tepe (blanket mound, the ancient Nuzi), land could not be sold. Hence it was acquired by means of a process of adoption. Thus, a man who wished to obtain property had himself adopted by the owner of that property. The property was then willed to him and became his, in return for which he was to offer the owner a gift. Very often, the man who desired the property took advantage of the owner, particularly if the latter was poor or in need. Many such cases are seen in the activities of one Tehiptilla, one of the most notorious of those who in ancient Nuzi acquired property by this means. Cf. Wilson, *A Scientific Investigation of the Old Testament* (Chicago, 1959), pp. 167-73, in which the present author has discussed the Nuzi texts.

"field to field" — Seneca in one of his letters writes; *"qui agros agris adiiciant, vicinos pellendo."*

206

lay field to field — The sin consisted in the general multiplication of property, and so was one that violated the spirit of the Year of Jubilee. When all this property was purchased, there was no room left for others to dwell. They had no room for a house of their own, and so must live on the property of the owner as servants or slaves. Inasmuch as the land had been promised to the descendants of Abraham, each descendant should have had a place in which to reside. As a result of some persons obtaining all the property the owners must now live alone. This condition has been brought about by their own actions. Upon them the responsibilities of ownership now rest; their condition is not to be envied.

9 The sin has been described; the punishment is now stated. The prophet is speaking, and he proclaims that the LORD of hosts is in his ears.[10] This is indeed a strange statement, but what Isaiah means is that the LORD is at the moment revealing to him His word. God is in his ears, and what Isaiah speaks, he hears from God.

Men had been joining house to house, so runs the divine message. These houses — for that matter, many houses — will certainly become a desolation. The houses were great and high, pleasant and comfortable, and were owned by those who were constantly acquiring property for themselves. Yet they would not last, but would become a desolation with no inhabitants. Jerusalem was to be a ghost town.

10 The houses will be without inhabitants because the land will lose its productivity and will not yield enough to support a large population. Surely as much land as ten yoke of oxen can plough in one day should be expected to bring forth a tremendous produce. As a matter of fact, a vineyard which is of such a size

---

10 Isa. 22:14 is a similarly constructed sentence. Rosenmüller thinks that here we should understand, "and it was heard." Others would propose other verbs to be understood. The style, however, is good Semitic. The word, "ears," is separated from what follows, and also, through the *qametz*, has somewhat of a pausal force. Thus, "in my ears is the Lord," i.e., the Lord hath spoken in mine ears. Cf. 1 Sam. 9:15 for the idea of revelation through the ear.

"however" — These houses had been mentioned in 8a. Just as v. 10 reflects upon 8b so does v. 9 upon 8a.

"without inhabitant" — Lit., "from not (being) a dweller."

will yield only about eight gallons of wine.[11] What a considerable piece of land this was! Ten yoke of oxen working hard for a day, yet a vineyard of that size would produce only eight gallons. How poverty stricken the land has become! The same was true of the seed that was sown. It would give an ephah, which was only the tenth part of a homer, one-tenth as much as it should have brought forth. The homer amounted to about ten and one-half bushels, and ten ephahs would have equaled a homer. It was as though both seed and land had conspired against the nation.

11 As we contemplate the desolation which the first woe announces, we hear again the cry of the prophet, Woe! The second woe is directed against those who engage in drunkenness and dissipation.[12] These people begin early in the morning their pursuit of strong liquor. It is not the fact of drinking in itself

---

[11] Benzinger measured the bath at about 36.44 liters, Josephus at about 40 and the Rabbis at about 20 (*Antiquities*, 8:57—72 ξέσται). צמדי — The *daghesh* is striking; is it a later and artificial development? When *daghesh* occurs contrary to rule, it is generally in כ ד and פ· The const. represents the following change, in which *daghesh* is not to be expected: *tzᵉmādim* > *tzᵉmādē tzemedē tzimdē*. As a punishment for sin Moses had promised sterility of the land; Lev. 26:14ff., Deut. 28:17ff.

[12] Ecclus. 10:16ff.; *Pirqe Abot*, 3:10b; Acts 2:15 condemn wastefulness of early-morning time through drinking. But in the *Moallaka* of Amr ibn Kelt, early-morning drinking was praised, the drinker being designated *sabchān* "praised." In the classical writers we have Juvenal 1:49, "*ab octava hora Marius bibit*"; Catullus, 47:5; Cicero, *de Senectute*, 14; Propertius. IV:6:85,

> Sic noctem patera, sic ducam carmine, donec
> Iniiciat radios in mea vina dies.

Horace: *Carmina*, 1:1; 19:20.

"rise up" — The two participles are const. plurals followed by preps., a regular Heb. construction.

"strong drink" — Cf. Isa. 28:7. In the OT the word, which is doubtless related to Gk. *sikara*, denotes an intoxicating drink. ורדיפו — The imp. subordinates the verbal idea which is complementary to that expressed by the part.

"twilight" — The period after sunset. The word is also used of the dawn (1 Sam. 30:17) and night (Isa. 21:4; Job 3:9). Here it forms a contrast to "morning," and hence does not indicate morning (Rosenmüller) but either twilight or night.

"inflames" — An affirmative circumstantial verbal clause. To paraphrase, "delaying in the twilight while (or, until) wine inflames them." Each clause begins with a part. in const. followed by a prep. and concludes with a finite verb in imp. having the force of a circumstantial clause.

which is here condemned, but the debauchery and waste of time that is connected with it. Those condemned rise early in the morning, not thereby to glorify the Lord in their daily work, but to satiate themselves with strong drink and so to render themselves unfit for their proper tasks. "Woe to thee, O land, when thy king is a child, and thy princes eat in the morning! (Eccl. 10:16).

Some men pursue riches; some fame. The inhabitants of Judah chased after strong drink. They hunted for it and pursued after it. At this drinking they stayed until it was late, even to the twilight, and while they remained late at their drink, the wine inflamed them.

12 Not only drunkenness, but also riotous merriment characterizes the feasts of the revelers. In the celebration of these revelries there were wind, string and percussion instruments. [13] The zither

---

[13] The force of the sentence is "and the zither and the viol, the drum and the pipe, and wine are (will be) their feasts." The verb form suggests something that recurs often; cf. Gen. 29:3; 1 Sam. 1:3-5. The boldness of the subject should be noted, for in effect it identifies itself with the object. Cf. Ps. 45:9; 120:1; Song of Sol. 1:15; *GKC*, no. 141d. Hammond (*Isaiah Statesman Prophet*) has translated,

> Lyre and harp, timbrel and pipe,
> And wine, are in their feasts.

This is poetic, but does not actually bring out the force of the Hebrew.

"zither" — Josephus thought it had ten strings. Possibly it was a general designation of stringed instruments, plucked with the hand. The word appears in Hittite as *kinirri*, "lash," Sanscrit, *kinari*, Gk., *kinura*.

"harp" — According to Josephus it had 12 strings; cf. Egy. *nfr*, "lute."

"timbrel" — Drechsler calls attention to the Spanish *aduffe*, which may be etymologically related.

"their feast" — Pred. nom. to the preceding. I regard this form as a singular, the *Tzere yod* representing the *ay* diphthong in an unaccented syllable.

"regard" — We may render, "and the work of the Lord they do not regard, and the work of His hands they have not seen." Some restrict the work of the Lord to judgment. Dillmann takes it as God's working in history to accomplish His purposes of salvation. To this Duhm retorts that Isaiah would know nothing of Protestant dogmatics. But what Duhm disparagingly designates Protestant dogmatics is simply the teaching of the OT itself. Ginsberg proposes for this and the preceding verse three emendations: (i) *yadliqû* in the sense "to chase after"; (ii) omit "and wine"; (iii) For *mištēhem* either *mš 'tm* or *mš 'tēyhm* or *mš 'eyhm* or singular absolute *maš 'it*. We cannot accept these emendations, for they are without objective textual support. There is no reason for emending *mištēhem* into some form of *š'y* "to turn, to look," and the opinion that *weyayin* is hypermetric is surely no warrent for removing it.

had strings which ran over a bridge and were plucked by hand. Likewise the harp was an instrument played by the fingers, and the timbrel was held and struck by the hand. The small flute or pipe may be heard even today in the Holy Land. Isaiah expresses himself in a strange and forceful manner. His words may be rendered literally, "And the zither, etc., are their feast." Thus, the objects which are first named are so prominent that they characterize the feast and may be said to be identical therewith. Amos speaks of those "that chant to the sound of the viol, and invent to themselves instruments of music like David; that drink wine in bowls, and anoint themselves with the chief ointments: but they are not grieved for the affliction of Joseph" (Amos 6:5, 6).

Isaiah is not condemning music as such. Music is one of God's greatest gifts to man. What is condemned is the usage to which musical instruments are put at the drunken carousals, so that the noise of these instruments, as it were, would drown out the voice of conscience. The songs that were sung and the music that was present at such occasions were not of an ennobling nor elevating kind. Isaiah later predicts that such singing will come to an end, "The mirth of tabrets ceaseth, and the noise of them that rejoice endeth, the joy of the harp ceaseth. They shall not drink wine with a song; strong drink shall be bitter to them that drink it" (24:8, 9).

and the work of the Lord do they not regard — What is this work of the LORD that is ignored? It is the on-hastening judgment. At the same time, inasmuch as the LORD was about to bring judgment upon the nation which had been so rebellious against Him, it is evident that the destiny of the nation lay in the LORD's hands. And the judgment was necessary in order that God might accomplish His plan of salvation. In the fullest and broadest sense, then, the work here referred to is that of God in history to accomplish His purposes of redemption. Inasmuch as it was too preoccupied with those very sins which were speeding it on to destruction, the sinful nation does not regard this work of God. If men are too preoccupied with sin, their horizon is so restricted and narrowed that they cannot see sin's final consequences.

and the work of his hands they do not see — The sinner does not see God's hands at work. According to Psalm 19:1 the very firmament declares that it is the work of God's hands, but the eyes of his understanding being blinded, the sinner does not perceive God working about him. Likewise, when the hands of God are fashioning the judgment, the obtuse sinner does not see it.

13 Inasmuch as the debauchery of the people was so great, they would go into captivity. Speaking in his role of prophet, Isaiah beholds the people of God, already taken away by a hostile nation. He describes the entire event as though it had already occurred in the past. Time and time again he had depicted Judah's sins and had warned against sin. Frequent, however, as his warnings had been, the people had paid no heed, and the judgment was now about to fall. The exile, therefore, which was a manifestation of the judgment, was clearly a punishment for sin. At the same time, the judgment was not limited to the exile. It was basically the final and universal judgment which would come upon the world, and upon the inhabitants of Judah. Of that judgment, however, the exile was a part; indeed, now a prominent part, which would fall upon those whom God even now regards as "my people." It is a sad and tragic designation. My people, chosen of Me, nurtured by Me, to be a blessing to the world, are now subject to the forces that come from without, and exile is the result. My people — they are now in the hands of those who will take them into exile.

for want of knowledge — "without knowledge." It is not ignorance which has caused the exile, but sin.[14] In a certain sense, of course, ignorance might be regarded as a cause of the exile. Through sin the nation knew not the working of God and so, not knowing this working, heeded it not and exile was the result. Whereas, however, this is a true thought, nevertheless the great emphasis of the context is that the continued, steady sinning of the nation was what brought on the banishment. The nation has become so steeped in sin it does not know that the catastrophe which is to come upon it is the result of its own doings, and that in this catastrophe the judging and punishing hand of God is to be seen. In other words, the nation cannot rightly interpret the

---

14 "are gone" — Heb. uses the prophetic perf. The exile has not yet actually occurred, but it is so vivid to the prophet's eye that he speaks of it as though it were already an accomplished fact.

"without knowledge" — Cf. Job 9:5. A similar thought, expressed by a *ḥal* clause is found in the Koran, 16:28, *walā yash'arûna* (and they do not surmise it, i.e., before they surmise) ; Loqman: *wahuwa lā ya'lamu* (and he does not know). Here too the clause is best taken as circumstantial. "glory" — von Rad (*TAT*, p. 238) thinks that the people's glory is its upper classes.

signs of the times. Of the true nature and meaning of what will befall it, Judah will be ignorant.

and their glory is famished men — The glory of the nation is to be found in the famished men which compose it. It is that in which the nation's honor is to be found, and here consists simply of men who are perishing from hunger.

and their multitude dried up with thirst — In Judah there was a multitude, which lived in idleness, rioting and reveling. The multitude which had tarried long at wine would now be parched with thirst. As the people go away into captivity, they will be without knowledge, their nobility will starve of famine, their multitude will be parched with thirst. These are the three conditions which will accompany the exile, and they express not only the sinful condition of the nation, but also the outward effects which will result from the punishment.

By means of a pagan manner of living the nation has profaned the holy and promised land. Consequently, the people will continue to live in a heathen manner in a foreign land. Eating and drinking had been made to serve their evil purposes; they would therefore face hunger and thirst. Living sensually like animals and without the use of their understanding, they were now to go into their punishment without an actual understanding of the true nature of what was taking place. So the LORD had promised: "The LORD shall bring thee, and thy king which thou shalt set over thee, unto a nation which neither thou nor thy fathers have known; and there shalt thou serve other gods, wood and stone" (Deut. 28:36).

14 Over the entire picture hangs a cloud of distress or suffering. The captivity will surely come, and with it hunger and thirst. Following in such a wake will be a huge mortality. There is a great monster with wide-open jaws, ready to receive those who die.[15] With the famished men and the thirsty multitude this

---

[15] "herself" — Her appetite; cf. Hab. 2:5; Prov. 10:3; Isa. 29:8; *Aeneid*, 6:273, *"Vestibulum ante ipsum primisque in faucibus orci."* Von Rad (*TAT*, p. 157) would take the word in its basic meaning *Kehle, Gurgel*. Cf. L. Durr; *ZAW*, 1925, p. 262. Eitan appeals to Akk. *napištu,* "neck," and would render "throat." He goes on, however, to remark that the nether world is mythologically pictured as a dragon. This conclusion does not necessarily follow.

"opens wide" — The perf. with *waw* cons. may express a definite assurance or expectation. The co-ordination of the two perfects is somewhat loose and

monster is ready to satiate herself. It is sheol, the underworld, and what Isaiah has in mind here is simply the entrance into sheol, or death itself. It is death which is ready to receive those who perish from the captivity, for death has an appetite, and to satisfy it the jaws are opened wide ready to receive all that fall therein.

and opens wide her mouth without measure — By such a forceful figure the enormity of the mortality is indicated. Without ceasing the monster opens wide her mouth.

and there shall descend — As though by attraction. Sheol opens wide her mouth, and the nation goes down into it. That in which Jerusalem glories and in which her glory expresses itself, together with the uproar of her revelers, will go down into the jaws of the monster.

and he that rejoiceth in it — This completes the picture. The one who is in Jerusalem and there rejoices, unmindful of the work of the LORD, will go down into sheol. Thus, the entirety of the city will be swallowed up in death.

Are then the promises of God to go down to destruction and oblivion in the throat of a wide-jawed monster? Will the Christ not come? Will the blessings promised fail? If the Christ is to come, Judah must abide in her land. She was to be the theocracy, the nation in which God ruled, and which had received His promises and blessings. From this nation in the fullness of time the Messiah was to be born. Now, however, all seems to fail. Before this nation there is a horrible monster, a monster which had been summoned by the sins of Judah. This monster was willing, and opened wide its jaws so that it might swallow up the people. What was this monster? Isaiah speaks of it as sheol, a designation which usually refers to the grave. The thought is that the people would go into captivity, and so out of the promised land. This was a judgment, and such a judgment would simply bring about death. Hunger and thirst, as well as the

---

usually occurs when the reference is not to some definite or specific act but to that which may take place at any time.

"pomp" Lit., "roar," the uproar caused by the revelers.

"he that rejoiceth in it" — In the city, the place of reveling. Note the omission of *nasog ahor;* the ultima retains the accent says Delitzsch, "to cause the rolling and swallowing up to be heard as it were." Note *Baal,* 1,1,7, *bnpš. bn. elm. mt. bmh mrt. ydd. el. ġzr* (into the throat of Mot son of El, into the miry gorge of the hero loved of El).

sword, would kill the people. Others, carried away from the land
of promise would die in a strange land, and such death would
really be a judgment, leading only to the bottom of the pit, to
hell itself. Could then this monster thwart the purposes of the
Lord of hosts?

A new beginning had to be made. The nation to which the
promises had been entrusted could no longer serve as the theocracy. The land could no more be called the land of promise.
There must be purification in order that from the decayed nation
a new seed of life might by God's grace be created and come
forth. Had not victory been swallowed up by death? So it might
have seemed, but God, who carries out His plan, would so work
that one day, inasmuch as from Judah the LORD had sprung, the
triumphant message of salvation might be proclaimed, "Death
is swallowed up in victory" (1 Cor. 15:54b).

15 Reflecting upon the language of chapter 2, Isaiah emphasizes the design and ultimate purpose of the punishment, namely,
the complete and utter humiliation of man and the exaltation of
the LORD.[16] In that sheol had opened her mouth, and in that
man and the city were to be completely destroyed, man is seen to
be humiliated. In the preceeding verses the activity of sheol had
been presented, and with the present verse the ultimate end of
the punishment is set forth. The prophet then proceeds in verse
16 to mention the exaltation of the Lord, seen through the exile,
so that the blessings which he describes in verse 17 can be possible.

---

[16] ‎וישח‎ — The imp. with *waw* cons. in this instance serves to represent a
future action in dependence upon the perfect with *waw* cons. and the earlier
simple perf. of v. 14. It is also used as a parallel to the later simple imp.
without *waw*. Driver (*TT*, p. 93) suggests that the imp. without *waw* represents the event as "*flowing* naturally *out of*, being an *immediate consequence*
of, the situation described in the preceding sentence." The simple imp. *tišpal-
nah* stresses a particular feature of the description. We may diagram as follows:

v. 14 *hirhîḇāh* simple prophetic perf., "will enlarge."
     ûfāʿarāh co-ordinate perf. with *waw* cons., "and will open wide."
     weyāraḏ co-ordinate perf. with *waw* cons., "and there will go down."
v. 15 *wayyiššah* imp. suggesting consequences, "so there will be bowed down."
     wayyišpal imp. suggesting consequences, "and there will be humbled."
     tišpalnāh vivid simple imp. "are being humbled."

Driver (*Von Ugarit nach Qumran*, pp. 42, 43) would emend the text and
render, "and their splendid ones, their multitude and their noisy throng, shall
go down and suffer pangs therein." This is unnecessary.

16 The lofty ones shall be brought low, and the LORD will become lofty. Isaiah seems to play upon the word "lofty" of the preceding verse. Those who acted as lofty ones will be brought low, and the LORD alone will be shown to be truly lofty. The judgment which humbles man and brings him low at the same time raises high and elevates God as alone truly exalted. He is thus seen to be the LORD of hosts, the omnipotent One, who controls the events of history, and who when He executes judgment manifests Himself as glorious. It is, then, by means of the judgment that He makes Himself known as righteous. In the punishment of sin the righteousness of God is seen.

and the holy God — What an instructive phrase![17] When God is designated *el* in prose, an adjective usually accompanies the designation. Thus we read of the jealous God, the mighty God or the most high God. In Isaiah this word *el* is employed of the God who is sovereign, and this fact stands out here from the parallel expression "the LORD of hosts." To say that God is holy is not to say that His acting as manifested in the judgment and the accomplishment of His purposes is His holiness. His holiness, rather, is an attribute. He is God who is holy. The Scripture here intends to predicate something of God that is true. He is holy; He possesses holiness as an attribute; and inasmuch as He Himself is holy, He desires a people that are holy. "Ye shall be holy: for I the LORD your God *am* holy" (Lev. 19:2b).

At the same time there is here a pregnant expression of the concept, namely, that the God who is holy reveals or declares that holiness in the accomplishment of His righteous judgments. The thought is typically Isaianic, and that is one reason why this verse is not to be regarded as an interpolation. Not only does it make preparation for the following passage but it also leads us to the account of the prophet's call given in the sixth chapter.

shall be sanctified in righteousness — The prophet's thought is

---

17 Herntrich, for example, writing from the standpoint of modern neo-orthodoxy declared that holiness was not an *Eigenschaft* (attribute) of God's being, but His acting as manifested in judgment and the accomplishment of His purposes. Cf. Jacob, *"Il ne peut s'agir ici du torrent qui apporte la vie, mais de la rigeur de Yahweh qui anéantit ceux qui manquent de foi à son égard, et la manifestation de sa sainteté par la justice n'apparaît pas dans le contexte où elle se trouve mentionnée comme une intervention particulièrement salvifique (Es. 5:16)"* (p. 80). Vos, however, rightly remarks that "the divine righteousness is explicitly named as bringing the judgment on sin" (*BT,* p. 273).

that in righteousness the LORD will be manifested as holy. When men see the righteous punishment of sin they will acknowledge that God is truly holy, truly divine. In the day of judgment all will confess that God is God; some from a willing heart, some from compulsion. May our acknowledgment and confession of Him come from a heart that loves Him for the manifestation of His righteousness in the punishing of our sins in Jesus Christ.

17 The enlarged mouth of sheol has swallowed up the famine-stricken and thirsty men, and now lambs graze where once the vineyard of the LORD had been.[18] Complete is the desolation; the judgment has wrought its work. In this devastated vineyard the lambs graze as though they were in their own pasture. Once the rich vineyard of the LORD — now the grazing place of lambs.

Likewise the rich and prosperous ones who had once possessed lands now have only devastated land. This devastated land had at one time been theirs. Because they had had plenty, they are described in line with Semitic idiom as the fat ones. This wasted land is to be devoured by temporary sojourners who do not even make it a permanent home. Formerly the people of God had themselves been sojourners in this land; now, the land is traveled through by foreign sojourners.

When the theocracy ceased and the nation went into captivity, the first fulfillment of this prophecy took place. Archaeology has

[18] "feed" — The verb is generally followed by the place in which animals pasture.

"in their pasture" — Some derive this word from *dibrāh* (custom) and render, "according to their custom," e.g., Vulg. (*iuxta ordinem suum*), and Sym. Others, "according to their leading," i.e., either their being led by shepherds, or their own leading. Others, "in their pastures," as in Mic. 2:12. Fischer, *"auf ihrer Trift"* (in their pasture). Some render, "wilderness, desert." Jarchi vowels the word to read, "as it was spoken to them." Ug. does not help, but I incline to the view that the word is to be rendered "pasture." Note the order of 17b, obj., subj., verb.

Ginsberg would translate, "And lambs shall graze upon the pasture of the stout (sheep) and kids shall feed upon the (wastes) of the fat (goats)." He finds a parallel between Isa. 5:14-17 and Zeph. 3:1-13. He would emend *hrbôt* to *rhbôt* (wide spaces); *g'ym* to *gdym; kdbrm* to *brym* or *b^eri'im* (stout ones), and the first two letters *kd* he takes as meaning pasture. This is ingenious, and the text is truly difficult; the evidence of 1Q, B, and the minor Greek versions, however, points toward M, and it is the course of prudence not to discard M merely because of its difficulty.

"fat ones" — Ug. also uses the word *dasm*, "fatness," in the sense of well-being, and *Iliad*, 18:342, "we wasted rich cities of mortal men."

216

shown how clearly desolation followed in the wake of the captivity. It may be, however, that the judgment which the prophet pictures is one greater than the exile, even all the punishments which culminate in final judgment. Following such judgments only desolation can remain.

18 A strange sight. A heavy cart is being laboriously drawn, not by work animals but by men; yoked, straining, tugging men.[19] They are yoked like beasts and hitched to a heavy wagon, and, just as beasts are wont to do, so these men draw after them the heavy wagon. This wagon is their own iniquity and sin, and so by such a figure we are made to see the close connection between the sin and the one who commits that sin.

The ropes with which one drags his sin are cords of vanity. "His own iniquities shall take the wicked himself, and he shall be holden with the cords of his sins" (Prov. 5:22). The cords are those which consist of vanity. By means of vanity men are dragging iniquity after them. Vanity is nothingness; it is without being and reality; it is the lie. With the lie men draw iniquity after them. It is not a pleasant picture, but it is a clear illustration of the fact that the way of the transgressor is hard. By means of the falsehoods which characterize his life, the transgressor is bound to a cart of iniquity and drags this cart after him. Some men strain and struggle to accomplish a good end; the inhabitants of Judah strain and struggle to have iniquity follow them and to draw it to themselves. Iniquity is a severe taskmaster. No taskmaster of Egypt ever ill-treated the Israelites more severely than did their own iniquity. These cords of vanity could be broken only by the LORD. Man can weave these cords, but he cannot unweave them.

---

19 Some interpret 18a of laboriously drawing sin unto oneself (Alexander, Kittel, Gesenius, etc.). Appeal is made to Job 40:25, and particularly Hos. 11:4. In Deut. 21:3, however, the reference is to an animal that draws in the yoke.

"cords of vanity" — when Kissane says that these bounds of wickedness can be loosed by repentance, he is really introducing Romish theology into the text. Penna likewise: *"Essi dovrebbero, invece, strappare questi legami per ottenere il perdono con la penitenza (58, 6)."* Only the Lord, and that through the suffering of the Servant, can loose the cords of wickedness and free the bound sinner (cf. Isa. 53).

"cart" — Delitzsch seems to engage in overrefinement when he asserts that the burden is iniquity and the cart sin. The two words are practically synonymous.

217

Sin also is drawn as with the rope of a cart. The verse reaches its climax in the word "sin." The whole thought is that the people draw iniquity with cords of lies and sin with ropes of a cart. The chiasm of the verse must not be overlooked.

a	b	b	a
Iniquity	with cords of vanity	With the rope of a cart	sin.

19 If in Judah there were those who drew iniquity with cords of lies a woe was pronounced over them. For them judgment would surely come; they were in a grave predicament. Were there actually such? There were indeed, and in the verse before us the prophet identifies them. He was not speaking in vague generalities. The sinners whom he had in mind were plentiful in Judah. They were practical atheists, who would not believe unless they could see and have a discerning of God's working. They were those who sought and required a sign. They spoke of God in mocking terms, even using some of the prophet's own phrases, so parodying him as well as his message. Perhaps in conscious reflection upon this and similar taunts, the prophet would name his own son Maher-shalal-hash-baz, "Speed the spoil, hasten the prey."[20] The taunt of these sceptics may be rendered, "Let his work speed, and hasten — let the counsel draw nigh." Possibly a touch of sarcasm is also indicated, so that we may render:

> let his work speed and indeed hasten —
> let the counsel draw near and indeed come —

What is this work of the LORD? It is the already mentioned judgment. "If the LORD is going to work judgment upon us,"

---

20 The *Paseq* after יְמַהֵר separates two verbs which are practically synonymous in meaning.

יה שֶׂה — Note cohortative ending with 3rd pers. twice in this verse. 1Q omits the first of these, but adds a cohortative ending to the first verb in 19b. The principal exegetical question in 19a has to do with the manner of translation, either "let his work speed and hasten, let the counsel draw near," or "let him speed his work, let him bring near his counsel," etc. In 19a the verbs may be either transitive or intransitive, but in 19b they can only be intransitive. Hence it would be well to maintain consistency throughout and to take all the verbs as intransitive.

וְנֵדְעָה — The cohortative expresses a consequence after the preceding jussives. The verb introduced by the prep. is a weaker expression of purpose than the corresponding form in 19a. Von Rad (*TAT*, p. 452) identifies the work of God as "*die heilsgeschlichtlichen Taten Gottes in Vergangenheit und Gegenwart*" (his deeds of holy history in the past and present).

we may paraphrase the thought, "let the judgment hurry and come. If there is such a judgment as you, Isaiah, constantly aver, let it speed and come more quickly, so that we may see it. If we see it, of course we shall believe it. You cannot expect us to believe if we do not see for ourselves. If it is coming, why does it not hasten?"

The depth of depravity is reached when the taunting unbelievers mention the Holy One of Israel. "They have despised the Holy One of Israel" (Isa. 1:4). Their use of this designation is clear evidence that they had often heard it from the lips of Isaiah. Of course they use it derisively. Thus to employ the name which had made such a deep impression upon the prophet was a mark of heinous wickedness. What about that counsel of the Holy One of Israel? That purpose which He has purposed to carry out with respect to our punishment? Why does it not come to pass? If it should eventuate, then we might truly know that the judgment was a reality. We should then have seen and experienced the judgment, and through such practical experience we would know of the judgment's reality.

20 Irreverence and deep wickedness are close partners. [21] Those who mockingly ask why God does not carry out His purposes are also those who overthrow and obliterate all moral distinctions. Doctrine and ethics are also close partners. When one no longer believes the doctrine of a judgment one turns aside from moral distinctions. The condemnation may apply to a large segment of the population and may have included people from all walks of life. Those who would subvert all moral distinctions in effect introduce chaos and in place of true ethics substitute expediency and utilitarianism.

Such people recognize the evil and address it. They speak to that evil as though it were a person. "Thou art good," they say to it. They also address the good, "Thou art evil." This they do, not through actual words but through their actions. They are ignorant. Of course, even the most depraved of men will pay

---

[21] Gesenius interprets of those judges who received bribes and so perverted justice. Jarchi of those who followed idols and rejected the worship of the true God. Cf. S. Aalen: *Die Begriffe Licht und Finsternis im Alten Testament, im Spätjudentum und Rabbinismus* (Oslo, 1951).

"placing" — They make darkness into light; cf. 13:9; 23:13; 25:2; 41:15; 42:15; 49:11 and Juvenal, *Satires, "qui nigrum in candida vertunt."*

lip service to the truth and to right, but in their actions will eradicate all moral distinctions. The man who is engaged in an evil course very often proclaims the importance of the true and the good. At the same time, not only did men approve of the evil, they manifested a positive antipathy toward the good, for they called it evil. In their hearts they hate the good, to them the only good is evil. What fallen men need is the regenerating power of the Spirit of God who causes old things to pass away, and all things to become new.

These people also make darkness to be light. In the place of light they put darkness, so that it is regarded by them as light itself. As great as is the contrast between darkness and light, so great is that also between good and evil. Between bitter and sweet also is a great disparity, but these men of Judah will pervert the two. Perversion is of the very essence of sin; for sin is the transgression of the law. He who transgresses the law thereby tacitly proclaims that the law is wrong and that the opposite of the law is right. In so transgressing the law a man is declaring good to be evil and evil to be good, darkness to be light and bitter to be sweet.

With this verse there begins a series of three uninterrupted woes, which may remind of the three woes of Revelation 8:13, "And I beheld, and heard an angel flying through the midst of heaven, saying with a loud voice, Woe, woe, woe, to the inhabiters of the earth by reason of the other voices of the trumpet of the three angels, which are yet to sound!"

21 The prophet has cried woe, and has made no mention of punishment. The tones of the first woe have barely died away, before we are face to face with another. The two woes are closely related, and herein probably is to be found the fact that no punishment has been inserted between the two. The breakdown in moral distinctions is probably to be found in the fact that the nation no longer relied upon the wisdom of God but upon its own wisdom. This may very likely have been done under the guise of practicality. True wisdom derives from God and is to be found alone with Him. To neglect the source of true wisdom leaves open only one other source, namely, the unaided human mind, and that wisdom which comes from the human mind does not originate with God. What we have here is a general condemnation of reliance upon the supposedly autonomous mind of man. Utterly lacking is a heeding of the command, "Be not wise in thine own eyes: fear the LORD, and depart from evil" (Prov. 3:7).[22]

22 Here is an ironical tone. In Judah there were mighty men, heroes, men of valor. This valor was not directed to battle or war, wherein they might have brought profit to their country, but to the drinking and mixing of wine. In defending their country they were not heroes, but only in mixing drinks. They were, it would seem, drunken, unjust judges. Here, if anywhere, mighty men were needed; these mighty men were at hand, it is true, but their might lay in the direction not of goodness, but of wickedness. Against such a woe is certainly deserved, and a severe woe at that!

In the field of drinking wine the might of the judges manifested itself. At the same time the sin which they committed was not that of drinking wine; it was the sin of dereliction from duty. It was not that they drank wine, but that in drinking they were mighty men; they drank to excess. Wine drinking became with them a habit and took from the time which should have been devoted to duty. They were engulfed by the sin of drunkenness. To make the drink more stimulating they mixed it, probably with roots and spices.[23] "I would lead thee, and bring thee into my mother's house, who would instruct me: I would cause thee to drink of spiced wine of the juice of my pomegranate" (Song of Sol. 8:2).

23 Here is no introductory woe, but one is not necessary. The thought of the preceding verse is continued and at the same time those over whom the woe had just been pronounced are identified. By means of a participle the prophet continues the

---

22 "eyes" — Cf. Akk. *ina ramanišu*, as opposed to the wisdom of God; cf. Prov. 3:7. The reference is not primarily to the priests and prophets (Duhm), nor to those who wished to appeal to Egypt for help against Assyria (Drechsler), nor to the ruling classes (Kissane), nor to those who pervert justice (Gesenius), nor those who are blind and deluded. All these classes are doubtless included, but the reference seems to include all, not merely a particular group, in the nation.

23 "to mix" — So as to make the drink more stimulating. It was not therefore a mere mingling of water and wine. The mixing may have been with roots or spices; cf. S. of S. 8:2; Ps. 75:9; Prov. 23:30; Amos 6:6; Pliny, *Natural History*, 14:13; Amr el-Quais, *Moallaka*, 5:81.

description of the men upon whom he had pronounced his woe. The interesting chiastic order of the verse must be noted:

The justifiers of the wicked for a reward — and the righteousness of the righteous they turn aside from him

Here is a further example of calling light dark and day night. The judges justify the wicked; they declare that the wicked person stands in a right relation to the law; they pronounce upon him a sentence of justification. This they have no right to do. There is only One who can tell the wicked that he stands in right relation to the law, and that is God Himself, and God can only so declare when it is the truth. Only when the claims of the law have been satisfied, and the wicked man actually possesses righteousness, may God tell him that all is well. This He can do on the grounds of the perfect righteousness of Christ. For a man to declare a wicked person righteous, however, when such a wicked one possesses no righteousness, is to do a heinous thing.[24]

The wicked one is the man who has broken the law and consequently stands condemned. He is the one who in fact is actually guilty and so in a wrong relation to the law. The judges, however, tell such a one that he stands in a right relation to the law, and hence are declaring what is contrary to fact. Their sentence of justification consequently is false. When God pronounces a sentence upon the wicked, He pronounces a sentence that accords with the facts; for the wicked whom God justifies possesses the imputed righteousness of Christ.

for the sake of reward — These mighty men are bribed judges, and from such one cannot expect just judgment. The drunkenness was not necessarily the reason why the judges took bribes. Men who carouse and men who take bribes are likely to belong together. The whole picture is that of complete disregard for the serious work of the judge.

and the righteousness of the righteous — Those who, because they have not broken the law, are actually in a right relation with the law, have that condition taken away from them. From each

---

[24] After a part. or inf. it is common to change the construction and to employ a finite verb, here the simple imp.

"righteousness" — Lit., "the righteousness of the righteous they turn aside from each of them." The pl. subj. is viewed distributively, and regard is had to each particular included in it, hence the suffix of ממנו is s. B has τοῦ δικαίου, however, and Ginsberg also prefers the s. taking the final consonant as enclitic -ma.

one that comes with a complaint, his innocency is, as it were, taken away. Justice is completely perverted, and we have a picture of what the writer of Proverbs condemned. "He that justifieth the wicked, and he that condemneth the just, even they both are abomination to the LORD" (Prov. 17:15).

c. *The judgment of abandonment* (5:24-30)

24 Therefore as the tongue of fire devoureth the stubble and the dried grass of flame fades away, so their root shall be as rottenness, and their blossom shall go up as dust, because they have despised the law of the LORD of hosts, and condemned the word of the Holy One of Israel.

25 Therefore is the anger of the LORD kindled against his people, and he hath stretched forth his hand against them and hath smitten them; and the hills did tremble, and their carcass was like refuse in the midst of the streets. For all this his anger is not turned away, and his hand is stretched out still.

26 And he will lift up an ensign to the nations from afar, and he will hiss for him from the ends of the earth, and behold! he will come in haste swiftly.

27 There is none weary and none stumbling among them, none shall slumber nor sleep, neither shall the girdle of his loins be loosed nor the thong of his sandals be broken.

28 Whose arrows are sharpened, and all their bows bent, their horses' hoofs are reckoned as flint and their wheels like a storm wind.

29 His roaring is like a lion, and he shall roar like young lions; and he shall roar and seize the prey, and he shall carry it off, and none shall deliver.

30 And in that day he will roar against him like the roaring of the sea; and one will look to the land and behold! darkness! affliction and light! It is dark in the clouds.

24 Israel has abandoned the LORD, she herself will therefore be abandoned to the most severe judgments, and these will culminate in the coming of an enemy from afar. Here is the conclusion and also an announcement of the punishment to be meted out for the sins mentioned. These sins, we now learn, are equivalent to a rejection of the LORD of hosts.

Therefore — A reference to what has immediately preceded, and also an introduction to a general conclusion. Because of the sins which Isaiah has so clearly delineated, an announcement

223

of doom is made. Isaiah begins as though he were introducing a conditional sentence. "As the tongue," he says, and we might expect him to continue with a conclusion such as, "so will the judgment devour the people." This, however, he does not do. He begins with a simile, "as the tongue of fire devoureth the stubble," and from this simile he passes to a metaphor, "so their root shall be as rottenness," and from this metaphor he goes on to give a general reason for the punishment of the people. His style is abrupt, but it is forceful; his sharp, staccato utterances are in keeping with the rapidity of the coming judgment. In broken expressions his urgency finds its utterance. The darting tongue licks up and consumes what is left of the grass that had already been cut, and the flaming grass falls down, sinking into ashes.[25]

In the root of the tree lay its strength, but the root has decayed and hence the entire tree is done for. The flower also will be lifted up and carried away by the wind. Hence, both root and flower — the entire tree will be destroyed.

for they have despised the law of the Lord — Here is the sinful action of the nation set forth in a general statement, and, inasmuch as the apodosis of the preceding has been omitted, it has all the greater force. It is by means of the sins already described, these and others also, that the nation has forsaken God. Hence, the general ground for the condemnation, one which in no way excludes the individual grounds which had been previously mentioned. It is a despising of God's law.

and condemned his word — Now Isaiah reverts to the thought of 1:4, with which he had begun his prophecy. The word of which he here speaks is that which has come to the nation both through the written law and the words of the prophets; it is therefore a synonymn for His revealed will. As Calvin says, the nation was in open rebellion against God. And here the doctrine of retaliation or reprisal meets us; as the nation has rejected the Lord and His goodness, so now He gives them over to the consequences and punishment of their sins. "My people are destroyed

---

25 "flame" — Note *Metheg* with a vowel in an apparent distant open syllable. The form *le-hā-ḇāh* represents an original *lah-ha-bah*, for unaccented *ah-ha* becomes in Heb. *eha*. Cf. *Georgics*, 1:84ff.; *Aeneid*, 2:684. The construction is either "and the grass (in respect to flame) falls," or "and the grass of flame falls."

"their blossom" — Gray calls attention to the curse of Eshmunazar, "let him have no root below or fruit above" (*CIS*, 1:2; 11:12).

for lack of knowledge: because thou hast rejected knowledge, I will also reject thee, that thou shalt be no priest to me: seeing thou hast forgotten the law of thy God, I will also forget thy children" (Hos. 4:6).

25 *Therefore* — Isaiah's expression reminds of verse 24, and refers generally to the entire preceding section. With this word we are given the reason why the anger of the LORD is against His people.[26]

In what manner, however, is this verse to be interpreted? If Isaiah is speaking of the past, to what is he referring? Surely the reference is not restricted to events such as the earthquake under Uzziah. Rather, it would seem to include all the past judgments of God, judgments which had been sent in order to turn the nation from its sins. It is in this light that the last clause should be understood. The thought is that despite all that has occurred, God's anger is still not turned away. Stroke after stroke

---

[26] The verbal tenses are perf. and hence some would refer all to past events. Kissane and Ridderbos interpret of the earthquake in Uzziah's day (cf. Amos 1:2; Zech. 14:5); Bewer, either a plague or an earthquake; *De Bijbel in Nieuwe Vertaling*, the Syro-Ephraimitish War.

Drechsler takes the verbs as prophetic futures, for (1) v. 19, and indeed the entire chapter, shows the nation as standing in a condition of security; (2) the opening parable teaches that the nation has already received its blessings and now can look forward only to judgment; and (3) v. 24, which summarizes the chapter, is stated in the future, and (4) the 1st and 2nd woes belong to the future, yet are partly given in prophetic futures.

These are cogent considerations, and it is difficult to be dogmatic. Certainly, however, the verbs do most naturally refer to the past. But the reference need not be restricted to events such as the earthquake under Uzziah. It could include all the past judgments of God which had been sent in order to turn the nation from its sins. It is in this light that the last clause is best understood. The thought would then be that, despite all that had been done, God's anger is not turned away. The phrase would also have force, if the reference were to the future, but that force would be greatly diminished. While therefore we incline toward taking the verbs as past, we do admit that the essential meaning of the prophecy is not greatly altered, if the future sense be retained. In the one case, the judgments which have already occurred are not sufficient to produce repentance; in the other, even though the judgments will come, God will still stretch forth His hand in punishment.

"tremble" — Cf. Isa. 13:13; Joel 2:10.

"like refuse" — Duhm aptly calls attention to the filth of oriental cities. Cf. Jer. 8:2; 16:4; 25:33. *Kaf* is best taken as a prep. and not as the *kaf veritatis*. B. κοπρία Vulg. *stercus*, Syr. *sᵉyoho*, "mud."

has fallen; Israel remains unrepentant, and God's anger is still directed against His people.

This anger is like a fire which has been kindled and so will burn toward His people. In punishing judgment, not in love or in grace, God's hand has been stretched out. By His hand God accomplished His purposes, and that hand is now still at work. In judgment He had smitten them, possibly through famine, pestilence, earthquake and war. And when God performs a work of judgment, even nature is affected. "Therefore I will shake the heavens, and the earth shall remove out of her place, in the wrath of the LORD of hosts, and in the day of his fierce anger" (Isa. 13:13). Palestine was a land of mountains; hence, to mention mountains is to give the impression of a general upheaval or commotion. It is not the trembling of the mountains which causes the death of the people, but in this trembling the effectiveness of the judgment is shown. It is the judgment itself which brings death, so that the carcasses of the people are like refuse in the streets of the cities. The judgment has struck; the people are dead; their bodies lie unburied as offal in the midst of the streets. Filthy are the streets of an oriental city under normal conditions; the grievous hand of death now adds to that filthiness.

In the midst of the streets, where there should be and normally was free passage for carriages and beasts of burden, the refuse which death had brought is lying. Despite all that has happened, however, God's anger is still abroad accomplishing its purposes; it has not yet returned to Him. It is a thorough messenger which, despite the severity of the judgments already wrought, is still engaged in accomplishing His will. The preceding judgments had all been insufficient. God's outstretched hand, the symbol of His power and strength, will still carry out His purposes, inflicting new judgments beyond those which had already been executed.

26 God's outstretched hand is at work. He will raise up an ensign (note the paronomasia, *nasa nes*). On a height where it would be conspicuous this pole will be raised as a rallying point for the nations.[27] These were nations outside of Judah and

---

27 וּבָשָׂא — The accent is affected by the principle *nasog ahor*. The נֵס is used in Num. 21:8 of a pole; in Isa. 33:23 the sense seems to be slightly different; here it may designate a sail (cf. 18:3; 30:17; 11:10; 13:2). The raising of the ensign served as a signal for the approach of the hostile armies. Cf. Caesar, *Gallic War*, II:20: "*Caesari omnia uno tempore erunt agenda: vexillum propo-*

hostile to her. Of them one in particular is chosen as the enemy to come. This is the great Assyrian nation, which had been growing and increasing steadily in its power. It was to come from afar, indeed, from the ends of the earth. With this poetical expression Isaiah simply wishes to indicate that the enemy is at a great distance from Palestine.

As the Lord raises the standard, so also does He whistle as though He were swarming bees. As Cyril had early remarked, "He [Isaiah] takes this [figure] from the custom of calling the bees, for the beekeepers are accustomed to whistle to them, thus to bring them from the beehives to the flowers and herbs, and to call them back from the fields, and that they may stay at home."

and behold! — When God acts, the response is immediate. Indeed, quickly, as a swift one, does the enemy come. The mockers had asked, "Why does God not hasten?" Isaiah reflects upon their taunt. "Quickly, as a swift one," so the enemy will appear. The courses and destinies of the nations are in the hands of God. A nation may deceive itself into thinking that it is taking matters into its own hands. We need but reflect upon Nazi Germany, Fascist Italy, Soviet Russia, and all too often our own country. The Assyrians thought that in entering upon a course of aggression they were on their own. They did not consider that they were but tools in the hands of the sovereign LORD of hosts. Actually, they moved only because God in His providence permitted them to move. This is the first reference in Isaiah to their coming, and its vagueness supports the idea that this is an early prophecy.

27 Who is this enemy? With hyperbolical expressions Isaiah now describes him. A weary army is an easily defeated one. "How

---

nendum, quod erat insigne, cum ad arma concurri oporteret." Note Quintus Curtius with respect to the army of Alexander (V:2), *"Tuba, cum castra movere vellet signum dabat, cuius sonitus, plerumque tumultuantium fremitu exoriente, haud satis exaudiebatur. Ergo perticam, quae undique conspici posset, supra praetorium statuit, ex qua signum eminebat, pariter omnibus conspicuum."* The philosophy which underlies this verse makes clear that the movement of the enemy armies is due to the working of God in His providence.

"ends of the earth" — There is no reason to doubt that Isaiah knew the existence of lands and nations beyond Mesopotamia (cf. 13:5; 49:12). Livy speaks of the Gauls (5:37), *"ab oceano terrarum ultimis oris bellum oriente,"* and Thucydides of the Medes (1:22) *ek peratōn gēs.* Gesenius pointed out that the Ethiopian ruler bore the title *aznaf sayed,* "honored by the ends of the earth."

he met thee by the way, and smote the hindmost of thee, even all
that were feeble behind thee, when thou wast faint and weary;
and he feared not God" (Deut. 25:18). Although coming a long,
weary distance, it is not a weary enemy that comes against Judah.
It is in fit condition. In that army none is exhausted, so none
must fall behind. Nor do any stumble, ready to fall and unable
to fight. This army does not sleep; it does not even slumber.[28]
So great are the desire and the eagerness for battle that the army
does not even sleep for refreshment.

The girdle which bound together the cloak and provided a hold
for the sword or dagger is not opened. It was an army strictly
intent upon business. Even the thong of the sandals was in good
condition for the battle; it was not broken in two.

28 Turning from the army itself, Isaiah now gives us a glimpse
of the arms and weapons of war which that army possessed. The
arrows had already been sharpened, and are ready to be used in
the battle.[29] The language calls to mind the description of
Psalm 45:5, "Thine arrows are sharp in the heart of the king's
enemies; whereby the people fall under thee." The bows also
were ready for usage, having been bent so that they could cast
the arrow. Arrian describes how the warriors stepped on the

28 "slumber nor sleep" — These words are needed as a parallel to 27a and
so should not be omitted. Between the two verbs a distinction is probably
to be noted. The army does not sleep; it does not even slumber.

29 "whose arrows" — Lit., "which, its arrows." The relative refers to the preceding, the word "army" being understood but not expressed. שבובים is a
passive part.

"sharpened" — The arrows have already been sharpened, and so are now
ready for usage in battle (cf. Ps. 45:6).

קשתותיו qaš-še-tô-ṭāf. The pl. is qe-sā-tôṭ, but when suffixes are added,
Dagesh forte (dirimens) usually appears in the *Sin* (cf. Jer. 51:56; Ps. 37:15).
This *Daghesh* is generally placed in sonants, sibilants or emphatic *qof*.
The development of this particular form is probably (1) qešaṭôṭ; (2) qe-še-ṭô-ṭāf;
addition of the suffix causes the *qāmetz*, being in a distant open syllable to drop
to *Šewa*. (3) We should normally expect a *Hireq* under *q*, but instead the original short *a* appears (cf. Akk. qaš-tu). (4) Probably to make the *Šewa* more
audible, the *daghesh* is now inserted.

"are reckoned" . . . Calvin takes the verbs as futures, but it is more forceful
to continue the description in the present. The perf. indicates that the hoofs
have been and still are reckoned. The verb is pausal and hence to be separated from what follows. For classical references cf. *Iliad* 8:41 and *Odyssey*
21:30. Gesenius adduces further examples from Arabic literature.

bow with the left foot and then drew back the string to a great distance.

In antiquity the hoofs of the horses were not shod. A horse, then, which had hard hoofs could endure heavy and difficult travel; it was greatly prized for purposes of war. Xenophon demanded horses with hard hoofs, and Homer praises such horses as having strong-ankled and bronzed hoofs. Flint is unusually strong and so forms a fitting comparison. The Assyrians needed horses whose hoofs could stand any kind of difficult travel. The Assyrian chariots had two wheels, and these stirred up the dust like a whirlwind. Isaiah later uses the figure in a different sense, "For, behold, the LORD will come with fire, and with his chariots like a whirlwind, to render his anger with fury, and his rebuke with flames of fire" (66:15). Against such an army who can stand? God was using an effective, well-prepared instrument to carry out His purposes.

29 Capable is the enemy and ready for attack. He is also fierce and bold, and one who will have success.[30] Like a wild lion who roars and carries off to safety his prey, so that he may devour it undisturbed, no one being present to deliver it, is this enemy. Like the lion, he, too, is roaring. On the prowl, in search of his prey, the lion roars. Across the desert a lion was now marching, roaring as he came, searching for a prey to devour. Like the lion, he is aggressive. Ready to defend himself, to be sure, but more than that, he is prepared for the offensive.

As the young lions roar which have been weaned from their mother, so this army also roars. When about to spring upon his prey, the lion utters a low growl, and this enemy is also growling. Isaiah hears the low growling and murmuring of the approaching army; the time for the attack is drawing nigh. When the attack has been made, the lion will carry off his booty to a place of safety where he may devour it at his leisure. This spoil is the land of Judah which will be so mastered by the enemy that it will do all that this enemy desires. God could deliver; He is the only

---

30 Gesenius adduces an interesting parallel from the *Hamasa*, "a wilderness overgrown with reeds, in which there are lions," i.e., an army filled with war-thirsty enemies.

In the preceding verses there had been an admixture of the perf. and imp. In this verse the imp. alone is employed. The passage turns from mere description to prediction.

one that can do so. God, however, will not deliver, for it is better that Judah should be punished. In His strange providence God would bring the theocracy to an end. Its day is to be over, and the enemy is permitted to do according to its will until it has accomplished God's own purposes.

30 Night has fallen, and all about is heavy, unrelieved gloom.[31] Against Judah Assyria will roar like the roaring of the sea. It is a time of roaring; first that of a lion, now that of the sea. When the judgment falls, then the enemy will roar. The unrelieved darkness, however, suggests that a heavier judgment may also be indicated, namely, that time when there will truly be no one to deliver, and the wicked will go away eternally into the outer blackness.

The sea roars and threatens destruction; no help is to be found there. Hence, one will look to the land; can there be help or escape on the land? If one should look to the land, he will see only darkness. Light will have utterly vanished. No, not utterly. There will be light, but it will be mixed with affliction, so that it too will be as darkness. Light, then affliction; light, then affliction, until the light gives way entirely and only the absolute darkness remains. Clouds overshadow the land, and in these clouds is darkness. The land of Judah is covered; the light has gone; the darkness reigns, black and still and heavy.

[31] This verse bristles with difficulties. Some regard it as a prophecy of salvation, and hence, as not genuine.

"he will roar" — Ewald took the verb impersonally, one will roar.

"and one will look to the land" — The words may be taken conditionally, "and if one look to the land." The verbal form is either *nifal* or *piēl*, probably the latter, and, as far as I am able to determine, this is the only passage in which the verb appears outside the *Hifil* stem.

"darkness" — The word is accented with *zaqef-qaton* and is to be separated from what follows.

"in its clouds" — Cf. Akk. *irpitu*.

C. JUDAH'S TRUE HOPE: THE MESSIANIC KING
(6:1—12:6)

1. ISAIAH'S VISION OF THE HOLY GOD (6:1-13)

a. *The vision itself* (6:1-7)

1 In the year that king Uzziah died I saw the Lord, sitting upon a throne, high and lifted up, and his train was filling the palace.

2 Seraphim were standing above him, each with six wings; with two he covered his face and with two he covered his feet and with two he did fly.

3 And one cried unto another and said, Holy, holy, holy is the LORD of hosts; the fullness of all the earth is his glory.

4 And the posts of the thresholds moved because of the voice of the one crying, and the house was being filled with smoke.

5 Then said I, Woe is me, for I am undone, for I am a man of unclean lips, and I dwell in the midst of a people of unclean lips, for mine eyes have seen the king, the LORD of hosts.

6 Then there flew unto me one of the seraphim, with a live stone in his hand, which he had taken with the tongs from off the altar.

7 And he caused it to touch my mouth and said, Lo! this hath touched thy lips, and thine iniquity is turned aside, and thy sin is atoned for.

Several questions of unusual interest revolve around this chapter. Some have maintained that chapter 6 is the account of an inauguration in preparation for a particular ministry. Calvin, for example, thinks that the vision is necessary to the prophet in order to confirm and to strengthen him in the discharge of his office. He compares the ministry of Isaiah with that of the Apostles, who after their original call nevertheless received further inaugurations from God, e.g., John 20:21, 22 and Acts 2:3. On this view the chapter is to be regarded simply as the introduction to a specific mission.[1]

---

1 Sebastian Schmidt remarked, "*Adunum specialem actum officii.*" Vitringa and others have also adopted this position, and Alexander seems to favor it.

On the other hand, the view is now more generally held that the chapter presents Isaiah's original call to his prophetic ministry, and thus corresponds to the calls given to other prophets. The reading of this chapter, as had already been noted by Umbreit, gives the impression of a solemn original call, and it is difficult to escape from this impression. The fifth verse seems to support the idea that this is an inaugural call. The vision of the Lord produces upon Isaiah the feeling that, since he has seen the Lord, he is undone and will perish. It seems to imply that this is the first vision of the Lord that Isaiah has had. Had he engaged in previous speaking and prophesying, he would have known that the One whom he served was gracious and merciful toward him and would not have shown that fear of which we read in verse 5.[2]

If, however, this sixth chapter is indeed the account of the prophet's call, why is it found at this point rather than at the beginning of the prophecy?[3] For our part we do not believe that

---

Kaplan (*JBL*, 1926-27, Vols. 45-46, pp. 251-59) thinks that chap. 6 merely pictures the sense of despair that came over Isaiah during his ministry. Kaplan does not do justice to the content of vv. 5ff. which seems to presuppose that the prophet had not yet engaged in prophesying. Penna remarks of Kaplan's view, "*Tale opinione, che agevola la soluzione del problema suscitato dalla successione dei capitoli 1-5 e 6-12, non sembra fondata su alcun motivo oggettivo.*"

[2] Engnell (*The Call of Isaiah*, Uppsala and Leipzig, 1949) opposes Kaplan (see n. 1) and holds that chap. 6 is the inaugural call. So also Kroeker, Bentzen, Kissane, Fischer, Penna, Steinmann. Also Balla, but he places chap. 6 on the level of accounts of heroes of religion who have had ecstatic experiences in their calls.

[3] It has been maintained that the position of the chapter indicates that Isaiah's prophecies were originally found in small collections, and that chap. 6 stood at the head of one of these collections. Budde would place it at the beginning of the small group, 6:1-9:6, Hempel, Herntrich and others at the head of 2:1-4:6. It has also been held that chaps. 1-5 were added to the collection 6-12, and that they were placed first because they were actually earlier in time. Likewise, it has been held that chap. 6 originally was followed by chaps. 1-5. We agree with Penna in saying that the explanation that the chapter found its present place by chance is one of ignorance. Perhaps we can never tell exactly why the prophet put the chapter where he did, but there is a line of thought that at least should not be neglected.

Isaiah's intention was not to stress a chronological arrangement of his prophecies but, at least at this point, to bring prophetic emphasis to the fore. The arrangement then would be one of emphasis and not of chronology. At the beginning of the entire book, Isaiah places the introduction which is now

the present position of the chapter is due to haphazardness or carelessness in the collection of Isaiah's prophecies. Rather, there appears to be a very definite reason why the chapter is in its present position. Isaiah's purpose apparently is first to present the heart of his message, and only then to relate the account of his own prophetic call. To accomplish this end he places at the head of all his prophecies a general introduction (chapter 1) in which he sets forth in germ form the themes which he is later to develop. From this he plunges immediately into his message, beginning with a note of hope (2:2-4) and concluding on the same note (4:2-6). In this first utterance he announced the sinful depravity of the nation and the certainty of coming judgment. From this judgment the only refuge was to be found in God and His redeeming grace. In order to reinforce the message a picture of the loving care of God in the choice of Israel and in the gifts which He gave to her is found in chapter 5, a chapter which leaves no doubt as to the justice of God in sending judgment upon sin. It is only after this initial proclamation that the prophet is ready to relate the call to the prophetic office, an account which reinforces what he has already proclaimed.[4]

---

there. This is an introduction to the book, and not to the prophet. It presents to us in germ form the truths which later are to be developed. Immediately following this introduction we are given specimens of Isaiah's preaching to the Judah of his day.

Two parallel lines run through this section. The prophet must proclaim the hardening of the people and also the coming of the Messiah. To prepare for the proper understanding of this little section of Messianic prophecies, the great trilogy, as it has been called, Isaiah places his inaugural call where he does. It is therefore not only an inaugural vision, but, by its present position in the prophecy serves to introduce the reader to the Messianic trilogy which immediately follows.

L. J. Liebreich regards the chapter as the conclusion of what precedes and the introduction to what follows. In chap. 6 God is King, and in the following chapters there are three human kings (cf. *HUCA*, Vol. 25, 1954, pp. 37-40). F. Frühstorfer (*TPQ*, Vol. 91, 1938, pp. 414-24) thinks that Isaiah decided to publish the chapter several years after the events in order to satisfy doubts among some of his hearers. Variations of this position are quite old.

4 That chaps. 2-5 are a unity may be seen from the following considerations: 1:10 is taken up again in 3:9 (cf. 1:19, 20 with 3:10, 11). 3:14 is developed in 5:1-7 and 3:9b, 11 in chap. 5 generally. Compare 3:14 with 5:5; 2:9, 11, 17, with 5:15, 16; 5:9, 10, 13, 14, 17 with 6:11-13; 5:9 with 6:11; 5:5 with 6:13; 5:24 with 6:13b; 5:26 with 7:18; 5:5, 6 with 7:23-25; 5:30 with 8:22.

The general character of chapters 2-5 makes it clear that they belong to the very first part of Isaiah's ministry. This character shows that they were written down before the Assyrian power had reached the height of its threatening menace. They furthermore prepare us for an introduction to the man who had uttered them. They are thus greatly strengthened by this account of the prophet's call to his ministry. He has preached a final judgment and the perishing of the nation because this was the message given to him by God Himself.

Chapter 6 contains a vision and a message, and scholars have been divided as to the proper relationship between the two. Is the vision merely introductory to the message, or is the message somewhat of an appendage to the vision? The present writer inclines to the position that the two complement one another, and that the chapter would be bereft of its full strength if either one were missing. The vision is necessary for a proper understanding of the message, and the message itself cannot begin to receive its proper force apart from the preceding vision. The two belong together and should not be separated.

Thus there emerges a significant difference between Jeremiah and Isaiah. In his prophecy the person of Jeremiah is prominent. Not so in Isaiah. Here it is the message which stands out, and the person of the prophet recedes in the background. Once we have been made familiar with the heart of the prophet's message we may learn of the prophet himself and his call.

1 The king had died.[5] Uzziah had brought many benefits to the country and had introduced an era of prosperity and peace. But now Judah was without *the* king.

It was a critical time. Three years before Jeroboam II of Is-

[5] Opinions as to the date of Uzziah's death range between 748-734: Mowinckel (735-734); Bentzen (739/8? 747/6?); Kissane (740-741); Feldmann (737); Boutflower (736); Engnell (748); Fischer (c. 738); Thiele (between Tishri 740 and Tishri 739); Steinmann (c. 740). The chronological questions are difficult of solution; for an introduction, see Edwin F. Thiele: *The Mysterious Numbers of the Hebrew Kings* (Chicago, 1951).

A gravestone from near the time of Christ, written in Aramaic, reads: "Hither there were brought the bones of Uzziah, the king of Judah — not to be opened." This stone was found in the Russian archaeological museum on the mount of Olives. In all probability the bones of the king had been removed and this stone erected over their new resting place. It shows the respect which the Jews of Christ's time paid to the kings of their nation of old. See *BA*, Vol. I (May, 1938), p. 8, for an illustration.

rael had died, and now Menahem was ruler. Under Jeroboam and Uzziah the boundaries had been extended to their ancient extremes; commerce and agriculture flourished, and the two nations were at peace.

As with Solomon's death, so with Jeroboam's, it was followed by anarchy. Judah likewise declined. More and more Assyria increased. A weak and decaying Judah it was that Isaiah had to face. In this year of moment the prophet Isaiah had a vision. He does not tell us whether the vision occurred before or after the death. The important point is that the year in which Isaiah saw God was that of the king's death. In the year in which the old order ended God appeared to the prophet. The great glory and national pride of Judah were now facing an end, never to rise again. The year of Uzziah's death (possibly 739 B.C.) may not have been the actual year of the founding of Rome, but according to tradition, the great city on the Tiber arose about this time. From now on Judah declined more and more, and Rome increased.

In this year, the twelfth of Jotham's co-regency, the thirteenth year of Pekah of Israel, the prophet Isaiah saw the Lord.[6] But Scripture says that no man can see God at any time (John 1:18; 1 Tim. 6:16). This, however, was no seeing with the bodily eye, for God is invisible. No physical eye can see Him. At the same time, despite the fact that God is a spiritual, invisible Being, the Bible does say that men will see Him. "Blessed are the pure in heart: for they shall see God" (Matt. 5:8). It is not the essence of God which Isaiah sees, for, inasmuch as God is spiritual and invisible, that essence cannot be seen by the physical eye of the creature. At the same time it was a true seeing; a manifestation of the glory of God in human form, adapted to the capabilities of the finite creature, which the prophet beheld! "There was therefore," as Calvin puts it, "exhibited to Isaiah such a form

6 According to 2 Kings 15:1, 2, Uzziah (Azariah) began to reign in the 27th year of Jeroboam of Israel and reigned for fifty-two years. The year of his beginning was 767 B.C., and apparently he ascended the throne after Tishri of that year. In the 41st year of his reign Jotham ascended the throne as a co-regent. This (750-751 B.C.) was the 2nd year of Pekah of Israel. Jotham reigned as sole king from 739-735, a total of four years. All told he reigned 20 years.

The name of the king appears as (1) *uzziayahu;* 1:1; 7:1; 2 Kings 15:32, 34; 2 Chron. 26:1ff. (2) *uzzah,* 2 Kings 21:18, 26. (3) *uzziyah,* 2 Kings 15:13, 30; Amos 1:1; Zech. 14:5. (4) *azariyah,* 2 Kings 14:21; 15:1, 7, 17, 23, 27; 1 Chron. 3:12. (5) *azariyahu,* 2 Kings 15:6, 8.

as enabled him, according to his capacity, to perceive the inconceivable majesty of God; and thus he attributes to God a *throne,* a *robe,* and a bodily appearance."

Isaiah saw the Lord, but in a vision. In mysterious manner the power of God came over the prophet, so that he became unconscious to the outside, external world, and yet with the inner eye saw what God revealed to him. It was thus a divinely imposed vision, one that was objective to Isaiah in that it was not the product of Isaiah's mind. Inasmuch, then, as it was a vision, it is beside the point to seek to determine whether the palace described was either the earthly Temple or the heavenly. For that matter, we have no means of knowing where Isaiah was when the vision came to him. He may have been in the Temple, but he may also have been in his own home.[7] We are not therefore warranted in saying that as Isaiah looked toward the Holy of Holies in the Temple he alone of all those standing about saw

[7] To insist that Isaiah must have been in the Temple as he received the vision does despite to the visionary character of the message. Nevertheless, most moderns seem to think that the Temple was the scene in which the vision occurred. Cf. Rowley, *FI,* p. 136. Steinmann suggests that he was standing in the Oulam where fire burned on the altar of incense. Hyatt *(Prophetic Religion,* p. 47) thinks that as a layman Isaiah could have had access only to the outer court, not to the sanctuary which was restricted to the priests.

This is the only actual vision recorded in Isaiah. From 2 Chron. 26:22 it need not be inferred that Isaiah had actually begun his prophetic ministry before this time. He may have written the acts of Uzziah at a later time, for they do not constitute a part of the present book.

"that I saw the Lord" — The imp. with *wāw* cons. is used to express the temporal sequel of what has just been stated by the inf. for the inf. here has the force of a perf. The conjunction is omitted in 1Q. According to Marti, Isaiah enters the Temple and stands in the outer court; he is probably alone, deep in thought. In this state of meditation he looks to the most holy place. There, in the earthly Temple he sees the Lord. Duhm thinks the scene is the heavenly Temple. Gesenius contends that Isaiah's vision must have taken place before the death of the king, otherwise the text would read, "In the first year of Jotham." But it is clear that Jotham served as co-regent. Bentzen thinks that the vision must have occurred after the death, otherwise the death would not be mentioned. Both these views miss the basic reason for the mention of the death (see exposition).

Schmidt points out that in Egypt private men had copies of their deeds inscribed to serve as proofs in the next life. Isaiah writes in the first person, however, not to glorify himself, but to record his experience with God. Nor did he merely describe external events, as others, writing autobiography, had done. Not even in a formal sense has any document from antiquity been the equal of chap. 6, as far as the relation of inner, spiritual events is concerned.

God. Isaiah did not see God because he was more spiritually attuned than others; he saw God because God had revealed Himself to him.

He whom Isaiah sees is the Lord (*Adhonai*), the God who is able to carry out His purposes. In this vision the power of God is to be manifested in His hardening of the hearts of men. He who can harden men's hearts is truly sovereign, and it is God as the sovereign One whom Isaiah sees. At the same time the appearance is in a human form, so that man can behold it. Calvin rightly remarks that "John tells us that it was Christ (John 12:41), and justly, for God never revealed himself to the Fathers but in his eternal Word and only begotten Son." The prophet, however, simply gives an indefinite designation of God; he does not stress the person of Christ. He sees God as sovereign in human form, and this appearance we learn from John was an appearance of Christ.

It is therefore a vision which Isaiah has, but it is nevertheless a real and genuine seeing of God. The mention of the palace would most naturally call to mind the Temple at Jerusalem, but since the revelation is by vision, there is no attempt to confine the description and the measurements to this Temple. It is simply the Temple as such to which attention is drawn.[8] The Temple of the vision certainly reflects upon that at Jerusalem, but is not confined either to its precise arrangements or directions. By means of this vision it may be made clear to the people that the Lord is there in the Temple, and so even by the reference to the word "temple," the nation will see that He is present in their own midst ready to proclaim judgment.

seated upon a throne — God is both king and judge.[9] He is

8 In some passages the word היכל refers to the heavenly Temple: Ps. 11:4; 18:7; Mic. 1:2. For this reason certain exegetes wish to place the vision in the heavenly Temple (e.g., G. A. Smith). The word is of Sumerian origin, *E-GAL* (large house), and comes to Heb. through the Akk., *ekallu* (*bitu rabbu*). Feldmann regards the term as post-Isaianic. But the term does occur in Ug. where it refers to the palace of some particular god. The word may designate the entire building, 1 Sam. 1:9; 2 Kings 20:18, or the largest room, 1 Kings 6:17. With respect to the Solomonic Temple it would designate the holy place.

9 Appealing to Amos 1:5, 8 Engnell thinks that we have here a technical term for king (cf. Isa. 10:13). The word is also employed of the Lord when He sits as king or judge (cf. Ps. 29:10; 2:4). Engnell also thinks that the representation here is that of the LORD as a high god. It may be that certain features of the description have their counterparts in the ancient religions of the Near East, but such resemblances are at best but accidental.

ready to exercise His kingly prerogative of pronouncing judgment upon the people in whose midst He had appeared. Solomon said that God would be found of His people in the Temple. "And hearken thou to the supplication of thy servant, and of thy people Israel, when they shall pray toward this place; and hear thou in heaven thy dwelling place; and when thou hearest, forgive" (1 Kings 8:30).

The Lord was seated upon a throne, high and lifted up, and so, very high. As judges and kings sat upon their thrones, so the Lord is sitting upon His. He is thus seen as One who is already king, engaged in the act of judgment. The long, loose, flowing robes or skirts of the robe were filling the palace, so that there was no room left for anyone to stand.[10] It is a scene of glorious majesty. As the vision is seen by Isaiah, he is silent, and his silence simply focuses attention upon the unspeakable exaltation of the Lord. Isaiah is to be called to a ministry in which the sovereign power of God will be displayed, and in which judgment is to be prominent. In preparation for such a ministry there must be a vision of God's holiness. Indeed, the entire scene befits the solemnity of the message. Our attention is directed immediately to the Lord as Him who alone is sovereign, who can both create and destroy, and in whose hands are the times of all men and nations.

2 Earthly monarchs are accompanied by their magnates and retinue, but the vision which Isaiah saw is unique, and its lines are not necessarily drawn from earthly customs. The God of creation was attended by His heavenly court long before there were any earthly monarchs. In fact, human kingship is derived from the divine King and the idea of earthly retinues from that of the divine retinue. It is true that in the ancient Near East

---

[10] In placing a *Tiphcha* with כסא the Masoretes separate that word from the two adjectives, and apparently construe them with "the Lord." In Isa. 57:15 these two epithets are used of God, and in 52:13 both roots are employed of the Servant of the Lord. In view of the word-order, however, it is more natural to apply the epithets to the throne. In thus emphasizing the majesty of the throne, the prophet is really calling attention to the majesty of the One who sits thereon.

"his train" — Lit., his skirts, the long, "loose flowing parts of the robe or the upper garment" (Gray). Ibn Ezra applies the word to the throne, and Calvin, by his translation, does the same, *"Cuius extrema replebant templum."* The Vulg. reads, *"quae sub ipso erant,"* and B, evidently desirous of avoiding an anthropomorphism, "and the house was filled with his glory." Engnell points out that the royal robes play a significant role in the *akitu* festival.

two figures were often present with the deity as his special tutelary deities.[11] This was true in Egypt as well as in Assyria. Are
we then to make the assumption that the contents of this vision
were derived from similar arrangements found elsewhere in the
ancient world?

As we have insisted, the vision was a divine revelation. It was
a revelation given to the prophet in time and space upon this
earth, and not in a vacuum. It is to be expected, therefore, that
in a formal sense it would have a point of contact with the
religious paraphernalia which the prophet would understand.
In a formal sense there are relations between the contents of this
vision and practices and customs to be found in other religions
of antiquity. What was essentially new was the fact that this
vision was a revelation from God. It must also be remembered
that the pagan religions of antiquity were degenerations from
the true, and indeed were imitative of it.

The heavenly attendants are described as seraphim, or burning
ones. This is the only passage in the Old Testament in which
they are mentioned.[12] The seraphim are personal, spiritual beings, for they have faces, feet and hands, they employ human

[11] Cf. H. Ringgren: *Word and Wisdom* (1947), pp. 11f.; Schräder, *KAT*
(1903), p. 310. The Akk. king had two tutelary deities, *shedu* and *limassu,*
also designated *kettu* and *mesharu* (cf. Engnell, *op. cit.,* p. 34). Cf. also
Béguerie: *La Vocation d'Isaiae,* p. 20. In Egypt the designations were
Hu and *Sia* or *Kike* and *Sia.* It is not clear that this phenomenon was actually
present in Ugarit. Cf. 1 Keret, 1, lines 12ff.

[12] The seraphim had wings, countenances, feet and hands and could speak
in human language. The word "seraph" is also employed of poisonous serpents
(Num. 21:4ff.) which could fly (cf. Isa. 14:29; 30:6). Hence, some have sought
a connection with the Serapis (serpent) cult of Egypt, although this cult was
not introduced until the time of the Ptolemies. Duhm thinks that the seraphim originally had the bodies of serpents, for he can see no reason for not
identifying these seraphim with the poisonous serpents of the wilderness.
More cautious commentators, however, have recognized that the only relationship is to be found in the name. König, for example, who is at his best
in the discussion of this passage, points out that the seraphim are spiritual
beings which have moral conceptions. Kimchi considered them to be messengers of fire, taking the root in the sense "to shine." Others have sought
a connection with the Ar. *sharif,* "noble."

Those who favor the identification with serpents appeal to statements of
the classical writers; e.g., Herodotus (2:74) mentions holy serpents found at
the temple of Jupiter at Thebes. I cannot agree with Bentzen that the representation stands in connection with ancient mythology. Nor, as Herntrich
suggests, are the seraphs half men and half animal, nor does the mention of
wings necessarily imply mixed forms.

speech and understand moral concepts. The only relation which they sustain with the fiery serpents is that they have wings and are burning creatures.

Nor are the seraphim to be identified with the cherubim, for the functions of both were quite different.[13] The cherubim are over the mercy seat, and in Ezekiel they are represented as having four wings. The seraphim are simply those creatures that were standing about the throne in the vision, and Isaiah immediately recognizes them as attendants. They are seen as standing above the throne, and thus the relative position of those who are sitting and those who are standing is expressed. In that the seraphim stand above they are not to be thought of as superior to Him, but simply as being in the position of waiting upon Him as His attendants.[14]

each with six wings — The expression is distributive, each seraph had three pair of wings. We may literally render, "six wings, six wings, to each one."[15] As a sign of reverence and awe before the holy Lord, each seraph covered his face with two of his wings. The sight of God wrought humility in the beholder, and the covering of the face would also preclude any irreverent be-

---

Inscribed Hebrew seals from the ninth and eighth centuries B.C., made of semi-precious stones, often represent winged creatures, such as winged lions with human heads, winged sphinxes with human heads, etc. See Thomas: *Documents from Old Testament Times*, 1958, p. 218.

Nor are the seraphim mere symbolic personifications of divine qualities; they are set forth as actual beings, true personalities, whose function was the praise of the majestic Lord.

[13] The cherubim surround God's throne, Ezek. 1:22; Rev. 4:6. Some think that they are a reminiscence of Babylonian mythology, perhaps suggested by the winged stone monsters *(qaribu)* which stood in guard over palaces. Another view is that they are symbolic figures and not angels. This apparently was held by some of the church fathers. It has also been suggested that they are a personification of the storm cloud, and the flaming sword (Gen. 3:24) of the lightning. Leupold (*Commentary on Genesis*, Grand Rapids, 1950, p. 184) maintains that the cherubim are beings like angels, for in Ezek. 1:22 they are described as living. He also suggests that the Israelites remembered how the cherubim looked, for when they are commanded to make two cherubim no further description of them was deemed necessary. Cf. *BA*, I, 1 (Feb., 1938), pp. 1-3.

[14] Engnell suggests that עַל is the regular preposition to point out the attendants upon one who is seated; cf. Gen. 18:8, Exod. 18:3. Drechsler maintains that עַל is sharper than the mere מֵעַל and should be rendered "*bei ihm.*"

[15] In 1Q the phrase is written only once. Here it has distributive force, i.e., each seraph had three pairs of wings; cf. Num. 14:34; 17:21; Lev. 24:8.

holding of the Lord. Perhaps also we may not be wrong in assuming that the glory of the Lord was so great that just as one cannot look directly at the sun for its brightness, so one could not look directly at the majestic figure seated upon the throne.

with two he covered his feet — This action does not necessarily imply sinfulness, but was perhaps done as an expression of humility and unworthiness. We need not assume that the feet are mentioned as an euphemism for sex, but rather simply as a less noble part of the body. With two wings also the seraphs flew in order to carry out the will and orders of the Lord.

This picture of the heavenly retinue is one that is common to the Scriptures. The seraphs are standing, as though they were ready to serve.[16] They were ever at hand, prepared for obedience. It is a strange picture. Perhaps we cannot say that they were hovering, yet, on the other hand, they were not standing upon a solid surface. These were ready, obedient servants. With their wings they were accustomed to serving the Lord.

3 The continuous occupation of the seraphim is the blessed work of praising God.[17] They are engaged in the unbroken task of chanting His praises. We are not told how many of the seraphs there were.[18] Perhaps there were two rows, one on either side of the throne, but of this we cannot be sure. We do not know whether the seraphs were in groups or choirs. It is probably safe to assume that the singing was antiphonal, for the seraphs cry out to the other seraphs, as though proclaiming to them and declaring to them that the LORD is holy. That the chanting was

16 Cf. Dan. 7:10; 1 Kings 22:19ff.; Job 1 and 2.

17 After a part. the perf. with *wāw* cons. has frequentative force, "and each kept crying." On the basis of an appeal to Isa. 40:3 and the usage of Ar. *qara*, Engnell asserts that the verb has the "proximate specially cultic meaning, 'recite, intone'." In Egypt the high priest, addressing the enthroned Pharaoh, proclaimed, "Pure, pure is the king of the south and of the north. Thy purity is the purity of Horus, of Seth, of Thoth and of Sepu [*sopou*]" (A. Erman: *The Religion of the Egyptians*, p. 59). In Isaiah's vision, purity and holiness are united.

18 Some of the earlier interpreters believed that there were only two of the seraphim. Origen held that these were the Son and the Holy Spirit, who cover the face and feet of the Father upon the throne. They reveal the Father, yet they conceal the beginning and the end of His eternity. Jerome rejected this. Drechsler held that there were two rows of seraphim, one on either side of the throne. Rosenmüller divides the seraphs into choirs; first one choir sings, then the other and finally both together. Others have held that there were two groups of the seraphim.

241

actually antiphonal cannot, of course, be proved. To the end that Isaiah might understand them, they called out in human language.

Holy, holy, holy — As here used, *qadosh* signifies the entirety of the divine perfection which separates God from His creation.[19]

[19] In 1Q the word is written only twice, but thrice in B. Note the *Paseq* which here separates two identical words from each other. The root קדש is generally taken in the sense "to separate, cut off." However, Bunzel (*Der Begriff der Heiligkeit im A.T.*, 1914) appealed to a root *quddushu*, "to shine, be pure." The following considerations would support the first position: (1) "The transition from majesty to purity seems easier than that from purity to majesty" (Vos); (2) The opposite of *qdš* is *ḥol* (open, accessible). This favors the idea that *qdš* denotes something not open or accessible, but set apart and separated. (3) There is a certain similarity between the concept of *qdš* and that of *ḥerem*, "the thing devoted" (see Vos). (4) A number of sacred places in the ancient Near East bore the name *qāḏēš*. These were set apart and not accessible to the ordinary mortal. (5) The *qeḏešîm* and the *qeḏešôṯ* were men and women set apart from ordinary life to a particular religious function, namely, prostitution.

Thus, originally, the root seemed to express the concept of separateness, or as Vos puts it, "unapproachableness," and this is due to the fact that the divine is separate from the human. This is not to say that the person or object under the influence of "holiness" was under the influence of a force that could be either good or harmful, a force somewhat akin to *mana* or *taboo*. Even though moral and ethical conceptions may have been lacking in the general Near Eastern conception of "holiness" and it may have been something apparently quite impersonal (Von Rad), nevertheless it was the belief that the "thing holy" was divine or possessed divine nature that rendered it separated from the ordinary human sphere.

In Israel this concept was greatly enriched and deepened due to the fact of special revelation from God. God is holy, for He is completely separate from the creature. Holiness is then ". . . something coextensive with and applicable to everything that can be predicated of God . . . " (Vos). ". . . I am God, and not man; the Holy One in the midst of thee . . . " (Hos. 11:9).

Inasmuch as the Lord is holy, He is separate not merely from the creation but also from sin. Thus the concept "holiness" also possesses an ethical quality. Being thus separated from sin, holiness is opposed to sin and determined upon its punishment. "The LORD of hosts is exalted in judgment, and God the Holy One is sanctified in righteousness" (Isa. 5:24). While we should perhaps not actually identify God's zeal and His holiness (Von Rad), nevertheless God's zeal is the expression of His holiness in action. Von Rad has rightly pointed out that three ethical prohibitions are justified by an appeal to God's zeal (Exod. 20:5; 34:14 and Deut. 6:14ff.).

When Isaiah beheld the "Holy One" in the Temple, he was before the One who alone is truly God, utterly separate from His creation and from all that is sinful. I cannot agree with the definition of Jacob, influenced by Pedersen, that "from the phenomenological point of view, holiness is a supernatural and mysterious force which confers a special quality upon certain

God is the Creator who exists in absolute independence of the creature. He is the Lord, and not a man. Although the creation depends upon Him, He Himself is entirely independent thereof. This is the heart and core of Isaiah's theology. Also included in the word holy is an ethical element, the thought of complete freedom and separation from what is sinful. The prophet seems to acknowledge this when in reaction to the cry he confesses his own sinfulness and unworthiness. The One upon the throne is God, who exists distinct from and in complete independence from those whom He has created, and from all His creation. He is also One whose eyes are purer than to behold iniquity, and who will in no wise clear the guilty.

In their song of praise therefore the seraphim set forth what was the distinguishing characteristic of God, namely, His holiness. Their hearts burst forth in praise of His very essence. Our greatest service to Him also is to be found in praising His name. To praise His name involves more than the mere repetition of the word qadosh. It includes deep meditation upon God and His attributes and the living of a life of humility in accordance with the precepts laid down in His Word. It is, in other words, the life of faith in Jesus Christ, lived for the glory of God.

Why is the word holy uttered three times? An ancient answer is that this has reference to the Trinity, and in the New Testament different parts of this chapter are indeed referred to the three Persons of the Trinity.[20] Delitzsch interestingly remarks:

persons and certain things" (p. 69). Rather, God is said to be holy because He is God. Certain objects are regarded as holy because they are thought to be under the divine influence. The best recent discussion is found in Vos, pp. 264-70. Cf. also M. Garcia Cordero: "El Santo de Israel" in *Mélanges Bibliques redigés en l'honneur d'André Robert* (Paris, 1957); A. Friedrichsen: *Hagios-Qadosh* (Oslo, 1916); J. Hanel: *Die Religion der Heiligkeit* (Gütersloh, 1931); H. Ringgren: *The Prophetical Consciousness of Holiness* (Uppsala, 1948).

Liebreich (*op. cit.*) points out that the word qadosh occurs once in 1:4, three times in chap. 5, namely, vv. 16, 19, 24, and three times in 6:3. In the first six chapters there are two favorite designations of the Lord, "the Lord of hosts" and "the Holy One of Israel." The first of these is found in every chapter except 4, whereas the second appears only in chaps. 1 and 5. In 5:16, 24 the two names appear in parallelism, and in chap. 6 they are equated. Hence chap. 6 forms a suitable climax to the preceding.

20 The primary thought is that of emphasis; cf. Rev. 4:8; 2 Cor. 3:18. Appeal has been made to the Latin, *Ter Optimus Maximus; Ter Geminus*, etc., and the Greek *Trismegistos*. Engnell takes this *trisagion* as a burden from the Jerusalem Temple cult, belonging "obviously" to the New Year's ritual.

"The fact that three is the number of developed and yet self-contained unity has its ultimate ground in the circumstance that it is the number of the trinitarian process and consequently the trilogy (*trisagion*) of the seraphim (like that of the cherubim in Rev. iv. 8), whether Isaiah was aware of it or no, truly pointed in the distinct consciousness of the spirits themselves to the tri-une God." At the same time we must be cautious, and Calvin is correct in remarking " . . . that the passage is not as clear as might be, and that to deduce the Trinity from this passage would only be to give occasion to the unbelievers to boast." The number three seems to be employed primarily for the sake of emphasis. In thus stressing the word *qadosh* we find the unwearied perseverance with which the seraphs cry out and perform their work. God is the threefold Holy One.

The vision made a tremendous impression upon Isaiah, and his favorite designation of God was "the Holy One of Israel." Twelve times in chapters 1-39 he employs this designation and fourteen times in chapters 40-66. "It forms an essential part," says Delitzsch, "of Isaiah's prophetic signature." Apart from the book of Isaiah it occurs in 2 Kings 19:22; Psalm 71:22; 78:41; 89:19 and Jeremiah 50:29 and 51:5, these last two passages revealing an Isaianic influence. Luzzatto makes the interesting observation that ". . . the prophet, as if with a presentiment that the authenticity of the second part of his book would be disputed, has stamped both parts with this name of God, 'the Holy One of Israel,' as if with his own seal."[21]

Herntrich asserts that men can make no assertions (*Aussagen*) about God's essence. The best that they can do is to experience God's working in their lives. Hence he exclaims about the wonder of this vision that a man who is bound to space and time may perceive this confession (*Bekenntnis*) which is essentially free of time and space. "Isaiah receives a glance into eternity. In this seeing even time stands still for him; for, what he sees, he truly sees at a definite point of history (v. 1), but it is at the same time (*doch*) the powerful anticipation of all coming time. It is God's eternity."

These words, however, confuse the question. God Himself is independent of time and space, but His creatures are not. The vision which God gave was a vision which took place in history.

---

[21] This is a nominal sentence in which "the Lord" is subject and an adjective is the predicate.

It was one of God such as only a creature could receive. It was not a vision of God as He is in Himself, but as He had accommodated Himself to the capacities of finite man. And so it will ever be. Even in eternity, man will be but a creature with the limitations that necessarily accompany anything created. He will always behold God as a creature and with the restrictions which his creaturehood imposes upon him.[22]

Herntrich, however, is right in his statement that in Psalm 2 we have an echo (possibly a forerunner) of the seraphs' song: "Yet have I set my king upon my holy hill of Zion," and Duhm rightly reminds us of the Lord's Prayer, "Hallowed be thy name."

the fullness of all the earth is his glory — The sentence may be rendered, "his glory is the fullness of all the earth." in which case the word "glory" is taken as subject and "fullness" as the complement. On this construction the thought is that the glory of God consists in all that is found in the created universe. On the other hand, the word "fullness," etc. may be taken as the subject, and this is the more natural order of the Hebrew words. The meaning is essentially the same, except that this view does not limit the glory of God to creation. It asserts that the entirety of creation, not merely the whole earth, is His glory. The reference is to the declarative glory of God. Theologians have rightly distinguished between God's essential glory, that glory which He has in and of Himself as God, and the glory which He has displayed in the created universe.[23]

What is God's glory? It is the revelation of His attributes.[24] By regarding the universe which He has created we behold His glory, His perfection and His attributes. The revelation of God in the created universe, His declarative glory, is sufficient to convince men of God's holiness, righteousness and justice as well as of His almighty power, so that man is without excuse. The

---

22 Cf. Cornelius Van Til: *The Defense of the Faith* (Phila., 1955). Reference should also be made to the standard theological treatises of Bavinck, Hodge, etc.

23 Cf. Ashbel Greene: *Lectures on the Shorter Catechism*, 2 vols., Phila., c. 1841.

24 An Akk. hymn to the moon god reads, "O Lord, thy divinity fills the wide sea with awe, as well as the distant heavens" (*ANET*, p. 385d). With respect to the relation between v. 3a and 3b, I follow König in asserting that 3b is not a causal clause and does not give the reason for the utterance of 3a; it rather is correlative, or parallel. 3b also contains a hint of rebuke to those who thought that the glory of God was to be displayed only in the Temple and only to the Jews.

entirety of creation, visible and invisible, speaks with voices clear and positive of the glory of the Holy God. Wherever we turn our eyes, we see the marks of His majesty, and should lift our hearts in praise to Him who is holy. This is His world, the wide theater in which His perfect glory is displayed.

all the earth — It is the theater, not of all the land, but of all the earth, in which His glory is disclosed and in which the great struggle between the powers of light and darkness was to take place and in which the Son, who is His perfect and final revelation, would vanquish the Prince of Darkness.

4 There were effects of this crying. The foundations of the threshold shook.[25] It is a scene of incomparable majesty. We need not assume with Calvin that no human voice could thus shake the temple, and that the crier must on that account be a divine being. The entire scene occurs within a vision, and it is the very glory and strength of the song of praise that the seraphs constantly utter which causes the thresholds to tremble.[26] In using the word *nuah* Isaiah is preparing us for what he is to say in the next chapter about the swaying of Ahaz' heart. Here, we may look at the posts of the building, swaying as it were. Later, even the heart of the king would sway as the trees before the wind.

The reason for this shaking is to be found in the voice which the criers make, as they chant the praise of the Holy One who

[25] In reading אמות 1Q supports M. Engnell would compare with the late Heb. *'ametz, ell* (the handle of a hand mill; Berachoth 18a). Cf. also the Akk. *ammatu, ell,* "cubit." Engnell thinks that if the word is connected with *'ēm,* it is used in a metaphorical sense; cf. 2 Sam. 20:19, and he interprets "pivots of the doorposts."

ימלא The imp. expresses an action which is continuous in nature and of progressive duration. We may paraphrase, "and the house was constantly being filled with smoke." The first verb is m. pl. whereas the subj. is f. It may be that m. and f. are regarded as common as in Hos. 14:1; it is also possible that, similar to the construction in Gen. 4:10, the verb is influenced by the *nomen rectum (sippim),* rather than by the *nomen regens.*

[26] For this reason I do not think that the oft-adduced words of Virgil are appropriate,

> . . . *iuga coepta moveri*
> *adventante Dea . . . (Aeneid,* VI, 255) .

Bentzen maintains that the earth under the prophet shook because of the crying, much as in 1 Kings 1:40, " . . . so that the earth rent with the sound of them." But it is not said that the ground moved, merely the posts of the threshholds.

246

sits upon the throne. In addition to this shaking, the house itself in which the scene took place, the Temple, was being filled
with smoke.[27] In the Bible smoke is often represented as a con-
comitant of the presence of God. Have we not already read,
"And the LORD will create upon every dwelling place of Mount
Zion, and upon her assemblies, a cloud and smoke by day, and
the shining of a flaming fire by night: for upon all the glory shall
be a defense" (Isa. 4:5)? Possibly the smoke is here also to be
regarded as a natural attendant of the fire upon the altar, from
which it was arising and filling the Temple. In the beholder the
smoke would have produced a solemn reverence and awe. Isaiah
is in the presence of God.

5 "But who may abide the day of his coming? and who shall
stand when he appeareth" (Mal. 3:2a)? "Who shall stand in his
holy place? He that hath clean hands and a pure heart" (Ps.
24:3, 4). But who has clean hands and a pure heart? Not
Isaiah, for when he has seen God upon the throne, he can think
only of his own uncleanness. He bursts out into an agonizing
cry. "Woe," he cries, using a word which in itself may either
indicate that calamity has fallen or is about to fall upon him.[28]
In this one piercing utterance lies his whole self-condemnation.
And he immediately appends the reason why this woe will come
upon him.

I am undone — In one word, *nidmeti*, Isaiah expressed his
thought; I have been made to cease, I am cut off, undone, doomed
to die.[29] What a terrifying evaluation, since it is true. But what

[27] The smoke did not come from the mouths of the seraphs (Duhm). The
context opposes this view. Nor does it permit Engnell's interpretation that
the smoke is simply typical of the LORD, the "atmospheric high god." Delitzsch
maintains that the smoke was the immediate consequence of the seraphs'
song of praise. Smoke, however, often appears as a consequence of or in connection
with the divine presence; cf. Isa. 4:5. It does not, however, necessarily indicate the anger of God (König).

[28] There does not seem to be much difference between אוֹי and הוֹי. The
latter may generally be rendered "oh!" or "ah!" with a tinge of sadness, or "alas!"
whereas the former is more the equivalent of "woe is me!" Cf. *'alwailu li* (so
often found in Loqman's fables). Isaiah's cry reminds one of Gideon's; cf.
Judg. 6:22; 13:22.

[29] The perf. expresses a condition that is thought to be imminent and therefore already in existence (*perfectum confidentiae*). In much of the discussion
of this word there seems to be a confusion beween the two roots *dum* and
damah. The root *dum* appears in the nouns *dumah*, "silence," e.g., Ps. 94:17,
and *dummiyah*, "silence," e.g., Ps. 39:3 and also in the word *duman*, "silence,"

caused the prophet so to speak of himself? The answer immediately follows. "I am a man," says Isaiah. A man, for he has heard angelic beings praise God, and he is but a man. His entire utterance may be rendered, "a man — unclean of lips am I." The seraphs had praised God with pure lips, and this Isaiah could not do. His lips were unclean, and that means that he as a man was unclean.[30] A sinful man, he cannot praise God, and his sinfulness manifests itself at the lips. What Isaiah must do is praise God as the seraphs were doing, but because of his depravity, he could not do this. Those whose natures are sinful cannot praise God as they should. There must first be a cleansing of the heart. The prophet must first of all be made conscious of his own sin and unworthiness before he can praise God as he should.

---

which may also appear as an adverb, Isa. 47:5. On the other hand, *dumah* means "to cease, to cause to cease," and in the *Nifal*, as here, "to be cut off, ruined, destroyed, undone." From this root is derived the noun *domi*, "quiet," Isa. 62:7. Furthermore, there is a root *damam*, "to be or to grow silent, dumb." In the light of this multiplicity of words, it may be seen how difficult it is to determine precisely the force of the present verb. Drechsler, for example, suggests that the root has original reference to the holding of the breath and then of all activity of life. Calvin likewise takes it as signifying that the prophet had been reduced to silence — so terrified as to resemble a dead man. It is perhaps better to take it in a stricter sense; lit., "I have been made to cease, i.e., I am cut off, undone, doomed to die." Vulg. translates as a causal: "because I have been silent" *(quod tacui)*, either when Isaiah should have spoken (Grotius, following an old Jewish tradition, and Jerome, *"quia tacui et non audacter Oziam regem corripui, ideo labia mea immundi sunt")* or else when he heard the song of the seraphim (Lowth). A guilty silence, on this construction (Vitringa) is the cause of the destruction. There was an ancient Rabbinical tradition to the effect that the prophet had been deprived of his office for failure to rebuke Uzziah in his presumption (2 Chron. 26: 16ff.). These are mere exegetical curiosities. Why, then, did Isaiah feel himself doomed? Bentzen, following Duhm, thinks that the reference is not to sin in the ethical sense, but only to cultic impurity. It was as one uninitiated that Isaiah saw the Lord; hence, he feared death. But the Bible nowhere teaches the necessity for initiation into divine mysteries. The reason for Isaiah's fear, which he himself gives, is far deeper.

[30] "unclean lips" — The part of the body affected by some condition, here a spiritual one, is expressed by an epexegetical gen., following the const. Note the word order of the final clause, namely: obj., verb, subj., thus emphasizing the obj. Whether this exclamation expresses a suspicion that the work to which God will call him is that of declaring His Word, that is, employing the lips in God's service, we cannot say. It may be that there is such a surmise, but the predominant thought is that of the utter unworthiness of the prophet to praise His God.

and in the midst of a people — Not only is Isaiah unfit to praise God, but the same is true of the nation in whose midst he dwells and which he represents. Because of its sinfulness, the entire nation is unfit to praise God. The theocracy, the kingdom that was intended to be the servant of the Lord, was not fit to utter His praise. Praise is a privilege, not granted to all, but only to those whose guilt has been removed.

A second reason why Isaiah believes himself to be undone is that he has seen the King.[31] The Lord is the King, the true King of the theocracy, who will further manifest His kingdom in the reign of the Messiah and the subjection of all nations. In these two expressions, "the King" and "the LORD of hosts," there is united the thought that God is the covenant God, the King of the theocracy, as well as the fact that He is the Creator, the living and true God. It is not only that Isaiah has seen God, but it is the infinite distance between the Holy God and the sinful creature which produces this prostrating effect. Indeed, even pure beings such as the seraphim must veil their faces before God.

6 Even though recognizing his sinfulness the seraphim do not banish Isaiah from the presence of the Lord. Rather, they give to him a symbolical assurance that his sins are forgiven. They were doing God's bidding, but Isaiah does not state, nor is it particularly necessary for us to know, whether this flight was suggested through a nod or beckoning of the hand, or whether it was by a direct command. One from among the number of the seraphim left that number and flew to the prophet.[32] This seraph flew and there was a hot stone in his hand.[33] It is not

---

31 כִּי is causal. This clause gives a second reason why the prophet believes himself to be undone. It was believed that men could not see God and live, Judg. 13:22; Gen. 32:31, etc. When Engnell declares that the earthly king in the cult represents and corporalizes the heavenly king, we can only reply that he has turned aside from the fact that the revelation herein recorded is supernatural. It is not a projection of the earthly king, but rather a vision of the heavenly Lord, seated upon the throne, thus revealing that He is the one true ruler, who in sovereign majesty, must subdue all His and our enemies, and to whom all men must bow.

32 "There were therefore," says Delitzsch, "a large and indefinite number."

33 "and in his hand" — A noun clause expressing the circumstances existing at the time of the action of the main verb.

רצפה . . . Hitzig thought that the seraph first took the stone with the tongs

that the seraph first flew and then with the tongs took the stone, finally taking it in his hands. Rather, he took the stone with the tongs from the altar, the stone was in his hand as he was flying.

The *ritzpah* was a stone on which the incense was placed and burned, and hence it would seem that the scene reflects upon the altar of incense rather than that of burnt offering, inasmuch as it is difficult to account for the presence of the stone upon the latter. The stone would be for the burning of the incense, and hence would be taken from that altar. At the same time, we must remember that these details of the vision are not important. As has already been remarked, the idea of the Temple is derived from the well-known earthly Temple, and merely serves as a background for the vision.

The passage clearly teaches that purity of lips can come alone from God. Isaiah had been a true believer and he had served the Lord. We are not here reading the account of his conversion. Now he is to be promoted, as it were, so that he can serve the Lord in greater measure than heretofore. "It was because the Lord intended to enlarge and extend his favour towards him, and to raise him to higher dignity, that he might have greater influence over the people; and this was rendered necessary by the character of the times, and the change which had taken place in the state" (Calvin).

In a symbolical sense fire is regarded as having purifying power. The application of fire to the lips, therefore, symbolized the fact that those lips were cleansed. This cleansing, however, is not the work of fire, but of the Lord; it rests upon the fact, as is brought out in the next verse, that a sacrifice for sin has been offered. Consequently, this passage is not simply another

---

and then with his hand. But the seraph took the stone from off the altar with the tongs, and as he flew, the stone was in his hand, probably being held by the tongs. B ἄνθρακα followed by many rabbis who render "live or glowing coal." Vulg. rightly, *calculus*, "small stone," possibly a glowing, incandescent stone. The word is a *nomen unitatis* of *retzeph*, appearing in Ar. as *ridfah*.

"tongs" . . . lit., "the takers." We should expect a *qametz* under the *q* and not *pathach*.

Some suggest that even the seraphs cannot directly touch the altar, since it has been consecrated to God. The sentence is relative in character, even though the relative pronoun is omitted; " . . . a hot stone which he had taken from the altar with the tongs."

illustration of the ancient belief that fire was regarded as possessing purifying power.[34]

7 The action of the seraph in touching the coal to the lips of Isaiah symbolized the fact that, the necessary propitiatory sacrifice having been made, his sins were forgiven. Acting in accord with God's behest, the seraph caused the stone to touch the lips of the prophet. This stone, taken from the altar, was merely a symbol of forgiveness; the fire in itself could naturally not cleanse from sin. The cleansing and purifying work is not that of the fire, but of God alone. "There is no reason to believe," said Calvin, "that the coal possessed any virtue, as superstitious persons imagine that in the magical arts there is some hidden power." God alone is the Author of forgiveness, and the seraph is but His messenger, flying to do His bidding.

Lo! this hath touched thy lips — Can a symbolical action have meaning without a verbal explanation?[35] Can revelation be by acts alone divorced from words? The prophet must be made to understand the truth itself, in distinction from the signs which symbolize that truth, and for this end words must be employed. At the same time the signs and the truth which they signify must

---

34 Gesenius has called attention to some of the ancient views. In Persian mythology, for example, the soul would have to go through fire, to be purified and to become a partaker of blessedness. In Egyptian mythology Isis placed the son of the king of Byblos in the fire to purify him from earthly impurity. Probably the doctrine of purgatory goes back to these ancient superstitions. It is a doctrine of foreign importation, not of Biblical origin. Kittel appeals to the *Fasti*, 4:785, "*omnia purgat edax ignis.*" There were similar purification rites in both Egypt and Babylonia, and among the Hittites. For the *bit rimki* rites in Mesopotamia, cf. R. Dussaud, *Les Religions de Babylonie et d' Assyrie* (Paris, 1945). In Egypt at the purification of the dead the opening or purification of the mouth was considered to be of first importance. Among the Hittites, to reconcile a person, his lips and mouth were purified. Cf. also the *surpu* rite among the Babylonians. The root *srp* is similar to that of seraphim, *srf*.

35 The fire symbolized forgiveness and cleansing. The actual cleansing was accomplished by an offering upon the altar. The touching of the lips does not signify prophetic inspiration, nor may we assume that the seraph of himself could take the initiative toward the forgiveness of sins (Duhm).

"and so [as a result of the touching] thy iniquity shall pass away" — The perf. with *wāw* cons. serves to announce a future event after the two preceding verbs which contain the reason for what is expressed by the perf. Engnell takes the verb as an emphatic perf., and renders, "Lo! when this toucheth now thy lips, thy guilt certainly departs, thy sin being expiated." This translation is possible.

not be separated. The meaning or explanation of the sign must be conveyed by words, which bring the truth to Isaiah's mind, and at the same time serve as an accompanying explanation of the sacraments and signs. Let us listen again to Calvin: "Let us therefore learn that the chief part of the sacraments consists in the word, and that without it they are absolute corruptions, such as we see every day in popery, in which the sacraments are turned into stage plays."

First of all, a verbal explanation is necessary in order to guard against false interpretations of the action. Secondly, the accompanying words are essential in order that the truth itself may be known. The seraph first calls attention to the symbol, which is important, for the symbol directs the thought to the thing symbolized, namely, the fact that Isaiah's iniquity is turned aside, and his sins forgiven. Without the spoken word the prophet would have no understanding of what was transpiring.[36]

To what sins does the seraph refer, and what is the iniquity of which he speaks? He speaks of sin in the ethical sense, sin which could preclude Isaiah from the active service of God. The seraph is not alluding to some particular sin but to sin in general. Isaiah had been a sinful man and, like all sinners, needed the forgiveness which God alone could give. He who would serve God must be one whose sins are forgiven and whose iniquity is pardoned.

and thine iniquity is turned aside — The guilt which is involved in Isaiah's iniquity is turned aside so that it no longer stands as an obstacle in the path of divine forgiveness. If iniquity stands in the way, there can be no forgiveness. That iniquity must be removed or turned aside, so that God may forgive.

and thy sin is atoned for — The necessary sacrifice has been offered upon the basis of which there may be forgiveness.[37] From

36 What I have written in the exposition is in conscious opposition to the view that the revelation of God is found in acts and not in words. Cf. e.g., G. Ernest Wright: *God Who Acts* (London, 1952).

37 "The word כפר , standing at the heart of the Hebrew sacrificial system, reveals that the worshipper felt the need of escaping the divine displeasure at sin. In this respect it appears to have had a basic propitiatory connotation, although the grammatical construction varies. The non-religious use of this verb confirms this (Gen. 32:21; Prov. 16:14) ," (Roger Nicole, "C. H. Dodd and Propitiation," *WThJ*, Vol. XVII, No. 2, May 1915, p. 152) . The basic meaning of כפר is "to cover," and this is supported by the cognate languages. With reference to sin the thought is that the person is so covered by means

this we learn that without shedding of blood there is no remission. Forgiveness is based upon propitiation.

b. *The mission of Isaiah the prophet* (6:8-13)

8 And I heard the voice of the Lord saying, Whom shall I send, and who will go for us? Then said I, Here am I, send me.

9 And he said, Go! and thou shalt say to this people, Hear ye indeed, but perceive not, and see ye indeed, and know not.

10 Make the heart of this people fat, and make its ears heavy, lest it see with its eyes, and hear with its ears, and perceive with its heart, and turn and be healed.

11 Then said I, Lord, how long? And he said, Until cities be made desolate without inhabitant, and the houses without man and the land shall be utterly desolated.

12 And the LORD will have removed men far away, and the forsaking in the midst of the land will have become great.

13 And yet there shall be still in it a tenth; it shall again become wasting like the terebinth and like the oak which in their fallen state have substance in them, the holy seed is their substance.

8 For the first time in the vision the Lord speaks.[38] Up to this point He has been seated upon the throne, as it were, in the background. He is the Lord, *Adonai,* the sovereign One, and He speaks. His question directs attention to the one who is to be sent. Whom? that is the question of the Lord. Among all the inhabitants of earth, among all the men of Judah . . . whom? It is God Himself who gives this commission, and this He does by means of a rhetorical question designed to elicit a response upon the part of Isaiah.

---

of a sacrifice that the sin can no longer be seen; the sin is atoned for. God does not see the sin and hence it is propitiated. That which covers the person (namely, the sacrifice) God regards as sufficient. He is satisfied. I cannot follow Engnell (*SDK*, p. 32, n. 2) in his appeal to the *mishpi-* rites in the Akk. royal *kuppuru* ritual, or to the *stj. r'* rites in the Egy. *pr dw.'t* ritual. Cf. Driver: *JTS,* 34, pp. 34-38; Koehler Baumgartner, *BK,* pp. 451, 452.

[38] וָאֶשְׁמַע — Engnell regards the word as introducing a "temporal-hypotactical" clause, and renders, "And when I heard the voice of the Lord saying, etc., I answered, Here am I, send me." It is possible that Engnell has detected a nuance of Hebrew syntax not heretofore noticed, but I still incline to the view that the two clauses are parallel or co-ordinate, and that *wa'omar* should introduce an action which is consecutive (either logically or temporally) to the first verb. Hence, "And I heard . . . and then I said."

Why, however, does the Lord speak of Himself in the plural?[39] Is He simply employing a plural of majesty or is He also including the heavenly seraphs in His question? In carrying out His sovereign purposes God consults only with Himself. He has no need of counseling with His creatures, even with angelic creatures. Hence, it would seem wise to adopt the time-honored interpretation of the church and to regard the Lord as using the plural form to indicate that in the Speaker Himself there is a plurality of persons.[40] Let us not fear to acknowledge that here is an adumbration of the doctrine of the Trinity which in the New Testament receives its fuller revelation. It is this great God who here permits Isaiah a glimpse into the very nature of His being, who cries for a messenger that will go for His benefit.

Isaiah's response is immediate. A moment before he had feared that there was no hope for him; now, however, that he has received the assurance of the forgiveness of his sins and understands that God will not banish him from His presence, he is ready to do service for the sovereign Lord. It is the readiness of true faith. Indeed, even before the prophet knows what God's bidding is, he is willing to do that bidding. Here in this matchless passage we find the reason why so few are willing to serve God. They need above all the conviction of sin. Only when a man has been convicted of sin and has understood that the Redeemer has borne the guilt of his sin is he willing and ready joyfully to serve God, to go wherever God may call him. Does our day and age have any greater need than the preaching of the law, that men may know of their sin, and the gospel, that they may look to Him who has turned aside their iniquity and pardoned their sin? *"Then* will I teach transgressors thy ways; and

---

[39] "for us" — The most commonly accepted view is that the seraphim are included as members of the heavenly court. In favor is the naturalness of the view and the fact that the seraphim have just been mentioned. But nowhere is God represented as deliberating with creatures as to His purposes. The passages which are usually adduced to support such a position are really irrelevant; cf. 1 Kings 22:19ff. and Dan. 4:14. An Assyrian text reads, *"mannu lushpur,"* cf. Tallqvist: *Die assyrische Beschwörungsserie Maqlu* (1895). Does this show that the LORD's question is a "consecrated formula" (Engnell)?

[40] This statement must be guarded. We are far from saying that the doctrine of the Trinity, in its fullness, was revealed in the Old Testament. All we are saying is that this particular passage and others, e.g., Gen. 1:26, suggest that there is a plurality of persons in the Speaker. It is a foreshadowing of the doctrine which God graciously revealed in fuller measure to the saints of New Testament times.

sinners shall be converted unto thee. Deliver me from blood-guiltiness, O God, thou God of my salvation: and my tongue shall sing aloud of thy righteousness. O Lord, open thou my lips; and my mouth shall shew forth thy praise" (Ps. 51:13-15).

9 Upon the expression of Isaiah's willingness, the command follows immediately. Messengers of God are sent, and they are sent that they may speak. God's message to mankind comes in words, and the proclamation of those words is the task of those who go. The accomplishment of the work of God is missionary throughout. "This prediction," remarks Alexander, "is clothed in the form of an exhortation or command addressed to the people themselves, for the purpose of bringing it more palpably before them, and of aggravating their insanity and wickedness in ruining themselves after such a warning."

Of particular interest is the form of the prophecy. In most prophetic language (in accordance with what is taught in Num. 12:1-6) there is likely to be somewhat of obscurity. In the present prophecy, however, this obscurity is removed (even though the message itself was received in vision) and the doom of the people is foretold in words that cannot be misunderstood. The guilt of the nation, as a result, stands out in bolder relief. The people are commanded to do the very thing that will bring about their ruin. Probably there is a certain amount of irony. "Hear," we may envision the prophet crying, "but of course you will not hear." It was thus that our Lord spoke to the Jews of His day, "Fill ye up then the measure of your fathers" (Matt. 23:32). We may listen again to Alexander: "This form of speech is by no means foreign from the dialect of common life. As J. D. Michaelis well observes, it is as if one man should say to another in whose good resolutions and engagements he had no faith, 'Go now and do the very opposite of all that you have said.'"

to this people — Of the people God had already said, "My people doth not consider." This people is My people. Here, however, He does not identify them. Here He does not call them, "My people." They are His, but they are untrue to Him and a people which had contemned Him (1:4). It may be that in this designation there is a tone of depreciation. This people is one that no longer cares for Me.[41]

---

[41] Cf. Exod. 32:9; Isa. 9:16; etc. The phrase seems to indicate the nation as superstitious or in unbelief (Duhm). Boehmer ("Dieses Volk," *JBL*, 1926-

Hear ye indeed — Employing what may well have been a proverbial form of expression Isaiah gives these words a depth of
meaning which they never had before.[42] To whom does he
speak? To the entire nation, to Israel alone, or to Judah alone?
These questions may be difficult to answer, but primarily at
least Judah is in view. What the prophet commands of this
people is a continual hearing, an ever renewed hearing. Hear
ye continually. What is the nation to hear? — the words of the
prophet, the written Scriptures, the revealed commands of God.
That there might be no excuse for not understanding them,
these messages were to be heard. At the same time, the nation
was forbidden to understand. "Israel does not know: my people
do not understand." These words from the first chapter stand
out in the background. "The doom of the people," remarks
Gray, "is inevitably fixed; there is to be no further healing of
their sick state (cp. 1:5ff.); let them now persist in their insensi-
tivity (cp. 1:3) to the voice and will of God: even the prophet's
preaching is but to render them blinder, deafer, and more in-
sensitive."

Likewise the nation was to behold wondrous miracles and works
of deliverance that God would accomplish and had accomplished
on behalf of His people.[43] The meaning of the great things that
they had seen, however, they would not understand. "And Moses
called unto all Israel, and said unto them, Ye have seen all that
the LORD did before your eyes in the land of Egypt unto Pharaoh,
and unto all his servants, and unto all his land: the great temp-
tations which thine eyes have seen, the signs, and those great
miracles: Yet the Lord hath not given you an heart to perceive,
and eyes to see and ears to hear, unto this day" (Deut. 29:2-4).

---

27) rejects Duhm's view and claims that the phrase never has a derogatory
sense but expresses the LORD's pity for the nation.

42 Demosthenes, *Contra Aristogenes*, I, "ὥστε τὸ τῆς παροιμίας, ὁρῶντας μὴ
ὁρᾷν, καὶ ἀκούοντας μὴ ἀκούειν.

"hear" — After a finite verb the inf. abs. expresses continued, intensive action. Thus, "hear ye continually." This is really an adverbial usage, and the
inf. is to be regarded as adverbial. The Akk. inf. has the adverbial *u* ending,
ka-ša-dum ik-šu-du. Kissane tones down the force of the imper. by saying,
"The imperatives are really equivalent to indicatives — 'you hear . . . you
see'." The strengthening of the imper. by the inf., however, militates against
this interpretation.

43 ראו . . . note the orthography. The vowel corresponds precisely with
the *a* in the Akk. inf. *pa-râ-sum*.

It was not darkness and a famine of hearing the word of God that would destroy the nation; it was light, too much light. It was this very light which would blind the people.

10 It is to Isaiah himself that the Lord now utters His command. He is charged to work in such a manner that his labors will bring about a hardening of heart and sensibility upon the part of the nation, so that there will be no possibility of its being saved. The heart with which men understand is to be made fat so that it is gross and callous and hence cannot perceive nor understand the divine message. In the Bible the heart is generally conceived as the center not merely of the understanding but indeed of the entire man.[44] It is the man himself, then, that is to be made callous when he hears Isaiah's preaching, so that he will not believe. Again, God simply speaks of the nation as "this people." He no longer refers to them as "my people."

The ears, the normal organs of hearing, are also to be made so dull that they cannot even hear the spoken word, and the message of truth, which should bring light, is to bring light so blinding that the eyes will not be able to see.[45] It will, as it were, have the effect of placing a veil over the eyes. Preaching is thus compared to the act of smearing something over the eyes.

lest it see with its eyes — Interesting and forceful is the chiastic arrangement.

> Heart   ears   eyes — eyes   ears   heart.

In the second half of the verse there is another chiastic arrangement;

> lest it see with its eyes — and with its ears it hear.

It is of course a metaphorical seeing; it is nevertheless a seeing

---

[44] השע — 1Q *hshm*. Note the *Patah* which is present because of the guttural, but is surprising in pause. ושמע also in pause with *Rebi 'a;* inasmuch as it brings to a close the first member of the group, there should be a small pause made with this word. Thus:

    a. lest it see with its eyes and with its ears it hear;
    b. and its heart perceive and it turn,
    c. and there be healing unto it.

The first member (a) relates to the outward means of perception. In (b), however, it is the heart which perceives, and the result of this perception is the repentance of the nation. Hence, (a) and (b) are to be separated. Furthermore, in (a) itself there is a chiastic arrangement, namely a—b : : : b—a. For these reasons we see why there should be a pause after (a).

[45] This description is used elsewhere of the tongue, Exod. 4:10; of the eyes, Gen. 48:10 and of the ears, Isa. 59:1.

of things as they actually are: the nation's sinfulness and its need for repentance. If the eyes of the people behold its true condition, it will abhor that condition and turn from it. One will not repent of sin until he first sees that he is a sinner. Such "seeing" is a gift of God, but that gift would be withheld from this people.

How often God had commanded the world to hear His word. In this hearing which is enjoined upon all people there is included an understanding and a willingness. Isaiah's ministry, however, is to counteract this command. He is to preach so that men cannot do what they have been commanded to do. And yet, the responsibility and guilt lie upon the nation. Zechariah later comments on them (7:11, 12), "But they refused to hearken, and pulled away the shoulder, and stopped their ears, that they should not hear. Yea, they made their hearts *as* an adamant stone, lest they should hear the law, and the words which the LORD of hosts hath sent in his spirit by the former prophets: therefore came a great wrath from the LORD of hosts. Therefore it is come to pass, *that* as he cried, and they would not hear; so they cried, and I would not hear, saith the LORD of hosts."

The entrance of the words of God giveth light, and the preaching of the gospel should result in the opening of the eyes of the understanding. Hence it appears that those who are in need of conversion are also in need of and are without a true understanding. Only to those who have been delivered from their sins is there understanding. If there is to be understanding there must be a change of heart. But when Isaiah preaches, the heart will not understand and consequently will not turn.

In all this activity and proclamation of Isaiah there is an end to be achieved. It is a negative end; the people must not turn from their sins to God, for if they turn they will be healed. Strange indeed are the ways of the great God. He commands that all men hear His word and walk in His paths. At the same time He sends forth a messenger to prevent this result from occurring. He opposes the Word of God with the Word of God. How can this be explained? Surely God's great command that all men should hear and obey His word has not been abrogated! Those who do not hear that word will be held guilty of disobedience. At the same time, if God would abide true to His promises, it was necessary that some do not hear that word. The nation had so sinned and hardened its heart that it contained within it the seeds of its own destruction. The theocracy must come to an end. But if the theocracy must come to an end, it must be a theocracy which will have no concern for God, that is, it must in actual fact no longer be a theocracy. Isaiah's ministry was to preach to stony soil, so that it might be apparent that the people were no longer the theocracy, and that they were rightfully ripe for banishment from their land. God's work of hardening therefore attests the fact that the time for the banishment from Palestine was at hand.

Another problem confronts us. What is the relationship of these verses to the Scriptural doctrine of reprobation? Some would apparently think that there is no relation and would take the imperatives as futures.[46] On this interpretation we are simply to understand that the people will refuse to hearken and so will lose their spiritual receptivity and will not repent. Isaiah, on this construction, will simply preach to rebellious people who will harden themselves in their hardheartedness. But this interpretation does not do justice to all the facts of the case. It is apparent that the result of Isaiah's preaching is foreseen by God. Isaiah is commanded to preach in such a manner that a particular result will be the consequence. Now, if God foresees that such a particular result will be the consequence, it is clear that that particular result is certain and that it has already been determined by God. From this conclusion there is no escape. In His mysterious wisdom God had foreordained that this people would not respond to the blessed overtures of the gospel. In His sovereign good pleasure He had passed them by, not ordaining them unto life eternal, and for their sin had ordained them to dishonor and wrath.

We must then note the theological implication of the passage. The blindness of the nation is to be ascribed to its own depravity. When the prophet commands the people to hear, he commands them to do something which would bring salvation, and at the same time testifies to the fact that the message which he proclaims is designed for and is suitable for the instruction of the hearer. In preaching, Isaiah is offering hearing, sight and understanding to a deaf, blind and ignorant people. These blessings come with the message as its fruits, when the Spirit of God applies that

[46] Gesenius regarded the imperatives as having future force. Bewer wrote: "But they will continually refuse to heed and thereby lose their spiritual receptivity and capacity to repent and the possibility of being saved." We should see rather the result of Isaiah's preaching, which was, of course, foreseen by God. Nor is it correct to render, "Preach that the heart is fat," etc.

message to the heart. It is therefore not the content of the message itself which is a savor of death unto death. "Such blinding," says Calvin, "and hardening influence does not arise out of the nature of the word, but is accidental, and must be ascribed to the depravity of man." The ungodly, Calvin goes on to say, have no right to object to the preaching of the Truth as though the proclamation of that Truth in itself brought evil effects. The evil effects come not from the Word, but from the heart of man, which stands in desperate need of regeneration. "The whole blame," Calvin continues, "lies on themselves in altogether refusing it admission; and we need not wonder if that which ought to have led them to salvation becomes the cause of their destruction."

"Yet if you inquire into the first cause, we must come to the predestination of God." Jennings seeks to explain the situation by means of the following illustration. He speaks of carrying a lantern into a dark barn at night. At once all the unclean creatures of darkness, the rats and the mice to whom darkness is congenial, will flee from the light and will scatter to the darkness, but creatures of the light, such as the birds, will fly to the light. "The lantern comes into the darkness for judgment, and exposes the true state of all — what they really are, and what must be their natural place according to that nature." This illustration is, however, woefully inadequate. The gospel does far more than bring to the light the fact that some men love darkness and others the light. It would be more in keeping with Scripture and hence more accurate to say that all men love the darkness; all men, in the language of the above illustration, are creatures of the darkness, and when light appears, rather than fly to it they seek deeper darkness. Some of these creatures of darkness, however, are transformed by the gospel so that they love the light. A new heart is given to them, a heart that is the gift of the Spirit of God. That which makes a distinction among men is grace, sovereign grace, and sovereign grace alone. According to the teaching of the Old Testament — we need not even turn to the New — salvation is of the Lord. Calvin therefore is right when he says that the "first cause" of the condition of the nation is the predestination of God.

At the same time we must make a distinction between the proximate and the ultimate cause of the hardened condition of the heart. The proximate cause of the nation's callousness was to be found in its sinful heart. The ultimate cause, however, was the reprobating decree of God. The elect are not saved because they are creatures of light; they too were creatures of darkness and in them there was no goodness, nothing that would attract the light. God, however, out of His mere good pleasure did choose them and ordain them to life eternal, and when the blessed gospel was heard by them, they were given a heart that was then willing and able to hear and to respond. Those, however, whom God did not ordain to life eternal, He passed by and for their sin ordained to dishonor and wrath.[47]

One cannot but admire and even love Isaiah for his willingness and readiness to serve God, even though he was told that his labors would appear to be fruitless. From this we learn the necessity for continuing in the work of the gospel, even when outward success does not appear to attend our work. It may be that apparent lack of outward success is in part due to our own inefficiency; our task, however, is to be faithful. May God grant that His church may have ministers who, above all else, are faithful, even as was Isaiah.

11 *Lord, how long?* — Out of love for and concern over his people Isaiah raises the question.[48] It is really a prayer uttered

---

[47] Several passages speak of God hardening the heart: Exod. 4:21; Deut. 2:30; Rom. 1:28; 2 Thess. 2:11. For a recent Scriptural presentation of the doctrine of reprobation, cf. Van Til, *op. cit.*, pp. 413ff.

"and be healed" — Lit., "and there be healing to it." The indefinite subject is expressed by the 3rd person m.s. For the N.T. usage of this passage, cf. Young: *Thy Word Is Truth* (Grand Rapids, 1957), pp. 157-61.

[48] Cf. Ps. 94:3; Zech. 1:12; Ps. 6:4; etc. Kittel, following Hitzig, thinks that Isaiah asks how long this preaching *(Verstockungspredigt)* must continue. The phrase corresponds to the *adi mati* of the Akk. supplications.

"How long, O my Lord,
will mine enemies cast evil glances at me . . . .
How long, O my Lord,
will the miserable lillu come towards me . . . .
How long, O my Lord,
art thou angry and thy soul in anger?
How long, O my Lord,
art thou enangered, and is thy visage turned away?
Turn thy neck toward him whom thou hast rejected.
For a word of grace, set thy face."

The text is found in Dhorme, *Choix de textes religieux Assyro-Babyloniens* (Paris, 1907). Engnell regards this expression as a "technical term from the phraseological fund of the lamentation psalms." On the other hand, Isaiah may have asked how long for the simple and uncomplicated reason that he wanted to know how long.

261

on behalf of his people. Will there be no end to this hardness of the people? How long will they continue to be hard of heart? When will the period of grace begin? Will God always chide? Will He keep His anger forever? How great will the wrath be? It is a question that the prophet must ask. He cannot defend his people. God's judgment upon them is true; that Isaiah knows. Nor does he even dare suggest that God modify His judgment. That he cannot do. God's pronouncement is true; it cannot be modified. But Isaiah is concerned for the nation, and his concern is prompted from his own affection toward the people.

Thus he is placed in a twofold position. With eager desire and true faithfulness he must proclaim the message of God, even when that message involves the announcement of the nation's hardening. On the other hand, in no disloyalty to his message and with the utmost concern that it be declared in its fullness, he must manifest anxiety and love toward those to whom he is called to preach. "These two feelings," says Calvin, "though they appear to be inconsistent, are in full harmony." They must supplement one another. On the one hand, natural affection toward those to whom one must preach will prevent a cold and harsh, or even cruel presentation of the truth. On the other, natural feelings and affections must not prevent the minister from declaring the entire truth. Here is the problem that must be faced by all true ministers of God. And the deepest, the truest, the most sincere and earnest love for the people to whom we minister will be shown only when we declare to them in loving, yet firm, fashion the whole counsel of God. Anything less than full proclamation of the truth is a manifestation of a spirit of self-interest, not of true love. Genuine love to our people demands that we tell them the truth.

Again Isaiah addressed God as *Adhonai*, thus acknowledging His supreme power. It is a fitting designation in this connection, for it admirably expresses the sovereignty which is manifest in the disposition of the welfare of both nations and individuals.

and he said — The answer of God continues until the close of verse 13. Until the condition be fulfilled that cities be desolate, the hardness of the nation will abide. These cities of Judah, now populous, filled with those who now have no time for God, will at that time be utterly desolate, for they will have no inhabitants. They will become ghost cities, no cities at all. Likewise the individual houses will have no one within them, and for that reason the cities will be without inhabitants. The cultivated

262

land, fruitful and exuberant, will become a *shamamah*, a desolated land.[49] Such will be the ravages of war, and this will occur at the time of the exile. But there is a deeper fulfillment than the exile. The inspired writer of the Gospel says, "Therefore they could not believe, because that Esaias said again, He hath blinded their eyes, and hardened their hearts; that they should not see with their eyes, not understand with their heart, and be converted, and I should heal them" (John 12:39, 40). From this we may see that a prophecy is capable of more than one fulfillment. Before these judgments are completed the land will be wasted completely.

12 The judgment will be carried out in that men will be brought into exile.[50] This is a specific example of the process of purification. The LORD, who chose Israel and gave her the land of promise, will now remove her from that land. Indeed He will remove her far, to a great distance, and thus we have a general description of the exile. "The children also of Judah

---

[49] "until" — Cf. Gen. 28:15; Num. 32:17. *ad* alone is found in Gen. 24:19, **33**; Ruth 2:21. שאו — The *futurum exactum;* the perf. serves to express a condition which is fut. and yet which is regarded as certain of coming to pass, "shall have been made desolate."

[50] Because of the change in subject Marti and others think vv. 12 and 13 are a later addition and not an integral part of the prophecy itself. Also, inasmuch as in v. 11 the people were removed from the land, there was nothing remaining to be taken far away, hence v. 12, even as far as contents are concerned, is said not to belong after v. 11. In answer it may be pointed out that in the midst of a passage in which God is speaking, God often appears in the third person, cf. 3:17 (König gives over forty examples in his *Stylistik*, p. 154). Bentzen takes vv. 12 and 13 as Isaiah's own interpretation of the vision. Since the discovery of the Qumran manuscript, which gives these verses essentially the same there has been less of a tendency to regard them as out of place, or M as corrupt, ורחק . . . . König thinks that the verb is not dependent upon the "until" of v. 11. Grammatically, it need not be, and hence may be taken as explanatory or illustrative of what had been stated in v. 11.

"men" — Here is the heart of the removal. Man as such, will be taken away. The first instance of such a removal is seen in the exile; cf. 5:13; Deut. 28: 63-67; etc.

"and great will be the forsaking" — If עזובה is similar in form to *melûkāh* it may be regarded as a noun.

"forsaking — If it is a *Qal* pass. part., however, it should be rendered, "forsaken" or "unoccupied." It may refer either to the land as forsaken, or else to the act of forsaking itself. The root appears in 7:16; 17:23; 27:10 and 62:12.

"the midst of the land" — Where the population had been thickest, the emptying will be greatest.

and the children of Jerusalem have ye sold unto the Grecians, that ye might remove them far from their border" (Joel 3:6).

When God removes men far from their own land, there will be a great forsaking: either that the land itself will be unoccupied, forsaken land, or a forsaking as such will take place.

13 Despite the tragedy of the desolation, there will come forth a new Judah from the holy seed. In the "and yet" we may see a "there shall be."[51] A tenth is a small proportion indeed, and even this tenth will again become a wasting.[52] Even though a tenth should survive the exile, it itself will again be subject to a wasting, and in this wasting it is compared with the oak and terebinth trees. The *elah* is an old and durable tree, and as such is often mentioned in Scripture, and the *allon* is an oak. Hence, the tenth will not be completely destroyed. "However frequently," says Alexander, "the people may seem to be destroyed, there shall still be a surviving remnant, and however frequently that very remnant may appear to perish, there shall still be a remnant of the remnant left, and this indestructible residuum shall be the holy seed, the true church" . . . (Rom. 11:5).

[51] The reading of 1Q has caused some interesting interpretations. Hvidberg, "The Masseba and the Holy Seed," in *Interpretationes (Mowinckel Festschrift)*. Oslo, 1955, pp. 97-99, interprets, "which lie flung down upon the pillar in the high place." Albright, "Like the terebinth goddess and the oak of Asheriah, cast out with the stelae of the high place" ("The High Place in Ancient Palestine," *VTS*, 1957, pp. 242-58). S. Iwry ("Masseboth and Bamah in 1Q ISAIAH 6," *JBL*, Vol. lxxvi, Part III, Sept. 1957, pp. 225-32) first takes the relative as a noun and translates Asherah. The word *bamah* he also takes as a noun and construes it with *matzebet*, thus obtaining the rendering, "like a terebinth, or an oak, or an Asherah, when flung down from the sacred column of a high place." This requires the omission of the last three words of the verse, and these words are retained in 1Q. B may be translated, "when it falls from its vault (chest) tomb." Cf. Millar Burrows: *More Light on the Dead Sea Scrolls*, 1958, pp. 146ff.

[52] "and yet" — These words may also be rendered as a hypothetical clause, "and if there be still in it a tenth part, it shall again be consumed." Cf. Isa. 4:2; etc. "in it" — I.e., the land.

"it shall become" — Lit., it shall return and be for a wasting, etc. In the *Piel* בער may mean both "to burn" and "to waste, consume"; cf. 3:14. The inf. with *lamed* after a form of *hyh* expresses destination. Note also that the perf. with *wāw* cons. may introduce an apodosis after a nominal sentence which acts as a protasis. The two verbs introduced by *wāw* cons. are co-ordinate one to another. With respect to the last clause Kissane well remarks, "The final clause is necessary to represent the prophet's teaching with complete accuracy — the destruction of the nation, and the survival of a remnant to be the nucleus of a glorified Sion."

When the tree has fallen or even when it has been cut down, there may yet remain life within it. This substance is in both teil and terebinth when they are lying in a felled state.[53] This life is that which endures. Just as the fallen tree has life and substance within it, so in the tenth which has again become a burning there is also substance, and this substance is the holy seed. This seed is holy. It is the elect, those who are preserved by the mercy of God. A remnant which can be called holy, as earlier in the chapter God Himself was designated holy, is one which can survive. Hence, it is a spiritual seed, partaking of holiness, and in such a holy seed the promises of salvation are to be realized. God's blessed purposes were those of salvation, and although judgment must come upon the chosen people in blow after blow, nevertheless no judgment would utterly wipe out the nation until the promises were fulfilled in Christ.[54]

[53] אֵלוֹן is a species of quercus, the oak. In Palestine it has narrow leaves and blossoms without corollas and does not drop its leaves.
"in their fallen state" — Probably a *Piel* inf. with f. ending; cf. Lev. 26:18. The word designates the state or condition of the tree after it has been felled. An active sense does not well fit the context. The comparison of the nation to a tree does not go back to ancient mythology. Engnell thinks that there is reference to the Tammuz pole.
[54] Very different, however, is the view of Herntrich. It is a return, he says, not to life, but to destruction. There is no remnant, cf. Amos 3:12. Hope and promise are hidden in chap. 6 and have their basis in the song of the seraphs. It is the question "how long?" proclaimed by one who had himself been saved as by fire, which is a mark of hope. Thus, by their exclusion of a remnant, even the last words include a promise of hope. Herntrich regards chap. 6 as a witness to the God who forgives sins and saves from death, whose majesty once for all became revealed in Jesus Christ. Thus, this chapter is a witness to the eternal Word. The forgiveness is an eternal forgiveness, which surpasses (*umspannt*) the year of Uzziah's death, as it transcends all dates. Isaiah is a witness of the eternal Word and yet already in the years 739-738 before Christ's birth he is a member of the community which was founded through the Word.
But this language in reality divorces the Word of God from history and makes the proclamation of the Christ-event, or Christ-moment, something divorced from the actual saving work of the Jesus Christ of history. Isaiah 6 is not merely a witness to some eternal Word; it is rather a direct prediction and prophecy of the historical Jesus Christ. "These things said Esaias, when he saw his glory, and spake of him" (John 12:41). The chapter, we believe, closes on a note of hope, a remnant which is holy will be preserved, and this remnant will find salvation because once in history our Lord died on the cross.

2. The Crisis and the Promise (7:1-25)

a. *Ahaz the fearful* (7:1-9)

1 And it came to pass in the days of Ahaz the son of Jotham, the son of Uzziah, king of Judah, that Rezin the king of Syria, and Pekah, the son of Remaliah, king of Israel, went up to Jerusalem for war against it, but could not prevail against it.

2 And it was told the house of David, saying, Syria is resting upon Ephraim; and his heart was moved and the heart of his people as the trees of the forest are moved from before the wind.

3 Then the LORD said unto Isaiah, Go out now to meet Ahaz, thou and Shear-yashub thy son, unto the end of the ascent of the upper pool, unto the way of the fuller's field.

4 And thou shalt say unto him, Take heed and be quiet, fear not, nor let thy heart be soft, for the two tails of these smoking firebrands, the burning anger of Rezin and Syria and of the son of Remaliah.

5 Because there has devised evil against thee Syria, Ephraim and the son of Remaliah, saying,

6 Let us go up against Judah and destroy her and let us make breaches in her for us, and let us cause a king to reign in her midst, even the son of Tabeel.

7 Thus saith the Lord God, It shall not stand neither shall it come to pass.

8 For the head of Syria is Damascus, and the head of Damascus is Rezin, and within sixty-five years will Ephraim be broken, that it be not a people.

9 And the head of Ephraim is Samaria and the head of Samaria is the son of Remaliah: if ye will not believe, it is because ye are not established.

1 Uzziah is dead, but Isaiah has seen the true king, the Lord of hosts. As His prophet he must face a recalcitrant and hardhearted nation, one headed by a recalcitrant and stubborn king. The ministry of hardening is beginning. Quite possibly Isaiah wrote down the contents of this chapter after Ahaz had died, and

266

now simply draws our attention to the most prominent event that had taken place during the days of Ahaz.[1] The Syrian king Rezin had come up against Jerusalem, and with him was Pekah of Israel.[2] Their purpose was to wage war, but they were unable to fight against the holy city.

During the reign of Ahaz, Syria and Israel had formed an alliance for the purpose of overthrowing the Judean king. According to 2 Kings 15:37 they had actually begun the siege of Judah during the days of Jotham. During the reign of Ahaz the northern enemies also came against Jerusalem but were unable to overcome it (2 Kings 16:5). According to 2 Chronicles 28:5 Ahaz was delivered into the hands of the Syrians who smote him, and one hundred twenty thousand men in Judah were slain. What is the relationship of these various passages?

Apparently the book of Kings gives an account of the beginning and conclusion of the campaign, whereas Chronicles presents the intervening events. It may be noted that 2 Kings 16:5 and Isaiah 7:1 are very similar. Rezin of Syria and Pekah of Israel came up against Jerusalem for war, they assert, but failed to take it.

According to 2 Chronicles 28:5 the Lord gave Ahaz into the hands of the king of Syria. There has been question as to whether this event belongs to the same campaign or to a different phase of the same campaign. It is also possible that, even though the king Ahaz was temporarily taken, the enemy could not conquer the city itself. If this were the case it would have been parallel to Nebuchadnezzar's siege of Jerusalem in which the king Jehoiakim was captured but not the city itself. To determine the precise relationship between the accounts in Kings and Chronicles

---

1 "Ahaz" — For *Yeho'achaz;* cuneiform, *Iauhazi.*

2 "Rezin"— Doubtless the instigator, hence the verb is s. Gray points out that the conjunction before Pekah is *wāw concomitantiae,* which in Ar. is followed by the acc. Thus, "Rezin, together with Pekah [he] came up." "came up" — Employed of ascent to Jerusalem from Israel, 1 Kings 22:2; 2 Kings 8:29; Acts 8:5, 15. The idea of the verb applies to Jerusalem in all the senses in which Jerusalem may be said to be exalted and lifted up. "Pekah" — Cf. 2 Kings 15:27-31. "for war against her" — Jerusalem was the principal object of their advance. The noun serves in place of an inf. עָלֹיה is not to be deleted, for the author of 2 Kings is not slavishly following Isaiah, and the minor variations in the two accounts are typical of Semitic writing; cf. G. Douglas Young (*OS,* Deel VIII, 1950, pp. 291-99). For the phrase "to fight against" cf. Jer. 34:22; 37:8.

is probably not possible with our meagre knowledge of the war. It is clear that both speak of the same war, but whether they distinguish different phases of that war we cannot be sure.

At any rate Ahaz was smitten and a great number of captives were taken from his army and they were brought to Damascus. The text does not state that Ahaz himself was taken to Damascus, and it may refer only to the prisoners of war. Apparently Ahaz was given into the hand of the king of Israel who struck him with a great blow. The spoil which had been taken from Judah was brought to Samaria.

At Samaria, however, there was a prophet named Oded, who went before the returning army, advising the return of the captives, and in this advice he was joined by certain chiefs of the Ephraimites. Consequently the prisoners were taken to Jericho, a city of Judah, and were there dismissed.

About this time Ahaz appealed to the king of Assyria for help. In the language of 2 Kings 16:7, "Then Ahaz sent messengers to Tiglath-pileser king of Assyria saying, Thy servant and thy son am I, come up and deliver me from the hand of the king of Syria and from the hand of the king of Israel who have risen up against me."

It is at this point that we must consider the relationship of Isaiah 7 to the passages in Kings and Chronicles. With slight variations 2 Kings 16:5 and Isaiah 7:1 are practically identical. Isaiah 7:1 gives a summary of the entire situation. Ahaz had already been captured and released, and the huge spoil mentioned in 2 Chronicles 28:5ff. had been taken. The meeting with Isaiah described in Isaiah 7:2ff. occurred, it would seem, after these events and before Ahaz made his appeal to Tiglath-pileser for help. Apparently what induced him to turn to Assyria was the report that Syria was resting upon Ephraim. The hostile intentions of the two enemy kings had not yet been abandoned, despite the fact that they had once released Ahaz.[3]

Objections to this reconstruction of events will of course be raised. It may be argued that Ahaz would more likely make his appeal at the first sign of threat from the north. Such need not, however, necessarily have been the case. Without doubt the measures of the north convinced Ahaz that his enemies were much stronger than they actually were. They had indeed taken much spoil; they had taken Ahaz himself; Rezin had returned

---

[3] See Introduction, "The Historical Background."

Elath, which formerly belonged to Judah, to Syria, and had driven out the Jews from there. All of this would have impressed Ahaz with the strength of his enemies.

It must furthermore be pointed out that the whole purpose of Isaiah's message was to dissuade the king from embarking upon a wrong course of action, namely, that of relying upon Assyria rather than upon the Lord. If, however, the king had already made his appeal to Assyria, Isaiah's prophecy would seem to have come too late. What point would there be in urging Ahaz to trust the Lord rather than man after the king had already placed his trust in Assyria? Why urge him to choose a sign after he had already made his decision and embarked upon his fatal course of action? If he had then reversed his decision he would have Assyria to contend with.

It may of course be maintained that as soon as the first tidings of the north's purpose had been announced and before the actual invasion had begun Isaiah was sent to Ahaz with his message. In opposition to this, however, we may note that the hostilities had evidently begun during the reign of Jotham, and so were not entirely new to Ahaz. More important, however, is the fact that both Kings and Chronicles seem to place the appeal for help after the invasion of Judah had taken place.

We assume therefore that the appeals to Tiglath-pileser occurred after Ahaz had been released from Samaria. Syria and Ephraim were evidently determined not to give up their purpose of deposing Ahaz from his throne. What had led them to repent of having followed Oded's advice we can but conjecture. Word was brought to Ahaz that Syria was resting upon Israel, and it was the announcement of this fact which brought consternation to the king so that "his heart trembled, and the heart of his people, as the shaking of the trees of the forest from before the wind." It was, in other words, a time when all appeared to be lost, and at such a moment God intervened with an announcement of hope.

2 We are not told how word came to the Davidic court that Syria was reposing upon the land of Ephraim, but this news brought great consternation to the heart of the king and his court.[4] Syria is resting upon Ephraim. In these words the heart

---

4 Some ancient interpreters understood this to mean that Syria and Ephraim were allies. Recently, De Bijbel: "*het vijandelijke leger is aangekomen en heeft zich met Ephraim verenigd.*" Kraeling: "But could not the author

of the message is to be found. In a friendly manner Syria had halted her homeward march and was still encamped in Israelitish territory. To the mind of Ahaz these tidings could be a foreboding of evil, and consequently his heart was filled with terror.[5] As the wind sways the trees of the forest, so fear swayed his quaking heart.

3 It is a time of desperate need; hence it is a time when the Lord intervenes with gracious help. Ahaz was concerned about the condition of the city. The Lord was far more concerned. How God conveyed His words to Isaiah, whether by dream or vision, we are not told. Isaiah writes in the third person and so objectifies himself and renders himself less conspicuous.[6] He is commanded to go out, not merely from his own dwelling, but from the city itself, for the king is outside the city and the prophet is to meet him where he is.[7]

In ancient times prophets had ready access to royalty. In the world generally this was true of soothsayers and diviners, but in the Old Testament the prophets are to be regarded as guardians of the theocracy.[8] When a king is about to make a foolish or sinful move, it is often the duty of the prophet to restrain him and to declare unto him the will of the Lord. Isaiah himself

---

imagine the Aramaeans as a swarm of bees or flies, who could 'alight' exactly as in the case with Egyptians and Assyrians in v. 18?" In support of this interpretation appeal is sometimes made to Exod. 10:14 and 2 Sam. 21:10. Gray, however, thinks that the passages to which appeal is made do not quite correspond to " . . . what the context seems to require, the friendly and temporary halt of an army in the country of allies."

The verb may be employed in the sense "settle down" or "alight." Such passages as Gen. 8:4; Exod. 10:14; Isa. 7:19 seem to prove this. At the same time the verb may also have the connotation, "to rest," "to repose," "to be quiet." We may appeal to Esth. 9:16, 17, 18, 22, and note that *nwh* is thus used in Ug. 95:14; 49:III:18; 2 *Aqht* II:13. This connotation fits in well with the requirements of the context, namely, that the resting of Syria in Ephraim was of a friendly nature. (The word then does not designate the relative position of armies on the field of battle.)

[5] נחה — The Masoretic accentuation makes clear that the stress falls upon the penult, and therefore the word can only be the perf. There is paronomasia between this word and נוע which follows. The f. form is probably due to the fact that the subj. is collective; cf. also 1 Sam. 17:21; 2 Sam. 8:6; Job 1:15.

[6] Isaiah uses the third person elsewhere; cf. chaps. 37 and 38.

[7] There is no implication that the king is returning from any place.

[8] I have tried to develop this thought in *My Servants the Prophets* (Grand Rapids, 1952).

270

in this instance is to go to Ahaz but he is also to take with him his son who bears the symbolical name "A remnant will return," a name which calls to mind the promise of 6:13. The presence of this son will bring vividly before the king the fact that, great as the judgment might be, there would nevertheless be a remnant delivered. The boy's very presence was to serve as a sign of hope, and would probably prepare the king for a prophecy from the Lord.[9]

It is a striking name in which the stress falls upon the remnant rather than upon the returning. There is to be a remnant, we may paraphrase, and what is significant about this remnant is the fact that it will return unto the Lord.

unto the end — Detailed instructions are given the prophet as to where he is to meet the king. Detailed as is this instruction, however, we today cannot with assurance locate the precise spot.[10] Apparently it was the same place where the Assyrian Rabshakeh later stood. "And he stood by the conduit of the upper pool in the highway of the fuller's field" (36:2b). At the point where the water left the pool Isaiah was to meet the king. How important these historical details are![11] The revelation of God was given in history and is historical in nature.

Ahaz may well have gone to this spot for the purpose of ascertaining the situation of the water supply. Would the two northern enemies be able to cut off from the city its life-supply of water? At this spot could also have been found the men who

[9] In an ordinary narrative sentence the verb should precede the subject. The rendering would then be, "a remnant will return." Koehler renders, "the remnant that will return" (*VT*, III, 1953, pp. 84ff.). As Lindblom points out, however (*A Study on the Immanuel Section in Isaiah*, Lund, 1958, p. 8), this is ruled out by Isa. 10:21, 22. I agree with Lindblom in regarding the sentence as nominal, with "remnant" as the subj. and a verbal sentence as predicate (*op. cit.*, p. 9). Lindblom is also correct in rejecting Blank's interpretation of the verb as referring to a return alive from the struggle (*JBL*, 68, 1948, pp. 211ff.). It is a return to the Lord, as is shown by the usage in 6:10, "and return and be healed."

[10] Some would place the upper pool on the northern side of the city (cf. Dalman: *Jerusalem und seine Gelände*, Gütersloh, 1930, p. 38ff.), and some would place it near the present Sitti Miriam, southwest of Jerusalem; at the foot of the so-called Zion in the Hinnom valley is a flowing spring, Siloah (8:6), also called Gihon, I Kings 1:33; 2 Chron. 32:30. It has been held that the stream from this spring divides itself, forming two pools (Neh. 2:15), the upper and lower (Isa. 22:9).

[11] Without warrant Jennings spiritualizes these descriptions. The upper pool is said to be "blessing of the Most High."

tread upon cloth, beat it and kneaded it in cold water, thus cleansing it. These were the fullers, and the field in which they worked was approached by a way or road, this way being where the king was now to be found.

4 By the upper pool stands quaking and trembling Ahaz. But the man who approaches him is not trembling. Daring to come into the very presence of kings, this man, Isaiah, cries out with the bold voice of authority. He dares in God's name to command kings, "Take heed," he enjoins, "and be quiet."[12] These are not the words of suggestion but of command. They are to be obeyed unquestioningly. Why should Ahaz tremble? Let him rather stand in quiet confidence, his trust placed not upon Assyria but upon the Lord. He should see to it that he is calm. An agitated spirit does not comport with true faith; when one rests upon the Lord, there is no need to fear what man will do. Faith involves calmness and serenity.

Absence of fear brings calmness of spirit; indeed faith and fear are contraries one of the other. Faith in God removes fear of heart.

> Be not afraid of sudden fear,
>   neither of the desolation of the wicked when it cometh.
> For the Lord shall be thy confidence,
>   and shall keep thy foot from being taken.
>
>   (Prov. 3:25, 26)

When God says "Fear not," there is nothing to fear. Ahaz was doing something foolish. He was fearing what was not there. The dangers which he thought were present were really not present at all. Isaiah's command is deeply practical, based upon true knowledge of reality. A second negative command, indeed, a prohibition, is given, so that Ahaz may see clearly that after all there is nothing to fear and that his conduct has been foolish. Rather than shake, his heart must not be faint and timid. An agitated mind belongs to disbelief; Ahaz was the theocratic king, and of all people he should be calm and depend upon the true Ruler of the theocracy.

---

[12] השמר — The form with *Tzere* is probably for the purpose of establishing assonance with השקט; cf. 30:15. Two positive and two negative commands are given the king that he may see that he has nothing to fear. בחרו — *BH* suggests emending to *min*, which is unnecessary, for *beth* may mean "from," like Akk. *ina,* Egy. *m,* and Ug. *b.* If so, the preposition sets forth the reason, "because of."

272

from the two — Because there are two smoking tails of fire-brands — they are not even firebrands — there is no reason for fear.[13] The strength of the enemy is practically played out. Once there had been fire and a flame; now only smoking tails of wood. Gone is the strength; and the wood is charred. Burning pieces of wood — charred and smoking. What then is there to fear from Rezin and his people and that man of ignoble descent, the son of Remaliah? Against the son of David, to whom the throne and kingdom rightfully belonged, the son of a certain Remaliah, without divine authority and promises, would raise his hand.[14] The son of David need not fear any son of Remaliah.

5 Syria has decreed, and the nature of her decree is evil, for it does not bode well for Ahaz.[15] Aiding Syria is the northern kingdom with its insignificant king, that son of Remaliah.

Isaiah does not hesitate to use scorn. By omitting the actual name and merely referring to the king as the son of Remaliah, he expresses his disdain.

6 Here we are told what Syria's evil counsel is. To reach Jerusalem the enemy had to ascend, and so they purposed to do. When they had ascended to the capital city they intended to destroy it[16] and thus to break its defenses, so that it would be theirs. Back of this program of evil stood out the ultimate purpose. Over Jerusalem there was to reign a man whom Syria and Ephraim chose, a man who would support them in their opposition to Assyria. This man, the son of Tabeel, would be their ally. In place of the son of David, the son of Tabeel was to reign; in place of the legitimate king, a usurper.[17]

---

13 "firebrands" — Amos 4:11 shows that this was a piece of burning wood. Cf. Zech. 3:2.

14 V. 4b is explanatory of 4a. The preposition *b*, "from," is parallel to *min*, "from," of 4a.

15 The principal actor is Syria, and hence the verb is placed in s. The Israelitish king is again designated "the son of Remaliah." Were it not for the first verse, his name would not be known, an incidental evidence of genuineness. Note 1 Sam. 20:27, 30; 22:12.

16 Eitan compares Ar. *qāda* and *baqaʿa* and would render, "Let us go up to Judah, and break it up, and make it over to our side, etc." S. Speier (*JBL*, March 1953, p. xiv) also renders, "let us destroy." He points out that verbs beginning with *qa* have the notion of "cutting off." Inasmuch as Judah is mentioned, the verbal suffixes probably refer to it.

17 See Introduction, "The Historical Background."

7 We have heard the counsel of Syria; let us now hear the counsel of the Sovereign One, Yahweh, who alone has power to carry out His designs. In a word we are told that the plans of Syria and Ephraim will not be fulfilled.[18] The general denial of Syria's counsel is first given, and then the details follow, the verses 7 to 9 forming an apodosis to verses 5 and 6. It is Yahweh, not Syria and Ephraim, nor for that matter Ahaz with his eyes toward Assyria, who disposes of the destinies of nations. He alone can frustrate the designs of men to bring them into conformity with His own will.

Abrupt and to the point is the message. The plan will not stand. It will fail and it will not eventuate. It cannot be carried through. True, it may originate; it has, indeed, already originated, but it will not be continued through to fruition. The negative is strong; for it is a direct denial. Thus Ahaz is graciously given an insight into the future. It is not the opinions of a fellow man with which he is confronted here; these are the revealed words of Almighty God.

8 God is good to Ahaz. Instead of giving him a mere denial, absolute as is that denial, He goes on to give him a reason for the denial. "The counsel will not stand," so we may paraphrase, "for the capital of Syria is Damascus, and will continue to be. That situation will continue without the addition of Judah. And the head of Damascus, the capital, is the king Rezin, and he shall continue as king over the land as it was then organized without the addition of Judah."[19]

---

18 "it shall not stand" — The 3rd f. is used as the predicate of a f. subj. which has not been mentioned but which is in the mind of the speaker. Cf. also Isa. 14:24. תקום may signify "to come into being" as well as "to continue permanently." In the light of the parallel verb it is perhaps to be understood in this sense.

19 Lindblom suggests that the king was tendentiously called Resin, "pleasure," suggesting the root rṣṣ, "crush." Possibly so. Procksch, Herntrich, Mowinckel, Steinmann, etc. would add something like, "but the true king of Judah is Yahweh." Vischer proposes: *"Das Haupt von Juda ist Jerusalem, und Jerusalems Haupt der Sohn Davids"* (*Die Immanuel Botschaft im Rahmen des königlichen Zionsfestes*, Zollikon-Zürich, 1955, p. 18). Vriezen takes *ki* as concessive, *"mag auch das Haupt von Aram Damaskus, usw."* (although the head of Syria is Damascus, etc.).

As the text stands the basis for the assertions made in v. 7 are found in 8a and 9a. On the other hand, both 8a and 9a are complemented by 8b and 9b respectively. 9b is somewhat of a parallel to 8b, standing in relationship to 9a as 8b to 8a. There is thus given a symmetry which should not be de-

Syria is the more prominent of the two enemies. As long as Syria stands, Damascus will be her capital, and Rezin the head of Damascus. As for Ephraim, however, we may note in passing that within sixty-five years she will cease from being a people. While she does exist, Samaria will be her capital, and the son of Remaliah her head. The thought may be expressed by the following arrangement of the lines:

> For the head of Syria is Damascus,
> And the head of Damascus is Rezin.
> (And in sixty-five years Ephraim
>   shall cease from being a people.)
> And the head of Ephraim is Samaria
> And the head of Samaria Remaliah's son.
> If ye will not believe, it is because
>   ye are not established.

In this arrangement Syria is given the position of priority, and Ephraim is introduced almost as an afterthought. What did Isaiah mean by the reference to the sixty-five years until Ephraim's destruction?

It would seem that at least three events were to be included. In the first place there is the invasion of Tiglath-pileser, which took place at about this time (2 Kings 15:29, 16:9). Secondly, the conquest of Samaria itself and the consequent deportation of the ten tribes (2 Kings 17:6). Even after this event, however, the nation Israel was yet regarded as standing. During the reign of Manasseh another race was introduced by Esar-haddon (2 Kings 17:24; Ezra 4:2; 2 Chron. 33:11). From the Bible itself it would seem to be impossible to determine precisely the year in which the deportation of Manasseh occurred. According to Esar-haddon's own inscription (681-669), however, Manasseh was listed as one of the kings of the Hittite country who were in vassalage to him. If the present prediction were uttered in 734, as is probably the case, and Manasseh were carried away captive in

---

stroyed. Syria is elevated to a position of prominence, and Ephraim is thrown in almost as an afterthought. Fullerton (*JBL*, Vol. 35, p. 140-42) takes the text as follows. 8a is Ahaz' thought, and to this Isaiah responds, "Within . . . Damascus will be destroyed." 9a is also Ahaz' thought, and this is followed by a response of Isaiah, "Within . . . Damascus will be destroyed." This again involves a drastic and unwarranted reconstruction of the text.

יחת is *Niphal* imp; *yinḥaṯ* $>$ *yi(ḥ)ḥaṯ* $>$ *yēḥaṯ*. מעם — that it be not a people, lit., *from* the status of a *people*.

669, the 18th year of Manasseh's sole rule, and the 27th year if the years of co-regency with Ahaz be counted, we have exactly sixty-five years. Manasseh might then have been permitted to continue his reign in Palestine, after he had been brought in bonds to Babylon and made a subject of the Babylonian king.

On the other hand, it may be that Isaiah is simply employing a round number, and merely intends to say that by about 670 B.C. the nation Israel would cease to exist as a separate people. If that be the case, the difficulty practically vanishes. The message which we are now considering probably was delivered in the year of the beginning of the Syro-Ephraimitish war. At this time too Tiglath-pileser was probably in Philistia (2 Chron. 28:18-20). In 733 Tiglath-pileser made his campaign against Damascus. In 732 he placed Hoshea on the throne, and Ahaz began his first year as sole king.

It may be objected that the time measure sixty-five years does not place its emphasis upon the destruction of Samaria, a catastrophic event. In reply we would say that the catastrophic event is not the event which actually brought to an end the existence of Israel as a people. It is further objected that Isaiah did not use such preciseness in his prophecies as is found in this mention of a definite number. Such is not a weighty objection. Must a writer do something more than once before he can be said to have done it at all? In sixty-five more years, we are taught, Ephraim would cease from being a people, and, as a matter of fact, precisely this occurred.

9 Although within sixty-five years Ephraim will come to an end, as far as Judah is concerned, Ephraim will continue as she now is without the addition of Judah. Thus God has spoken. The truth is clear. Will Ahaz believe? If he does not believe, there can be only one explanation; he is not established so that he can believe. If Ahaz does not believe, there are others standing about who must believe. Isaiah turns to the assembled group. "If ye," he says, addressing them all, "do not believe."[20]

---

[20] כִּי – "It is the case that"; cf. Job 12:2. The word may simply be employed in the apodosis to express the certainty with which a result is to be expected, in which case the apodosis becomes a mild form of exclamation. Even better, perhaps, is to take the apodosis as expressing cause, giving the reason for the disbelief, "it is that." אמן – A recent study of the root is by J. C. C. van Dorssen (Amsterdam, 1951). See Lindblom, *op. cit.*, p. 12, for references to other literature.

276

To believe! How fundamental and all-penetrating this concept is in Isaiah! It involves accepting as true the words which the prophet speaks and acting in accordance with those words. Credence and trust! These are what the prophet demands. He calls upon the entire court to trust in the Lord, and such trust involves belief in the truth of what he is saying.

The root is used in both the *Hifil* and *Nifal* stems. In the *Hifil* it has the significance of showing oneself firm or steady. But this must be done with respect to something. Hence, Lindblom is not correct when he remarks that it "does not only mean a special physical function in the sense of 'believe, and least of all an intellectual function."[21] When Abram believed the Lord he showed himself firm with respect to the promise, committing himself with the entirety of his being to the truthfulness of that promise and acting in accord therewith. Likewise, with respect to Isaiah's prophecy, Ahaz is to show himself filled with steadfastness; he is to believe that word, not wavering in doubt. If he does not believe, it is because he is not in a condition of firmness, in which alone he is able to believe.

Suppose, however, that men do not believe! What then? In that case, it is due to the fact that they are not established. "You are not to believe, and so you do not believe." Only established men, those who have been brought into a believing condition, are able to believe, for faith is the fruit of constancy, stability and steadfastness, and these qualities are gifts of God alone.

A ruler on the throne of David must be a "faithful" man. "Thy house is established," God had declared with respect to David's dynasty. It had already been prophesied by Abigail that David would have an established house (1 Sam. 25:28). And to Jeroboam Abijah declared that God would give an established house as He had given it to David. But Ahaz refused to act as a true heir of the Davidic throne. In the house which God established he was himself not established. Hence he could not show himself firm toward Him who alone could give firmness and constancy.

b. *The Lord's sign* (7:10-17)

10 And the LORD spake again unto Ahaz saying.
11 Ask for thyself a sign from the LORD thy God, make deep the request or make it high above.

---

[21] *Op. cit.*, p. 12.

12 And Ahaz said, I will not ask, and I will not tempt the LORD.

13 And he said, Hear ye now, O house of David; is it too little for you to weary men, that ye weary also my God?

14 Therefore the Lord himself will give to you a sign. Behold! a virgin is with child and will bring forth a son and she shall call his name Immanuel.

15 Butter and honey will he eat when he knows to reject the evil and choose the good.

16 For before the child knows to reject the evil and choose the good, the land which thou abhorrest will be forsaken of her two kings.

17 The LORD will bring against thee and against thy people and against the house of thy father days such as have not come since the day of Ephraim's turning aside from upon Judah, namely, the king of Assyria.

10 Strange and wondrous statement! Yahweh spake. How could He, a Spirit, speak to a human being Scripture means that He spoke through the mouth of His prophet. The speaking of God and that of the prophets are equated. Here Yahweh speaks by means of Isaiah. What an instance of goodness! Yahweh speaks, and He speaks to Ahaz. The all-merciful One approaches the rebellious one. The message is from God, who would make abundantly plain to the king that there was no cause for fear. Ahaz had not been moved by the revelations of God spoken by Isaiah; hence, God speaks again. His gracious revelations are varied. If we are not moved by one, He speaks again to touch our cold hearts.[22]

11 Tender as is the speech of Yahweh, it is nevertheless couched in the imperative. Ahaz has no choice. He must obey and ask. It is God who speaks and His commands cannot be dismissed.[23]

[22] There is no warrant for substituting "Isaiah" for "LORD" as suggested in *BH*. Nor should the verb be emended to the first person. See *SII*, 1954, for a discussion of the evidence. Both B and Vulg. support M; as does 1Q apparently also, although only the final *h* of the divine name appears. I cannot agree with Procksch, Fischer, Steinmann, Kissane, Lindblom, etc., that the scene here has shifted to the royal palace. If v. 10 introduces a new oracle, unconnected with the preceding, the entire force of vv. 1-9 is lost. Verse 11 is pointless apart from a reflection upon the events of vv. 1-9.

[23] Both Delitzsch and Drechsler rightly take Hitzig to task for his statement that the prophet is playing a dangerous game, since, had the king asked for a sign, Yahweh would probably have left the prophet in the lurch. De Lagarde remarks that Isaiah must have been either a fanatic or a deceiver, to which

At the same time, the sign is one which is to be for Ahaz' benefit. It is designed to convince him. The choice is placed in Ahaz' hands, and we have every right to assume that, had he asked for the performance of a miracle, it would have been granted to him. How magnanimous God is toward unbelievers! Those who resist His will have no excuse whatever for the punishment that is sure to follow their sinful course.

The words of God came through the lips of Isaiah, and Ahaz heard Isaiah speak. What right, he might have asked, did this prophet have to make such a demand of him? Ahaz was king; dared this mere prophet stand before him and command him? But the prophet does command for he knows that God will not forsake him. Isaiah stood boldly before men; he bowed in humility before God. Hence he enjoins Ahaz to ask a sign, some kind of pledge which can be known by the senses that will attest the truth of his message. A sign is not necessarily a miracle.[24] Inasmuch, however, as in this particular instance the sign should be of such a nature that it would substantiate the message of Isaiah and produce faith and belief in the king, it may be that a miracle could have been requested.

This sign is to be asked, for only Yahweh, who is Ahaz' God, can give it. To request this sign from Yahweh would have been a manifestation of faith, an evidence that Ahaz believed in the power of the Lord to fulfill the word which He had spoken already through His servant the prophet. God still recognizes Ahaz as His own and is willing so to reveal Himself. With gracious love He draws near to this unbelieving king. Yahweh is "thy God," and with that phrase the shadow of the Ten Commandments comes before us. "Thy God" is the God of love, but the words also contain the tone of authority.

Authoritative as is the command, yet God gives the king much leeway. The sign may be in the depth or in the height, on earth

---

Duhm replies that until the eighteenth century the world has consisted of "fanatics." Thus men show how little they understand the Word of God.

[24] A sign may consist of a prophecy that something will take place in the future or it may be a reminder that something has already occurred, e.g., 1 Sam. 2:34; Jer. 44:29. It may also belong to the class of miracles, e.g., Exod. 4:8ff.; 7:8ff.; Deut. 13:2ff.; Isa. 38:7. Here, the sign is probably a miracle. Only a sign, such as the darkening of the sun or the recession of the shadow on the sundial will convince the king. König cites *Odyssey* 20:103c., for an example of appeal to thunder as a sign.

or in the sky.[25] But Ahaz will not ask; he has no intention of obeying. He turns from God, but he turns knowing precisely what God's will is and what God requires of him. He is commanded to believe; the gospel is preached to him. That he refuses to believe is to be attributed to the fact that he hates the Lord and leans upon his own understanding.

12 Ahaz is nothing, if not direct. He will have no part in such things.[26] He is direct, but he is also stubborn, defiant and rebellious. His refusal indicates a complete lack of trust in the power of God and in the faithfulness of God to stand by His prophet. Faith shows itself in obedience; unbelief in disobedience. Here is a "practical" man to whom the worship of Yahweh has little meaning. In a time of crisis he is too busy for Yahweh; he would rather follow the dictates of his own "practical" reason than to walk in dependence upon his God.[27]

Obedience to God's commands is dismissed by the hypocritical king as a tempting of God. But Ahaz had no serious concern over whether or no he was tempting God. If he had had such concern, he would have been advised by Isaiah. He knew well enough that if he were to ask for a sign, it would be granted to him, and as a consequence he would have been compelled to believe the Lord and to place his trust in Him. This he did not wish to do. Not Yahweh but Assyria was his desire. Yet in his refusal he reflects upon Scripture: "Ye shall not tempt the

---

25 Vulg., Aq., Sym., Targ., Luther read "to Sheol," which stands in contrast to "above." The form would then be a locative, the *o* representing an original long *a*. On the other hand, the word might be pointed שאלה a paragogic imper. as in Dan. 9:19. The preceding word is then to be construed as a *Hifil* inf. abs. used adverbially. "By making deep ask." It is placed first for emphasis. The contrast appears in the infinitives; "making deep do thou ask," or "making high above." The sign is to be asked either on the earth or in the heaven; cf. Matt. 16:1.

26 Guthe thinks that the refusal displays the king's modest holding back. Procksch thinks that the king could have been neutral, Bentzen that Ahaz was not a hypocrite but a syncretist in religion. He was, of course, a syncretist; the worship of the true God meant so little to him that he could introduce into his land the worship of other gods as a course of political expediency.

27 Welch (*Kings and Prophets of Israel*, London, 1953, p. 213) says that Isaiah's thought was "moving along an entirely different plane" from that of Ahaz. But the question is not which of two human opinions is wisest, for Isaiah gives the revelation from God, a revelation which Ahaz must obey. Not to obey God is to be impractical.

LORD your God, as ye tempted him in Massah" (Deut. 6:16). To tempt the Lord is to put Him practically to the test.[28]

Here, there would seem, was an impasse; the defiant will of a hypocritical man was set against the revealed will of the sovereign God. But actually there was no impasse. The situation was in God's hands. Refusing to ask for a sign was no way to escape from receiving a sign. As a matter of fact, what Isaiah commanded Ahaz to do was not a tempting of God. Isaiah's command was to obey God, to act the part of a believer, to carry out the dictates of faith. In his refusal Ahaz deliberately set himself up as wiser and better informed than God. This was serious; to clothe the refusal with the hypocritical guise of not wishing to tempt the Lord was despicable in the extreme.

The sign for which Ahaz was to ask was intended to be an aid to faith. At times believers have asked for signs, and their requests have been granted. "And this shall be a sign unto thee from the LORD, that the LORD will do this thing that he hath spoken" (Isa. 38:7). Probably God gives signs because the recipients are weak in faith, and we may agree with Calvin when he remarks that "we ought to grieve and lament, that the sacred truth of God needs assistance on account of the defect of our flesh." He goes on, however, to point out that since God has so graciously given such aid, it ought not to be despised. "In like manner," he continues, "fanatics of the present day disregard Baptism and the true Lord's Supper, and consider them to be childish elements." To a true believer the sign would be a confirmation and strengthening of his faith. In that he rejected the offer, we must assume that Ahaz had no true faith. He speaks merely of the Lord, *Yahweh*, and not of "my God," in contrast to the "thy God" of Isaiah. God would own Ahaz; Ahaz will not own God. Deep indeed is his depravity. "He studiously," remarks Delitzsch, "brought down upon himself the fate denounced in ch. vi., and indeed not upon himself only, but upon all Judah as well. For after a few years the forces of Asshur would stand upon the same fuller's field (ch. xxxvi.2) and demand the surrender of Jerusalem. In that very hour, in which Isaiah was standing before Ahaz, the fate of Jerusalem was decided for more than two thousand years."

Ahaz was not the only one who used the language of Deuteron-

---

28 Cf. Exod. 17:7; Ps. 78:18, 19. The contrast between Hezekiah and Ahaz is great. One was willing to obey; the other not.

omy. There was also another. Speaking to the devil, Jesus Christ said, "It is written again, Thou shalt not tempt the Lord thy God." Our Lord accused the devil of tempting; Ahaz in effect accused God of tempting.

13 How objective! Isaiah writes of himself as though he were writing of another. No longer does he speak to the king alone, but to the king as the representative of the court which was standing about him. All must hear what he has to say, for all are responsible. Hence, he speaks in the plural. Again he breaks forth with a command. The faithless house of David must still listen to the word which God speaks through the mouth of the prophet. His question is one which reveals the faithlessness of those to whom it is addressed. "Is the wearying of men too little for you, that ye weary also my God?[29] You have been wearying men in that you have not listened to God's prophet. That is too little a thing for you, so now you must weary God also." God is long-suffering and slow to anger, and because of this very fact we begin to see how heinous was the sin of Ahaz. Ahaz had tried the patience of God. He had also tried Isaiah's patience in insulting the prophet by not giving obedience to his demands. That was serious enough, but apparently it did not satisfy the king. To try the patience of Isaiah was a small thing, and Ahaz, not being content with that must go on to vex the patience of God also. In thus speaking Isaiah shows that his own words were also those of God and that, consequently, Ahaz' stubborn and hypocritical refusal to obey was an insult directed not merely against men but also against God. "He that heareth you, heareth me; and he that despiseth you despiseth me; and he that despiseth me despiseth him that sent me" (Luke 10:16).

Isaiah speaks of the LORD as "my God," but Ahaz had refused to acknowledge God in such a manner. Thus to identify oneself with the cause of God as Isaiah does is a strengthening and blessed consolation and encouragement.

In this approach to Ahaz we discern the goodness of God manifested toward those that are reprobate. No man can say that he perishes because he does not know what God's will is. What God requires of Ahaz is made very plain; Ahaz knows precisely

---

[29] The subject of the question is the phrase "the wearying of." "Is it too little for you, namely, the wearying of men, that ye weary my God also?" The prep. has comparative force; cf. Gen. 18:25; Num. 16:9; Job 15:11.

what he is required to do. The gospel was preached to him, and he rejects it. Knowing clearly the will of God, he refuses to obey that will. Can any tragedy be greater?

Calvin sets forth Isaiah's action as an example of the true method of dealing with sinners. His words are worthy of quotation: "for we ought not to begin with severe reproof, but with doctrine, that men may be gently drawn by it. When plain and simple doctrine is not sufficient, proofs must be added. But if even this method produce no good effect, it then becomes necessary to employ greater vehemence."

14 Inasmuch as the wicked king in hypocritical fashion rejects the opportunity of asking for a sign, the Lord Himself gives the sign, one of His own choosing, announcing the birth of a wondrous Child as the sign of deliverance, and making the infancy of that Child the measure of the time that Judah is yet to suffer affliction.

Ahaz has refused to ask for a sign and he has gone on with his court to weary God; therefore, for that reason, the Lord takes the matter out of his hands, withdrawing, as it were, the offer, and Himself gives the sign.[30] Ahaz might have asked for any sign that would have satisfied him. By hypocritical unbelief, however, he cast away this privilege and so wearied God. Therefore, he is no longer to enjoy the privilege, but will have to receive whatever sign God chooses to give. A sign which Ahaz might have asked for would have been for his benefit. No longer, however, is there any choice. He must receive such a sign as God will give him, one which will have a relationship to his own lack of faith and hence will be a pledge of doom.

Ahaz' wickedness is seen in the fact that by his stubbornness he was in fact rejecting the very foundation of the covenant. God had promised to be a God and a Deliverer to His people. Syria and Israel, therefore, will not overthrow the Davidic dynasty, for if they could succeed in so doing, the promises of God would be rendered void and salvation would not ultimately be accomplished through the Messiah. In effect, Ahaz, by his re-

---

[30] The particle most naturally introduces the ground for something that has just been stated. In itself it does not insure that the following must be ominous. It serves to introduce a sign of different character from what had previously been offered. When taken in connection with v. 13 we see that the particle introduces a sign of doom and not of blessing.

fusal, is asserting that God is not faithful to His promise. In fearing that Syria and Israel could actually depose him, he is expressing disbelief that "there shall not fail thee a man in my sight to sit on the throne of Israel" (1 Kings 8:25). A son of David is willing to reject the covenant. God therefore must take over, and give a sign of the greater deliverance, as well as of the proximate deliverance from Syria and Israel.

He who will give the sign is *Adhon*.[31] Possibly Isaiah deliberately uses this designation instead of the covenant name Yahweh. He wants to bring to the fore the might and omnipotence of the One who will give the sign. He who alone can give a sign, whether it be in heaven above or on the earth beneath, will now exercise his prerogative. *Adhon* has control over all things, and Isaiah may have used this word by way of rebuke to the king. It is *Adhon,* even He, who will give the sign.

We may paraphrase Isaiah's words: *"Adhon* will give to you a sign, and the sign which He will give is this: Behold! a virgin. . . ." But the sign is not for Ahaz alone. Previously, Ahaz had been commanded, "Ask for thyself." Now, leaving Ahaz, Isaiah addresses the nation generally. "To you," he says, turning not merely to the king, but also to the court and all the nation. The sign, therefore, is intended for all the people and not for Ahaz alone. Inasmuch as it is given to all the nation, all the nation must receive and believe it.

In language of deep beauty and mystery, the prophet directs us to the virgin and her Child. He uses a form of language similar to that which had been spoken to Hagar in the wilderness, "Behold thee — pregnant, and about to bear a son, and thou shalt call his name Ishmael" (Gen. 16:11). Somewhat similar is the declaration made of Sarah, "Sarah thy wife shall bear thee a son indeed; and thou shalt call his name Isaac" (Gen. 17:19). To the mother of Samson also an announcement was made, "Behold! now, thou art barren and hast not borne, but thou shalt become with child and thou shalt bear a son" (Judg. 13:3).

Behold! — The language introduced by *hinneh,* "behold!" is employed in the Scriptures to announce a birth of unusual importance and significance. It has also appeared upon the texts

[31] 1Q and some mss. have the Tetragrammaton, but the preponderance of mss. do not have it, and inasmuch as their reading is the more difficult and also in keeping with the fact that Isaiah often uses אדני when he wishes to stress the sovereign power of God, that reading is to be preferred.

from Ugarit.[32] This does not mean that Isaiah is simply taking over a phrase that was common to the ancient Orient; it does mean, however, that because of the solemnity and importance of the announcement which he was to make, Isaiah did take over as much of this ancient formula of announcement as suited his purpose. His reason for so doing was to attract attention to the announcement itself. If Ahaz and others who were present were at all familiar with this formula, they would immediately realize that an announcement of supreme importance was about to be made. Isaiah is not going to declare the birth of just any child, but of a significant Child.

Even though Isaiah may have employed this formula for his own ends, he nevertheless gave to it, or more accurately, God through him gave to it, a dignity of function such as it had never before enjoyed. In Ugarit it had been used to announce the birth of gods, nonexistent beings who were a part of that web of superstition which covered the ancient pagan world. On Isaiah's lips, however, this formula is lifted from its ancient pagan context and made to introduce the announcement of the birth of the only One who truly is God and King. No longer must this phrase serve the useless purpose of heralding the birth of beings who had never existed and never would exist. The formal similarity fades into the background, and a tremendous contrast in the usage of the phrase emerges into the foreground. What is important, in other words, is not that the prophet employs a phrase which has also been found in Ugarit; what is important is that he uses this phrase in a context which in significance differs completely from that in which it was found elsewhere. Granting, therefore, the similarity in language, we nevertheless insist that the words of Isaiah must be interpreted upon their own merit and not as bound by the same connotation which they bore in Ugarit.

Divine authority commands us to look where the prophet points.[33] The word serves to arrest the attention and to stress the

---

[32] *hl. ǵlmt tld b(n).* (*Nikkal and Yarih,* 1:7). In Ug. *harah* is missing, and hence Isa. 7:14 cannot be regarded as a mere quotation. At the same time *hl* or *hinneh* appear to have been used to announce a birth of particular significance.

[33] הָרָה — The form is not a part. which would be *hôrîāh,* but a verbal adj. whose m. would be *hareh.* The *a* vowel of the part. is naturally long; cf. Ar. *qā-til* and Akk. *qā-ti-lum.* On the other hand, the vowel in the penult of *hārāh* is short (tone-long) and is reduced to *Shewa* in a distant open syllable;

importance of what is to be announced. "It means here," says Barnes, "that an event was to occur which demanded the attention of the unbelieving monarch, and the regard of the people — an event which would be a full demonstration of what the prophet had said, that God would protect and save the nation." The thought has been beautifully paraphrased by Machen: "I see a wonderful child, the prophet on this interpretation would say, a wonderful child whose birth shall bring salvation to his people; and before such a period of time shall elapse as would lie between the conception of the child in his mother's womb and his coming to years of discretion, the land of Israel and of Syria shall be forsaken." With the physical eyes it would of course have been impossible for Isaiah to have seen the mother. Only in vision could he see her, and commend her to the attention of those about him. But this did not absolve anyone from his responsibility to receive the sign, nor can it be urged as an argument against this interpretation, for in seeking to understand the prophecy we must be guided not by how we think Ahaz would have been affected, but only by the text itself. In vision Isaiah was allowed to see the virgin, and it is the announcement of what he is permitted to see in vision that he declared unto Ahaz and the nation.

a virgin is with child — Can we tell who this virgin is?[34] Isaiah uses the definite article in speaking of her. It might seem then that she were some well-known virgin, whose identity everyone would recognize. Indeed, some have assumed that this was actually true. Gressmann, for example, held that in ancient Israel

---

cf. Jer. 20:17. In the pl. however, the *a* is long. Cf. Amos 1:13 and 2 Kings 8:12. Matt. 1:23 reads 'έξει, which does not prove that the Heb. must be read as a future, but simply that here Matthew found B more suitable for his purpose, in that he simply regards the words as a prophecy.

וקראת — Perhaps this orthography is simply due to the analogy of certain *l″h* forms. After the verbal adj. the perf. with *wāw* consecutive expresses the future.

34 The word is not a vocative (Briggs, Hoffmann). It occurs in the pl. 5 times and 4 in the s.; see Song of Sol. 1:3; 6:8; Ps. 68:26; 46:1; 1 Chron. 15:20; Gen. 24:43 (cf. v. 16, which shows that the word may be used of a virgin); Exod. 2:8; Prov. 30:19. I have discussed this biblical evidence in *SII*, pp. 171ff. See also Robert Dick Wilson: "The Meaning of Alma (A.V. 'Virgin') in Isaiah VII. 14," *PTR*, vol. xxiv (1926), p. 316. In the light of the Ar. cognate the word *almah* may refer to one who is sexually mature. Here, it is not etymology, however, but usage, which plays the decisive role.

there was a widespread belief that a particular virgin would bear a son. In the Old Testament, however, there is only one other explicit reference to the mother of the Messiah, and that is in Micah 5:3, "Therefore will he give them up, until the time that she which travaileth hath brought forth. . . ." Here the definite article is missing.

More natural is it to maintain that the definite article is used with the word *almah* in a generic sense, and serves to designate some particular unknown person. Isaiah's purpose is to distinguish the *almah* from some other kind of woman. As though he were to say, "It is not an old woman, or a married woman which I behold in vision, not a bride or a girl, necessarily, but an *almah*." Hence, in our English translation we may best bring out Isaiah's force by the indefinite article. By this means the prophet focuses the attention upon the *almah*.

At the outset we may confidently assert that the word *almah* is never employed of a married woman.[35] At least one of these occurrences makes it clear that the word may designate one who is truly a virgin (Gen. 24:43). Rebekah is called an *almah,* but she is furthermore designated a *bethulah,* and it is said of her that a man had not known her. In one passage, namely, Proverbs 30:19, the word *almah* may possibly signify an immoral girl, but it does not indicate a married girl. Perhaps the closest equivalent in English is the word *damsel* or *maiden.* Neither of these is generally employed of a married woman. Yet even these words may not be precise equivalents, for whereas they could possibly refer to married women, *almah* does not do so. For these reasons it may be wisest, after all, to render *almah* in English by "virgin."

Particularly striking are the extra-Biblical references. On the texts from Ugarit *ǵlmt* is employed of an unmarried woman. We may note in particular the phrases:

tld,btl (t

hl glmt tld b (n

In Ugaritic the word *glmt* is never used of a married woman.[36]

---

[35] Vischer mentions Luther's offer to give a hundred *Gulden* to anyone who could show that *almah* ever referred to a married woman. In characteristic fashion Luther added that the Lord alone knew where he would get them. Says Vischer: "So far no one has collected the hundred gulden."

[36] It is not accurate to say with Coppens (*La Prophétie de la 'Almah*, Bruges: Paris, 1952, p. 24) that *ǵlmt* is applied to Ashirat, the daughter and wife of El. The word used of Ashirat is *ǵlm,* e.g., *aṭt.il. aṭt.il. w'llmh* (52:42) and

In the light of the oft-repeated statement that *almah* can designate a young woman, good or evil, married or unmarried, it is well to ask why this particular word was chosen to designate the mother of the Messiah. Obviously the word *yaldah* would not be suitable, inasmuch as it is used for one who is but a child. Nor is the word *naarah* appropriate, for it can apply to any woman indiscriminately. This word is so indefinite in its force that, unless Isaiah had wished to express the thought that a "young woman" would bear a son, he would not have found it suitable.

Often it has been said that had the prophet desired to designate the mother as a virgin, there was at his disposal the word *bethulah*.[37] At first sight this might seem to be a perfectly good word; upon closer examination, however, it proves to be most unsatisfactory. True enough, *bethulah* may designate a virgin, but it may also refer to a betrothed virgin (*bethulah meorasa*). In Deuteronomy the laws make clear that betrayal of the state of betrothal was as heinous as adultery and punishable with death. In Joel 1:8 the *bethulah* is clearly a married woman, and in later Aramaic incantation texts, the Aramaic equivalent of *bethulah* refers to a married woman. If Isaiah had used this word *bethulah*, he would have left us in confusion. We could not have known precisely what he had in mind. Would he have been speaking of one who was truly a virgin or would he rather have had in mind one who was betrothed or one who was actually a wife? In the light of these considerations it appears that Isaiah's choice of *almah* was deliberate. It seems to be the only word in the language which unequivocally signifies an unmarried woman. No other available Hebrew word would clearly indicate that the one whom it designates was unmarried. Consequently, no other word would have been suitable for fulfilling the requirements of the sign such as the context demanded. None of these other words would have pointed to an unusual birth. Only *almah* makes clear that the mother was unmarried.

If, however, the mother is an unmarried woman, a question

---

also *bt.il bt.il. w'lmh* (52:45,46). Cf. *UH,* p. 144. The expression *bǵlmt* is difficult. It may mean "son of Galmat, the goddess," and thus serve as a proper name. It is used as a parallel of *źlmt,* which may mean "darkness." Cf. *CML,* p. 101. In any case the word does not offer an objection to the argument presented above.

37 As late as 1959 Schilling (*Isaiah Speaks,* New York, 1958-59) makes this claim. Cf. Bratcher (*The Bible Translator,* July 1958, p. 102).

arises. Was the child illegitimate or not?[38] If the child were illegitimate, would such a birth be a sign? The whole context, indeed, the whole Biblical context, rules this out. On the other hand, if the mother were a good woman, then the birth was out of the ordinary, an unusual birth. The mother is both unmarried and a good woman. When this fact is understood, it becomes apparent that in all history there is only one of whom this can be predicated, namely, Mary, the mother of the Lord.

and will bring forth a son — As the prophet beholds the virgin in vision she is with child, but the birth is to take place in the future. When Isaiah sees her, she has not yet brought forth her son. The one to be brought forth is a son, and the birth of that son is the sign that Ahaz has nothing to fear from the northern kingdoms.

and she will call his name — The mother herself gives the name of her child. She calls him Immanuel, for in a unique way God is present with His people.[39] The hope that Yahweh would be present was expressed in Psalm 46, "The LORD of hosts is with us." Now, however, it is not Yahweh, but God (*El*) who is present.

---

38 Vischer remarks (*op. cit.*, p. 50) that when an *almah* bears it does not necessarily imply a virgin birth, but he goes on to say that it is not normal and bears the stamp of the illegitimate. Isaiah stresses that the mother will name the child, whereas in the 8th century B.C. the father normally did this (8:3). The regent is not normally and legitimately born in the royal family at Jerusalem.

39 Lindblom (*op. cit.*, p. 22) says that the name is taken from the cultic terminology and does not belong to the stock of ordinary Hebrew names exemplified by Isaiah's and Hosea's children. The name indicates that with the expected prince, Hezekiah, a period of good fortune and bliss would ensue in Judah. The arguments against the identification with Hezekiah, however, are cogent. (1) The chronology cannot be dismissed offhand, as even Holwerda is willing to do (*De Wijsheid die Behoudt*, 1957, p. 39. Cf. Coppens: *op. cit.*, p. 17). (2) To identify Immanuel with Hezekiah is to rob the prophecy of that aura of mystery and wonder in which it is couched. (3) The mother of Hezekiah, unless she is some woman not yet married to Ahaz, cannot be designated an *almah*. (4) The unique name Immanuel does not apply to Hezekiah. While it was true that God was with this ruler on the Davidic throne, Immanuel, on the other hand, will be Himself the one who brings God to His own. (5) The birth of Hezekiah is not such a sign as is demanded by the context. (6) What warrant is there for expecting that Ahaz would have permitted his wife to name the child? Why would not he himself have given this name? (7) The introductory *hinneh*, "behold!" points to the future. The birth has not yet occurred.

At times of crisis God was present *with* His people. (1) He had been with Abraham and Isaac (Gen. 26:3) and Jacob (Gen. 28:15). (2) He was with Joseph, and Joseph prospered (Gen. 39:2, 3, 21, 23). (3) He was also with Joshua (Josh. 6:27), and Joshua's fame became spread abroad. (3) When David suffered from the jealousy of Saul, God was with him (1 Sam. 18:14). (5) In establishing the Davidic dynasty God declared that He had been with David, and hence David had received a great name (2 Sam. 7:9). So also would He be with Solomon (1 Kings 1:37). Had Jeroboam acted like David, God would have been with him also (1 Kings 11:38). In 2 Samuel 23:5 we have the combination "my house is with *El*." In the birth of the Child God would be with His people in One who should sit upon David's throne.

Gray, however, suggests that "the name Immanuel asserts that God will be present with the Jews, that they will experience success, deliverance, freedom from danger and anxiety; the meaning and result of God's presence can be gathered from such sayings as, 'I fear no evil for thou art with me,' Ps. 23:4, etc."

According to this interpretation, the presence of God is seen in His providence. In the delivery from Syria and Israel, for example, the presence of God is to be manifested. There is, however, a point which is too often overlooked. The deliverance from Syria and Israel will not occur for some time after the birth of the child. The child cannot be just any child, but only such a child as would serve as a sign. No mother would have the right to name her child Immanuel in the mere hope that within a few years Judah would be saved. How could she possibly know apart from divine revelation that her particular child would be the child intended by the prophet? How could she be warranted in naming her own child Immanuel, unless there was some revelation to her to that effect?

The presence of God appears, then, not in the deliverance from Syria and Israel, but in the birth of the Child Himself. When the Child is born, God is seen to be present with His people. In the light of the fact that the birth is to be a sign and also in view of the unusual character of the mother, we cannot regard the child as a contemporary. His birth is surrounded with the mysterious and the supernatural. Again in 9:6 the Child is called *El,* the same word that is used here, a word which in Isaiah always signifies deity.

290

Isaiah, therefore, is not announcing some contemporary birth, neither that of Hezekiah, nor of any unknown, obscure child. Rather, in dim and strange vision he looks forward to the birth of One whose very presence brings God to His people. When that Child will have been born, then God will have come to His own. "I will be their God," He had promised, and now, in the time of their deep need, He would come to His own, not by might nor by power, but in the birth of a little Child.

In any interpretation of this passage there are three points which need to be stressed. (1) The birth must be a sign. (2) The mother of the Child is one who is both unmarried and a good woman. This fact simply cannot be glossed over, and in itself rules out those interpretations which regard the mother as a married woman. (3) The very presence of the Child brings God to His people. Calvin rightly maintains that the name cannot be applied to anyone who is not God. No one else in the Old Testament bears this name. For these reasons, the prophecy must be interpreted only of that One to whom these conditions apply, namely, Jesus the Christ, the Son of the Virgin and the Mighty God.

15 The infancy of the promised Messiah is made the measure of the time that Judah will be in danger from her two enemies. This thought, namely, the duration of a period of difficulty, is expressed symbolically in that Immanuel is pictured as subsisting during His infancy on curds and honey, which was symbolical royal diet.[40] From the time of His birth, supposedly, the Child will eat this peculiar food, and at the time when He can discern between good and evil, rejecting the one and choosing the other, He will be eating these things.[41] At an early age a child learns to reject evil and to choose good, or at least to distinguish between

---

[40] חמאה — "Curds"; thickened, sour milk, like the laban of modern Syria. Lindblom (op. cit., pp. 23ff.) argues that the mention of this food is to indicate a period of prosperity and bliss. Immanuel, he claims, was not a god, but a wonder-child. But how could Hezekiah possibly be regarded as a wonder-child?

[41] Following B, some would render, πρὶν ἂν γνώναι, "until he knows." Others take the clause as expressing purpose. John Rea (The Connection Between Isaiah 7:14 and 7:15-17, unpublished) holds that the infancy of the Messiah is made a measure of the time elapsing between the issuance of the prophecy and the beginning of the desolation. But the climactic point seems rather to be the forsaking of the land by the two kings, the immediately present enemies.

the two. Thus, by means of this measure, we learn that the affliction or desolation of threat of the two enemy kings is short-lived, possibly only two or three years.

For what reason is such an unusual diet mentioned, one which obviously could not sustain an infant? It was a widespread ancient belief that one who subsisted upon the "food of the gods" was himself a supernatural being. Perhaps Isaiah deliberately employed such language for the purpose of stressing and bringing to the fore the regal character of the Messiah. At the same time this interpretation cannot be pressed, and it is best not to be dogmatic. Whether Isaiah deliberately hints at the divinity of the Child or His kingly character may be difficult to prove. It would, however, at least seem to be the case that by mentioning this royal food the prophet does draw attention to the fact that this birth and infancy are not normal and that a period of difficulty will endure the length of time that it takes a child to reach the age when he knows the difference between good and evil.

What is the meaning of good and evil? There is a phrase in the Egyptian language, *nfr-bn,* "good-bad," which means "everything"). One who knows good and evil knows everything. It is not that, however, which Isaiah at this particular point wishes to stress. He is not concerned to tell us that the Child will know all things, but simply that the Child will reach an age in which He can distinguish between good and evil, rejecting the evil and choosing the good. Immanuel will possess knowledge, a knowledge which consists in choice of good as over against evil. Unlike our first parents, He does not choose the evil. His nature is such that He rejects evil.

The reference may be to what is injurious or useful in life but in the light of the usage of this phrase in Genesis 2, it clearly refers also to what is morally good and evil.

16 Ahaz should be quiet, and not fear. His enemies are but the smoking tails of firebrands. The threat that they can provide will at best be short-lived. Indeed, before the boy even knows to despise the evil and choose the good the land will be forsaken. When a boy (*naar*) knows the difference between good and evil, he may be very young. The word is also used of the baby Moses (Exod. 2:6). Even before such a time shall have arrived, the threat will have come to an end.

But what land is to be forsaken? Probably it is Syria and Israel considered as a unit, for the two kings are identified as belonging to the land. Isaiah speaks of "her two kings," and it is difficult to see how that could apply to Judah. To Isaiah it had been already told that in the midst of the land there would be a great forsaking. The punishing hand of God would come. Judah, however, was not the only land to experience a forsaking. Syria and Israel would also have a forsaking; they would be forsaken of their two kings. They would no longer be in a position to threaten the people of God in Judah. Before these two kings the unbelieving Ahaz stood in fear and dread. They wanted to harrass ($qitz$) Judah; it is their land which Ahaz abhors ($qatz$).[42]

As a summary of these three verses we may say that in verse 14 Isaiah announces that the Lord will give a sign. "I see," we may paraphrase his thought, "a virgin, and this virgin is with child." We are reminded of the words of Balaam, "I see him, but not now; I behold him, but not nigh" (Num. 24:17a). This seeing of the virgin is not with the physical eyes, but in vision. In vision, then, the prophet beholds the virgin with child, "She is about to bring forth a son and she will call his name Immanuel." In the birth of this son, the presence of God is manifest in a most unique way. The fourteenth verse constitutes a definite prophecy of the birth of Immanuel.

With verse 15 the prophet proceeds to make the infancy of the Messiah a symbolical representation of the fact that the threat which overhung Judah would be short-lived. This he does by picturing the child in vision eating royal food. The child will

---

[42] According to Duhm v. 15 was inserted from the margin. Probably the composer thought that the child was the Messiah and through a combination of our passage with vv. 21ff. thought that he had found an interesting detail about the child. Hence, the verse is more recent than the redactor, who, since it described a later time, would have added it after v. 16. This is pure supposition. When we come to sum up the teaching of the verses, it may be clearly seen that v. 15 is in its proper place. Again, in vv. 18ff. the eating of cream is set forth as a result of the devastation of Judah, whereas in v. 15 it is the result of the devastation of Israel and Syria. Well and good, the two are not talking about the same thing. Duhm's attempt is only a part of the modern *Zerstückelungssucht*, and is best refuted by an analysis of the verses in question. For a summary of modern literature see Coppens, *op. cit.*, pp. 3-5. In *SII*, I have discussed certain recent interpretations, including the collective view. Rignell (*Studia Theologica*, xi, 1957) advanced the idea that the *almah* was a designation of Israel. Gottwald (*VI*, viii, 1958, pp. 36ff.) has revived the view that the mother is Isaiah's wife, who, however, is called "the prophetess" in 8:3. Perhaps the most widely accepted position is that which identifies the *almah* as Ahaz' wife and the child as Hezekiah (see note 39).

eat this royal food, symbol of threat and desolation; yet before He reaches the age where He knows the difference between good and evil, the two kings which Ahaz dreads will forsake the land of Israel, and there will be nothing more for him to fear from them.

Upon this interpretation there is a change in the nature of the prophecy between verse 14 and the two following verses. In verse 14 the birth of the Messiah is present to the prophet's vision. This is prediction, and in the birth of Jesus Christ it found its fulfillment. Verse 15, however, is of a different character. We should remember that the language of prophecy is filled with mystery and is sometimes obscure. It is not simple history written in advance, but is language of profound and beautiful symbolism, clothed in an aura of mystery. Who are we to set limits upon the categories and devices which the prophet might employ? We cannot circumscribe and define the bounds which must contain the prophetic inspiration; rather we are to come to the prophecy, as indeed to all the sacred Scriptures, ready to accept it as it is and to yield to it our obedience.

17 Ahaz has asked for the king of Assyria; he shall have the king of Assyria. Sometimes the greatest punishment that can come to us is to have our own desires and prayers granted. Isaiah turns directly to the king. "You, Ahaz," he says in effect, "have refused to choose a sign. The Lord therefore will give a sign, and this sign is to be found in the birth of the Messiah Himself, who will bring salvation to His people. Upon thee, however, the Lord will bring the king of Assyria, for whom thou hast been seeking."[43]

To state the matter in a slightly different fashion, verse 14 presents the sign which the Lord will give. Verses 15 and 16 constitute the conclusion of the prophecy and verse 17 the announcement of the punishment which is to overtake Ahaz and his house. Verses 18-25 form somewhat of an excursus to the

---

[43] The sentence is asyndetically joined to the preceding. By the omission of the copula a certain effectiveness is secured, providing a forceful climax to the Immanuel prophecy. Rosenmüller aptly compares 1:3: "Israel does not know."

"will bring" — With the prep. the verb has the sense of bringing misfortune; cf. Job 2:11.

"have not come" — Lit., "such as have not been." The days which the Lord would bring would be seen to culminate in the exile and the consequent destruction of the theocracy.

present verse, singling out and developing one particular aspect of the promised threat.

will bring — For emphasis' sake, the verb is placed first. The threat is directed against Ahaz, but also against his people and the house of his father. It is to be fulfilled, then, so it would seem, not in the coming of one particular king alone, but in the coming of a period of depression and affliction caused by Assyrian kings generally. Days are to come, days which these kings will introduce. These days would culminate in the exile which would bring the theocracy to an end. Since the time when the ten northern tribes apostatized from Judah no calamity had come upon the nation such as that which the Lord would bring with the coming of the Assyrian king.[44]

the king of Assyria — The verse concludes in a tremendous climax. What Ahaz had desired, that he was to receive. As Delitzsch well remarks, "It is with piercing force that the words 'the king of Assyria' are introduced at the close of the two verses." The nature of the evil days to come is to be found in the presence of the king of Assyria. Something of grandeur pertains to the manner in which the verse works up to this climax. There are two great coming figures. To the people of God Immanuel will bring salvation; to Ahaz and those who followed him the king would bring destruction. With the coming of the Assyrian king an entire new order of things is introduced. With Tiglath-pileser III the destruction of the theocracy began and a new period was introduced. What set in motion the train of events leading up to the exile and the abolishing of the theocracy was the coming of this particular Assyrian king. From this time on, nothing would be as it had been before. The end of the theocracy was now in sight. By his refusing to obey the Lord, Ahaz was responsible for the introduction of this entirely new order of things.

c. *The coming desolation* (7:18-25)

18 And it shall come to pass, in that day the LORD will hiss for the fly which is in the end of the rivers of Egypt and for the bee which is in the land of Assyria.

19 And they shall come and rest all of them in the gullies and in the clefts of rocks, and in all thorn bushes and in all pasture.

---

[44] After an indefinite object the objective particle may be employed to introduce an object that is more definite; cf. Gen. 6:10; 26:34.

20 In that day the LORD will shave with a razor that is hired in the parts beyond the river, with the king of Assyria the head and the hair of the feet, and it shall also sweep away the beard.

21 And it shall come to pass in that day that a man will keep alive a young cow and two sheep.

22 And it shall come to pass that from the abundance of making milk he shall eat butter, for butter and honey shall everyone eat that is left in the midst of the land.

23 And it shall come to pass in that day that every place where there shall be a thousand vines at a thousand pieces of silver, it shall become briers and thorns.

24 With arrows and with bows will one come thither, for the whole land will be briers and thorns.

25 And on all the hills which are digged with the hoe, thou shalt not go there, for fear of briers and thorns, but it shall become a sending place for bulls and a trampling place for sheep.

18 As in 2:2 Isaiah pointed to the future, so here also. It is necessary properly to understand the force of his language. He is not saying, "It shall come to pass in that day that the Lord will whistle," but rather, "and it shall come to pass — pause — in that day the Lord will whistle." The whole picture, in other words, is set in the future. The day mentioned is that in which the dangers just threatened will become a reality, the time characterized by the presence of the king of Assyria. At that time, when the threatened danger has become a reality, the Lord will hiss for the enemy. By means of hissing, bees and flies were called.[45] Earlier, Isaiah has stated that the Lord would hiss for faraway nations; now he identifies those nations.[46]

the fly which is in the end of the rivers of Egypt — Egypt is a land filled with flies, and the Egyptian enemy is thought of as being as multitudinous as flies. From the ends of the streams and rivers, (lit., "the Niles"), that is, from even the most remote parts of the nations the Lord will hiss for the armies of Egypt.

Ancient testimonies speak of Assyria as a country of beekeeping. The bees are a picture of cruelty and danger. "And the Amorites, which dwelt in that mountain, came out against you,

---

[45] A similar example is found in *Iliad*, 2:87 (bees) and 2:469 (flies). Cf. Aeschylus, *Persians*, 128ff., and *Georgics*, 4:64. In 5:26 it had already been stated that the Lord would hiss for faraway nations; now the prophet names and identifies those nations.

[46] ובאו — The accent is *mil 'el* because of *nasog ahor*. As to the historical fulfillment, without question Assyria is the prominent figure.

and chased you, as bees do, and destroyed you in Seir, even unto Hormah" (Deut. 1:44). Mighty in number will be the coming enemy; mighty, but also cruel and harmful. The Lord need but hiss, and this powerful and mighty army could come from Egypt and Assyria. To arouse these great countries was no more diffi- cult for the Lord than to hiss for flies and bees. A mere hiss, a whistle, and mighty Assyria and Egypt obey.

Ahaz had sought for an ally in the Assyrian. By his actions he wanted to rule the movements of nations. As a matter of fact, however, since it was subject to the Lord's control, Assyria could not have come to Palestine apart from the Lord's permission. Even the mighty Tiglath-pileser could not act upon his own. The exile, brought about by the Lord, was the punishment of Judah inflicted by Assyria and Egypt, and these two powers were simply the instruments of the Lord's working.

19 Bees and flies will swarm into the land and devastate it com- pletely. The Lord's hissing will be successful. The bees and flies will come and they will settle in the land. It is no temporary invasion. Judah is a land of dry watercourses, wadies or gullies, and these are precipitate and steep. On such high-walled wadies flies and bees might most naturally settle. Even such supposedly inaccessible places will not be free from the insects. Not only the deep valleys but also the high crags, the wild places and pastures will be taken by the insects. From this enemy there is to be no escape. The coming Assyrians cannot be eluded.

20 Egypt is now left out of the picture, and Assyria alone is mentioned, for she was the leading foe with whom the people of God had to do. At the time when the flies and bees come in and settle down upon the land, then the Lord will shave the entire body, head and feet, for the devastation to come over Judah rests ultimately in His hands. Judah is a human body in which there is no soundness (1:6). With a razor that is hired, the Lord will shave this body.[47] This hired razor of Assyria is to do his bid-

---

[47] "a razor that is hired" — The razor of the hired; the adj. apparently serving as a subsequent explanation of the noun in const. "hired" — The translation "drunken," e.g., Cyril, "with a great and drunken razor," goes back to B, which must have confused the word for *škr*, "strong drink." Such shaving would have been regarded as shameful; cf. 2 Sam. 10:4, 5; Isa. 50:6. The instrument to accomplish these things is expressly said to be the king of Assyria.

ding. Ahaz had paid tribute and in that sense had hired the Assyrians, in order that they might shave Syria and Israel. This hired razor now serves as the agent of God to shave Judah herself. From beyond the Euphrates this razor was brought. From a great distance it was to come and at a great distance it had its origin. The river, however, was no obstacle to those who intended to come and to despoil Judah. To them it would be no hindrance to prevent them from shaving the entire body. Complete would be the devastation, and its height of insult and disgrace appears when the beard is shaven away. No insult could be greater than this. A shorn, disgraced, devastated theocracy; a hired razor, Assyria; a sovereign God who is no respecter of persons or of nations.

21 How often the prophet speaks of "that day" (vv. 18, 20 and 23) ! It will be a day of complete devastation and it will be a day in which one will keep or preserve alive his sheep, protecting them from the invaders.[48] A great change, wrought by the invaders, will be introduced. No longer will the land be agricultural, but rather pastoral. Life will be simple, and men so few that uncultivated grounds will abound. The few remaining animals will be sufficient for the few remaining men.

22 The future is determined. The punishment will come. For the second time in a series of three Isaiah utters, "and it shall be." Only a few men remain in the land, and with respect to them there will be an abundance of making milk. Because there is an abundance of making milk, men will eat the products of milk, namely, curds. In this can be seen the change from the agricultural to the pastoral mode of life. Natural was this abundance, and not one which man's toil had brought about. Of tilling the soil there was none; it was a time of poverty. The great majority of Judah had gone into exile, and only a few were left.

23 A new phrase of the devastation is introduced. Wherever there could be a thousand vines the price would be a thousand silverlings. Growing of grapes had been one of the most, if not

48 "keep alive" — As a consequence of the devastations the agricultural nature of the land will change, and it will become pastoral. Life will be simple, and men so few that the uncultivated grounds will be many. The few animals will provide ample sufficiency for the few people remaining.

the most, important of Judah's industries. A good-sized vineyard possibly contained a thousand vines, and the vineyards were valued according to the individual vine. How much were these silverlings?[49] Probably not much, for the vine is not very valuable. Instead of a vineyard, the land will become briers and thorns.[50]

24 Arrows and bows![51] Into a desolate land men come. They come to hunt but they come also to protect themselves from the wild animals.[52] Briers and thorns again. We have been told how the vineyards would become briers and thorns. Now the land itself is briers and thorns. Men will enter the land, if they enter it at all, with arrows and bows. To keep themselves alive they come to hunt. No longer is it a cultivated land, and they must be armed. It is a wilderness: briers and thorns.

25 The mountains, the glory of Palestine, were inaccessible to the plow, but were digged with the hoe. The hills are terraced, and even they were places of cultivation. But into the hills, out of fear of the briers and thorns, men are not to go.[53] Into these once carefully and tenderly cultivated places, mankind will not enter. In these places the oxen will be sent, and the sheep will trample. A complete change has been made. Places once assiduously cultivated by man are now the trampling spots of oxen and sheep. The invading foe had done his work well. The hired razor has shaved clean. The land is desolate. Men are gone, and we are left with the oxen and the grazing sheep in full possession of what had once been man's. The dwelling place of the theocracy is briers and thorns.

49 The prep. expresses price, but the denomination is not stated. Burckhardt declared that in his day (1817) a vine sold for a *piastre*. Today the value would be about fifty cents. After numerals certain specifications of weight or measure are usually omitted. Probably we are to understand the word shekels.
"it shall become" — The disjunction between the rich vines and the future desolation is made very prominent. Note that in this verse the frequentative and future senses of the imp. meet.
50 The repetition of *hayah* and *yihyeh* heightens the heavy and tedious nature of the description. Cf. Delitzsch; *com. in loc.*
51 The words are first, for emphasis' sake; cf. 32:13, 14.
52 The verb is indefinite, "will one come." Cf. *Georgics* III:341-45.
53 "fear" — Best construed as an acc. of cause or reason. Cf. *GKC*, No. 1181; Wright: *Arabic Grammar* (vol. ii, p. 121 A). Hence, the rendering of AV is incorrect, "there shall not come thither the fear of briers and thorns."

3. THE ASSYRIAN INVADER (8:1—9:7)

a. *Maher-Shalal-Hash-Baz* (8:1-10)

1 And the LORD said unto me, Take for thyself a great tablet and write upon it with the pen of a man, To Maher-Shalal-Hash-Baz.

2 And I shall take to witness for me faithful witnesses, Uriah the priest and Zechariah the son of Jerebechiah.

3 And I drew near unto the prophetess, and she conceived and bore a son, and the LORD said unto me, Call his name Maher-shalal-hash-baz.

4 For before the child knows to cry, My father and my mother, they shall take away the wealth of Damascus and the spoil of Samaria before the king of Assyria.

5 And the LORD proceeded to speak to me further saying,

6 Because this people hath despised the waters of Shiloh which flow slowly and rejoice with respect to Rezin and the son of Remaliah.

7 And therefore, behold! the LORD is about to bring up upon them the waters of the river, strong and many, even the king of Assyria and all his glory, and he shall come up upon all his channels and flow over all his banks.

8 And he shall sweep on into Judah; he shall overflow and go over, he shall reach unto the neck, and the outstretching of his wings shall be the fulness of the breadth of thy land, O Immanuel.

9 Be wicked, ye people and be ye broken, and give ear, all ye remote parts of the earth, gird ye and be ye broken, gird ye and be ye broken.

10 Take counsel and let it be frustrated, speak a word, and it will not stand, for Immanuel.

1 "At sundry times and in divers manners" God "spake in time past unto the fathers by the prophets." The prophets presented their messages in different ways. Isaiah had already declared the coming of the Assyrians and the overthrow of Judah. Now by means of a symbolical name, he repeats his message. "But because the wicked," says Calvin, "are not terrified by any threatenings, it was therefore necessary that this prediction should be repeated and demonstrated by some outward sign."

How God spoke to Isaiah we are not told. The prophet was commanded to take for his own benefit a tablet which was great, both in proportion to the writing upon it and also because it was to be exhibited in public. A large, smooth surface would have suited his purpose, and upon this he could write letters of sufficient size so that they would be easily legible to the passer-by,[1]

In 1953 at Nimrud sixteen ivory writing boards and about the same number of wooden boards were discovered where they had been thrown in a well. The wooden boards were larger than the ivory ones and seem to have been often repaired. The ivory boards were intended for the royal palace of Sargon II at Khorsabad and may be dated from 707-5 B.C. (during Isaiah's lifetime). An inscription reads:

> The palace of Sargon, the king of the world,
> The king of the land of Assyria./ The series "When the
>   gods Anu and Enlil" on a tablet of ivory he had
>   written/ and in the midst of his palace in Dur-
>   Sarrukin he had placed it.[2]

and write upon it — Jeremiah had been commanded to employ an amanuensis; but Isaiah himself is enjoined to write.[3] In writing the prophet was to use a stylus of iron or lead with which one usually wrote on a hard surface. It was the kind of stylus that ordinary men used. What the prophet had experienced in the sphere or realm of vision he is now to carry out with material implements in the realm of the senses. The pen of a man is a pen that is common and ordinary, and the writing such as simple, everyday men could understand. We are not told where the tablet was to be erected, whether in the Temple court or in the house of the prophet. It was, however, to be set up so that the inhabitants of Jerusalem could see it. Hence, it was not to con-

---

[1] "tablet" — Cf. 3:3 and Exod. 38:8.

[2] For the text see Donald J. Wiseman: "Assyrian Writing-Boards," *Iraq*, Vol. xvii, Pt. 1 (1955) pp. 3-13.

[3] "with the pen of a man" — Not "with a pen, oh! man" (cf. Job 19:23). "man"— Weak, frail man. Stade would contrast the writing herein mentioned with divine writing (Exod. 32:16) and introduce the parallel between the Egy. hieroglyphs and demotic (language of the people). Cf. Herodotus 2:36 The phrase is not as clear as we might wish. But the genitive "man" appears to indicate what is ordinary, common or simple.

tain secret writing but such as could be understood, so that "he
may run that readeth it" (Hab. 2:2).

The content of the inscription is the phrase, "belonging to
Maher-shalal-hash-baz."[4] But is this compound expression at this
particular point a proper name? True enough, it is so used later,
but in this verse it is the meaning of the sentence itself which
is of primary importance, "Hastening is the booty; speeding is
the prey." Two kingdoms, Syria and Israel, are involved. To
them a doom is speedily coming. In this symbolical act of writing, then, we have the general announcement of the same un-
happy destiny that had been predicted in the previous chapter.
Perhaps this chapter is to be regarded as chronologically subsequent to the seventh, inasmuch as it sets forth in more detailed
fashion the events of the future.

2 It is Yahweh who speaks. He will take for Himself faithful witnesses so that His prophecy, uttered through the mouth of
Isaiah, may be accredited and His honor upheld.[5] These witnesses would be able to testify that the prophet had written and
exhibited the prophecy a long time before its fulfillment. When
the fulfillment did come, then they could point out that Isaiah
had already written thereof. There were some men whose word
the nation could trust, and such would these witnesses be. In
the eye of the people, they were faithful and trustworthy. Although we today do not know their identity, they must have
been well known to the nation of the time, for they are named.
Uriah cannot be identified, but Zechariah may have been the
father-in-law of Ahaz.[6] At any rate, he was someone acceptable

4 The *lamed* of inscription is used, and may be rendered, "to" or "for." Old
Canaanite seals have been found containing names prefixed with *lamed*,
"belonging to Shema" (Megiddo, 9th cent. B.C.). Cf. *NSI*, p. 360ff.

מהר — Not an inf. nor an acc. nor an inf. abs. or imper., but a verbal adj.
"hastening," for *memahar*. שָׁשׁ is a part. and so the whole may be rendered,
"hastening is the booty, speeding is the prey." Cf. Humut-tabal (remove
hastily), the name of a boatman, *ANET*, p. 109.

5 As it stands the verb is imp. with weak *wāw* and may be rendered, "And
I shall indeed take as witnesses." The final *hē* expresses a strong determination or fixed, definite purpose and intention. Cf. Jer. 32:10-44. The ethical
dative has reference to God. God will do this thing for Himself that His
prophecy, uttered through the mouth of the prophet, may be accredited and
His honor upheld.

6 These men were to witness the fact that Isaiah had written and had
exhibited the prophecy so long before its fulfillment. Is Uriah to be indenti-
fied with the Uriah of 2 Kings 16:10ff.? Kittel denies it, and Gray assumes it.

302

to the people, someone who was truly known, someone who was faithful.

3 After the announcement made in the first verse, the wife of Isaiah became pregnant, and later gave birth to a child.[7] We need not necessarily infer that Isaiah's wife herself actually exercised the gift of prophecy. Her character as the wife of the prophet was public, however, and it may be that for this reason she had received the designation "the prophetess." The wife of a *nabi* would be a *nebiah,* like the later designations *episcopa* and *presbytera;* at the same time, we cannot shut out the possibility that Isaiah's wife may also in her own right have been a prophetess.

call his name — Immanuel was to be named by His mother; here it is the father who is to name the child. The strange name which Isaiah had been commanded to write upon the public tablet is now to be transferred to his own son, so that, like the tablet, this son may be a reminder of the prophecy to the nation.

4 As in 7:15, 16 the infancy of the Messiah was made the measure of the time that Judah would suffer from her two adversaries, so here the infancy of Maher-shalal-hash-baz is made the measure of the time that would elapse before the king of Assyria would devastate Damascus and Syria. In the length of time that it would take an infant to reach the age where he could stammer out, "my father," and, "my mother," the Assyrian king would come and devastate the two northern powers. What was prophesied in 7:15, 16 is thus here confirmed. It was a simple cry, *abi* and *immi;* not full-blown speech but the *pappazein* of a child.[8]

We cannot be sure. For Zechariah cf. 2 Kings 18:2; 2 Chron. 29:1, 13. The Zechariah of 2 Chron. 26:5 seems to have died before Uzziah. 2 Chron. 24:20, 21 mentions Zechariah the son of Jehoiada, but he was put to death before the time of Uzziah. The name was common, and we cannot identify Zechariah more exactly.

[7] As in Gen. 20:4; Lev. 18:6, the verb is euphemistic. It is not necessary, however, to render, "I had drawn near."

"the prophetess" — Not a designation of the *almah* of 7:14 (Gesenius) but of Isaiah's wife. Tertullian applied the prophecy to the Virgin Mary. "call his name" — Other examples of long names in Scripture are 1 Chron. 3:17; 25:4. Cf. Gesenius for interesting names from Eth. and from the time of Cromwell.

[8] Cf. *Iliad,* 5:408. The Vulg. and certain Heb. codices read 3rd person suffix, *patrem suum et matrem suam.*

There is thus a formal relationship between the two prophecies. There is, however, an even deeper relationship. Men could verify the prophecy concerning Isaiah's son; they could witness its fulfillment. It would thus become as it were a pledge or earnest of the prophecy of the virgin's Son. Seeing that Maher-shalal-hash-baz had been born in accordance with the prophecy, they could be sure that in His own good time God would fulfill the promise concerning the virgin, and that she would bear a son.

When this child can lisp *abi* and *immi* the wealth of Damascus will be snatched away by force. Together with this wealth all the spoil that could be found in Samaria would also be taken. Two years later, in 732, Damascus was plundered by Tiglath-pileser, and twelve years later Samaria itself was taken. Probably, however, Samaria may have been depredated by Tiglath-pileser earlier than this (cf. 2 Kings 15:29). The booty of these two cities would be before the Assyrian king; all would be at his disposal. The two enemies of Ahaz were but the smoking tails of firebrands; they would soon lose their power to hurt. They would be destroyed by the coming of the one whom Ahaz desired to have for an ally.

5 One cannot help but be reminded of the similar structure of chapter 7.[9] In 7:10 Yahweh spoke to Ahaz; here He addresses Isaiah. There verses 10-17 bore a special relationship to 2-9. Here verses 5-8 sustain a particular connection with 1-4. What follows has a close bearing upon and association with what has preceded.

6 In the message of Yahweh a reason and a conclusion are given, and we may paraphrase the arrangement of this and the next verse as follows: "Inasmuch as this people hath despised . . . , therefore, behold! Yahweh is about to bring up. . . ." But to whom does Yahweh refer when He speaks of "this people?"[10] When God revealed Himself to Isaiah in the inaugural vision, He

---

[9] It may be that as in 7:10 an interval of time had elapsed. The language serves to show that what follows bears a close relation to what precedes.

[10] Three principal interpretations have been held: (1) The entire nation (Hengstenberg) ; (2) the ten tribes; (3) Judah (Alexander, Vitringa, Drechsler). Jennings argues that Judah was trembling, not trusting, and so refers the words to Israel. Fullerton refers the words to Judah, but regards 6b as a gloss. He thinks that the whole passage has been revised in eschatological interests to show that, whereas Israel may perish, Judah, Messiah's land, cannot be destroyed.

spoke also of "this people," and there the reference was to Judah. Here also it is primarily Judah. Because of Judah's lack of trust in Yahweh, the attack of the Assyrians was brought on. In Ahaz' rejection of Isaiah's prophecy, Judah had despised the Lord and had also turned to Assyria for help. The protection of God is symbolically expressed by a reference to the waters of Shiloh.[11] To despise these waters is to despise Yahweh. Perhaps Isaiah has in mind the spring which today is known as *En sitti Miryam,* from which the city receives its water.

Certain is the coming judgment, and two reasons are given therefor. First of all Judah has despised Yahweh, and secondly she has rejoiced in the defeat of her northern enemies.[12] This rejoicing manifested itself in particular with respect to Rezin, and the son of Remaliah who, again, is not named.

7 The condemnation is just. Judah has despised the Lord and she has rejoiced over the defeat that would come to her neighbors. For these reasons the Lord will act.

behold! — The Lord, the sovereign God, the One who had the power to give Ahaz a sign, that powerful Lord is about to act. He will bring up — for only He can move nations at His will — upon those who with contempt have rejected His mercies something that Judah did not wish. From the waters of Shiloh Judah had turned away. Well and good! Judah should have waters, not those of Shiloh which flow slowly, but waters of the Euphrates. No slowly flowing waters, but great and powerful waters, which will not nourish Jerusalem but will overflow her, bringing harm and damage in their wake.

Who this enemy is, is not left in doubt. It is the king of Assyria.[13] In chapter 6 that enemy had not been named; in

---

11 Cf. Neh. 3:15. Kittel thinks the reference is to the tunnel connecting *En sitti Miryam* and *En Silwan.* While we cannot be positive, it does seem likely that inasmuch as the *En sitti Miryam* seems to be connected with waters which flow from under the Temple area, the reference is to this spring.

12 The present reading is difficult, but there is no objective warrant for emending the text. *Sis* is not followed by a direct acc., and את should be taken as a prep., "with respect to." The thought is that the rejoicing of the people had to do with Rezin. It was not a rejoicing on his part, but a rejoicing with respect to him. Note the paronomasia between *mā'as* and *mesôs.*

13 Certain critics have only to see this expression to cry, "gloss!" As Ewald pointed out, however, the more an expression occurs, the less likelihood that it is a gloss.

chapter 7 and at this point he is named. Thus there is brought home to Ahaz the name of the one who will set in motion the chain of events which is finally to accomplish the downfall of Judah. In himself, however, this king of Assyria was only the first step, the first blow to be struck against the nation. The coming of this king would herald the coming of Judah's downfall.

Accompanying the king of Assyria would be all his glory.[14] In their historical inscriptions the Assyrian kings often spoke of the power of the glory of their might as overwhelming the enemy. In all its strength the mighty river of the east would send its waters, and these would overflow into all the river beds and all their parts.[15] After the melting of the winter snows in Armenia's mountains, the Euphrates in spring and summer overflows its banks. Now, however, it will also overflow all its canals and banks and so with a vast inundation will destroy Judah. Slowly flowing waters of blessing Judah will despise; overflowing floods of destruction she will receive.

8 We see the mighty flood gaining force, beginning with the Euphrates overflowing its own banks and canals and then approaching with ever increasing power until it sweeps on into Judah, a mighty flood of destruction. Either he must sink or swim, for the flood will reach to his neck. Ezekiel later was to speak of waters in which a man must swim.[16]

Abruptly Isaiah changes the figure and speaks of the outspread wings of a bird.[17] Like a great bird of prey, the approaching

---

[14] A genuine Isaianic touch; cf. 10:16; 16:14; 17:3, 4 and Micah 1:15.

[15] The river symbolizes the invasion of the Assyrian army; cf. Jer. 47:2 with respect to Philistia. The two epithets "great" and "powerful" are often employed together; cf. Deut. 9:14.

[16] In Ezek. 47:3-5 the waters are first measured until they reach the ankles, then the knees, then the loins, then they are waters that cannot be passed over. Many expositors apply the figure of the neck here to Jerusalem, but it is not necessary to carry out the details of the description. Probably Jerusalem would be first attacked, for once it was taken, the remainder of Judah would easily fall.

חלף — To pass over, sweep on. The two verbs together may be rendered, "to overflow." Cf. Dan. 11:10, 40; Nah. 1:8; Isa. 28:2; 30:28. Weak *wāw* serves to co-ordinate the ideas expressed by the two verbs.

[17] Isaiah frequently changes his figures, e.g., 5:24; 9:17ff.; 28:16, 20.

מֻטּוֹת is a *Hofal* verbal noun (cf. vv. 23; 14:6; 29:3; Ps. 89:3). It is a f. pl. after the verb. When the pred. precedes the subj. such variations in gender are often found. The suffix in "his wings" refers to the invading army, and the thought is that like a bird of prey the army will completely cover the

army spreads out its wings over Judah. Wherever the land extends, there also will be the wings of the bird. The extent of the land, in all its fullness, will be covered, so thoroughly will the Assyrian do his work. But the bird does not belong there, for Judah belongs to Immanuel; but it is to be devastated by those who know not Immanuel. The climax of the verse is a prayer, addressed to the Messiah.[18] Who cannot but weep that such an enemy should completely devastate thy land, O Immanuel? The land which Thou alone couldst promise to Thy people, Thy land, devastated by the Assyrian!

9 Immanuel! Uttering that blessed name, the prophet has become emboldened, and addresses the nations with fresh courage. He can well be bold, for God is with him. Evil are the nations which are to come against Judah, and ironically Isaiah addresses them, "Be ye evil."[19] As a representative of his people, yet speaking in the name of his God, he says in effect, "Do the worst that you can; do your very worst." Such a command, reminding us of that in the inaugural vision (6:10), in fact contains a prophecy. An interesting assonance characterizes Isaiah's two commands, *ro-u wahottu* (cf. 31:14).

Enemies intent upon destroying Judah are in the offing. They think that they are acting in their own strength and power. But they are deceived, for they are merely instruments in the control of the Lord which He is using to punish His own people of Judah. In His own good time, these evil nations will be broken. He in Judah who trusts in the Lord need not fear, for God is with us. His watchword can be, "Immanuel." Well might Isaiah cry aloud, "Do your worst, O ye peoples, and the result will be that you will be broken!"

---

land. "thy land" — The suffix refers to Immanuel. When one speaks of a land as belonging to someone he generally is designating the fatherland; cf. Gen. 12:1. It was the Messiah's land and also the land that was to be devastated; cf. 2 Kings 15:29; 17:3ff.; 18:9-19, 37.

18 "To base a far-reaching construction of Messianic belief on so ambiguous a passage is a mistake" (Gray). But would Isaiah have named the land after one of his own sons or after some hypothetical person? There is a seriousness in the passage that is overlooked by those who refuse to accept the Messianic reference.

19 The *Qal* imp. of רעע assumes two forms, a) *yārō' frangere,* and b) *malum esse, yērā'.* The former is not applicable here.

In beginning his prophecy Isaiah called aloud to heaven and earth as witnesses. Now he speaks to the remote parts of the earth. All the nations who are regarded as God's enemies are addressed. Whoever he may be that would attack the people of God, let him now give ear. "Ye remote parts of the earth, gird yourselves."[20] A contest is to take place, and the nations must be ready therefor. In this contest, however, they will be broken.

10 Broken in pieces! The mighty armies from the east, overflowing the land like a flood. Evil they had planned,[21] but broken they would be. Syria and Ephraim had taken evil counsel together, but their counsel was frustrated. Like that of Rezin and Pekah, so the counsel and purposes of the evil enemies would also come to nought.[22] God is with us! Just as earlier the fact of coming doom was symbolically expressed in the name of Isaiah's child, so here the fact of deliverance is given symbolical clothing in the name of the virgin's Child. To contemplate the declaration that God is with us brings us face to face with the Child, who is the source of power and consolation. If there is to be deliverance and consolation, it is the Child to whom we must turn.

Isaiah shows a holy boldness, a prophetic courage. He is well aware of the machinations of the enemy nations; he knows that they will to a certain extent be successful in their plans. But he does not fear, for in the person of the virgin's Son, God is present. Immanuel! That is his cry and watchword. May it be the true watchword of all who trust in God.[23]

20 This expression seems to have found its origin in the ancient practice of wrestling with a belt. Cf. Note 11 to Chapter 11.

21 עֻצוּ — As the normal pointing we should expect *Hatef-patah* under the ע. The very strangeness of the pointing, however, may indicate that the form is not an error. "speak a word" — The expression seems to have primary reference to the enemy's plan. Eitan, however, would construe it like Ar. *dabbara*, "to manage, arrange."

22 "and let it come to naught" — The jussive in an apodosis after the hypothetical imper. in the protasis. The form is *tu-far*, the vowel with the preformative is naturally long. Possibly this is the reason for the naturally long vowel in the preceding imper. The two forms would then give a striking sound.

23 The relationship which this section bears both to the preceding and to the following chapter should be noted. Let the reader compare carefully the following references: 8:9, 10 with 7:3-9; especially 8:9 and 7:8; 8:10 and 7:5-7, 46:10.

b. *Confidence in God* (8:11—9:1)

11 For thus saith the LORD unto me in strength of hand, and instructed me from walking in the way of this people, saying,

12 Ye shall not call conspiracy everything which this people calleth conspiracy, and its fear ye shall not fear, nor treat with awe.

13 Sanctify the LORD of hosts himself, since he is your fear and he is your dread.

14 And he shall be for a sanctuary and for a stone of striking and a rock of stumbling to the two houses of Israel, for a gin and for a snare to the inhabitants of Jerusalem.

15 And many shall stumble against them, and they shall fall and be broken, and they shall be snared and taken.

16 Bind up the testimony, seal the law, in my disciples.

17 And I shall wait for the LORD, who hideth his face from the house of Jacob, and I shall look eagerly for him.

18 Behold! I and the children which the LORD hath given to me are for signs and wonders in Israel from the LORD of hosts who dwelleth in Mount Zion.

19 And when they shall say unto you, Seek unto the spirits and unto the familiar spirits, which chirp and which mutter, should not a people seek unto its god? for the living unto the dead?

20 To the law and to the testimony, if they do not speak according to this word, there is no dawn to them.

21 And they shall pass through it hardly bestead and hungry; and it shall come to pass that when they are hungry, they shall fret themselves, and curse their king and their God and shall look upward.

22 And they shall look unto the earth, and behold! distress and darkness, dimness of anguish, and thrust out unto darkness.

9:1 For there is no darkness to her that is distressed. As in the former time he degraded the land of Zebulun and the land of Naphtali, so in the latter he glorifies the way of the sea, the bank of the Gentiles.

11 Isaiah's boldness has been holy, but it has been well founded.[24] He now appeals to divine authority to show that he was not merely speaking on his own. God's power had come upon the prophet for the purpose of assuring him of the truth of what had been revealed and to warn him from walking in the way of the people who would perish. The message was a divine revelation. God's hand had come upon Isaiah and he

24 What has been stated in v. 10 is now grounded or justified by an appeal to divine authority.

had felt God's power.[25]   When this hand of God comes upon a man, that man is completely subject to God's power.   This is not ordinary prophetic inspiration, but a power of God to constrain Isaiah.   The seizure was in order to instruct Isaiah so that he would not walk in the way of the people of Judah and bring condemnation upon himself.[26]

12 This people again!   Now they were crying, "Conspiracy." But who was conspiring?   It was Isaiah himself who had been attempting to dissuade Judah from seeking foreign aid.   That was to go contrary to the policy of the court.[27]   Isaiah, Jeremiah and other prophets advocated a policy of dependence upon the Lord and not upon foreign powers.   Surely that was treason! But Judah was the theocracy and should have been governed in all policies by God Himself.   Ahaz, the son of David, of all men, ought to have understood this.   His first question should always have been, "What does the Lord command?"   The nation was so low, spiritually, however, that when the prophets advocated that the theocracy act like the theocracy, they were accused of conspiracy.   So it has always been.   Throughout the history of the church, those who have sought to call the church back to her God-given mission and away from her man-made "programs" have been treated as troublemakers.   A man such as Ahaz could

[25] "in strength of hand" — The phrase, "the hand of the LORD" occurs often in Scripture; cf. Ezek. 1:3; 3:14, 22; 37:1. The phrase indicates that a peculiar force is exerted upon the prophet which is to be distinguished from ordinary prophetic inspiration. This does not paralyze the prophet nor render him unconscious. He was able to receive and to understand the message that was given him. The understanding of this warning presupposes a condition of clear consciousness (Herntrich).

[26] ויסרני — This is an extremely difficult form. Gray suggests that it may be Hifil imp. of sûr. But the basic Hifil form would be ya-ser, and when the qametz in a distant open syllable drops to Shewa, it cannot be replaced by Hireq followed by Daghesh. This would involve an open syllable becoming closed. The form may be an imp., but it may also be a Piel perf. with an anomalous connecting vowel. We should expect patah instead of Tzere in the perf. "from walking" — From carrying on my manner of life in the way of this people. The final word introduces the discourse which God Himself had spoken to the prophet.

[27] קשר — A conspiracy with treasonable intent; cf. 2 Chron. 23:13. It was more than a mere alliance, such as that of Syria and Israel against Judah or any agreement with Assyria. Cf. 2 Kings 11:14; 12:21; 14:19 and 15:30.

not understand what prompted Isaiah's actions and hence would simply conclude that Isaiah was in the service of the enemy and one who was conspiring for the overthrow of the land.

As a matter of fact, Isaiah was rendering the highest form of service to his country. He was not to call his action a conspiracy but was to interpret it in a fashion diametrically opposite to that in which the nation interpreted it. "And what this people fears, you need not treat with awe. They fear the two northern enemies, but you need not regard with awe those two tails of smoking firebrands. There is one place alone where your fear should be placed; put your fear in the Lord; fear Him."

13 "No, Isaiah, you and others who believe like you are not to fear what this people fears. Rather, you are to fear Yahweh." Had there been a proper fear of the Lord there would not have been this present distrust. If one had sanctified Yahweh in his heart, he would not have regarded Isaiah's work as a conspiracy. But how does one sanctify the LORD of hosts? So to set God apart in the heart that He is regarded as highly exalted and acknowledged to be omnipotent is to sanctify Him, and one who has so sanctified Him will rejoice in the work of His servants (cf. 1 Pet. 3:15). When times of fear come upon us we must remember that He is the Yahweh of hosts, and so able to deliver all those who put their trust in Him. Calvin rightly says " . . . for if we are not convinced that innumerable methods, though unknown to us, are in his power for our deliverance, we conceive of him as a dead idol."

"And fear not them which kill the body, but are not able to kill the soul; but rather fear him which is able to destroy both soul and body in hell" (Matt. 10:28). God alone is the One whom we must fear, the sole object of our fear.[28]

14 God's command continues. Sanctify yourselves, He commands, for He will be a sanctuary. If you sanctify Him, He will in His turn be a sanctuary to you also. The Lord is the Holy

---

[28] "and he is your fear" — The development of the noun is probably as follows: *mô-rā-'e-ḵem* > *mô-rā-'a-ḵem* or possibly *mô-rā'-kem* > *mô-ra'-ḵem;* then compound *Shewa* under *aleph.* At any rate the vowel under the *resh* should be accompanied by *Metheg.*

מערצכם . . . with long *i*. The word may either be a *Hifil* part. or a verbal noun, "the object of your dread."

One to His people. If, in the fullest sense, they regard Him as holy and so sanctify Him, He will be to them an object of holiness, and in Him there will be true protection. About them He will be a wall of holiness and a place of refuge.[29] As Delitzsch puts it; "All who sanctified the Lord of lords He surrounded like temple walls; hid them in Himself, whilst death and tribulation reigned without, and comforted, fed, and blessed them in His own gracious fellowship."

On the other hand, a stone of striking and a rock of stumbling which will cause those who bump against it to fall[30] — such He will be to the two kingdoms, Israel and Judah. The schism was never regarded as legitimate, and the two kingdoms are here set before us as a unit. To those in both the north and south God will be a stone; to some a sanctuary, but to others, a stone of stumbling. The leaders in the kingdom were the inhabitants of Jerusalem whose lives set the pace for the remainder. The divided condition of God's people and all the sad consequences which came from that division were in reality the result of the way that the inhabitants of Jerusalem acted. Had it not been for the folly of Rehoboam and his advisors, the schism might have been averted. The prophecy, therefore, has reference primarily to the responsible ones at Jerusalm, but also to the people of God in its entirety. Unfortunately, when Isaiah prophesied, the people was a divided one, and hence the designation, the two houses of Israel.[31]

Not only a stone of stumbling but also a bird trap which snares and a spring trap will God be to the people.[32] In the first part of the verse we see the results of godly fear; in the second, those of ungodly fear.

---

[29] "for a sanctuary" — That which is holy, as in Luke 1:35. Cf. also 1 Pet. 2:7; Rom. 9:33. In ancient times altars were sometimes recognized as places of asylum; cf. Appian, *de bello civili*, II.

[30] אבן, "stone," and צור, "rock," but no essential difference between them is intended. The variety is probably due to the desire to avoid tautology.

[31] Herntrich, however, would follow B, "to the house of Israel." The two houses are now separated but Isaiah here speaks of the one kingdom which is withstanding its Lord.

[32] פח — A trap which catches but does not harm the prey. מוקש — Catches by means of a spring. Cf. Driver: *JBL* (Sept. 1954), p. 131. Philby (*The Empty Quarter*, London, 1933, p. 12) notes that the Arabs near Hufuf use the term *fakh* to designate a bird trap.

15 The figure is completed. The wicked in Israel will actually stumble over the stone, the gin and the snare.[33] Because of the stone many will stumble and fall and be broken. They will be caught as in a gin and a snare. Those who meet the stone and the snares will be completely destroyed. Five verbs are used to state this destruction. Stumbling, they will fall and be completely destroyed; the gin and snare will be effective, for the Lord Himself will be the occasion for the destruction of those who fear Him not. Peter reflects upon this verse when he says, "Unto you therefore which believe he is precious: but unto them which be disobedient, the stone which the builders disallowed, the same is made the head of the corner, and a stone of stumbling, and a rock of offence, even to them which stumble at the word, being disobedient: whereunto also they were appointed" (1 Pet. 2:8; cf. Luke 2:34; Matt. 21:44; Rom. 9:33).

16 It has been a message of utter doom. God now utters a command to the prophet himself. Isaiah is to bind up God's revelation in the sense that he is to close it spiritually in the hearts of his disciples and to leave it there.[34] This revelation may be the inscription mentioned in the first verse, but more likely it is the entire preceding message recorded in this chapter.[35] This testimony then is the revelation which God has given to Isaiah, a revelation in spoken words. How significant and im-

---

33 The first three words are in 1Q and evidently in B. Cf. Isa. 28:13 and Hos. 14:10. The word בם seems to refer not to the people, but to the stone, gin and snare. The first three verbs may have more immediate reference to the stone, and the second two verbs to the traps. At the same time this may be somewhat of an overrefinement. All five verbs indicate that those who meet the stone and snares will be completely destroyed.

34 An inf. followed by a perf. with *wāw* cons. The thought is, "there is nothing left for me but to bind up the testimony," etc.

35 "in my disciples" — One who is taught, instructed; cf. Song of Sol. 3:8; 1 Chron. 25:7. The prep. should have its natural force, the reference being to the sealing of the law *in* the hearts of the disciples. The modern view is that the disciples were those whom Isaiah had gathered about him and who were trained of him. They saved his writings for posterity, and their activity led to the beginnings of the canon (cf. Mowinckel, *Jesaja Disciplinen*). This interpretation may in part be correct, but the suffix refers in the first place to God. The disciples are those among the people who are truly enlightened in that they are taught of God Himself; cf. Isa. 54:13. It may be that this activity was carried out through the prophet, so that in a certain sense these enlightened ones might also be called the disciples of Isaiah. To assume that there was a specific narrow group that collected Isaiah's writings is an assumption for which there is no evidence.

portant are these words! They are a testimony, not in the sense that they are pointers or witnesses to some vague, nebulous revelation or Word of God, but in that they themselves are the testimony, the revelation of God. The words which God speaks to man are revelatory words; they are themselves revelation. This testimony is also described as the law, the teaching in words which has been revealed by God. The two words, neither of which has the definite article, describe the content of what Isaiah was to bind up. Perhaps, therefore, it was testimony and law in a general sense which he was to bind up; more likely, it was simply the message or content of the chapter before us.

Who are these disciples, however, in whose hearts the message is to be sealed, and how is this testimony to be sealed in their hearts? First of all, we should note that they are God's disciples and not Isaiah's. They are the elect; the ones among the nation who are taught of God and who learn of Him. They were taught of Him, however, by means of the instruction of the law and of the prophets, and here particularly by means of the teaching of Isaiah. In this derivative or secondary sense, then, they may also be denominated the disciples of Isaiah. In their hearts he would seal the teaching by means of faithfully proclaiming it to them and explaining it. Such, indeed, is the work of every faithful minister of the testimony and law. In teaching and preaching the truth (not some pointer to the truth) they are sealing in the hearts of God's elect the testimony and law. When truth is thus sealed in the heart, it is in a certain sense hidden from others. It is put away in order that the one in whose heart it is sealed may benefit therefrom. God's truth must be deposited in the hearts of His people.

17 The one who waits does so with eager and patient expectation. The Lord has hidden His face, as He had promised when revealing Himself to Isaiah in the inaugural vision. When punishment and devastation came upon the nation, then the face of Yahweh was hidden. The entire nation, but specifically the southern kingdom, felt His wrath and was shut out from His countenance. But this is a difficult verse. Who is it that speaks, and declares that he will patiently await the Lord? There are three principal interpretations, which we must briefly consider.

A. The Targum regards verse 16 as a command from God to the prophet, as we also have done, and then considers verse 17 as Isaiah's response. We may paraphrase:

16. "Prophet, preserve the testimony, do not bear witness against them, because they do not hearken; seal and conceal the law, for they do not wish to learn in it."

17. The prophet said, "Concerning this I prayed before the Lord, who said that he would remove his dwelling from them of the house of Jacob, and I sought from before him."

On this interpretation Isaiah may be pictured as one who does not lose hope and belief, even though the nation itself can no longer hope, because Yahweh has covered His face. The predicted judgment has fallen, and during this time one can but wait in patience while God hides His face. Isaiah's words have fallen on stopped-up ears; he must grieve like Moses or Paul for his people, while his message goes unnoticed.

B. A second view finds the subject of the verbs of verse 17 to be the Messiah. In verse 16, according to this position, the speaker is God who there addressed the prophet. In verse 17, it is claimed, there is no change of speaker, and inasmuch as verse 18 is quoted in Hebrews 2:13 of the Messiah, it is assumed that here also the Messiah is the speaker. Upon this construction the Messiah announces that He will await expectantly, while the face of God is hidden. This hiding of the face is seen not only in the outward calamities which come upon the nation but also in the withholding of the divine illumination, which was alluded to in the preceding verse. For a time, when the face of God is concealed, the meaning of the promises is hid from the many and known only by the few. During this time the Messiah will wait in patience until the time be passed, and the fullness of time come, when He is openly to appear.

C. The third view is closely related to the first with the exception that it pays more attention to the New Testament interpretation of the passage and regards Isaiah as a type of Jesus Christ. For the unbelievers among the nation there is a period of punishment, but for the true believers the prophecy has another meaning. Isaiah suffers not only as a sinner among sinners, but he also suffers through them. He is comparatively innocent, yet he must suffer through the guilty. He thus assumes the position of a mediator. In verse 11 the singular was employed, but in verses 12 and 13 the plural, where Isaiah includes himself or represents the entirety of the believers. In verse 16, then, on this view, Isaiah is represented as interceding and in verses 16-19 he appears as a mediator between the God of Israel on the one hand

and those among the people who are aroused, on the other. As Christ before His suffering prayed the prayer recorded in John 17, so Isaiah, according to this interpretation, facing the period when the countenance of God would be hidden, prayed the words recorded in these verses.

The reader must study these interpretations carefully for himself. It is not easy to be sure precisely what the prophecy intends. The present writer inclines towards the second of the above views but cannot be dogmatic.

18 As is so often the case, the prophet directs attention to the prophecy with an introductory "Behold!" And the speaker places himself first. "Behold I!" The speaker and his children are signs and wonders. As signs, they would be pledges of something that was to be accomplished. As wonders, they were special manifestations of the power of God or tokens or symbols of future events. They are thus set apart in Israel as manifestations of the power of God and pledges of the fact that God will be true to His promises. But who is intended? Again, there are three principal interpretations.

A. The prophet has reference to himself and to his own children, Maher-shalal-hash-baz and Shear-jashub. The children are in this interpretation Isaiah's actual sons. The children were signs in that the name Shear-jashub signified that the nation would not be destroyed entirely, but that a remnant would be delivered. On the other hand, the younger son bore a name which pointed to the speedy coming of the destruction of the nation. Even the prophet's own name is said to signify that salvation is found only in Yahweh.

B. A second interpretation applies the passage to Isaiah and to the disciples who followed him and believed in God. On this view the disciples would be true followers of God. It has even been suggested that they were in a sense forerunners of the apostles who were gathered around Christ. It was an *ecclesiola in ecclesia*.

C. A third view applies the reference to Christ and to those whom the Father gave Him. The disciples would be a spiritual seed, as in 53:10 we read, "He shall see his seed," and they would be given of the Father (John 6 and 16). Calvin remarks: "By *given* he means those whom God drew by an inward and secret operation of his Spirit, when the sound of the external voice fell on the ears of the multitude without producing any good effect." He goes on to remark: "Thus we see that readiness to believe does not depend on the will of men; but that some of the multitude believe, because, as Luke tells us, *they had been foreordained,* (Acts xiii. 48). Now, *whom he foreordained he likewise calls* (Romans viii. 30), and efficaciously seals in them the proof of their adoption, that they may become obedient and submissive. Such, therefore, is the *giving* of which Isaiah now speaks." It is the application of this verse to Christ in Hebrews 2:13 which supports the Messianic interpretation.

If, however, the reference is to Christ, there need not necessarily be excluded a secondary reference to Isaiah. The Spirit of Christ was in Isaiah, and in a certain sense we may say that the prophet was a type of Christ to come.[36]

whom the Lord gave me — Children are regarded as gifts of God, and believers are as children. "My little children," writes John (I John 2:1), and they too are given to the Messiah by the Father. In Israel the Messiah and His own serve as signs and wonders. Their very presence in the midst of an unbelieving church (Israel) is a portent of the fact that God will fulfill His promise and send the Redeemer. At the same time, they are the objects of derision and abhorrence. The unbelieving multitude, as Calvin points out, is concerned with material advantage and possessions. When it sees the true people of God despise these things and cleave unto the Lord, it despises that people. Here we may learn that one mark of the true Christian is his willingness to sacrifice material possessions for the kingdom of Christ.

from the Lord of hosts — It is from the Lord that the Speaker and His children are as signs and wonders. The thought is not merely that there are signs and wonders from the Lord, nor that the Speaker and His children are from the Lord, but rather that the Speaker and His children as signs and wonders are from the Lord. Inasmuch as the position of believers with their Messiah is from the Lord of hosts, they need not fear the calumny of the entire world. There is in these words, as Calvin remarks, a lofty defiance.

who dwelleth in Mount Zion — The wicked majority of the nation appealed to the Temple. Outwardly they were worshipers of Yahweh. Isaiah now points out to them that their confidence

---

36 Drechsler points out that these verses are a short summary of the Lord's high-priestly prayer in John 17. Cf. v. 18 with John 17:6, 9, 11, 12, 24; 6:37, 39; 10:29; and v. 19 with Luke 17:23; Matt. 24:4.

is vain, for it is this very Yahweh who dwells in the Temple on Zion that has set forth the Messiah and His own for signs and wonders. Many there are who make an outward profession of orthodoxy whose hearts are in reality far estranged from the Lord. Such a condition is about us today in the fact that the great Protestant denominations, while retaining ancient creeds, have nevertheless for the most part departed far from the faith once for all delivered unto the saints.

19 The Messiah continues to speak. The ever present temptation to idolatry was at hand. Unbelievers were tempting the believers by suggesting that they consult the spiritualistic media. It is no mere hypothetical suggestion. The Messiah is not merely advancing the supposition that someone might conceivably make such a suggestion. Such suggestions, rather, were constantly being made, as they are constantly being made today. When the temptation to such idolatry is presented to them, what should true believers do?

It is a deceitful suggestion. Seeking is important; the people should seek unto God. But the tempters suggest that they seek unto the spirits. Just like the witch of Endor, there were others who made it their nefarious business to call up the dead.[37] And there were ghosts who supposedly had knowledge of the future and of various events, ghosts who may have been known to the enquirer.[38] Like birds, these familiar spirits chirp and twitter. Apparently the reference is to the manner in which the soothsayers invoked their spirits or possibly delivered their messages. Like the mourning of the dove, so the voice of the medium was mournful as it called forth the spirit.[39]

[37] "to seek unto" — Cf. Deut. 18:11; Job 5:8. The verb may be used of seeking unto God through the prophet or oracle and also of seeking unto the spirits.

[38] אוֹב — A necromancer who calls up the dead. The word may also refer to a ghost itself, as in Isa. 29:4.

יִדְּעֹנִי — Those who had a knowledge of the future and of various events; ghosts of knowledge; cf. Lev. 19:31; 20:27; Deut. 18:11. It could also be that the spirit was one known to the enquirer.

[39] "and which mutter" — Used of the mourning of a dove; Isa. 38:14. Here the root suggests the mournful voice of one who calls forth the spirit. Cf. *Aeneid* 3:39:

> *gemitus lacrymabilis imo*
> *auditur tumulos et vos reddita fertur ad aures*

and Horace: *Satires*, L.I.VIII. 40. The Ar. term *tzaftzaf* indicates the piping of sparrows. Cf. Procopius, 29:4. Rosenmüller gives classical references.

should not a people — Here is the response to be given to tempting suggestions. A nation should not seek unto spirits; rather, it should seek unto its God. When wicked persons suggest that you, the people of the Messiah, should consult the spirits, just as the nations seek their gods, so you should seek your God, who is the LORD. Other nations seek their gods which are vain; you, the people of the true God, should seek Him.

Why go to the dead on behalf of the living?[40] Should we seek the dead for the benefit of the living? Perhaps there is a touch of irony in these questions. This temptation to turn to the dead on behalf of the living is ever with us. The wickedness of such a practice is always before us. In times of calamity and personal sorrow, God's people must not forget Him. The abominable practice of consulting the spirits is a forgetting of God; it is a denial of His very existence. These spirits mutter and chirp; they do not come out openly with clear-cut information. They are utterly different from the candid "thus saith Yahweh," of the prophets.

If other nations consult their gods, gods which are not real, we who know the Lord should at all times consult Him. In Old Testament days this might be done through the prophets; in these latter days, God has given to us His infallible Word, the Bible. When we wish to consult Him, let us turn to the Bible, for its words are the words of God Himself. Not only is spiritualism wicked; it is also foolish, for it is foolish to consult dead people on behalf of the living!

20 If any seeking is to be done, it should be unto the law and the testimony.[41] The law (note that the words from verse 16 are here inverted) is the revelation of God expressing His will for man's obedience, and the testimony is His revelation expressing His will as a system to be believed. These are the standards by which all opinions and utterances are to be judged. If anyone does not speak in accordance with the law and the testimony, he is the one to whom there is no dawn.[42] Whoever speaks not in

[40] In reality this is a second question and so, grammatically, need not depend upon the interrogatory particle.

[41] The clause is elliptical and we are probably to understand the words "seek unto the law."

[42] In support of the translation adopted we may remark: (1) The Ar. word *sahr* may mean "enchantment," but that cannot determine the meaning

accordance with these standards is one that still abides in the darkness of sin and unbelief, and hence, one who cannot give light.[43]   Even in times of calamity God's people are to hearken to the law and the testimony.   There is extant a written revelation which at all times may be consulted.   It is the law, for it tells man precisely what God requires of him, and it is also testimony, for it speaks forth God's will and bears witness to the fact that it is from God.   Even in times of distress there are many whose messages do not agree with the Word which God has given.   If such speak words that are not in harmony with the objective revelation of God, the reason is that there is no light of salvation in them.   It is also true that to them who thus speak there is no such light.   To hearken to a message which finds its origin in darkness rather than in the clear light of the law of God is folly.

Light is found in the law of God, the written revelation, the Scriptures.   Those who speak contrary to Scripture have no dawn. They remain yet in the darkness of deep night.   Upon them the morning light has not broken, nor will it break until they turn as little children to the law and submit all their thinking and their opinions to it.   Then will the early rays of morning light shine, and the full light of the sun break forth in their hearts. More than anything else today there is need that all our thinking be based upon and in conformity with the Holy Scriptures.

21 There have been those who have not spoken in accordance with the law and testimony.   Indeed among those who have not thus spoken, some shall pass through the land.   Traversing the land, however, will be difficult.   Those who journey through will be destitute both of physical and spiritual good.   The hard condition of the passers-through manifests itself in hunger and

---

of the Heb. word in this passage.   (2) The pronoun suffix in *lô* need not be restricted in its reference to "word."   It may be employed in a distributive sense to refer to the ones who speak.   (3) אשר indicates the apodosis, and may be used in the sense of *ki* as is shown by 2 Sam. 2:4, etc. (4) The words "to the law and the testimony" constitute a cry such as is found in Judg. 7:18.   They are to be taken as the words of the Messiah.

[43] The rel. pro. is equivalent to "he it is who."   The copula must then be supplied; thus, "he it is to whom there is no dawn."   It is also possible to take the relative as a substitute for *ki* and to render, "it is that there is no dawn to them."

famine.[44] When famine comes, it brings with it fretting. The people will work themselves into a frenzy, exciting themselves to anger, and this anger will burst out in cursing. In anger they will curse their king and their God. The uncontrolled anger leads to cursing, and this cursing is not merely turned against the king but, more than that, against God. All that is their proper and rightful help, the people turn upon in cursing. Desperation has gripped the people, and they are willing to take leave of the true God, in wrath uttering curses against Him. All they can do is to look upward in complete desperation (cf. Rev. 16:11, 21). Whether they look upward to God or to the earth, all that meets them is darkness. Rejecters of king and God have no gleam of light to encourage them. These are forsakers of God, but more than that they are forsaken of God.[45]

Forsaking the Lord brings certain definite consequences. Having given counsel that is contrary to the law and the testimony, they will one day forsake the Lord Himself. In desperate need they will go through the devastated land, and there will be none to help.[46] When one forsakes the Lord, he will become forsaken of the Lord. When times of calamity come, the wicked are often hardly bestead. Hunger may cause a man to arouse himself to anger, and being beside himself in rage, to curse everything that could give him help. When one adopts the attitude of "curse God and die," he has clearly lost all confidence in God.

22 To look upward brings no help.[47] Nor is there help if one looks to earth. No matter where the wicked looks, he finds no hope. The gloom about him is unrelieved. Ahaz would not look above for a sign; his descendants will look above, but all is black.[48] There is for them no sign, for the sign has already been

---

[44] "hungry" — An adj. which expresses a state may be placed after the verb to describe a bodily condition more accurately. The conj. is *wāw specificum*.

[45] Cf. 5:30 and note Koran 2:17.

[46] בה — Has reference to a concept previously understood, namely, "land." Jennings refers it to the gloom itself, which is without warrant from the context.

[47] König suggests that the descendants of Ahaz will do what he had spurned doing; they will look above for a sign, for any sign that would promise relief.

[48] I am inclined to regard אֲפֵלָה as an acc. (of specification or place) and to render, "and with respect to darkness, it [the people] is cast out." Reider ("Contributions to the Scriptural Text," *HUCA*, Vol. xxiv, 1952-53, p. 87).

given. Only light can dispel the gloom of despair and desperation, but that light is not to be seen. There is distress of soul
and distress in physical circumstances, and this distress speaks
out in darkness.

All may be summed up in the words, "dimness of anguish."[49]
It is a dim or gloomy anguish, a gloom that consists of anguish.
Gloom, inward and outward; compressed or straightened circumstances which reflect themselves in a corresponding state of mind.
The people are cast out into darkness. He who consults dark
omens and does the deeds of darkness can only expect an affliction that is characterized by darkness. In the Bible sin is described as darkness. Gloom is oppressive and constraining. Those
who regard it as light and freedom are deceived. The end of
those who live in the dark is to be driven into the darkness.
Sinners think that they are in the light and that they possess
freedom, independence, truth, an unprejudiced mind; actually
they walk in darkness and are the slaves of gloom, subject to
falsehood and prejudiced in favor of evil.[50]

9:1 (In Heb. 8:23) Darkness and gloom all about! But they
will not last forever. For the sinners of the people there is to be
perpetual darkness, but for the people of God, for the nation itself,
the all-encircling gloom will pass away. Now she is in distress, but
she will not always have darkness. We may paraphrase Isaiah's
meaning: "For to the land to which there is now distress there
will not always be darkness."

A blessed contrast explains why the darkness is not to be
permanent. According to the former time, the extended pe-

---

suggests the following, "and behold distress and darkness making it impossible
to flee, distress and darkness making it impossible to depart." This verse
is not corrupt. The learned arguments which Gray adduces amount to saying that the verse does not fit the strophic arrangement, or that they are
not the best words to express the thoughts. These are not weighty arguments.

[49] מוּצָק, "darkness," and מוּעָף, "distressed," are both verbal nouns of the
Hofal stem. We may paraphrase, "For to the land to which there is now
distress, there will not always be darkness." As in 5:30 the designations "now —
then" are omitted.

[50] According to Kissane vv. 21, 22 are out of place and belong rather after
5:30. In answer to this we must point out that all textual evidence, including
1Q, places the verses where they now are. Secondly, a good and consistent exegesis of these verses is possible, as the above has sought to show. The very difficulty of the verses argues for their genuineness. If they are so completely out
of place at this point, why did anyone ever place them where they are?

riod during which the degradation lasted, God degraded the land and brought darkness over it.[51] The latter time, however, the period of glory, will occur but once and will endure forever. God will honor the land. Zebulun and Naphtali, the two north-eastern tribes of the land west of the Jordan (later known as upper and lower Galilee), were first devastated and depopulated by Tiglath-pileser. "In the days of Pekah king of Israel came Tiglath-pileser king of Assyria, and took Ijon, and Abel-beth-maachah, and Janoah, and Kedesh, and Hazor, and Gilead, and Galilee, all the land of Naphtali, and carried them captive to Assyria" (2 Kings 15:29).

A time of distress was the former time, the latter is one of glory, and the way of the sea, the way along the western side of the sea of Gennesaret, Galilee of the Gentiles, is to be honored.[52] The circuit of the nations is the northern boundary of Palestine in which there was a large mixed population. Throughout, the same district is designated. It is first identified by the names of the two tribes, Zebulun and Naphtali, which dwelt therein. It is next identified by its relation to the Sea of Galilee and to the Jordan River.[53] Being most remote from Judah it was nearest to the foreign countries and so subject to heathen influences. Not only the location of the district contributed to its disgrace, but it had been the first to tremble in awe before the might of Assyria. This despised district, despised even in New Testament times, was glorified when God honored it, and the fulfillment of the proph-

---

51 "the former time" — The following arguments are used to support the view that this phrase is subj.: (1) *Ki* is to be rendered "even as." (2) In the poetry of the OT and also of the Arabs a designation of time is often the subj. of a verb (cf. Job 3:5; Ps. 19:3); *yaum bashir*, "a day which brings good news." But the prep. is placed before the phrase "the former time" to empha-size the fact that the time of degradation lasted over an extended period. On the other hand, the phrase "the latter" is a simple acc. indicating that the period of glory will occur but once and that forever. The verb has the force of a prophetic perf. עֵת — Is usually f. but it does occur as m. and takes a m. pl.

52 "sea" — The word could designate the Mediterranean and the reference could then be either to the road from Acre to Damascus, or it could also be interpreted "toward" the sea, or westwards. Most modern commentators refer it to the Sea of Gennesaret.

53 Galilee of the Gentiles (or, the circuit of the nations) is the northern boundary of Palestine, in which there was a large mixed population (cf. 1 Kings 9:11; Josh. 20:7; 21:32). It was most remote from Judah and next to the foreign lands and so subject to heathen influences. In the NT we may note John 1:46; 7:52; Matt. 26:69; Acts 1:11; 2:7.

ecy occurred when Jesus Christ the Son of God dwelt in Capernaum (Matt. 4:13ff.) .

The sin of Israel brought upon her as a nation the darkness of punishment. Nevertheless, inasmuch as the God of Israel is a God of light, and faithful to the words of His promise, the darkness which came upon the nation would one day be dispelled. We receive at the Lord's hand punishment and affliction but also honor and glory. The glory which we receive is the result of His own presence in our midst.

c. *The Messianic King* (9:2-7; in Hebrew, vv. 1-6)

2 The people that walked in darkness have seen a great light; they that dwell in the land of the shadow of death, a light hath shined upon them.

3 Thou hast enlarged the nation, thou hast increased its joy; they joy before thee as the rejoicing in harvest, as men rejoice when they divide the spoil.

4 For the yoke of his burden and the rod of his shoulder, and the staff of the one oppressing him thou hast broken, as in the day of Midian.

5 For every boot of one trampling is with a sound, and garments rolled in blood, and it shall become a burning, the fuel of fire.

6 For unto us a Child is born, unto us a Son is given, and the government is upon his shoulder, and his Name is called Wonderful Counsellor, Mighty God, Everlasting Father, Prince of Peace.

7 Of the increase of the government and of peace there is no end, upon the throne of David and upon his kingdom to found it and to establish it in judgment and in righteousness from now and forever; the zeal of the LORD of hosts will accomplish this.

2 The inhabitants of Galilee, those to whom reference has just been made, are walking in darkness.[54] Their manner and course of life, their very existence, is one that is in the darkness.[55] Darkness without and darkness within, ignorance, distress, misery and

---

[54] "the people" — The noun is collective and so may be followed by a part. in the pl. "that walked" — The walking ones. Life is conceived as a journey; the verb indicates the course of life, hence the NT usage of καθήμενος as a *quid pro quo*. Cf. Ps. 1:1 where the two conceptions are practically synonymous.

[55] "darkness" — In the darkness. The word means "deep shadow," and is poetical for intense darkness. If it be derived from *tzel* and *mawet̲*, it is difficult to explain the shift of the *i* vowel in *tzel* to *a*. If it be derived from *tzelem*, the difficulty is explained; cf. *zalima*, "to be dark," and the Eth. *salema*.

sin. By the Assyrian invasion the darkness may have been brought on, or possibly was simply intensified by that invasion. Far deeper than any darkness brought on by an invasion, however, was the inward condition of the nation, the plight of sin and misery in which it carried on its life.

To these people, walking in darkness, a great light appeared. When the prophet wrote, they had not yet seen this light, but its occurrence was so certain and vivid to Isaiah's mind that he described it as though it had already dawned.[56] In place of the darkness of calamity the people saw the light of peace and blessedness; in place of the darkness of death, the light of life; in place of the darkness of ignorance, the light of knowledge; in place of the darkness of sin, the light of salvation. Salvation in its widest sense had shined upon these people; a complete reversal of their condition had occurred.

The darkness was a shadow of death, for it was deep and of death, such as could be removed only by a light of life.[57] Only a Light which was able to bring life and immortality to light could dispel this deep darkness, and such a Light appeared when Christ, departing from Nazareth, went down to Capernaum and dwelt there (Matt. 4:12-17). The darkness of sin can only be dispelled by something that is its very opposite, namely light. Light is a gift of God; it cannot be produced from a human heart which itself is in darkness. The whole work of Christ and all the blessings which He brings may be characterized by the one word "light."

3 The blessed thought that light has shined upon the darkened Galileans causes Isaiah to address the One who is the source of the light, and in whose light alone we may see light. When the Light came, God brought the Gentiles into the true Israel, the household of faith, in fulfillment of the promise which He had made to Abraham, "I will make of thee a great nation [got]." Thus, with the addition of the Gentiles, the people were made

---

[56] A description of the fut. may begin with a verb in the perf.; la may be regarded as a type of *casus pendens,* lb forming a strong balance and parallelism. "that dwelt" — The dwellers in the land. The const. before a prep. usually occurs with the part.

[57] The light of the divine law had already shone over Galilee. Now, however, the sun of righteousness will arise, Mal. 3:20 (4:2); John 1:9; 8:12; Isa. 42:6; 49:6; 60:1-3. Christ is the fullness of light; cf. also Luke 1:78, 79. Note that "light" is contrasted with "men who walk in darkness."

greater in number.[58] "Sing, O barren, thou that didst not bear; break forth into singing, and cry aloud, thou that didst not travail with child: for more are the children of the desolate than the children of the married wife, saith the LORD" (Isa. 54:1).

With the enlarging of the nation, joy itself is increased.[59] The result of the mighty act of God in multiplying the nation is a true joy before God in the hearts of those who receive and who have received His blessings. It is a marvelous joy; one such as is found when men have harvested the grain and when as victors they divide the spoils of war.[60] The salvation of sinners produces exultation in the hearts of God's people, and such jubilation is a gift of God Himself. Israel's blessings were truly from God. To rejoice in God is the highest form of rejoicing, indeed, it is the only true rejoicing. Man's chief end is not only to glorify God, but also to enjoy Him forever. Only by means of a God-induced response to His own mighty work of salvation do men truly joy before Him as they should.

[58] Continues with the prophetic perf. The increase is of the people of Israel. Jer. 32:22; Isa. 54:1ff., a commentary upon this passage. After the captivity there was an increase of the people, which pointed forward to the great increase when the Gentiles were to be included in the household of faith (cf. Acts 15:13ff.).

[59] "thou hast increased" — M has the negative. Various attempts have been made to explain this negative, "thou didst multiply the nation which thou didst not increase" (Sym.); "thou hast increased the nation [the Jews] but thou hast not increased the joy" [of the Gentiles] (Luther); "thou multipliest the nation to which thou didst not increase the joy" (Hengstenberg); "thou hast made the nation great, but thou wilt not therewith make the joy great" (Hoffmann).

Selwyn (*Horae Hebraicae*, 1860) proposes to emend to לו and to render, "the joy to him." Krochmal, Robertson Smith, Cheyne, etc., would read, "the rejoicing," ("thou hast multiplied the rejoicing, thou hast increased the joy"). It is, however, questionable whether this reading is permissible. Furthermore, this would twice mention the increase of joy with no mention of the increase of the people. It seems best to read לו in place of the similarly sounding negative. This is really supported by B, Syr., Targ., and Saadia, whereas the negative is supported by 1Q, Vulg. and Sym. Perhaps לו was replaced by the negative as in 2 Sam. 16:18, Isa. 63:9 and 1 Chron. 11:20. Cf. Drechsler, *in loc*. The position of לו is for emphasis' sake, as in Prov. 24:8; Lev. 7:7; etc. "the joy" — The last, final decisive joy of victory.

[60] "in harvest — Cf. Ps. 4:8; 126:5. Note the const. before the prep. "when they divide the spoil" — Cf. Ps. 119:162; Isa. 33:23; Judg. 5:30. "before thee" — A religious rejoicing, a delighting in the Lord such as is described in Isa. 65:18. וגילו — The imp. may assert facts which are likely to occur at a particular period, as when the reference is to a habit or custom, "as men are wont to rejoice."

4 *For . . .* with this word the prophet presents the reason for the great rejoicing. It is a word which introduces this and the following two verses. There is reason for the rejoicing, for God has wrought a mighty deliverance. Israel was like an animal of toil over whose neck a heavy wooden bar lay.[61] This was a burden; it was not, however, a literal wooden bar that bore down upon Israel's neck. It was a more grievous burden. It was the heavy burden of sin and corruption, of departure from God, and of the evil consequences of such departure. At one time the people had been under burdens in Egypt when cruel taskmasters oppressed them; now they are still in bondage for the yoke of their sins rests upon them. As every beast of burden and toil is beaten with a rod so Israel also had a rod with which it was beaten on the neck or shoulder.[62] There was also, as in Egypt, an oppressor who used a staff to strike the beast. This oppressor was the Assyrian enemy, but in a far deeper sense it was the bondage which sin itself had brought on.

Mighty is the victory, so great that it may be compared with that over Midian wrought by the Lord through Gideon. Human strength in that day had been unavailing, and Gideon had to recognize that the battle was the Lord's to be won only by His power. This present victory was similar, for it was won against a foe over whom human hands could have no power, and it was won by God alone. It was a spiritual battle, won because a Child would be born, and the victory consisted in the deliverance of

---

[61] "the yoke of his burden" — His burdensome yoke. Cf. Ar. *fiy riqbatihi ghol min chadiyd,* "an iron yoke lies on his shoulder." The suffix in "his burden" is s., but has a collective force and refers to the people. We should normally expect the form *sob-lô.* The *daghesh dirimens* makes the consonant more distinct. Thus, *quṭl > quṭlô > quṭelô > quṭ-ṭo-lô.*

"the rod of his shoulder" — His shoulder rod, with which the shoulder or neck of the animal was beaten. The word need not refer exclusively to the shoulder, but may refer to the back (in a human body the upper part of the back between the shoulders). Here the reference is probably to the shoulder side or flank. Hence, there is no need for emendation of the text.

[62] "the staff of the one oppressing him" — The suffix in בֹ may refer to the rod, but more likely to the subject of נֹגֵשׂ or to the object. "thou hast broken" — The ח is virtually doubled, and hence a *pathah* instead of an *i* vowel appears in the first syllable. The *Holem* represents long *a,* and the form is similar to the Akk. permansive, *šakin-ât-ta.* "like the day" — After the manner of the day; cf. 1:26. Usually, it is a day on which there has been a victory in war. Cf. Koranic *yaum Bdr* (the day of Beder). Note Hos. 2:2, the day of Jezreel; Ezek. 30:9, the day of Egypt, and Ps. 137:7, the day of Jerusalem.

God's people from all that had oppressed them. Sin is a burdensome yoke, for it subjects man to a slavery in which, like the beasts of toil, he is under a taskmaster that beats him. There is only One who can set man free from the yoke in which he has been bound, and that One is God. The act of delivering man from sin is a mighty victory, so mighty in fact that man could never have won it any more than Gideon, unaided, could have conquered the Midianites.

5 Again the word "for," and with this word we are given a second reason for the great rejoicing.[63] Following the victory which has just been mentioned, there is to be complete peace. This thought is expressed in a negative manner, in that the accoutrements of warfare are said to be utterly consumed. All these will be burned because they will no longer be needed. The footgear of the soldier appears in the thick of battle, for in the noise and tumult of war the soldier comes ready shod.[64] If even his shoes are destroyed, the actual weapons of war will also perish. Along with the shoes the upper garment, stained in the blood of battle and rolled in the blood of the slain, will be burned.[65] It will become the food which fire devours. There is no need to mention the destruction of the implements and weapons themselves, for if the shoes and garments of the soldier are burned, the weapons will be also.[66]

They are no longer needed, for a Child will be born, and His

[63] The introductory "for" is really parallel to that of the preceding verse, inasmuch as it assigns a second reason for the joy depicted in v. 3. It does not explain the reason for the victory of v. 4, nor is it to be translated "when" as suggested in the margin of AV.

[64] סְאוֹן is related to Akk. senu, "a boot." It is not necessarily a heavy shoe and yet is to be distinguished from na‘al. The reference here seems to be to the footgear of the Assyrians without any particular reflection upon the type of that gear. "with a sound" — The noise of tumult of battle rather than the sound which the warrior makes as he marches along.

[65] The expression suggests that the garment had actually been rolled in the blood of the slain; cf. 2 Sam. 20:12. "and it shall become" — The nouns standing before the apodosis are so arranged that the predicate takes the number and gender of the nearest noun; cf. Job 19:15; Isa. 1:7b. There is not necessarily an allusion to the burning of weapons after wars, although that custom may lie at the basis of what is said. The picture rather is of the utter destruction of all the accouterments of war. Cf. Livy, 1:37; 38:23; and Aeneid, 8:562. Note Josh. 7:25; 11:6, 9.

[66] The purpose of this verse is to show that following the destruction of v. 4 there will be complete peace. The accouterments of warfare will be consumed because they will no longer be needed.

birth will bring peace to His people, for He will Himself be the Prince of Peace. "Glory to God in the highest, and on earth peace among men of his good pleasure" (Luke 2:14).

6 A third and climactic sentence introduced by "for." The thought of the argument may be paraphrased as follows: "There is great rejoicing among God's people, because God has broken the yoke of burden and oppression, and the burden and oppression are removed because the weapons and garments of the warrior are destroyed, and the basic reason for these blessings is that a Child is born." In contrast to the mighty foe of Assyria and also to the Syrian Ephraimitic coalition, a Child brings deliverance to the people of God.

A Child — The word occurs first in the Hebrew, for all the weight and emphasis fall upon it. We must note again how impressive this fact was to Isaiah. He speaks of the birth as though it had already occurred, even though from his standpoint it was yet to take place in the future. It will be well, then, if we render the verbs literally, so that their true force may be apparent.

has been born .... will be born
has been given .... will be given
and has been .... and will be
and has called .... and will call

We know that Isaiah is not speaking of a past occurrence, for the simple reason that to do so would not yield a good sense. Whose birth, prior to Isaiah's time, ever accomplished what is herein described? To ask that question is to answer it. Furthermore, we must also note that the Child whose birth is here mentioned was also the One whose birth had been foretold in chapter 7. In that chapter His birth was a sign; here it brings salvation to His own.

The form of the verb (the perfect) really emphasizes the historical nature of the birth. The deliverance which brings rejoicing to the people of God is not something vague but something to be brought about by a birth in history upon this earth at a definite time and at a definite place. The birth of this Child is a gift of God. He is a Child, but He is also a Son. But must not a male child, a *yeled*, be a son?[67] Why then, inasmuch as it

---

[67] ילד — May be employed of a youth, as in Gen. 37:30; 42:22, and also of a small child; Exod. 1:17; 2:3,6. "is born" — Drechsler was probably one of the first to identify this form as a passive *Qal* rather than a *Pual.* "unto us" — Cf. Luke 2:10-12. "is given" — Cf. John 3:16; 4:10; 6:32.

is so obvious that any male child born is a son, is this Child also designated Son? He is of course a son of David, a legitimate heir to David's throne, for He is to bear the government with all its responsibilities, and this He will do upon David's throne. "And the key of the house of David will I lay upon his shoulder; so he shall open, and none shall shut; and he shall shut, and none shall open" (Isa. 22:22).

Hengstenberg points out that the Messiah early became known not only as the Son of David but also as the Son of God. "Thou art my son, this day have I begotten thee" (Ps. 2:7b), and the designation of the Messiah as "Mighty God" in this present passage should also be connected with the thought of the second Psalm.[68] Isaiah has already prophesied that the Virgin would bring forth a Son, and John states that "God so loved the world, that he gave his only begotten Son" (John 3:16a).

If this child is to be a legitimate ruler upon David's throne, it is redundant to say that He is a son of David. When, however, Isaiah does call Him Son, it must be with a larger reference in mind. It is the fact of sonship itself which here receives the emphasis, as is also the case in the second verse of Hebrews 1, "God has spoken in a Son." The Child to be born is a Son, a unique Son, a Son par excellence.

And it is for us that He is to be born. The prophet here groups with himself all those who are to be the recipients of the blessings which the Son's birth will bring. Isaiah had already pointed out (7:14) that the Messiah would be with us (*Immanuel*) to bring us blessing; here He is to be for us (*lanu*). At the same time this *lanu* is to be contrasted with the *lakem*, "to you," of Isaiah 7:14. There the Son was a "sign" given to those round about Ahaz; here the birth of the Son is for the benefit of those who are included in the *lanu*.

Upon this Child the government with all its responsibilities lies.[69] Like a burden it rests upon His shoulders. Isaiah had

---

[68] Kittel thinks that this interpretation is forced (*fingiert*), but a little reflection will show that such is not the case. If in this passage the term "son" simply indicated that Messiah was a son of David, it would be redundant. It is then in some other sense that the term must be understood. It is used in the sense of "my son" in Ps. 2:7, the Son begotten of God. The Messiah is a Child, a descendant of David; He is also a Son, the Son of God.

[69] "the government" — The thought is not that the Child actually comes to the reins of government (Marti), but that the government itself, i.e., its responsibilities, rests upon his shoulders. Cf. *"bene humeris tuis sedet imper-*

earlier inveighed against child rulers; one of the punishments which was to come upon Judah was that children would be its princes (3:4). Here, however, not only is a Child to be the ruler, but the entire responsibility for the good administration of the government is said to rest upon His shoulders. The Child is to be a King, a Ruler, a Sovereign.

This government is the kingdom of grace, but also in widest extent the kingdom of nature and power. All the world is subject to the rule of the Child. "All power in heaven and in earth is given unto me" (Matt. 28:18; 11:27; John 5:22). World powers were threatening the very existence of the people of God; the government of the Child is a spiritual rule, but for that very reason more embracing and world-wide. "My kingdom is not of this world" (John 18:6).

Who is this Child? In chapter 7 the mother named Him Immanuel. Here, the subject is impersonal and the verb may be rendered in English by the passive, "and his name will be called."[70] Isaiah does not intend that we should understand that in actual life the Child would bear or be addressed by these names, anymore than in actual life He should bear the name Immanuel. As a matter of fact, in fulfillment of the Immanuel prophecy He was named Jesus. "And she shall bring forth a son, and thou shalt call his name Jesus: for he shall save his people from their sins" (Matt. 1:21). The thought is that the Child is worthy to bear these names, and that they are accurate descriptions and designations of His being and character.[71] In the Bible the name indicates the character, essence or nature of a person or object. When, therefore, it is stated that He shall be called, we are to understand that the following names are descriptive of the Child and deserve to be borne by Him.

---

ium," Pliny, *Panegyric*, 10; "*rempublicam universam vestris humeris sustinetis*," Cicero, *Pro Flacco*, 95. The emphasis in this passage is not upon a *Thronbesteigungsfest*, but upon the *birth* of a Child.

[70] "is called" — Probably better to construe impersonally than to take God as subject. The 3 mss. may often express an indefinite personal subject. Note the similarity of the language between 7:14, "and she shall call his name," and 9:5, "and his name shall be called."

[71] To maintain with George Adam Smith that the text merely says he will be called, not that he actually will be what the names indicate would be a gross misunderstanding of the nature of the prophecy, indeed, of the nature of Biblical language generally. Smith, *The Book of Isaiah*, Vol. I (New York), p. 137.

Both Isaiah 7;14 and the present passage lay stress upon the Child's name. That we may more correctly ascertain what the name is and what the name means, we must consider various views of the name, some of which are erroneous."

A. The Targum rendered the passage, "And there was called His name from of old, Wonderful Counsellor, Mighty God, He who lives for ever, the Messiah, in whose days peace shall increase upon us."[72] This closely parallels and supports the Masoretic text; nevertheless, upon the basis of the Targum, Jewish commentators have produced other renderings. Thus, Kimchi, "The God, who is called and who is Wonder, Counsellor, the mighty God, the eternal Father, calls his name the Prince of Peace."[73] This translation at least has the merit of giving to the individual words of the name their proper force and significance. The order of the words, however, is a fatal objection to this rendering of Kimchi. The words "his name" cannot be separated from the name itself by the subject of the sentence. Calvin was one of the first to point out the objection to this construction. It should also be noted that in this context we expect to find attributes of the Child and not of God, inasmuch as it is the Child who is the agent in bringing about the peace described.

B. Samuel David Luzzatto took all the titles together and read them as one word, "A wonderful thing is counseling he who is the mighty God, the everlasting Father, the Prince of Peace."[74] The thought is that "God the Strong, the Eternal Father, the Peace Prince resolves upon something wonderful." On this construction the first word *pele,* "wonderful," constitutes the object, and is emphasized, whereas the remainder of the sentence forms the subject of the participle *yoetz,* "counselling." It is of course true that names are composed of sentences in the Old Testament, but one may well wonder why such a sentence as this should con-

[72] Text in J. F. Stenning, *The Targum of Isaiah* (Oxford, 1949), which also has an English translation. According to B the name of the Child is μεγάλης βουλῆς ἄγγελος. 1Q supports M, save that it inserts an article before *peace.*

[73] Louis Finkelstein, *The Commentary of David Kimchi on Isaiah* (1926), p. 62.

[74] Samuel David Luzzatto: *Il Profeta Isaia volgarizzato e commentato ad uso degl' Israeliti* (Padova, 1855). He renders, "*Decreta prodigi Iddio potente, il sempre-padre, il signor della pace.*

stitute the name of the Child.[75] Why should the participle be employed instead of the imperfect? And if the purpose of the prophet, as this name would suggest, was to stress God's wisdom, why does he heap up epithets which do not contribute to that object? And finally, as may clearly be seen from the context, the designation "Prince of Peace" applies not to God, but to the Child. Dillmann called this name an unparalleled monstrosity, and Delitzsch labelled it a sesquipedalian name.

C. The Vulgate finds here six names: *Admirabilis, Consiliarius, Deus, Fortis, Pater futuri saeculi, Princeps pacis.*

D. The common English versions give five names to the Child.

E. The Child is probably given four names, and that for the following reasons:

1. The last two names consist each of two members, the first of which in each instance is in the construct state followed by the dependent genitive. The first two names also stand closely together, the first in each instance being in the position of an appositional genitive.

2. The Masoretic accentuation supports the position that there are four names.

3. If there are four names, a remarkable symmetry is obtained. Each name thus consists of two members, and each half of the verse of two names.

4. At this point note should be taken of the remark of Herntrich that in each name one of the two words always describes the earthly side and the other the "metaphysical" side of the government. In the first two names, the designation of deity is first, whereas in the last two it is the second member of the name. This point may be illustrated, if we print in capital letters the designation of divinity, leaving in smaller letters the designation of humanity. Thus:

PELE   yoetz   EL   gibbor   abi   AD   sar   SHALOM.

Wonderful Counsellor

This is the first of those wondrous and precious names of the Messiah, which, to use Reichel's language, constitutes the Church's

---

[75] Cf. Ps. 88:12 (11 in M) ; 119:129. In the Bible the word *pele'* is employed of what God, never of what man, has done. The accent is *Teliša*, one of the weakest of the disjunctives.

monumentum aere perennius. They are a healing balm in which the Christian soul will find comfort and strength throughout time and eternity. It is one of the saddest points in the entire history of exposition that so many have refused to see the true import of these glorious names.

Isaiah begins by using the abstract for the concrete, "wonder" for "wonderful." In reality this is stronger than if he had used an adjective. Not merely is the Messiah wonderful but He is Himself a Wonder, through and through.[76] The root of the word *pele* occurs in Psalm 78:12, where we may obtain an idea of its force. "Marvellous things did he in the sight of their fathers, in the land of Egypt, in the field of Zoan." The root is used to describe the miracles which God performed in Egypt, namely, the dividing of the sea, the safe crossing of the Red Sea, the leading by pillar of cloud and fire, the cleaving of the rocks in the desert and the providing of water. All these mighty miracles are characterized as wonders. The word refers to what God has done and not to the work of man.

Of particular interest is Judges 13:18, where the Angel of the Lord replies to Manoah that His name is *peli,* i.e., incomprehensible to man. This is a clear indication of the deity of the Angel. The Old Testament usage of this word compels us to the conclusion that it here designates the Messiah not merely as someone extraordinary, but as One who in His very person and being is a Wonder; He is that which surpasses human thought and power; He is God Himself. To designate the Child with the word *pele* is to make the clearest attestation of His deity.

The position of this word as the first in the series is striking. His name shall be called Wonder. We are brought head on, as it were, with God Himself as we hear the names of the Child.

---

[76] The relationship of these two words is the same, I believe, as *pere' 'āḏām* in Gen. 16:12. Why Alexander should call this construction ungrammatical I am at a loss to understand. יוֹעֵץ is an appositional genitive to פֶּלֶא and the two may be rendered, "a wonder of a counselor," "a wonderful counselor." Such counseling was given by God; cf. Ps. 16:7; 32:8; Prov. 1:30 and 8:14. Notice Isa. 28:29, "he caused counsel to be a wonder," i.e., wonderful.

The concept of wisdom was significant in the ancient East; the Babylonians spoke of the king as *re'u itpešu,* (wise shepherd) ; Hammurabi, for example, spoke of himself as a god among kings, wise, understanding *(mu-di ḥasīsim).* He speaks also of the wisdom with which Ea has imbued him *(ḥasīsim);* cf. Col. 3:16, 17 and R24, 26, 27).

It is our first encounter with Him. All the following designations are influenced by or stand under the shadow of this first majestic name. This Child who is born for us is Wonder.

The second word of the first pair may be rendered, "Counsellor." To sit upon the throne of David as the Messianic King requires wisdom such as no mere man possesses. The Counsellor Himself must for that reason be a Wonder in order that He may establish and administer His kingdom. In this King there will be hid all the treasures of wisdom and knowledge, for He must be properly equipped to redeem His people. Upon Him the Spirit of wisdom is to rest (Isa. 11:2). Wisdom and the ability to give counsel are necessary for a king, and hence, the words "counsellor" and "king," are used as synonymns in Micah 4:9. There is a certain uniqueness about the word, for it suggests that this One has no need of being surrounded with counsellors and advisors as is the case with mere human kings; He is Himself Counsellor. Such counselling is characteristic of God. "This also cometh from the LORD of hosts, which is wonderful in counsel, and excellent in working" (Isa. 28:29). In the manner in which He renders decisions the Messiah will remind of God and the reason why He will so remind is that He Himself is of the same nature as the Lord: He *is* God.

The Mighty God

"We should hesitate," writes George Adam Smith, "therefore, to understand by these names a God in the metaphysical sense of the word."[77] Smith himself would simply render "God-Hero," and there are many others who refuse to see in this designation a genuine attribution of deity. Ilgen, for example, had thought of the language as mere court flattery, and the title as a play upon the designation Hezekiah, "the strength of Yahweh." If we hold to an incarnation of Yahweh, he maintained, in the person of the Messiah, it is to be compared with incarnations of India and China. Later, indeed, the concept of Messiah did include the idea that He was a higher, super-earthly being, sent from heaven, but not an incarnate Yahweh. Such a transfigured representation appeared only at the time of Christ, and we must not look for it here at the very childhood of the conception.

Duhm takes the expression as an example of popular hyperbole.

[77] *Op. cit.,* p. 135.

335

Just as Esau, he maintains, appeared to Jacob as a God (Gen. 33:10), so will the king, prepared and equipped with the Spirit of the hero, appear as an *el* to His people, as one of those war-like transcendentals of whom the army of Yahweh consists. But the word used in Genesis 33:10 is *elohim* and not *el*. To understand properly this name, we must pay attention to the usage of the word *el* in the Old Testament. In prose the word *el* usually appears in connections such as *"el shaddai," "el elyon,"* etc. Likewise the word *gibbor* also occurs elsewhere as an epithet of *"el,"* sometimes alone and sometimes with other epithets. We may note *"el gibbor"* (Isa. 10:21); *"hael haggadol haggibor wehannorah"* (Deut. 10:17; Neh. 9:32); *"hael haggadol haggibbor"* (Jer. 32:18).

In the plural *"el"* may have reference to men, but its usage here in Isaiah must be based upon other considerations. In Isaiah it is found as a designation of God and only of Him. "Egypt is a man (*adam*) and not God (*el*) (31:3). The name of the Messiah teaches that God is present with man (Isa. 7:14). Isaiah 10:21, however, settles the question, for it states that a remnant of Jacob will return to *el gibbor*. In verse 20 it had been asserted that the remnant of Israel would no longer lean upon its own staff, but would lean upon Yahweh, the Holy One of Israel in truth. This thought is then summed up in the statement that the remnant of Jacob would return to *el gibbor*. In other words, from the context itself, we see that the Lord, the Holy One of Israel, and *el gibbor,* are one and the same.

Such a designation of God was traditional, as the above references show. Even on the Ugaritic texts we have the phrase *"el. gzr,"* which is an equivalent in construction to *"el gibbor,"* and which was the designation of an *el,* a god, who was distinct from man.[78] With these considerations we are brought face to face with the questions: Does the phrase *"el gibbor"* designate a God in the metaphysical sense of the term? Is *el gibbor* God

---

[78] B ii:viii:31, 32 *tny. lydd el.gzr.* There is, of course, an exegetical question. Are we to render: "Repeat to the hero, loved of El," or, "Repeat to the one loved of El, the hero"? Cf. B ii. vii. 46, 47. iii. vi. 31. It is possible that the word *gzr* is a designation of *el,* and if so, we have a parallel to the Isaiah passage. Marti says that the word indicates nothing about the divine origin of the Child. König claims that the phrase need not have the same sense here as in 10:21, for the precise significance must be determined from the immediate context. But if ever a context pointed to the fact that it was speaking of One who is God in the metaphysical sense, this is that context.

in distinction from man, or is the purpose of the phrase merely to suggest that the Messiah was endued in an unusual measure and to a superhuman degree with godlike qualities?

One factor that cannot be overlooked is the fact that the easy transition between gods and men so common to ancient mythology is completely foreign to the Old Testament and to Isaiah's prophecy. We have but to read the sixth chapter or the first three verses of chapter 31 to note how carefully the distinction between God and man is guarded. Whereas the word *elohim* in the Old Testament may sometimes apply to beings lesser than God, such is not the case with *el*. This designation is reserved for the true God and for Him alone.

Gibbor simply means "hero."[79] We may connect the two words in either of the following ways. They may be translated "a heroic God," or else "a God of a hero," a hero whose chief characteristic is that he is God. The Messiah thus, on this latter rendering, is a Wonder of a Counselor and a God of a Hero. In 11:2 also the thought of strength or might follows that of counsel. Likewise in 36:5 we read, "I have counsel and strength for war. . . ." The New Testament lays stress upon the power of the Messiah. "In the world ye shall have tribulation, but be of good cheer, I have overcome the world" (John 16:33b). The Child is a God, a God of Might; He is the Mighty God. Therefore, we may be of good cheer.

Isaiah here brings out an important contrast. By means of the words *yeled*, "child," and *yullad*, "is born," he has called attention to the Messiah's humanity, but by the phrase *el gibbor* we are brought face to face with Messiah's deity. This interpretation is strengthened by the word *pele* in the first name. He is a Wonder, and in the light of this strong designation, we may well expect that in the second name also the prophet is attributing deity to the Messiah.

What then did Isaiah mean by his use of the term *el* and why did he employ it? In answering these questions we must remember that the wondrous prophecy which we are now studying was not primarily the product of Isaiah's own thought. It did not come to him as the result of private interpretation (see 1 Pet. 1:21). It was a revelation of God. Isaiah penned these words

---

[79] If גבור is an appositional genitive, the rendering would be, "a god of a hero," a divine hero. If it be used adjectivally, we may render, "a heroic god." The term generally serves as a descriptive epithet.

concerning the Messiah for the reason that he was borne of the Spirit of God. To what extent he himself understood the import of what he was writing we have no way of knowing. The revelation was made to him, however, that the Messiah was a divine Person. In the light of the New Testament we learn that this revelation was an adumbration of the doctrine of the Trinity. Isaiah, in other words, is now given a glimpse of the fact that in the fullness of the Godhead there is a plurality of Persons. Hence, in obedience to the revelation of God, he wrote of the Messiah that He was *el gibbor*. With this revealed truth may our hearts delight, for He who is born the mighty God is therefore able to save all those who put their trust in Him.

The Father of Eternity

To discover the precise significance of this epithet is not easy.[80] The word *ad* signifies perpetuity or duration. It may have the sense of eternity, as when Isaiah speaks of the "high and lofty One that inhabiteth eternity . . ." (57:15). Possibly that is the force here, for it is stated that there will be no end of the Messiah's kingdom. In what sense, however, may the Messiah be designated the Father of Eternity? We may perhaps bring out the thought by paraphrasing, "One who is eternally a Father."

The word "Father" designates a quality of the Messiah with respect to His people. He acts toward them like a father. "Thou, O Lord, art our father, our redeemer; thy name is from ever-

---

[80] Some render the third name, "father of eternity," or, "eternal one," as though the words had the force, "possessor of eternity." This usage is common in Ar. (cf. Rosenmüller), but it is questionable whether it is permissible in Hebrew. König renders, *"Urheber von Beute"* (author of booty). Cf. Gen. 49:27; Isa. 33:23; Zeph. 3:8. But this does not fit in well with the context, where the Messiah is shown to be the Prince of Peace. Gesenius took the sense as constant father, or, constant protector of His people; cf. Job 29:16. The Persians thus spoke of Cyrus; cf. Her. 3:89. Calvin, *"pater saeculi."* Calvin thinks that the word denotes eternity, but is willing to render it as "perpetual duration" lest anyone should limit the reference to the heavenly life. Ridderbos, *"die eeuwigheid bezit"* (the one who possesses eternity). Cheyne wished to emend to *"hod,"* (glory) and Sellin "der Vorzeit", (father of previous time), to show the Davidic descent of the Messiah. But this would be better expressed by the phrase "son of former time." Kittel applied the reference to the ruler of the new world period (*Hellenistische Mysterienreligionen*, pp. 73ff.). The word *'ad* is not necessarily late, for it appears in Ug. in the sense "period, cycle of time."

lasting" (Isa. 63:16). "Like as a father pitieth his children, so the LORD pitieth them that fear him" (Ps. 103:13).

The quality of fatherhood is defined by the word eternity. The Messiah is an eternal Father. If this is correct, the meaning is that He is One who eternally is a Father to His people. Now and forever He guards His people and supplies their needs.[81] "I am the good shepherd," said our Lord, and thus expressed the very heart of the meaning of this phrase. What tenderness, love, and comfort are here! Eternally — a Father to His people!

The Prince of Peace

Restoring peace to the world He reigns in peace. War and oppression were the factors which in the first instance directed the prophet's eyes to the Messiah. How climactic and emphatic, then, is this name! This One is a Prince, and He seeks the greatness of His kingdom and of Himself not in war, as do ordinary rulers, but in peace. He establishes peace; He seeks it and pursues it. In active vigor He is the true David and in love of peace the real Solomon. As under David, so His kingdom will increase, and as under Solomon so will it prosper. Like the three utterances of the Aaronic blessing, the names of the Messiah die away in the word "peace." "To elevate the Davidic government to a government of eternal peace is the end for which he is born, and for this end he proves himself to be what he is named and is" (Delitzsch).

Inasmuch as the peace to be established is eternal, it is clear that this peace includes more than a temporary cessation of hostilities among nations.[82] The cessation of warfare in itself does not bring about a desired condition of existence. There must

---

[81] Cf. also 11:6, 7, 8 and Vergil's picture:

> Ille Deum vitam accipiet, divisque videbit
> Permixtos heroas, et ipse videbatur illis,
> Pacatumque reget patriis virtutibus orbem.

Hammurabi speaks of himself as one who is like a natural father for his people, "ša ki-ma a-bi-im wa-li-di-im a-na ni-ši" (col. 25, reverse, lines 21-23); who has established perpetual safety for his people, "ù ši-ra-am ṭa-ba-am a-na ni-ši a-na da-ar i-ši-im" (col. 25 reverse, lines 34-36). See Gesenius for references to the Persian kings. But designations such as this would not have been attributed to a mere Judean king.

[82] "peace" — Cf. Leon Morris: The Apostolic Preaching of the Cross (1955), pp. 210-17, and The First and Second Epistles to the Thessalonians (1959), p. 49, n. 8.

also be removed the cause of war, namely, human sin. When this cause of war is removed, then there can be true peace. For human sin to be removed, however, there must be a state of peace between God and man. Not only must man be at peace with God, but what is more important, God must be at peace with man. The enmity which had existed between God and man must be removed. It was human sin which had kept God at enmity with man. When that sin has been removed, then there can be peace, as the Apostle says, "Therefore being justified by faith, we have peace with God through our Lord Jesus Christ" (Rom. 5:1). The Prince of Peace is One who is the very embodiment of peace. He is the Prince who has procured that peace. He procured it by removing the handwriting of ordinances that was against us and nailing it to His cross. He has satisfied the claims of absolute justice so that God in perfect justice can declare that the sinner stands in a right relationship with Himself. Being at peace with the sinner, God could pardon that sinner, and give to him the peace which is a divine gift. From the peace of God which passeth all understanding there flow the blessings which find their origin in such a peace. When the peace of God is in the human heart, then there will be manifest in the world peace among men.

True peace comes to us because a Child was born. That Child, and He alone, is the Prince of Peace. Would we have peace, it is to Him that we must go.

SPECIAL NOTE ON THE TITLES OF THE CHILD

The titles themselves, it has been argued, need not bear the higher interpretation. Some say that two of the names are capable of being used of an earthly monarch: *Wonderful Counsellor* and *Prince of Peace*, which are within the range of human virtue, in evident contrast to Ahaz, at once foolish in the conception of his policy and warlike in its results. With respect to the title *Everlasting Father* it is said to be similar to oriental titles. The best refutation of this kind of argumentation of course is a study of the titles themselves.

It has also been claimed that Isaiah stressed the unity of God. In opposition to the polytheism of the people and its ruler, he asserted that only the LORD is God. Says George Adam Smith: "It would have nullified the force of his message, and confused the generation to which he brought it, if either he or they had conceived of the Messiah with the conceiving of Christian theology, as a separate Divine personality." In answer to this, however, it is sufficient to point out that a proper exegesis of this passage does present a Messiah, who, although a legitimate heir to the Davidic throne, is, nevertheless, a "separate Divine personality." As Davis well remarks: "It is enough to know that in the days of the prophets the conception of identity with, yet distinguishableness from, Jehovah was present in Hebrew thought and was consistent with the pure monotheism which was taught in Israel."

It has further been declared that the Messianic King was to perform only the ordinary duties of the kingdom. His work was simply that of an earthly king, and that was all Isaiah expected of him. In the New Testament, however, the work of salvation is spiritual. If therefore our understanding of Jesus' work is truly spiritual, we shall be less inclined to appeal to the prophecies of Isaiah as proof of His deity. This thought, however, is simply wishful thinking representing a liberalism which wished to remove as much as possible of the supernatural from the Bible. Certainly v. 6 makes it clear that the work of the Messiah is spiritual in nature.

When, it is further claimed, the actual reigning king was worthy, Isaiah felt no need for another king, but simply laid his stress upon the inviolability of Jerusalem. If, on the other hand, the actual king was an unworthy one, then Isaiah felt compelled to predict an ideal king. Hence, the expected king was not a supernatural being, but a human person. But Ahaz was the only evil king and Hezekiah the only good one. Furthermore, the Messianic prophecies uttered during the reign of Ahaz were basic for the understanding of those uttered under Hezekiah. The objection which we are considering presupposes that there was a whole list of good and bad kings. Such was not the case. This objection cannot be demonstrated to be valid.

Later in the prophecies Isaiah is silent about a divine Messiah, and so, it is claimed, he is also silent here. The other prophets also at a later time were silent about a divine Messiah. But whatever later prophets may have done, and we cannot entirely agree with the statement of this objection, the fact remains that in this particular prophecy the deity of the Messiah is clearly taught.

Mention has been made of the view that the passage simply represents the flattery of a poet. In times of distress, however, such flattery would not likely be heard. Furthermore, there is an earnestness and seriousness about this passage which does not well comport with the view that this is merely the flattery of a court poet. It is easily understandable that such an interpretation has not gained wide ground. The same is true of the view that this is mere popular hyperbole. In such hyperbole, it would have been most unlikely that the king would have been identified with God. That might have been the case in Egypt, but not in a monotheistic land such as Judah. Furthermore, when human beings are compared with God, the term employed is not *el* but *elohim*.

341

Upon the basis of a study of the accents Norman H. Snaith ("The Interpretation of EL Gibbor in Isaiah 95 [EVV 6]" in *The Expository Times,* 52, No. 1, Oct. 1940, pp. 36, 37) derives the following rendering: "And the Mighty God hath called his name Wonderful Counsellor, The Everlasting Father (hath called his name) Prince of Peace." Cf. also G. R. Berry: "Messianic Predictions" in *JBL,* 1926-1927 and Alt ("Befreiungsnacht und Kronungstag," *Kleine Schriften,* pp. 206-25) who proposes a reconstruction of the text of 8:23. He holds that at the moment Galilee is freed from Assyria a new David ascends the throne and has the announcement of his ascension proclaimed even in Galilee. An excellent defense of the Messianic interpretation of these verses will be found in the article of John D. Davis, "The Child Whose Name Is Wonderful," in *Biblical and Theological Studies* (Princeton Centenary Volume), New York, 1912, pp. 93-108.

7 Being established upon the double foundation of justice and righteousness, the Messiah's reign will be perpetual and progressive.[83] The government belongs to the prince, and the text may even make an intended play upon the words *sar,* "prince," and *misrah,* "government."

Perhaps in the reuniting of the divided houses of Israel and certainly in the inclusion of the Gentiles this government will increase, and corresponding to an enlargement of the government there will also be an increase in peace. This peace existed in opposition to war and involved well-being, welfare and prosperity in general as opposed to want and need. God only can give such a peace, and in giving it shows that He is well disposed to man.

These blessings of the increase of the government and of peace are connected with the One who sits upon the throne of David

---

[83] "increase" — Fanciful explanations have been offered for the closed *mem.* It has been said to designate the recession of the shadow on Ahaz' sundial, the secret progress of Christ's kingdom among men, the perpetual virginity of Mary, etc. But the copyist had just written a closed *mem* in the word "peace." שלום — He now repeats the *lamed* and *mem.* The *lamed* may be taken as dative, "with respect to." *Marbeh* is then to be regarded as a *Hiphil* part. which passes over into an impersonal meaning. The word reminds us of the "thou hast increased" of v. 2. "the government" — Of the Child; cf. Mic. 5:2ff. Possibly there is an implication that the Child will reunite the divided house of Israel. Reichel notes a play upon words and renders, "*Vermehrer der Herrschaft, der etwas vermehret.*"

plausibility to find another subject; and until that is done which all the Rabbis and a Grotius could not do, we may repose upon the old evangelical interpretation as undoubtedly the true one." A Child is born and that Child is Jesus. He is the true King and Shepherd of Israel and in Him alone is to be found the peace that mankind needs.

DOES THIS PROPHECY TRULY COME FROM ISAIAH OR NOT?

a. It is claimed that this passage does not fit well into any period of the prophet's life. In answer we may say that this is no reason for denying the words to Isaiah. Into whose life does it fit well? We really know very little about Isaiah. How can anyone claim that this passage does not fit into Isaiah's life, when so little is known about that life?

b. In Isaiah 8:16-18 the prophet is said to place his hope on the Lord and upon a religious community without political organization. He does not place it in the Davidic dynasty or in a political rule. The Messiah who is prophesied in 9:1-6, on the other hand, is said to be a political figure, who has no direct bearing upon religion. This latter prophecy might be said to suit the Jews, who hoped for freedom from the Roman yoke, but to Isaiah God's kingdom was not of this world.

This argument is both subjective and shallow. To think that the Child presented in Isaiah 9:2-7 is merely a political Messiah is to fly in the face of the clear teaching of the passage. He pursues peace by righteousness in His reign. But righteousness implies rightness before God. If this concept is not spiritual, what concept is?

c. The "zeal" of the Lord is said not to have been a sign of comfort, but first became a basis for comfort only in Ezekiel. It is hence concluded that this present passage must be exilic. In 2 Kings 19:31, the word is used of comfort. We may furthermore ask how often this word "qinah" is used in the prophets? Let the reader compare Jer. 7:29; 9:9, 19 and Amos 5:1; 8:10. Apart from these and the present passage the word appears only in Ezekiel of all the prophetical books.

d. It has been claimed that other prophets such as Jeremiah, Ezekiel and the "second" Isaiah know nothing of this prophecy. Whether these other prophets knew this prophecy or not, we have no means of telling. The fact that they do not mention it is no proof that they did not know it. Nor does their silence in any way disprove Isaianic authorship.

e. In Isaiah's day, it is claimed, only a portion of the nation was in danger, whereas this prophecy presents the whole people as in need of salvation. Here again, we would reply, exegesis, and not preconceived opinions and prejudices, must settle the question.

This righteous judgment is not merely external and outward.[86] There is justice because the King is Himself just. To this justice man will be willingly subject, for he will have received the righteousness which the King alone is able to bestow and so will stand in right relation to the King and will endeavor to respond to the just government of that King and to obey His precepts and commands. The blessings follow because of the Child who is to sit upon the throne and only because of Him.

Isaiah places himself at the beginning of the Child's reign and would have us understand that from that time on justice and righteousness will be employed in the establishment of this kingdom for eternity.[87] When the Son appears in life with the attributes here assigned to Him, then the kingdom will be founded and established. The kingdom of the Son continually progresses. Justice and righteousness are its foundation; oppression and injustice have no part in its progress and growth. Unlike the temporal kingdoms of this earth, it is eternal. "And in the days of these kings shall the God of heaven set up a kingdom which shall never be destroyed" (Dan. 2:44a). "He shall be great and shall be called the Son of the Highest; and the Lord God shall give unto him the throne of his father David: And he shall reign over the house of Jacob for ever; and of his kingdom there shall be no end" (Luke 1:32, 33).

With this passage we have made a distinct advance over the prophecy upon which it is founded, namely 2 Samuel 7:12-17. In that latter prophecy we were told that there would be a Davidic throne and a successor of David. His throne would continue and there would always be a man to sit upon that throne. We have now made an advance, for the blessings herein depicted are brought about by a solitary figure. The eschatological stage of history has been reached, and Isaiah sees the Child upholding the kingdom. The thought of Messiah's reign coming to an end,

---

[86] The prep. indicates the means by which the kingdom is to be established. If the conjunction is *wāw explicandi*, the words may form an *hendiadys* and be rendered, "through righteous judgment." His obedience and suffering is the basis and foundation of His eternal kingdom.

[87] עוֹלָם denotes indefinite duration. When applied to human life it should be taken in its fullest sense unless specifically restricted. Here the context makes clear that the kingdom is everlasting in nature. It is inconceivable that a kingdom founded in justice and righteousness, ruled over by One who bears the names of v. 5, which will increase peace without end, should be thought of as in any sense having only a temporal duration.

or of successors to the Messiah is foreign to the Old Testament.

The zeal of the Lord of hosts will accomplish this — Judah is in desperate condition. On the horizon looms the Assyrian oppressor. Who will bring it about that the divine kingdom shall be founded? Nothing other than the zeal which Yahweh of hosts has for His own honor will bring about this result.[88] In itself this zeal or energy designates the deep love which God has for His people and also His jealousy on their behalf, His profound desire to protect and guard them and their welfare. But even more the word signifies a determination jealously to protect the divine honor and to vindicate the divine purposes. God's partiality to His people and His jealous disposition to vindicate His honor will accomplish the establishment of the kingdom over which the Child will reign. "The astonishing effects," Alexander well says, "produced by feeble means in the promotion, preservation and extension of Christ's kingdom, can only be explained upon the principle that the zeal of the Lord of Hosts effected it."

In the mention of Yahweh of hosts and of the Child as Mighty God there is no incongruity. In this remarkable passage there is an adumbration or foreshadowing of the later to be revealed doctrine of the Holy Trinity. The Child to be born is God (in the metaphysical sense, as distinct from man) and yet His birth and the establishment of the Kingdom is the work of the Lord of hosts.

Isaiah uses the verb "will accomplish" to show that the kingdom will be established and prosper, and thus introduces a further striking contrast with the present condition of the Davidic kingdom.

When we say that this passage refers to the Messiah, we must be more specific. We have in mind none other than the true Son of David, Jesus the Christ. He and His kingdom alone fulfill the description of this prophecy. Let us again hear Alexander. "Upon the whole, it may be said with truth, that there is no alleged prophecy of Christ, for which it seems so difficult with any

---

[88] In itself the word קִנְאָה means "ardor." It is sometimes used to signify not merely God's deep love for His people, but also His jealousy in their behalf, and His jealousy for His own honor. God's zeal is manifested in His punishment of sin and displeasure against sinners, as well as in His furthering of His purposes in the bringing of blessing to His people. Cf. Exod. 20:5; 34:14; Deut. 4:24; 5:9; 6:15.

and apart from that throne they will not be found.[84]   He who sits upon this throne, therefore, is a legitimate descendant of David. It had earlier been promised that David's throne would endure forever, and hence the description of Messiah's reign is identified with that of David.   This identification of the two reigns is not merely due to an external resemblance or even to a typical relation, but to the fact that Messiah's reign was really a continuation or restoration of David's kingdom.   David was a temporary and temporal king; the Messiah an eternal King. Both ruled over the same kingdom.

Peace and the government are mentioned together.   This is striking, for most governments find their increase through war. Unlike other kingdoms, this one will grow through the means of peace, through the gracious working of the Spirit of God in the hearts of men and through the preaching of the gospel.

Its prosperity and increase are neither temporal nor local, for the kingdom is itself eternal.   That interpretation which would apply this prophecy to a literal throne of David to be established in Jerusalem during a "millennium" must be rejected for the following reasons: The reign begins with the birth of the *yeled,* who sits upon the throne of David and reigns eternally.   To limit this reign to a period of one thousand years is to neglect the words, "there is no end."   And to make the beginning coincide with the beginning of a millennium is to ignore the fact that it begins with the birth of the Child.

to found it and to establish it — Upon the throne of David the government will increase and will thus be made sure by means of judgment and righteousness.[85]   Tyrants and dictators of the world make their kingdoms sure by oppression and tyranny; this King will found and establish His kingdom through righteousness in government and the people will joyfully obey such a righteous rule.   The righteousness which the Child accomplishes for the subjects of the kingdom is the basis and the foundation of the kingdom.

[84] "throne" — We may paraphrase: "For the increase and for peace upon the throne of David, there is no end." The promise recapitulates and expands what had been revealed in 2 Sam. 7:11-16. For this reason the Messiah is practically identified with David.

[85] "to found it" — To make it sure. Cf. Isa. 16:5 and 54:14. For the fulfillment cf. Luke 1:32, 33.

4. The Threat of Assyria (9:8—10:34)

a. *The approaching destruction* (9:8-17)

8 A word did the Lord send into Jacob, and it fell in Israel.

9 And all the people will know; even Ephraim and the inhabitant of Samaria, in haughtiness and greatness of heart, saying,

10 The bricks have fallen, let us build with hewn stone, the sycamores are felled, and we shall substitute cedars.

11 And the Lord has set on high the enemies of Rezin upon him, and he will instigate his own enemies.

12 Syria from before and the Philistine from behind, and they devour Israel with open mouth. For all this his wrath does not turn back, and still his hand is stretched out.

13 And the people have not turned unto the One who smote them, nor have they sought the Lord of hosts.

14 And the Lord will cut off from Israel head and tail; branch and rush in one day.

15 The elder and the favorite, he is the head, and the prophet who teaches falsehood, he is the tail.

16 The leaders of this people have been seducers, and those who are led of them are swallowed up.

17 Wherefore the Lord will not rejoice over their young men, nor will he have pity over their orphans and widows, for everyone of them is profane and an evildoer, and every mouth speaketh folly. For all this his wrath is not turned back, and his hand is outstretched still.

8 **A word!** It was that with which Isaiah's soul was full. Here it was a threatening word, probably the prophecy contained in verses 14-17 of chapter seven, the mother of all these threatenings.[1] Sometimes God sends plagues; sometimes He sends help; now He

---

[1] This verse introduces a new section which bears no title. דבר is often used of messages of threatening. B reads θάνατον, probably having understood *deḇer*, "pestilence." *it fell* — Note the unusual use of the perf. with weak *wāw*.

sends a word, and this word was sent into Jacob. It was directed against Jacob, but Jacob is here conceived primarily as the recipient or the place where the word was sent. Like a thunderbolt, it fell down upon Israel. Jacob and Israel are two terms designating the northern kingdom. From heaven, or from Jerusalem, the word takes its origin and is sent as the messenger of God.

Men are still opposing God's activity, and so He must send His Word; His hand is outstretched still. What, however, is a word? Is it something, which after its utterance, gains a power of its own? Balak apparently thought that Balaam could utter a word which had the power of bringing either blessing or cursing. Balak, however, lived in a superstitious environment and believed in the power of magic as was so common in his day.

There is truly a power which accompanies the Word of God, but it is a divine power. In that Word itself there resides no magical efficacy. The Word of God is truth itself, and God blesses that Word so that it does not return to Him void but accomplishes the purpose for which it was sent. The Word is thus itself sometimes thought of as a working power which accomplishes its end. "Therefore," says the LORD, "have I hewed *them* by the prophets; I have slain them by the words of my mouth: and thy judgments are as the light that goeth forth" (Hos. 6:5). Ben Sirah expressed the truth when he said, that, "in the words of the Lord are His deeds." God has sent forth this prophecy, and because it was His Word, He would bring to pass the threatenings which it contained.

9 All the people, the entire Israel, will know as a result of experience.[2] The word has reached them and accomplished its end. Until now they have paid no attention to God's threatenings, but the word has reached them. Experiencing the divine chastisement, the entirety of the people will obtain knowledge, but even so will continue in hardness of heart. Ephraim itself and the inhabitant of Samaria, because of their haughtiness, were the hardest to convince.

---

2 "will know" — Through experience; cf. Hos. 9:7; Ps. 14:4; Job 21:19. Cf. Koran 26:49 *falasaufa ta'lamouna*. "the people" — The noun is s. but contains a collective idea and so may be construed with a pl. pred. even when that pred. precedes. When *kōl* with a suffix follows the noun it is more emphatic than when it precedes; thus, "the people, all of it," or "all of the people." "in haughtiness" — "and all of the people shall know, who in haughtiness and pride of heart are saying," or "the ones who in haughtiness are saying."

Here is no humility, no repentance for sin. Rather, in haughtiness and in greatness of daring of heart, they speak.

10 Here is haughtiness indeed! "Let the judgment come, we can more than make good the losses that we may sustain." Bricks were not strong; they were made of clay dried by the sun and hence could easily crumble to pieces.[3] Eliphaz spoke of the weakness of houses of clay, "How much less in them that dwell in houses of clay, whose foundation is in the dust, which are crushed before the moth" (Job 4:19). Very well, if the bricks had fallen, there is always hewn stone available. Amos had denounced the wealthy, "Ye have built houses of hewn stone, but ye shall not dwell in them. . ." (5:11). The haughty and daring Ephraimites had forgotten Amos, however, and now would vauntingly build houses of hewn stone. Suppose that Tiglath-pileser should take away the brick houses, the Ephraimites were confident of their powers to meet any loss. The sycamores were not valuable trees; they could be replaced with cedars.[4] As brick stood to stone, so stood these sycamores to the cedars. Boasting and vaunting, the people think that they have the control of the situation in their own hands. They refuse to acknowledge that things are in God's hands.

11 In the progress of God's judgments there is a second stage.[5] For three verses Isaiah has been making a digression dealing with Ephraim, and in verse 11 he continues his discourse. Yahweh has determined to make high and so secure and safe those who were to conquer Israel, namely the enemies of Rezin, and these enemies of Rezin he will exalt over Ephraim. Who are these enemies? The

---

3 "the bricks" — It may be that the losses described are those resulting from the depredations of Tiglath-pileser and the period following the death of Jeroboam II.

4 "sycamores" — A common tree, growing in the Shephelah (*ficus sycomorus*). "we shall substitute" — Cf. 40:31; 41:1.

5 "has set on high" . . . the action is to take place in the future, but the revelation and revolution are already past (cf. 5:15; 9:5). "'The adversaries" —Those who oppress Rezin. Thus the Israelites are reminded of their alliance with Rezin and it is intimated that they who had so lately conquered Syria were soon to conquer Israel. These were the Assyrians. We may paraphrase: "The Lord will set on high above Ephraim the victorious enemies of Rezin (Assyria), for Rezin had been the late ally of Ephraim, and in addition God will also instigate against Rezin those who had long been his own enemies, even Syria and Philistia." יסכסך an intensive form of *śkk*, "to incite, to prick up." The imp. gives a particular force and vividness to a particular phase of the action.

enemies of Rezin are also those of Ephraim, for Israel had entered into alliance with Rezin. They were the Assyrians who had lately conquered Syria and would soon conquer Israel. Hopes had been concentrated in Rezin, and hence, he rather than Ephraim is mentioned, but God will instigate even Rezin's own enemies, Syria and Philistia, against him.

12 Isaiah now returns to his main theme and names Rezin's own enemies.[6] They are the Syrians; possibly, those from the east. If this is so, then these Syrians are to be understood as the enemies of Rezin. They come from the east, and the Philistines from the west, in other words, from opposite directions. The term Israel probably designates the entire land, inasmuch as there is no recorded attack of the Philistines on northern Israel. The Syrians had come against Ephraim, and the Philistines against Judah. Like wild animals they came with open mouth ready to devour the prey.

Notwithstanding all this, there was no repentance on Israel's part, and the wrath of God was therefore still directed against the people. The punishing hand of God was yet outstretched. As long as the people did not repent, that hand would be outstretched to punish, and wrath would be manifested.

13 *The people* — Isaiah brings them first before our attention. God's hand is still outstretched, but the people — they do not repent. They must turn and go to God, for sin is a departure from Him, and repentance is a returning of the One that has been afar. To turn to God involves a complete conversion, a turning away from the former walk of life and a turning unto a new walk. There was One whose wrath had not turned, and whose hand was upraised to smite. He was the Smiter.[7]

Nor had the nation sought God. They had sought the idols, and the spirits, but not God. To seek God is a communion with Him

6 Even in Saul's day, Syria had been an enemy; cf. 1 Sam. 14:47. Possibly the reference is to those Syrians who had been subjugated by Assyria and were now tributary to it. "Philistines" — Earlier they had been Israel's most dangerous enemy; Isa. 14:28-32; 2 Chron. 28:18. "they devour" — Continues the standpoint of the first imp. in the preceding verse. The *Moallaka* (v. 32) speaks of a battle as a meal. The Assyrian inscriptions are replete with examples of the readiness of kings to exact vengeance. "from behind" — From opposite sides. "with open mouth" — Lit., "with whole mouth," i.e., with mouth fully open to devour the adversary.

7 Note the chiastic arrangement of the verse, which continues the description of the preceding. המכהו — This form is correct even though one codex (Rossianus) gives the form without suffix; cf. Isa. 24:2; Prov. 16:4; Deut. 13:6, 11; 20:1; Isa. 63:11. Cf. *GKC*, no. 116f.

that involves prayer, coming for help and guidance and walking with Him. A man is known by the object of His seeking. An idolator seeks an idol and consults it; a superstitious man consults an astrologer, and a Christian goes to Jesus Christ.

14 A new, higher measure of punishment will come. Using a proverbial manner of speaking, the Lord announces the full destruction of the people. He will cut off head and tail, branch and rush in one day.[8] Small and great will be cut off. The branch formed the head of the crown of the palm, and the rush grew in the marsh. Every class among the people, superior and inferior, would at that time be cut off, and that suddenly. One day! A brief expression — a brief time. It is as though Isaiah were to say, "At one time, at once." So Rebekah had used it of her sons, "Why should I be deprived also of you both in one day?" (Gen. 27:45b). The phrase does not necessarily exclude the thought of an extended period of time over which destruction might endure, but indicates rather that at once the destruction will take place. All together will perish. Even though the nation does not seek after its God, He is still in control of its destiny and welfare.

15 The head and the tail, all classes of the people! In excitement Isaiah adds an explanation. The head is the elder and the favorite and the tail the false prophet.[9] It is a brief explanation, and the prophet explains only the first description; he makes no attempt to explain branch and rush. His brief words direct the thought to those who are causing the nation to fail and to perish. The leaders were in the government, but the false prophets were not at the head of the people. No leaders were they but, following where the leaders led, they simply flattered and fawned, a wagging tail on a dog.

---

[8] ויכרת — Continuing the description begun by the first verb of v. 10, and hence to be rendered by the future or present. "branch and rush" — Proverbial expressions. Gesenius compares the Ar., "some were the nose; the remainder the tail."

[9] For the following reasons this verse is to be regarded as genuine: 1) It fits into the sectional arrangement. The first two sections each contain five verses and the last two four verses, so that if this verse is stricken out, the structural arrangement is destroyed. Section 1: 9:8-12; Section 2: 9:13-17; Section 3: 9:18-21; Section 4: 10:1-4. 2) The verse does not break the train of thought, but rather advances it. 3) The verse can hardly be criticized as too prosaic. But even if it were, Isaiah's concern was not to write esthetic poetry. 4) Isaiah customarily supplied his own explanations.

16 Why had Isaiah mentioned the leaders and the false prophets specifically? The reason now appears.[10] They were the ones who had been seducers, blind leaders of the blind. Those who were led of them were led astray, swallowed up in ruin. Promising to lead in a straight way they led astray, and those who were led by them were swallowed up. Those led astray are not themselves without fault, for they have permitted themselves to be led astray.

17 This terrible description carries us back to the time before the flood. Men were then evil in every imagination of the thoughts of their hearts, and judgment was impending. Now there is a similar situation. The people of Judah are impenitent.[11] The young men, chosen for warrior service, in whom the nation might place confidence, will find no rejoicing at the hands of God. They cannot stay the doom. Inasmuch as conditions actually are such as have been described in verses 13-15 God will not rejoice in the chosen soldiers of the people. What, however, about the widows and orphans, over whom God had expressed concern and to whom He had shown mercy? The time will come when He will no longer have pity over them, for they too are responsible in guilt. Can judgment be harder than this? Yet it is a righteous judgment, for all the people, widows and orphans as well as the leaders, are profane. In their thoughts and hearts they are irreligious and alienated from God. Wickedness, however, is not confined to the inward man. In their outward deeds every one of them does evil, and their inward character and nature appears in the folly which without exception they all speak. This is not mere foolishness or jesting, but wicked speech directed against God in which ethical perversity rises to full madness. "For the vile person," said Isaiah later (32:6) "will speak villainy, and his heart will work iniquity, to practise hypocrisy, and to utter error against the LORD, to make empty the soul of the hungry, and he will cause the drink

---

10 This verse arises naturally out of v. 15, which would support its genuineness. וַיְהִי — This verb should be taken in connection with the preceding verse, as adding a point of information and hence should be translated by the past. "seducers" — The root *'tr* appears in Ug. in the sense "to march."

11 "Therefore" — Replaces the *wāw* cons. of the two preceding verses. The dependent part of the sentence appears first for emphasis. "will not rejoice — The futures indicate the course that from now on God will take with His people. "evildoer" — The word "profane" refers more to the inner disposition and attitude, whereas the word "evildoer" refers to the actual overt acts. "folly" — Wicked speech directed against God; cf. 32:6; Ps. 14:1; Job 2:10.

of the thirsty to fail." It is God-blaspheming speech, and hence there is reason why God punishes. His hand is still outstretched and consequently there will follow stroke after stroke and blow after blow. The judgment must run through many stages and courses before its final end is reached. Each day will bring new plagues, new blows, new strokes. What appears to the people to be the end will be followed by still more punishments. Judgment in its completeness will finally come, for the hand of God is still outstretched (cf. the promise of Lev. 26:27-41).

b. *The punishment* (9:18—10:4)

18 For wickedness burneth as the fire, the brier and thorn it devoureth; and it kindles in the thickets of the forest, and they are borne along upwards, a column of smoke.

19 At the wrath of the LORD of hosts the earth reeled, and the people were as the fuel of fire; no man shall spare his brother.

20 And he shall consume on the right hand and is hungry; and he shall eat upon the left, and they are not satisfied; every man shall eat the flesh of his own arm.

21 Manasseh, Ephraim, and Ephraim, Manasseh, and they together against Judah. For all this his wrath is not turned back, and his hand is stretched out still.

10:1 Woe unto them that decree decrees of injustice, and write prescriptions of travail,

2 To turn aside from judgment the weak and to snatch away the right of the afflicted ones of my people, that widows may be their spoil, and the orphans they plunder.

3 And what will ye do in the day of visitation, and of the ruin which cometh from afar? Unto whom will ye flee for help, and where will ye leave your glory?

4 There is nothing left but to bow beneath the prisoners, and under the slain they fall. For all this his wrath is not turned back, and his hand is stretched out still.

18 *Wickedness* — godlessness, the curse which Israel's apostasy bears within itself. Here is the reason why the punishing hand of God is yet stretched out.[12] Wickedness — untamably it burns. God's restraining grace will be removed, and wickedness will then burst forth, devouring like a fire both brier and thorn, the individual

---

12 Herntrich remarks that the fire of God's wrath devours them, and their own evil devours them like a fire. וַיִּתְאַבְּכוּ — Cf. Akk. *abaku*, "bring, turn," i.e., the twigs are borne or roll themselves upward as a column of smoke.

and the thickets, the whole mass of people. The thickets are those of the forest in contrast with the briers and thorns. In them the mass of the people are bound together by iniquitous cords and plaits. All will thus perish, both individuals and the mass. Starting in the lower places, the fire burns, consuming at last all things.

19 A rising, whirling, turning column of smoke. God's wrath continues and burns.[13] Such wrath poured out is more than the earth can bear. Like a weak, tottering man, the earth reels, and the people become the prey of licking tongues of fire. When this wrath was poured out, men acted in cruel self-destruction, each turning upon his brother and close relation. It will not do to say that in this civil war men acted like beasts for even the beasts seem to spare one another. Rather, it was the man in man that appeared; not a beast, but man in his depravity. God had blinded them and given them up to a reprobate sense, and their monstrous wickedness bursts forth against one another.

20 Ravenous men even devour their own flesh. They look to the right and bite what they can find, but they are not satisfied.[14] Brethren should defend each other; this civil war is so severe that they seek to devour one another. One turns to the right and one to the left, but there is no satisfaction. Members of one's own tribe or even family were designated the arm, for they were its stay and support. To such lengths did this cannibalism go that men thus turned upon one another. Surely the punishing hand of God was

---

13 בעברת — 1Q reads *mem*. It may be that the prep. *bet* is to be rendered "from," and so expresses cause: "because of the wrath of the Lord," etc. Isaiah continues his description of the general burning but introduces an account of the miseries which the internal war of the nation produced. נעתם·
— Probably to be derived from n (w) ', "to reel." The *m* stands for an enclitic *mi*. The form is then 3 f.s. agreeing with "earth." Cf. Wm. L. Moran: "The Putative Root '*TM* in Is. 9:18" in *The Catholic Biblical Quarterly*, Vol. XII, No. 2, April 1950, p. 153. Cf. also *JBL*, June 1957, p. 94. For Ug. examples cf. *UH*, p. 101, #13.91. Note the Amarna text 69:10 "*iltiku-mi*," (they have taken) and "*nadnati-mi*" (I have given), 85:24. This interpretation removes the difficulties which Gray finds in this verse. "shall spare" — The pl. refers to the people as subj. understood.

14 "consume" — The idea is that of cutting or tearing with the teeth and then devouring. The Kamus explains this root by *akala*, "to eat." Cf. Metamorphoses 8:877. Dillmann takes the word in the sense of cutting a piece of meat at the table. The people eat what is its greatest help. "left" — On all sides. "arm" — Man's most necessary help; cf. Jer. 17:5. The word also serves as an expression for help, Isa. 33:2; Ps. 83:9. Codex A reads "his brother."

present. After the death of Jeroboam II the judgment fell and continued, until the enemy came and bore the northern kingdom away.

21 The people of God, the holy nation, the light to the Gentiles, devours itself.[15] Most closely related were the two sons of Joseph, Manasseh and Ephraim, and now the tribes which bore their names, the two principal members of the north, are fighting one another. Jealousy between these two had broken out before, and now when they can unite, it is only for the purpose of attacking Judah. How wicked is an evil union! Herod and Pilate were friends at one time, when Christ was crucified. Only one thing seems to have exceeded the mutual enmity of Ephraim and Manasseh, namely, the hatred of Judah. Civil war may easily lead to foreign war. All these woes were but the beginning of strife; the end was not yet. The hand of God was stretched out still. The nation had not turned, and God's hand had not turned.

10:1 Cannot the prophet's description be too harsh, too unreal? Will the people of God really sink to the depths that he has described? Has he not allowed his imagination to run away with him? With fine dexterity Isaiah mingles announcement of doom with a description of the reasons for that doom. The rulers had acted unrighteously, and even the administrators of the laws enact unrighteous decrees.[16] The laws were not made with regularity, and hence Isaiah here has in mind not lawmakers as such but rather those into whose hands the administration of the laws came, namely, judges and other administrators of law. The decrees of

---

[15] Cf. Judg. 8:1ff.; 12:1ff. These two tribes were descendants of the two sons of Joseph and were the two chief representatives of the northern kingdom. The verse probably constitutes a prophecy of the general internal destruction that will grip and devour the nation. The northern kingdom will be torn by internal dissension and this kingdom in turn will direct itself against Judah. Thus, Isaiah's purpose is to show that the sinful condition of the nation has wrought its own destruction. Gray refers to the legend of Dibbarra (*in loc.*).

[16] The root חקק means "to cut, carve." It is employed of the hewing out a hole in the rock, Isa. 22:16, of engraving a writing in stone, Isa. 30:8. It also comes to mean "to design," Isa. 49:16. The *Piel* would have frequentative force. For unjust decisions with respect to Judah, cf. Isa. 3:14, 15; 5:7, 8, 23; 1:17, 23, 26 and with respect to Ephraim Mic. 2:1, 2 and Amos 2:7. "decrees" — Cf. Judg. 5:15. The form is *qitl;* cf. Ar. *hiqq,* and *GKC* 93bb. Reichel, however, would render, "legislator," appealing to such forms as *'illēm,* "a dumb person." עמל seems to be related to און as the effect to the cause. The decrees are unjust and so involve travail.

these people resulted in unrighteousness, and the prescriptions in unjust oppression.[17]   The result of their activity was to produce hardship and suffering.   How can such a nation continue?   In this very description a ground for the coming judgment is given.

2 These were judges whose only purpose was to harm weaker people.   They would stretch away from judgment the poor who did not have the means to institute legal proceedings.[18]   How did they do this?   Did they refuse to exercise judgment at all, or were they simply so concerned to receive all that they could that in whatever way possible they precluded the poor from receiving justice in court?   Certainly these afflicted ones did have at least the right to just judgment.   That right, however, the judges snatched away as though it were held by a child.[19]   Whatever was in the hands of the poor became their prey.   Yet these afflicted ones belonged to God's people; upon them He had set His love and had exercised His concern.[20]   It is always an evil thing to defraud anyone; it is unusually heinous to defraud those who belong to God's people.

There was indeed one spoil which these unjust men desired, namely, widows.   Weak, helpless, defenseless, widows could not stand up and defend themselves.   Whatever they had was not prey of thieves that roamed the streets at night, but of men who sat upon the so-called bench of justice.   In the one place where these widows should have been defended they were defrauded.[21]   It was not a place of justice, but of plunder, and the objects of that plunder were orphans.   A nation in which such things could be carried on was ripe for destruction.

3 Three questions!   They cry for an answer from all those who seek to flee God's avenging wrath.   Three unanswerable questions!

[17] מכתבים — This form should not be emended, BH. It is acc. construct with enclitic *mi-* (cf. note 13 on 9:18). The concept of writing is employed elsewhere for denoting the decrees and purposes of God; cf. Isa. 65:6; Job 13:26. We may compare the written decisions that were rendered at ancient Nuzi.

[18] The inf. makes the verse dependent upon the preceding, and the third inf. connects the two halves of the verse.

[19] "to snatch away" — Either strictly or figuratively in the sense of doing violence to justice; cf. Jer. 5:28.

[20] The words "my people" refer not alone to the poor (Marti); the thought rather is that the poor ones who belong to my people are being afflicted.

[21] "they plunder" — The imp. lends vividness to the description in singling out one particular phase or aspect for emphasis. From now on we shall simply refer to this as the imp. of vividness. Cf. comments on 2:8.

for from God's avenging wrath there is no escape. Isaiah does not ask, "What will you do if a day of visitation comes?" That day will come; on that question Isaiah entertains no doubts. That day will come in which God will visit wrath upon the people and with it desolation.[22] That is the first question, What will you do? The day is one of visitation,[23] but it is also a storm, a desolating, rumbling tempest, gaining strength in the distance.[24]. It comes and breaks in hail and thunder. From afar it comes, from the place whence come evils upon Judah.

To whom will ye flee for help? The only One who can give help is the One who controls the breaking storm of judgment.[25] Ye will not flee to Him. To whom then will ye flee?

Where will ye deposit your glory,[26] and whatever else you glory in? During the breaking tempest of wrath, who can hold those things in which you now boast? "All the instances of punishment," says Calvin, "that now produce fear or terror, are nothing more than preparations for that final vengeance with which he will thunder against the reprobate, and many things which he appears to pass by, he purposely reserves and delays till that last day."[27]

How majestic this picture is! Before a whole nation stands the lone Isaiah. "What will you do?" he asks. You who are confident that you can meet every situation, who think that all wisdom resides in man alone! Judgment is coming, mighty and gathering force. What will ye do? Oh! that Isaiah's words could be heard today! What will you do, you who trust in man? The day of judgment is coming. Flee unto Him who alone can save from the wrath to come!

22 The conjunction "that" may be rendered "but."

23 "visitation" — From God. The word may be used both in a favorable and unfavorable sense.

24 שׁוֹאָה — Devastation, ruin, sudden destruction. The *lamed* should be rendered either "at the time of" or "with respect to." It is not necessary to insert the phrase "in the day of" before either of these nouns. Gray remarks that the day is thought of as a desolating storm already brewing in the distance, noisy with thunder and hail; men would fain flee from it to some place of refuge for themselves and their glory, but the true Refuge is the cause of the storm.

25 עַל with *bet* seems to lend a particular nuance distinct from that expressed by אֶל.

26 "glory" — the word refers to what is weighty; i.e., whatever they now boasted of and placed their trust in. It is not necessarily riches acquired unjustly, though such may have been the case.

27 *Commentary on Isaiah,* I, 335.

4 Not only do you not save the glory that is yours but you
yourselves will sink beneath the prisoners.[28] You will sink down
on your knees before the conqueror, who puts his foot upon the
neck.[29] And you will fall under those who are slain. Isaiah describes a full end and destruction. But God's wrath is still out-
poured. This is not the end but the prelude to greater judgments.

c. The boasting of Assyria (10:5-19)

5 Alas! Assyria, the rod of mine anger, and the staff in their hand is
mine indignation.

6 Against a profane nation will I send him and against a people
will I command my wrath to take spoil and to seize prey, and to
place it a trampling like the mire of streets.

7 But he is not thus inclined, and his heart does not so consider;
for to destroy is in his heart, and to cut off nations not a few.

8 For he saith, Are not my princes altogether kings?

9 Is not Calno like Carchemish, or Hamath like Arpad, or is not
Samaria like Damascus?

10 As my hand hath found the kingdoms of the idols, and their
images were more than Jerusalem and Samaria,

11 Shall I not, even as I have done to Samaria and to her idols, so
do to Jerusalem and her idols?

12 And it shall come to pass that when the Lord finishes all his work
in the mount Zion and in Jerusalem, I shall visit on the fruit of
the greatness of heart of the king of Assyria, and on the beauty of
the loftiness of his eyes.

13 For he saith, By the strength of my hand I have done it, and by
my wisdom; for I am prudent: and I have reached the bounds of
the people, and have robbed their treasures, and I have put down
the inhabitants like a mighty man.

14 And my hand hath found as a nest the riches of the people; and
as one gathereth eggs that are forsaken have I gathered all the

---

28 "nothing left" — *bilti* is used in Num. 11:6; Dan. 11:18, in the sense
"except to," i.e., "there is left nothing but to." The negative thought is not
actually expressed, but must be understood. B continues the preceding verse
by rendering "lest" or "that not." The word may form a negative composite
as in 1 Sam. 20:26 with an adj. and in Isa. 14:6 with a noun. It serves to
strengthen the negative concept as in Amos 3:3, 4. Lagarde and Euting had
proposed to render, "Belti breaks together; Osiris is broken." But there is
certainly no evidence of the worship of Egyptian deities in Judah in Isaiah's
day. Gray rightly rejects this erroneous proposal.

29 The preterites serve as prophetic perfects. "under" — Not only do the
Judahites receive the same destiny, but their destiny is even less desirable
than that of the prisoners. They, as it were, fall beneath the prisoners.

earth, and there was none that moved a wing or opened a mouth or chirped.

15 Shall the axe glorify itself over the one using it? Or shall the saw magnify itself above the one handling it? It is as though a rod wields those who wield it, like a staff's lifting that which is not wood.

16 Therefore the Lord, the LORD of hosts, will send upon his fat ones leanness, and under his glory shall burn a burning like the burning of fire.

17 And the light of Israel shall become a fire, and his Holy One a flame, and it shall burn and devour his thorns and briers in one day.

18 And the glory of his forest and of his garden land, from soul unto body he will consume, and it shall be like the wasting away of a sick man.

19 And the remnant of the trees of his forest will be few, and a child will write them.

5 Marvelous is God's work of Providence, His "most holy, wise and powerful preserving and governing all His creatures and all their actions". In His hands He raised up an instrument to punish His people Judah. That instrument was the mighty nations of Mesopotamia, Assyria and Babylon.[30] But they thought that they were acting in their own strength. All that we do has been foreordained of God, and to Him we are responsible. When we are employed in some momentous task we should look to Him and acknowledge His greatness for using us as He has. This Assyria did not do. Puffed up with pride, she thought that she was conducting affairs in accordance with her own wishes. Instead of recognizing the sovereignty of God, she believed herself to be sovereign. Judgment was indeed to come to Judah, but woe to that nation that brings the judgment. Instruments of God who measure their task by their own lusts and desires are the objects of woe. Assyria is the rod by which the anger of God is manifested, the rod with which He strikes. In the hand of Assyria also there was a staff, and that staff which was in Assyria's hand was God's anger.[31] Not only the nation itself, but also its

---

30 הוֹי — Here an expression of indignation which serves to introduce the declaration that judgment will fall upon the person named. "staff" — The staff of my anger is the staff wherewith my anger is exercised, not "my anger is a staff."

31 "and the staff" — Either we should render, "the staff, it is in their hand, it is my anger," and thus the last word stands independently; or else, "the

power and might were controlled by the wrath and anger of God. When a nation is thus charged with the execution of God's wrath and looks not to God, it itself can only become the object of woe.

6 God alone could send.[32] He could send plagues and He could send prophets. Now He sends Assyria against an irreligious nation, even Israel and Judah. Once He had called them "my people"; now He speaks of them simply as "a people." It is a people that provokes and deserves His wrath. The tempest will come, and wrath will be poured out upon Israel and Judah with the result that there will be a great despoliation. The enemy will trample the land just as the mire in the streets is trampled.[33] It would be difficult to discover a figure more adapted to express the utter lack of concern of Assyria for the inhabitants of Israel and Judah. Let the reader note the strength of the parallelism in 6a, a parallelism which even advances to rhyme.

7 In God's hand the Assyrian was an unconscious and unwitting instrument. To claim that Isaiah thought that the Assyrian knew God's commission is mistaken.[34] At the same time Assyria was without excuse. Assyria should have realized, and all nations should realize, that in all that they do they are instruments in God's hands.

---

staff, it is in the hand of my anger." On this last construction, the final *mēm* is to be taken as the enclitic (see note 1 on 9:8). The verse thus teaches that Assyria is the rod which God uses to express His anger, and the staff of Assyria (that with which Assyria strikes the enemy) is His anger. Assyria is the rod which smites by a staff, yet that staff is God's anger.

32 "will I send" — As the prophet had been sent against his people, so will the Assyrians be sent. The expression had been used in the sending of the plagues. The *Piel* is stronger than the *Qal*; cf. 9:7; Ezek. 7:3; Amos 1:4ff. The mission is many-sided and already partially carried out, so the verbs should be rendered by the past. König refers 6b to the time immediately after the Syro-Ephraimitic war. "profane" — Cf. 1:4, "a sinning nation." A profane nation is one that is irreligious.

33 וְלָשׂוּמוֹ — Qere, "*ûlᵉśûmô,* and 1Q, *wlśym.*" חֹמֶר . — "*clay*"; cf. Mic. 7:10; Zech. 10:5; etc. Note how this passage refers to previous sections; cf. 5:5; 5:25; 8:1, 3.

34 Verses 6 and 7 form a contrast between God's action (v. 6) and Assyria's reaction (v. 7). "yet he" — The emphasis brings out the contrast. "not so" — The Assyrian does not think that he is a mere tool. He ought so to think, for he was indeed in the hand of God an unconscious instrument. "inclined" —The root means "to be similar," and hence, "to think similarly, to be inclined"; Num. 33:56; Judg. 20:5; Isa. 14:24. "his heart" — Cf. 1 Sam. 14:7; Isa. 63:4.

For Assyria this was a special providence, which, inasmuch as it was directed against the nation and the city where Yahweh dwelt, should have caused heart-searching. Assyria, the great power, has here become personified, and Isaiah speaks of this power as purposing and thinking in its heart. Here, as Dillmann suggested, we are given a graphic picture of the heart of a dictator. Assyria does not think that she is in the hands of God. Her purpose, rather, is to destroy and to conquer many nations.[35] To this pattern of thought the courses of tyrants and dictators have been true from the days of Assyria down to our own times, to Hitler, Stalin, Mussolini and Khrushchev. God's purpose was to have Assyria cut off Judah: Assyria would purpose to cut off many nations.

8 Assyria speaks and gives expression to her philosophy of war.[36] She too has a word. I have princes, she says, princes who are subject to me and over whom I am lord, but these are kings as far as the rest of the world is concerned. I am the great king. Thus Assyria arrogates to herself a position that belongs alone to the true King of kings and Lord of lords. Her war philosophy came to outward expression in her incursions and expeditions and in the words of Rabshakeh which were later addressed to Judah. "Hath any of the gods of the nations delivered his land out of the hand of the king of Assyria? Where are the gods of Hamath and Arpad? where are the gods of Sepharvaim, Hena, and Ivah? have they delivered Samaria out of my hand? Who are they among all the gods of the countries, that have delivered their country out of my hand, that the LORD should deliver Jerusalem out of my hand?" (2 Kings 18:33-35). These are the words of defiance, not of a consciousness that one is an instrument of the Lord.

9 The language of braggadocio continues. The world power had boasted of its princes, now of its conquests. It is not any one

---

[35] The inscriptions are replete with statements in which the Assyrian kings boast of their supremacy and destructive acts.

[36] "saith" — He has said on former occasions, and now continues to say. "princes" — Perhaps the word *sar* is deliberately chosen to reflect upon the Akk. *šarru*. Some of the conquered satraps were designated kings; cf. 2 Kings 25:28. In antiquity the chief king was often designated "the great king," (*šarru rabu*); in Greek, "great king, king of kings," and Persian *shahinshah*. Under this king others may also have been designated king. Cf. Hattusilis' Inscription. Gesenius adduces many examples. Belshazzar is accurately designated king, although he was not a monarch. Cf. Cooke, *NSI*, 174, 181. Merodach-baladan was a vassal of Assyria and yet was designated king, Isa. 39:1 and 23:8. Cf. the description of the Assyrian army in 13:1ff., 29:7; 30:28.

particular Assyrian king who is to be thought of as speaking but the Assyrian thought or spirit as such. The conquests had been speedily achieved. One nation gave way before Assyria just as did another. Calno was the same as Carchemish. First the one had been taken, and then the other. Neither could withstand. Hamath was like Arpad, and Samaria like Damascus. The enemy speaks as though Samaria had already fallen, so that Jerusalem would have to give earnest heed to this boast. Would Jerusalem be the next to fall? Could Jerusalem be any exception? The Assyrian thought not, but what would Judah herself think?

All these were fairly nearby kingdoms which in Isaiah's time had been destroyed. Calno was taken in 738 B.C., Carchemish on the Euphrates in 717, Hamath on the Orontes in 720, Arpad in 740 and 720, Samaria in 722 and Damascus in 732. It is an interesting enumeration, one that seems to come closer and closer to Jerusalem. It begins with the most distant and most northern places and concludes with the nearest and most southern. These, however, are not the conquests of a single Assyrian king; they are the conquests of Assyria.[37]

10 Here is Assyria at the height of her boasting, directing words of conviction to Israel so that Israel would feel the necessity for surrendering.[38] It is Assyria vaunting herself, but she uses Israelitish forms of speech. "Why," she addresses Israel, "do you think that Yahweh your god can protect you? The nations round about, whose gods you have called idols, have each had gods, but they have all been deceived in their gods.[39] With you too it will be the

---

[37] "like Carchemish" — Note *Daghesh lene* in the prep. despite the fact that a vowel precedes and the accent is conjunctive. "Calno" — Cf. Amos 6:2. Generally located in N. Syria, at the southern environs of Unki, on the Mediterranean coast. "Carchemish" — Also in N. Syria, a former capital of the Hittite empire. Probably the modern Jerablus. This is the most remote city from Jerusalem, some 360 miles distant in a straight line. "Arpad" — North of Aleppo, the modern Tell Erfad, near Hamath. "Hamath" — Located on the Orontes River in N. Syria. It was taken by the Assyrians and its inhabitants located in Samaria; cf. 2 Kings 17:24. Antiochus named it after himself, Epiphania, but its ancient name survives in the modern Hama; Akk. *amatu*. Gods were actually taken from captive cities. Cf. the language of Rab-shakeh in Isa. 36:19, and " . . . the king of Akkad and his troops went upstream against the towns of Mane, etc., and took spoil from them and carried off many of them as prisoners, and led away their gods." (Cf. D. J. Wiseman: *Chronicles of Babylonian Kings*, London, 1956, p. 55).

[38] "hath found" — Has had power over; cf. v. 14.

[39] "than Jerusalem" — Whose graven images were more numerous than those of Jerusalem.

same. Just as my hand, my powerful hand, has found the idol kingdoms, kingdoms whose images exceeded those of Jerusalem and Samaria, much more will it find Jerusalem and Samaria themselves." In boasting blasphemy Assyria designates the holy Yahweh of hosts an idol.

11 The boasting continues. The rod by which God expressed His anger now vaunted itself above Him.[40] In this perverted reasoning of Assyria there are two stages. First, other nations have easily fallen. Secondly, Samaria, the sister kingdom, has also easily fallen, and Samaria trusted in Yahweh. Actually Samaria had not yet fallen, but Isaiah allows the Assyrian to speak as though the conquest were already past.

What, however, about the Judahites' relationship to Yahweh? Was He to them anything more than an idol? Should they have taken offense at the blasphemous reference of the Assyrian, when they themselves by their practices ignored His being?

12 We have listened to the boasting heart of Assyria. The Lord now speaks and announces what He will do.[41] The persecution of Zion and Jerusalem represents in essence the substance of all the persecutions that would come upon the Church, and the declaration and description of this punishment prepare the way for the announcement of the coming of the end of the days, the period of blessing to be ushered in by the Messiah. The work to be accomplished on Zion may seem to be the Assyrian's, but in reality it is the Lord's, who is in control of all that is done. The Assyrian must also be punished, but before he is punished the Lord intends to complete His work on Zion.

When this is completed then the Lord, the Sovereign One — Isaiah does not use the tetragrammaton — will turn His attention to

---

[40] This verse reverts to the standpoint of v. 9 and expresses the conclusion that after Samaria came the turn of Jerusalem. Verse 11 really forms a second protasis with v. 10, the apodosis following in v. 12. Cf. Rom. 5:12. "her idols" — Note daghesh in the bēt.

[41] A conclusion or apodosis to the preceding, and also a short summary of the contents of the following. "all His work" — All the Lord's work. "fruit" — Note the unusual heaping up of genitives. Four members of a series are determined by the concluding genitive "Assyria." Cf. "fruit" in Matt. 3:8 and Luke 3:8. "loftiness" — There are two principal interpretations. One would make the Lord's work of completion on Zion identical with the punishing of the Assyrian king. The other would make it a previous condition for the punishing. On this latter view, adopted in the translation, the word ki is best rendered in English "when."

Assyria. The vainglorious blasphemy of the true God is Assyria's fruit. It is the fruit of his self-glorification and swelled-up heart, whereby he overestimates his own significance, a fact which gives itself expression in the lofty look of his eyes.

13 Assyria counted on two things, strength and wisdom[42]. Yet her strength was weakness, and her wisdom folly. True strength and true wisdom are necessary for a successful ruler, and Assyria thought that she had both of these. These two attributes were manifested in removing the bounds of peoples, thus taking them to be a part of herself. No one like Assyria had mixed up nations before. Those who had been on the throne Assyria brought down so that they must now go about without a fixed dwelling.

14 To find an unprotected nest, with the mother bird away, and to take the eggs from that nest, is not difficult.[43] The young birds cannot defend themselves, neither by moving a wing nor by opening the mouth. To the Assyrian the whole world is but a nest, an unprotected nest, and he has taken and will take what he desires. With the exception of Tyre, Arabia and Egypt, Assyria had conquered the then known world. To her it was no more difficult than taking eggs from a bird's nest. The earth, however, did not belong to Assyria; it belonged to the Lord. "The earth is the Lord's, and the fulness thereof" (Ps. 24:1). Wrongfully, Assyria had taken what did not belong to her. Her actions therefore were really an assault upon God Himself. When we take what belongs to God, we are assaulting Him and His Name.

15 Assyria's boasting cannot go unchecked. Like Amos his predecessor, Isaiah asks some pertinent questions, and these bring

---

42 "by my strength" — By position these words receive the emphasis. "I have done" — Accomplished, partly through forming a world kingdom and amalgamating other kingdoms into it and partly through the deportation of other peoples to distant lands. "and I have removed" — Or, "I am wont to remove." "their treasures" — The word refers to things laid up or kept in store for future use. "I have plundered" — The form is *Po'ēl* perf. and the *Tzere* should be noted. "the inhabitants" — The sitting ones (upon thrones). Eitan points out that it means enthroned ones, and refers to Amos 1:5, 8 where this root is parallel to the phrase "those who hold the sceptre."

43 "nest" — *Continens pro contento;* cf. Deut. 32:11. ʽI understand the construction of v. 14a to be, "and my hand has found like a nest with respect to the wealth of peoples," i.e., "with respect to the wealth of peoples my hand has found that to take them is like taking the eggs from a nest." "as one gathereth" — The inf. is substituted for the finite verb, lit., "as the gathering of eggs." "eggs" — A f. pl. in -*im;* the adj., however, takes the normal ending.

out the true nature of things. Assyria was only an axe in the hands of God. Should Assyria exalt herself over God who was employing her?[44] That were truly a perversion of the right order of things. Should a mere saw, held in the hands of a carpenter, vaunt itself, as though it were acting without the hand of the carpenter, as though it were independent and greater than the hand that held it?

How lifeless a mere rod is! Can a lifeless rod actually wield those who hold it and wield it? That were folly indeed, but that was the way in which Assyria was acting. And a staff, made of wood, a mere material object, shall it lift that which is immaterial, which is not wood like itself? Shall finite, human Assyria, move the mighty God? Can we for a moment accept this philosophy of Assyria? Yet, so do sinners constantly act, perverting the true nature of things. Sin involves perversion. He who sins, by that very fact shows that he regards himself as greater than God. God forbids. Man disobeys. Does it not then follow that man considers himself of greater authority than God? "Whenever men ascribe to themselves," says Calvin, "more than is proper they rise against God." Here are only a couple of examples taken from daily life, but they show the folly of Assyria's attitude.

16 Folly is the counsel of Assyria and that counsel cannot stand. The sovereign God will act. This sovereign God is the Yahweh of hosts, and He will again send.[45] He had already declared (v. 6) that He would send the Assyrian against a profane nation. Now He will send against the Assyrian, whose warriors are designated fat ones, a leanness which will destroy them. Just as fat animals are thought to be the best, so the army of Assyria was the best; it was a fat army in that it was rich and strong and in good, healthy

---

44 For the construction of the sentence cf. Judg. 7:2. "using" — Lit., "the one hewing with it." The change of tone from the preceding verses is to be explained by the fact that the verse begins a new section in which the prophet himself is the speaker. "not wood" — When the staff lifts itself against something that is not wood, i.e., non-material, it is lifting itself against something greater than itself. The basic contrast is between wood and non-wood.

45 "the Lord" — This particular epithet serves to call the attention of the Assyrian to the position of the God of Israel. The accumulation of titles is in no sense pointless. "Therefore" — Connects this verse with the preceding. Inasmuch as its haughtiness was unbearable, the Sovereign One must act against Assyria.

condition.[46]   Upon this strong army God sends consumption or leanness, so that the whole army will be weakened unto death and will then know that the God of Israel is truly the Sovereign One.   The condition of the Assyrian army will be completely changed.

The glory of Assyria! Her might and magnificence; her civil and material greatness! Could anything withstand them? Under this glory in which she boasted the One who has all power will kindle a burning, which will burn like the burning of fire. As under thorns and thistles men kindle a fire, so that fire reaches up, crackling and devouring, till the thorns and thistles are gone. Lighted under the glory, it towers up in flame, until the glory is entirely consumed.[47] "In accordance with Isaiah's masterly art of painting in tones," says Delitzsch, "the whole passage is so expressed, that we can hear the crackling, and spluttering, and hissing of the fire, as it seizes upon everything within its reach. This fire, whatever it may be so far as its natural and phenomenal character is concerned, is in its true essence the wrath of Jehovah."

17 To Israel God is a light, for He is pure, and the source of knowledge and salvation; to Assyria He is a fire that devours and consumes.[48] To His people He is a light that shines in the darkness of their hearts and brings them saving truth; to those whom He would punish this light becomes an omnivorous fire. Israel's Holy One, the Light, will be to the enemy a flame. Before this fire of burning wrath — this destructive might of God's penal righteousness — the glory of Assyria was like a mass of thorns and briers. They had grown up in the place where the once

---

[46] "his fat ones" — The warriors of Assyria. For the sense we may compare, Dutch, *hij heeft geen pit,* no power; and Ar. *ma bihi tirqun,* there is no fat (strength) in him.

[47] "glory" — The word refers to general grandeur and magnificence, whether inward or outward. The Paronomasia in 16b should be noted. Duhm thinks that the figure of consumption in 16a is not good, because the Assyrian was defeated at one stroke. But the point is not to stress a slow wasting away but simply that a complete change will occur. From being a strong army it becomes one that is its opposite. The reference is not necessarily to the plague that visited Sennacherib's army, but rather to the general weakening of the now strong army.

[48] "light" — The reading is attested by B and 1Q. God is Light, for He is pure, and from Him comes the light that brings life and salvation. To the Assyrians He is a burning fire. "thorns and briers" — We should have expected שׁיתוֹ; cf. *'îrô* from *'ayir.* The reference is to the lower classes of the people. Fire begins at the lower parts of the forest and reaches the tops of the trees. Rapid changes of figure occur in Isaiah; cf. 5:24; 8:7ff., 28:18.

theocratic nation dwelt. Now, they crackle and burn up. It is swift and sudden. One day! As God has raised up nations, so He can swiftly consume them.

18 Burning first the thorns and briers, the flames leap higher and consume even the high trees of the forest.[49] Using figures borrowed from the world of plants and trees, Isaiah represents the greatness of the Assyrian enemy. Sennacherib himself had used similar language. "By the multitude of my chariots am I come up to the height of the mountains, to the sides of Lebanon; and I will cut down the tall cedars thereof, and the choice fir trees thereof; and I will enter into the height of his border, and the forest of his Carmel" (Isa. 37:24b). Composed of various nations, the Assyrian army was a forest. Possibly too there is a reflection upon the fact that the Assyrians had brought beautiful trees from other lands. On the other hand, the *carmel* was the cultivated land in contrast to wilderness and forest. In its entirety the glory of the Assyrian, all in which he could place his boast, would be consumed by the fire of God's punishing justice.

Assyria was also like a man about to waste away. His soul would consume and with it also his body, so that nothing would remain. This consuming would not be accidental, but was to be imposed by God who would cause both soul and body to waste away.

Sickness and fire are mixed together in the description, and a proverbial manner of speaking is introduced. Assyria's decaying will be like the wasting away of a sick man. This is the conclusion of the whole matter. God will so act that Assyria will be like the consuming of a consumptive. How proud, how boasting was that philosophy of Assyria! What were gods to such a nation! One of these gods, however, One indeed whom Assyria called an idol, was the Sovereign God, and when He acted, Assyria was reduced to a languishing consumptive, pining away to nothing.

19 Assyria's forest will not be completely destroyed, for there will be a remnant.[50] A few trees will remain. These, however,

---

[49] "forest" — Isaiah's purpose is to set forth the greatness of Assyria under figures which have been taken from the vegetable world. "from the soul" — Cf. Gen. 14:23; 1 Sam. 15:3. Note the triliteral infinite cons. We may render, "like the wasting away of a sick man."

[50] "few" — Lit., a number. Inasmuch as it can be numbered, i.e., is a definite number, it is not regarded as large. Cf. Gen. 34:30. Cf. also Cicero, *Philipp.* II: 97, c. 38. "will write them" — In the sense of taking a register.

will be so few in number, that a child could write them down. A little child who cannot count very high will find no difficulty in writing down the few remaining trees of this forest.

d. *The deliverance by the Lord* (10:20-34)

20 And it shall come to pass in that day that the remnant of Israel and the escaped of the house of Jacob shall no longer again lean upon his smiter, but will lean upon the LORD, the Holy One of Israel in truth.

21 A remnant will return, the remnant of Jacob, unto the mighty God.

22 For though thy people, O Israel, shall be like the sand of the sea, a remnant of them shall return. A consumption is decreed, pouring forth righteousness.

23 For a determined end is the Lord, the LORD of hosts, about to make in the midst of all the earth.

24 Therefore, thus saith the Lord, the LORD of hosts, O my people that dwelleth in Zion, fear not from Assyria; he will smite thee with the rod and his staff he will lift up against thee in the manner of Egypt.

25 For yet a little while, and the indignation has ceased, and my wrath in their destruction.

26 And the LORD of hosts will rouse up against him a scourge like the smiting of Midian at the rock of Oreb, and his rod will be over the sea and he shall lift it up after the manner of Egypt.

27 And it shall come to pass in that day that his burden will turn aside from upon thy shoulder, and his yoke from upon thy neck, and the yoke shall be destroyed by reason of fatness.

28 He is come to Aiath, he is passed to Migron; to Michmash he entrusts his baggage.

29 They have crossed over the pass, in Geba they have made their lodging; Ramah trembles; Gibeah of Saul flees.

30 Cry aloud, O daughter of Gallim; give ear, O Laish, O thou poor Anathoth.

31 Madmenah wanders; the inhabitants of Gebim flee.

32 Yet today he is to stand in Nob; he will shake his hand against the mountain of the daughter of Zion, the hill of Jerusalem.

33 Behold! the Lord, the LORD of hosts will lop off the boughs with a clash, and those that are high of stature will be cut down, and the lofty ones shall be brought low.

34 And he shall strike the thickets of the forest with iron, and Lebanon will fall as a mighty one.

20 Here grace breaks through! The promises of God have not failed. Ahaz had leaned for help upon Assyria, and Assyria had

set free from the danger that threatened him. As a result, however, there came a train of worse evils. Assyria marched in mighty power against Judah, but Assyria would be brought to an end, and then the people of God would turn to the only One upon whom they could safely lean for support, the Holy One of Israel.

Assyria had been a smiter, not a protector. Duhm tells us that "Ahaz leaned for support on Assyria (2 Kings 16), but was not smitten; Hezekiah was smitten, but did not lean for support on Assyria." This is not quite accurate. The point of Isaiah is that the genius of the Mesopotamian power, not any particular ruler, is one that would afflict the people of God. To lean upon this smiting power for support is folly. There is to be a return, however, when Jacob will lean upon the Lord in truth, and so in a saving sense. All who have been left over from persecution and bondage will gradually turn unto the Lord. This is not a hypocritical turning, nor one characterized by capricious vacillation, but a turning in sincerity and constancy, a turning in truth. There will thus be fulfilled the promise found in the name Shear-jashub, "a remnant will return." Assyria's remnant was a few scattered trees of the forest, and there was no hope: Jacob's remnant had hope as broad as the promises of the God of truth.

21 Herein is graphically expressed the truth which was taught in the name of Isaiah's son, Shear-jashub.[51] Salvation had been promised, the seed of the woman would bruise the serpent's head. If this is to be accomplished there must be a remnant. A remnant will indeed return, and this is the remnant of Jacob. It is the true Israel, the elect people of God, who will lean not upon the smiter Assyria but upon the Mighty God. This Mighty God has already been introduced. He is One that will sit upon the throne of David. To turn to *el gibbor* is to turn to the Lord Himself. "Afterward," said the Lord through Hosea, "shall the children of Israel return, and seek the LORD their God, and David their king; and shall fear the LORD and his goodness in the latter days" (Hos. 3:5).

22 What is the meaning of "remnant"? As though speaking directly to the ancestor of the nation, the prophet now explains

---

[51] In returning to the mighty God, the remnant will return to God as manifested in a descendant of David. The foundation of the passage is 9:6, and hence the reference is Messianic.

the term. "For," he says in effect, "if thy descendants, the people of Israel, become, as they now have become, like the sand of the sea, then a remnant will return."[52] Is this not strange, however? Had it not been promised that the seed of Abraham would be as the sand upon the seashore for multitude? True enough, but the principle herein stated is for the purpose of confuting a false reliance upon the promise. It will not do to say, "We have Abraham for our father," as though mere physical descent from Abraham were sufficient to ensure deliverance. Whenever the people became over-numerous, then there would be a remnant, and a deliverance. The remnant, and that alone, would return to the Lord. Thus, the nation is reminded of the true force of the promise once made to Abraham. "The bold address to the patriarch," says Calvin, "has a striking effect. God, addressing a dead man, declares to the living what he had formerly promised."

For the mass of the people a consumption has been decreed.[53] For them there will be no salvation or deliverance, but the wrath of God, overflowing with a punitive righteousness, will bring them to their deserved end. Descent from Abraham will be no stay at the time when the punishment and judgment of God overflow. Eternal punishment is a manifestation of justice against which no valid objection can be raised. Our sins have brought it upon us. Only in the return of the remnant to the Mighty God Jesus Christ can there be deliverance!

23 Here is the justification or grounding of the threatening just made, and like the preceding verse this one also begins with *ki*.[54] An end is coming, not an end which the Assyrians will accomplish, but one wrought by the Lord. It is a determined end, for it has been decreed of God and is irrevocable. The Sovereign One alone can make such an end, and that He does as

---

52 "for although" — "for, although thy people should be," not, "though thy people were." The words provide a general rule of the divine economy which would be applicable in each particular case. Whenever the people became numerous this rule came into effect.

53 "consumption" — The principal part of the complicated subj. is placed first for emphasis. We may render, "a consumption (which has been decreed), pouring out righteousness."

54 "a determined end" — Lit. "an end, a determined one." The two words form an hendiadys. The connection appears again in Dan. 9:27 and Isa. 28:22. "the earth" — Not the promised land, but the whole earth. Paul applies these verses (Rom. 9:27, 28) to the saved remnant, not to the Jews as such.

Yahweh of hosts. It will be made in the midst of the earth and so will affect the whole earth. It is the last judgment, from which no man can flee. It is not some local judgment, confined to the boundaries of Palestine, but one in which all the earth is involved.

24 *Therefore* — Isaiah would probably have us return to the thought of verse 19, in which he had pictured the remnant of the Assyrian forest as so small that a child could number it. Hence, there is no need for fear. After verse 19, Isaiah breaks out into a parenthesis in which he describes the fact of salvation and the certainty of the coming judgment. Now he introduces his wondrous conclusion.[55]

"Fear not," He says. How often this phrase appears in the Bible! It is a favorite word of comfort. Later Isaiah told the servants of Hezekiah, "Fear not" (Isa. 37:6). All these commands are but preludes to the majestic "Fear not: for, behold, I bring you good tidings of great joy" (Luke 2:10), and to the Lord's "Fear not, little flock, for it is your Father's good pleasure to give you the kingdom" (Luke 12:32). Once more God addresses His own as "my people." They dwell in Zion where the Temple is. They are His elect. From Assyria they have nothing to fear, for the might of Assyria will soon be reduced to nothing. The juxtaposition in the Hebrew is striking! *Dweller of Zion — from Assyria.* The one need not fear the other.[56]

True enough, Assyria will smite. She has a rod with which she will strike, and a staff which she will lift up against Israel. This she will do as Egypt did at the time of the bondage. The Assyrian is cruel and, like Egypt, intends thy destruction, but he will only wound, not slay thee, Israel. Therefore, fear not.

25 When God commands His people not to fear, there is always good reason. Fear not Assyria, He is now enjoining, for soon they

---

[55] "Therefore" — The logical connection is really with v. 19 and the discourse is resumed as though there had been no interruption. "my people" — In contrast with the "this people" of 6:9; 8:11, 12. "Zion" — The words are a title of honor, a pledge of all comfort and a sign of all help.

[56] "he will smite" — The future may be taken as permissive, "he may smite." The word introduces a verbal, circumstantial clause. For the suffix, cf. 2 Sam. 2:24. The form וכבהו has *zaqef-qaton*. In rapid speech there is generally a *Shewa* in place of *Segol*, the fuller forms standing either in pause or before a break. "in the way of Egypt" — In the manner of Egypt. Egypt was the house of bondage. Assyria's smiting will be similar to that of Egypt.

will be destroyed.[57] From the time of Tiglath-pileser to Sennacherib was roughly about thirty years. In the prophetic view, it was a short time. It may be, though, that Isaiah envisions not merely the destruction of the Assyrian Sennacherib, but the destruction of the Mesopotamian powers as such. Even if this is so, viewed from the standpoint of God, the time until this foe would be done away was very little.

Indignation will cease! These are words of promise. The entire period of the exile was known as the Indignation. It may be that Isaiah here is announcing that the period of such indignation will be short, and that the punishment to fall upon the enemy is the final judgment. When the indignation is completed, God's wrath will then manifest itself in the enemy's destruction.

Babylon was like a grave, and exile to Babylon was like burial in a grave. But the period of indignation continued until the restoration was complete and Christ had come. Indignation was then the prelude of blessing to God's people and of wrath for His enemies.

26 God has announced the definite destruction of the enemy. The prophet now seems to explain this prediction and hence speaks of God in the third person. Against Assyria God would raise up a scourge,[58] against Israel Assyria had been a rod, but against Assyria a scourge is to be raised up. The scourge could bring not only pain but shame. It will be like the smiting of Midian at the rock Oreb. At this rock the princes of Midian who had escaped from the battlefield were slain by Gideon. So Sennacherib, although he might escape death in Palestine, would die at home. Oreb was

---

57 "a little" — Lit., "yet a trifle, a very little while." "for" — Is founded upon the basic thought, "fear not." "has ceased — The preterite shows that the change has already occurred in the prophet's view. After a determination of time the perf. with *waw* consecutive is often used. "indignation" — The word coincides with "his work" of v. 12, the "consumption" of v. 22 and "decreed end" of v. 23. Dan. 11:36 reminisces upon this word. Note also Matt. 3:7 and Rom. 1:18. It is the indignation directed towards Israel which will soon be over.

58 "will rouse up" — "awaken, arouse, incite." The word is used both in a literal and figurative sense. "scourge" — May denote divine judgments. It is stronger than *šēbeṭ* or *maṭṭeh,* and so indicates a difference between Israel and Assyria as to punishment. "Oreb" — "The rock Oreb is particularly mentioned because one of the Midianitish princes, who had escaped from the field of battle, was there slain by Gideon, and so Sennacherib, although he should survive the slaughter of his host, was to be slain at home" (Alexander). "his rod" — Moses' rod over the sea; Exod. 4:20.

truly a place of significance. There had been a long previous period of servitude. Here at the rock, however, the deliverance was final and complete, and moreover, it was a deliverance of such a nature as only God could accomplish. If the enemy is to be defeated as Midian fell at Oreb, surely that would be a grand and final defeat.

Once Egypt had driven Israel to the sea. Likewise, Assyria has driven Israel into a sea of affliction. Over the Red Sea Moses' rod had been lifted, and now over the sea of Israel's affliction God would raise a rod. As the waves of the Red Sea had swallowed Pharaoh and his horseman, so also the waves of this sea would engulf and devour the Assyrians. Assyria in the manner of Egypt had lifted up the rod over Israel; now God in the Egyptian manner would lift up the rod over Assyria. Like Egypt Assyria has carried and used the rod; like Egypt Assyria will also feel that rod.

27 Speaking in the vigorous language of predictive prophecy Isaiah declares the certainty that Assyria's yoke will be removed from Israel.[59] How great that day will be! It will be the day of deliverance and of vengeance for God's enemies. Israel is a slave upon whose shoulder a heavy burden rests, and that burden is Assyria. Over the paths of Judea trod men bearing heavy burdens. Unenviable is their lot! Like them Israel is trudging a difficult path and carrying a heavy burden.

Israel is also a domestic animal of labor. Upon his neck is a collar or yoke. But Israel is a fat animal, so fat indeed, that his very fatness breaks the yoke. The figure signifies that Assyria cannot subdue Israel. It is not Israel's superiority, however, which overthrows Assyria. The figure of fatness does not imply that Israel in herself can be free of Assyria, but only that Israel is such a nation that cannot be destroyed by Assyria. Not Assyria, but the Lord, will bring to an end the theocracy.

28 Inasmuch as the final overthrow of the enemy was sure, let that enemy come, let him do his worst! Isaiah stands upon the wall of Jerusalem, as it were, and describes Assyria's approach, by men-

---

[59] The principal difficulty of the verse is found in the conclusion, "and will be pulled down (destroyed)." The yoke (Assyria) will be brought to nothing, because of the fatness of Israel. It is the fatness of the animal which leads to the destruction of the yoke; cf. Rom. 11:17; Deut. 32:14; Hos. 4:16. Many emendations have been proposed, but both B and 1Q support M. Penna reads, "*il distruttore viene da Rimmon.*" He has changed the verb to *hôbēl.*

tioning the main points which one must attain in an approach to Jerusalem.[60] "We may conceive the prophet," says Alexander, "standing in vision on the walls of Jerusalem, and looking toward the quarter from which the invasion was to come, numerating certain intervening points, without intending to predict that he would really pass through them." There would be obstacles in the way, and the more difficult the route which the enemy had to traverse, the clearer it would be that despite all the obstacles this enemy would come. As a matter of historical fact, Sennacherib approached Jerusalem from the south. "And the king of Assyria sent Rabshakeh from Lachish to Jerusalem unto king Hezekiah with a great army" (Isa. 36:2a). We are not then to understand Isaiah as seeking to delineate the actual route by which the Assyrian would come, but rather as simply setting forth the approach of that Assyrian as he comes nearer and nearer to Jerusalem, passing over one by one the obstacles and difficult places which he would have to face, and outlining the principal points that lay between him and his ultimate object Jerusalem. It is therefore an ideal picture, and seems designed by the prophet to express the thought that the enemy when he comes will take over the whole land. And yet we may also agree with Delitzsch when he says, "What the prophet here predicts has, when properly interpreted, been all literally fulfilled. The Assyrian did come from the north with the storm-steps of a conqueror, and the cities named were really exposed to the dangers and terrors of war. And this was what the prophet depicted, looking as he did from a divine eminence, and drawing from the heart of the divine counsels, and then painting the future with colors which were but the broken lights of those counsels as they existed in his own mind." The sublimity of Isaiah's description is incomparable!

Vividly Isaiah sets forth the approach. He has fallen upon Aiath, about thirty miles northeast of Jerusalem and here he first entered Benjamite territory. Then he deviates from the main route and

---

[60] "he is come" — Note this usage of the prophetic perf. which is continued by a second verb in the perf., and the description is then made more impressive by an imp. of vividness. The tenses correspond to the progressive stages of the march of the army which Isaiah followed in spirit. "Aiath" — Possibly identical with Ai or with Khirbet Hayyan. After the exile the city was repopulated; Neh. 11:31. "Migron" — Tel Miryam, near Michmash? "Michmash" — Mahmas, about 7½ miles north of Jerusalem. It was separated from Gibeah by the deep wadi Suwenit. The enemy's last stopping place would be at this gorge, the implements on the north, and the army on the south.

passes over into Migron, and in Michmash, on the eastern side of the valley of Migron, he deposits his equipment. This he does so that he may pass through the pass of Michmash as unencumbered as possible. At Michmash he is about seven and a half miles away from his object, Jerusalem.

29 At Michmash they have already crossed over the well-known pass.[61] Isaiah switches from the singular to the plural for now he is thinking not so much of the approaching enemy as a unit, but rather of the men of the army. They have made a lodging in Geba. They have acted; but the places where they pass also act. Ramah, a short distance to the west of Gibeah, trembles, but Gibeah herself flees.

30 Hitherto description; now the language of address.[62] It is the voice of lament and complaint. The command is to cry shrilly, to neigh, out of fear at the enemy's approach. Let the daughter or population of Gallim so cry; let Laish hear, and let Anathoth be truly pitied. She is near Jerusalem.

31 Madmenah flees in madness and the dwellers of Gebim (the water pits) seek for cover. The enemy approaches closer and closer to Jerusalem and the desperation of the local inhabitants becomes greater and greater.[63]

32 So near to Jerusalem has the Assyrian come that he may now defy it from where he is.[64] Nob was close at hand, a priestly city

---

61 "the pass" — The definite article shows that it is a well-known pass. Note the paronomasia. "Geba" — Modern Jeba, about 6 miles northwest of Jerusalem. It belonged to Benjamin. "Ramah" — Modern er-Ram, 5 miles north of Jerusalem. This city was repopulated after the exile; Neh. 7:30; 11:33. "Gibeah of Saul" — Modern Tel el-Ful, about 3 miles north of Jerusalem.

62 "Gallim" — Possibly the modern Khirbet Ka 'kul. "Laish" — Modern el-Isawiyeh? north of Jerusalem. "Anathoth" — Modern Ras el Kharrubeh, near Anata, the home of Jeremiah, northeast of Jerusalem. "cry aloud" — Lit., "let thy voice neigh" (from fear). On the basis of the Syriac some would render, "answer her."

63 "Madmenah" — north of Jerusalem; possibly the modern Shufat. "Gebim" — The cisterns north of Jerusalem and possibly just southwest of Shufat. הָעִיזוּ — "Take refuge," cf. Koran II:67, "I take refuge in Allah."

64 "Nob" — Possibly modern Ras Umm et Tala on the eastern slopes of Scopus, northeast of Jerusalem. לַעֲמֹד — It may be that this form is not an inf. but an imp. with the emphatic particle "la"; cf. Ar. la (verily). If so, it would be a contracted form of le-ya'a-mōd and the contraction would be due to vowel recession (Eitan). If taken as an inf. the form may be rendered, "it is to stand," i.e., "one must stand." Today he is to stand in Nob.

of Benjamin near to Anathoth. This day the enemy is to take his stand even there at Nob, possibly within sight of Jerusalem, there to make ready for the attack upon the Holy City. Here he will rest and regain strength for the attack. Now he can shake his hand in threat against Jerusalem. He is ready for final action. The power of the world is aligned against the city of our God. Twelve names have been mentioned, and each of these twelve becomes as it were a symbol or byword of terror. Each brings the judgment closer at hand. Rapidly the enemy comes, choosing bypaths in order to make a sudden onrush. The blow is ready to fall, but the outcome is known. God is in the midst of the city, and no world power can be victorious against the Lord of hosts who dwells in Zion. The earthly Zion may go, but the Zion of the people of God abides forever.

33 Will the blow fall? Will Assyria reach Jerusalem in surprise and destroy her? We are ready to hear of her victorious attack, but Isaiah interrupts our expectation.[65] Look! he tells us, breaking into our eagerness. Look! the Lord, the Sovereign One is again before us. He will act. The matter is not in Assyria's hands at all. The Sovereign One has allowed her to come almost to the gates of Jerusalem . Enough about Assyria, however; let us notice her no longer. The Lord who has her in His control is now ready to act. He will let us see the enemy no longer as a mighty approaching army. Rather we again see that enemy as a forest. The figure which had been dropped in verse 19 is taken up anew.

The high branches of the trees will be suddenly lopped off, branches that are beautiful and ornamental. The lopping off, however, will not be the quiet work of a cultivator, but will be done with sudden and terrific violence. The trunks, denuded of branches, will not stand alone, for they too will be felled and brought low. Thus Sennacherib and his hosts will be destroyed. Can anything be more beautiful than a majestic tree? So stood the might of

---

[65] "will lop off" — The primary reference would seem to be to the downfall of Sennacherib, although ultimately to the complete defeat of the Mesopotamian enemy of God's people. פארה — "boughs," i.e., the branches considered as the ornament or glory of the tree. The Qerē and about 40 mss. read "pŭ-rāh." I do not think that this is an alternate form for pŏ'-rāh, for this latter has a naturally long vowel, cf. pô- rŏ- ṭāw, whereas pŭ- rāh, appears to contain a short vowel. Possibly it is a defective writing, but 'ālēf seldom quiesces with qibbutz.

Assyria, the product of long and slow growth, the splendor of the glory of might. But in one swoop, He who alone is truly sovereign, cuts the trees down, and Assyria is destroyed completely.

34 The forest in its entirety will disappear, for the thickets which usually grow in forests will also be cut down. Whether these thickets have particular significance as a figure or no is questionable. Some refer them to the common people, but it seems more likely that Isaiah is merely attempting to complete his figure. The whole forest, both great trees and the accompanying thickets, will be cut down.[66] To cut down these thickets iron will be used, and from this we are to understand that the work is to be thorough. When the iron has completed its work, no thicket will stand, and any remaining trees will be so few in number that a child can note them.

As elsewhere the Assyrian is compared to Lebanon. "Behold, the Assyrian was a cedar in Lebanon with fair branches, and with a shadowing shroud, and of an high stature; and his top was among the thick boughs" (Ezek. 31:3). But great as Lebanon was, it would fall by means of a mighty One, and that mighty One is the punishing God of Israel. The forest, mighty like Lebanon, is gone. The trees are felled, the thickets cut down. The Mighty One remains, Lord over all. He has protected His people and demonstrated His faithfulness.

---

[66] "and he shall strike" — Piel. Some would construe as *Niphal* and render intransitively, "will be stricken." "thickets" — Note the *Metheg* with a const. Its presence apparently shows that the following *Shewa* is vocal, and that the syllable is not closed. Cf. Zech. 11:1-3 where the different categories of vegetation are used to describe those who are noble and those less noble. Kissane thinks that the thickets represent the common people, but Alexander suggests that they are mentioned merely to complete the picture of a forest totally destroyed. Kimchi referred the thicket to Sennacherib's counselor by whose devices he had been entangled. "with iron" — With an instrument of iron.

5. JUDAH'S HOPE IN THE MESSIAH (11:1—12:6)

a. *The shoot of Jesse* (11:1-5)

1 And there shall go forth a shoot from the rootstock of Jesse, and a branch from his roots will be fruitful.

2 And there shall rest upon him the Spirit of the LORD, the Spirit of wisdom and perception, the Spirit of counsel and might, the Spirit of knowledge and the fear of the LORD.

3 And he shall delight in the fear of the LORD, and not will he judge according to the sight of his eyes, nor will he render decisions by the hearing of his ears.

4 But with righteousness will he judge the poor and decide with equity for the oppressed of the earth, and he will smite the earth with the rod of his mouth, and with the breath of his lips will he slay the wicked.

5 And righteousness will be the girdle of his hips, and faithfulness the girdle of his loins.

1 Great and lofty was the forest of Assyria, but it would be cut down by a mighty One. What, however, had become of David's house? That now was but a tree, and at that a tree which had been felled. It was only a stump or rootstock. To emphasize its mean condition, Isaiah looks to its lowly origin, not even referring to it as the house of David, but merely as the rootstock of Jesse. Jesse had lived in Bethlehem, and Bethlehem was least among the thousands of Judah.

What possible contrast, however, could there be between that mighty Assyrian forest and the lowly stump of Jesse? Just this: Assyria would perish and come to a complete end, but in the rootstock of Jesse there was yet life. From that stump a twig was to come forth,[1] and from the roots which furnish the stump with life a branch would grow,[2] and would derive its life from the roots so

---

[1] "and there shall go forth" — The verb connects the following with what precedes; 10:33, 34 should be compared with Dan. 2:34, 35. יצא is used of human genealogy, Gen. 17:6, but here, as also in Job 5:6; 14:2, it is taken

378

that it might be fruitful. David's dynasty, then, is not completely exterminated; its roots are in the ground, and a stump[3] remains. Having reached the height of its power, Assyria is cut down forever but David's house, reduced by its apostasy to the condition herein described is suddenly exalted. The branch[4] from the roots will bear fruit, a figure which suggests that the dynasty will no longer continue as a fallen tree, but will truly prosper. Life is in the roots, and that life, in God's own time, will manifest itself.

In what sense, however, will this branch bear fruit?[5] Isaiah is obviously not speaking of mere outward prosperity or material welfare. Under Uzziah there had been such prosperity, but in the year of Uzziah's death Isaiah could speak of the nation as a people of unclean lips. All that is stated in the remainder of this present chapter shows that the prophet is not concerned with material welfare but with something far more important. Once again there will be a great ruler on the throne of David. It is this branch which promises to supply the place of the crown and trunk to which one would ordinarily look for the life and fruitfulness of a tree. And the dynasty will prosper as before in that it will fulfill the ideal of the true theocracy. The fruitfulness, therefore, is of a spiritual nature, one that has to do with obedience to the Lord of creation,

---

from the realm of plant life. Isaiah's purpose is to show that the kingdom has sunk to so low a point that there must be a new beginning. The mighty Assyrian power was about ready to destroy the Davidic kingdom, but actually the Assyrian power would perish, and the Davidic kingdom would arise again.

2 חטר — "Shoot, twig"; cf. Akk. *huṭaru,* "scepter"; Ar. *chitrun,* "twig, shoot." B ῥάβδος. Cf. Prov. 14:3 where the word has this force. The grammatical relation of the words can best be brought out by rendering, "the shoot which belongs to Jesse." This twig promises to supply the place of the crown and trunk.

3 נצר — "Rootstock, stump." In Job 14:8 the word refers to the stump of a fallen tree; cf. Isa. 40:24. It is the stump, or part of the tree remaining above ground when the tree is felled.

4 נצר — "Shoot, twig, sprout." In Isa. 14:19 it refers to a growth from the tree that is despised in the eyes of man. Here it is a new hope coming from the already felled tree. "from his roots" — I.e., from Jesse's roots.

5 "will be fruitful" — M is supported by 1Q. Hitzig, followed by many, would emend by substituting a *Het* for *He* as the final radical and thus translate, "will sprout." This appears to be supported by B, ἀναβήσεται. Kissane thinks that it offers a better parallel to "shall go forth" than the rendering "will be fruitful." Eitan suggests that the word may possibly be compared with Egy. *pry,* "to come up, ascend, sprout." This might also fit in Isa. 45:8.

the actual ruler of the theocracy. On the throne there will be a Son of David, One who will in Himself embody all the ideals of the real Davidic kingdom. At the outset then we are faced with the fact that the blessings about to be depicted are to be realized because of the shoot and branch which comes from Jesse's stump. This is Immanuel, the true Messiah, who is to be the Hope of His people.

It is true that some Jewish expositors found here a reference to Hezekiah and others to Zerubbabel, but the Targum applies the passage to the Messiah. Hezekiah, of course, was already born, so that the passage does not refer to him. And the descriptions do not apply to Zerubbabel, or, for that matter, to Hezekiah either. This passage is dependent upon the fountain prophecy in Isaiah 7, and hence is to be interpreted in the light of that revelation.

2 Not unprepared does the shoot come out of Jesse's roots! He who is to sit upon the throne of David is rich in gifts and accoutrements. In His human nature, as the Messiah, He is equipped for the tremendous task of bringing peace upon earth. It is the goal for which many strive! When the second world war was still in progress men spoke as though, once the war were concluded, they would be able to establish a just and lasting peace. That end has not been attained. Not by might nor by power, not by human wisdom and means will it ever be achieved. Peace will come only by the One who issues forth from Jesse's roots. In the first part of his prophecy Isaiah depicts this Messiah as Immanuel, the Prince of Peace. In the second part he sets forth the Messiah as the Suffering Servant and shows that this wondrous peace is to be obtained because the Servant suffered. "The chastisement which procured our peace was upon him." The thought of suffering does not appear in the first portion of the prophecy, but only the lowly beginnings of the Messiah.

Upon this Messiah the Spirit of Yahweh is to rest.[6] Not the spirit of prophecy, not a mere influence is this Spirit, but rather the Spirit that belongs to Yahweh, and who works for Yahweh.[7] He

---

[6] ונחה — With *waw* cons. the tone is shifted to *milra*. Cf. Isa. 7:19 as distinguished from Isa. 7:2. Cf. also Num. 11:25; 2 Kings 2:15; Acts 2:3; 1 Pet. 4:14 and John 1:33; 14:16, 17.

[7] "spirit" — Best taken generally as in 1 Cor. 12:8-11. Kittel well remarks that all that is good in Israel's life has been accomplished by the Spirit; cf. 1 Sam. 10:6; 16:13ff. He will endue others for their service; cf. Isa. 28:6; and will come in greater measure upon the Messiah. Examples of those whom the Spirit has equipped and endued for work: craftsmen, Exod. 31:3; 35:31;

is therefore a person. Furthermore, He is distinct from the Messiah. Isaiah is not speaking of the human spirit of the Messiah, but of the Spirit which comes from Yahweh. This Spirit had already wrought good and blessing in Israel. A portion of the Spirit had been placed upon the elders who assisted Moses; the Spirit of the Lord was to come upon Saul in order that he might be changed into another man; and at his anointing the Spirit of the Lord came upon David. Assyria's ruler had boasted of his own wisdom; but the Branch receives His gifts from the Spirit.

When the Lord was upon earth it was said of Him, "Upon whom thou shalt see the Spirit descending, and remaining on him, the same is he which baptizeth with the Holy Ghost. And I saw, and bare record that this is the Son of God" (John 1:33b, 34). "For in him dwelleth all the fulness of the Godhead bodily" (Col. 2:9).

To be endued for the Messianic work an anointing of Yahweh was necessary, and this anointing consisted in the impartation to the Messiah of the Spirit. "The Spirit of the Lord GOD is upon me; because the Lord hath anointed me to preach good tidings unto the meek; he hath sent me to bind up the brokenhearted, to proclaim liberty to the captives, and the opening of the prison to them that are bound" (Isa. 61:1). In the resting of the Spirit upon the King we see a Messianic trait. This Spirit of Yahweh is the Spirit who brings all these gifts. Some of these gifts have appeared in individual men individually, but all of them appear together in Immanuel, the Messiah, and all of them serve as a remarkable preparation for fulfilling the duties of the Messianic office. Nor need we think that Isaiah mentions all the preparation which Messiah had. "He does not mention, therefore," says Calvin, "all the gifts which were bestowed on Christ, for that was unnecessary; but only shows briefly that Christ came not empty-handed, but well supplied with all gifts, that he might enrich us with them."

Isaiah does not intend to state attributes or qualities of the Spirit Himself. When he speaks of the Spirit of wisdom, he is not saying especially that the Spirit is wise.[8] True enough, He is a wise Spirit,

---

warriors, Judg. 6:34; 11:29; 13:25; 14:6; prophets, Num. 11:25ff. The grammatical relationship of the words may be brought out in translation, "The Spirit of the Lord who is the Spirit, ..."

[8] Genitive of causality, hence, "the Spirit who produces or gives wisdom, etc." The gifts are stated in three pairs, and hence the Spirit is mentioned only three, instead of six times. The reference is not to seven spirits nor to a sevenfold spirit. The qualities mentioned cannot all be entirely separated

but the emphasis rather is that the Spirit is the source or cause of wisdom. After the mention of the Spirit three pairs of qualities are stated, and we are reminded of the seven-branched candlestick and the three pairs of arms which proceeded from it.

Wisdom and perception — Gifts of the Spirit, which have to do with the realm of theoretical power. None of the terms employed is entirely exclusive of the others, and all together denote true piety or fear of God. Wisdom belongs to God and is derived from Him. It is the ability to render right decisions at the right time so that one may act in accordance with the right. It includes therefore intelligence, but it comprehends far more than that. Certainly the Messiah is intelligent, but this word suggests that He also has the ability rightly to appraise situations and to render right decisions in all matters.

Perception — Refers to insight into the true nature of things, and this, in particular, as it has respect to the human heart. Of Christ we read, "And needed not that any should testify of man: for he knew what was in man" (John 2:25). "And Jesus increased in wisdom and stature, and in favor with God and man" (Luke 2:52).

Counsel and might — Here we enter the practical sphere. The Messiah can discover wisdom and so advise and contrive that all his decisions are the manifestation of wisely-laid plans. In every given case this King chooses the right means and renders the right decisions. Together with such counsel there was present a power to carry out His wise decisions. We are reminded of the beautiful names of the Messiah in 9:5 where the terms "counsellor" and "mighty" are found in close conjunction. Our Lord was spoken of as "—a prophet, mighty in deed and word before God and all the people" (Luke 24:19b). Having chosen the right means and made the right decisions, the Messiah exhibits a firmness and constancy in executing these decisions.

Knowledge and the fear of the Lord — Here we meet the content of the Messiah's gifts. This knowledge has to do with the theoretical sphere but it includes more, for "The fear of Yahweh is the beginning of knowledge" (Prov. 1:7). There can be no knowledge unless one knows God, for knowledge comes from

---

from one another. " . . . none of these terms is entirely exclusive of the others. Wisdom, understanding, the knowledge of God, the fear of God, are all familiar scriptural descriptions of religion or piety in general" (Alexander).

God. To know God is the first principle of all true religion. Did the Messiah know God? It is well to remember the words which the Branch of Jesse spoke when He was here upon earth, ". . . and no man knoweth the Son, but the Father; neither knoweth any man the Father, save the Son, and he to whomsoever the Son will reveal him" (Matt. 11:27b). The fear of the Lord is the heart and core of Biblical religion. It involves a recognition of the absolute holiness of God; it is a fear based upon the recognition of that holiness and coupled with full reverence before Him. Such a holy fear had been manifested in the attitude of the seraphs above the throne of the Lord. The phrase itself is the practical equivalent of true piety and devotion. True religion is a reverent and godly fear, for it recognizes that the creature is but dust before the holy Creator, and it prostrates itself in His presence, expressing itself in reverential awe. The Spirit produces the fear of the Lord in those to whom He gives this gift. Even the Messiah will be imbued with the fear of the Lord in order to accomplish His mighty work.

3 In view of His utterly unique equipment, the possession of the Spirit without measure, how will this King stand out in distinction from others? He will have infallible knowledge and so will find His delight in the presence of true piety in others. Kings for the most part look for strength and wisdom in others; they seek men with those attributes which they themselves can use for their own advantage. This King, however, finds His delight when there is true devotion to Yahweh. His power of perception which is graphically expressed as His sense of smelling, with the implication that He actually receives pleasure therefrom, is exercised in that sphere where the fear of Yahweh is to be found.[9] This is the true nature of a Davidic king as ruler of the theocracy. Insofar as a king had deviated from this particular principle of cherishing and delighting in true piety, he had failed as a ruler in the theocracy.

The principal function of a ruler is to judge, and to reign with authority. How will this King, one who so delights in the fear

---

9 ריח — "To smell," construed with the acc.; Gen. 27:27. With the prep. it denotes a perception with pleasure; cf. Exod. 30:38; Lev. 26:31. Drechsler states that the Messiah rejoices in the fear of the Lord just as in an offering which has been brought to Him. The form is not a finite verb but an inf. const.; lit., "and his smelling with delight will be in the sphere of the fear of the Lord." M is supported by 1Q.

of Yahweh, carry out His function of judging? To ask that question is to answer it, for His judging will be completely unlike that of previous rulers on David's throne. His judgments will not be based upon the ordinary sources of information open to men, namely, what men see and what they hear. Such means, the eyes and the ears, can bring at best but an outward impression. For absolute justice, there must be absolute knowledge, one that cannot be derived merely by these two regular and ordinary sources of information. Step by step, as it were, the veil is being removed from the figure of this King, and we are learning that not only in His human nature is He miraculously equipped, but that He is also Himself a divine person.

4 No obstacle can stay the reign of this King; completely He carries through His rule.[10] Those who are in greatest need of righteousness are the poor and the oppressed, for they have been trampled under foot and neglected by men, particularly by human rulers at whose hands they should have obtained justice. If any needed righteousness in judgment, it was the poor. We are not to understand that the Ruler will have nothing to do with those who were rich in material possessions, but Isaiah mentions the poor because they serve as a fitting symbol for all the poor in spirit, those who have laid aside their haughtiness and lofty dispositions and are truly humbled by a conviction of their spiritual poverty before God. Such will be judged with righteousness. Here is no taking of bribes, but a just administration of the law, in which truth and honor are upheld.

What characterizes the judgments of this King is their absolute fairness. Before men the oppressed ones had sought for fairness,

---

[10] "will he judge" — What stands out is the contrast to human kingdoms, principally Assyria. In v. 3a the Messiah manages His rule perfectly with respect to the fear of the Lord, in v. 3b with respect to the means of obtaining information which are His; in v. 4a in respect to the judgment that He pronounces and in 4b with respect to the infallible execution of that judgment. "poor" — Note absence of the definite article in Hebrew. ארץ — As a parallel to "the wicked," the word may take on the secondary connotation "wicked earth." It is better, however, to regard "earth" as forming a contrast with Messiah, and so the reference is not to earth's inhabitants, but to the earth as that which, because cursed through human sin, is to be smitten. M is supported by both B and 1Q. "rod of his mouth" — Cf. Ammianus Marcellinus, 18:3; 29:1. Gesenius points out that in the Qamus 'ṣan, "stick," is rendered lisan, "tongue."

and found it not; from the Shoot and Branch, the true Messiah, they will be judged with equity. The decisions which He as the King is called upon to render will be such as manifest perfect equity.

As for the earth itself, that earth upon which the poor and the oppressed lived, He will smite it. He is above that earth, a supra-earthly, supra-natural Being; and He can do with that earth what He will. The very breath of His mouth, as it were, is a rod, with which He can chastise and smite. ". . . and out of his mouth went a sharp, two-edged sword . . ." (Rev. 1:16b). What comes forth from His mouth is His Word, and that Word is a judging, smiting Word. How powerful and efficacious is the breath of God's mouth! By that breath the hosts of heaven were made. The breath which goeth out of the mouth of the Messiah accomplishes the end for which it is designed; it slays the wicked.

The earth and the wicked are the objects of Messiah's wrath, and hence we are probably to understand, inasmuch as "earth" is parallel to "wicked," that Isaiah actually conceives of the earth as itself wicked. The inhabitants of the earth are under Messiah's power and will feel His wrath. His judging work could be seen in His pronouncement of doom upon Assyria through His prophet. It is seen today in the proclamation of His Word through His ministers, for He said to the disciples, "He that heareth you heareth me; and he that despiseth you despiseth me; and he that despiseth me despiseth him that sent me" (Luke 10:16). Finally, this breath of the Messiah will destroy that Wicked One, ". . . whom the Lord shall consume with the spirit of his mouth, and shall destroy with the brightness of his coming" (2 Thess. 2:8b). At the great last day of judgment, the voice of God will speak and the wicked will perish everlastingly.

5 At the outset we have learned of the full accoutrement of the Messiah and of the sure outcome of His work, the destruction of the wicked and the deliverance of the poor and afflicted. His work will not be easy, and He must meet foes. For the encounter He girds Himself, as a warrior ready for the battle. Some have claimed that the girdle was the garment which bound the other clothing together, and for that reason is mentioned. Others have thought that the girdle was the symbol of power and preparedness or that it was an emblem of royalty or a sign of royalty. Kittel was near the truth when he said that the girdle was the requirement of the warrior. Archaeology has now explained what lies in back of the figure.[11]

In ancient times the belt was worn by one who was ready to engage in a bout of wrestling with an opponent. The object of the bout was to wrest the belt from that opponent. Later, this conception took on a figurative meaning and came to be used of any who were ready to face a contest or struggle. When, therefore, the Messiah is described as so girded, we are to understand that He is to face a foe and to engage in a struggle, and that He is fully equipped for that struggle.

What wonderful preparation is His! He comes not with the ordinary weapons of war, but girded with the greatest of prizes,

---

[11] Drechsler holds that clothes serve as a picture of the qualities mentioned; cf. Isa. 59:17; Col. 3:12 and 1 Sam. 2:4.

אזור — "loin cloth"; Ug. *m'zrt*, "that which binds about the loins." Wrestling with the girdle or belt was well known in the ancient world. One example is seen on the paintings in the tombs of the Beni Hassan; another is the statute of the Khafaje wrestlers from Mesopotamia, third century B.C. Cf. Cyrus H. Gordon, "Belt-Wrestling in the Bible World," in *HUCA*, Vol. xxiii, Part One, 1950-51, pp. 131-6, Cincinnati. The practice seems also to be attested in the *Iliad*, 23:710. "When the two had girded themselves, they went into the place of gathering," and *Odyssey*, 24:89, "The young men gird themselves and prepare the contests." Of particular interest is a cuneiform text found at Nuzi in which wrestling with the girdle is a form of ordeal. Two brothers find themselves in a suit at law. One, Gurpazah, accuses his brother Mateshub of assaulting and injuring his wife. Mateshub denies the truthfulness of this charge, and the judges prescribe as an ordeal a form of belt-wrestling. The pertinent portion of the text follows:

ik-ta-bu-u a-lik (ma? a-na?)	
m*Ma-at-te-šub ilani i-ši-iš-mi*	
im-ma-ti-me-e m*Gur-pa-za-ah*	"They said, 'Go! carry the gods to Mat-
a-na ilâni i-la(?) -ak-mi ù	teshub!' When Gurpazah goes to the gods,
m*Ma-at-te-šub* m*Gur-pa-za-ah*	then Matteshub is to seize Gurpazah and
iṣ-ṣa-bat-mi ù qa-an-na-šu	he is to wrest (i.e., try to wrest) his belt
i-na qa-an-ni-šu he-is-mu-um-ma	in his belt. Gurpazah prevailed in the
i-pu-uš u i-na di-ni	suit. And the judges sentenced Matteshub
m*Gur-pa-za-ah il-te-e-ma*	(that he should pay) one ox to Gurpazah
ù daiiani m*Ma-at-te-šub*	for his belt."
a-na qa-an-ni-šu it-ta-du (uš).	

The text is found in Chiera: *Proceedings in Court*, Publications of the Baghdad School, Texts, Vol. IV, Philadelphia, 1934, No. 331; cf. Young, *The Study of Old Testament Theology Today*, 1959, pp. 53-55. It was probably this conception which underlay the common expression, "to gird up one's loins." The double occurrence of אזור is typically Isaianic, as Gesenius long ago pointed out (see text). I thank Gesenius for this additional bit of support for the unity of Isaiah, for many of these passages he denies to Isaiah.

prizes which none can wrest from Him. He faces His foe girded with righteousness and faithfulness.[12] Elsewhere this pair of qualities is ascribed to God and His judgments, "I know, O Lord, that thy judgments are right, and that thou in faithfulness hast afflicted me" (Ps. 119:75). Christ is the righteous judge and the One who maintains faithfulness. "For the Father judgeth no man, but hath committed all judgment unto the Son" (John 5:22), and "And I saw heaven opened, and behold a white horse; and he that sat upon him was called Faithful and True, and in righteousness he doth judge and make war" (Rev. 19:11).

There is a strong and forceful repetition of the word *ezor,* "girdle," in this verse, and for a word to occur twice is characteristic of Isaiah, who delights in using again a word that he has just written. In order that the reader be not tempted to think that an emendation of the text at this point is necessary, we urge him to read the following passages: Isaiah 14:4; 15:1, 8; 16:7; 17:12, 13; 19:7; 31:8; 32:17; 42:19; 44:3; 54:4, 13; 59:10. He who is girded with righteousness and with faithfulness can be ready for any foe.

b. *The coming peace* (11:6-10)

6 And the wolf shall dwell with the lamb, and the leopard shall lie down with the kid; and the calf and the young lion and the fatling together, and a little child shall lead them.

7 And the cow and the bear shall pasture, their young ones will lie down together, and the lion like the ox will eat straw.

8 And the suckling shall play upon the hole of the viper, and upon the den of the viper will the weaned child put his hand.

9 They shall not hurt nor destroy in all my holy mountain, for the earth shall be filled with knowing the LORD, as the waters cover the sea.

10 And it shall come to pass in that day that the root of Jesse which is standing for an ensign of the peoples: unto him the nations will seek, and his rest shall be glorious.

6 Wondrous indeed is this Messiah! In verses 2-5 we have seen Him completely distinguished from all earthly and temporal rulers. In verses 6-9 we learn that His kingdom also is to be contrasted with all earthly kingdoms. His is the kingdom as that kingdom

---

12 This same pair of qualities is applied to God: Ps. 33:4, 5; 36:6, 7; 89:15; to the Messiah: Jer. 23:5, 6; 33:15, 16. Christ is the Judge who maintains righteousness: John 5:22; Acts 17:31. He is also the Faithful: 2 Cor. 1:20; John 1:17; Rev. 19:11.

should be. It will be the very opposite of what now is found in human kingdoms. All enmity will disappear, not only from among men, but even from among beasts, and even between men and beasts all will be in harmony.

There is a remarkable chiasmus in 6a. "And there will sojourn the wolf with the lamb, and the leopard with the kid will lie down." The wolf is well known as an enemy of the lamb! Phaedrus, for example, tells us of the wolf who, standing abovestream at a brook, nevertheless accused the lamb downstream of muddying the waters. Then, upon that pretext, he seized the lamb and slew it. Now, however, the old hostility is removed, and the lamb, who once lived in dread of the wolf, now entertains that wolf in his dwelling.[13] The wolf is the lamb's guest and sojourns with him.[14] The lamb was young and tender, one that would ordinarily have been peculiarly tempting to the wolf. The leopard, too, equally rapacious as the wolf, would now lie down in peace and rest as one that was satisfied with food, and this he would do with the kid. No longer would the enmity between them be found. Both could live together.

Indeed, in the day of this kingdom we may see a wonderful trio. On either side is a tame animal, a beast of burden, and between them a beast of prey. In the names themselves there is a remarkable contrast, namely, wolf and lamb, and leopard and kid. And the contrast even extends to the name of the wild beast and to what is said about it; thus "the wolf" and "lying down." The verbs describe actions which are not normally thought of as characteristic of these wild animals. With respect to the tame animals, the calf is the weakest and hence the most accessible to the lion. The fatling is the ox that has been fattened and so is particularly desirable to the lion. Between them is the young lion, which neither seizes the weaker calf nor longs for the fatter ox.

More remarkable yet, a young, inexperienced boy leads them. A little child can scarcely be trusted with tame animals, but like

---

13 Cf. Lev. 26:6; Isa. 65:25; Hos. 2:20; Ezek. 34:25-31. Virgil, *Eclogues*, 4:21, 24. 5:60; Horace, *Epodes*, 16:53, 54; Theocritus, *Idylls*, 24:84; Lactantius, 7:24; Martial, *Epigrams*, 9:73; etc. These extra-biblical references and others are appealed to by some in support of the view that the passage in Isaiah simply expresses the same type of hope for a return of Paradise.

14 Between the calf and the fatling, the two domestic animals, stands the young lion, the wild beast. They are together; Isaiah's point is not that they are doing something together but that they are together. Hence, there is no need to insert any verb.

a shepherd that drives his flock, he leads these without fear and in perfect safety.

7 Perhaps we have reached somewhat of a climax. Not merely does the nobler lion, the king of beasts, find itself at peace with the domestic animals, but the bear, more ferocious and less noble, also is at peace. Indeed, the nature of the bear, here probably the female, is completely changed, for the bear pastures.[15] It even acts no longer as a bear but as a domestic animal, in that it grazes and does so in company with the cow. Permanent and perpetual is this peace, for it extends to the young of both bear and cow, which lie down in rest together as friends and show no sign of enmity. Likewise the lion, losing his lion nature, pastures like an ox, eating the straw which sledges had cut to make it suitable for the tame beasts.

8 How far will this reversal of nature extend? Will it obliterate that most ancient of enmities, the one between the serpent and man? So great is the Messiah's power that even this fundamental enmity will be wiped out. Indeed the most helpless of human beings, the child that has just been weaned, will be unharmed by mankind's deadliest enemy. At the creation the animals were a help to man. With the fall, however, enmity was introduced, and although the animals are still helps, they must be subdued by man. Enmity with the serpent was the first of all enmities, whereby man's relationship with all the animal world was really thrown out of joint.

The suckling child, probably at the age at which children were about to be weaned, will put his hand over the opening of the snake's den, thus closing the opening for the snake. In thus putting his hand over the opening, the suckling was playing and enjoying himself.[16] His actions would not draw forth the terrible bite of a serpent. Perhaps we may not be able to tell precisely

---

[15] "shall pasture" — The verb is f. although the subj. is m. In Heb. animals which are strong and courageous are usually regarded as m. whereas those that are weaker are considered f. Here the word "bear" may have feminine force; cf. German *Bärin*. Elsewhere it seems to be used for common gender, cf. 2 Sam. 17:8; Hos. 13:8; 2 Kings 2:24. The gender would also be determined by the preceding word and by the following suffix. "straw" — Cf. Pliny: *Natural History*, 18:30.

[16] ושעשע — "to sport, take delight in." Cf. Isa. 5:7; Ps. 119:70. Gray points out that the verb suggests the idea of playing, not merely with impunity, but also with delight; cf. 66:12. The Syriac cognate is used of diverting oneself with balls, hounds, etc.

what serpents are intended, but the context shows that they were regarded as poisonous and deadly. If there were any serpents from which mothers would wish their children to be kept away, it was these.

The weaned child also had no fear of putting his hand over the cave or hole[17] in which the viper[18] lived, for the fruit of Messiah's righteous rule is a deep peace, a world-revolutionary peace, so that all hostile relations between men and animals are removed.

How are we to understand the words of this glorious prophecy? Some think that this passage simply depicts a return to Paradise such as was taught by the ancients generally (see note 13 for references). According to the older expositors these expressions of a change in the animal world were simply figures to express a change in man himself. So Calvin, for example, remarks: "By these images, the Prophet indicates that, among the people of Christ there will be no disposition for injuring one another, nor any ferocity or inhumanity." And without question the prophet does desire to teach that there will be a change in human nature, inasmuch as this future time of blessing will be one in which the knowledge of the Lord will cover the earth as the waters cover the sea.

At the same time it must be noted that Isaiah has placed great stress upon the animals themselves, and this very fact shows that it is impossible to carry through in detail a figurative interpretation. If all is merely figurative, what is the point of such detailed statements concerning the change in animals? It would appear also that we have here a parallelism or comparison with the condition before the fall of man into sin. Before the entrance of sin into the world the animals were the helps of man and were named by him. All that God had made was good. Hostility between man and the animals, at least, was unknown. Hengstenberg says rightly, I believe, and in accordance with Scripture, "Where there was not a

17 מאורת — Lit., "a place of light." 1Q has pl. and B κοίτην. Kittel attributes to the word the force of "shining" (*leuchtendes*). He refers it to the bright, shining eye of the serpent. Probably, however, it is the entrance of the hole, where the hole reaches the light, that is in view. The child places his hand upon the opening, and stops the light from entering the hole in which the serpent lives.

18 "viper" — Isa. 14:29; 59:5. The reference doubtless is to a particularly poisonous kind of snake, but it is impossible to tell what kind is intended. Cf. the discussion in Rosenmüller and Gesenius. Jerome thought that this verse predicted the casting out of devils by Christ's disciples; Vitringa, the conversion or destruction of heretical teachers; Cocceius makes it a specific prophecy of Luther, Calvin and Huss, as the children who were to thrust their hands into the den of the anti-Christian serpents. If the last word is a verb we have the order: subj., obj., verb. Cf. Reider in *VT*, 2, 1952, p. 115, for a proposed emendation.

Cain, neither was there a lion."[19] May it not be that in Isaiah's language, "The lion shall eat straw like the ox," there is a reflection upon the command and permission granted to the animals that every green herb should be to them for meat?

Other passages of Scripture also indicate that when evil will cease in the rational creation, the reflection of evil will disappear from the non-rational creation. Cf. Isa. 65:25 and 66:22. This change in the non-rational creation implies of course the more wondrous change among men themselves. The animals no longer are at enmity one with another, because evil has departed from men. Men will know the Lord, and the reflection of that fact appears in that even among the animals there will also be a full and complete cessation of hostility.

It may be noted also that even upon this more or less literal interpretation we need not be compelled to press all the details. We need not assume that there will be physiological changes in the structure of the lion, for example. All that is clearly taught is that the animals will not prey upon one another. This, as Hengstenberg says, is the outermost limit of the changes to be wrought by the blessed rule of the Christ. If here there is a change, how much more among men.

When, however, is this change to appear? In answer it should be noted that Isaiah has emphasized the fact that the Messiah is the Prince of Peace. When the Messiah has completed His Messianic work, peace is introduced into the hearts of men, and insofar as men are true to the principles of peace which they have received from the Messiah, so far do the blessings herein depicted obtain. In its fullness, however, this condition will not be realized until the earth is covered with the knowledge of the Lord, and that condition will only obtain in the new heavens and the new earth wherein dwelleth righteousness. "Wherever there is sin," says Bracker, "there is lack of peace. Only where righteousness reigns, is there peace." For this reason the condition herein described cannot apply to a supposed millennium. Advocates of a millennial theory maintain that even during the millennium there is sin, for after the millennium the nations will again gather for battle. The picture before us, however, is one in which there is no sin, but in which the fullest manifestation of peace is to be seen. We read these words with grateful hearts for we know that one day we too shall enjoy these blessings in their fullest sense. And we shall enjoy them only because of the work of Immanuel, that One who was born from Jesse's root, and who in the great battle of Calvary slew the wicked in that He gave Himself a ransom for sin. To His name be all praise, honor and glory given.

---

[19] *Christology of the Old Testament*, 1856, II, 120.

9 The description now becomes more general.[20] It is the complete opposite of the Judah of the present. Now men do harm, but in that day they will not do so. The subject is indefinite, and Isaiah gives a reason why men will not harm one another. At that time the earth will be filled with the knowledge of Yahweh. Inasmuch as the earth is filled with the knowledge of Yahweh, there will be no harm nor evil action. Hence, it is of men primarily that the prophet speaks. Today men do harm one another; they defraud, they cheat, they steal from one another. Then, however, when they know Yahweh, they will no longer do evil to one another. God's holy mountain is Zion, the symbol of His presence. In the future Zion will be the dwelling place of God's people, and He will be in their midst.

The reason for this absence of harm is to be found in the knowledge of Yahweh. Men will know God, which involves first of all a theoretical knowledge, but it includes practical knowledge also. Indeed, the two cannot be separated. One can hardly know God without knowing about God, nor can one really know about God without knowing Him. Men will know Yahweh in that they will know that He truly exists, and they will act upon that knowledge in that they will give to Him all their love, obedience and devotion. He will be their God. This knowledge will be so extensive that it will fill the land, as the waters cover the sea. Isaiah does not mean that the earth will be divided into two parts, the earth and the sea, but would merely say that just as the sea to the fullness of its capacity is filled with waters so the earth will be filled with the knowledge of Yahweh. When once the land will be thus filled, then men will cease to harm one another. Before there can be peace there must first be knowledge.

---

[20] "they shall not hurt" — The subj. is impersonal, and refers to men, not animals. The subj. is really limited by the phrase, "in the mountain of my holiness" and cannot refer to the animals. It is questionable whether expressions such as "holy mountain" and "God's mountain" are used in the O.T. of any mountains other than Sinai, Zion and Jerusalem. "the earth" — Some take this as equivalent to "my holy mountain." But it would rather seem that the word is the opposite or contrast to the sea, mentioned in the second member of 9b. As the waters cover the sea, so will the knowledge of God cover the earth, the dry land. "filled" — A prophetic perf. "knowing" — A verbal noun strong enough to take an acc. "the sea" — Lit., "as to the waters, with respect to the sea, are covering." The prep. serves to introduce the direct obj., as in Num. 10:25. Cf. Koran, 15:9, *"inna lahu lahafizuna"* (verily we are its guardian). Perhaps we may simply render, "with respect to."

10 With the beloved introduction, "and it shall come to pass in that day," Isaiah directs us to that wondrous time in which the following blessings will be found. Jesse's root is the basis or foundation which produces the trunk.[21] Thus, the Messiah is seen to be a support or stay for Jesse's family. After the tree has been cut down, only the root itself remains in the ground, and from this root alone can new life come. Hence, the Messiah is truly the restorer of David's line. It is this root itself, equivalent to the shoot and branch of verse 1, which becomes the rallying standard for the peoples. This root is no longer under the ground and invisible, but standing to such a height that it can serve as a point about which the peoples will meet and rally. As the Root the Messiah was unknown and disregarded; as the Standard He is lifted up that all men may gather about Him. "And as Moses lifted up the serpent in the wilderness, even so must the Son of man be lifted up" (John 3:14) ; "And I, if I be lifted up from the earth, will draw all men unto me" (John 12:32) . His being lifted up, His standing, is therefore for the benefit of the peoples.

Unto Him the Gentile or heathen nations, who know not Yahweh, will seek for the purpose of obtaining religious instruction. He stands permanently unmovable, and the Gentiles will turn to Him, for they will regard Him alone as the One who is able to give them the religious help and knowledge that they need. Whenever they come, He will be there, a rallying and gathering point. Indeed, He alone is that standard which unites men and brings them together.

21 "root" — The construction is "and it shall come to pass that the root of Jesse." After the tree has been felled, the root remains in the ground, and from it alone new life can come. The Messiah is the restorer of the house of David, the Root of Jesse, Rom. 15:12; the Root and Offspring of David, Rev. 22:16: "stands" — The part. indicates that the Root is already standing. It is standing firm; cf. Mic. 5:4. "ensign" — A standard which was erected in a conspicuous place for communicating information, Jer. 50:2; for gathering troops together, Isa. 18:3; Jer. 4:21; for the gathering of fugitives, Jer. 4:6; for gathering people together, Isa. 5:26; 11:10, 12; 49:22; 62:10. It was often erected upon a high place or eminence, Isa. 13:2. In contrast to the dispersion of Gen. 11:8, the Messiah stands as a central rallying point. He is here depicted as a king, and a king that is lifted up. He was first lifted up upon the cross, John 3:14, and then will be lifted up as judge, John 12: 32; Phil. 2:9; Heb. 7:26. Note the contrast between "root" and "ensign." The root hidden deep in the earth becomes the ensign lifted up high. "will seek" — Cf. Job 5:8 and 8:5; in the sense of doing homage and showing reverence, cf. Matt. 2:2.

His place of rest, where He has settled down to rule and to live, is glory itself.[22] How forceful Isaiah's language is! Glory! Instead of saying glorious, the prophet merely employs the noun. "His resting place is glory." Here indeed is a vivid emphasis.

c. *The future of Israel* (11:11-16)

11 And it shall come to pass in that day that the Lord will add his hand a second time to gather the remnant of his people which is left over from Assyria and from Egypt and from Pathros and from Cush and from Elam and from Shinar and from Hamath and from the isles of the sea.

12 And he will lift up a standard to the nations, and will gather the dispersed ones of Israel; and the scattered ones of Judah will he gather from the four corners of the earth.

13 And there will turn aside the envy of Ephraim, and the enemies of Judah will be cut off; Ephraim will not envy Judah, and Judah will not vex Ephraim.

14 And they shall fly shoulder to shoulder upon the Philistines towards the sea; together they shall spoil the sons of the east, Edom and Moab the stretching out of their hand and the children of Ammon their obedience.

15 And the LORD will destroy the tongue of the sea of Egypt, and he will wave his hand over the river, in the violence of his wind, and smite it into seven streams and make men tread it in shoes.

16 And there shall be a highway for the remnant of his people which is left over from Assyria, even as there was for Israel in the day of his coming up from the land of Egypt.

11 That day will be a day of action. Once before the sovereign Lord had lifted His hand in punishment. Once before there had been a deliverance, when the nation lay captive to Egypt. Isaiah mentions the Lord's hand, which reminds us of the Exodus, for then it was that with a strong hand and a stretched-out arm the Lord brought deliverance to His people. Now He will add to the sending out of His hand but this time it will be to gather His

---

22 "his rest" — Lit., "place of rest." Used of Zion, Ps. 132:8, 14; 1 Chron. 28:2. It is the place where God has settled down to rule. "glory" — A noun does duty for an adj. The Vulgate apparently understood this of Christ's burial, *"et erit sepulcrum eius gloriosum."* As the Temple of the Old Covenant had its glory, even the glory of the Lord (1 Kings 8:11), so in the time of fulfillment there will be a comparably greater glory. Cf. Isa. 4:5; Hag. 2:7, 9. This glory is specified in Isa. 60:19; 44:5; 55:5; Zech. 2:14, 15; cf. Rev. 21:23.

people unto Himself.[23] A first time for chastisement; a second time for deliverance. It is the same hand, but the hand that Pharaoh felt in chastisement the remnant will feel in deliverance.[24]

Only a remnant, however, will be delivered, and this remnant will consist in what Assyria and the other named nations have left over. They will have done their work, and they will have destroyed, but they will have left some remaining. This remaining lot the hand of the Lord will gather unto Himself. Of all the oppressors, Assyria appears as the chief. In Isaiah's day it was Assyria, more than any of the others, who constituted the great danger to the people. Egypt also was a threat, but of the two Assyria was the greater. Having mentioned Assyria, Isaiah next turns to the south and mentions Egypt, Pathros and Cush. Then he looks to the northeast, mentions Elam and Shinar, following with Syrian Hamath and the coast lands of the Mediterranean Sea.

In Isaiah's day there was no such dispersion as is here described. As yet the people had not been so widely scattered. True enough, there were the forerunners of such a dispersion. The Galileans had been taken away by Tiglath-pileser. There had been wars and skirmishes. Forerunners there were, but actual dispersions, on a scale so grand as here, had not really occurred in Isaiah's day. We are faced therefore with the language of prediction. Here Isaiah speaks as a prophet who discloses the future. The dispersion

---

23 שֵׁנִית preceded by *paseq* which serves to separate the two words, a purpose which is also partially accomplished by the disjunctive *yetib*. By itself the form *yôsîf* may be somewhat weak, and the addition of *šēnit* strengthens it. A somewhat similar usage is found in the *Annals of Mursilis* II, col. III, 58, "*da-a-an KAS-ŠI nam-ma pa-a-un*" (for the second time again I went). "the Lord" — God is designated the sovereign One in view of the great work of gathering in the Gentiles which is ascribed to Him.

24 "to gather" — The inf. is best construed with the entire preceding. rather than with the verb alone. Note the prominence of the combination *sr.* in v. 11b. "Pathros" — *p-to-res*, "south land," means Upper Egypt. König thinks that all the names following Egypt are added later, inasmuch as in Isaiah's day there was no such wide dispersion. But the language is that of prediction. Cf. Pliny, *Natural History*, 18:18. "Cush" — Ethiopia. "Elam" — In southern Media. "Shinar" — Babylonia; cf. Gen. 10:10; 11:2. "Hamath" — See note on Isa. 10:9. "the isles of the sea" — The coast lands, Gen. 10:5; Zeph. 2:11. This term, says Gray, is never used by Isaiah, but is a favorite of deutero-Isaiah. As a matter of fact, the expression "isles of the sea" occurs only in Isa. 11:11 and 24:15 and never in the latter portion of the prophecy. The pl. "isles" alone is found in Isa. 40:15; 41:1, 5; 42:4, 10, 12, 15; 49:1; 51:5; 59:18; 60:9; 66:19. The s. occurs only in Isa. 20:6 and 23:2, 6.

to come will be world-wide in its extent; but from every nation, kindred and tongue God will a second time stretch out His powerful hand to regather His people.

12 The Messiah would be a standard to which the Gentiles might rally.[25] Here also we learn that the Lord will lift up a sign for the benefit of Israel. The Messiah will be a drawing point for the heathen, and through the work of Christian preaching and Christian missionaries He will draw them unto Himself. How important, particularly in this day and age, therefore, that the church send forth to the four corners of the earth missionaries who are aflame with the truth that apart from the true Messiah, Jesus, there is no salvation!

By means of this Standard, God will also gather the dispersed ones of Israel. Indeed, apart from the Messiah they have no future and no hope. The dispersed ones of Judah God will also gather, and so Israel and Judah will again be together. Strangely, Isaiah speaks of Judah's dispersed ones in the feminine, and so, by an admixture of the genders, seems to reflect upon the divided condition of the nation. The Messiah's work will be one of unifying and bringing together those that were separated through strife and schism.

Great has been the dispersion! To the four corners of the earth the people have been scattered. Isaiah does not intend us to understand that the earth actually has four corners. He is merely employing a manner of speaking taken over from the idea of referring to the four corners of a garment as indicating the entirety of the garment. Our Lord was reflecting upon this passage when He said, "And he shall send his angels with a great sound of a

---

25 Note the paronomasia in *"nasa nes."* Note also the mixing of genders in נדחי (with omitted *daghesh*) and נפוצות. Cf. 3:1; Zech. 9:17. The *daghesh* is omitted because of the following guttural. Cf. also Isa. 56:8 and Ps. 147:2. "standard" — A signal will be raised so that the Gentiles may know that the Jews are to be set free. Cf. Caesar, *de bello Gallico,* 2:10, *"vexillum propenendum quod erat insigne, cum ad arma concurri oporteret"*; Ammianus 27:10. In the actual fulfillment the Lord's purpose was made known through the course of history by means of events such as the downfall of Babylonia. A similar picture is given in 49:22 and 62:10. Passages which speak of the Gentile nations as assembling the dispersed of Israel are Isa. 14:1, 2; 49:22, 23. "four corners of the earth" — Cf. Deut. 22:12; Zech. 8: 23ff. In Rev. 7:1 both expressions are combined. The basic passage is Deut. 30:1ff. Isa. 5:26 forms a contrast to this passage. In Matt. 24:31 Christ takes traits from this passage as well as from Isa. 27:13 for the description of the universal judgment.

trumpet, and they shall gather together his elect from the four winds, from one end of heaven to the other" (Matt. 24:31).

13 How great and tragic are conflicts among the people of God![26] Ephraim had envied Judah and had sought to achieve the position of pre-eminence among all the tribes. Originally there were other objects of this enmity, but it finally concentrated upon Judah. In his great blessing Jacob had given pre-eminence to Judah, and the tribe of Judah was more numerous than Ephraim and also first in war. Enmity was the source of quarrel, and quarrels produced wars between the northern and southern tribes. How often envy has been the source of disruption in the church! Those who name Christ's name must keep the heart, that no envy or jealousy ever be permitted to appear therein.

When Ephraim's envy of Judah is turned aside, Judah's enemies, who vex and afflict her, will also be cut off. Where were these oppressors to be found? Doubtless within Ephraim, but Isaiah may have in mind all who are the afflicters of Judah. When the Messiah reigns, Ephraim will no longer live with envy directed toward the southern kingdom, and Judah will no longer act in such a way as to provoke her northern neighbor to anger and vexation.

The great scandal in Israel's history was the schism under Jeroboam. Indeed the latter is known to us as the man who caused Israel to sin. Involved in this schism was an apostasy, a complete rejection on the part of the northern tribes of the promises which had been made to the house of David. Such a condition of things was wrong, and throughout her history God sent prophets to the apostate nation, to call it to repentance and to point it to the Messiah who alone could heal the breach. The prophets delight to picture as one of the blessings of the Messianic age the healing of the breach between the northern and southern kingdoms. Is there not a lesson here for our ecumenically minded age? True union and unity will be produced only through the historic Mes-

---

[26] Note the mildness in "will turn away" in contrast to the strong "will be cut off." It is difficult to tell whether the genitives are objective or subjective. The first gen., "the envy of Ephraim," I take as subjective: "the envy which Ephraim exercised toward Judah." Luther took it as objective, "*und der Neid wider Ephraim wird aufhören.*" "enemies of Judah" — Not those whom Judah oppresses, but as Eitan translates, "they that harass Judah (among the Ephraimites)." Thus, 13ba interprets 13aa, but 13bb does not interpret 13ab.

siah. What man, even churchmen, cannot do, the Messiah alone can accomplish. Unity must be in the truth.

In Christ all national, sectional and regional distinctions will be abolished, and through the figure employed in this verse we learn that in Christ there is a true unity and place for all men of whatever race or color. In Christ alone can they be one.

14 What great things can be wrought by true unity![27] Israel and Judah are together; their ancient enmities have been put aside, never to be remembered again. In the Christ they have a unity that cannot be destroyed. From the mountains of central Palestine they swoop down like a great bird, down over the shoulder of sloping coast land toward the sea. With one accord, concertedly, they come. Gone is the division, and they are together. Here is the true unity of the faith in opposition to the hostility of the world. This true unity does not hide itself in cringing self-defense, expecting attack. It takes the offensive; the enemies of the Messiah must be destroyed, and in the strength of the unity that the Messiah gives, the people fly upon the Philistines, representatives of the enemies of God and His church.

27 "they shall fly" — Eitan would emend the verb on the basis of Ar. *'akka*, "to assault." He would then render, "and they shall assault concertedly the Philistines on the west; together they shall spoil the children of the east." But it is not necessary to assume a *Pe* incorrectly written for *Kaf*, and we should retain the derivation from *'wf*. The figure is that of a bird of prey; cf. Hab. 1:8. "shoulder" — Eitan renders "concertedly." ASTh supports M, as does 1Q. but B reads ἐν πλοίοις ἀλλοφύλλων. Jerome: "*et volabunt in humero Philisthaeorum per mare.*" Ships are conceived as flying over the sea. Note Syr. *plh,* "they will plough." As it stands the form is not const. which would have to be *keṭef* (BH suggests *keṭef*), but absolute. If the punctuation be retained we may understand the word "one" following, i.e., "with one shoulder," or "shoulder to shoulder." Cf. Zeph. 3:9. The indefinite form may even admit this interpretation, "with a shoulder," i.e., "concertedly." It must be noted, however, that the absolute can stand for the const. as in Josh. 8:11. "towards the sea" — This expression contrasts with the following "sons of the east" to express the thought of inclusiveness. "children of the east" — Inhabitants of the desert east of Palestine, ancient enemies of Judah; cf. Judg. 6:3, 33; 7:12; 8:10. As they had plundered Israel, so would they also be plundered. "Edom" — Cf. Isa. 34:5; 63:1; Joel 4:19; Amos 9:12. "Moab" — Isa. 25:10; Zeph. 2:8ff. the stretching out of their hand" — Lit., "the place of sending out their hand." "sons of Ammon" — Judg. 10:17ff.; 2 Sam. 10:13. "their obedience" — Their hearing regarded as obeying. Of the five enemies here named, four appear in the opening threatenings of Amos; Mic. 5:4, 5 is a parallel passage with relation to Assyria and vv. 6-8 in general. Deut. 30:7 is the mother passage. All these people are taken from the realm of Davidic rule.

What Isaiah is here describing cannot, of course, be understood in a literal sense. Rather, here is a beautiful picture of the unity that is the possession of the saints of God, obtained for them not through their own works, but through the blood of Christ, and of the vigorous, active participation in the work of conquering the enemy world, a conquering which is brought about through the sending of missionaries and the constant, active, vigorous, faithful proclamation of the whole counsel of God to every creature.

Among the inveterate enemies of Judah were the children or sons of the east. How often they had invaded and plundered Palestine! How often they had deprived the land of what was rightfully its own. The land had become filled from the east, and now against these sons of the east the people will engage in plunder. But it will be a different kind of plunder! The glorious hope here held out for God's people does not consist in a literal despoliation of nomad Arabs of the desert. It rather consists in the blessed task of making the saving power of God known even to those who, like the apostle Paul, had once been persecutors of the church. Our constant prayer should be that the sons of the east will be despoiled so that, being deprived of false riches and possessions, they may instead have the Christ of God.

Upon Edom and Moab also, two inveterate enemies, the people will stretch their hand to grasp them. Even the sons of Ammon will hear and obey.

All these figures are drawn from the existing condition of things. The people of God had been surrounded by external foes, which had been conquered by David, and which had rebelled and at one time or another had vexed Israel and Judah. The picture is of a complete reversal of conditions, not to take place in Palestine, but in the greater field of the world, a reversal which would consist in the people of God reaching out to bring all men and make them captive to Christ.

15 Remarkable as is the unity of Israel and Judah, the secret of their victory is that the Lord fights for them.[28] There was an

---

28 "will destroy" — M is supported by ASTH and 1Q. Cf. Isa. 34:2. *BH* adopts the ancient suggestion that the word be read as *he-ḥe-rîb*, as evidently understood by B ἐρημώσει. Granted that the interchange between *b* and *m* does occur, such an emendation here is not necessary. It is possible also that B does not presuppose a reading different from M, but has translated according to sense, as in Jer. 25:9. "tongue" — Drechsler compares the German *Erdzunge*. Used of the Dead Sea, Josh. 15:2-5; 18:19; of a promontory in Ovid, *Met.* 15:724; Livy, 37:31; Ammianus Marcellinus, 14:8. Ar. uses the

ancient obstacle, the tongue of the Egyptian Sea, that body of narrow water that extended north from the Red Sea, and this obstacle must now be devoted to destruction. It is put under the ban, and by the Lord set apart for ruin. No longer can it hinder the redemption of the people of God. To the east lay a river which had shut off the Israelites from their homeland, the great river Euphrates. Over this river God will wave His hand as a gesture of threat and destruction. With this upraised hand there will come a violent wind, and the river will be divided into seven streams. Thus the power of the river will be broken, so that men wearing shoes will be able to walk in it.

The Egyptian Sea and the Euphrates were far apart, yet they were two obstacles that the people of God in olden times had to face. When God acts, however, all obstacles will be removed, just as they had been in former times. When God leads His people, He brings them in safety through all hindrances and difficulties into the land of promise.

16 When Assyria has furnished her work, there will be a remnant of the people of God remaining.[29] For them there will be a highway on which they may return to the land of promise. It is a way that the Lord Himself will erect, a way formed by the casting up of the earth. "And I will bring the blind by a way that they knew not" (Isa. 42:16a); "I will even make a way in the wilderness, and rivers in the deserts" (Isa. 43:19b); "And they

---

word to describe both ends of the Dead Sea. "the sea of Egypt" — An absolute before the genitive. "the river" — the Euphrates. Kimchi refers the Sea of Egypt to the Nile. "in the violence" — Luzzatto, Krochmal, Perles, etc., would emend, b^e-o-tzem, "in the strength of." Reider points out that עוים may be the equivalent of Ar. *ghayyamun*, "cloud, anger," "in the violence of his wind." The Jewish version reads, "with his scorching wind." "and smite it" — The suffix refers both to the river and to the tongue of the sea. Cf. Zech. 10:11. "seven streams" — For the number cf. 4:1 and note Ps. 136:13. The streams are the small channels that form when the large river dries up. Cf. Her. 1:189 who relates that Cyrus, in order to punish the Gyndes River, which had swallowed up one of his white horses, has it divided into 360 canals. "shoes" — Possibly one will not even need to put on shoes to wade through the stream. Cf. Isa. 47:2.

[29] "a way" — A road which has been constructed by casting up the earth, like the Latin *agger,* and so to be distinguished from an ordinary path worn by the feet. "Assyria" — Named here as a representative of all the enemies. Parallel passages to this verse are 42:15, 16; 43:19, 20; 48:21; 49:10, 11; 55:13; and with reference to Egypt and the miracles of deliverance, cf. Isa. 48:21; 51:9, 10. Cf. also Zech. 10:10, 11.

thirsted not when he led them through the deserts" (Isa. 48:21); "And I will make all my mountains a way, and my highways shall be exalted" (Isa. 49:11).

Isaiah is not here speaking primarily of the return from Babylonian exile, although it may be that the thought of such a return lies at the foundation of what he says. Rather, he is thinking of a deliverance so great that it can only be performed by God. As once in former times God had brought up His people out of the land of Egypt through desert regions until finally they came to Palestine, so once again He will bring them up out of the house of spiritual bondage and prison of sin over a way which is the Messiah, the Way, the Truth and the Life, until He finally brings them through many difficulties into the City of God.

d. *A victorious song of praise* (12:1-6)

1 And thou shalt say in that day, I shall praise thee, O LORD! for though thou wast angry with me, thy wrath hath turned and thou hast comforted me.

2 Behold! God is my salvation, I shall trust and not be afraid, for my might and strength is Yah, and he has become my salvation.

3 And ye shall draw water with joy from the springs of salvation.

4 And ye shall say in that day, Praise the LORD, call upon his name, cause to be known among the peoples his deeds, cause them to remember that his name is exalted.

5 Ascribe strength unto the LORD, for he hath done excellent things. Known is this in all the earth.

6 Cry out and exult, thou inhabitant of Zion, for great in thy midst is the Holy One of Israel.

1 Redemption results in praise.[30] As once the Israelites sang the praises of God for the mighty deliverance from Egypt, so in the future the people as one man will again praise God for His wondrous redemption. Isaiah is speaking as though his own contemporaries would experience the redemption. Actually he is depicting the people of the future in terms of his contemporaries. He does this by using the singular and writing as though the entire nation were but one man. The people are thus seen to be united in their praise of God. So it is that Paul enjoins Christians, "That ye may with one mind and one mouth glorify God, even the Father of our Lord Jesus Christ" (Rom. 15:6). To praise God is to acknowledge Him as worthy and to bless Him for

---

[30] "I shall praise thee" — Cf. also Ps. 75:2; 139:14; Dan. 2:23. Note our Lord's words in Matt. 11:25. The imp. expresses continuance of action.

what He is and what He has done. Here it is one voice that acknowledges the worth and greatness of the redeeming God.

This gratitude is expressed to Yahweh not because He was angry, but because He had been angry, and yet turned His wrath aside from the suppliant and instead showed comfort.[31] Yet, we must not misunderstand this expression. The Bible never teaches that the wrath of God is removed in that it is simply turned to love. The wrath of God was not removed and turned into comfort. If that were the case it would present a low picture of the integrity of God. God is wrathful against sin, and that wrath must be visited upon sin. "The soul that sinneth it shall die." That wrath of God will fall upon the guilty one and he will be punished. If, however, the wrath of God is removed from a man, it is visited in the punishment of sin not in that particular man but on One who in his place bears the guilt of that man's sin. Then, God may justly show His comfort to the man upon whom His wrath had formerly rested. Although God had indeed been angry and rightly so, His anger had turned. In that thought lies the heart of redemption. God's anger has turned, but turned from me to Christ. And I who deserved the anger of God to be poured out upon me have received His comfort instead.[32]

2 Now the brightness of the LORD God's reconciled face shines forth. Behold! at last the long-awaited deliverance has arrived. My salvation is God Himself.[33] Now the great truth is clearly

[31] "thou wast angry" — For the same manner of expression, cf. Rom. 6:17. König gives a concessive sense to the verb, "although thou wast angry." It is for our comfort to know that God's anger is of short duration; cf. Ps. 30: 5, 6. וישב — Note the jussive form. As it stands it should probably be rendered, "let it return and show mercy to me." It may be that the jussive is simply to be substituted for the imp. (cf. GKC, no. 109k). Note also that the jussive without wāw may be used to express events in past time. Perhaps it is more accurate to regard the jussive as characterizing the apodosis of the sentence, "Thou wast angry, let thine anger return (i.e., thine anger must return), and do thou show comfort to me."

[32] "thou hast comforted me" — "to console, ease one's grief, to relieve one from hardship and suffering." The basic thought is expressed in Gen. 5:29 in the hope that Noah would comfort God's people because of the curse which had been placed upon the ground, rendering their labor grievous toil. It was this comfort which Isaiah later stressed, 40:1, 49:13; cf. Phil. 2:1; John 14:16, 26; 16:7.

[33] "Behold" — To announce a momentous truth; cf. 40:9. Marti takes 'ēl as a const. But it is this word upon which all the emphasis is to be placed. Isaiah has been working up to this word. All his hope and all the hope of the nation is to be found in 'ēl. 1Q repeats the word as though to read, "Behold God! the God of my salvation."

stated. How wondrous had the preparation been for its announcement. With us is God. *El* is my salvation! A remnant will return unto mighty God! Blessed is that nation whose God is the LORD. How happy that one who can say, "God is my salvation. I shall trust and not be afraid." Here is a striking paronomasia, *evtach* and *afkad*. If God is one's salvation, there is need only of trusting; no need of fearing.

What is meant when the prophet states that God is his salvation? It means that God is the author, the cause, the agent, the accomplisher of that salvation. Salvation apart from God is unthinkable. In the counsels of eternity God the Father ordained unto life and salvation His people; in time God the Son wrought that salvation by His death upon Calvary's cross, and also in time God the Holy Spirit applies to the hearts of His own the blessings which Christ has obtained for them by His death. In obtaining salvation for man God was active. In salvation we are delivered from the guilt and the pollution of our sins, and we receive the wondrous and blessed righteousness of the eternal Christ. God is our Father, and by an act of His omnipotent grace adopts us as His own children. In the fullest and deepest sense, we receive God. What more can we have — what more do we need than God Himself? He is our salvation.

"If God were not my salvation," the people of God might reason, "there would be everything to fear." Man is lonely, man is despondent; he lives in the blackness of long night. There is everything to fear until God becomes his salvation. Then there is nothing to fear. Only one may speak with such boldness and confidence; he is the one to whom God has become salvation. With full security and assurance he may proclaim, "I will trust and not be afraid." This is a God-given certainty of hope which may be possessed only by the redeemed.

Every man must have might and strength in order to live.[34] Unless there is something upon which one can base his life, he will go to pieces. Some lean on drink; some on narcotics; some on dogged willpower; some on bravado; some on "religion"; all with a single exception lean on man. That exception consists of those who find

---

[34] זמרת — B ἡ αἴνεσίς μου. The word means "strength"; cf. Ug. *ẓmr*. It is the *qametz* in the ultima which causes difficulty, and some would read *zim-rā-ṭî*. If so, then the final *yod* has been omitted because of the following *Yah*. It is also possible that the form has a f. ending, and is correct as it stands. When *'oz-zî* has *holem* in the penult, the word is always written in combination with *zimrāh*. Elsewhere the orthography is *'uz-zî*.

their might and their strength in God. When therefore they say that they will trust and not be afraid, they are not vainly boasting. How enviable are those who have Yahweh, the covenant God who has redeemed Israel, for their strength and might! He is as a rock indeed, and only those who have Him have a strength upon which to lean in confidence. All other might and strength is illusory.

The prophet reflects upon the language of the Exodus (15:2). After the great deliverance at the Red Sea, Moses and the delivered people sang, "The LORD is my strength and song, and he is become my salvation." Isaiah, however, adds a word. He identifies the redeemer as Yah, Yahweh, for he is looking forward to the Christ, to the new covenant, to the antitypical redemption of which that under Moses was but a type. It is well to speak of the redeemer not merely as Yahweh — that was the typical designation — but as *Yah*. How suitable to conclude this verse with the utterance, "And he has become my salvation." To render literally, "And he has become to me for salvation."

3 In the burning wilderness of Sinai the people had murmured because there was no water. In response to their murmuring, Moses had smitten the rock, and from it water had gushed forth. Here was grace in the desert! "And did all drink the same spiritual drink: for they drank of that spiritual rock that followed them: and that rock was Christ" (I Cor. 10:4).

If Sinai was a desert, how much more dreary is the desert of life! Yet even in this barren wilderness there are life-giving springs of water. From these wells the redeemed will draw that which gives and strengthens and sustains their life, even the waters of salvation.[35] From the rock in Sinai water gushed forth; from the springs of salvation also men will draw waters. Waters! It is an intensive plural, for it indicates the fullness and all-sufficiency of the blessings which come from these springs.

Water is a beautiful figure of salvation and its attendant blessings.[36] How refreshing and reviving to a wanderer in a thirsty and dry land. How fit an emblem for salvation! "When the poor and needy seek water, and there is none, and their tongue

---

[35] This verse sets forth the content of God's comforting. The s. with which this passage begins now passes into the pl. to express the fact that the people will be the recipients of God's comfort.

[36] Note that the pl. appears again in Rev. 7:17. In the early history of the nation water had served as a type of salvation; cf. Exod. 15:27; 17:1ff.; Num. 20:2ff.; 33:9. These passages illustrate the nation's need for water, and they are interpreted by 1 Cor. 10:4. For the true fulfillment, cf. John

faileth for thirst, I the LORD will hear them, I the God of Israel will not forsake them. I will open rivers in high places, and fountains in the midst of the valleys: I will make the wilderness a pool of water, and the dry land springs of water" (Isa. 41:17, 18). Continuing the Old Testament figure our Lord said, "But whosoever drinketh of the water that I shall give him shall never thirst; but the water that I shall give him shall be in him a well of water springing up into everlasting life" (John 4:14). "For the Lamb which is in the midst of the throne shall feed them, and shall lead them unto living fountains of waters: and God shall wipe away all tears from their eyes" (Rev. 7:17).

As the water in the wilderness had been provided by the goodness of God, so the water in the wells of salvation is a gift of His goodness.[37] Salvation is entirely of grace. As Calvin says, "By a figure of speech, in which a part is taken for the whole, he declares that everything necessary for supporting life flows to us from the undeserved goodness of God." It is with joy that we draw water from these blessed springs. We are to enjoy God forever. And the life of the believer is one of joy for he knows that the terrible burden of his guilt which had separated him from God has now been removed and no longer stands between him and his God. And all because of the work of Christ! Truly we may rejoice in the Lord, now and always.

4 What is described in this verse is not only a consequence and result of drawing water from the wells of salvation; more than that, it is also the outworking of such drawing.[38] When men enjoy the blessings of salvation they must make known the glories of the

---

4:14; 7:37; Rev. 7:16, 17; 21:6; 22:17. As hunger and thirst so often represent spiritual need, so food and drink stand for spiritual blessing; cf. Isa. 41:18; 55:1; Ps. 23:2.

[37] "springs" — With two *paṭaḥs*, but cf. 1 Kings 18:5 where *Shewa* appears under the *'ayin*. The form is probably to be explained like *ya-'a-mō-ḏû*. The pl. indicates the fullness of blessing; included are all the blessings of God's grace. From His fullness we all draw, for we are as a dry land; cf. Ps. 143:6 and John 1:16.

[38] "call upon his name" — Marti thinks that the phrase comes from cultic usage when a man was accustomed to call aloud the name of the god whom he worshipped. He takes the phrase as meaning to call aloud the pronunciation of the god's name; cf. Ps. 43:1. But the name of God is the sum of His attributes. The phrase means to invoke or call upon God. "his deeds" — The word may be used both in a bad and in a good sense; cf. Ps. 9:12; 77:12, 13. Parts of this verse appear in Ps. 105:1 and 1 Chron. 16:8.

redeeming and pardoning God. When the heart overflows with
the bounties of the Lord, the tongue speaks forth His praises. In
that day, so different from the day in which Isaiah lived, when
men oppressed one another and despised the holy name of Israel's
God, men would speak to one another, enjoining upon each other
the holy duty of praising the Lord. In calling upon His name —
and there is no other name upon which men should call — men are
acknowledging Him to be what He is. His name is Himself,
His very being. It is His infinite, eternal and unchangeable
Being, Wisdom, Power, Holiness, Justice, Goodness and Truth.
Under this designation of calling upon God, the entirety of
true worship is included.

Here is the content of true missionary preaching; it is the
mighty deeds of Yahweh. But it is not possible to tell of the
mighty deeds of God without also giving an interpretation of
these deeds. We cannot merely speak of a man Jesus who died
on the cross. We must tell *who* that Jesus is and what He accomplished by His death. And when we do that, we are preaching
doctrine. Doctrine, then, must be the content of what we preach
to the heathen. "Ye turned to God from idols," says the apostle
Paul, in what may be regarded as a summary of his missionary
preaching, "to serve the living and true God, and to wait for
his Son from heaven, whom he raised from the dead, even Jesus,
which delivered us from the wrath to come" (1 Thess. 1:10).

Exalted is the name of God, for He Himself is the high and
Holy One. Men forget that His name is exalted, for they do
not magnify Him in their hearts. They live as though He were
not. The task of the church is to cause men to remember
that His name is exalted. Therefore the church does not exist
to give the opinions of men, or to teach that all religions are
equally good, or to beg men to unite with her. Her one supreme
task is to cause men to remember that the name of God is
exalted. This she can do only through the divinely appointed
task of proclaiming the truth of God, namely, through preaching.

5 By singing and playing upon stringed instruments men may
praise Yahweh, and in so praising Him may ascribe strength to
His name.[39] In ascribing strength they are declaring that He

---

39 זמרו — Possibly the *Piel* has declarative force, and the verb may be regarded as cognate with *zimrāt*; "declare the Lord to be strong, ascribe
strength to the Lord." "excellent things" — Lit., "majesty." Note the reflection upon Exod. 15:1. "known" — *me-yud-da-'at* is a *Pual* part. with the

406

truly is the Strong One, the Mighty God, and that He only has strength. There is a reason why men should do this. Yahweh hath done excellent things, in that He has delivered Israel and set His people free from bondage. Nothing can be compared with the great deliverance that He accomplished when He offered up His only begotten Son. The things that He has done are high and exalted; truly, they are excellent, and they are known; they were not done in a corner.

6 The inhabitant of Zion is personified as a woman, and this inhabitant is the people that have been redeemed. In speaking to her, the prophet is addressing all the people of God personified. He commands her to give a shrill cry and to break forth in exultation.[40] In the midst of His people, God resided in the Temple, and by means of this residence in their midst God shows Himself to be truly great. In Old Testament times this residence was in the Temple and the presence of God also appeared in the performance of miracles. Today He dwells in the midst of His people in His Word and in His Spirit whose temple is our bodies.

How symmetrically constructed this chapter is! In verses 1 and 2 we have the language of the redeemed, in verse 3 the prophet speaks and again in verses 4 and 5 the words of the redeemed, closing in the last verse with Isaiah's own command. It is an interesting interchange between the words of the people and those of Isaiah.

---

force of the Latin gerundive, "it is to be made known." The *Ketib* is rarer and is to be preferred over the *Q* which would make a *Hofal* of the word, *mŭ-da-'at̩*. Marti, however, prefers the *Hofal*.

40 "cry out" — Lit., "give a shrill voice, neigh"; cf. Isa. 24:14; 54:1; Jer. 31:6; Esth. 8:15. "inhabitant" — The f. part. is used, for the redeemed are personified as a woman. The church is the bride of Christ. "great" — Not "the Holy One in thy midst is great," but "in thy midst the Holy One has shown Himself to be great."

II. The Theocracy and the Nations (13:1—39:8)

A. JUDAH AND THE WORLD POWER (13:1—27:13)

1. The Growth of the Mesopotamian Power (13:1 — 14:32)

a. *The judgment will come* (13:1-8)

1 The oracle of Babylon which Isaiah the son of Amoz did see.

2 Upon a bare hill lift up a standard, raise up a voice for them, wave the hand and let them come to the gates of the nobles.

3 I have commanded my sanctified ones; also have I called my mighty ones for my wrath, my proudly exulting ones.

4 The sound of a multitude in the mountains, the likeness of much people, the voice of a tumult of kingdoms of nations gathering themselves together; the LORD of hosts is mustering a host of war.

5 Coming from a land afar, from the end of the heavens, the LORD and the instruments of his indignation, to ruin all the land.

6 Howl ye! for near is the day of the LORD, as ruin from Shaddai will it come.

7 Wherefore all the hands will sink, and every human heart will melt.

8 And they shall be confounded, pangs and throes shall they seize, like the travailing one they shall writhe, each at his neighbor they shall wonder, faces of flames shall be their faces.

1 According to this title we are faced with a *massa*,[1] i.e., a divine oracle or declaration, which has to do with Babylon.[2] It

---

[1] The מַשָּׂא is an oracle or divine declaration. As a superscription the term is found in 13:1; 14:28; 15:1; 17:1; 19:1; 21:1, 11, 13; 22:1; 23:1; Nah. 1:1; Hab. 1:1; Zech. 9:1; 12:1; Mal. 1:1 and Lam. 2:14. It designates an exalted style of speech in Prov. 30:1 and 2 Kings 9:25. B renders ὅρασις, ὅραμα and λῆμμα, the first two of which, although not really inaccurate, are free renderings. Targ., A, Syr., and Vulg. rendered "burden," and Jerome explained it as designating threatening oracles, which has been adopted by Luther, Calvin, Hengstenberg, etc. The minatory element, however, is not necessarily present.

[2] "Babylon" — An objective genitive: the oracle respecting or concerning Babylon.

is not a declaration which Babylon herself has made, but one which concerns her.[3] Babylon is the object of the prophecy. From the context it appears that a *massa* may be minatory in nature, although it would be going too far to claim that such was always the case.

Inasmuch as this chapter introduces the second great division of Isaiah's prophecy, it has a special heading; and lest we should think that because the content concerns Babylon, a nation far removed in time from Isaiah, the prophet himself could not have written the chapter, we are expressly told that it was seen (i.e., in vision) by Isaiah, the son of Amoz. If Isaiah was not the author, it is strange that his name should appear in the heading. What would cause a redactor to think that Isaiah could have had a vision concerning Babylon? We may note that the style is Isaiah's, and that both Zephaniah and Jeremiah, who lived later, used portions of this chapter. The verse before us then is a divine revelation which has to do with Babylon and which was revealed by God to Isaiah the prophet of the eighth century B.C. How all important it is for Isaiah to declare that his message is divinely revealed! Dazzled by the power of the massive world forces, men's eyes would turn to look at the prophet's words only if they were convinced that those words have come to their speaker from God.

SPECIAL NOTE

With the thirteenth chapter we are plunged into the midst of nations. "Woe to the multitude of many people, which make a noise like the noise of the seas; and to the rushing of nations, that make a rushing like the rushing of mighty waters! The nations shall rush like the rushing of many waters: but God shall rebuke them and they shall flee far off, and shall be chased as the chaff of the mountains before the wind, and like a rolling thing before the whirlwind" (Isa. 17:12, 13).

Just as in Jeremiah and in Ezekiel the prophecies of the foreign nations are grouped together, so also in Isaiah. This section, therefore, may be compared with Jeremiah 46-51 and Ezekiel 25-32. The prophet speaks concerning Babylon, Assyria, Philistia, Moab, Damascus, Ethiopia, Egypt, Elam, Media, Arabia, Tyre, and then concludes the prophecies with a description of judgment of the world and of the last things (chaps. 24-27).

---

3 Because of the presence of מַשָּׂל in 14:4a Fischer and others have argued that 13:1 cannot be original. But the מַשָּׂל is an integral part of the entire passage; it refers only to 14:4ff. and not to the whole section which begins with 13:1.

By the majority of modern critics these chapters are denied to Isaiah. Pfeiffer for example attributes to Isaiah only 14:28-32; 17: 1-3; 18:1-6; 20:1-6; 22:1-14, 15-25. The remainder of the section, he thinks, was written long after the time of Isaiah. 13:17-19 was written before Cyrus conquered Babylon, presumably about 550 B.C. 14:4b-21 was written some time within the period 580-250 B.C. The oracle against Moab (15:1-9a; 16:7-11) probably dates from 550-540 B.C. The prophecy against Egypt (19) probably falls within the period 600-300 B.C. (19:1-15). 21:1-10 contains an oracle against Babylon and is said to have been composed probably about 550, but by a different author from that of chapter 13, because in that chapter the Medes were said to conquer Babylon whereas here it is the Medes and Elam. The original poems of the fifth and sixth oracles, namely, 21:11ff., and 21:13-15, probably come from the fourth and fifth century, whereas the prose appendix to the second poem (21: 16ff.) could have been added in the third century. With respect to the seventh oracle, that addressed against Tyre, it may have been composed between 550-300, and the appendix (23:15-18) was written shortly after 274 B.C. (cf. Pfeiffer: *Introduction to the Old Testament,* pp. 443-47).

Why should these prophecies be denied to Isaiah? The principal reasons are the following: 1) Babylon appears as a world power, towering over other nations, "the glory of the kingdoms" (13:19). In Isaiah's day, however, Babylon had to struggle for existence, for at that time Assyria was the greatest of the powers. 2) Over Babylon's downfall the entire earth is said to rejoice and glory (cf. 14:7). Even the trees of Lebanon join in this rejoicing. This, it is said, does not suit Isaiah's day, since Lebanon then belonged to Tiglathpileser. 3) In Isaiah's day the Medes were not enemies of Babylon but its allies against Assyria.

Some scholars, consequently, think that chapters 13 and 14 referred originally not to Babylon but to Assyria, and in support of this, appeal is made to the passage directed against Assyria, which occurs in 14:24ff. Kissane, perhaps the leading advocate of this view, argues as follows: A late writer may have substituted Babylonia for Assyria in the text. After 612 Babylonia succeeded Assyria as oppressor of Israel, hence the change in names would be a natural one. In 2 Chron. 33:16 the name has been changed to Babylon and in Mic. 4:10 the name Babylon, if not more, is the work of a later hand. In Isaiah 23:13 the name Assyria has again been supplanted. Lastly, everything here agrees with the other prophecies of Isaiah on the ruin of Judah and the downfall of Assyria. Earlier H. Grimme (*Th. Q,* 1903, p. 1ff.) and Feldmann (p. 186ff.) held that the prophecy did not originally refer to Babylon. Against this, however, we have the title which mentions Babylon expressly by name, and even if this title were the work of a redactor, it would show that he thought that the passages had to do with Babylon. Furthermore, in

410

the passage itself, Babylon is named as the object of the judgment (13:19a).

Must this section really be denied to Isaiah? For one thing, the title explicitly speaks of Isaiah the son of Amoz (13:1). Gray calls this the "singularly unfortunate guess" of some editor who thought that the entire oracle was a prophecy of Isaiah's and that this guess for some two thousand years led to an unquestioning acceptance of Isaianic authorship (Gray, p. 233). If the editor really was so ignorant of Isaiah's times as to think that Isaiah could have prophesied concerning Babylon, we wonder how he came to develop the prophecy into such a marvelous composition (this applies even to chapters 13 and 14 alone). He must have been somewhat of a genius, and yet he apparently made such a bad guess. The title is very clear. It speaks of an oracle concerning Babylon which Isaiah the son of Amoz did see. What would have led an editor to insert such a title? Would not the editor have known at least that much history — that in Isaiah's day the great world power was Assyria and not Babylon?

Another explanation of the heading is that it is genuine and means what it says. On this assumption, which is embraced in this commentary, Isaiah himself composed these chapters. If we assume the genuineness of the title we are not shut up to the conclusion that Isaiah thought that in his own day Babylon was the great world-power. It is perfectly possible that toward the close of his life, after 700 B.C., Isaiah may have gone into retirement and may have put together his entire prophecy. The spirit of prophecy may then have carried him to an ideal speaking point, so that from that standpoint he spoke of the greatest of Israel's enemies, Babylon, an enemy so great that in the Revelation it is made a type of the Antichrist, the spirit that opposes the working of God.

The heading of the section, the fact that the section is found in the book of Isaiah, and the epilogue, namely 14:24-27, point to Isaianic authorship. It was Isaiah's custom to append epilogues to larger prophecies, e.g., 8:1-4 to chapter 7; 16:13ff. to chapter 15-16:12; 20 to chapter 18, 19; and 22:15 to chapter 22:1-14. This is done in such a way that the prophecy and epilogue bear an integral relationship to one another.

Jeremiah has imitated 13:1-14:23 step by step in chapters 50 and 51. Attempts have been made to avoid this conclusion by an hypothesis of interpolation, but against this is the fact that Zephaniah 1:7; 2:14 and 3:11 contain reminiscences of Isaiah 13. Stähelin sought to overcome this by making the author of Isaiah 13 an imitator of Zephaniah and of Ezekiel. But Isa. 13 is original and only reproduces words of Joel (cf. 13:6, 9, 13 with Joel 1:15; 2:10ff., 4:15). A number of Isaianic expressions are found in Isa. 13:1-14:23. Cf. Isa. 13:2 with 5:26; 11:10, 12; 18:3; 10:15-33; 11:15; 19:16 and 30:32. Cf. Isa. 13:3 with 10:5; Isa. 13:5 with 5:26; 10:5, 25; Isa. 13:6 with

411

18:1 and Isa. 14:20 with 1:4. (Cf. Karl Budde, "Jesaja 13" in *Festschrift von Baudissin,* Giessen, 1918, pp. 55-70, for an attempt to reconstruct the text on the basis of metrical considerations.)

It should, however, be noted that the vocabulary and style are consonant with those passages which are generally recognized as Isaianic. Secondly, these passages are based upon what precedes and, indeed, are really not understandable without the preceding. Thirdly, Zephaniah and Jeremiah presuppose these passages, and hence they are not exilic but must at least be earlier than Jeremiah and Zephaniah.

An older defense of Isaianic authorship is found in Uhland *(Vat. Jes. cap xiii. . . . prophetae Jesaiae vindicatum,* Tübingen, 1798). For more recent defenses see von Orelli, Delitzsch, Alexander.

It is necessary at this point, however, to discuss more fully the position which these chapters occupy in Isaiah's prophecy and their purpose. Such a consideration will lead to the conclusion that it is only upon the assumption of Isaianic authorship that they yield a good sense.

Within the compass of chapters 13-27 there are certain sections which when taken by themselves are somewhat obscure. Such, for example, is true of 24:1-15. It is also true of 17:12-14 and 18:4-6. The same thing may be said of 14:32 and 18:3. Passages such as these presuppose something that has gone before. If they be lifted from their context (particularly that of chapters 1-12) they do not yield a clear sense. Obviously they are rooted in something preceding. The same is true of the brief statements of promise and blessing which are scattered throughout these chapters, such as 14:1, 2; 14:29, 30; 16:1, 4b, 5; 18:7. These brief notes appear suddenly. What is their justification and explanation? If they stand alone, they are difficult to interpret. When will the Lord have mercy on Jacob? How will He do so? Under what circumstances? These Messianic elements, for so we may rightly denominate them, rest upon a mother prophecy, a previous announcement of more detailed and clear-cut character, that God will save His people, and how He will do it.

The flowering tree of 13-23 his its roots in chapter 7. Indeed, this chapter is foundational for an understanding of what is to follow. In this great seventh chapter two basic thoughts are presented in seed form. First there is to be a deliverance for God's people through Immanuel, the Son of the virgin. Immanuel is to bring to the true Israel an exaltation in God Himself. At the same time, the world powers were to come more and more upon the horizon, for they would increase in strength and power until they had accomplished God's purposes with them.

It was a time of trouble. The theocracy, because of its sin, was to come to an end. In bringing it to an end, God would employ a great world empire, even Assyria and Babylon. Looking to Assyria for help, Judah would discover that Assyria was the cause of her downfall. From this time on these great world powers would loom large upon the horizon of human history, and they would represent the spirit of opposition to the people of God, and so to the coming of the Christ and the carrying out of God's purposes of redemption. At the very beginning of this period the prophecy of Immanuel was uttered, so that the consolation which that promise could bring would extend throughout the period for the blessing of God's true people. And for this reason the prophecies and oracles concerning the heathen nation are connected essentially with this prophecy of Immanuel.

The idea of the world empire is developed somewhat in 8:9, 10, which gives us the heart of the entire concept. "Do your worst, O ye people, and ye shall be broken in pieces; and give ear, all ye of far countries: gird yourselves, and ye shall be broken in pieces; gird yourselves, and ye shall be broken in pieces. Take counsel together, and it shall come to nought; speak the word, and it shall not stand, for Immanuel (God is with us) ." The peoples will seek to carry out their plans, but they shall not ultimately prevail against the purposes of God, the true counsellor, for Immanuel is present to deliver His own.

With 10:5-34 we reach a further stage in the revelation. Now the enemy power is individualized and identified. We know who that enemy is, namely, Assyria. Chapters 13-27 carry us on to a third stage in that they serve as an exposition and enlargement of 8:9, 10. Assyria is the enemy, but the work of Assyria will be carried on by one that is far more powerful than she, even Babylon. Hence, Isaiah first turns to Babylon. He then discusses the neighbors on all sides of the chosen people, somewhat in the manner that Amos had used. Beginning with Philistia, he works his way till he comes to Syria-Ephraim. Twice, however, namely in 14:24-27 and 17:12-18:7 he looks again at Assyria, and so we see that after all Assyria is very much present.

The spirit of the world power is to be found in Babylon. In the first place Babylon is introduced as a center of world power, and secondly, as the center of idolatry (13:1-14:27 and 21:1-10) . But even this apex of human power, directed against God and His purposes, is to be cut off. To illustrate these truths Isaiah uses passages of somewhat similar construction. In 8:6-18, for example, we have a rather long-drawn-out description of that power which overflows Immanuel's land. Then follows in verses 9 and 10 the sudden announcement of destruction. At once, as it were, the strength of the enemy is cut off and he disappears.

This procedure is repeated in 10:28-34, where step by step we watch the enemy approach the holy city. Closer, closer he comes with hand raised in threatening gesture. Suddenly, however, the Lord strikes, and the enemy is gone. Again in 17:12-14; 18:4-6 and 24:1-15 we have the same manner of statement. This is an interesting phenomenon, and points toward the unity of the book.

Another phase of the development must be noted. Judah was to be brought to judgment at the hand of the world powers. When this thought, introduced in 7:17-25, appears again in 8:5-9:6 and 10:5-12:6 more is said about Assyria. Egypt, however, is left unsettled. What is Egypt to do? It is in 13-23 that we learn more about Egypt.

Indeed, the very manner in which Assyria is mentioned in these chapters presupposes that there has been previous information given concerning Assyria. Why would the powerful Assyria be introduced in so cursory a fashion and in the manner in which she is, unless something concerning Assyria had already been said?

What about the promises of the exaltation of God's people through Immanuel which were introduced in chapter 7? This thought also is developed in chapters 9 and 11, but the full explanation of how the Messiah is to accomplish His work is left until the second portion of the prophecy. At the same time, against the dark background of the raging nations, there appear, as a gleam of bright hope, references to the coming salvation which Judah is to enjoy at the hands of the Lord. Grace — this is the bright beam that shines through these chapters. Fragments which in a broad sense may be called Messianic are the following: 14:1, 2, 29-30; 16:1, 4b, 5; 18:7; 19:16-24 and 23:15-18. We may note that 14:1a reflects upon 11:11, 12; 14:1b on 11:10; 14:2a on 11:12a and 14:2b on 11:14.

We have said that chapters 13-23 carry out more fully the prophecies of world power and its downfall. In this line we may now notice that 13:1-14:27 is in general an expanding continuation of 10:5-34. Even 14:28-32 puts on a broader basis the removal of the world power. The judgment is seen not to be confined to one nation but to all the powers which have stood in opposition to God's people. In chapters 15 and 16 the judgment is broadened into a world-wide one. We may compare 16:1, 2 with 11:10; 16:3, 4a with 11:12; 16:4b with 9:3, 4; 11:6-9; 16:5a with 9:5, 6; 16:5b with 9:6 and 11:2, 5, 14; 17:7, 8 with 10:20-23; and 18:7 with 11:10. Chapter 19 parallels 10:5-34; although it speaks of a spiritual subjection. Cf. 19:16, 17 with 11:15, 16; 16:16 with 11:15; 19:18-22 with 11:10; 19:18, 23-25 with 11:6-8; 19:23 with 11:6; chapter 20 and 18:1, 2, 7 with 11:11; 21:11, 12 with 11:14; and 21:13-17 with 11:14.

Note also the similarity of treatment of the following themes:
Israel is to become a remnant: 10:21, 22 with 17:4-6; 24:1-13.
The return of the remnant: 10:20, 21 with 17:7, 8; 20:5, 6; and 27:9.
A cry of deliverance in darkness: 9:1 with 11:1 and 24:14.

414

The destruction of the oppressor: 10:16-19, 33, 34 with 14:25; 16:4;
    17:12-14; and 18:4-6.
The regathering of Israel: 11:11-16 and 14:1 with 27:13.
The turning of the nations: 11:10 with 14:1b; 16:1, 2; 18:7.
The nations serve Israel: 11:11 with 14:2.
They partly experience Israel's rule: 11:14-16 with 14:29.
The coming peace: 9:4-6 and 11:2-5, 6-9 with 14:1, 2, 7, 8, 29, 30;
    16:4, 5.
The redeemed sing hymns of praise: chapter 12 with 24:14-16; 25:1-
    5; 26:1, 2.

    The purpose of chapters 13-27 is to develop more fully one aspect
of thought which Isaiah had already introduced. Even as early as
2:2-4 he had mentioned a judgment, but only in the most general
terms. No instrument or agent of judgment was named. In 5:26ff.
Isaiah advances a step further and gives in a general manner a description of those who are entrusted with carrying out the work of
judgment. Chapter 7 introduces us to the world power which
God intends to employ, naming it according to its two poles, namely,
Assyria and Egypt. In chapters 8 and 10 there is a broadening
out of identification and description of the world power, but it is
reserved to chapters 13-23 for the further development of this theme
which had earlier only been sketched.

    That these prophecies appear in the Biblical book of Isaiah was
not for the benefit of the Babylonians but for the people of God.
From them they would learn that the hostile power of the world in
its most powerful manifestation would finally be brought to ignominious defeat and ruin. No power that sets itself against God,
be it as haughty and pretentious as was Babylonia, can prevail.
Thus, Israel would learn that God does not permit to go unpun-
ished the wickedness of those who have set themselves against the
Lord and against His anointed, and who oppose His people.

    To see the opponents of God's purposes punished would bring
consolation and encouragement to the Jews, for it would teach them
how precious their salvation was in God's sight. But they would
also learn that they too were deserving of punishment, and that only
by God's mercy had a remnant been spared. Then, too, the raging
of the nations is but a carrying out of God's purposes. He is in
control of all things. A topsy-turvy world is not really topsy-turvy.
Even the darkest moments are in God's providential control and rule.

2 By means of a command, Isaiah plunges us immediately into
the heart of the matter. Who, however, issues this command?
Isaiah does not actually answer the question, but it is probably
Yahweh Himself who through His prophet addresses those whose

task it is to raise a standard.[4]   Likely they were warriors or soldiers rather than angels.   Because it may be easily seen a mountain is chosen,[5] one that is to be bare, and hence especially suited for visibility.[6]   On a lofty and conspicuous spot it was the custom in ancient times to arrange signals for the purposes of summoning troops.

On such a mountain a standard was to be raised,[7] and about this the soldiers were to gather.   It would be their rallying point.   For those to be summoned, the voice needs also to be raised in shout, and a gesture[8] made.   Three means of bringing the troops together are mentioned, and all three show the need for haste, and exhibit the zeal of the prophet who utters the commands in the Lord's name.   The raised standard would serve to call those who were afar, and the voice those that were near.   And the gesture, as Drechsler suggests, would give character to the call as being one of spirited liveliness.   Hence, the highest degree of urgency is indicated.   The meeting place is designated as "the doors of the noble ones," the Babylonians or Chaldeans at whose gates the soldiers will gather and into which as victors they will enter. How beautiful and noble were the gates of Babylon!   And the men — they were nobles indeed!   But the captor is to come[9] and take possession of Babylon.   The greatest of Israel's foes — but her doom is sure.   At the head of the prophecies directed against the foreign peoples stands Babylon, and if she is to fall, so also will foes who were less powerful than she.

---

[4] Jerome held that angels were addressed; Knobel thought they were captive Jews; Kissane refers to the leaders of Yahweh's host and thinks that the reference is probably to the campaign of Sennacherib which began Judah's desolation. The reference is best taken as indefinite, the command being uttered to those whose responsibility it is to obey.

[5] Vitringa thought that Isaiah had in mind the Zagrian mountains; Feldmann thought that Nineveh was intended. According to Haller, Yahweh is the old god of battle, who now summons his hosts in the eastern mountains.

[6] נשפה — As the Syr. shappî "smooth, bare," shows, the word should be rendered "bare." Cf. the usage in Isa. 41:18; Jer. 3:2; 4:11.

[7] נם is Isaianic; cf. 5:26; 11:10, 12; 18:3; 49:22; 62:10. Indeed, the threefold command is itself Isaianic. For the beginning of this verse cf. Isa. 40:9.

[8] Cf. 10:32; 11:15; 19:16.

[9] The rendering, "and let them come," rather than "that they may come" is probably more suitable, inasmuch as the action of coming is really correlative with the three preceding commands. Cf. König for the opposite position. The army, summoned by the Lord, will enter Babylon as conquerors. "nobles" — Of Babylonia.

3 It is God who speaks. "I," He says — and the pronoun is emphatic — "I have called." Those whom He calls are His warriors,[10] already solemnly consecrated and set apart for His warfare, as instruments appointed and chosen. To designate them "sanctified" is not to refer to their moral character, but only to the fact of their having been set apart. Having been specially dedicated by God, the "sanctified ones" are now commanded by Him to execute His will.[11] They are His proudly exulting ones,[12] in whom He glorified Himself. The war is thus truly a holy one, led by God who commands His soldiers to carry out His purposes of wrath against the enemy, even Babylon.

4 It is the prophet who speaks and in language reminiscent of Joel describes the approaching army. "The voice,"[13] he cries, and the word is almost an ejaculation, as though he had said, "Hark! there seems to be the noise of an army." One continues to listen and learns that it indeed is an oncoming army; battalions are on the mountains. Here are no staid prosaic sentences, but lightning-like exclamations breaking forth from the prophet's mouth as in vision he sees the troops draw near. The absence of verbs lends great vividness to the description. The approaching army; it is like much people, people that have come together from all over Persia.

What is this voice to which Isaiah alerts us? It is the tumult of

---

10 The construction with the dative is rare. לְמְקֻדָּשַׁי — Those already consecrated by the Lord to do His service. The root here has no reference to moral character, but signifies merely "to set apart." In 2 Chron. 26:18 it is employed of the priests. It does not contain any reference to religious ceremonies performed before going to war, as is suggested by some who appeal to 1 Sam. 7:9; etc. Dependent upon this passage are Jer. 22:7; 51:27, 28. Note that Zeph. 1:7 clearly presupposes this passage. For references to setting apart, cf. Isa. 42:1; 44:28; 45:1; Mic. 3:5; Jer. 6:4; 22:7; 51:27ff.; Josh. 4:9. Despite these references, however, the present word in itself designates nothing more than those who are set apart to a particular work.

11 "for my wrath — To my anger, to obey God in carrying out His command to punish; cf. 1 Sam. 28:18.

12 "the exulters of my pride" — My proudly exulting ones. If the governed noun qualifies the preceding noun by denoting an attribute, the suffix attached to it properly belongs to the preceding word in the const. Cf. Deut. 1:41; Judg. 18:16; and Ps. 2:6. Zeph. 3:11 presupposes this passage. The allusion is to the haughty character of the Persians, to which attestation is also given by the classical writers; cf. Ammianus Marcellinus 23:6:80; Her., 1:89; Aeschylus, *Persae*, 8:27; and cf. E. Herzfeld: *Altpersische Inschriften*, 1938.

13 קוֹל practically has the force of an interjection, for it introduces a sentence interjectional in nature, as in 52:8; 66:6; Jer. 50:28.

kingdoms of nations. In Cyrus' armies there were mixed peoples, many nations, coming from the various governments which went to make up Persia. One after another Cyrus had conquered the states of Persia; one after another they had joined themselves to his army. Step by step the army grew and now in the mountains, overlooking, as it were, the Mesopotamian plain, the forces are gathering themselves together[14] for the final onslaught.

What a remarkable gradation! A sound is heard — a sound distant, far away in the mountains! What makes the sound, indistinct as it is? Kingdoms gathering themselves together cause the sound. Yahweh, who controls all hosts, is mustering His army for war. As once He had brought the Assyrian against Judah, so now He musters the Mede against the land of Babylon.

5 Who is this foe that comes from the most distant places,[15] even the end of the heavens? His origin and identity are not revealed, and the Babylonians, ignorant of these things, would look upon his approach with greater terror. From a point remote as the eye can see, even where the vault of heaven seems to touch the earth, comes the enemy host. Persia is this land afar: to Isaiah in Palestine a most distant land.

At their head is the God of Israel, Yahweh of hosts, and under His command are the instruments[16] wherewith He executes His wrath and ruins all the earth. Great was the Babylonian empire; indeed, in all world history it was the first of empires, and in its destruction all the earth had been involved. Before Yahweh, however, no world empire can stand, for Yahweh has control of all heaven and earth.

6 Standing upon the roof of his palace, Nebuchadnezzar could cry out, "Is this not great Babylon which I have builded?"[17] Incom-

14 The reflexive part. expresses action going on at the time of the speaker. Isaiah sees nations in the process of gathering themselves together.

15 "the end of the heavens" — The phrase accentuates the distance and unknown character of the land from which the enemies come. The thought of distance appears in 5:26; 33:17 and 46:11. Poetically conceived, the end of heaven would be the place where sky and earth meet, or where the sky seems to rest upon the mountains, i.e., the most distant of places. Cf. 2 Sam. 22:8.

16 In Rom. 9:22 Paul adapts this language. According to Paul, the vessels were instruments in which or against which the wrath of God was manifested.

17 Cf. Dan. 4:27. For Babylonian references see *Enuma Elish*, VI:57ff.; Prologue to Code of Hammurabi, line 13ff., Nebuchadnezzar II: Expedition to Syria, ix:1ff., *Keilinschriftliche Bibliothek*, iii, 2, p. 25, 39.

418

parable Babylon! World empire indeed, you must howl[18] and lift up your voice in wailing, for Yahweh, whom you despised, will in His day exalt Himself. The day of Yahweh was first of all a day which would manifest itself in the destruction of Israel at the hand of Assyria. That destruction, however, did not exhaust the wrath of God. In His own time He would pour out the vials of His anger upon Assyria and Babylon, and the ruin of Babylon would be but a prelude or type of the final destruction of all His enemies.

This day which belongs to Yahweh is near. That is, it is near not from the standpoint of Isaiah's own day, but from the standpoint of the proud world empire of Babylonia. There were to be various manifestations of this day, and the destruction of Babylon would be one of the most forceful. It would also be a type and even a beginning of the final judgment which was to come over all mankind. Isaiah sees both together. In the book of Revelation Babylon is portrayed as the type of the great enemy of God.[19]

Interesting is the paronomasia between *shod and shaddai*,[20] but it is difficult to bring out its force in English. "You shall know what Shaddai means," we may represent Isaiah as saying; "it means destruction so complete as though it were from the destroyer. How great then must be a destruction that comes from Shaddai!"

7 The enemy, led by Yahweh, approaches, and His day comes, bringing total ruin to Babylon. Because of this sudden and irresistible attack, the hands wherein man's power resides will become lax and slackened.[21] They will hang down helpless, un-

---

18 The address is to the Babylonians. Zeph. 1:7, 14 takes up the thought, as does Obad. 15 and also, in different fashion, Jer. 50:31. The imper. conveys the assurance that the punishment will come; cf. Isa. 10:30; 23:1, 4; 37:30; 60:1; 65:18.

19 The day of the Lord is the day of final judgment, but a forerunner of that judgment appeared in the destruction of Babylon. Cf. Kline: "The Intrusion and the Decalogue," in *WThJ*, XVI, No. 1, Nov. 1953, pp. 1-22. Mowinckel goes beyond the evidence when he claims that the day is depicted in the "traditional colours of cosmological mythology" (*HTC*, p. 147). Von Rad thinks that the imagery of the "day" goes back to the old Israelitish tradition of the holy wars of Yahweh. See *JSS*, Vol. IV, No. 2, April 1959, pp. 97-108.

20 Probably the prep. is the *kaf veritatis*, "a destruction from Shaddai." Dillmann seeks to retain the paronomasia in his rendering, *"wie Gewalt vom Allgewaltigen her kommt er."*

21 The hands will fall down as helpless. Courage will be gone. Instead of using their hands for fighting, men will let them fall to the side. Cf. Ovid, *Metamorphoses*, vii. 346, *"cecidere illis animique manusque."*

able to resist the enemy. Courage will vanish from the heart, which
will simply melt, without any will.[22] Dread terror is over all.
Who can abide the day of His coming?

8 It is a day of trouble. Convulsing agitation and desperate
perplexity[23] come upon the Babylonians, and they seize — for
there is nothing else to seize — pangs and throes.[24] Then they writhe
in bitter pain like the mother that is bearing her child.[25] Theirs is
the deepest anguish, for the day of Yahweh is breaking. And this
is the forerunner of that great last day of which the apostle
writes, "For when they shall say, Peace and safety; then sudden
destruction cometh upon them, as travail upon a woman with
child; and they shall not escape" (1 Thess. 5:3). Then will one
man look at another and will fall into wonder, for the faces of all
will be as flames, glowing red from embarrassment and lack of
counsel. Men are not alone. All are in the same predicament,
and one looks with stupefaction at their condition. All countenances are red, not merely from crying, but glowing from fear.
The enemy has come and with him destruction. Here is a picture
of the greatest fear which reveals a burning glow both within
and on the countenance.

b. *The outpouring of judgment* (13:9-22)

9 Behold! the day of the LORD cometh cruel, and wrath and heat of
   anger, to place the land a waste, and its sinners he will destroy
   from it.

---

[22] V. 6 has parenthetical force; v. 7 continues the argument. "Wherefore,
inasmuch as the land will be ruined, every hand will be lax, . . ." Note the
parallel between "every hand" and "every heart." The heart is weak. Ar. has
the term *ma'un*, "watery," to describe a fearful people.

[23] ונבהלו — The form has the disjunctive *šalšelet* followed by a vertical
stroke, which many call *paseq*. The correctness of this I question. The combination Great *šalšelet* is found only 7 times; Gen. 19:16; 24:12; 39:8; Lev. 8:
23; Isa. 13:8; Amos 1:2; Ezra 5:15. In each case this accent stands upon the initial word of the verse. The regular pause accents produce vowel changes, but
other accents do so also, which explains the pointing of this word; cf. Green,
Hebrew Grammar, no. 65:b.

[24] "pangs" — Due to physical and mental anguish. The word is probably
to be construed as object; cf. Job 18:20; 21:6, and Livy *"capere metum."*

[25] When one seizes hold of pangs, he writhes in pain. The faces are flame-
faces, because they burn red from embarrassment and lack of counsel as to
what to do. Cf. Joel 2:6 for a different description. Note the two parallel
paragogic *nuns*.

10 For the stars of the heavens and their constellations shall not give their light — the sun is darkened when it arises, and the moon will not cause its light to shine.

11 And I shall visit upon the world evil, and upon the wicked their iniquity, and I shall cause to cease the arrogance of the presumptuous ones, and the pride of tyrants I shall bring low.

12 And I shall make weak man more precious than pure gold, and a man than the gold of Ophir.

13 Wherefore I shall cause the heavens to tremble, and the earth shall shake from out of its place in the wrath of the LORD of hosts and in the day of the heat of his anger.

14 And it shall be like a roe chased, and like a flock with none gathering them, each unto his people, they will turn, and each unto his land, they will flee.

15 Everyone who is found shall be stabbed, and everyone who is captured will fall by the sword.

16 And their children shall be dashed to pieces before their eyes, their houses shall be plundered, and their wives ravished.

17 Behold! I am about to stir up against them the Medes, who will give no thought to silver, and, as for gold, they will not desire it.

18 And bows shall dash boys in pieces, and the fruit of the womb they will not pity; upon sons their eye will not spare.

19 And Babylon, the beauty of kingdoms, the ornament of the pride of the Chaldeans, shall be as when God overthrew Sodom and Gomorrah.

20 It shall not be inhabited forever, and it shall not be dwelt in from generation to generation; and the Arab will not pitch his tent there, and shepherds will not cause their flock to lie down there.

21 But there will lie down desert creatures, and their houses will be filled with jackals; and there will dwell the ostrich, and wild goats will play there.

22 And jackals shall howl in his palaces, and jackals in the temples of delight; and her time is near to come, and her days shall not be prolonged.

9 One Babylon after another will be destroyed until the last sinner is removed from earth. Apparently Isaiah is unaware of what some would teach today, when they say that it is poor psychology to appeal to the motive of fear. Isaiah thought differently, or, to speak more accurately, the Holy Spirit thought differently, for here the prophet not only mentions the coming day of judgment but commands men to look at that day. "Behold!" he cries out, as he was wont to do whenever announcing something of tremendous significance, "the day of Yahweh is coming." It

421

may well be that men do not wish to hear of the judgment, but Isaiah demonstrates that he is a true evangelist, with a love for the souls of men. The judgment is coming; to be silent about that fact is not to be wise, but is to exhibit a lack of love toward men. "Behold! the day," cries the evangelist, "and in beholding it, flee unto God for deliverance and salvation!"

Not only is that day about to come, but it is about to come as a cruel one.[26] It is hard and unfeeling, breaking out in vehement destruction, showing no mercy and sparing none. With that day there will be no sunlight of blessing but wrath and the heat of anger.[27] Over the world city the judgment deepens for the purpose of making the earth, represented by and affected by Babylon, a desolation. What is this desolation? It is the destruction of earth's sinners.[28] Here is no talk about the worth of the individual or the inherent value of the soul; here is the announced purpose of the day of Yahweh; sinners are to be destroyed from the earth. The world city was a sinful city; she had attacked Judah and Jerusalem and had countenanced a steady idolatry. She was a worldly city as well as the world city, and she gloried in her self-sufficiency. Yet the destruction of Babylon was but a small prelude of the ultimate ruin which the day of judgment was to bring. Isaiah speaks of the destruction of sinners from the earth; he uses language that seems to transcend a mere reference to Babylon. Over Babylon the judgment pours out, for it will also pour out over all the earth. The language, therefore, is also to be understood of the final judgment. Day of wrath and anguish! In that day who can stand? Are not we also, like the Babylonians, sinners who have turned against the holy Yahweh

26 "cruel one" — In opposition to "day," and thus the day is personified as something cruel. Jeremiah (50:42) applies this epithet to the enemies.

27 "and wrath" — The *wāw* should be rendered "with." Cf. Judg. 6:5; 2 Kings 11:18. וישמיד — Inasmuch as the verb is separated from the *wāw*, the imp. is used. This separation has the effect of placing "and her sinners" in the place of prominence. "and as for her sinners — he will destroy them from her."

28 Delitzsch would limit the reference to a particular historical catastrophe. but Babylon was the world-city, the supreme manifestation of worldly power in self-sufficiency (cf. Rev. 17 and 18). She was sinful in her haughtiness (cf. 13:11; 14:11; 47:7, 8) in her tyranny (14:12, 17) in her idolatry (Jer. 50:38) and in her mistreatment of God's people (Isa. 47:6). As the judgment deepens over the world-city, it proves to be a universal judgment. Reichel is correct in saying: *"Die ganze Beschreibung zeigt es, dass Jesaias von dem jüngsten Tage redet; von welchem die Zerstörung des alten Babels ein kleines Vorspiel gewesen."*

of hosts? We are such sinners indeed, but we have a refuge which God Himself has provided, even Jesus. How great is our deliverance, and how great the price paid for that deliverance! Ought not our blessed Redeemer ever to be the theme of our praise and song?

10 The day of Yahweh comes as a cruel one and as a day of wrath, for even the stars of heaven will give no light. Here we have the reason for what Isaiah had previously stated. Nature dresses herself in the clothing of wrath. When at the creation the earth was desolation and waste it was enshrouded in darkness. The first work of creation was the introduction of light. But now that light will vanish, and darkness will stand forth as a characteristic of the day of Yahweh. The stars had been created to give light, but they are now to withhold it. With them their constellations,[29] such as Orion and other brilliant constellations, also refuse to shed their light.

Even more, the sun in particular, which is the great light to rule the day, when it breaks forth from the darkness of night at morningtime, will itself be darkened.[30] Both halves of the day are therefore dark. The judgment is universal. No sun; and even the pale light of the moon is lost. Over all is darkness, deep, profound, still.

11 Again the Lord speaks and announces what He will do on this dread day. Over all the earth is darkness, but, as once the Spirit of God hovered over the dark waters to control, so now God acts to bring forth punishment. The earth on which men live, the earth in its whole circumference, will be visited with evil from God.[31] What is this evil?[32] It is the iniquity of wicked

---

[29] בכסיליהם — The s. is found in Job 9:9; 38:31; Amos 5:8. The *wāw* is augmentative; "and especially their (the previously mentioned stars) constellations." כסיל means "fool." The pl. may designate giant stars or constellations. Gesenius gives a thorough discussion of the views of the classical writers.

[30] Darkness is one characteristic of the day of Yahweh; cf. Amos 5:18; 8:9; Joel 2:10; 3:4; 4:15; Ezek. 32:7ff.; Zeph. 1:15. Note the usage of the verbs. First an imp. describes the failure of the stars to shine. A perf. then refers to the future, and views the matter objectively from an ideal standpoint. The sun is dark when it arises. The prophet then subjectively indicates his actual position and employs the imp. with reference to his own time of speaking. With יהלו we may compare *ellu* and Ar. *ḥalla*, "to begin to shine."

[31] פקד is used with the acc. of the thing visited and the prep. with the person upon whom it is visited; cf. Jer. 23:2. The earth is conceived as a mother or bringer forth of all things, in its entire circumference. Like Sheol

tyrants. By the mention of the wicked we are not merely to see a reference to the Babylonians, but rather to all the wicked who have done iniquitously against the Lord our God. Sinners are presumptuous, and what identifies them is their haughtiness. Tyrants in particular show haughtiness; indeed, it elevates them to the point where they would lord it over their fellow men.

12 The beginning and the conclusion of this verse form a striking assonance. Here we face again the doctrine of the remnant.[33] Isaiah and the other prophets present this doctrine in different ways, and in this verse it is done by means of a more specific and particular threatening. Through the destroying judgment men will become so scarce that they cannot even be bought or redeemed with gold.[34] Indeed, they will become rarer than gold, than the finest gold, gold from Ophir. This was a district, probably in South Arabia, which was known for its fine gold. An ostracon discovered at Tell Qasileh bears the inscription, "Gold of Ophir for Beth Horon, thirty shekels."

13 Wherefore,[35] in order to accomplish and fulfill His purpose, God will even shake the heavens, and the earth will be removed from its place. God will judge, and the heavens and earth will tremble (cf. Matt. 24:29; 2 Pet. 3:10; Rev. 6:9-17; 20:11). In order to show the size and severity of the judgment, Isaiah depicts the forces of nature as being in upheaval. The judgment is world-shaking, for the upheavals are the result of the anger of Yahweh, Israel's God.

We are not to understand these upheavals in the realm of nature as necessarily demanding a literal fulfillment. But through figures of speech such as these Isaiah is permitting us to perceive how

---

and Tehom, *tebel* is not used with the article. When Babylon is punished, the entire earth is affected; cf. Isa. 24:4; 26:9.

[32] The visitation of the evil of a person's deeds is a punishment, not merely because the natural consequences of those deeds result in evil, but because a judicial punishment is meted out.

[33] For other ways of depicting a remnant cf. 10:16-19; 17:4-6; 24:13; 30:17.

[34] בז — "refined or pure gold." כתם — "gold," possibly goes back to Sumerian. Ak *kutimmu*, "goldsmith," is a Sumerian loan word, from which Canaanitish *kotemt* comes, and this appears in Egyptian as *ktm.t*, "gold." The exact location of Ophir is disputed. Probably it was a district in south Arabia, although some have held that it was in western Abyssinia or in India.

[35] "Wherefore" — The words probably have a general reference to the preceding.

424

great is the judgment which God will bring. Can there be doubt as to the power of our God to move the universe with His judgment? Let us rather fear before Him in whose hands is all power.

14 A tender description is introduced, one which even arouses pity. The roe is shy and fleet of foot (cf. 2 Sam. 2:18; I Chron. 12:8; Prov. 6:5). Alone, it must dart away from its pursuers. All men are against it.[36] And without the shepherd the sheep are easily dispersed and lost.[37] They are objects of pity. How helpless too is man without God! He thinks that he is sufficient unto himself, but in the day of God's visitation he is as helpless as the sheep and the roe. He is a foreigner who seeks to flee to his own land. Indeed, Babylon was composed of many peoples, whose flight to their own houses serves as a type of the terrible fear that will grip men when the judgment falls.

15 Not all will flee; some will be found. They are those who have remained behind in the city and are captured. A general massacre sets in. Those who are captured are pierced through to death, and those who in their flight are caught[38] will be stabbed with the sword. Slaughter reigns over the captured city.

16 War in all its brutality and cruelty is set before us.[39] Only the fallen heart of man can do what the Medes are here depicted as performing. The aspect of a universal judgment is now pushed into the background, and Isaiah describes the appalling deeds of an army of depraved men. The little children of tender age will be dashed to pieces, for the invaders, despite their "civilization,"

---

[36] *mud-dah* — a *Hofal* part. for *mun-dah*.

[37] Babylon was a melting pot of the ancient world. At the coming of judgment, the foreigners would scatter to their own places. Note the pl. verbs in 14b. Jer. 50:8, 16, 37; 51:9, 44 casts light upon the condition in Babylon. Aeschylus (*Persae*, 52) speaks of the πάμμικτον ὄχλον of Babylon. The *wāw* has the force of a relative, "like a flock which has no one to gather it."

[38] In distinction from those who flee successfully, the one who is found (article with *nifal* part.) in the city by invaders will be stabbed, and the one who is caught or snatched away will fall. In the *Cyro.* (vii. 5:31) Xenophon describes how Cyrus made a distinction in the conquest of Babylon. Those found in the streets were to be killed; those who remained in the houses would be safe, but if any came outside, they should be put to death. There is no warrant for Gray's assumption that behind this passage lies a Jewish aspiration for vengeance.

[39] וישסו — *nifal* of שסס, a secondary form of שסה. Both words seem to have been introduced into Canaanite from Egyptian *šāsu*, "marauders, nomads." Cf. Coptic, *šōs*, "shepherd."

are barbarians. This wicked work they perform in front of the anguished parents. Wrath knows no bounds; the house of the captives must be burned, and their own wives ravished.[40] In this judgment there is no mercy shown.

17 Who are these destroyers of Babylon who show such revenge and cruelty? They are the Medes, a people from Persia, and are now mentioned by name for the first time. Of all the nations of Persia they were the most powerful, and hence they alone are named. It is not, however, in its own strength that this cruel eastern enemy comes. The Medes have been lying dormant as it were, but now they are to be aroused by God to strike against Babylon.[41]

Booty and money do not interest the Medes, but only revenge, and a nation activated by revenge can wreak great cruelty. Offer them silver,[42] and they do not even stop to think about it. Tempt them with gold; they do not desire it. Mere payments of money will not suffice to turn them aside. Give them revenge. That they will regard and think about.

18 The Medes were men of the bow, and their bows would send out arrows with such force that boys, the hope of the people, would be destroyed. Isaiah uses a strange figure. How can bows dash boys to pieces?[43] What he means is that the bows would be the means of the boys' destruction. Even against the fruit of

---

[40] "ravished" — The *Ketib* is deliberately chosen to show the horror of war and the merciless character of the judgment. Cf. Hos. 10:14; 14:1.

[41] Cf. Isa. 41:2, 25; 45:13. "Medes" — The only proper name in the oracle.

[42] For classical illustrations, cf. *Iliad*, 6:68 and 6:46ff.; *Aeneid*, 10:526; and *Cyro.*, 5:10:10.

[43] Grammatically the sentence must be rendered, "and bows will dash youths in pieces." תרטשנה — The form is pausal. Note *patah* before a sibilant. In an accented closed syllable *i* often shifts to *a*. The meaning of the text is difficult, but we must abide by it as it stands. W. G. Lambert: "Three Unpublished Fragments of the Tukulti-Ninurta Epic" in *Archiv für Orientforschung*, 1957, Band xviii, Erster Theil, pp. 38-51, offers this line on p. 40, " . . . the weapon of Assur, it threw down as corpses the aggressors, the fierce, the destroyer." (. . . *qiskakku! dAšur ti-ba! dap-na uš-har-mi-ta ša-lam-da id-di*). In this passage the description is figurative. The *kakku* did not literally cast down (*id-di*) the destroyer, but by means of weapons the destroyer was thrown down. So, the bows do not literally dash young men to pieces, but by means of the bows, in war, the young men are dashed to pieces. Assurbanipal (*Rassam Cylinder*, iv. 65-76) speaks of an offering in which he smashed people by the figures of protective deities (the *shedu* and *lamassu*, stone winged bulls) between which they had smashed Sennacherib. In the light of these examples we may assume that the text is correct and not in need of emendation.

the womb, little children, they will show no pity. "What destroyed the empire of the Medes?" we read in Diodorus Siculus, and the answer is given, "Their cruelty to those beneath them." Sons, the delight of fathers, will not be spared before the cruelty of this enemy. The eye, in which the soul is mirrored, sees boys, but the soul is cruel, and the eye does not spare.

19 Now we reach the heart of Isaiah's message. The judgment is directed against Babylon, the ornament and beauty of many conquered kingdoms.[44] But just as God had overthrown Sodom and Gomorrah, so He would overthrow Babylon. The judgment is thus seen to be supernatural. In the first line of this verse Babylon is highly exalted; in the second, she is brought low. Babylon is beauty, ornament, pride, says the prophet in one breath; Babylon will be like God's overthrowing the cities of the plain, he concludes.

20 Desolation is the result of the judgment, but the situation herein described did not immediately take place. Cyrus left the walls and the city of Babylon itself still standing. Later, in 518 B.C., the walls were destroyed. Then Xerxes ruined the temple of Belus. As Seleucia rose, so Babylon declined, and in Strabo's time Babylon was a desert of which he says, "a great desert is the great city." Here then is a complete destruction (cf. Isa. 47:1; Rev. 18:7). Babylon must be wiped off the face of the earth. She will not sit as an inhabited city, not even a solitary city like Jerusalem, after the banishment. Neither will she be inhabited from generation to generation. How truly this prophecy has been fulfilled!

Not even for a transitory dwelling place will Babylon be sought. The nomads who wander in the desert will not choose her,[45] nor will shepherds use her for a pasturing place. Can there be a stronger picture of utter forsakenness? The world city is gone, and only wilderness remains. When we doubt the power of our God, let us look to the wilderness where Babylon once was. So will He judge the wicked.

[44] In the course of the first millennium before Christ Aramaeans came and overspread the Babylonian plain and finally with Nabololassar, who with the Medes overthrew Nineveh in 612 B.C., came into the rule of Babylon. Strabo speaks of Babylon as a desert and Pausanius says there is nothing there but a wall.

[45] 'arābi seems to express the nomadic way of life (Jer. 3:2 is an exception) and 'arbi the distinction from other groups of people; Neh. 2:19; 4:1; 6:1; etc.

21 Using the very word of the preceding verse, Isaiah brings in a strong contrast. Shepherds will not cause their flocks to pasture in Babylon (*yarbitzu*), but there will lie down there (*rabetzu*) desert creatures, animals of the steppe and wilderness. Isaiah does not have in mind any particular animals or class of animals, but rather animals generally whose home is in the desert. There will also be houses, but they will be the houses of desert beings.[46] Yelping creatures[47] will fill them. There too will be the ostriches,[48] and demons[49] in the form of goats will dance there.

22 Once in Babylon's palaces there was song and merriment, now the shrieking and howl of wild animals.[50] In similar language Milton[51] describes the flood:

And in their palaces,
Where luxury late reigned, sea-monsters whelped
And stabled.

---

[46] צִיִּים inhabitants of the צִיָּה, the dry steppes. Sometimes they are men, Isa. 23:13; Ps. 72:9; sometimes animals; cf. Isa. 34:14 and Jer. 50:39. The reference is not to any specific animal.

[47] אָח — Possibly Ar. *'ahha,* "to groan, sigh," is instructive. Cf. Akk. *aḫu,* "jackal." The context seems to demand reference to some animal.

[48] Cf. Isa. 34:13; 43:20; Mic. 1:8; Job 30:29. The reference is probably to the ostrich or to some unclean bird. Ar. *wa'nah* is the rocky, hard land, hence, "daughters of the wasteland."

[49] שָׂעִיר — A he-goat or a hairy being. In some passages it apparently designates a demon in goat-form, e.g., Lev. 17:7; 2 Chron. 11:15, where they were objects of idolatrous worship. B here renders δαιμόνια and both Targ. and Syr. "demons." Calvin thinks the reference is to devils who will produce terror in solitary places and will there deceive by their tricks. Alexander rules out all reference to demons as being an accommodation to superstition. But the prophet may use poetical language without sharing in popular superstition. The passage does not teach the actual existence of such creatures. For examples of popular superstition, cf. *Ta 'abata Sharran* (the goat becomes a demon); Horace, *Odes,* I:1:31; Vergil, *Eclogues,* 5:73. Gesenius gives testimony to the belief in the existence of such beings near Samara on the Euphrates.

[50] "to answer" — Probably "to shriek"; cf. Exod. 32:18; a s. verb with following subj. in the pl. m. This is genuine Semitic usage, and there is no need for emendation to the pl. (*BH*). The reference is to the howling animals, probably jackals. Wiseman ("Secular Records in Confirmation of the Scriptures," *Victorian Institute,* 1954, p. 36) renders, 'Moles (?) shall be in their desolated places and lizards in their (once) luxurious palaces.'" But if the verb be retained, both nouns should indicate a howling (answering) animal. In both instances, therefore, I have retained the rendering, "jackal," although aware of the difficulties.

[51] *Paradise Lost,* Book XI, Lines 750-52.

Babylon's palaces! Those houses of pleasure have long since departed. Once they were temples of delight,[52] but when judgment strikes, jackals[53] will howl there. Babylon's time for judgment is near at hand. It will not delay. Yet a little, and it will be present. Will Babylon take warning? The days of her existence, in which she may continue as a mighty city, are numbered days. They will not continue, and they will not be lengthened. Nor will our days be lengthened. Our time has not yet come, and now is the day of salvation. May all who read these lines turn to the Lord of all power in humble supplication for mercy. Whosoever calleth upon the name of the Lord will be saved.

---

[52] Delitzsch points out that the use of ל was a sarcastic turn. Cf. Rev. 18:2.

[53] תנים — Generally taken of jackals, although, according to Gesenius, Abu-l-walid applied it to a snake.

Special Note to Chapter Thirteen

Donald M. Wiseman has published the text of the inscribed prism of Sargon II from Nimrud, discovered in the excavations of 1952-3.[a] Lines 7-44 are of miscellaneous content. They describe rich offerings brought to the deities of Babylon and other Babylonian cities. Two distant islands[b] send tribute, for they have heard of the great prestige of the Assyrian king. The king has his deeds inscribed upon a stone stele in Cyprus. The account of the ruin of Babylon may be rendered as follows:[c]

At that time[d] the way which leads from (....)
To come to Babylon the fortress[e] of —
Was not open, not passable (was) its road.
The land was desert[f] from days long past
In its midst travel was quite cut short
Its way was quite difficult and
There was no path in existence[g]

---

[a] "Iraq," 14 (1952), p. 28.

[b] These were Dilmun and Ia', a district of Iadnana (Cyprus).

[c] The description of the ruin of Babylon, possibly taken from some larger account, was probably written in 710-709 B.C.

[d] Note the emphasis upon the "day" in Isa. 13:6, 9, 13, 22.

[e] maḫazu — the center of the worship of Enlil and Ninlil. Isaiah calls it the glory of kingdoms.

[f] ma-ad-bar — Heb. miḏ-bār. Short a may shift to short i in a closed, unaccented syllable; cf. Isa. 13:20ff.; 14:17.

[g] la šit-ku-nu da-rag-gu; cf. Isa. 13:20.

As for the inaccessible parts thorns
Thistles and jungle
Had prevailed over them, and dogs
And jackals in their recesses
Assembled and huddled together (?) like lambs.
In that desert country Arameans
And Suti, tent dwellers,[h]
Fugitives, treacherous, a plundering race[i]
Had pitched their dwellings, and had
    blocked passage.
There were settlements in their midst
Which for many days past
Had fallen into ruin
Over their cultivated ground channel and
    sown land
Did not exist, but was woven over with spiders' webs
Their rich meadows had become like a
    wilderness
Their cultivated grounds (were forsaken of)
    the sweet harvest song[j]
Grain was quite cut off.
The jungle I cut down, the thorn and thistle
With flames I burned, the Arameans, a
    plundering people
With arms I cast down; as for the
    lions
And wolves, I slaughtered them
The districts of the former wilderness
    — I took
And people of hostile lands, captives
    of my hands
I placed (?) — in their midst.

[h] Cf. Isa. 13:20.
[i] Cf. Vergil in speaking of the Aequi: "A plundering race, still eager to invade, On spoil they live, and make of theft a trade."
[j] Cf. Isa. 16:10 *zi-im-ru ta-a-bu.* Cf. A. Leo Oppenheim: "Assyriological Gleanings," in *BASOR*, No. 103, pp. 11-14.

c. *The fall of the Babylonian king* (14:1-11)

1 For the Lord will have mercy upon Jacob and will choose again Israel, and will cause them to rest upon their land; and the stranger will be joined unto them and they shall be attached unto the house of Jacob.

2 And peoples shall take them and shall bring them unto their place, and the house of Israel shall take possession of them upon the land of the Lord, for slaves and maid servants; and they shall be captors of their captors and shall rule over their oppressors.

3 And it shall come to pass in the day of the Lord, causing thee to rest from thy toil and from thy disquietude, and from the hard service which was imposed upon thee.

4 Then thou shalt raise this proverb against the king of Babylon, and thou shalt say, How hath the oppressor ceased; the haughty city hath ceased.

5 The Lord hath broken the staff of the wicked, the scepter of rulers.

6 He who smites the people in wrath without cessation — ruling nations in wrath as the hunted one without restraint.

7 At rest, quiet is the whole earth. They burst forth into singing.

8 Yea, the cypresses rejoice at thee, the cedars of Lebanon, saying, Now that thou art lain down, the feller shall not come up against us.

9 Sheol from beneath is moved for thee to meet thee at thy coming; it rouses for thee the giants, all the he-goats of the earth; it raises from their thrones all the kings of the nations.

10 All of them will answer and will say unto thee, Also thou hast become weak as we, thou hast become like unto us.

11 Thy pride is brought down to the grave, the music of thy harps: the worm is spread under thee, thy covering is maggots.

1 With what word of blessing and comfort does this chapter begin! In the previous chapter we learned that, because of her sin, Babylon must and will fall. Now, the prophet gives us a second reason: Babylon must perish because it was the purpose of God to raise and exalt His people. Babylon had been but an instrument in the hands of God for the accomplishment of His sovereign purpose of redemption. Toward Israel He had love, and it was His particular love which is now declared to be at work. In order that the Redeemer may come, Babylon must be destroyed. Thus, God's people may return from bondage, and the way lies open for the advent of the Saviour.

In this first verse we have in germ form the entire blessed message of comfort which Isaiah develops in the last twenty-seven chapters of his book. Again Yahweh will show mercy,[54] he declares, and again He will choose His people.[55] Once before He had shown mercy and once before He had chosen them when they were suffering under the oppression of Egypt. Now they are in captivity to Babylon but the Babylonian captivity is merely a type or symbol of the deeper degradation that covered the people. The great bondage which held them captive was that of sin from which, Isaiah was later to declare, there could be deliverance only through the Servant of the Lord.

There must be a second beginning. When they were in bondage to Egypt, the first great hostile world power, God formed His people into a theocratic nation. So great was their sin, however, that the theocracy had to be disbanded, and once again the people, in more or less disorganized state, were in bondage to a foreign hostile power. Babylon is a type of the great enemy of God's people, the Antichrist. There must be another deliverance and a new beginning. The beginning this time, however, was not to be under Moses. It would consist rather in a return unto the land of promise,[56] followed by a period of gloom. When the nation had all but lost the true understanding of the purposes of God, Christ would come to sit upon the throne of David and to reign there forever. The mercy of which Isaiah here speaks and the choice to which He refers are those which bring us to Christ.

God's choice and mercy will involve causing the nation to rest in its own land. The verb which the prophet employs signifies the placing of a person in a particular spot after his removal from elsewhere. But what is meant by placing the people in their land? Does the prophet merely have in mind the restoration from

54 Duhm thinks that vv. 1-4a are not historical, for the idea of Israel's receiving mercy because of Babylon's destruction is said to be characteristic of later Judaism. This loses sight of the Biblical-theological significance of the passage.

55 In reality there is no second choice. Having elected His people God never repents of His choice (Rom. 11:29). When, however, He punishes that people it may seem to them that He has cast them off (Ps. 74:1). The exile was so great a punishment that its end may be graphically termed a second choice. Both in the deliverance from Egypt (Deut. 7:6, 7, etc.) and in the second deliverance (Zech. 1:17; 2:16) the term בחר is employed (note the use of עוד in these latter passages).

56 As God caused man to rest in the garden (Gen. 2:15), He causes His people to rest upon their land. The expression "to cause them to rest in their land" is figurative for a return to the establishment of the Davidic dynasty in the Messianic age.

432

Babylonian exile? In Palestine the old theocracy was not to be re-established, and the people would still be under a foreign rule. Many, indeed, were content to remain in Babylon. Possibly their physical lot there was just as satisfactory as it would have been in Palestine.

If we read the text more closely, we shall see that something more is intended than a mere return to Palestine. In this promise God shows mercy and choice, and He fulfills to the nation the ancient promises made to the patriarchs. Unto these people the sojourner is to incline, and they are to be attached to the house of Jacob. Here is the heart of the matter. In being attached to the house of Jacob, the people would align themselves with the promises made to the ancient patriarch. The being attached to the house of Jacob was wrought through the coming of Christ in whom the house of Jacob came to its fullest and truest expression.

When the Lord showed mercy to His people, then the sojourner would join himself to them.[57] The sojourner was a person who lived outside his own homeland. In Israel he formed a distinct class. He enjoyed certain privileges at the hands of the Jews, and in turn adopted certain of the Jewish religious practices. Using the ideas which characterized the Old Testament dispensation, Isaiah thus teaches that at the time when God shows mercy to His people, the sojourner will be joined to those people. Here, in other words, is a prophecy of the inclusion of the Gentiles into the kingdom.

2 When God shows mercy, the relation between the captive and the captor will be reversed. The Babylonians[58] will take the Jews and bring them to their homeland. Isaiah does not name the Babylonians, but here merely designates them as "peoples." The Jews will be brought to their own homeland, the place that had been promised to them afore by God Himself. This is an emphatic designation of Canaan. Palestine is their land. Isaiah now makes Israel the subject of his sentence, and not merely

---

[57] Cf. Isa. 56:3, 6; Zech. 2:15; Num. 18:2. That God's purposes of the inclusion of the sojourners into the kingdom should be accomplished, the preservation of the chosen people was necessary.

[58] Note the *m* sound in 2a. The people are not the Jews, but persons distinct from the Jews, who proved to be the Babylonians. Lit., "and they will appropriate them unto themselves for a possession." Note the acc. suffix with the reflexive stem. The verb might be active; cf. Lev. 25:46; Num. 33:54; Rom. 15:26, 27.

Israel, but the house of Israel, the nation as chosen by God, the true Davidic dynasty, and the true people. They cause their captors to inherit the land of Yahweh. The promise had been made to Israel, but the land which she was to inherit was the Lord's, and only those could dwell therein to whom He gave permission. Israel is to bring enemies into the Lord's land and to cause them to inherit it. This promise was not fulfilled in the return of the Jews from Babylonian bondage, but is being fulfilled when the Gentiles who oppose God are conquered through the house of Israel, the Israel of God, the church, and are subdued by the Holy Spirit and made heirs of the promises. The deliverance from Babylon is made the basis of the promise, for the deliverance from Babylon was but typical of Christ's greater salvation.

The enemy will dwell upon the land as slaves and as maid servants.[59] Israel will not serve them, but they will serve her, and through her will serve her God. They had led her captive, but now Israel will act toward them as a captor. Once they had oppressed Israel, but now she will rule over her former oppressors. Through Christ the heathen are being spiritually subdued; that is to say, through Christ working by means of His ministers and missionaries, they are being subdued. Only in that last great day will everything be fully subject to Him.

3 In the time of the deliverance the people will sing a song in which the downfall of the king of Babylon is celebrated. By means of this song of the redeemed, the overthrow of the king is made more vivid and graphic. In the present verse, we are given merely a protasis, the conclusion or apodosis of the sentence appearing in verse 4.

Rest will be given to the people, and it will be given by the Lord. At the time that He gives them rest, they will sing, for they will rest from their tormenting trouble[60] and suffering, and from vexations of all kinds. As in the first bondage, so in this one, there was a hard work of slavery from which deliverance was needed. This hard work that they were made to serve was the condition

---

59 It is an enduring condition, and the concept is based upon Lev. 25:43, 46, 53. 14:1, 2 goes back to chap. 11, which in turn is based on Deut. 30:1-10.

60 Note the sharpened pointing of the prep. in מַרְגֵּזְךָ. Cf. 1 Sam 23:28; 2 Sam. 18:16. *GKC*, #22s describes M as exhibiting a kind of virtual strengthening. "From the long period of Israel's toil, and the disquieting mental agitation of the bondslave the Lord has wrought deliverance."

of their servitude.[61] To be delivered therefrom would be the work of God. Here is then a second exodus, a second deliverance, only one far greater than that from Egypt or even from Babylon.

4 Now follows the apodosis of the preceding sentence. When God gives to His people rest, then they will take up on their lips this proverb.[62] Isaiah addresses the people as though it were an individual. In that day, he says to them, thou shalt raise, in a musical sense, this satirical poem. It is the song which they will sing over the downfall of the enemy, even the king of Babylon.[63] This king is not an individual, historical person, but rather the Babylonian dynasty conceived as an ideal person. The standpoint seems to suppose that the Babylonian dynasty has been completely destroyed. Are we then to understand the song as actually having been sung by the exiles on their way home to Palestine? No, for at that time the enemy had not been destroyed in fullness and entirety. Perhaps we can approach an understanding of the situation somewhat as follows: When Isaiah wrote, the great might of Babylon had not made itself fully manifest. Assyria at that day was in the ascendancy. But Babylon would come, the agent of God in bringing about the overthrow of the theocracy. With Babylon the ancient order instituted at Sinai would be done away. No longer was there to be a nation of God. Babylon, therefore, was the great foe, far greater even than Assyria. But Babylon had been a proudly exulting foe.[64] She had acted as though her own hand and prowess had given her the victory. She, therefore, must fall, and fall completely. Her overthrow would thus signalize that the way was fully open for the Redeemer to come, and for the promises of God to be fulfilled. Babylon's destruction betokened full victory for God's people. For that reason it is here celebrated in such strong terms.

---

61 עָבַד — "wherewith it was worked with thee." The subj. is an indefinite nominative understood, and the prep. serves to render the verb transitive. Cf. Ar. *ba litta 'diah*. אֲשֶׁר is not subj. but equivalent to the internal object.

62 וְנָשָׂאתָ — The accent *mil 'el* is in accordance with the general rule that with *wāw* cons. remains *mil 'el*. The same is true of וְאָמַרְתָּ, although, when the penult is closed, or when both penult and antepenult are long syllables. Here the penult is a long syllable, but the antepenult short, so the accent with *wāw* cons. remains *mil 'el*. The same is true of וְאָמַדְתָּ, although, when the word is in pause, the accent does not shift to *milra'*.

63 "oppressor" — Cf. 9:3. Fischer thinks the reference is to the last king of a dynasty, but the whole description tends to preclude such a reference.

64 Years ago Drechsler pointed out that 3:5 really supported the reading מַרְהֵבָה now attested by 1Q, and supported by all the old versions.

The proverb begins as a lamentation, "How hath the oppressor ceased," and the people's astonishment takes the form of a question. There is reason for astonishment and surprise. The oppressor who had made life bitter for God's people has ceased to exist. He who had dealt so haughtily has come to an end.

5 Here is the answer to the previous question. Yahweh, the God of all creation, has acted. There was a rod,[65] and it had been used by wicked ones against God's people; and there was a scepter wielded by rulers and tyrants, but Yahweh has broken them both. By the rod and staff the wicked and the rulers exercised their authority. To accomplish their will they had to strike and to smite. Their power, however, is gone, for Yahweh, whom they despised, has intervened and acted. He had broken their power.

6 Now we learn about the tyrant of Babylon. Incessantly he was smiting peoples in his wrath.[66] His blows were not reasoned, but were the manifestation of his unreasoning anger. He was unfit to rule. Babylon can do nothing more than destroy the people of God. There was no turning aside of these blows; they fell continually. Nor was the reign one of wisdom, for it was conducted in anger. The one who was hunted[67] was ruled without restraint. The ruler without restraint hunted out people and smote them. A true picture indeed of Babylon's conquests.

7 How powerful and mighty must the enemy have been, for his death now brings joys to all the earth. No longer need the earth

65 Note the reflections upon Egyptian bondage, Exod. 2:11; 5:14, 16. Note the asyndetical placing together of staff and scepter. The genitives may be appositional, e.g., staff of the wicked ones — wicked staff.

66 The participles of v. 6 may be construed with "oppressor" or with "rod" and "scepter." Note the const. before the adverbial phrase containing a negative. The const. מכה is also a second object cognate to the verb, "striking peoples in wrath a blow without withdrawal."

67 מרדף forms alliteration with מכה . *Kibbutz* appears in place of *Qametz-hatuf,* probably because of the following *daghesh.* Döderlein proposed to read מרדת , making the noun cognate with the verb. This seems to be supported by Targ. and possibly by B. 1Q has the consonants of M, and Syr., Saadia, and Vulg. take the form as active. Alexander favors the emendation, but he makes the sage observation, "And yet the point in which the parallelism fails may sometimes be the very one designed to be the salient or emphatic point of the whole sentence." I propose to accept the consonants of M and to render by the passive. If taken as a *hofal,* the form is a *hal* acc. of specification, "as the hunted one without sparing."

be stirred up by the machinations and movements of the tyrant, but rather she is at rest.[68] Not only Israel, but the entire world begins to breathe. People break forth, not in hostility, but in song.[69] Isaiah uses a favorite expression, and one which the Arabs also employ when they speak of persons breaking forth in speech. Song cannot be repressed; when the enemy has been removed by the goodness of God, the heart bursts forth into singing.

Isaiah's description reminds of the language of the so-called 'Israel Stele' of Merenptah (c. 1223-1211 B.C.) after he had quelled revolts in Palestine, and had made his western borders secure against attacking invaders. We render a few lines:

"There is great rejoicing in Egypt,
Exulting has come forth from the towns of To-meri;—
One may walk freely on the way, without fear in men's hearts.
Fortresses are left to themselves;
Walls are open, available for the messengers."

8 How Isaiah loved trees, and how characteristic of him to bring them into the picture of general, world-wide rejoicing.[70] Well could the trees rejoice, for they had good reason so to do. Here, too, is gradation. Not only does the world break forth into singing, but even the trees do so, for among them the Babylonians had wrought damage.[71] The cedars gave to Lebanon her greatest renown, but after them came the cypresses. In the Wady Brissa in Lebanon, Nebuchadnezzar had built a road for obtaining cedars, and it may be that some such activities as this lay at the base of the prophet's thought, even though the Babylonians were to carry

[68] "quiet" — The root is used in Judg. 3:30, "for the rest that the people had after deliverance." Cf. Isa. 18:4. The *Hifil* appears in 7:4; 30:15; 32:17. For the Israel stele, cf. *ANET*, pp. 378a.

[69] These are Isaianic expressions; cf. 44:23; 49:13; 52:9; 54:1; 55:12. Arabic uses the phrase *shaqshaqa 'lkalam*, "to let speech break through or to speak loudly." The pl. verb seems to refer to earth's inhabitants as distinct from earth itself.

[70] To mention the trees is Isaianic. They form part of one great universal picture in which all nature rejoices. Cf. Isa. 35:1, 2; 44:23; 49:13; 52:9; 55:12; Ezek. 31:15-17; Ps. 65:13 and note the *Eclogues* 1:49; 5:20, 27, 62.

[71] The absence of a word such as "saying" makes the speech more lively. The particle introduces a clause subordinate to and dependent upon the main sentence. The verb יַעֲלֶה may be taken as a future, "will never come up," the imp. expressing a fact of definite occurrence. Brockelmann, however, p. 151, renders as a preterite, "*kam kein Holzfäller über uns.*" This is not necessary. The definite article, "the feller," indicates the well-known enemy of the forest.

on their activities long after Isaiah's death.[72] Once the enemy is dead, the trees need fear no longer that a woodsman will come to cut them down. Their enemy, too, has been removed, and so with the remainder of creation they join in song.

9 On earth all was quiet and still and there was singing. One place, however, was agitated. Sheol,[73] where the departed spirits go, and where the wicked await the judgment under the reign of death, was agitated with respect to the tyrant. Inhabitants of earth had thought that he had merely lain down. As a matter of fact, he was coming to Sheol, and Sheol awaited his coming. In the preceding verse Isaiah had led us to the heights; now he brings us to Sheol beneath the earth. This place has a lively interest in the tyrant and looks with expectation to his arrival. The shadows of the underworld, the shadowy corporeity of the spirits, have aroused themselves, even they who once were princes, the he-goats[74] of earth. The kings of the nations who have departed this life await in expectation the king of Babylon, the king who above all others had caused trouble for God's people. He is now to take his place among them as one of them.

10 No one of these departed kings will miss the opportunity of addressing the new arrival.[75] With no exceptions, all will take up the taunt. "Thou, even thou," they will say. "Thou hast been

---

72 Tiglath-pileser I says, "To the Lebanon I went. I cut timbers of cedars for the temple of Anu and Adad, the great gods, my lords, and transplanted (them) to Assyria." Cf. Luckenbill: *Ancient Records of Assyria and Babylonia.* 1926, Vol. I, p. 98.

73 Life in Sheol is pictured according to the analogy of life on earth. The kings, for example, sit on their thrones, and so the distinctions of this life seem in some sense to be perpetuated in Sheol. Cf. Ezek. 32:21ff. and 1 Sam. 28:15ff. "Sheol" may be either m. or f. and so may be construed with both verbs. The nearer verb agrees with the subj. as f. Render "Sheol beneath," not "Sheol from beneath." רפאים — Ug. *rpum.* Driver (*CML*, p. 10) believes that the root is to be found in *rapa'*, "bound up, healed," and that the words describe the dead as a bound-up community of the nether world. Here (and also in Isa. 26:14, 19; Prov. 2:18; 9:18; 21:16; Job 26:5) the word denotes the shades of the departed. Ug. *rpu* may denote a ghost or shade. I can see no warrant for comparison with the εἴδωλα καμόντων of Homer (*Iliad* 23:72). Rowley suggests that behind the conception of Sheol lay the Babylonian Arallu, a subterranean cave in which all the dead without distinction were gathered. Cf. Jastrow: *Hebrew and Babylonian Traditions,* 1914, pp. 197ff.

74 Cf. Zech. 10:3 and *Hamasa,* "I fought with their goats (*kabshahum*), nor did I see any escape from fighting with the goats."

75 The answer amounts to a retort. Cf. Ezek. 32:21. The words of the shades are found only in 10b. There is no need to turn this into a question.

brought down from strength into the condition of weakness, like ourselves." What a contrast! From the peak of the development of power to the weakness of shadowy life — there lies the history of the enemy of God's people. Thou hast become like us! The kings now make themselves the standard of comparison. Between them and the newcomer there is no difference. Thou — us. "Thou, of all kings; thou, the great enemy of God; thou — at the pinnacle of power; thou hast become like us."

11 Again Isaiah brings us to the central point of the proverb.[76] The haughtiness of Babylon, the pride which had been her governing and motivating power, is brought low to the grave, even to Sheol. And with this pride disappeared the beauty of Babylonian life. Daniel tells us about the music of the Babylonians. This music was a symbol of the luxury found in the royal court; it meant pleasure and ease. No longer, however, is there spread under the king a carpet of luxury, but in its stead only the worm. This is a picture of decomposing bodies in the grave. At one time there was a variety of coverings, rich and varied garments. Now there is only one — worms. Pomp, glory, and pride can lead not to God, but only to worms. Isaiah wisely uses this strong language that we may ponder our own condition, and align ourselves not with one whose doom is sure but with Him in whose hand is all power and strength.

d. *The end of the boastful king* (14:12-21)

12 How art thou fallen from heaven, Helel, son of the morning, thou hast been felled to the ground, thou who didst weaken the nations.

13 And thou, thou saidst in thy heart, I shall ascend to the heavens; above the stars of God I shall raise my throne, and I shall sit in the mount of meeting, in the sides of Saphon.

14 I shall ascend upon the high places of the clouds; I shall make myself like the most High.

15 But unto Sheol thou shalt be brought down, unto the sides of the pit.

16 They who look at thee will gaze, they shall look at thee attentively, saying, Is this the man who made the earth to quake, who caused kingdoms to tremble?

17 Who placed the world a wilderness, and its cities he has overthrown: its captives he did not set free to go homewards.

---

[76] יצע — pual perf. If the noun is not properly a collective, but is used as a collective, the verb may be s. Here the verb is m. but the noun f.

18 All the kings of the nations, even all of them, lie in glory, every one in his own house.

19 But thou, thou hast been cast from thy grave like a despised branch, the raiment of the slain, those pierced with the sword, those going down to the stones of the pit, like a trampled carcass.

20 Thou shalt not be joined with them in burial, for thy land thou hast destroyed, thy people thou hast slain; let the seed of evildoers be named no more for ever.

21 Prepare for his sons a place of slaughter, because of the iniquity of their fathers. Let them not arise and inherit the earth, and fill the face of the world with cities.

12 The Babylonian king had boasted. Yet, he, the morning star,[77] the shining one who is son of the morning, has fallen to the

---

[77] To fall from heaven is to fall from a great political height. So Cicero, *ad Atticum*, 2:21; *Philippicum*, 2:41; Horace, *Epodes*, 17:41; Her. 3:64. Note what is said of Antiochus in Dan. 8:10. In Num. 24:17 the star designates the Messiah. Cf. Rev. 22:16. Note also Ar. *kaukab 'lqaum* (star of the people or princes), the designation Bar Kochba (son of a star) and Ecclus. 50:6. König suggests that the description of the king as a fallen star reflects ironically upon his own boastful claims, 10:8-11, 13ff. Cf. 47:8 and Ezek. 28:2, 6, 9.

The proper name is Helel ben Shachar (not to be emended to Helal). In Ugaritic *shahru* (dawn) is the name of one of the children born to a woman seduced by the god El (*Shachar and Shalim*, 2:18). Possibly he is to be thought of as the god of dawn. Heb. *shachar* ("dawn"; actually the instant just before dawn) and the cognates (Ar. *sahar;* Akk. *šêru;* Aram., *šahrâ*) have about the same meaning.

The form *helel* has been derived from a root, "to howl," which is followed by A, Peshitto and Jerome. In the light of Ug., however, the word is best derived from *hll*, "to shine." Cf. 13:10; Job 29:3; 31:26; 41:10. Cf. Akk. *ellu*, f. *ellitu*, which is applied to Ishtar. Grelot suggests *halilu* > *elilu* > *ellu*, and that *elil* (*u*) comes into the Bible through Phoenician (cf. *VT*, 6, 1956, pp. 303-4). He thus identifies Helal with Ishtar, as does Albright (*ARI*, p. 84), who thinks that we have here a quotation from Canaanite poetry. Note also Ar. *halla*, "shine," Vulg. *lucifer*, and B ἑωσφόρος. Venus was regarded by the Arabs as *zahra*, "the bright shining one." According to Jacob, p. 161, and Childs (*Myth and Reality in the Old Testament*, 1960, pp. 67ff.), Helel was certainly a divine person. Jacob says he was reduced to the proportions of a historic individual, and Childs thinks that he was an upstart against El who was thwarted. This is mere conjecture. Isaiah may simply use the phrase to indicate the morning star. Of all the stars it would be the brightest, but that clear star, unique among the stars of heaven, would fall upon carcasses.

Verse 12b changes the figure and pictures the king as a tree that is felled. In triumphing over nations, thus bringing defeat upon them, the king is himself cast down.

We may note a bilingual text — Hattic and Hittite, *KUB*, xxviii, 5 — which speaks of the moon or moon-god falling from heaven. No one, however, saw him. Then the storm god sent rain after him — "so that fear took hold of him [and fright seized him]"; cf. *ANET*, p. 120a.

ground. From the height of heaven where he had shone in glory and splendor, he has tumbled in disgrace to the depth of earth. Like a stately cedar, he has been felled. His reign had been one that threw away and weakened the nations, now he himself is weakened and thrown away. "As a star," the prophet addresses him, "thou hast brought an overthrow over nations, so now thou thyself art overthrown."

Tertullian, Gregory the Great, and others have referred this verse to the fall of Satan, described in Luke 10:18. But the present passage pictures the end of a tyrannical reign. The Babylonian king had desired to be above God, and so fell from heaven. He falls to Sheol, and his power is done away. Not so Satan. His fall was against God, but he continues yet his tyrannical acts against God's people. "His doom is sure," for Christ has died, but not until the final judgment will he be confined to the lake of fire. Inasmuch, then, as this passage describes a king's downfall and removal from the scene, it cannot apply to Satan.

13 What a contrast! "But thou," we may paraphrase the thought, "thou hadst intended a different end for thyself.[78] Falling from heaven was not in thy plan; rather, thou didst purpose to ascend to heaven to be like God." Only one can rule in heaven, even God, and when the Babylonian king wanted to place his throne there, even above God's stars, he was planning to exalt himself against and above God. No man would give this king his throne;

---

[78] The stars of El, thinks Jacob (p. 34) express the idea of divinity as subordinate to that of power. What is powerful, he holds, is divine. But in the véry fact that the stars belong to El (note the const.) God shows that He is superior to them. Cf. Ibn Doreid 5:111, "if anyone would rise higher in generosity, and glory, unto the heaven let him mount."

The imperfects without *wāw* cons. give distinctness to the enunciation of separate particulars: "I shall ascend — I shall raise — I shall sit." The mountain is not Zion but Mt. Zaphon or Mons Cassius, the modern *Jebel al 'aqra*, the bald or snow-capped mount about 25 or 30 miles northeast of Ugarit, from where it is visible. In Ug. Baal is the god of this mountain, and is designated *b 'l spn* and also *el spn*.

Among the ancients there was widespread belief in a mountain where the gods gathered. Among the Indians the mountain was Meru, among the Persians Albordsch and among the Babylonians Esarra.

The pagan mythology best known to the Hebrews would be the Canaanitish. Hence, Isaiah places in the mouth of the king the language of Canaanitish paganism and polytheism that the men of Judah may learn the extent of his boastful pretensions. This would seem to militate against Babylon as the place of composition of Isa. 14. The boasting typifies that of the man of sin, 2 Thess. 2:4.

441

he intended to erect it himself, and to do so where he pleased. To reign from any ordinary earthly city was not sufficient; the haughtiness of Babylon had to reign from above the stars which belong to God Himself. Exalted as are these stars, this king's throne must be even more exalted. Where the gods meet upon their holy mountain of Saphon, he purposed to take his place. The king speaks as a heathen. He believes in many gods and he is perfectly ready to place himself as an equal in the council of these gods. Against the true God he manifests enmity — he would be above that God — but with the gods of the day he is ready to be an equal. His language calls to mind the description of the man of sin (II Thess. 2:4), of whom the Babylonian king is a type: "Who opposeth and exalteth himself above all that is called God, or that is worshipped; so that he as God sitteth in the temple of God, shewing himself that he is God." When we thus look back at his plans for his self-deification, we may understand why God acted and why such a king should finally have worms as his covering.

14 Here is unbounded arrogance.[79] How could the Babylonian spirit ever plan such a thing? The answer is that Babylon had sought to render void the work of God. God's plan was to bring salvation to the world through the coming of a Saviour. Babylon had set herself in opposition to God; she would thwart His plans by means of self-exaltation against the true God. We are not to understand any of the individual Babylonian kings as specifically ever having uttered precisely these words, but what they express is rather the intention of the Babylonian power or spirit.

In the last analysis it was to be either Babylon or God. Almost every word in this and the preceding verse is designed to emphasize the concept of height. Even the high places of the clouds, as high as one could go, the king purposed to scale. The most High is exalted, but the king intends to become yet more exalted. To ride upon the clouds is God's prerogative, and the king thus shows that he wishes to be equal with and to rival God. Intentions such as these are the prelude to downfall. "Ye shall be like God," the

---

[79] במתי — To the normal f. pl. ending a second const. ending is added, *bâ-mô-ṭê*. Apparently the *Ḥolem* is regarded as representing short *u*, and hence, a *hatef-qametz* is inserted in const. But the f. pl. has naturally long *a*. A consistent writing would seem to be *bâ-mô-ṭê*.

Probably there is a Canaanitish flavoring in the language of the king. Cf. Ἐλιοῦν in Philo-Byblous and Eusebius; *Praeparatio Evangelica*, 1:10. אדמה is *Hiṭpael*, "I shall regard myself to be like."

serpent had said in the garden. Whenever men have designed to raise themselves to an equality with God, a downfall follows.

15 Again we have the awful contrast between what the Babylonian spirit desired for itself and the end for which it was destined. Twice before the prophet has mentioned this contrast, and we may compare verses 14 and 15 with 8 and 9 and also with 11 and 12. Isaiah begins the verse with an adversative particle. The king would ascend to heaven, but, as a matter of fact, he will be brought low to hell. The language of the nation of Israel, who took up the lament, has imperceptibly passed into the mouth of the prophet himself, who now directly addresses the enemy king. In the nation's song, the downfall of the king was regarded as already having taken place. In Isaiah's own address, the downfall is future. There is no contradiction, for the people are idealized as singing over the fall of a mighty enemy, and it is to be expected that they would describe that fall as already having occurred. Isaiah, on the other hand, looking to the future, naturally describes the fall as not yet having taken place.

Sheol is set in the greatest contrast to the heights of heaven, and not only is the king to be brought down to Sheol but even to its deepest parts. Indeed, every word that is used in this verse seems to have been chosen in order to accentuate the opposite of height. The "pit" is employed sometimes as a synonym of Sheol, as in the expression, "They that go down to the pit." Isaiah refers not merely to the grave but to Sheol itself, and the expression, "the sides of the pit" even implies that there are distinctions of position in Sheol, and that this king was to be brought to the lowest part. We may then note the following contrasts between this verse and verse 13:

Sheol — mount of meeting — depths of the pit — extreme parts of Saphon.

The contrast is again shown by the brevity of the present verse. Both 13 and 14 were long verses, for the aspirations of the king were long and pretentious. To tell of his end, however, only a few words are needed. The deeper in Sheol one falls, the more awful his condition.

16 Where do men behold the fallen king? Do we here have a description of what takes place in Sheol or, rather, of how men on earth will regard the fallen corpse of the king? The latter view is probably correct. What takes place here is not in Sheol but

above ground, when men look with astonishment at the one who
was once so haughty and powerful. The mighty king now lies
on the ground, a fallen corpse. "Thy seers," says the prophet,
for they are the only ones who still belong to the king, "unto thee
they will gaze."[80] Here is an emphasis. The king's seers gape at
him. He is the object of their fervent stare, a contemplation filled
with unbelieving, uncomprehending surprise. To this king, lying
on the ground, they pay full and complete attention. All other
objects will be shut out from their view. "Is it possible," they will
ask, "that this man, who ruled in such splendor and glory, now
lying a vile corpse on the earth, is actually the same one that
was going to shake the earth and cause kingdoms to tremble?"
When that question is asked, the beholders realize how impossible
the king's claims had been. What misplaced ambition; only God
can shake the earth and cause kingdoms to tremble!

17 An enumeration of the king's triumphs continues. The cultivated, inhabited world he turned into a wilderness and he up-
rooted its cities. His prisoners he did not set free so that they could
go to their own homes.[81] That had not been his intention.

18 How different was the end of the Babylonian king from that
of other rulers! In the ancient East much stress was placed upon
the importance of burial monuments. All kings — and in order
that he may stress that there are no exceptions, Isaiah uses the
word twice — all of them,[82] indeed lie in state and honor in their
tombs. Honorable burial was the last honor to be paid to royalty.
The deceased kings lie in state, not far from their own land, but
in their own burial vaults. To be left unburied is a disgrace even
for a private person; how much more so for a king.

19 *But thou!* . . . again we have emphasis. How different from
the stately burial of most rulers is the disgrace which comes upon

80 Cf. Ezek. 28:17-19. The participles without the article, yet modifying a
definite noun, have the force of a relative clause.

81 The sentence continues with an anarthrous participle concluding with a
finite verb, an additional clause being added, as in Isa. 44:26b. We may render: "his prisoners he let not loose, nor sent them back to their home." Cf.
GKC, #117o, p. 366. Possibly there may be a reflection upon Babylon's
refusal to allow the people of God to return home, whereas Cyrus did so
permit them; cf. Jer. 50:33.

82 ביתו is probably not a palace, but a mausoleum, the grave; cf. Job 30:
23; Ecc. 12:5 and the Phoenician inscriptions.

For Egyptian belief, cf. *ANET,* p. 417, "Make rich thy house of the west
and adorn the place where thy tomb is."

the Babylonian king.[83] He has been cast away from his grave. Isaiah does not mean that he has been cast out of the grave that had been rightfully his, that he had been in that grave and then later thrown out of it. He means that the king had been thrown out in a direction away from the grave. He had in fact never been in that grave. Men cut off a despised branch from the tree because it deprives the tree of vitality. Inasmuch as it is injurious to the growth of the tree they cast it away in disgust. The rejected king is of no more value than the cast-away tendrils. He is clothed with the slain, for they cover him, even they who had been pierced by the sword and who go down into the stones of the pit. Sheol is here conceived as in the deepest rocks of the inner earth. One climactic thought finishes the verse. The king is like a body that has been trampled. Can one conceive of deeper degradation?

20 Babylon's king lies covered over with the bodies of those that have been slain. They shall be buried,[84] but not he; he will not be buried as they. Other kings may have done evil, but not like this one. The ruler of Babylon destroyed the land. He had been entrusted with power for a different purpose, but he had misused that power. His reign was one of cruelty. For him there is to be no monument which will cause his name to be remembered. It is better that all remembrance of the seed of evildoers be forgotten for ever.

21 The Babylonian seed must be completely cut off.[85]. To whom is this command addressed? Is it to the Medes? Probably not; in

---

[83] The *hofal* form has *qametz hatuf*, but in Dan. 8:11 is written with *Qibbutz*. The king was cast out in the direction away from the grave in which he was appointed or intended to lie. Cf. *Gilgamesh Epic*, XII:61, "he did not fall on the battlefield of men (for) the underworld had seized him." Note the const. followed by a prep.; cf. 5:11; 9:1, 2; 28:9 and 56:10. "stones of the pit" — The phrase suggests that Sheol is in the deepest rocks of the inner earth, bound in the silence of death (Drechsler).

[84] Verse 19 is a description of the king's unburied condition in contrast to the different state of other deceased rulers. Verse 20 infers that the latter cannot be united with the former in burial. Cf. *Gilgamesh Epic*, XII:150-152. 1Q and A support M, but B goes its own way.

[85] "cities" — Some follow B, Targ., and Syr. and render "enemies." *ASTh* and Jerome support M. The negative in 21b negates three verbs and not merely the verb with which it is immediately construed. Fischer thinks that there may be a reflection upon Nebuchadnezzar's cruelty against Zedekiah, but the passage does not refer to a historical individual as such except in so far as such individuals form part of the entire picture. It is the entirety of the Babylonian kingdom, conceived as the haughty human spirit opposed to God,

fact, probably to no one in particular. The command is general, serving to show that there will be no continuing Babylonian seed. There will never be a revival of the Babylonian empire.

Our understanding of the command will be clarified if we note Alexander's statement: "The dramatic form of the prediction is repeatedly shifted, so that the words of the Jews, of the dead, of the Prophet and of God Himself, succeed each other, as it were, insensibly, and without any attempt to make the points of the transition prominent." For the sons of the Babylonians there awaits only a place of slaughter prepared at God's direction. The prophecy does not deny the truth of individual responsibility. It purports rather to teach that in Babylon enmity against God had grown to such a degree that the empire represented by Babylon had to be wiped out if the purposes of grace were to be realized. It was either Babylon or Christ. Hence, because the fathers had done iniquitously, the sons must be slaughtered. If salvation was to come of the Jews, there could be no continuing Babylonian line.

The sons are not to take any initiative. If they arise, they will possess the earth, for they are insatiable. But they are not to inherit the earth, for that is reserved for the meek, those of God's own choice. If the sons arise, they will build cities throughout the earth, and in that sense will take possession thereof. The Babylonian spirit and culture must cease, for it stands in full opposition and hostility to the kingdom of God.

e. *The destruction of Babylon, Assyria, and Philistia* (14:22-32)

22 And I shall arise against them, saith the LORD of hosts, and I shall cut off from Babylon a name and remnant and progeny and offspring, saith the LORD.

23 And I shall place it for a possession of the porcupine, and pools of water, and will sweep it with a besom, even bringing destruction, saith the LORD of hosts.

24 The LORD of hosts hath sworn, saying, Surely! even as I have planned, so has it come to pass, and even as I have counseled, it shall stand.

---

that is in the prophet's picture. Concerning the downfall of Babylon cf. Dan. 5; Her. 1:191; Xenophon, *Cyro.* 7:5, 15ff. Cf. Isa. 14:19 with *Cyro.* 7:5, 30; and Hengstenberg, *Authenticity of Daniel*, pp. 325, 36. For a survey and discussion of the cuneiform material, cf. J. C. Whitcomb, Jr., *Darius the Mede*, Grand Rapids, 1959.

25 To break Assyria in my land and on my mountains I will trample him, and will turn aside from upon them his yoke, and his burden from off his shoulder shall depart.

26 This is the counsel that is counseled upon all the earth, and this is the hand that is stretched out upon all the nations.

27 For the LORD of hosts hath counseled and who will frustrate him, and his hand is that which is stretched out, and who will turn it back?

28 In the year of the death of king Ahaz was this oracle.

29 Rejoice not, O Philistia, all of thee, because the rod that smote thee is broken, for from the root of the serpent there will go out a poisonous snake, and its fruits will be a flying fiery serpent.

30 And the first-born of the poor will feed, and the needy will lie down in security, and I shall kill thy root with famine, and it shall slay thy remnant.

31 Howl! O gate! cry, O city! dissolved is Philistia, all of thee; for from the north there comes a smoke, and there is no one isolated in his ranks.

32 And how shall one answer the messengers of a nation? That the LORD hath founded Zion, and in it shall the afflicted of his people seek refuge.

22 Babylon is not to arise, but Yahweh, the true God, will arise.[86] And He will arise, not to possess the earth, for the earth is already His — He is Yahweh of hosts — but to cut off Babylon's posterity. His initiation will be directed in a hostile sense against those who belong to Babylon. Those who bear the name of Babylon will be no more, and Babylon will have no remnant. Israel had a remnant, hence, for Israel there would be no complete destruction. Babylon had no remnant, hence, for her, complete destruction was inevitable. The last four nouns of this verse express in the most general and fullest manner the idea of posterity. Each of the two pairs of words forms an alliteration, and the last pair is emphatically all-embracing. No Babylonian empire will ever rise again After the worst of catastrophes, there is usually some survivor, but after this one there is none. Babylon is to be utterly cut off. As though to render this fact the more emphatic, the Scripture adds the words, "saith Yahweh." God has spoken, and His word is irrevocable. Babylon will not rise again.

---

[86] For the use of קוּם cf. 2:19, 21 and the preceding verse. This language is not part of the "burden," as may be seen by the insertion of the words, "thus saith the Lord."

23 If Babylon is to have no descendants nor posterity, what will she have? God now states what He will do with the city.[87] Babylon had wanted to possess the earth; now the very place of Babylon itself will become a possession, not of Babylon's posterity, but of hedgehogs or porcupines which inhabit the desert. There will be stagnating, marshy waters, where only animals, not men, can live. And that Babylon may be swept clean of all traces of its past, the Lord announces that He will sweep the place with a broom which brings destruction. Thoroughly and completely will God sweep it, so that it will be as though there never had been a city there. The once glorious city will be as sweepings. Again the asseveration is made that Yahweh of hosts hath spoken. We have here no mere prognostication of a man; God Himself has uttered His voice, for Babylon was the great enemy of His kingdom.

24 Three times God has spoken, and the threefold recurring *neum,* "oracle," now climaxes in a glorious asseveration upon the part of Yahweh of hosts.[88] Three times in the entire prophecy of Isaiah it is stated that God has sworn; cf. 45:23 and 62:8. The opening of this verse is striking when compared with the closing words of the preceding. We should compare the two statements which stand together: "Hath said Yahweh of hosts — hath sworn Yahweh of hosts." The words of the oath are then given. "Even as I intended, so it has come to pass, and even as I counseled, so will it stand." Of what, however, is the Lord speaking? Isaiah now takes the thoughts which had just been expressed and transfers them from the Babylon of the future to his own present. In this way the whole body of the prophecy is placed in the future. The destiny of Assyria which is now discussed becomes a pledge of the future destiny of Babylon. From this we see that what has just

---

[87] קפד — porcupine, hedgehog; cf. Isa. 34:11; Zeph. 2:14; Ar. *qunfudun;* Eth. *qwenfaz.* 1Q has קפץ, arrow snake. Cf. Strabo 16:1 for a statement concerning hedgehogs on the Euphrates' islands, and Dio. Sic. 2:7. Kimchi states that the rabbis did not know what מאטא meant in this passage, until they heard a woman say, "Fetch a broom and sweep out the house." Note the inf. abs. "and I shall sweep it with a besom, even bringing destruction."

[88] "surely" — "if not." Underlying this formula appears to be the thought, "If I do not do this, then may the Lord do such and such to me." But in actual usage the formula simply means "surely."

The speaking of God is represented by the prophets as coming with varying degrees of emphasis. Here God swears in an oath, a clear evidence that the revelation was verbal. היתה — The f. verb is used with a f. subj. which has not actually been spoken but is in the mind of the writer. The subj. is "what I have planned."

preceded is not intended to have a reference contemporary to Isaiah but describes what is to occur in the future. Verses 24-27 serve as a conclusion to the former passage concerning Babylon in the same manner as 16:13, 14 forms a completion to what has just gone before, or 21:16, 17 to what just precedes it. With this verse therefore we are not beginning a new prophecy.

If we note the two verbs, we see that one of them is a perfect and one an imperfect. What God has intended has come to pass already in the destruction of the Assyrians and what He has counseled will be fulfilled in the future destruction of the Babylonians. This is not to say that when Isaiah spoke Assyria had already been destroyed. That was not the case. `Sennacherib had not yet come. The first verb is a prophetic perfect, and the thought is that just as the doom of Assyria is sure so also is that of Babylon.

25 Here is contained the content of what God has counseled.[89] Assyria was a staff that could be broken. "O Assyria, the rod of mine anger, and the staff in their hand is mine indignation" (Isa. 10:5). Palestine, the promised land, was mountainous, and upon the mountains of the land that peculiarly belongs to God, God will trample His enemy. He will not only break, but He will tread upon the adversary. Assyria's yoke had rested upon the people of God; now God would bend that yoke, and turn aside from their shoulder the burden which Assyria had placed thereon. The deliverance will be of God, and hence, wholly of grace.

26 What has just been stated in the two preceding verses is the counsel which God had counseled.[90] Both the Assyrian and the Babylonian overthrow are partial carryings out of one general all-embracing decree directed against all hostile and opposing powers. Sometimes a large empire is hyperbolically represented as being the entire earth, and in so far as that is the case, the determination of God to destroy Assyria may be called a determination against the entire earth. The counsel which God had taken was of a threaten-

---

[89] Cf. with Isa. 9:3. It is not necessary, however, to follow B, Vulg., *BH*, Duhm, etc., and read a pl. suffix, "their shoulder." The s. may be for dissimilation after the prep. Cf. König, *Syntax*, #348u. The relation between 25b and 26 is similar to that between 1:2b, 3 and 1:4. There is a differentiation between the speaking of God and that of the prophet.

Hendewerk had remarked that Assyria had never been in Palestine. Mowinckel attributes the hope of Israel to the enthronement festival (*HTC*, p. 146). Cf. Appendix III.

[90] Note the paronomasia between noun and attribute.

ing nature. It is God's hand that is stretched out in threat and punishment. If such is the hand stretched out, who can withstand it?

27 Can the sureness and certainty of God's avenging power be more strongly expressed? Who will frustrate His counsel? To ask that question is to answer it. None can frustrate it. Hence, this question clearly shows that Yahweh of hosts is the sovereign God. As Gill remarked: "There's nothing comes to pass but he has purposed, and everything he has purposed does come to pass."[91] Many will seek to frustrate His purpose and to turn back His hand. How tragic to be found fighting against God!

28 The reference is to the prophecy which follows, not to what precedes. The year was probably 727 B.C. which seems also to have been the year of the death of Tiglath-pileser. We are not explicitly told whether this burden was seen before the death of Ahaz or not. Jerome thinks that the message came during the first year of Hezekiah's reign, but the point of importance is not whether it was seen before or after the death, but that the year in which it was seen was the year of Ahaz' death.

29 If Assyria was to be smitten so that she should be destroyed, could not those nations which had suffered at her hand rejoice, and regain their strength so as once again to turn against Judah? One of these nations, close to Judah, who might well rejoice at Assyria's defeat was Philistia. But Philistia is not to rejoice, for what she has suffered under the temporary subjection of Sargon stands only in a preparatory relation to the permanent subjection under God's people which the prophecy declares will come.

David had subdued the Philistines, and later we are told that under Jehoshaphat they paid tribute. Under Jehoram they rebelled, to be again subdued under Uzziah. During Ahaz' reign, however, they shook off the yoke. Philistia was divided into five principal city states, and so the prophet addresses the entire land. "All of thee, Philistia," he cries, "thou art not to rejoice. The rod which smote thee is broken." Assyria had been that rod, the rod of God's agency, the smiting, punishing rod, the rod of cruelty. That rod is now broken and there is no longer a threat. But that is no reason for rejoicing. The oppressor was a serpent, declares

---

91 Quoted by Alexander, *ad loc*. Cf. Amos 3:8. Note force of the article, "his hand is that which is stretched out." The sense requires that the predicate be definite; cf. Gen. 2:11; 45:12.

the prophet, and that serpent has a root. Strange expression, one taken from the plant world! The thought of a root suggests something of durability and permanence. From the root of the serpent, then, there will come out a poisonous snake, and its fruit will be a burning, fiery serpent. We may note the contrast between root and fruit. From one snake will come a poisonous serpent, and that poisonous serpent will produce another that is burning and flying. There will now be an enemy far more serious to conjure with than Assyria had been.[92]

It is not Isaiah's intention to teach that the enemy to come must necessarily be a physical descendant of Assyria, but merely to show that spiritually that enemy will be even more severe in its attitude toward Philistia than Assyria had been.

30 When God speaks, blessing often flows from His mouth for His people! Here is a prophecy of certainty. The first-born of the poor ones, the poorest of all, who do not have sufficient for their daily lives, will feed. Isaiah uses figures taken from pastoral life. The people of God are here conceived as sheep which pasture and lie down. In pasturing and lying down in comfort and security they truly are safe. They have security because God has protected them, for in God and not in men is true security to be found.

Not so the future of the Philistines. What a contrast between their future and that of God's people! The root of the Philistines from which the nation derives its life will be destroyed by God's wrath. It will receive no nourishment, and famine will cause it to perish. God employs the same contrast in 65:13, "Therefore thus saith the Lord GOD, Behold, my servants shall eat, but ye shall be hungry: behold, my servants shall drink, but ye shall be thirsty: behold, my servants shall rejoice, but ye shall be ashamed."

There is alliteration between "root" and "remnant" (both in Hebrew and in the English). Unlike Babylon there will be a remnant to Philistia, and the flying serpent will kill[93] that remnant.

---

[92] Various indentifications have been made: Shalmanezer V, Hezekiah (Jerome), death of Uzziah, death of Tiglath-pileser, etc. Freedom from Assyria, whenever it may have occurred, was no cause for rejoicing. Note the gradation: serpent — poisonous snake — fiery flying serpent. The צפע is a poisonous variety of serpent whose exact identity is not known. Isaiah is simply using a figure of speech, much as we do when we speak of someone being a dragon or fiend. Cf. Amos 1:6-8; Zeph. 2:4-7; Ezek. 25:15-17; Zech. 9:5-7.

[93] "I shall kill" — Used of the death that God brings through famine, sickness, etc., Exod. 16:3; 17:3.

31 Well known were the city gates of Philistia. To mention the gate is to mention the city itself.[94] One city here cries as a representative of the rest. All of Philistia, the entirety of the five city states, is dissolved, for she is destroyed. Good reason there is for lamentation! "Rejoice not over the destruction but howl over thy own dissolving." Smoke, and with it the oncoming enemy, has come from the direction of the north, whence later the Babylonians did appear. In this approaching enemy there is no one separated or isolated. All in its armies are together, for it is well organized, well trained, ready to fight and to destroy. Before it Philistia cannot stand.

32 When messengers of any nation — not necessarily those of Philistia or of Assyria, for the phrase is indefinite — ask, the answer to be given is that although Philistia or any other nation may perish, the Lord has founded Zion, and Zion remains.

This is the gospel. When any enquire, they are to be told that Zion is God's work and in Zion the afflicted of the people may find refuge. This spiritual truth is here expressed in terms of the Old Testament dispensation. Zion has been founded by the Lord, the God of hosts, and for that reason cannot be destroyed, and those among the people of Judah who have been afflicted may find refuge there.[95]

In this prophecy we are taught that the purposes of God will be fulfilled. Inasmuch as Assyria, the present threatening foe, will certainly be destroyed, so also will that far greater foe, even Babylon, the type of Antichrist, be completely brought to ruin. When she sees Assyria perish, Philistia may think that it is a time for rejoicing, in which she may again direct attention toward Judah. Judah, however, is the nation of God, and an enemy will come against Philistia, far greater than were the Assyrians, so that Philistia in her entirety will be destroyed. The work of God is sure, and the refuge which He provides in Christ will stand firm when

---

94 "gate" — A parallel expression for city; cf. 3:26. "smoke" — Symbol of an approaching, destroying and consuming enemy. Cf. *Aeneid*: 11:909: "*Ac simul Aeneas fumantes pulvere campos Prospexit longe, Laurentiaque agmina vidit.*"

95 Verse 32b, although often regarded as fulfilled in Hezekiah's time, is really Messianic; it reflects upon 11:1-12:6. Cf. 14:29b with 11:1, 10; 14:30 with 11:4. In v. 31, the destruction of 10:28-32 is applied to the Philistines and the salvation of 10:33, 34 to Zion in v. 32b. Jeremiah 47:2-4 is to be compared with 14:30, 31 and 5:28. Verse 32 gives a conclusion to the Philistine prophecy similar to that which 14:24-27 gives to the preceding.

all enemies are done away. What comfort and consolation we find here! How great were those enemies which sought to prevent the coming of Christ! But Babylon is gone; Christ has come; and in Him the afflicted may find refuge.

THE POSITION OF ISAIAH 14:24-27 IN THE PROPHECY

Marti denies this section to Isaiah largely because of its content. Isaiah, he argued, was not concerned with world judgment but only with salvation and judgment as they applied to Israel. Belief in world judgment was too theoretical a conception to have been held by Isaiah. While the verses do contain some Isaianic parallels, they also parallel "non-Isaianic portions of the prophecy." Marti would attribute the passage to the Maccabean age.

Duhm rejects all of this and treats the verses as a "side-piece" belonging to the time of Sennacherib, but its author, he thinks, is unknown to us.

To understand the passage we must recognize that it purposely takes up an already presented message and places that message in a new context. Somewhat in the same manner as 16:13, 14 brings to a close the oracles concerning Moab, or 21:16, 17 that concerning Arabia, so do these verses conclude the preceding oracle. They turn the thoughts on Babylon to the present and so push the whole prophecy into the future, to show that what was uttered in 13:1-14:23 did not have an immediate relation to the present. And the destruction of Assyria, so soon to be accomplished, thus stands as a pledge that the further distant destruction of Babylon will also come to pass.

Jeremiah writes (50:17, 18) "Israel is a scattered sheep; the lions have driven him away; first the king of Assyria hath devoured him; and last this Nebuchadnezzar king of Babylon hath broken his bones. Therefore thus saith the LORD of hosts, the God of Israel; Behold, I will punish the king of Babylon and his land, as I have punished the king of Assyria."

Thus, the destruction of Babylon becomes a confirmation and seal of the earlier ruin of Assyria.

2. The Downfall of Moab, Syria, and Other Nations (15:1—18:7)

a. *The oracle of Moab* (15:1-9)

The oracle of Moab, that in the night that Ar of Moab is laid waste, it is destroyed; that in the night that Kir of Moab is laid waste, it is destroyed.

2 They go up to the house and Dibon, to the high places for weeping. On Nebo and on Medeba, Moab howls, on all his heads is baldness, every beard is cut off.

3 In its streets they are girded with sackcloth; on its roofs and in its squares all of it howls, coming down with weeping.

4 And Heshbon cries and Elealeh, even to Jahaz is their voice heard; wherefore the warriors of Moab cry, his soul is distressed unto him.

5 My heart shall cry out for Moab; her fugitives are as far as unto Zoar, a heifer of three years; for he who ascends to Luhith with weeping goes up by it, for in the way of Horonaim they raise a cry of destruction.

6 For the waters of Nimrim shall be desolations; for the herbage is withered, the grass faileth, there is no green thing.

7 Wherefore the remainder of what one has made and their acquisitions over the brook of the willows they carry them away.

8 For the cry has gone round about the border of Moab, unto Eglaim its howling, even to Beer-Elim its howling.

9 For the water of Dimon are full of blood; for I will bring upon Dimon additions, for the escape of Moab a lion, and for the remnant of the land.

1 Moab is a region east of the Dead Sea whose inhabitants are descended from Moab, a son of Lot and his eldest daughter (Gen. 19:31-37). It has been claimed that the kingdom of Moab was not founded until the thirteenth century B.C. (cf. *WHAB*, p. 436), but excavations have shown that civilization in Moab far antedated the thirteenth century.

454

On their way to the promised land the Israelites were opposed by Balak (Num. 22:24), who hired Balaam to curse them. During the period of the judges Eglon, king of Moab, attacked Israel, capturing Jericho and holding Israel in subjection for eighteen years (Judg. 3:12). Under David Moab was conquered and its inhabitants compelled to labor on royal projects (2 Sam. 8:1).

After the death of Ahab Moab's king Mesha rebelled against Israel, but this rebellion was suppressed, the Israelites stopping the wells of water and cutting down the trees (2 Kings 3). A little more than a hundred years before Isaiah's prophecy concerning Moab (c. 840 B.C.) Mesha the king erected a stele which was discovered in 1868 at Diban. On this stele Mesha mentions Omri, king of Israel, and tells of taking the vessels of Yahweh and placing them before Chemosh.[1]

Against Moab there is an oracle, which in this place has a tone of threat and doom, because in a night of wasting the cities of Moab will be destroyed.[2] Again, Isaiah adopts an ideal standpoint. Moab has not yet been destroyed, but the event will surely occur, for God has decreed it, and the prophet employs the prophetic perfect to indicate the certainty of what he is prophesying. And Isaiah enters into the suffering of Moab, for his own heart is painfully affected and grieved by what he knows must come to pass. What a picture of the true evangelist! Here is no vaunting oneself over the sinner, but a compassionate tenderness for those against whom one is called to preach.

Destruction comes in the night, which may simply mean that it is sudden, or that it comes as a result of the raids that were commonly held during the nighttime. First the northern boundary, Ar Moab, situated on the Arnon, was destroyed.[3] Perhaps there is somewhat of sympathy when Isaiah says Ar is "destroyed," for it is the same word that the prophet had used of himself in his inaugural vision, "Woe is me, for I am undone." So, Isaiah now sees Moab

[1] The text of the Mesha inscription is found in *TGI*, pp. 48, 49. For further literature see *ANET*, pp. 320-21; *NSI*, Lidzbarski: *Ephemeris für semitische Epigraphik*, I, 1900; R. Smend and A. Socin: *Die Inschrift des Königs Mesa von Moab*, 1886.

[2] Mowinckel attributes this section (with Isa. 33 and 34) to a post-exilic period (*HTC*, p. 154).

[3] Ar is another name for the territory of Moab (cf. Num. 21:15, 28; Deut. 2:9, 18, 29). Inasmuch as the consonants are the same as those of the Hebrew word "city," the reference may be to the capital, possibly modern el-Misna.

completely perished. Likewise, in a night, Kir Moab,[4] which was south of Ar Moab, was also destroyed. Thus, the prophet uses these two particular cities to give a general picture and to show that the destruction had extended to the entire country.

2 Moab howls in lamentation. In every place and in every way, the voice of crying is heard. Dibon[5] was north of the Arnon,[6] and had once belonged to the Israelites. These were the high places, the temples or houses where idolatrous worship was conducted.

[4] Kir is probably Kir-hareseth, modern El-Kerak, east of El-lisan (the tongue), which extends as a peninsula into the Dead Sea. It was located on a high, easily fortified hill (elev. 3690′), and may have been Moab's capital, 2 Kings 3:25. כי is taken as asseverative (Alexander, *IB*, Gesenius), interjectory as in Gen. 18:20 (Duhm), or explanatory (Delitzsch, Drechsler, as in Isa. 6:5).

Delitzsch takes ליל as absolute, "in a night," as in 21:11. Others take it as const., "in the night of — laid waste was Ar." The *Gerashayim* would support the absolute, but this accent is missing in the second occurrence of the word. For the absolute we should expect *layil*. The unaccented dipthong takes the form *leyl*. Here in both instances the word is accented, and the form may be regarded as stereotyped. In the second instance at least, however, I prefer to take it as a const.

שדד is perf. m. because the verb seems to reflect upon the destruction of the inhabitants, so also the following verb.

[5] Dibon was rebuilt by Gad, Num. 32:34; and in Num. 33:45, 46 it is called Dibon-gad. Jerome comments: "*usque hodie indifferentur et Dimon et Dibon hoc oppidulum dicitur.*" In Josh. 13:17 it is assigned to the Reubenites. Here it is possibly the seat of a sanctuary. We should render either "one goes up to the house and to Dibon," adverbial acc., or "the house and Dibon ascend." But Maurer renders, "*Adscendit Moab in templum et Dibon in loca edita.*" It is best to understand "people" as subj. and to construe the verb impersonally. It is possible that *waw* is pleonastic, "Dibon has gone up to Bayith, to Bamoth to weep." Cf. Dan. 11:6 and Isa. 57:11. Cf. Wernberg-Møller, *JSS*, Vol. III, No. 4, p. 324.

The text is difficult, but 1Q supports M. On the Mesha inscription *bt*, "house," is used as a place name, '*ank. bnty. bt. bmt* (line 27); *bmt* is therefore in apposition to *bt*. Cf. Num. 21:19. Sanctuaries were usually on high places; cf. 1 Kings 11:7; Isa. 65:7. וייליל — The preformative has been added to the contracted form; cf. Job 24:21; Ps. 138:6. גרועה — "shaved, clipped." Several mss. have *daleth* instead of *resh*. 1Q supports M. But cf. Isa. 14:12 and note Jer. 48:37a.

[6] "Arnon" (*Wadi el Môjîb*) — One of the four main streams which divides the plateau of Transjordan, crossed by the Israelites, Num. 21:13ff.; Deut. 2:24. It formed the northern boundary of Moab, Judg. 11:18, and the southern boundary of Transjordan, Josh. 12:1ff.; Deut. 3:8 and 4:48. Mesha speaks of the road by the Arnon, *hmṣlt b 'arnn* (note const. and article followed by the prep.).

There the people go up, but for the purpose of weeping and lamentation. If we look to Nebo,[7] the great mountain, or to Madeba,[8] where there were idols, we find the same thing — Moab howls. It is a weeping of bitterness and anguish, for the land is destroyed. But can weeping before idols provide any help or relief? Isaiah personifies his enemy Moab. The reason why there is weeping is that the entire head of Moab is baldness, and so disgrace, and his beard has been cut off so that he is humiliated and unable longer to raise his head and face the world. Humiliating, shameful defeat has come to Moab.

3 Men go to the streets to see what is happening. In the streets of Moab's cities people have girded themselves in sackcloth, as a sign of lamentation and mourning. On the flat roofs of the houses and in the public squares and plazas of the cities there is the same howl of anguish that the whole country raises. The whole country howls and comes down with weeping.[9] As water runs down, so the nation comes down entirely with its weeping.

4 Nine cities have been mentioned in verses 1 through 4, and six words of complaining have been used. Complaint and lament characterize these verses. Heshbon[10] and Elealeh[11] cry also. For this, Isaiah has really prepared us, with his command to Phil-

---

[7] "Nebo" — Modern Jebel en-Neba, 2740' elevation, 12 miles east of the Jordan's mouth. Here Moses died, Deut. 32:49; 34:1. Some have referred this to a city which had become Moabite. Chemosh commands Mesha, "Go! capture Nebo from Israel." Cf. Num. 32:3, 38; 33:47. Jerome remarks: "*In Nabo erat Chamos idolum consecratum, quod alio nomine vocatur Beelphegor.*"

[8] "Madeba" — It formerly had belonged to Reuben, Josh. 13:9, 16; Num. 21:30; 1 Chron. 19:7. Mesha speaks of the building of Madeba. The city is now known for the remarkable mosaic map discovered there; cf. *BA*, Vol. XXI, No. 3, pp. 50-71; John D. Davis: "Medeba or the Waters of Rabbah," *PTR*, xx., 1922, pp. 305-310.

[9] Both number (3a) and gender (3b) change surprisingly, depending upon whether Moab is conceived as an individual or a plurality, or whether the concept of land or people predominates; cf. Jer. 48:37, 38. Note the Ar. expression, *warada 'el-bika*, "to flow down in weeping."

[10] "Heshbon" — Modern Heshban, once the capital of Sihon, Num. 21:25ff. Its fishpools are mentioned in Song of Sol. 7:4. Pliny, V:11, speaks of *Arabes Esbonitae.*

[11] "Elealeh" — Modern 'el- Al, north of Heshbon, built by the Reubenites, Num. 32:3, 37. Eusebius says it is one Roman mile from Heshbon. "wherefore" — Because of the general lamentation of the country, the warriors cry.

istia, "Howl, O gate; cry, O city" (14:31a). The voice of their lamentation is heard even as far as Jahaz.[12]

Therefore, as a result of this general cry of the men of Heshbon and Elealeh, the warriors, those girded to defend the country, cry out, not in joy and confidence, but in complaint. As the heart of Hannah was grieved because she had no sons, so the soul of Moab is grieved. To that soul all is evil.

5ᐧ How true an evangelist was Isaiah! Often he expresses his feelings for sinners (cf. 16:11; 21:3,4) and here he enters into Moab's suffering and anguish. How compassionate he is! He does not merely say, "I cry out for Moab," but, "My heart shall cry out for Moab." It is a matter that concerns him in his inmost being. Men wish to flee from such a land of lamentation; indeed, Moab's fugitives have gone as far as Zoar,[13] the city that their ancestor Lot sought when he fled from Sodom. Were they seeking eventually to come into Judah? Hitherto unconquered, Zoar is now their destination from an oncoming foe from the north. Moab is simply a calf of the third year, untamed, new to the yoke.[14] As such an animal rebels when the yoke is placed upon it, so Moab feels now the weight of the yoke of suffering that is imposed upon her.

So great is this yoke that the one who goes up to Luhith[15] must go up in crying. For this reason the heart of the prophet cries; indeed, it is the first reason given. Three other reasons follow, each being introduced by a *ki*, "for." The second reason is that

12 "Jahaz" — Possibly modern Khirbet Umm 'el Idham. Mesha relates that he took Jahaz from the Israelites and annexed it to Diban. At Jahaz Sihon fought against the Israelites, Num. 21:23; Deut. 2:32; Judg. 11:20. It also served as a Levitical city, Josh. 21:36; 1 Chron. 6:78.

13 "Zoar" — One of the cities of the plain. It is probably to be located, not north of the Dead Sea, but with ruins near Bad ed-Dra.

14 The language is very difficult, and is the subject of discordant explanations. a) Some of the older writers took the words as a place name; e.g., Josephus, *Agalla;* Ptolemy, *Nekla;* Abulfeda, *Ajlun.* Döderlein thought that Eglath consisted of three towns. b) Other writers take the words as appellations, B, δάμαλις γάρ ἐστι τριετής; Vulg., *"vitulam conternantem;* Targ., Syr., Ibn Ezra. But the word is not an adj. and hence it is better to render, "a cow of the third year"; cf. Gen. 15:9. Thus. Moab is compared to a heifer still young and strong (cf. Jer. 46:20; 50:11).

15 "Luhith" — Location unknown. "Horonaim" — Location unknown, although it is mentioned by Mesha, 1. 31, *"whwrnn. yshb. bh."* Galling, *TGI,* p. 49, remarks that it is near El-Kerak, Jer. 48:3, 5, 34.

in the way of Horonaim men raise such a cry as is wont to be raised in times of destruction.

6 Isaiah gives two more reasons why his heart cries out for Moab. Not only will the cities be taken and the inhabitants caused to flee, but the country itself will suffer. The waters of Nimrim,[16] to the north, are to be made desolations. The springs which used to supply water for the river had been stopped up by the enemy. In place of the once beautiful meadows of the watery land, there is now nothing but withered, dry places. It is difficult to represent the full force of Isaiah's language in English, but possibly even the mere statement of the words in their Hebrew order may give a glimpse of the strength which appears in this sentence.

"For the waters of Nimrim — desolations they will be."

Isaiah now gives a further reason for his lamentation. When the streams are dried up, the herbage perishes. The grass has come to an end. With what short, tiny sentences does the prophet gasp out the sad condition of Moab! Greenness is gone; desolation has come.

7 Wherefore in the light of all that has previously been stated about Moab, and of the fact that the country can no longer be inhabited, the Moabites carry away into the neighboring country of Edom all that has been left over from the depredations of the enemy. Included are the things that they have been storing up for themselves, to take away with them over the Wadi el-Hesa which they had to cross in order to come to Zoar.[17]

8 *For* — How often Isaiah uses this word! He is not carrying us through a logical argument, step by step, but is grounding the reason for his statements in the general condition of the nation. Inasmuch as so great a tragedy has come to Moab, each of his utterances rightly follows.

The pitiful howling reaches unto Eglaim, which was probably at the northern end of the Dead Sea, and even to Beer-Elim,

---

[16] "Nimrim" — A Moabite oasis near the Dead Sea, possibly Wadi en-Numeira. Cf. Num. 32:3, 36; Josh. 13:27.

[17] "Brook of the willows" — Possibly Zered (?), modern Wadi el-Hesā, which formed the boundary between Moab and Edom. יתרה — A noun without the article in the absolute state, "what remained of what they (each one) had made (acquired)." Cf. Jer. 48:36 where the const. is followed by a finite verb.

459

Moab's boundary toward the wilderness.[18] We might have expected place names which would show the two opposite boundaries of the land, such as Dan and Beersheba do for Palestine, but Isaiah merely chooses two names to indicate the extent to which the wailing was heard.

9 Good reason there is for howling! The land is filled not only with tumult and confusion, but also with blood. The waters of Dimon[19] have become waters of blood. Sufficient blood has already been shed, but now new carnage is to appear. We are back with the waters of Arnon, where the descriptions began. They are filled with blood, no longer rivers of life, but of death and carnage. Additional things will be brought upon Dimon, as though there were not already enough evils. Those who escape from Moab will meet a lion, that beast of the wilderness which will destroy and finish the work of the invader. There will, however, be a remnant, and hence destruction will not be absolute and complete. But the lion will meet the remnant.

b. *Moab's suffering* (16:1-14)

1   Send a lamb to the ruler of the earth; from Sela to the wilderness, to the mountain of the daughter of Zion.

2   And it shall be like a bird wandering, a nest cast out shall be the daughters of Moab, the fords of Arnon.

3   Give counsel, form a decision, make thy shadow as the night in the midst of noon, hide the outcasts, do not betray the one who wanders.

4   Let mine outcasts dwell with thee, O Moab! be thou a hiding place for them from the face of the spoiler; for the extortioner has come to an end; violence has ceased; the tramplers are consumed out of the land.

5   And there shall be established in mercy the throne, and he shall sit upon it in truth in the tent of David, judging and seeking judgment and prompt in righteousness.

6   We have heard the pride of Moab, the very proud, his haughtiness, and his pride and his wrath; vain are his pretensions.

---

18 "Eglaim" — Exact location unknown. "Beer-elim" — Possibly a stopping place of the Israelites in Moab, Num. 21:16, exact location unknown.

19 "Dimon" — Possibly to be identified with Madmen, Jer. 48:2. The proper name forms a play on the following "dam, blood." Cf. H. Orlinsky: "Studies V," *Israel Exploration Journal*, IV, 1954, pp. 5-8 and *JBL*, Vol. lxxviii, March, 1959, p. 28, in which it is convincingly argued that Dimon is the correct reading.

7 Therefore Moab will howl for Moab; all of it will howl; for the raisin-cakes of Kir-hareseth shall ye moan; surely they are smitten.

8 For the fields of Heshbon are withered, the vine of Sibmah; the lords of the nations have broken down its choice plants; unto Jazer they reached, they wandered to the wilderness; as to its branches, they were stretched out, they reached over the sea.

9 Wherefore I shall weep with the weeping of Jazer for the vine of Sibmah; I shall wet thee with my tears, Heshbon and Elealeh! For upon thy summer fruit and upon thy harvest a cry has fallen.

10 And joy and gladness is taken away from the fruitful field; and in the vineyards there will no more be sung, will no more be shouted; wine in the presses shall the treader not tread; the cry have I stilled.

11 Therefore my bowels shall sound like the harp for Moab, and my inward parts for Kir-hareseth.

12 And it shall come to pass when it is seen that Moab has wearied himself on the high place, then he shall enter into his sanctuary to pray and shall not be able.

13 This is the word which the Lord hath spoken unto Moab from that time.

14 And now the Lord hath spoken, saying, In three years, like the years of a hireling, the glory of Moab shall be discredited, with all the great multitude, and the remnant shall be small and few, not mighty.

1 Can there be no salvation, no deliverance for Moab? Her rulers take counsel together, and see only one way open. Deliverance can be found in the house of David. Moab should look to the Davidic dynasty and pay the tribute that was demanded. In ancient times that tribute consisted of sheep and goats. Moab therefore is to send the lamb for tribute, for the Davidic dynasty is now the ruler of the earth.

This tribute would be sent from Petra[20] in Edom to the wilder-

---

[20] "Sela" — Capital of Edom. Greek, *Petra*. Cf. 2 Kings 3; 2 Chron. 20; Amos 2:1-3; 2 Kings 14:7 and possibly 2 Chron. 25:12. Isaiah mentions it again in 42:11 and cf. Jer. 49:16; Obad. 3. Classical references: Strabo, xvi:4; 21; Athenodorus mentioned the laws of the city; Pliny: *Natural Hist.*, vi. 28; Josephus: *Archaeology*, 4:4:7; Dio Cassius 68:14; Dio. Sic. 19:55. Hadrian had coins stamped *Hadriane petra Metrapolis*. Bishops from the churches of this region were called *hai petrai*. The city has become known in modern times through Burckhardt's journeys.

It is now located at Wadi Musa, and its entrance is through a narrow defile known as Es-Siq. It was the present author's privilege to visit Petra in April, 1930. I quote from my diary respecting Es-Siq: "A little stream flows

ness and through that wilderness until the mountain on which the Temple was located was reached. The Moabites know how to send the tribute to Zion; they are well aware of how God can be reached.[21] In historical times the tribute had been sent to Samaria; now it is to be sent to Jerusalem herself, for in Jerusalem the Lord may be found.

2 A bird[22] that is gone astray, that flutters about here and there, not knowing where its nest is, such was Moab. Wherever she turned there was no help, no refuge. Her nest had been thrown away. Thus will be the daughters of Moab, the women of the land.[23] They will lament and seek safety at the fords of Arnon, the boundary of the land. Crossing these fords, can they find deliverance?

3 The Moabites speak.[24] Once haughty, once proud, once confident, now they are willing to place themselves in the hands of their former enemy, Judah, and they beg to be covered over with Judah's shadow so that they will no longer be visible to the enemy. Isaiah uses short utterances, corresponding to the sense of importunity and urgency of the speakers.

Only Zion can give counsel, for the Messiah is in Zion, endued with the Spirit of counsel. "Give us right and righteousness," asks Moab. But counsel and right decisions are not sufficient. Moab needs deliverance, and hence prays that Zion will act. "Cover us with thy shadow as the night," she beseeches. The shadow is protection; it obscures, it hides, it prevents the enemy from seeing.

---

through the Siq, and little green bushes grow on each bank. It is a beautiful place. We killed one viper and saw another, and saw their tracks in the sand constantly. Lizards were running all over the place. Twenty minutes walking through this magnificent gorge brought us to Ed-Djerra. This is the façade of a temple cut out of the solid rock."

21 These words are the mutual exhortations of the Moabites. כֹּר — The lamb; cf. Ug. *kr*, "male lamb" and Akk. *kirru*. The word has collective force.

22 "like a bird" — When the object to be compared is defined by means of an attribute the article is omitted; the prep. is written only once but governs both objects to be compared; "like wandering birds (like) a scattered nest."

23 "daughters" — It is probably best to take this in the strict sense, the women of Moab. "fords" — An acc. of direction. As the women flee *towards* the fords, they are seeking the old boundaries and so safety (Num. 21:23).

24 I incline to take vv. 3-5 as the mutual entreaties and advice of the Moabites and v. 6 the refusing answer. For the figure of a shadow, cf. Hamasa 425 and Livy 7:30:32:11:34:9. פְּלִילָה refers to the function or work of a judge, "do the work of a judge," i.e., render a decision as a judge would do.

If there is to be deliverance Moab must be covered with Zion's shadow. Indeed, all who will find deliverance must be covered with Zion's shadow. For Zion's shadow is such that, if placed over one even at the heat of midday, it will nevertheless cover and protect.

Once Israel used to flee to Moab. Now the picture is completely reversed, and Moab flees to Israel. The reference is to a spiritual conversion of this ancient enemy of God's people. Moab is not to be utterly wiped out. When the enemy comes in upon her, she is to look to God, who is to be found in Zion, and to come with supplication for deliverance. "Hide me under the shadow of thy wing," is the essence of her prayer, as it is also of all those who flee for refuge to Jesus.

4 Moab desires refuge from the people of God. Moab, however, has oppressed them; she has spoiled them. How will she now act toward Israel? Are the Israelites to be safe with her?[25] They desire only to be sojourners, for they are faced with an extortioner who will soon cease to trouble them. Meanwhile, Isaiah commands Moab to be a shelter to Israel. While God's outcasts tarry in Moab, the extortioner will cease and with him the violence that he and the tramplers cause. May God's outcasts tarry then for a short time with Moab, the prophet prays, until the danger be past.

5 If there is perfect rapprochement between Israel and Moab, the throne of David will be established.[26] If the Moabites find shelter with Judah, and the dispersed of Judah can also be received by Moab, it will redound to the blessing of Judah. Hence, we have here not only the statement of a consequence, but also a promise of the establishment of David's throne. How important that we ever be reminded of the manner in which this throne is to be established! In gracious goodness will it be made firm. Grace will erect it. "But my mercy shall not depart away from him,

---

[25] "my dispersed ones" — Moab is probably to be taken as a vocative, for the accent separates the two words. "the spoiler" — The language is that of Isaiah whose purpose is to indicate by way of warning Moab's crimes against Israel that there may be a change of heart. כי — Introduces the reason why Moab should hear. All fleshly power will cease, and in its place a kingdom of a higher order will appear. Four nouns are employed to designate the foes of God's people.

[26] Cf. Ginsberg, *JBL*, March 1950, pp. 54, 55. 1Q supports M. Bentzen thinks that "in David's tent" is an addition (*en udsmykkende filføjelse*).

as I took it from Saul, whom I put away before thee" (2 Sam.
7:15). Founded, kept, and surrounded by grace! How different
from the thrones of this world, founded by might and power!

He who sits upon the throne will reign in truth, and this He
will do in the tent of David. Isaiah reverts to the time of the
beginning when David's dynasty ruled in nothing more than a
tent. It may also be that he is reflecting upon the low condition
of David's dynasty, in contrast to what it should have been and
was designed to be. The language obviously is based upon the
great Messianic passage of 9:6 and thus makes clear the superiority
of David's throne over a Moabitic dynasty. He who sits upon the
throne will exercise the judging functions of a king and will seek
for judgment and righteousness that his reign may be just and
perfect.

There is an indefiniteness in the manner in which Isaiah speaks
of a throne. When Moab and Judah come together as they
should, he says, a throne will be established. Here, Isaiah speaks
in indefinite and general terms, but his prophecy clearly rests
upon the more specific and definite prophecy which he had earlier
uttered. The throne is that of David upon which Christ sits.
Insofar, however, as previous kings, such as Hezekiah, could be
said to fulfill the terms of this prediction, they may be considered
as forerunners and types of the Christ.

6 Demands have been made upon Moab that she treat the
Judahites with kindness.[27] There is good reason why demands
should be made, for Moab has been a haughty nation, and her
haughtiness is well known. Isaiah continues to speak and asserts
that he and others have heard of this pride. Indeed, he heaps up
word upon word to express Moab's haughtiness. More serious is
it that God Himself has heard thereof. If Moab is to come to
Judah, there must be complete repentance and turning away from
pride. Moab possessed a pride that manifested itself in wrath, but
which also pretended and claimed for itself things that were not so.

---

27 Note the prominence of the combination נא in this verse. Isaiah answers
the previously stated demands and declares that Moab is ripe for judgment.
נא is a second acc., "as a very proud one." Note omission of the article.
"vain" — I do not construe this as an object of the verb. If this phrase were
a const., we should expect *Segol* and not *Tzere*. Better, therefore, to render:
"not so," or "nothing, are his pretensions." This verse is used in Zeph. 2:8-10
which proves that it is not post-exilic. It is repeated in Jer. 48:29, 30; cf. also
vv. 14, 26, 27.

7 Isaiah breaks out in vigorous sentences.[28]   Because Moab was what she was, there is to be lamentation. She will howl in grief and lament for herself, for she will be deprived of those things in which she had had her delight. The vineyards of Kirhareseth and the raisin cakes which could be made from the grapes and which were a delight to the Moabites are gone. The vineyards are smitten so that they bear no more grapes. Here is indeed a ground for mourning.

8 There is a reason for the mourning, for the vines of Heshbon no longer produce; they are withered and give forth no grapes.[29] Every vine of Sibmah has been broken down by the lords of the Gentiles. The tendrils of these vines crept along the ground, reaching even to Jazer and to the Dead Sea. The entire land was covered with vines, which the enemy destroyed.

9 Isaiah gives utterance to his own feeling of sympathy for a nation which is to be punished, and his heart bursts forth in grief at the thought of the destruction of Moab's vineyards. Upon a guilty people he was compelled to call down the punitive wrath of God, and for this guilty people he has compassion.

As the people of Jazer[30] weep, so the prophet will weep, actually sharing and participating in their sorrow. His wailing will be as bitter as theirs. He loved the vineyards, and realized that, because of human sin, these vineyards would be destroyed. All the country has suffered, and the prophet can but wet the land with his own tears. From this we learn that catastrophes destroying and mutilating the beauty of the world may be a result of man's sin.

10 Terraced hillsides covered with vineyards! Can anything be more beautiful, more picturesque? In such vineyards there

---

[28] Beginning with this verse we have three sentences, each consisting of two verses, 7, 8; 9, 10; 11, 12. Each sentence is introduced by לָכֵן or אֲשִׁישֵׁי עַל בֵּן — raisin cakes, of dried compressed grapes; cf. Hos. 3:1. Driver thinks that it refers to persons and renders, "ye shall moan for the luxurious dwellers in Kir-hareseth," in *Von Ugarit nach Qumran*, 1958, p. 43.

[29] "Sibmah" — Exact location unknown. Cf. Josh. 13:19; Num. 32:38. The predicate agrees in number with Heshbon; cf. Green, #293. On the other hand the f. pl. may be regarded as a collective.

תָּעוּ — Note the retraction of the accent to *mil 'el*. Delitzsch suggests that this is for the sake of assonance with *nā-gā-'ú*. I do not know.

[30] "Jazer" — Num. 21:32; 32:1ff.; Josh. 13:25; 1 Chron. 6:81; 2 Sam. 24:5. Possibly to be identified with Khirbet el-Jazzir, near Es-Salt. אֲרוּיֵך for אֲרוּיֵך. The second radical is doubled as *yod*, and the third appears as *waw*.

465

is rejoicing and gladness. God had increased the gladness, and men rejoiced before Him as when they gather the harvest. So it would be when Messiah should come. In Moab, on the other hand, the picture was to be different. For Moab too God had acted, and as a result gladness and joy had been removed from the fruitful field. Isaiah delighted to speak of the fruitful field, the Carmel. In Moab there is to be a Carmel without joy and gladness. In place of a fruitful field, desolation, grief-bringing desolation, would be found. In place of the former joy and song of the laborers there would be the ghastly reign of silence. Joy is departed; it has been gathered up so that it can no longer be seen.

In the fields lay great rocks which had been hewn out as vats for trampling the grapes. But there was no one to tread the grapes so that the wine would flow from the upper vat into the lower.[31] God had caused the cry of the worker to cease. Isaiah is speaking as God's representative. In so preaching he would not have us understand that he himself had caused the cry to cease, but that God had done so. Isaiah takes up God's words in his own mouth, and by employing the first person represents God's thought and words.

11 How much we learn from this passage both concerning Isaiah and concerning God! Already Isaiah had declared that his heart would cry out for Moab (15:5). Indeed, even with the weeping of Jazer he would weep, and so would identify himself with the afflicted nation (16:9). To carry out the gradation in thought, he employs a strong expression. As the hand that plucks the strings of a lyre gives forth a sound, so the threatenings and punishments decreed upon Moab would play upon the strings of his own inner heart and bring forth an echoing response.

Isaiah uses a strange word; that is, to us it is strange. He speaks not of his heart but of his bowels and inward parts, for the Hebrew considered these to be the seat of the emotions.[32] We today would prefer to speak of our heart and breast being moved. The shaking which moved Isaiah was one that agitated him to the very inmost depths of his being. It was no light "feeling sorry" for the con-

---

31 "the treader" — The one who walks on the grapes to crush them and cause the juice to flow out. In Salonika I have seen wagons filled with grapes and barefooted boys tramping on the grapes, the juice flowing into buckets at the back of the wagon. השבתי — Although in pause, this word has *patah*, probably because the syllable closes with *daghesh forte*, cf. 8:1 and 21:2.

32 מעי — The inward parts, intestines, bowels.

demned nation; it was a profound, soul-stirring emotion resulting from a deep affection for those to whom he was to preach.

At the same time the prophet is speaking as the representative of God, and if Isaiah thus exhibits concern, so also does God, for Isaiah declares only what God commands him. Within was a tumultuous agitation and raging, caused by affection and tenderness toward Moab. Did God also have such tenderness toward Moab, that ancient enemy of His chosen ones? At a later time Isaiah becomes emboldened sufficiently to ascribe bowels to God. "Where," he asks, "is thy zeal and thy strength, the wounding of thy bowels and of thy mercies toward me? are they restrained?" (63:15b). The speaking prophet is himself an evidence that God is merciful toward Moab and is profoundly moved at its desolation.

12 As the prophecy against Babylon had closed with a song of taunt or mockery, so this one closes with an elegy about Moab's fall. It is not a satisfying ending, but that in itself points to its genuineness. Moab did not know the God of Israel, and for that basic and ultimate reason she could find no rest. In times of distress, how tragic when one consults those that are not gods! Moab will go to its gods and be seen of them. It will appear before them, and will be completely wearied,[33] exhausted in vain striving to offer oblations upon the high places. Moab will also go into its temples where the statues of its gods are, there to pray. All in vain. It cannot pray. How desperate is the plight of such a nation or people! When a nation has sunk to the place where it cannot pray to the true God, its condition is not enviable. In Moab everyone went to "the church of his own choice." They could not pray, nor can anyone who does not come to God through Jesus Christ.

13 God had already spoken unto Moab, even from ancient time. Words of His against Moab are found even in the Pentateuch, and the present passage is but the conclusion of the message which He has all along been directing against Moab. There is thus no excuse for Moab's disobedience. She has known what the Lord has required of her, and she has known it from that time of old.

---

33 נלאה may be rendered "will have wearied himself." The perf. suggests a relation of priority to a future action, namely, "then he will come"; this latter thought being expressed by a perf. with *waw* consecutive. Note also the paronomasia in *nir'āh* and *nil'āh;* cf. Mic. 1:13.

14 The years of a hireling! He labors in hard servitude, looking forward to the time of release. Like those years are also the years of Moab until her glory, indeed, all in which she found glory, would be disgraced. Three years, precisely and exactly reckoned, just as the hireling reckons and keeps exact track of the time that he must serve until his period of service is over.[34] Moab will perish, but a small remnant — the prophet emphasizes its smallness — will be delivered. With Babylon there was no deliverance, for there was no remnant. On Babylon alone comes doom and judgment, final, full, all-embracing.

c. *Judgment over Syria* (17:1-14)

1   The oracle of Damascus. Behold! Damascus is removed from being a city, and is a heap, a ruin.

2   Forsaken are the cities of Aroer; they shall be for flocks, and they shall lie down, and none shall make them afraid.

3   And there shall cease the fortification from Ephraim and the kingdom from Damascus and the remainder of Syria. Like the glory of the children of Israel they shall be, saith the LORD of hosts.

4   And it shall come to pass in that day, there shall be made weak the glory of Jacob and the fatness of his flesh shall be made lean.

5   And it shall be like the gathering of the harvest, even the standing corn, and his arm will harvest the ears. And it shall be like one gathering ears in the valley of Rephaim.

6   And in it there shall be left gleanings like the shaking of an olive tree, two or three ripe olives in the top of a high bough, four or five in the branches of the fruit tree, saith the LORD, the God of Israel.

7   In that day shall man regard his Maker, and his eyes shall look to the Holy One of Israel.

8   And he will not show regard unto the altars, the work of his hands; and that which his fingers have made he will not look at, even the Asherah and the incense altars.

9   In that day will his fortified cities be like that which is left in the thicket and the branch, which they have left from before the children of Israel, and it shall be a waste.

10   For thou hast forgotten the God of thy salvation, and the rock of thy fortress thou hast not remembered; wherefore thou wilt plant plants of pleasantness and set it with a strange slip.

---

[34] The speaking of the Lord is assigned to a definite time. Verse 14 contains Isaianic language (cf. 10:25). I incline then to hold that Isaiah himself added these verses at a later time.

11 In the day of thy planting thou wilt hedge it in, and in the morning thou wilt make thy seed to blossom, a harvest heap in a day of inheritance and oppressive sorrow.

12 Alas! the noise of many nations! Like the noise of the sea they make a noise. And the rush of peoples! Like the rush of mighty waters they are rushing.

13 Nations, like the rush of many waters rush; and he rebukes it, and it flees from afar, and is chased like the chaff of hills before a wind, and like a rolling thing before a whirlwind.

14 At the time of evening, and behold! terror; when it is not yet morning, he is not. This is the portion of our plunderers, and the lot of our spoilers.

1 In these few words the heart of the entire oracle is contained. Once Damascus was a great and flourishing city. "Are not Abana and Pharpar, rivers of Damascus, better than all the waters of Israel?" Naaman had asked (2 Kings 5:12a). Now Damascus, named here for all that follows, has become something that is no longer a city. She is a heap, a mound of ruins, something that is fallen — indeed, an overturned heap and a fallen ruin.[35]

2 North of the Arnon and east of Ammon in the desert lies Aroer before Rabbah. The cities that belong to her will be forsaken, deserted, so that they will no longer be cities. Instead, they will be occupied not by men, but by flocks who will graze where once the cities stood. In quiet these flocks will lie down, and no one will be on hand to frighten them. A vivid picture of loneliness and desolation. Here indeed were ghost cities, occupied only by flocks.[36]

3 Step by step Isaiah brings the announcement of judgment closer to home. First Damascus, then Aroer, and lastly Ephraim. The fortified place, probably Samaria, will cease to exist for Ephraim and the kingdom will also be taken away from Damascus. Damascus and Ephraim, the two enemies who had threatened Ahaz, are now mentioned together. There will be a remnant of Syria left over by the invaders from Assyria, and from that remnant,

---

[35] "Damascus" — 1Q inserts an *r*. For discussions cf. E. A. Speiser: *JAOS*, No. 71, 1951, pp. 257-58, and C. H. Gordon, *Israel Exploration Journal*, Vol. 2, No. 3, 1952, pp. 174-75. Note the paronomasia and alliteration: *dammeseq* and *mûsār; mûsār* and *mē 'ir; me 'i* and *mappālāh*. Probably there is word play between *me 'i* and *mē 'ir*.

[36] "Aroer" — junipers. Four cities seem to have borne the name (Josh. 13:9; Josh. 12:2; 1 Sam. 30:28) and this Aroer in the territory of Damascus.

even the kingdom will be taken. What is left of Syria and Damascus will resemble what is left of the former glory of Israel.[37] In that word "glory" Isaiah comprises everything which the natural man would boast in. Included are fortresses, leading personalities, mighty troops, power and splendor of weapons. All in which men had vaunted will be taken. The glory will have departed.

4 Syria and Damascus now retreat into the background, and the reason for what Isaiah has been saying appears.[38] By Jacob the prophet has reference to the ten tribes, and by designating them Jacob he brings to their mind their illustrious ancestor. From Jacob's devotion to God the ten tribes have fallen far. Their glory is to become poor and weak, so that men will not delight in it any longer. The ten tribes are personified, and Isaiah may thus speak of the fatness of his flesh; the people's prosperity will be made lean. The richness, the wealth, the beauty — all will pass, and in their place will be hunger and leanness.

5 Through the field of standing corn the reapers go to pluck the harvest grain, and with their arms reach out to take the ears. Once the ears are taken, only the stalks remain. So will the glory of Jacob be at the time when the Lord visits it in judgment. Northwest of Jerusalem is the vale of Rephaim, noted for its richness.[39] But when the harvest is gathered there will be nothing left of that fruitfulness. So is the coming judgment.

6 By shaking the trees one gathered the olives.[40] A thorough shaking would leave gleanings of two or three berries remaining at the very top of the tree and four or five on the branches. The judgment was to be such a shaking up, distilling the nation and leaving only a few. No matter how fruitful and loaded with olives the tree might have been, the shaking would leave only a few gleanings remaining. The threatened judgment would thus

37 Note the alliteration of *m* in this verse.

38 The ten tribes are conceived as a person; cf. 1:5; their political downfall as sickness; cf. 10:18b. ומשמן — "the fat of his flesh," or "his fat flesh." The gen. is partitive, the noun in const. serving as an attribute, a construction found several times in Isaiah; cf. 1:16; 22:7.

39 Cf. Josh. 15:8; 18:16; 2 Sam. 5:18, 22; 23:13; 1 Chron. 11:15; 14:9.

40 Alternative numbers, two or three, are put together without a connective *waw*. Note the pleonastic use of the suffix followed by the noun to which it refers. בסעפיה — "In its branches, the fruit tree," i.e., "in its the fruit tree's, branches." גרגרים — Ripe olives; cf. Ar. *jar-jar*, thoroughly ripe olives and Akk. *gurgurru*, the name of a plant.

be great in extent, reaching to the top of the tree. Israel would be gleaned thoroughly.

7 "Nevertheless, divers of Asher and Manasseh and of Zebulun humbled themselves, and came to Jerusalem (2 Chron. 30:11). The judgments would be so severe that some would look in expectation for help to the God who had made Israel into a nation, the God who had established the covenant and formed Israel into the theocracy. Israel had forgotten that she was but a creature and that she owed to the Holy One all the blessings and the privileges which she had received. Sometimes it takes severe judgments to bring us to our senses so that our eyes look intently and steadily, not to man, but to God.

8 If there is to be a true looking unto God and dependence upon Him, there must be a turning away from idols.[41] "Ye turned to God from idols," writes Paul, "to serve the living and true God" (1 Thess. 1:9). In America we have our days of prayer in which everyone calls on his god for help, but we continue worshipping and serving our idols. There is no true repentance, no true resting upon and waiting upon God. If a man indeed trusts God, he does not trust altars. The conversion in Israel will be genuine. Looking unto his Maker, man will not pay regard or look with expectation to the altars of idols, altars which have been made by men themselves. The statues of Astarte and the sun images will be disregarded, for they are simply human creations, and in time of need, when the true God is acting, they will be of no avail. To trust in them and to depend upon them is the height of folly.[42]

9 Leaving the description of the judgment Isaiah has told us of a true conversion of the remnant. Now he returns and takes up again the figure of the olive tree, so that he may continue with his picture of judgment. Israel had gloried in her strong and fortified cities. In those days a strong city was a refuge and an object of glory. The strong and fortified cities of Israel, however, would be like ruins, grown over with thorns and bushes, and the

---

[41] Note the unusual pointing of the article. Cf. also Gen. 6:19 and Isa. 3:22. *Waw* as a copula often serves to explain; "even the Asherah."

[42] Cf. *BA,* Vol. I, Feb. 1938, p. 9. "Asherahs" — Apparently sacred trees or poles standing near the altars (cf. 1 Kings 16:33; 2 Kings 21:3). Cf. G. E. Wright: *Biblical Archaeology,* 1957, pp. 106-7. חרש — "wooded place"; cf. Akk. *ḥirśu.* The *mēm* in *'ārîm* may be enclitic; cf. Hummel, *JBL,* June 1957, p. 98.

whole land would simply become a desolation. What thicket and branch would leave was nothing more than a desolation.

10 There is a God with whom salvation may be found, even the God who chose Israel, but Israel has forgotten that God.[43] There was also a Rock which served as a true fortress, quite different from the cities of the fortress which had become a waste. That Rock, however, Israel had not remembered. Israel was unprotected; she had no fortress, no place of refuge. All that she did therefore would be subject to exposure. She would seek to plant plants of pleasantness, but her resolves could not be carried out. Plants of pleasantness would not grow because Israel would sow strange slips. Her purposes would be thwarted. What strange procedure, to plant plants of pleasantness but to sow strange slips! What kind of a gardener is he who plants thistles and expects roses! Folly is Israel's action; she turns to the idols and expects protection.

11 When one expends labor upon vanity, the result must also be vanity.[44] Israel will hedge in its planting at the time when she plants. She will thus seek to protect what she has planted, that no wild animals may trample it under and no harm may befall it. In the morning what she has seeded will be fruitful, breaking forth. The harvest, however, is not what was intended; it is but a heap. The day of inheritance will come, the day on which one expects to inherit what he has sowed and planted. It will be a day, however, of oppressive and tormenting sorrow. Israel strives for an inheritance; she will receive that inheritance, namely, oppressive pain. We reap what we sow. If we sow plants of pleasantness apart from God, we shall reap only the inheritance of tormenting pain.

12 We cannot contemplate the foolish dealings of Israel without sorrow of heart. The contrast between God's rich mercy and grace to Israel and her own stupidity and blindness stands out in strong relief. Yet the judgment must come, and in the background we hear the onrushing turbulence of many nations. Isaiah's own words roar and rush like mighty waters; they ferment like the

---

43 Snijders, *OS*, Deel X, 1954, p. 46, thinks that there is an allusion to the Tammuz-Adonis cult. The plants of pleasantness are compared with *n'mn* in Ug. Cf. *2 Aght* vi. 45; *Krt*, 40:61; 128: ii. 20. If men forget the true God, they will fall into idolatrous practices.

44 נֵד — If a verb, we should expect *Qametz*; if a noun, the pointing is in order; "a heap is a harvest."

waves of the sea. Yet he does not view the onrushing waves with joy; he hears them with sorrow. "Alas!" he cries. The judgment comes rushing on, and the judgment will be carried through by many lunging people. The Assyrians are coming. Great was their king and the multitude that was with him. They rage and bluster, not in some insignificant way, but like the thrashing waves of the mighty oncoming sea. Isaiah uses words of dark vowels and of droning, blustering consonants. One who reads aloud this verse in the Hebrew several times will be moved by the blustering, raging language in which is described the advance of the overpowering, overrushing sea.[45]

13 Mighty, onrushing waters! Mighty, lengthened sentences! In contrast Isaiah now speaks in short, chopped utterances. Thus he connects with the preceding verse, taking up its thought, and rendering it more effective. Not merely people generally, but nations rush, and thus we begin to understand somewhat the identity of the oncoming enemy. But Isaiah is too much in a hurry to identify or name the one who rushes on. Suppose one should rebuke it; who we do not know — Isaiah is too much in a hurry to specify a subject — a rebuke or check to its progress means nothing. This nation has exercised its own power and authority so long that none can check it. It flees from afar, and one cannot catch up with it. Let the chaff be blown away by the strong pure air of the mountains; it cannot be caught. Like the tumbleweed before the wind, so the enemy rolls on. What can man do with it?

14 It is eventime. The day of oppression is closing. As a prophet Isaiah speaks, calling attention to sudden terror. Has evening brought relief? No, it has brought terror, and thus night falls. The night will soon pass, and even before the morning approaches the enemy is destroyed. Threatening, menacing, Assyria shakes her punishing hand against Judah. When morning comes, where is the Assyrian? How simply Isaiah declares, "He is not." One night has removed the enemy. Well may the prophet conclude with the assertion that there is a portion for those who plunder and rob Judah. Those who spoil the people have a lot; within a night they disappear, and they are no more (cf. 14a with Ps. 30:6; 46:6; 90:6; and 14b with Job 20:29).

---

[45] Note the frequency of humming letters in v. 12, *m* and *n* and the *a* vowel.

d. *Distant effect of judgment* (18:1-7)

1   Alas! land of the buzzing of wings, which art beyond the rivers of Cush

2   Sending by sea ambassadors, and in vessels of papyrus on the face of the waters: Go, ye light messengers, to a nation tall and polished, to a people terrible, even farther than that one, a mighty nation, and trampling, whose land the streams divide.

3   All ye inhabitants of the world and dwellers of the earth, as the raising of a standard on the mountains ye shall see, and as the blowing of a trumpet ye shall hear.

4   For thus saith the LORD unto me, I will rest and will look on from my dwelling place, like a glowing heat in the light, like a cloud of dew in the heat of harvest.

5   For before the harvest when the bloom is furnished, and a ripening grape will its flower be, then he will cut down the sprigs with the pruning knives, and the tendrils he removes, he cuts away.

6   They shall be left together to the wild birds of the mountains and to the beasts of the earth, and the wild bird shall summer thereon, and every beast of the earth shall spend there the harvest time.

7   At that time there shall be brought a gift to the LORD of hosts, a people tall and polished, and from a people terrible, even farther than that one, a mighty nation and trampling, whose land the streams divide, to the place of the name of the LORD of hosts.

1 Taking up the woe expressed in 7:13, 14, Isaiah gives an example of how the nations are subject to God. His introductory word may be a cry of anguish or it may simply be designed to point out the great distance of the people of whom he is about to speak. At any rate, the language is arresting, and prepares the hearer for a description of the nation to be addressed. This nation is said to be a land of the rustling of wings, or "the buzzing insect of wings." We may not be able to identify this insect precisely, but it may be that the prophet had in mind the "tzetze" fly which is found in Ethiopia, a land that Fischer characterizes as an "Eldorado" of vermin. Whatever the insect may be, it was sufficiently obnoxious that Moses should mention it as a punishment to be brought against the Israelites (Deut. 28:42).

The prophet's purpose, however, is not to show that Ethiopia is an insect-infested land. His purpose rather seems to be to mention Ethiopia to show that its swarming hordes were like insects. For that reason he mentions the wings. When insects have wings they can fly and accomplish their devastating purposes.

Ethiopia's armies are equipped for foraging and conquering. They have all the capabilities of insects provided with wings.

This land which Isaiah mentions is said to be beyond the rivers of Cush, and hence, at a great distance. In Cush is the Nile with its tributaries, yet even beyond these, farther to the south, is the land which Isaiah mentions. It may be on the other hand that we are not to press the meaning of the word "beyond." It may simply be that the entire description is intended to be general and simply to convey the idea of great distance.[46]

2 This is a land in which there is a rustling of wings, a buzzing of insects, as it were, a land in which the hordes swarmed and buzzed, devastating regions about them, like swarms of obnoxious insects. Isaiah mentions some of the characteristics of these people and gives a certain air of mystery to the whole description. The land is in agitation and sends messengers from tribe to tribe, for on the horizon were the signs of an oncoming enemy; a conflict was in the offing, and the people are in an agitated condition.

by sea — Inasmuch as the vessels are of papyrus, it would seem that the sea must be inland. Pliny (*Natural History,* xiii. 72) mentions the Egyptians as constructing ships of papyrus, and it may be that the Ethiopians used the same method of transportation. Such light ships, however, would not be suitable for use on the Mediterranean, and it would even seem that the Red Sea was also out of the question. More likely the reference is to the Nile, for even today the Arabs speak of the Nile as the sea (*el-bahr*).

on the face of the waters — A parallel expression to "sea." These also must be inland waters. The messengers are sent in light vessels of papyrus so that they may quickly reach their destination.

The sending nation is introduced as speaking, and the ambassadors are to go as light messengers, for the message must be immedi-

---

[46] About 714 B.C. a new Ethiopian dynasty was established in Egypt. Because of Egyptian intrigue Philistia, Judah, Moab, and Edom rebelled against Assyria, but in 711 Sargon turned against Philistia. Judah's part may have been limited to receiving the envoys mentioned in this chapter if they actually did go to Jerusalem. צלצל — whirring, buzzing. Driver supports B, πλοίων πτέρυγες, Targ. and Th. He thinks the parallel demands the rendering "ships," which he finds confirmed by the Aram (*SOTP,* p. 56). Driver's evidence is strong, but the rustling sound of the word, followed by "wings," supports the traditional rendering. 1Q separates the word, which might support the rendering "double shade"; cf. A, Strabo, 2:2:3.

ately proclaimed. The ones to whom they are to go are not named, and this lends a certain air of mystery to the description. The people are described, however, as tall and polished. There is question as to the precise meaning of the words, but it is likely that the first adjective refers to the people as tall of stature, and the second as smooth because the hair has been removed. It may be then that there is some reflection upon a custom of removing the hair from the body. Herodotus (2:37) claims that on every third day the Egyptian priests shaved the entire body.

to a people terrible — This apparently refers to a different people from that just described as tall and polished. It is simply described as a people that can inspire terror.

and even farther than that one — To be taken in a local sense, not describing this second people as more terrible than the other, but as being farther away (cf. 1 Sam. 10:23; 20:22, 37). The language continues with further description, asserting that the nation is of great power and trampling, language which indicates that it crushes whatever is before it.

whose land — Apparently the reference is to the rivers (Nile and its tributaries) which divide the land.[47]

On the interpretation herein given the inhabitants of Cush send out their messengers to their tribes (the inhabitants of Meroe and of Abyssinia?) to prepare for the coming conflict. An ancient interpretation is that the messengers are sent to Jerusalem or Judah to seek for an alliance against the oncoming Assyrians, and Kissane even thinks that the reference is to the Medes.

3 Isaiah now breaks forth into his message. Unnecessary preparations for war should cease, for help will certainly come. On the mountains a standard of assembly will be raised, for the mountains are a most conspicuous and visible spot. The whole earth should hear, for there will also be a trumpet blown. Thus a prophet of Judah addresses the entire earth and speaks with confidence for he is the mouthpiece of the God of the earth.

---

[47] "papyrus" — Cf. Egy. Aram *gm'* and Eth. *gōmē'*. Lambdin suggests that in the light of Coptic *kam* the original Egyptian was *q/gim'û* > *gûm'û* > *gōme'* (*JAOS*, Vol. 73, No. 3, p. 149). "tall — "Long-drawn-out"; either tall or possibly long-living. "smooth" — "Scoured, polished of the skin." Cf. Her. III:20. "mighty" — Cf. Ar. *quw-qah* (strength). De Boer (*OS*, Vol. X, p. 225, 243) would render, "tension." מבוסה — The form is a f. *qal* part. but the word is evidently to be understood as a f. noun, "trampling, subjugation."

4 Isaiah now justifies his message. God has spoken to him. Standing in remarkable contrast to the agitation of Ethiopia with her swiftly traveling messengers, is the quietness of God who alone can control the destinies and movements of nations. Here is the explanation for His apparent inactivity. He was watching from heaven until the time had come to intervene. He rests serene and calm, not agitated as is man.

like a glowing heat — The language is difficult, but it may be rendered, "like heat glowing upon light." Possibly the reference is to the heat which accompanies the light that comes from the sun. The heat comes with the light for the heat too is derived from the sun, and such heat and light are for the benefit of plants. A cloud of dew is a cloud which gives dew. In the heat of harvest such a cloud is necessary that the plants may grow. So is God's waiting until the time is ripe for Him to act. In a certain sense it may be said that His waiting aids the power of the enemy nation to grow until the time has come for Him to intervene and bring that nation to destruction.[48]

5 Before the harvest actually arrives God will act. Isaiah does not use the word that specifically refers to the vintage (*batzir*) but one that has reference to harvest generally (*qatzir*). Whether the explanation given in this verse is that of Isaiah or rather is a continuation of the Lord's language is difficult to determine. The enemy nation, namely, Assyria, is represented under the figure of a vine. Before the complete ripening, at the time when the bloom of the flower is completed and over, and one would seem to be certain of a magnificent harvest and when the already formed grapes are ripening to become the flower, then the work of cutting will begin.[49] The enemy's growth is thus deceptive, and God awaits His time. When evil grows and grows about us, we must trust in God who controls all things and who permits evil to go only

---

[48] The speaking is personal. "God dwells in heaven, but he spoke unto me." אשקוטה 1Q also retains the *waw;* in 1Q the original *o* sound seems to be maintained. Thus, *eš-qōṭ eš-qo-ṭāh.* The paragogic imper. here expresses a determination. ב may be rendered "from."

[49] ובסר — "Grapes beginning to ripen." Cf. *busr* — "dates which are ripening." Note the sentence order; predicate complement first, "and a ripening grape will the flower be." וכרת — The perf. with *waw* cons. is often employed after a determination of time. התז — Pausal. The preterite occurs after a future to denote a later stage in the same transaction, an interval being assumed, "and he will cut the sprigs [i.e., shoots without buds] and [as for] the twigs [tendrils] he removes [them], he strikes [them] away."

477

so far. His purposes and plans cannot be frustrated. At that time the twigs will be cut away with pruning knives and with many cuttings this vinedresser will remove the tendrils. Assyria is indeed the vine, but she is under the eye of a vinedresser who pares down her strength at His appointed time.

6 With this verse a change of subject is introduced. It is a sudden change, for Isaiah leaves the metaphorical expressions which have characterized his utterances hitherto and now speaks in somber, even macabre fashion of the reality that is before him. The men of the enemy nation, all of them, will be left to lie in the open where the birds that build their aeries in the inaccessible spots of the mountains and the wild beasts of the field will devour them. From the mountains the wild birds come to spend the summer in devouring what is cast away and plucked off from the Assyrian vine, and the beasts who roam about the earth spend the time of harvest devouring what is left over from Assyria. It is a picture of ignominious defeat and destruction. The vine of Assyria grows not of itself, but is in the hands of One who can control its growth and strength as He will.

7 The Ethiopian ambassadors come with plans to meet the enemy. Yet these plans are not needed, for God will carry out His own infallible purpose. At that time when God cuts away the tendrils from the Assyrian vine and the bodies of the enemy lay exposed as a prey to the birds and beasts, tribute will be brought to the Lord of hosts. "Kingdoms of splendor shall come out of Egypt; Ethiopia shall stretch out her hands to God" (Ps. 68:3). Ethiopia is so impressed by what God has done to the mighty empire that she is represented in all her splendor as coming to Him now at Zion where He may be found. The language of verse 2 is repeated, almost in an ironical sense. The ones to whom ambassadors had been sent for help against the oncoming enemy will now themselves send tribute to the One who alone controls the hosts of war and might. Ethiopia's plans were not necessary, and now Ethiopia appears as a representative of the whole world in doing homage to the true God. It is a homage arising not merely out of fear and reverence of God, but also out of profound thanksgiving for the mighty deliverance that He has wrought.

The tribute is brought to the place where the name of the Lord dwells. During the Old Testament dispensation this dwelling place was Zion (cf. 1 Kings 8:29; 2 Kings 23:27). In the New Testament age, however, the dwelling place of the name of God is in Jesus

Christ. Jesus Christ is God incarnate, and no man cometh unto
the Father but by Him. This prophecy is fulfilled, not merely
in the conversion of the Ethiopian eunuch, but rather in the
turning unto the true God of all those that were and are scattered
abroad throughout the entire world.

Appendix I

THE TEXT OF ISAIAH

Until recently there was available only the Masoretic text, the oldest manuscript of which, the codex Petropolitanus at Leningrad, dated from A.D. 916. If one will consult the Ginsberg Bible, he will note that the variations in the different Hebrew manuscripts are not of a particularly serious nature. Difficulties could usually be resolved with the aid of the ancient versions.

In 1947 occurred the discovery of two manuscripts in the caves of Qumran (indicated in this commentary as 1Q and 2Q). These are now published and available for study. Inasmuch as the purpose of this commentary is not primarily textual, little use has been made of these manuscripts, save where a reference to them may be of help in understanding or in supporting the text. No attempt has been made to explain the divergencies of the Qumran manuscripts from the Masoretic text, inasmuch as such a procedure really lies beyond the purview of this work.

It may be said that essentially 1Q supports M, but it also in places supports the Greek text. Sometimes there are additions, e.g., 1:15, and omissions, e.g., 4:5; 7:2; 8:9. More difficult forms are at times substituted for those of M, 1:12, 20; 3:8. On the whole the manuscript possibly represents a tradition older than that of M.

In addition to the great Isaiah manuscript from Qumran (1Q) there is another (2Q) which follows M closely. This manuscript covers mainly chapters 38-66. At the Wady el-Murrabaat, a few miles south of Wady Qumran, another Isaiah manuscript was found which adhered closely to M. This manuscript would seem to indicate that M was much older than formerly had been thought to have been the case.

In this present commentary the position is adopted that M is a reliable text. For the most part even the versions, principally B, support M. M yields a good sense, and when there are divergences upon the part of the versions, these divergences can often be explained. Furthermore, difficult forms in M can now often be explained with the aid of the cognate Semitic languages. Examples of this will be found in the notes. When the orthography of M can be checked with ancient inscriptions, that orthography is often substantiated. To support this statement we would introduce the following considerations.

In the Hebrew language the position of the accent and the nature of the syllable are all important. In fact, the type of syllable and its relation to the accent determines the type of vowel that appears in the syllable. Let us take the following word:

APPENDIX I

הברים de-bā-rîm.

In this word there are three syllables. The accented syllable is closed, and we may simply designate it an accented syllable. The syllable preceding the accent is open, and because it immediately precedes the accent we may call it near open. The syllable immediately preceding the near-open syllable (the antepenult), even though it contains a vocal Seᵉwa rather than a full vowel, we may designate a distant open syllable.

In the Semitic languages there are three fundamental or basic vowels which appear in the various syllables in accordance with the following chart. The reader should examine this chart carefully, and refer to it frequently, for it will serve to explain many of the comments made in the notes to the text.

CHART OF SHORT VOWELS (NATURALLY SHORT AND TONE LONG)

Type of Syllable	A	I	U
Accented	ā	ē	ō
Near-open	ā	ē	ō
Distant open	e	e	e
Distant open with עחהא	ᵃ	ᵃ or ᵉ	ᵒ
Closed unaccented	a	e i[1]	o u[1]

The naturally long, unchangeable vowels appear as follows. If they are found in a distant open syllable, they do not change to Seᵉwa.

ו û

י î   sometimes   ê

ֹ ô   sometimes   â.

The following chart will explain the use of the diphthongs.

Type of syllable	AY		AW	
Accented closed	י	ayi.	ו	āwe.
Accented open				
a. at end of a word	ה	eh		
b. otherwise	י	ey	ו	ô
Unaccented				
a. at end of a word	ה	ēh		
b. otherwise.	י	ēy		

1 Usually before Daghesh Forte.

482

The regularity with which the vowels appear in the different syllables in accordance with the charts just given is astounding. When the orthography of the Masoretic text can be checked with cognate Semitic words, that orthography is usually in agreement with those words. One or two examples will suffice to illustrate this point. The proper name Megiddo appears as Ma-gid-dâ in the cuneiform texts. How should these vowels be rendered in Hebrew? Let us begin with the last and accented syllable. *Dâ* would appear in Hebrew as *dô* in accordance with the long vowel chart; *gid* would appear as *gid* (with Hireq because it precedes a dageš-forte) and *ma* appearing in a distant open syllable would be *mᵉ*. Thus we have mᵉ-gid-dô, מגדו, the orthography of M. One further example. The Arabic participle is qâ-ti-lun. In Hebrew the nunation disappears, leaving qâ-til. The ultima is accented, and hence the *i* vowel must appear in Hebrew in an accented syllable as Tsērē', *ṭēl.* The long *a* appears as *qô.* Thus, we have the form qô-ṭēl, קמל. If the reader will study the notes carefully in the light of these vowel charts, he will come to understand why the present writer entertains such a high regard for the Masoretic Text.

THE GREEK VERSIONS

The term "Septuagint" is likely to be misleading.[2] There is not one standard Greek translation appearing in many identical manuscripts to which appeal may be made. Rather there are many manuscripts and these offer significant variants. The principal uncial manuscripts are the following:

A. Codex Alexandrinus, 6th, 7th centuries, now in the British museum.

B. Codex Vaticanus, 4th century, at Rome in the Vatican library. It is this text to which we shall make frequent reference as B. It may be taken as the standard Greek Text for comparative purposes.

S. Codex Sinaiticus, 4th century, in the British museum.

Q. Codex Marchalianus, 6th century, at Rome, in the Vatican library.

V. Codex Venetus, 8th century at Venice, in the library of St. Mark's.

The Greek text of Isaiah appears to be represented by two different branches of tradition. On the one hand there are the uncial manuscripts A and Q, and often S, whereas on the other there are B and V which are the principal representatives of the Hexaplaric recension. Certain of the cursive manuscripts (minuscules), namely, Nos. 26-86-106-710[3] follow the Alexandrian uncials closely, and one of these in particular,

---

2 The following remarks are for the most part based on Ziegler.

3 No. 26 — 10th century; No. 86 — 9th-10th century, both at Rome, in the Vatican library; No. 106 — 14th century at Ferrara and No. 710 — 10th century, at Sinai (contains only 1:1-19:14).

No. 10b, is often very close to A. Peculiar readings therefore, seem to be shared between the cursives and A.

This Alexandrinian text is attested by Jerome in his remarks on Isaiah 58:11, "*Quod in Alexandrinis exemplaribus in principio huius capituli additum est; Et adhuc in te erit laus mea semper; et in fine: et ossa tua quasi herba orientur, et pinguescent, et haereditate possidebunt in generationem et generationem, in Hebraico non habetur, sed ne in Septuaginta quidem emendatis et veris exemplaribus; unde obelo praenotandum est.*" The Alexandrian text is not to be identified with the Hesychian recension, but is original, and is not influenced by the Masoretic text. It is also, for the most part, free of Hexaplaric additions.

In opposition to M, the Alexandrinian often has an addition that is lacking in the Hexaplaric text. Likewise its original word order is maintained, whereas in the Hexaplaric recension this has been brought into conformity with M. It also is a free rendering of the text which was later corrected in the Hexaplaric and Lucianic recension. In its principal representations A, Q, and Cyril of Alexandria, the Alexandrinian group preserves the old Septuagint text at its best, although it has become subject to various secondary influences. On the other hand in some places the Alexandrinian group has not preserved the original reading.

Inasmuch as it is not the purpose of this commentary to discuss fully each divergence of Greek manuscripts from the Masoretic text, only the principal divergences are noted. I have adhered to the Masoretic text, unless unusually good reason for not doing so appears. I am still of the opinion that M represents essentially the original Hebrew text. That the parent Greek text differed widely from the Hebrew is a position which I seriously question.

THE LATIN VERSIONS

The text of the Vetus Latina or Old Latin versions will be found in P. Sabatier: *Bibliorum sacrorum latinae versiones antiquae,* II, Paris, 1751. Of great importance for textual criticism is Jerome's Vulgate, to which rather frequent reference is made in the commentary. On the whole it may be said that the Vulgate is a witness in support of M. Cf. F. Stummer: *Einführung in die lateinische Bibel,* Paderborn, 1928, and A. Penna: "La Volgata e il manoscritto 1QIs^a," in *Biblica,* 38, 1957, pp. 381-397.

THE SYRIAC VERSIONS

Of particular importance is the Peshitto version, to which some references are made in this commentary. For samples of its language the reader may refer to the introduction of Gesenius' commentary, and for brief comments to Penna.

THE TEXT OF ISAIAH

THE TARGUMS

The Jewish tradition is interesting, and in the pages of this commentary I have sometimes translated the Targum on a particular verse.

Those who desire to make a study of textual questions, particularly as they have to do with the versions, may consult the following bibliography.

THE HEBREW TEXT

The Hebrew text of Isaiah is found in:

Rudolf Kittel: *Biblia Hebraica*, 3rd edition, Stuttgart, 1937.

C. D. Ginsburg, *Prophetae posteriores*, London, 1911.

M. Burrows, J. C. Trevor, W. H. Brownlee, *The Dead Sea Scrolls of St. Mark's Monastery*, I, *The Isaiah Manuscript and the Habakkuk Commentary*, New Haven, 1950.

Eleazer Sukenik, *Otzar Hammegilloth haggenuzoth*, Jerusalem, 1954.

I do not wish to give further literature on the Qumran scrolls, inasmuch as bibliographies on this subject are readily available. The reader may consult H. H. Rowley: *The Zadokite Fragments and the Dead Sea Scrolls*, Oxford, 1952, where he will find ample bibliographical material.

THE GREEK TEXT

J. Ziegler: *Isaias* (Septuaginta Vetus Testamentum graecum), Göttingen, 1939. I have found this work to be of inestimable value and have consulted it constantly in the preparation of this commentary.

I. J. Seeligmann: *The Septuagint Version of Isaiah*, Leiden, 1946.

A. Rahlfs: *Septuaginta*, II, Stuttgart, 1935.

R. R. Ottley: *The Book of Isaiah According to the Septuagint*, Vol. I 1904; Vol. II, 1906.

F. Field: *Origenis Hexaplarum quae supersunt*, II, Oxford, 1875.

Harry M. Orlinsky: "The Treatment of Anthropomorphisms and Anthropopathisms in the Septuagint of Isaiah," *HUCA*, Vol. 27, 1956, pp. 193-200.

THE LATIN VERSIONS

P. Sabatier: *Bibliorum sacrorum latinae versiones antiquae*, II, Paris, 1751.

F. Stummer: *Einführung in die lateinische Bibel*, Paderborn, 1928.

A. Penna: "La Volgata e il manuscritto 1QIsª," *Biblica*, Vol. 38, 1957, pp. 381-395.

THE SYRIAC VERSIONS

Biblia sacra iuxta versionem simplicem quae dicitur Peschitta, II, Beirut, 1951.

Appendix I

A. Ceriani: *Translatio syra Pescitto Veteris Testamenti*, Milan, 1876.
L. Delekat: *"Die Peschitta zu Jesaja zwischen Targum und Septuaginta,"*
Biblica, Vol. 38, 1957, pp. 185-99, 321-35.

The Targum

J. F. Stenning: *The Targum of Isaiah*, Oxford, 1949.
P. Churgin: *Targum Jonathan to the Prophets*, New Haven, 1927.

For the last two consult also E. R. Rowlands: *The Targum and the Peshitta Version of the Book of Isaiah*, V.T., Vol. IX, No. 2, pp. 178-191.

Appendix II

THE LITERATURE ON ISAIAH

1. THE EARLY GREEK FATHERS

a. In the early fathers before Origen there are scattered references to Isaiah and in particular to the Messianic prophecies. These were for the purpose of refuting the Jews. Didymus is said to have explained Isaiah 40-66 in 18 volumes, but his work is lost. In Apollinarius there are short explanations, and in the *Catenae* there are citations from works of Eusebius Emesenus and Theodorus Heracleota. These works, however, are lost.

b. Origen wrote a commentary in 30 books in which he covered the prophecy up to chapter 30:6. He also wrote homilies of which a few are extant. Apparently, many of the later commentators drew upon him for their material. As is well known, Origen's work is characterized by allegorical interpretation. I have not utilized it to any great extent in this commentary.

c. Eusebius wrote his *hypomnemata eis Esaian* and also explained many Isaianic passages in his *Demonstratio Evangelica*. He combined allegorical with literal or factual exposition. He used the *Hexapla* of Origen and compared the three minor versions with *LXX*. At times he is in agreement with, at other times in opposition to the Jewish exegesis of his day.

d. Basil the Great, d. 379. In expounding Isaiah 1-16 he used Eusebius. His remarks are allegorical and of a moral nature.

e. Chrysostom wrote his *Interpretations* (*Hermeneia*) of the first eight chapters of Isaiah.

f. Cyril of Alexandria, d. 441. On the whole Cyril follows text B rather than A and makes references to a pre-Origenic text. His interpretations are of a somewhat spiritual and mystic nature.

g. Theodoret, d. 457, used historical and linguistic explanations, referring to the other Biblical books and making comparisons with other Greek versions. Generally he follows the Alexandrian text, sometimes referring to the Hebrew (mainly in difficult passages) and once even to the Syriac, Isa. 8:21.

h. Procopius of Gaza (6th century) presents the heart of previous Greek expositions and also makes additional comments. He is significant for his use of the *LXX* and criticism of the Greek text.

2. THE EARLY LATIN FATHERS

Of these we can mention only Jerome, (his *Work on Isaiah* was written in 410) who of all the early fathers alone depended upon the Hebrew text. He uses Eusebius and also Origen and makes comparisons with the versions. Some of his historical and geographical allusions and comments are quite valuable. At times his exposition is historical and at times typological. I have found Jerome of considerable help and have used him frequently.

3. THE SYRIAN CHURCH

Ephraim Syrus, d. 378. Ephraim is known for giving the historical sense of the passage.

4. THE RABBINICAL INTERPRETERS

a. Of particular significance among Jewish expositors is Rashi (Rabbi Solomon Yizchaki) (1040-1105) who followed the Targum. He wrote on all the Old Testament with the exception of Chronicles. His style is clear and brief, for he sought to imitate the style of the Mishnah, and his comments are homiletical. He interprets Isaiah 9:6 of Hezekiah and refers the Servant passages to Israel. He eschews allegorical interpretation largely because if he employed it he would have to grant the same right to the Christians.

b. Abraham Ibn Ezra (1092-1167) of Toledo, Spain, was a man of encyclopaedic learning. All told he wrote 108 books, including many Biblical commentaries. He followed a grammatico-historical type of exegesis. Apparently he denied to Isaiah the authorship of chapters 40ff.

c. David Kimchi (1160-1235) was a more reliable commentator than Rashi. Many of his comments were polemics against the Christians. At the same time he wielded an influence upon Christian expositors. In his comments on Isa. 2:18 he had accused Christians of being idolators because they prayed to pictures of Christ. His comments, however, are helpful, and I have had occasion to make frequent reference to his commentary.

d. Don Isaac Abarbanel, born in Lisbon, died in Venice (1437-1508). He served in the governments of Portugal, Spain and Italy. A man of wide learning who knew Greek, Latin and Arabic, he quotes from those languages in his commentaries. He seeks for the plain meaning of the Scripture. He introduces each section by asking a number of questions which he seeks to answer.

e. Tanchum Jerushalmi. Tanchum ben Joseph probably lived in Jerusalem during the thirteenth century. Little is known of his life. He wrote in classical, flowing Arabic. He was not an original scholar although a capable grammarian. He rejects the Talmudic and Targumic expositions. Sometimes his own interpretation is striking, as, e.g., his interpretation of *ro-'eh* in Isa. 28:7 as "investigation." His commentary and dictionary were popular in Arabic-speaking countries, such as Yemen.

f. Solomon ben Melech of the 16th century was a factual interpreter. Born at Fez, he lived most of his life at Constantinople. His work is characterized by clear, grammatical exposition. Parts were translated into Latin. The title of his work was the *miklol yofi,* (*The Perfection of Beauty*).

5. THE REFORMATION

a. Martin Luther. The commentary on Isaiah appeared alone in 1528 and then bound with the other prophets in 1532, and in 1534 with the whole Bible. The work is typical of Luther; practical, with many digressions. At the same time the great reformer understood the message of Isaiah, which cannot be said of all commentators. I read Luther both with profit for the understanding and with blessing.

b. Zwingli (1529). The work is theological with insight into the true meaning of Isaiah.

c. Calvin (1570) wrote what in many respects may be called one of the greatest of the Isaiah commentaries. Calvin has deep insight into the great sweeps of revelation and of the relationship which the individual verses bear to the picture as a whole. Valuable homiletic and expository remarks abound. When Calvin is at his best, he is unsurpassable. He has been my constant companion in the preparation of this commentary.

6. EXPOSITION SINCE THE REFORMATION

a. Commentaries or expositions were also written by Oecolampadius (1525), Brentius (1550), Meusel (1570), Vatablus, a Catholic (1557), and comments of Sebastian Münster appear in the *Critica Sacra.* The following writers, whom I have not consulted, used the rabbinical learning: Castellio (1531), Foreirius (1553).

b. In the seventeenth century we may note Sanctius and Grotius (1644). The comments of Grotius are historical and factual. It has been said that he finds Christ nowhere. His comments are not satisfactory, for Grotius did not discern the profundity of Isaiah. His remarks border on the superficial. *De Dieu* (1648) employed a grammatical treatment, and appealed to the Syriac and Ethiopic. Of particular interest are the *Critica Sacri,* London, 1660, appearing in nine volumes. The fourth volume is devoted to Isaiah and contains the comments of Münster, Vatablus, Castalio, Clarius, Foreirius, Drusius and Grotius. This work is useful. Ludwig Cappellus (1689) made textual remarks on the variants in the manuscripts.

c. The eighteenth century. We may note Johannes Cocceius (1701), whose work contains some useful philological explanations. Cocceius refers the prophecies to events within Christian church history. Reference may be made also to the notes of Sebastian Schmidt (1702). Varenius (1708) used a scholastic method and introduced much irrelevant material in his work. His comments however, are significant.

(1) One of the greatest commentators was Campegius Vitringa whose work began to appear in 1714, a new edition being printed in 1732. The amount of learning displayed in this work is tremendous. Comments are made on the meaning of each word, and the treatment of the foreign prohecies is particularly helpful. The work is thoroughly orthodox, and must be consulted by every serious student of the prophet.

(2) In the margin of the Halle Bible (1720) occur the notes of J. H. Michaelis. In 1731 appeared Le Clerc's work, which is generally regarded as not as valuable as his comments on the historical books. Calmet (1724-26) gave a good treatment of the historical material, and C. F. Houbigant (1753) preferred the versions over the Masoretic text.

(3) Carl Rudolf Reichel (1759) wrote two valuable volumes on Isaiah. His work is thoroughly orthodox, and he makes a serious effort to bring out the meaning of the prophecy. I have found his work of great help.

(4) The commentary of Robert Lowth (1778) has an aesthetic and poetic emphasis. The notes are often quite valuable, because of their quotations from the classical writers. Kocher (1778) defended the Masoretic text as against Lowth.

(5) J. B. Koppe (1779-1781) edited the German edition of Lowth's commentary and supplied it with notes, some of which are reckless. He suggested that chapter 50 might be the work of Ezekiel or of someone living at the time of the exile.

(6) The comments of John Gill (1771), a Baptist minister, show a true understanding of the meaning of the prophecy. Gill was well versed in the rabbinical and talmudical literature.

(7) The remarks of Heinrich Eberhard Gottlob Paulus (1793) are of philological value, but his work is rationalistic. His students spoke of him as *"Paulus, der Nichtapostel."* We may mention also the work of G. L. Bauer (1794, 1795), and J. Chr. W. Augusti (1799), which latter was designed particularly for pastors.

(8) Of particular interest and significance is the commentary of E. F. Rosenmüller (1791-1793). These volumes are written in Latin and contain an elaborate exposition of the text with valuable philological comments. The standpoint is influenced somewhat by rationalism and the interpretation therefore is often disappointing.

(9) There were a number of translations into German with comments on the text. Eichhorn (1819) thought that the prophecy contained poetic descriptions of the present and not predictive prophecy. Döderlein first denied the entirety of chapters 40-66 to Isaiah and, as

may be said of Dathe, made many comments of a more or less superficial nature. Both these men change the text arbitrarily.

7. THE NINETEENTH CENTURY

a. The way for the criticism of the prophecy had been prepared by some of the eighteenth-century works. Among these we may note in particular that of J. D. Michaelis (1778), which was of independent tendency and may be regarded as a forerunner of the destructive criticism that characterized the nineteenth century.

b. One of the greatest commentaries was that of Wilhelm Gesenius (1821). The philological remarks are excellent, and there are many comparisons with the Arabic. Gesenius, however, did not appreciate the nature of prophecy and he has not really risen above the rationalistic level of some of his predecessors. Hitzig disagreed with Gesenius on many points, but his work is written on the same level. Hendewerk's commentary (1838, 1843) is no improvement as far as the spiritual interpretation of the prophecy is concerned. Umbreit's work is not satisfactory, for it is of rationalistic tendency. Ewald's comments (1841) are meagre, and Knobel also is of a "critical" bias.

c. Barnes's notes (1840) are conservative and useful, but his theological statements are not always in accord with Scripture. Henderson's work is also conservative (1840). Hengstenberg's *Christology* (1829) will ever remain one of the greatest works on the interpretation of the prophecies.

d. Joseph Addison Alexander (1846) produced a two-volume commentary that is exemplary. It is absolutely true to the Scriptures, rich in insight and in discussion of the Hebrew forms, and filled with valuable comment.

e. Moritz Drechsler (1845, 1849) has written what in the present author's opinion is one of the greatest, if not the greatest, commentary on Isaiah. The work exhibits a remarkable insight into the meaning of the prophecy.

f. Rudolf Stier (1850) defended the Isaianic authorship of chapters 40-66. The commentary is written in a devotional spirit.

g. Ernst Meyer (1850) covered the first twenty-three chapters of Isaiah. He regards the prophets as being concerned only with mankind's ethical freedom.

h. Samuel David Luzzatto expounded the prophecy from the standpoint of orthodox Judaism (1855).

i. Franz Delitzsch (1866), one of the greatest of the commentators on Isaiah. The work is orthodox, and gives full attention to the nature of predictive prophecy. Delitzsch wavered on the Isaianic authorship of the twenty-seven final chapters.

j. T. K. Cheyne (1868) produced a truly useful commentary on the prophecy. It is far more restrained than some of Cheyne's writings.

k. George Adam Smith (1888, 1890) wrote two volumes of popular lectures. These are written in beautiful style, but they lack an appreciation of the true nature of the prophecy. To the present writer they are most disappointing.

l. Bernhard Duhm (1892) suggested that the prophecy consisted of three main parts, and spoke of Isaiah, Second Isaiah and Third Isaiah. Stade before him had also suggested that certain parts were later than those normally attributed to the "second" Isaiah. Duhm's commentary is radical, and he is very free with textual emendations.

m. J. Skinner, ("Isaiah" in the *Cambridge Bible*, 1896-1898), for the most part adopted the position of Duhm. There are useful historical and introductory comments.

8. Recent Developments

a. Karl Marti (1900) spoke of Isaiah as a little library of prophetical literature. We have made frequent reference to Marti in the text, and from these references the reader may gain an idea of the type of approach used by Marti.

b. G. Buchanan Gray, in the *International Critical Commentary* (1912) makes philological comments that are usually excellent, but his approach to the book and his exegesis are not satisfactory when judged from the standpoint of those who hold to the trustworthiness of the Bible.

c. The school of form-criticism is represented in the Introduction of Herman Gunkel in *Die Schriften des Alten Testaments* (1914), and in the comments of Hans Schmidt in the same work.

d. Writing from the standpoint of historic Reformed theology J. Ridderbos (1922) has produced a useful commentary. In his larger work, *Jesaja,* appearing in *Het Godswoord der Profeten* (1932) he has discussed the entire prophecy.

e. Franz Feldmann (1924) produced a commentary in which a return to sober exegesis appeared. Feldmann was a Catholic and his comments are valuable.

f. Paul Volz (1932) discussed the second portion of the prophecy. His work is critical.

g. E. J. Kissane (1941, 1943) a Roman Catholic, wrote two volumes. Kissane is free with textual emendations, and his comments are not entirely satisfactory. They are brief, and the arguments are not always developed as fully as one might wish.

h. Johann Fischer (1937) has written two useful volumes. His viewpoint is generally conservative, although probably not as much so as Feldmann's. Fischer is Roman Catholic, and his best work deals with the Servant of the Lord passages.

i. The Danish commentary of Aage Bentzen (1944) covers the entire prophecy from the modern Scandinavian viewpoint. I have made frequent reference to it as well as to the work of Sigmund Mowinckel.

J. Writing from a neo-orthodox standpoint Volkmar Herntrich (1954) has expounded the first twelve chapters of Isaiah. There is much useful material in his book but, like many writers of this school, he is wordy.

k. Jean Steinmann (1955) has produced a study of Isaiah, hardly a commentary, which, although written from a Roman Catholic standpoint, is quite free in divisive criticism. There are useful historical notes, but the interpretation is not always satisfactory.

l. Sheldon H. Blank (1958) has produced an extremely radical study of the prophecy. Blank is so radical and changes the prophecy so frequently that I have been unable to derive much help from his work.

m. S. Paul Schilling, *Isaiah Speaks* (1958, 1959), is a popularization of the "three Isaiah" theory. There seems to be little grappling with the truly serious problems of the book.

n. Angelo Penna (1958), writing in Italian, has produced a remarkable commentary. He has useful comments on historical and geographical matters, and his exegesis is usually sound. A valuable work. Probably the best thing on Isaiah within recent years.

o. The Interpreter's Bible (1952ff.) covers the entire book with expository comments and practical applications. It approaches the work from a radical standpoint, assuming a multiple authorship for the prophecy.

NOTE: The above list is purposely limited. I have excluded reference to articles or essays and included only some of the commentaries. Those who desire a fuller discussion will find it in my *Studies in Isaiah,* Grand Rapids, 1954. References to articles and other literature will be found in the relevant places in the commentary proper.

Appendix III

THE FESTIVAL OF ENTHRONEMENT

In ancient Mesopotamia there was an annual festival of the enthronement of the king.[1] In Babylon it took place at the Esagila temple on the New Year in the spring. It lasted for twelve days of Nisan and served the purpose of celebrating the beginning of a new cycle of seasons. The god (in Babylon it was Marduk) had become inactive. The rains had ceased, and vegetation lay dying. Marduk was held captive in the mountain of the Netherworld.

On the first four days of the festival preparations were made, and on the eve of the fourth day the entire Babylonian epic of creation (the *enûma eliš*) was recited, for it was believed that there was a relation between the New Year and the day of creation. As at creation the world and man came into existence, so at the New Year the forces of life are released and overcome the obstacles which have led to the imprisonment of the god.

In some respects the most important point in the festival was the fifth day, which may be labelled a day of humiliation. In the morning the king offered his prayers of appeasement to the god Marduk. The temple was then subjected to purification, and incantations and offerings continued. The king entered the shrine of the god Marduk, and from the inmost recess or "holy of holies" where the statue of Marduk was, the high priest emerged, took the royal insignia, including the crown, from the king and placed them before the statue of the god. He then approached the king who was now divested of the royal insignia and smote him on the cheek. Following this the king was compelled to kneel down and to recite a prayer of confession. In return the priest pronounced what amounted to a declaration of absolution, assuring the king that Marduk would increase his dominion and raise his royalty. The royal insignia were then returned to the king, who was struck once more on the face in the hope of drawing tears, for these were regarded as a favorable omen.

The king seems then to have acted, in Babylon at least, as a master

---

[1] The literature on this subject is quite extensive. The reader may consult Henri Frankfort: *Kingship and the Gods*, Chicago, 1948, pp. 313-333; C. J. Gadd: *Ideas of Divine Rule in the Ancient East*, 1948; Svend Aage Pallas: *The Babylonian 'akitu' Festival*, København, 1926; Ivan Engnell: *Studies in Divine Kingship in the Ancient Near East*, Uppsala, 1943.

494

of ceremonies. In Assyria, however, he actually represented the god Assur. By means of the festivities the god was to be delivered from his imprisonment or condition of inactivity. The statues of other gods were floated on barges from different cities. These were brought into the Chamber of Destinies. Marduk was then liberated, and the combined power of the various gods bestowed upon him so that he would be victorius in his battle against the powers of death and chaos. There was a march to the Bit Akitu for the celebration of the god's victory over the chaos.[2] The sacred marriage then followed that the earth might be fertilized to bring forth new crops. On the twelfth day the gods assembled again to judge man and then were returned to their own cities and shrines.

Was this festival or anything akin to it celebrated in ancient Israel, and if so, is there any mention thereof in the pages of the Old Testament? In 1912 Paul Volz asserted that the Feast of Tabernacles was not merely a harvest festival borrowed from the Canaanites, but a festival of the New Year celebrated in honor of Israel's God, Yahweh, who had created the world and established the nation.[3] It is true, said Volz, that the festival did acquire a harvest character, but this was due to Canaanitish influence. In his study Volz made a comparison with both the Assyrian and the Babylonian New Year's festivals.

The thesis was more fully developed in 1922 by Sigmund Mowinckel who claimed that the cultic drama was more than a symbolical representation.[4] It was rather present and actual reality. Marduk was defeating the forces of chaos and death. The Israelites took this festival over from the Canaanites who in turn had received it from the Babylonians.

In 1927 Hans Schmidt tried to show from the Psalms that the first day of the great festival was celebrated by a procession in which an actual throne was carried on which the invisible God was to sit.[5] And in this same year Franz Böhl asserted that in the festival the ark was carried from the brook Gihon to the Temple.[6]

When, then, did the Hebrews take over this festival from the Canaanites? This question Mowinckel would answer by saying that it was just after their entrance into Canaan. On the other hand, Von Gall held that it was not until the Assyrian period, i.e., between 730-630 B.C., that they received it.[7]

---

[2] The meaning of *akitu* is not certain. Probably it is a Sumerian word in Akk. form. Cf. Pallas, *op. cit.*, pp. 191-193, for a discussion of the term.

[3] Paul Volz: *Das Neujahrsfest Jahwes*, Tübingen, 1912.

[4] *Psalmenstudien II, Das Thronbesteigungsfest Jahwäs und der Ursprung der Eschatologie*, Christiana, 1922.

[5] *Die Thronfahrt Jahves*, Tübingen, 1927.

[6] *Nieuwjaarsfeest en Koningsdag in Babylon en Israel*, 1927.

[7] A. von Gall: *Basileia tou Theou*.

A modified view of the enthronement festival appears in the writings of von Rad.[8] He holds that there were two acts to the enthronement. In the sanctuary the king was crowned and received the royal protocol, somewhat after the manner of the Egyptian Pharaoh. This legitimized his rule under the deity. Having been anointed king he was led into his palace, where he mounted the throne and in more or less threatening tone announced to all and sundry that he was about to rule. Messengers were then despatched to announce that the king was on the throne. It was a time of great joy. In Jerusalem it was doubtless understood as the promise of a new, divine order.

The basic point of the festival was the introduction of the Davidic ruler into the relation of childhood to Yahweh, which took place in the form of an act of adoption. In Israel, asserts von Rad, this adoption was never understood in a mythological sense, as was the case in Egypt, where the Pharaoh was regarded as the actual incarnate god who had been begotten by Amun and the queen mother.

The king now had the right to call upon the God, to sit at God's right hand and to advise with him about all matters of the kingdom. Indeed, he could now rule in God's stead. But the language of the enthronement stood out in sharp contrast with the actual person of the king and the actual realities of political life. This language is to be regarded as an old court style which served as a frame into which the faith in Yahweh was fitted, and thus the whole came to possess a new character.

This was a festival of the greatest joy and rejoicing for in a most dramatic manner it celebrated the commencement of Yahweh's rule over the world. Yahweh had overcome that which was chaotic in the world as well as political enemies. Von Rad acknowledges therefore a Babylonian influence, and this he believes came to Israel through Ugarit.

There are several considerations which compel one to reject the view that in ancient Israel a festival of the enthronement of Yahweh was celebrated.

(1) There is of course no explicit mention of such a festival anywhere in the Old Testament. To this Mowinckel retorts that such an argument is a perversion (*Verdrehung*) of the matter.[9] We are not dealing, he says, with a festival hitherto unknown, but rather with an aspect of the well-known Feast of Tabernacles which hitherto has been unnoticed. Well and good, let us rephrase the objection. Is there any mention or allusion to this particular aspect of the Feast of Tabernacles? To this we would reply with an emphatic negative, and our reply of course involves the question of exegesis. We cannot agree with the specific

[8] Gerhard von Rad: *Theologie des Alten Testaments,* Band I, Die Theologie der geschichtlichen Überlieferungen Israels, München, 1957, pp. 317ff.

[9] Sigmund Mowinckel: *Zum israelitischen Neujahr und zur Deutung der Thronbesteigungspsalmen,* Olso, 1952, p. 46.

interpretation of the individual Psalms where Mowinckel believes that he finds the necessary allusions, references and indications.[10]

(2) Hebrew kingship was unique. If we accept the statements of Scripture at face value, we recognize that kingship had been promised very early, even as early as the time of Abraham. At the same time, a king was not immediately given to the nation. It had first of all to learn its need for a ruler. When finally the request was made, it was made so that Israel might be like the nations about it. An emergency was at hand, and the nation recognized at last its need for a king.

(3) Kingship was not regarded in Israel as something which had originally dropped down from heaven and was an essential part of the nation's life. Rather, at a time when there was no king, the Lord chose Israel to be a nation. At that time the nation was in bondage to Egypt. Then God spoke, "Thus saith the LORD, Israel is my son, even my firstborn: And I say unto thee, Let my son go, that he may serve me: and if thou refuse to let him go, behold I will slay thy son, even thy firstborn" (Exod. 4:22b, 23). God is speaking to Moses in the wilderness. The nation is not organized, yet God addresses it as His Son. "For thou art an holy people unto the LORD thy God, and the LORD hath chosen thee to be a peculiar people unto himself, above all the nations that are upon the earth" (Deut. 14:2).

(4) In line with this thought that God chose the nation and honored it when it had no king, is the reaction of the nation itself. The Hebrews looked back to this time of the desert wanderings as the formative period of their national life. Then the Law of God had been given, and the great institutions were either established or promised. It was

10 A critique of Mowinckel's interpretation of the Psalms will be found in N. H. Ridderbos: De "Werkers der Ongerechtigheid" in de Individueele Psalmen, Kampen, 1939. Norman H. Snaith (The Jewish New Year Festival, London, 1947) has vigorously rejected Mowinckel's views, and to this Mowinckel has made partial reply, particularly as regards the date of the New Year (op. cit., pp. 39-52). In my opinion, however, the question of date is of a somewhat secondary nature. Even if Mowinckel's interpretation of the date were correct (and his argument is weighty), the arguments adduced above are sufficient to show that no enthronement festival was actually celebrated in Israel. Cf. also A. H. Edelkoort: De Christusverwachting in het Oude Testament, Wageningen, 1941, pp. 36-40, who gives a penetrating analysis of the weakness of Mowinckel's account of the origin of Israelitish eschatology. A useful discussion will also be found in Hans Joachim Kraus: Psalmen (Biblischer Kommentar Altes Testament, Neukirchen, 1958), pp. 201-205; J. J. Stamm: Theologisches Rundschau, 23/1, pp. 46ff. Three articles dealing with the interpretation of מלך יהוה are, Ludwig Kohler: V.T., 3, 1953, pp. 188ff., J. Ridderbos: V.T., 4, 1954, pp. 87-89 and D. Michel, V.T., 6, 1956, pp. 40-68. This last article is of particular value and is a cogent refutation of Mowinckel's contention with respect to the translation, "the Lord has become king." In connection with Isaiah 52:7 I plan to engage in a thorough discussion of this question.

this period which was formative and determinative for the life of Israel, and yet there was no king. If anything, it is correct to say that the kingship was an outgrowth of the basic nature of the theocracy which had been revealed by God to the nation in the wilderness of Sinai.

(5) In the light of the second commandment it seems inconceivable that any festival involving the usage of statues or emblems as did the Babylonian *akitu* festival could have been carried through in Israel. There were no statues of the Lord, no pictures of Him nor emblems of the religious cult. The ark was simply regarded as the abode of God. Its significance was quite different from that of the emblems employed in the *akitu* festival.

(6) It must be stated emphatically that the exegesis of the Psalms which characterizes the adherents of the view which we are considering is not tenable. It is precisely in the ninety-third Psalm, which has so often been closely connected with the nature myth of the renewal in creation, that we find the sovereignty and eternity of God stressed. "Thy throne is established of old: thou art from everlasting" (Ps. 93:2). The royal Psalms in particular emphasize the eternity of God's throne and His superiority and sovereignty over all false divinities. Nowhere is there mention of the Lord ascending the throne. Whatever celebration there may be appears to concern the choice of Jerusalem and David, not the Lord's ascending the throne.

(7) The whole concept of the enthronement is bound up with the changes in nature. In Mesopotamia the god became inactive. The forces of nature imprisoned him, and he had to be liberated by the king. This is wholly foreign to the Old Testament. Into what theological context could it possibly be fitted? The God of the Old Testament never loses His control over creation for an instant. He is the Creator in the truest sense of the word. In Babylon there was no true doctrine of creation. The forces of nature do not control the true God; He controls them. They obey His will. He laid the foundations of the earth, that it should not be removed for ever (Ps. 104:5). At His rebuke the waters fled. "He sendeth the springs into the valleys, which run among the hills." "He causeth the grass to grow for the cattle, and herb for the service of man; that he may bring forth food out of the earth" (Ps. 104:10, 14). If anything in the Old Testament is clear it is that God is not overcome by nature; nor does He have to do battle with chaotic waters. To think of Him losing His reign and being imprisoned is so far removed from the Old Testament thought that it sounds ludicrous.

(8) It should further be noted that among the Hebrews the functions of the king were primarily in the secular sphere. When Uzziah took upon him to offer incense he was smitten by leprosy in punishment (2 Kings 15:5; 2 Chron. 26:16-21). The king did have the prerogative of pronouncing judgment, but he could not take the place of the priests.

(9) The prophets had no hesitation in rebuking the king when they

thought he had deviated from the divine will. An outstanding example for our period is the meeting of Isaiah and Ahaz. Furthermore, nowhere do the prophets condemn an enthronement festival or those aspects of the Feast of Tabernacles which might be thought to allude to an enthronement festival. On this whole question the prophets are silent. They do not hesitate, however, to condemn other festivals. Isaiah, for example, has much to say by way of condemnation of the misuse of the festivals. And if there had been an enthronement festival, would he not have seized the opportunity to condemn it? Could he have tolerated the polytheism which it would have involved?

(10) The *akitu* festival stresses the oneness of man with nature. Man's life is bound up with that of nature, and so also is the life of the god. The god is really immanent in nature. In the Old Testament, however, the transcendence of the Lord receives the emphasis. It is the precise opposite of what we have in Babylon.

(11) One cannot escape the polytheism that characterizes the religion of Mesopotamia. Israel's monotheism on the other hand stands out as a fair flower in a barren desert. There is nothing similar to Israel's monotheism anywhere else in the ancient world. Polytheism and the *akitu* festival go hand in hand. Monotheism and the *akitu* festival have nothing to do the one with the other.

(12) Von Rad's interpretation of the enthronement festival is based upon the assumption that the Psalms, such as the second Psalm, are not speaking primarily of the Messiah, but merely of what was customarily done in the case of the Davidic kings.[11] Such an interpretation, we believe, is without warrant. For these reasons we are constrained to reject the view that a festival of the enthronement was held in ancient Israel and hence, we cannot accept those interpretations of Isaiah which would discover traces of such a festival in that book.

---

11 Cf. also Aubrey R. Johnson: *Sacral Kingship in Ancient Israel,* Cardiff, 1955. This is a thought-provoking book, but the phrase "sacral kingship" is essentially alien to the Old Testament thought. Cf. also the interpretation of Psalm 2 in Mowinckel, *HTC*, p. 67; Aage Bentzen: *King and Messiah*, London, 1955, p. 20; Helmer Ringgren: *Messias Konungen,* Uppsala, 1954 (English translation, Chicago, 1956). Ringgren thinks that the Psalm would belong to that part of the annual festival that represents the defeat of the enemies. The reader should consult the commentaries of Hengstenberg, Delitzsch, Alexander and Leupold for a presentation of the traditional interpretation of the Psalm.

Select Bibliography

(See also Appendix I and II)

Aalders, G. Ch., *Obadja, Jona* (Commentaar op het Oude Testament). Kampen, 1958.

Aalen, S., *Die Begriffe Licht und Finsternis im Alten Testament, im Spätjudentum und Rabbinismus.* Oslo, 1951.

Abu-l-walid, cf. Derenbourg, *Opuscules et Traités d'Abou 'l-Walid Merwan Ibn Djanah de Cordove.* Paris, 1880.

Abarbanel, Don Isaac; also Abravanel; cf. Rosenmüller.

Abulfeda, cf. H. O. Fleischer, *Historia anteislamica arabice edidit, versione latina auxit.* Lipsia, 1831.

Aeschylus, *Persae* (Loeb Classical Library).

————, *Aggardat Bereshith.*

Albright, William F., "Baal-Zephon," *FAB,* Tübingen, 1950.

————, "The Chronology of the Divided Monarchy of Israel," *BASOR,* No. 100.

————, "The High Place in Ancient Palestine," *VTS,* 1957.

————, "The Son of Tabael," *BASOR,* No. 140, Dec., 1955.

————, *Archives of the Religion of Israel.* 1942.

Alexander, Joseph Addison, *Commentary on the Prophecies of Isaiah.* 1846. Grand Rapids, 1953.

Allis, Oswald T., *The Five Books of Moses.* Philadelphia, 1943.

————, *Prophecy and the Church.* Philadelphia, 1943.

Alt, Albrecht, "Agyptisch-ugaritisches," *AfO,* 15, 1951.

————, "Galiläische Probleme," *Palästinajahrbuch,* 1937.

————, *Kleine Schriften,* II. Munchen, 1953.

————, "Menschen Ohne Namen," *Archiv Orientalni,* 18, 1950.

Amarna Text. J. Knudtzon, *Die El-Amarna-Tafeln.* Aalen, 1964.

Ammianus Marcellinus (Loeb Classical Library). Cambridge, 1935.

Amr el-Quais, *Moallaka,* cf. W. Ahlwardt, *The divans of the six ancient Arabic poets.* London, 1870.

Anderson, Robert T., "Was Isaiah A Scribe?" *JBL,* March, 1960.

Annals of Mursilis, text in Sturtevant and Bechtel, *A Hittite Chrestomathy.* Philadelphia, 1935.

Anspacher, Abraham S., *Tiglath Pileser III.* New York, 1912.

Apollinarius Appian, *de bello civili* (Loeb Classical Library).

Aqhat, see Gordon, *Ugaritic Handbook.*

2 *Aqht,* see Gordon, *Ugaritic Handbook.*

Arias Montanus, Benito, *Polyglot Antwerp.* 1569-1573.

501

Augusti, J. Chr. W., *Grundriss einer historisch-kritischen Einleitung ins A. T.* Leipzig, 1827.

Biblia Sacra iuxta versionem simplicem quae dicitur Peschitta, II. Beirut, 1951.

Biblical Archaeologist, The. New Haven, Connecticut.

Barnes, A., *Notes on Isaiah*, I. New York, 1840.

Basil the Great, in *Nicene and post-Nicene Fathers*, Second Series, VIII, 1895. Grand Rapids, 1955.

Baumgartner and Köhler, *Lexicon in Veteris Testamenti Libros.*

Béguerie, *La Vocation d'Isaiae*, Études sur les prophètes d'Israel. Paris, 1954.

Ben Melech, Solomon, *moklal yofi (Perfectio pulchritudinis).*

Bentzen, Aage, *Jesaji, Band* I, Jes. 1-39. Kφbenhaven, 1944.

——, *King and Messiah.* London, 1955.

Berry, G. R., "Messianic Predictions," *JBL* (1926-27).

Bewer, Julius A., *The Literature of the Old Testament.* New York, 1940.

Bijbel in Nieuwe Vertaling. Kampen, 1952.

Birkeland, H., *Zum Hebräischen Traditionswesen.* Oslo, 1938.

Blank, Sheldon H., *Prophetic Faith in Isaiah.* New York, 1958.

——, *JBL*, 68, 1948.

Bleeker, *Kleine Propheten*, II.

Böhl, Franz, *Nieuwjaarsfest en Konigsdag in Babylon en Israel.* 1927.

Boehmer, "Dieses Volk," *JBL*, 1926-27.

Boettner, Loraine, *The Millennium.* Philadelphia, 1958.

Bratcher, Robert G., *The Bible Translator.* July, 1958.

Briggs, Charles A., *Messianic Prophecy.* New York, 1886.

Brockelmann, *Hebräische Syntax.* Neu kirchen, 1956.

Bruno, D. Arvid, *Jesaja, eine rhythmische und textkritische Untersuchung.* Stockholm, 1953.

Budde, Karl, "Jesaja 13," *Festschrift von Baudissin.* Giessen, 1918.

Bultema, Harry, *Practische Commentaar op Jesaja.* Muskegon, 1923.

Burrows, M., Trevor, J. C., Brownlee, W. H., *The Dead Sea Scrolls of St. Mark's Monastery* I, *The Isaiah Manuscript and the Habakkuk Commentary.* New Haven, 1950.

Caesar, Julius, *de bello Gallico* (Loeb Classical Library).

Calvin, *Commentarii in Isaiam prophetam.* Geneva, 1570.

Campbell, Roderick, *Israel and the Covenant.* Philadelphia, 1954.

Cappellus, Ludwig, *Critica sacra.* 1650.

Caspari, Carl Paul, *Jesajanische Studien.* Leipzig, 1843.

Castellio, Sebastian, *Biblia Sacra.* 1531. Frankfurt, 1669.

Catullus (Loeb Classical Library).

Ceriani, A., *Translatio syra Pescitto Veteris Testamenti.* Milan, 1876.

Chafer, Lewis S., *Systematic Theology.* Dallas, 1947-48.

Cheyne, T. K., *The Prophecies of Isaiah*, I. 1868. New York, 1888.

Chiera, *Proceedings in Court,* Publications of the Bagdad School, Texts, IV, 331. Philadelphia, 1934.

Childs, B. S., *Myth and Reality in the Old Testament.* Napersville, 1960.

Chrysostom, *Hermeneia,* in Migne, *Patrologia.*

Churgin, P., *Targum Jonathan to the Prophets.* New Haven, 1927.

Cicero, *ad Atticum* (Loeb Classical Library).

———, *Definibus* (Loeb Classical Library).

———, *de Senectate* (Loeb Classical Library).

———, *Phillip,* II (Loeb Classical Library).

———, *Tuscalan Disputations* (Loeb Classical Library).

Clement, *Stromata,* ed. Hort and Mayor, *Clement of Alexandria.* London, 1902.

Cocceius, Johannes, *Opera Omnia Theologica.* Amstelodami, 1701.

Condamin, Albert, *Le Livre d'Isaie.* Paris, 1905.

Cooke, G. A., *A Textbook of North Semitic Inscriptions.* Oxford, 1903.

Coppens, *La Prophétie de la 'Almah.* Bruges, Paris, 1952.

Cordero, M. Garcia, "El Santo de Israel," *Mélanges Bibliques rédigés en l'honneur de André Robert.* Paris, 1957.

Corpus Inscriptionum Semiticarum.

Critica Sacri, ed. Edward Leigh. London, 1661.

Dalman, Gustav, *Jerusalem und seine Gelände.* Gütersloh, 1930.

D'Alpe, A., "Quis sit prudens eloquo mystici," *VD,* 23, 1943.

Dathe, Johann August, *Opuscula,* ed. E. F. Rosenmüller. Lipsiae, 1796.

Davis, John D., "The Child Whose Name is Wonderful," *Biblical and Theological Studies* (Princeton Centenary Volume). New York, 1912.

Davis, John D., "Medeba or the Waters of Rabbah," *PTR,* 1922.

De Ausejo, C. S., "El Problema do Tartesos,' *'Sefarad,* 2, 1942.

DeBoer, P.A.H., *Second-Isaiah's Message.* Leiden, 1956.

Delekat, L., "Die Peschitta zu Jesaja zwischen Targum und Septuaginta," *Biblica,* XXXVIII, 1957.

Delitzsch, Franz, *Biblical Commentary on the Prophecies of Isaiah.* 1866. Grand Rapids, 1949.

Demosthenes, *Contra Aristogenes I* (Loeb Classical Library).

Dhorme, E., *L'evolution religieuse d'Israel.* Bruxelles, 1937.

Dillmann, August, *Das Prophet Jesaia.* Leipzig, 1890.

Dio Cassius (Loeb Classical Library).

Diodorus Siculus (Loeb Classical Library).

Diringer, *Le Iscrizioni Antico-Ebraiche Palestinesi.* Firenze, 1934.

Döderlein, Christoph, *Esaias,* Altsofi, 1825.

Drechsler, Moritz, *Der Prophet Jesaja.* Stuttgart, 1849.

Driver, G. R., *Canaanite Myths and Legends.* 1956.

———, *A Treatise on the Use of Tenses in Hebrew.* 1892.

———, *Von Ugarit Nach Qumram.* 1958.

———, *JBL, Sept.,* 1954.

Driver, S. R., *Isaiah, His Life and Times.* New York.

Duhm, Bernhard, *Das Buch Jesaia*. 1892. Göttingen, 1922.

Dürr, L., *ZAW*, 1925, "Hebr. רגא = akk. napištu = Guroel, Kehle."

Dussaud, R., *des Religions de Babylonie et d' Assyrie*. Paris, 1945.

Eaton, J., "The Origin of the Book of Isaiah," *VT*, IX, No. 2.

Edelkoort, A. H., *De Christusverwachting in het Oude Testament*. Wageningen, 1941.

Eichhorn, Johann G., *Die hebräische Propheten*. Göttingen, 1819.

Eitan, *HUCA*, 12-13.

Engnell, Ivan, *The Call of Isaiah*. Uppsala and Leipzig, 1949.

————, *Studies in Divine Kingship in the Ancient Near East*. Uppsala, 1943.

Enuma Elish, cf. A. Heidel, *The Babylonian Genesis*. Chicago, 1951.

Ephraim, Syrus, *Opera Omnia*.

Erman, A., *The Religion of the Egyptians*.

Eusebius, *Die Griechischen Christlichen Schriftsteller der ersten drei Jahrhunderte*, VII-XXIII. 1913.

Euting, Julius, *Sinaitische Inschriften*. Berlin, 1901.

Ewald, H., *Die Propheten des alten Bundes erklärt*. Stuttgart, 1840-41.

Fahlgren, K.H., *Nahestehende und entegengesetzte Begriff im Alten Testament*. Uppsala, 1932.

Feldmann, Franz, *Das Buch Isaias*, I, II. Münster, 1926.

Field, F., *Origenis Hexaplarum quae supersunt*, II. Oxford, 1875.

Finkelstein, Louis, *The Commentary of David Kimchi on Isaiah*. 1926.

Firdawzi, cf. T. Nöldeke, *Das iranische Nationalepos*. Strasburg (Grundriss der iranischen Philologie, 1896-1904, II, 131-211).

Fischer, Johann, *Das Buch Isaias*. Bonn; I, 1937, II, 1939.

Frankfort, Henri, *Kingship and the Gods*. Chicago, 1948.

Freidrichsen, A., *Hagios-Qadosh*. Oslo, 1916.

Frühstorfer, *TBQ*, 91, 1938.

Fullerton, K., "Studies in Isaiah," *JBL*, 35, 38. 1919.

Gadd, C. J., *Ideas of the Divine Rule in the Ancient East*. 1948.

Gaebelein, Arno C., *The Annotated Bible*. New York, 1913.

Galling, Kurt, *Textbuch zur Geschichte Israels*. Tübingen, 1950.

Gesenius, Wilhelm, *Der Prophet Jesaia*. Leipzig, 1820, 1821.

Gesenius, Kautzsch, Cowley, *Hebrew Grammar*. Oxford, 1910.

Gilgamesh Epic, cf. A. Heidel, *The Gilgamesh Epic*.

Gill, John, *Body of Divinity*. 1771. Grand Rapids, 1951.

Ginsberg, "Some Emendations in Isaiah," *JBL*, 69, March, 1950.

Ginsberg, C. D., *Prophetae posteriores*. London, 1911.

Gordon, Cyrus H., "Belt Wrestling in the Bible World," *HUCA*, 23, Part One. Cincinnati, 1950-51.

Gray, George Buchanan, *The Prophecy of Isaiah*. Edinburgh, 1926.

————, *Israel Exploration Journal*, Vol. 12, No. 3, 1952.

————, *Ugaritic Handbook*. 1955.

————, *The World of the Old Testament.* New York, 1958.
Green, *Hebrew Grammar.* New York, 1898.
Greene, Ashbel, *Lectures on the Shorter Catechism,* 2 vols. Philadelphia, c. 1841.
Grelot, P., "La denière etappe de la redaction sacerdotale," *VT*, 6, 1956.
Gressmann, *Altorientalische Texte zum Alten Testament.* 1909.
Grimme, H., *Th.Q,* 1903.
Grotius, Hugo, *Annotata ad Vetus Testamentum.* 1644.
Gunkel, Herman, *Die Schriften des Alten Testaments,* 2 Abteilung, 2 Band. 1921, 1925.
Guthe, Hermann, *Geschichte des Volkes Israels.* Tübingen and Leipzig, 1904.

Haldane, Robert, *Commentary on Romans.* London, 1960.
Haller, Max, *Die Schriften des Alten Testaments,* II, 3. Göttingen, 1914.
Hamasa, ed. G. W. Freytag, *Hamasae carmina.* Bonn, 1828-1847.
Hammond, *Isaiah Statesman Prophet.*
Hammurabi, cf. A. Deimel, *Codex Hammurabi.* Romae, 1930.
Hanel, J., *Die Religion der Heiligkeit,* Gütersloh, 1931.
Hattusilis, *Apology,* cf. Sturtevant and Bechtel, *Hittite Chrestomathy.* Philadelphia, 1935.
Heidel, W. A., *The Day of Jahweh.* New York, 1929.
Henderson, Ebenezer, *The Book of the prophet Isaiah.* 1840. London, 1857.
Hengstenberg, E., *Authenticity of Daniel and Christology.* 1829.
Herntrich, Volkmar, *Der Prophet Jesaja, Kapitel* 1-12. Göttingen, 1950.
Herodotus (Loeb Classical Library) .
Hertzberg, H. W., *Der erste Jesaja.* Kassel, 1952.
Herzfeld, E., *Altpersische Inschriften.* 1938.
Hesiod (Loeb Classical Library) .
Hitzig, Ferdinand, *Der Prophet Jesaja.* Heidelberg, 1833.
Hölscher, G., *Geschichte der israelitschen und jüdischen Religion.* 1922.
————, *Die Ursprünge der jüdische Eschatologie.* Giessen, 1925.
Holwerda, B., *De Wijsheid die Behoudt.* 1957.
Homer, *Iliad* (Loeb Classical Library) .
————, *Odyssey* (Loeb Classical Library) .
Honeyman, A.M., *JAOS.*
————, *VT,* I, 1, Jan., 1951.
Hoonacker, A. Van, *Het Boek Isaias.* Brugge, 1932.
Horace, *Carmina* (Loeb Classical Library) .
————, *Epistles* (Loeb Classical Library) .
————, *Epodes* (Loeb Classical Library) .
————, *Odes* (Loeb Classical Library) .
————, *Satires* (Loeb Classical Library) .
Huffmon, Herbert, "The Covenant Lawsuit in the Prophets," *JBL,* IV, Dec., 1959.

Hummel, Horace, "Enclitic Mem in Early Northwest Semitic, Especially Hebrew," *JBL*, June, 1957.

Hvidberg, "The Masseba and the Holy Seed," *Interpretationes* (Mowinckel Festschrift). Oslo, 1955.

Hyatt, James P., *Prophetic Religion*. New York, 1947.

Ibn Hisham, ed. Wüstenfeld, *Des Leben Mohammeds*.

Ilgen, Karl David, *Die Urkunden des jerusalemischen Tempelarchivs in ihrer Urgestalt, als Beitrag zur Berichtigung der Geschichte der Religion und Politik*. 1798.

Interpreter's Bible. New York, Nashville, 1952ff.

Israel Stele of Merenptah, cf. Pritchard, James.

Iwry, S., "Masseboth and Bamah in 1Q ISAIAH 6," *JBL*, 76, Part 3, Sept., 1957.

Jacob, Edmond, *Theologie de l'Ancien Testament*. Neuchâtel, 1955.

Jastrow, *Hebrew-Babylonian Traditions*. 1914.

Jennings, F. C., *Studies in Isaiah*. New York. 1950.

Jerome, in Migne, *Patrologia*.

Jerushalmi, Tanchum, *Kitab al-Ijaz wa'l Bayan*, cf. Ed. Pococke, *Porta Mosis*.

Johnson, Aubrey R., *Sacral Kingship in Ancient Israel*. Cardiff, 1955.

Josephus, *Antiquities* (Loeb Classical Library).

Justin Martyr, ed. de Otto, *Opera quae feruntur omnia*, Ienae. 1876-80.

Juvenal, *Satires* (Loeb Classical Library).

Kamus, dictionary of al-Firuzabadi, 1329.

Kaplan, M. M., "Isaiah 6:1-11," *JBL*, XCV-XCVI, 1926-27.

Kaufmann, Y., "Bible and Mythological Polytheism," *JBL*, 3, Sept., 1951.

Kautzsch, *Die Derivate des Stammes tsdg im alttertamentlichen speauchgebeauch*. Tübingen, 1881.

Keil and Delitzsch, *Biblical Commentary on the O. T.* 25 vols. Grand Rapids, 1949-50.

Keizer, P., *De profeet Jesaja*. Kampen, 1947.

Keilschrifturkenden aus Boghazkeui, 1916, 1921.

Kimchi, David, ed. L. Finkelstein, *The Commentary of David Kimchi on Isaiah*.

Kissane, E. J., *The Book of Isaiah*. New York, 1926; Dublin; I, 1941, II, 1943.

Kittel, Gerhard, ed., *Theologisches Wörterbuch zum Neuen Testament*.

Kittel, Rudolf, *Biblia Hebraica*, 3rd ed. Stuttgart, 1937.

――――, *Hellenistiche Mysterienreligionen*.

Kline, Meredith, "The Intrusion and the Decalogue," *WThJ*, XVI, I, Nov., 1953.

――――, *Treaty of the Great King*. Grand Rapids, 1963.

Knobel, August W., *Der Prophet Jesaja*. Leipzig, 1872.

Köhler and Baumgartner, *Lexicon in Veteris Testamenti Libros*. 1953.

Köhler, Ludwig, *Theologie des Alten Testaments.*
————, "Syntactica, II, III, IV," *VT*, III, 1953.
König, Eduard, *Stylistik.*
————, *Syntax.*
————, *Das Buch Jesaja.* Gütersloh, 1926.
Koppe, J. B., 1779-81, editor of Lowth's commentary on Isaiah.
Koran, ed. Mavlana Muhammed 'Ali. Lahore, 1951.
Kraus, Hans Joachim, *Psalmen.* Neukirchen, 1958.
Kroeker, Jakob, *Jesaia der Altere (Cap. 1-35).* Giessen, 1934.

Lactantius, *Epitome*, ed. E. H. Blakeney. London, 1950.
Lambdin, *JAOS*, 73, 3.
Lambert, W. G., "Three Unpublished Fragments of the Tukulti-Ninurta Epic," *AfO*, 1957.
Landsberger, Benno, *Sam'al.* Ankara, 1948.
Le Clerc, *Ars Critica.* 1697.
Leupold, *Commentary on Genesis.* Grand Rapids, 1950.
Lidzbarski, *Ephemeris fur semitische Epigraphik*, I. 1900.
Liebreich, L. J., "The Position of Chapter Six in the Book of Isaiah," *HUCA*, 25, 1954.
Lindblom, *A Study on the Immanuel Section of Isaiah.* Lund, 1958.
Livy (Loeb Classical Library).
Löw, I., *Der Flora der Juden*, I-IV, 1924-34.
Löwth, Robert, *Isaia.* London, 1779.
Luckenbill, *Ancient Records of Babylonia and Assyria.* Chicago, 1926.
Luther, *Luther's Werke, Deutsche Bibel*, II Band, I Hälfte. 1528. Weimar, 1960.
Luzzatto, Samuel David, *Il Propheta Isaia volgarizyato e commentato ad uso degl' Israeliti.* Padova, 1855.

McClain, Alva J., *The Greatness of the Kingdom.* 1959.
Machen, J. Gresham, *The Virgin Birth of Christ.*
Manley, G. T., *The Book of the Law*, Grand Rapids, 1957.
Marriage of Nikkal and Eb, see Gordon, Ugaritic Handbook.
Marti, Karl, *Das Buch Jesaja.* Tübingen, 1900.
Martial, *Epigrams* (Loeb Classical Library).
Maurer, *Commentarius in Vetus Testamentum*, I. Lipsiae, 1835.
Megilla.
Meyer, Ernst, *Der Prophet Jesaja*, Erste Hälfte. Pforzheim, 1850.
Michaelis, J. H., Hebrew Bible with annotations, 1720.
Michel, D., "Studien zu den sogenannten Thronbesleigungs psalmen," *VT*, 6, 1956.
Milik, J. T., "*IL Rotolo frammentario di Isaia*," pp. 246-249, cf. also pp. 73-74, 204-225, *Biblica*, 31, 1950.
Milton, John, *Paradise Lost.*
Moallaka, see Amr 'l-Qais.

507

Möller, Wilhelm, *Die messianische Erwartung der vorexilischen Propheten.* Gütersloh, 1906.

Moran, William L., "The Putative Root TM in Is. 9:18," *Catholic Biblical Quarterly,* XII, 2, April, 1950.

Morris, Leon, *The Apostolic Preaching of the Cross.* Grand Rapids, 1955.

————, *The First and Second Epistles to the Thessalonians.* Grand Rapids, 1959.

Mowinckel, Sigmund, *He That Cometh.* Nashville, 1954.

————, *Jesaja Disciplinen.* Oslo, 1926.

————, *The Old Testament as Word of God.* New York, Nashville, 1959.

————, *Psalmenstudien, II, Das Thronbesteigungsfest Jahwäs under der Ursprung der Eschatologie.* Christiana, 1922.

Müller, W. E., *Die Vorstellung vom Rest in Alten Testament.* Leipzig, 1939.

Munch, P. A., *The Expression bajjōm hāhū.* Oslo, 1936.

Nägelsbach, Carl W. E., *Der Prophet Jesaja.* Leipzig, 1877.

Nicole, Roger, "C. H. Dodd and Propitiation," *WThJ,* XVII, 2, May, 1955.

Noth, *History of Israel.* London, 1958.

Nöttscher, F., "Entbehrliche Hapaxlegomena in Jesaia," *VT,* 1951.

Nyberg, H. S., *Hebreisk Grammatik.* Uppsula, 1952.

Oesterley, W. O. E., *The Doctrine of the Last Things.* London, 1909.

Oppenheim, A. Leo, "Assyriological Gleanings," *BASOR,* No. 103.

Orelli, Konrad von, *The Prophecies of Isaiah.* Edinburgh, 1899.

Origen, *Hexapla,* see Field, F.

Orlinsky, Harry M., "Studies V," *Israel Exploration Journal,* 4, 1954.

————, "The Treatment of Anthropomorphisms and Anthropopathisms in the Septuagint of Isaiah," *HUCA,* 27, 1956.

Osborn, A. E., "Divine Destiny and Human Failure, Isaiah 2," *Biblical Review,* 17, 1932.

Ottley, R. R., *The Book of Isaiah According to the Septuagint.* I, 1904, II, 1906.

Ovid, *Ex Ponto* (Loeb Classical Library).

————, *Fasti* (Loeb Classical Library).

————, *Metaporphoses* (Loeb Classical Library).

Pallas, Svend Sage, *The Babylonian 'akitu' Festival.* København, 1926.

Pap, L. I., *Das israelitische Neujahrsfest.* Kampen, 1933.

Paulus, Heinrich Eberhard Gottlob, *Philologische Clavis über das Alte Testament.* Jena, 1793.

Pausanius (Loeb Classical Library).

Pedersen, J., *Israel,* I, II. London, 1926, 1947.

Penna, Angelo, *Isaia* (La Sacra Bibbia). Torino, Roma, 1958.

————, "LaVolgata e il manuscritto 101s," *Biblica,* XXXVIII, 1957.

Pentecost, J. Dwight, *Things to Come.* 1958.

Perles, *Analecten zum Alten Testament,* 2 vols.

Pesikta de-Rab-Kahana.
Pfeiffer, *Introduction to the Old Testament.* New York, 1948.
Philby, *The Empty Quarter.* London, 1933.
Pirqe Abot.
Plato, *Phaedrus* (Loeb Classical Library) .
Plautus, *Poenulus* (Loeb Classical Library) .
Pliny, *Natural History.*
————, *Panegyric* (Loeb Classical Library) .
Polybius (Loeb Classical Library) .
Poole, M., *Annotations Upon the Holy Bible.* London, 1688.
Pratt, *The Religious Consciousness.*
Pritchard, James, *Ancient Near Eastern Texts.* Princeton University, 1950.
Procksch, Otto, *Theologie des Alten Testaments.* Gütersloh, 1950.
Propertius (Loeb Classical Library) .
Pseudo-Epiphanius, *De Vitis Prophetarum.*

Qumran, First Isaiah Manuscript, see Burrows, M.

Rahlfs, A., *Septuaginto,* II. Stuttgart, 1935.
Rashi, Rabbi Solomon Yizchaki, cf. the Rabbinical Bibles.
Rea, John, "The Connection Between Isaiah 7:14 and 7:15-17," unpublished.
Reichel, Carl Rudolf, *Der Prophet Jesaias.* Leipzig and Görlitz, 1755-1759.
Reider, "Contribution to the Scriptural Text;" *HUCA,* 24, 1952-53.
Ridderbos, J., *Jesaja in Het Godswoord des Profeten.* 1932.
————, "Jahwäh malak," *VT,* 4, 1954.
Ridderbos, N. H., *De "Werkers der Ongerechtigheid" in de Individueele Psalmen.* Kampen, 1939.
Rignell, "Isaiah, Chapter I" and "Das Immanuelszeichen," *Studia Theologica,* 11, 1957.
Ringgren, Helmer, *The Prophetical Consciousness of Holiness.* Uppsula, 1948.
————, *Word and Wisdom.* 1947.
————, *Messias Konungen.* Uppsala, 1954.
Robinson, *Studies in Old Testament Prophecy.* 1950.
Rosenmüller, E. F., *Scholia in Vetus Testamentum.* Lipsiae, 1791-93.
Rost, P., *Die Keilschrifttexte Tiglapilesers,* III. Leipzig, 1893.
Rowlands, E. R., *The Targum and the Peshitta Version of the Book of Isaiah, VT,* IX, 2.
————, *The Faith of Israel.* 1956.
Rowley, H. H., *The Zadokite Fragments and the Dead Sea Scrolls.* Oxford, 1952.

Saadia, see Gesenius' commentary for Saadia's exposition. Cf. also S. Landauer, *Kitab al-Amanat.* Leiden, 1880.
Sabatier, P., *Bibliorum Sacrorumlatinae versiones antiquae,* II, Paris, 1751.
Sallust, *Cataline* (Loeb Classical Library) .

Sanhedrin.

Schilling, S. Paul, *Isaiah Speaks.* New York, 1958-59.

Schmidt, Hans, *Die Schriften des Alten Testaments.* 1921, 1925.

————, *Die Thronfakort Jahwes.* Tübingen, 1927.

Schmidt, Sebastian, *Commentarius super illustres prophetias Jesaeae.* Hamburgi, 1702.

Scofield Bible.

Schräder, *Die Kielschriften und das Alte Testament.* 1883, 1903.

Seeligmann, I. J., *The Septuagint Version of Isaiah.* Leiden, 1946.

Sellin, E., *Israelitische-jüdische Religionsgeschichte.* Leipzig, 1933.

Selwyn, *Horse Hebraica.* 1860.

Shachar and Shalim, see Gordon; Ugaritic Handbook.

Skinner, J., "Isaiah," *Cambridge Bible.* Cambridge, 1925.

Smend, R., and A. Socin, *Die Inschrift des Konigs Mosa von Moab.*

Smith, George Adam, *The Book of Isaiah.* New York; I, 1888, II, 1890.

Smith, Norman H., "The Interpretation of El Gibbor in Isaiah 95 (EUV6) ," *The Expository Times,* 52, No. 1, Oct., 1940.

————, *The Jewish New Year Festival.* London, 1947.

Snijders, *OS,* Deel X, 1954.

Sophocles, *Antigone* (Loeb Classical Library) .

Speiser, E. A., *JAOS,* 71, 1951.

Speier, S., *JBL,* March, 1953.

Stamm, J. J., "Ein Vierteljahrhundert Psalmenforschung," *Theologisches Rundschau,* 23, 1955.

Stier, Rudolf, 1850.

Stenning, J. F., *The Targum of Isaiah.* Oxford, 1949.

Strabo, A. (Loeb Classical Library) .

Strachey, Edward, *Hebrew Politics in the Times of Sargon and Sennacherib.* London, 1853.

Stummer, F., *Einführung in die lateinische Bibel.* Paderborn, 1928.

Sukenik, Eleazer, *Otzar Hammegilloth hagenuzoth.* Jerusalem, 1954.

Tallgvist, *Die assyrische Beschwörungsserie Maqlu.* 1895.

Targum, see Stenning, J.F.

Tertullian, *De Patientia.*

Thiele, Edwin F., *The Mysterious Numbers of the Hebrew Kings.* Chicago, 1951.

————, *Journal of Near Eastern Studies,* III. 1944.

Thomas, *Documents from Old Testament Times,* 1958.

Thucydides (Loeb Classical Library) .

Trapp, John, *Commentary on the Old and New Testaments.* London, 1867.

Tur-Sinai, "Unverstandene Bibelworte I," *VT,* 1, 1951.

Uhland, *Vat, Jes, cap XIII . . . prophetae Jesaiae vindicatum.* Tübingen, 1798.

Umbreit, F. W. C., *Jesaja.* 1841.

Van der Flier, A., *De Profeet Jesaja*. Zust, 1931.

Van Imschoot, *Theologie de l'Ancien Testament*. Tournai, 1954.

Van Til, Cornelius, *The Defense of the Faith*. Philadelphia, 1955.

Varenius, August, *Commentarium in Isaiam*, Pars I-III. Rostochi, 1673.

Verhoef, P., *Die Dag van der Here*. Den Haag, 1956.

Virgil, *Aeneid* (Loeb Classical Library).

————, *Eclogues* (Loeb Classical Library).

————, *Georgics* (Loeb Classical Library).

Visio Pauli.

Vischer, *Die Immanuel Botschaft im Rahmen des königlichen Zionsfestes*. Zollikon-Zurich, 1955.

Vitringa, Campegius, *Commentarius in librum propheticum Jesaiae*. Leavadre, 1724.

Volz, Paul, *Das Neujahrsfest Jahwes*. Tübingen, 1912.

————, *Die Eschatologie der judischen Gemeinde im neutestamentlichen Zeitalter*. Tübingen, 1934.

Von Gall, A., *Basieilla Tou Theou.*

Von Rad, Gerhard, *Theologie des Alten Testaments*. München, 1957.

————, "The Origin of the Concept of the Day of Yahweh," *JSS*, IV, 2, April, 1959.

Vos, *Biblical Theology*. Grand Rapids, 1954.

————, *The Pauline Eschatology*. Grand Rapids, 1953.

Vriezen, Th. C., *Hoofdlijnen der Theologie van het Oude Testament*. Wageningen, 1954.

Wade, G. W., *Old Testament History*. New York, 1908.

Watts, J. D. W., *Vision and Prophecy in Amos*. Grand Rapids, 1958.

Weil, H. M., "Exégèse d' Isaie III, 1-15," *Revue Biblique*, No. 49, 1940.

Weiser, Artur, *Einleitung in das Alte Testament*. Göttingen, 1949.

Welch, Adam, *Kings and Prophets of Israel*. London, 1953.

Wernberg-Moller, "Studies in the Defective Spellings in the Isaiah Scroll of St. Mark's Monastery," *JSS*, III, 4.

Whitcomb, J. C., Jr., *Darius the Mede*. Grand Rapids, 1960.

Widengren, George, "Religion och Bibel," *Nathan Soderblom-Sälleskapets Arsbok*, II. 1943.

Wilson, Robert Dick, "The Meaning of Alma (A.V. Virgin) in Isa. VII:17," *PTR*, XXIV, 1926.

————, *A Scientific Investigation of the Old Testament*. Chicago, 1959.

Wiseman, Donald J., "Assyrian Writing-Boards," *IRAQ*, XVII, Pt. 1, 1955.

————, *Chronicles of the Babylonian King*. London, 1956.

————, "A Fragmentary Inscription of Tiglath-pileser III from Nimrud," *IRAQ*, XVIII, Pt. II, 1956.

————, "Secular Records in Confirmation of the Scriptures," *Victorian Institute*, 1954.

————, "Two Historical Inscriptions from Nimrud," *IRAQ*, XIII, Pt. 1, 1951.

511

————, *Vassal Treaties of Esarhaddon*. London, 1758.

————, *IRAQ*, XX, 1953.

Wright, William, *Arabic Grammar*, 2 vols. Cambridge.

————, *Biblical Archaeology*. Philadelphia, London, 1957.

Xenophon, *Cyropaedia* (Loeb Classical Library).

Yaha, *Shalshelet hak-kabbalah*.

Young, Edward J., *My Servants the Prophets*. Grand Rapids, 1954.

————, *The Study of Old Testament Theology Today*. London, 1958-59.

————, *Studies in Isaiah*. Grand Rapids, 1954.

————, *Thy Word Is Truth*. Grand Rapids, 1957.

————, *Who Wrote Isaiah?* Grand Rapids, 1958.

————, "Adverbial-u in Semitic," *WThJ*, XIII, 2, May, 1951.

Young, G. Douglas, *OS*, Deel VIII, 1950.

Zamaschari, 1075-1144, *Al-Mufassal*, ed. J. B. Broch. Cristiania, 1859, 1879.

Ziegler, J., *Isaias* (Septuaginta Vetus Testamentum graecum). Göttingen, 1939.

Zwingli, *Zwingli's Sämtliche Werke*, 14. Zürich, 1959.

Index of Scripture

Index of Persons

528

529

Index of Authors

530